WITHDRAWN

THE
COLONIAL HISTORY
SERIES

General Editor
D. H. Simpson
Librarian of the Royal Commonwealth Society

African Memoranda

Other titles in this series:

Beecham, John. *Ashantee and the Gold Coast*, 1841
New intro. by G. E. Metcalfe, reprinted 1968. £4 10

Buxton, T. F. *African Slave Trade and Its Remedy*, 1839–40
New intro. by G. E. Metcalfe, reprinted 1968. £7 10

Bridge, Horatio. *Journal of an African Cruiser*, 1848
New intro. by D. H. Simpson, reprinted 1968. £2 10

Letters of the Late Ignatius Sancho. An African, 1802
New intro. by Paul Edwards, reprinted 1968. £5 10

Proceedings of the Association for Promoting the Discovery of the Interior Parts of Africa, 2 vols. 1810
New intro. by Robin Hallett, reprinted 1967. £15

AFRICAN MEMORANDA:

RELATIVE TO AN ATTEMPT TO ESTABLISH

A British Settlement

ON

THE ISLAND OF BULAMA,

On the WESTERN COAST *of* AFRICA, *in the year* 1792.

WITH A BRIEF NOTICE OF THE

NEIGHBOURING TRIBES, SOIL, PRODUCTIONS, &c.

AND SOME OBSERVATIONS ON

The facility of COLONIZING *that part of Africa, with a View to*
CULTIVATION;

AND THE

INTRODUCTION OF LETTERS AND RELIGION TO ITS INHABITANTS:

BUT MORE PARTICULARLY

AS THE MEANS OF GRADUALLY ABOLISHING

African Slavery.

———

BY CAPTAIN PHILIP BEAVER,
OF HIS MAJESTY'S ROYAL NAVY.

———

London:
PRINTED FOR C. AND R. BALDWIN, NEW BRIDGE-STREET, BLACKFRIARS.
———
1805.

TO

THAT MAN,

OF WHATEVER NATION,

WHO,

WITH EQUAL MEANS,

SHALL DO MORE TOWARDS THE INTRODUCTION OF

𝕮𝖎𝖛𝖎𝖑𝖎𝖟𝖆𝖙𝖎𝖔𝖓,

BY CULTIVATION AND COMMERCE,

TO

THE INHABITANTS

OF THE

WESTERN COAST OF AFRICA,

THAN WAS EFFECTED BY THE ENTERPRISE

OF WHICH THE FOLLOWING SHEETS ARE DESCRIPTIVE;

THESE

MEMORANDA

ARE RESPECTFULLY INSCRIBED,

BY

PHILIP BEAVER.

CONTENTS.

	Page
Preface.	i
Introduction.	ix

PART I.

CHAPTER I.

Proceedings of the Bulama Society in England 1

CHAPTER II.

Proceedings of the Colonists from their leaving England to their arrival in the Bijuga Channel, on the Coast of Africa. 21

CHAPTER III.

Summary of the Calypso's proceedings from the time of her separation to her rejoining the Hankey 45

CHAPTER IV.

Proceedings from the rejunction of the ships to the abandonment of the island of Bulama by the major part of the Colonists, in the Ship Calypso 54

PART II.

CHAPTER V.

Lieutenant Beaver's Journal on the island of Bulama. 85

Contents.

PART III.

CHAPTER VI.

Apology for those parts of the preceding Journal which may appear either illegal or harsh—Objections foreseen and answered—Difficulties which we had to overcome stated—Natives opinion of the European character—Advantages resulting from our having remained upon the island. 284

CHAPTER VII.

Recapitulation of the principal causes of our failure—none of which can be attributed either to the difficulty or impracticability of the Enterprize itself.... 308

CHAPTER VIII.

Geographical outline of that part of the African Coast, which is comprized between the Rivers Gambia and Grande; with a brief notice of its Southern Inhabitants, its soil, and principal animal and vegetable productions........ 316

CHAPTER IX.

Of the Bijuga Islands, and its inhabitants. 332

CHAPTER X.

Of the Island of Bulama—its produce—animals—climate............... 341

CHAPTER XI.

Advantageous position of the Country sketched in Chapter VIII, for the purposes

Contents.

Page

of Cultivation and Commerce—its Colonization proposed—commodities intended to be there produced—how these might affect our West Indian possessions—what effect the colonization of this Country might have on the African character, particularly with respect to Slavery—and how far it may conduce towards the introduction of Letters and Religion into that Country, as well as to a more accurate Knowledge of its interior.—Reasons for fixing upon the territory between the Gambia and the Grande, and for beginning the plantations on the latter, instead of on the former River.—Conclusion. 373

Note, on a French work on the subject of the western coast of Africa........ 411

APPENDIX.

N° 1. Proposals of the Committee. 419
N° 2. Memorandum of agreement, and Constitution of Government, for the Island of Bulama 421
N° 3. List of the Colonists, &c., who sailed from Gravesend. 433
N° 4. List of the Colonists who remained with Lieutenant Beaver on the Island of Bulama 446
N° 5. Some account of the weather at Bulama 450
N° 6. Letter from Ghinala 2d August 1792 466
N° 7. Treaty between Lieutenant Beaver and the Kings of Ghinala and the Rio Grande, 3d August 1792 467
N° 8. List of the purchase goods of the Island of Bulama, &c. from the Biafaras. 469
N° 9. Extracts from the ship Hankey's log, to show that that ship was not sickly on her return to England, nor had been so for months before 470
N° 10. Letters and affidavits relative to the cutting off, and recapture, of the fisher schooner 472
N° 11. Depositions relative to an attack upon a Portuguese canoe 477
N° 12. Garden book 479
N° 13. Extracts from a letter, from the trustees to Lieutenant Beaver 485
N° 14. Instructions to Mr. Hood, on the evacuation of the Island being resolved upon. 487
N° 15. List of Grumetas, or free natives, employed, as labourers, on the Island of Bulama, by Lieutenant Beaver 490

Contents.

Nº 16. Lieutenant Beaver's opinion of the causes of the failure of the expedition, and of the probability of future success, laid before a general meeting of the subscribers, held at the Mansion-house by the Lord Mayor; with the resolutions thereat agreed to 494

Nº 17. Extracts from the ship Hankey's log, from London towards Bulama, from that ship getting soundings on the coast of Africa, to her anchoring in the east channel of Bulama 499

PREFACE.

THE following pages will make the reader acquainted with the melancholy, and unfortunate, result of an ill-contrived and badly executed, though well intended, expedition to the coast of Africa, in the year 1792: this expedition was proposed and undertaken by a few gentlemen, with a view to ascertain whether or not it were practicable to cultivate tropical productions on the coast of Africa, by means of its free natives. The question of the abolition of the slave trade had, at that time, for four or five years, been violently agitated; and some of those, who were advocates for its continuance, boldly asserted that the Africans were incapable of enjoying freedom, or being in any great degree civilized: and it was thought that this expedition would decide the injustice of such an opinion. Unfortunately however, for the Africans, it was so exceedingly ill conducted, that it was totally given up, ere the latter part of that opinion could be put to the proof; though the former part of it was unequivocally ascertained to be erroneous.

The ill success of this attempt, the report of the numbers killed by the natives, of those who had died from the unhealthiness of the climate, and of the mortality which had taken place on board the ship Hankey, all of which, moreover, were greatly magnified, were sufficient of themselves to deter others from engaging in such an enterprize; and would (if peace had even continued) have prevented those few, who remained upon the island of Bulama, from receiving any considerable reinforcement to their numbers, before the pernicious effects of these exaggerated reports had been considerably weakened. War however took place; and all hope of succouring the few who still kept possession of that island was at an end. Thus, without succour or assistance of any kind, after having maintained their position for nearly a year and a half, they were obliged to abandon the island, and the only two white men left, of those who had sailed on the expedition, returned to Europe.

If it be asked why these Memoranda have so long been kept back, and why they were not before made public—I answer that it never was my intention to make them so: but, if it had, they could not have appeared much earlier; for, soon after my return to England, I sailed on the expedition to the Cape of Good Hope, thence went to India, was afterwards, when in Europe, constantly in the Channel fleet, and latterly in the Mediterranean, from which I did not return till the summer of 1802. So that, for eight years after my return from Bulama, I had scarcely my foot out of a ship, and was very little in Europe; all which time my African papers were left in England. Had it therefore been my intention, it was not in my power to have published earlier than the beginning of 1803. Such intention however

I never entertained; I did not conceive these documents to be of sufficient interest, or sufficient importance, to give to the world. Accident, at length, has drawn them forth; and they are given, less with the hope of either informing or amusing my countrymen, than with a view to ward off a blow that is threatened to their interests.

In the latter part, of the summer of 1802, government, I suppose, had turned its attention towards Africa; for I was then requested, by the under secretary of state, to give my opinion on the best mode of opening a communication with, and of exploring, its interior. This naturally induced me to look over all my African papers; which brought that quarter of the globe, and its interests, again strongly into my mind. When full of these impressions, a friend of mine, early in 1803, put a French book on the subject of Africa, which had lately made its appearance, into my hands. Struck with the correct notions there formed of the importance of that country to France, and of the system there recommended for her to adopt; which if acted upon, would exclude for ever this country from a most valuable portion of it; and, vexed with, what appeared to me, the supineness of England towards her interests in Africa; I turned over in my own mind what would tend to open her eyes, to the danger she incurred of losing all influence and connexion with that country, north of the equator.

I had just then, for the first time in my life, sat down quietly in a house of my own: and for the first time in my life also, I had nothing to employ me. These leisure days, it was thought, might in some small degree be usefully employed, I, therefore, unqualified as I might be for the task, determined to translate this book, and make such remarks (in notes) on its tendency, as it was hoped would in some measure do away the danger apprehended. If the translation was bad, I knew that I should not be hanged for it, although I might be abused; however, this latter species of retribution I never cared much about, and the fear of encountering it will never, I trust, prevent my doing what I conceive to be useful. As a bad translation, it was thought, might do a little good, I determined to proceed. But I had scarcely begun, when my friend advised me, instead of translating this work, to give an account of the Bulama expedition; and my notions on the importance of cultivating that island and its neighbourhood; wherein I might take an opportunity of speaking of the book intended to have been translated; which he observed would have the more weight, as it would then be seen that I had resided in the country of which I was giving an opinion, and must therefore be supposed not totally incompetent to speak of it, and its inhabitants. Thus originated the intention of publishing the following sheets. I accordingly began on the 4th of March 1803 to arrange the Memoranda, preceding my Journal of our transactions on the island, when, four days after, a message to the house of commons announced the probability of the speedy commencement of another war: under which expectation it was impossible to

Preface.

remain quietly drudging at pen and ink; and all my papers were re-conveyed to their old musty box there to remain to the end of the war. However, the summer of 1804 having passed without any attempt on the part of the enemy to put his vain glorious threat of invading us in execution, and no chance remaining of seeing them on this side of the water, and my official situation not being the most active in the world, I again drew forth my African papers, to give me a little employment in the winter, in arranging them for publication. And I the more readily give them to the world, as it affords me, ere too late, an opportunity of expressing my opinion of the danger to be apprehended from French influence and intrigue; if, when peace arrives, they are suffered to retain such places, on the western coast of Africa, as will enable them to put in execution the projects of Mons. Golberry.

Of the sources whence these Memoranda are drawn it may be proper to give some account. Most of those preceding the 19th of July 1792, were written by myself as the circumstances occurred; those relative to the Calypso, after her separation from us, are given from the narration of those of that ship who remained behind with me on the island of Bulama; as well as from their journals, particularly that of Mr. Aberdein; all of which came into my hands, after their decease. And some are supplied by the correspondence, and the minutes, of the council; all of which, together with every document and paper relative to the expedition, from the first meeting of its proposers, to the final evacuation of the island, (except one of my own letters) are, either in the original, or in copy, now in my possession. After the 19th of July the occurrences of the day were always written in the evening thereof, till our arrival at Sierra Leone, where I ceased to keep either journal or minutes.

In speaking of the expedition, and of those who sailed in it, I have always spoken with unreserved freedom; but ever without prejudice, without malice; in the planning, and the conducting it, there was certainly much, very much, to blame; and, as one principally concerned in both, I take to myself my full share of it; my object has been to give an idea of the general conduct of the colonists, but not of individuals; therefore, when not obliged so to do, I have never named persons; in short I have said nothing from anger, nor withheld any thing from fear.

My opinions towards the latter end of the book are, I am aware, likely to be objected to by very good, well-informed, and well-intentioned men; they are too hostile to slavery to satisfy those who are advocates for its continuance; and concede too much toward that continuance to please those who are anxious for its abolition. So that most likely they will not please either party. Neither was it my object so to do. For, although I would not voluntarily give offence to any person in existence; yet am I not to be deterred, by a probability of that, from giving my free and unbiassed opinions on any subject, when occasion calls them forth. If they be erroneous, they are easily overturned by argument; but if just, they certainly deserve some attention, and finally will prevail; for, truth is eternal. Such as they are, however, they are my own, for no person whatever has yet seen the contents of the following book; no person has been consulted upon them; and I have studiously avoided, (what may appear very extraordinary) reading any work, or report whatever, on the subject of Africa, and the slavery of its natives; lest I might have been biassed and led away by others arguments, and might have formed my opinion from the reasoning of others, instead of my own observation. In as much solitude then, and with as little advice, as if I had been yet following my Robinson-Crusoe-like kind of life on the Island of Bulama, were my sentiments committed to paper. I consulted Edwards on the cultivation of cotton, coffee, &c., Labat, who wrote near a century ago; and Golberry, who gave rise to this publication, but no other author.

I may be accused of egotism in the narrative of the expedition. But alas! of whom else had I to speak? Things must be related as they were, and not altered, to appear more seemly: for truth, and not fiction, is the subject.

The most formidable objection, however, is yet to come; and that is as to the execution of my task. It will be seen, and by the candid probably remembered, that among all the trades which I was obliged to practise when on the Island of Bulama, that of book-making was *not* one; the title however which I have chosen for this, promises not much; that of

"Memoranda," giving only an idea of a book made up of *shreds and patches*. I forewarn the reader, therefore, not to expect entertainment. Information I promise, on the subject of the expedition, but nothing more.

A life almost constantly spent in the naval service of my country, since the period of my eleventh year, cannot but be considered as exceedingly adverse to the acquirement of either correctness in composition, or elegance in style. For whatever knowledge may be acquired by a salt-water education, it must be affirmed, that it is not very favourable to any considerable progress in literature.

I have therefore told my story in the manner and in the language which I should have used if telling it to a few friends in a room; without having used any art in its structure, or labour in its polish. I have never gone out of my way to seek a word, or round a period, with a view to elegance; and if I had, I know that I should have failed; but I have remained contented to express myself in the plain, open, and candid manner of a seaman. The first person is used instead of the third, because, unaccustomed to write, it was most convenient to me; and will not, I hope, be deemed an unpardonable fault, considering how much I am, of necessity, the hero of my own story.

To expect either emolument, or fame, from the publication of the following pages would be the height of presumptuous folly; but that they may render me liable to abuse and misrepresentation is not very unlikely. I should not, therefore, have published them, unless I felt convinced, that they tend to promote the interests of this country, and the happiness of the inhabitants of one quarter of the globe.

South End, Essex,
28th January, 1805.

INTRODUCTION.

WHEN that fleet was dismantled which, pending the differences between Great Britain and Russia relative to the possession of Oczakow, had been kept at Spithead during the summer of 1791, the ship to which I belonged, among others, was paid off. Without professional employment, young,* and not inclined to be inactive, I turned over in my own mind in what way my time could be completely, and, at the same time, usefully employed. Any thing I thought better than lounging about the capital.

I had a great wish to be acquainted with both our northern and southern whale fisheries, and therefore intended to go out, as a passenger, in some ship employed in those trades, in order to make myself master of the subject. The season was gone by for the former; I was therefore confined to the latter; and went, in consequence, to a house at Paul's Wharf, which owned a great number of ships in the southern whale fishery; and inquiring for the gentleman of the house, to whom I was totally unknown; " Sir," said I, " I understand that you have several " vessels employed in the southern fishery?" " Yes, Sir," he replied. " A young friend of mine," I continued, " wishes very " much to see your mode of killing the fish, cutting them up,

* At that time twenty-five.

"and melting them down, as well as the manner of killing seals, "and sea lions, on the Faulkland islands; where, if your vessel "be absent two seasons, he will have no objection to remain "one winter; and I come from him to propose his going out as "a passenger in one of them; he will pay any thing you choose "to demand for his possessing half the cabin; and taking with "him his books, he will have nothing to do with the ship, "where he will never be in the way, but, being a bit of a sea-"man himself, he may sometimes be of use."—" Sir," he replied, " we never take any such persons, I cannot therefore "comply with your request; he must be a very odd young man, "Sir."—" Yes, Sir," said I, " he is an odd fish."

My intentions being frustrated here; which probably might not have been the case, had I been a little more explicit; I was next divided between three subjects that occupied my attention.

The first was to endeavour to reach the North Pole; to this I was induced by reading a paper of the Honourable Daines Barrington, on the probability of its being practicable; this, though requiring perseverance, would not require much time, as, at the expiration of the first, second, or third summer, if not accomplished, it would be given up.

The next was to traverse Africa from the Cape of Good Hope, north; or from the Gambia, east. But this required, at least, three years preparation, and five more, in all probability, for its accomplishment. And the third was to coast the world.—This last I conceived might be usefully done in about twenty years.

I had seen the Dutch armament of 1787, the Spanish armament of 1790, and the Russian armament of 1791, terminate amicably; and I really began to think that war was at an end for our days. Having yet no serious cause to apprehend it from the French revolution.

Contriving the means, but undetermined as to which of these projects I should first undertake, I was in the autumn of 1791 introduced to Mr. Dalrymple. The Sierra Leone Company were at that time about commencing their settlement on the coast of Africa; and this gentleman I was informed was to be the governor of it. With him I frequently met four others; all military or naval, with whom I had lived one year in France, after the peace of 1783. These gentlemen had all agreed to go out with Mr. Dalrymple; and when he asked me to do the same I readily acquiesced. It was a plan so congenial to my mind, that a second was not required to hesitate; and my own plans being too expensive for my purse, were given up. I knew nothing of what would be expected from me, nothing of the plan, except that it was benevolent and humane. All that I knew was, that a colony was to be established; and among uncivilized tribes; and that was enough for me. Mr. D. always told us that the gentlemen who directed that company would consider us as a most valuable acquisition; as besides having persons of liberal minds and manners; they conceived that our military and nautical knowledge would greatly facilitate the success of their enterprize. Things went on thus for some days, when we observed to Mr. D. that it was necessary that we should see the gentlemen who directed the undertaking; and he accordingly fixed a day for introducing us. At length that morning arrived, when Mr. D. called upon me, and said, " I am no longer governor of Sierra Leone; I have disagreed with the directors; and have nothing more to do with them."—My disappointment was certainly very great; for I had conceived a very strong inclination to form a colony in Africa; with a view to decide a question at that time so much agitated. After some conversation, Dalrymple observed, that, " when " doing duty with his regiment at Goree, in the last war, he " had heard much of the fertility of an uninhabited island " near the mouth of the Grande, called Bulam;* and that " the account of that island given by a director of the French " Senegal Company at the commencement of this century " was exceedingly favourable, as a proper place for making an " establishment." " Let us then colonize it ourselves," said ,. " With all my heart," he replied; and thus originated the expedition to Bulama.

There appears to have been all this time some very unaccountable misapprehension on the part either of Mr. Dalrymple, or the Sierra Leone Directors. For in the end it turned out that so far from wishing persons of our description to go out, we were of all others those whom they most wished to avoid. Unacquainted myself with any one of them, except the Rev. Thomas Clarkson, who had written so ably on the inhumanity, and on the impolicy of the Slave Trade, I never sought to ascertain by what unaccountable misconception we had been led to believe that their sentiments towards us were so totally different from what they really were.

A resolution so prompt, so hasty, so unpremeditated, on so serious a subject, did not probably argue much wisdom; and may predispose the Reader to form no very sanguine ex-

* This island called Bulam, or Boulam, in old charts, I have invariably written Bulāma, as that is the way in which it is always pronounced by the natives.

pectations of an expedition, if conducted by persons, who so lightly determined on so important a point. Be that as it may, my mind was so completely fixed on the African scheme, as to be determined to undertake it, if I could only get half a dozen persons to accompany me. Not to anticipate, however, I shall only say here that we did what could not have been accomplished in any other country in the world; in little more than three months after this conversation with Dalrymple, we sailed with three vessels, and near three hundred persons for our intended island; whose proceedings from the meeting of the first committee to the final evacuation of the island, will be lightly sketched in the following pages; premising here only that the gentlemen who first met were all of them my friends and acquaintances, and that I had no idea myself of our increasing the number of the Committee to more than seven; or in other words of admitting more than one person, to be joined to us in the direction of the undertaking. Our proposals were public; and those who did not choose to accept of them on those terms might withhold their subscriptions.

When therefore the Committee was increased to nine, and afterwards to thirteen, I strenuously opposed both, conceiving that I therein saw the means of altering, or lukewarmly executing, our original intentions. But Mr. Young, for whose opinion I had great respect, urged that our keeping all the power in our own hands had the appearance, if it was not so in fact, of injustice; and that we ought to admit at least an equal number of the subscribers to be joined to the original proposers. His opinion prevailed; but mine I have not changed. The Reader will see which was right.

AFRICAN MEMORANDA.

CHAPTER I.

Proceedings of the Committee of a Society for establishing a Colony on the Western Coast of Africa, from the Period of its Institution, till the Departure of the Colonists from England.

IN consequence of the determination of Messrs. Dalrymple and Beaver, to attempt a settlement on the island of Bulama, they had made known their intentions on that subject to some of their military friends, who eagerly joined in their views, and in a few days the following gentlemen

1791.

Nov. 2.

  Messrs. HENRY HEW DALRYMPLE,*
    JOHN YOUNG,†
    Sir WM. HALTON, Bart.‡
    JOHN KING,§
    ROBERT DOBBIN,¶
    PHILIP BEAVER,¶

---

* Late an officer in some regiment stationed at Gorce.
† Late an Officer in the 42d regiment.   ‡ Late a Captain in the Militia.
§ A Lieutenant of Marines.   ¶ Lieutenants in the R. Navy.

B

1791.
Nov. 2. met at Old Slaughter's Coffee-house, and formed themselves into a society for the purpose of establishing a settlement upon an eligible spot on the western coast of Africa: and, being the original subscribers, constituted themselves a committee to open a subscription, and to form regulations for the purpose of carrying their views into effect.

The island of Bulama, at the mouth of the Rio Grande, on the western coast of Africa, in the 11th degree of north latitude, was the spot fixed upon as the best adapted to the commencement of our undertaking.

We knew that it was uninhabited, and had every reason to believe that there would be no difficulty in purchasing it from those neighbouring chiefs who might claim it as their property; to establish ourselves on an island, instead of on the continent, was thought most eligible, as we should be more secure from any hostile attack, if any quarrel should unfortunately arise with the natives; and quarrels with them would be less likely to occur, as our insular situation would put it out of the power of the colonists to wander into any of the native villages; moreover, Mr. Dalrymple, when serving with his regiment last war, on the island of Goree, had collected much information relative to this island—its harbours, productions, soil, &c. But what finally induced us to make this choice, was the very favourable account given of it by Mons. De la Brue,* who had been director-general of the French Senegal Company, and who had visited this island in the year 1700.

The views of the gentlemen who instituted this society were CULTIVATION; they conceived that the produce of the West

* Relat. de l'Afrique Occident. Par Labat, Vol. V. p. 141. Paris 1728.

African Memoranda.

Indian islands might be easily raised on the island of Bulama, and in its neighbourhood; but this was only a secondary object; at least I can aver it to have been so with *them*, though different sentiments might have actuated others, and certainly did,* to join in the enterprize.

1791.
Nov. 2.

But cultivation was considered by us only as the means which might lead to the CIVILIZATION of the Africans, and eventually put an end to their slavery.

Much had been said, and much had been written, on the subject of the slave trade for the last six years, and it had been strongly contended that the Africans were incapable of enjoying the blessings of liberty;† setting aside argument and debate on the subject, whether they are, or are not capable of enjoying that blessing, this is an experimental attempt to prove either the one or the other. To try therefore whether or not these poor degraded people are capable of holding that rank in the society of nations, which it is natural to suppose all people are capable of attaining, if they have but an opportunity of acquiring knowledge, was the end of our institution.

To purchase land in their country, to cultivate it by free natives hired for that purpose; and thereby to induce in them habits of labour and of industry, it was thought might eventually lead to the introduction of letters, Religion and civilization, into the very heart of Africa.

---

* Some confined their views to cultivation, others meant to unite it with commerce, while a great number had the latter in view only.

† It is with the utmost reluctance that I ever use the word " Liberty," since under its sacred name we have seen a neighbouring nation, after having committed every crime known either in savage or civilized life, reduced to the lowest degree of the most abject slavery.

1791.
Nov. 2.

The intention, it is hoped, is unexceptionable. It goes not to the invasion of any man's right; it trenches not on the privileges of any body of people; it endangers not any of our possessions; and has nothing to do with the abolition of the slave trade.*

It is merely an experiment to ascertain whether those Africans, already free, are capable, or not, of being drawn by industry, cultivation, and commerce, from their present debased situation to hold a respectable rank among the nations of the earth; if we fail, they will be just where they were; but if we succeed, it promises happiness† to myriads of living, and millions of unborn people.

At this meeting it was determined to draw up proposals to publish to the world; to hire rooms for the purpose of holding our meetings; and to meet again that day week. Accordingly on the 9th Nov. having hired rooms at No. 103, Hatton-Garden, the committee again met and issued their proposals. *(Appendix, No. 1.)*

Nov. 9.

It being impossible to sail this season if we should wait for application to parliament for a charter, it was determined to

---

* When I say it has nothing to do with the abolition of the slave trade, I mean to say that it has nothing to do with the question, whether that trade should be abolished or not by the legislature of this country.—No man is a greater enemy than myself to slavery—but at the same time I cannot help giving it as my opinion that it would be not only exceedingly impolitic and unjust, but exceedingly cruel to abolish it.—If the end proposed by such a measure be the increase of the general happiness of mankind, it would have a diametrically opposite effect. If Africans are destined to the enjoyment of freedom and happiness, it must be by very different means, as, I trust, I shall make appear in the sequel.

† I have nothing to do with the question whether a state of uncultivated nature or of civilization be most conducive to happiness. The man who prefers being a brute to a rational creature may put down the book.

make our intentions known to the prime minister; and, if not disapproved by him, to sail the moment our subscriptions would enable us, and take possession of the island; leaving to a committee at home the charge of taking the necessary steps to procure a charter, as soon afterwards as possible; in the mean time it was thought absolutely necessary that some temporary regulations should be drawn up, which every individual was to sign, prior to his embarkation; and by which we were to be governed until an act of parliament had framed for us a code of laws.

1791.
Nov. 9.

With these views it was agreed that we should draw up a form of a constitution for our government until one was provided for us by the legislature of our country.*

At the meeting on the 19th a secretary was appointed, and it was determined that each person who should receive land gratis should be obliged to remain one year in the colony, (unless it shall appear by the report of the surgeon that it is absolutely necessary for his health to return to Europe,) or forfeit all right to his allotment of land; and on the 22d it was resolved that no female should be admitted as a settler on her own account.

19th.

22d.

These restrictions were absolutely necessary at first, to prevent the colony from being weakened at its outset by the allotment of land, near the town, to either absentees or females.

We had already a great number of subscribers; it was therefore thought advisable to assemble them, and point out more particularly than could have been done in the proposals our views and intentions, which having done on the 28th the com-

28th.

---

* We were not at all aware at this time that we were acting illegally; but that we were so will hereafter be seen; as the expedition, on its arrival at Gravesend, was detained some days, by order of the secretary of state, on account of this constitution; nor were we permitted to depart until it was done away.

1791.
Nov. 28.
mittee submitted their proceedings to general inspection; and then dissolved themselves. The same gentlemen were re-elected, except Mr. Dobbin, and three added to their number, making the committee consist of nine instead of six persons.

Dec. 2. To avail ourselves as much as possible of any information possessed by those subscribers who were not of the committee, and to draw from them any hints or observations which might further our undertaking, they were informed that any objections, proposals, or remarks, which they might wish to make, would be taken into consideration by the committee, if transmitted to their secretary in writing; at the same time it was resolved, " that as soon as a sum should be raised sufficient to enable the society to charter one ship, and purchase a sloop, together with the necessary provisions, ammunition, &c. for the maintenance of forty families, and other indispensable articles of equipment, the vessels should be procured, and proceed, without delay, to the intended settlement."

5th. Fears having arisen in the minds of some of the subscribers, that they might become responsible for any debts which the committee might contract in establishing the intended settlement, it was resolved that no money could be borrowed for that purpose, nor debt contracted, without the consent of every individual subscriber.

20th. The time for receiving subscriptions was extended from the 20th to the last day of December for settlers* of the highest
21st. class of subscription only; and on the 21st a new committee was chosen for three weeks; which was chiefly employed in

---

* It was afterwards extended to the 25th of February, and subscriptions of twenty pounds received for 250 acres.—See Proposals, Appendix No. I.

drawing up a few plain and practical regulations for our government; in the mean time Mr. Dalrymple had, at the solicitation of many respectable inhabitants of Manchester, gone to that town to receive subscriptions and explain our views, and a correspondence was entered into by the committee in London, with one appointed by the subscribers in Manchester, on the general interests of the intended undertaking. 1791.
Dec. 21.

Another general meeting was held on the 13th January, when a new committee was chosen consisting of thirteen instead of nine members. Notice was given at Lloyd's Coffee-house, that the committee was ready to receive proposals for chartering five hundred tons of shipping and upwards; and two professional men were employed to search in the river for a small vessel, which it was the intention of the committee to purchase, and sail to the coast of Africa to answer the double purpose of a packet and a trading vessel.—It was also determined that, (as government ought to be officially apprized of the intention of this society to make their intended settlement on the coast of Africa,) a deputation of the committee should wait upon the minister, at any time that he might be pleased to appoint for that purpose. 1792.
Jan. 13.

18th.

The opinion of counsel having been taken upon the point of the responsibility of the absentee subscribers for any debt or loss that may be incurred by the joint adventurers in the undertaking; and it being decided (by the opinion of Sir John Scott, at that time solicitor-general) that such responsibility did attach to them in the case of their having any concern whatever in the purchase or sale of any joint investment, and in several other cases stated in that opinion—

1792. It was resolved,

Jan. 18. "That such gentlemen who have been hitherto denominated absentee subscribers, being desirous of getting rid of all possible responsibility on account of any debt or loss that may be incurred by this association, shall be considered only as purchasers of land, (with all the contingencies already agreed to concerning land,) from the persons going out as settlers."*

21st. The subscriptions were called in—two ships chartered, a cutter † purchased, and the committee divided into several separate ones for the purpose of expediting the purchasing of provisions, stores, plantation tools, and every thing that was thought essential to the success of our enterprize. It was agreed that besides the one ton which every subscribing settler was entitled to for his baggage, he should be allowed, if married, another for his wife, and that half a ton should be allowed for every child, apprentice, servant, yeoman, or labourer.

26th. A deputation having waited upon the Right Hon. William Pitt to state to him our views and intentions, they were told that government had no objection to our proceeding in the enterprize.

Feb. 2. On Thursday February the 2d, a general meeting was held

---

* The following gentlemen were appointed trustees to receive, and grant receipts for the subscription money.

Mr. Aldermen Le Mesurier.	Messrs. Harrison.
Messrs. Hartwell.	Ximenes.
Dickenson.	Wilson, and
	Clutterbuck.

† The Calypso of 298 tons burthen, for six months, at 10s. per ton per month—and the Hankey of 261 tons burthen for six or nine months, at £150 per month—and the cutter Beggar's Benison, a Gravesend boat, of 34 tons.

African Memoranda. 9

at the Globe Tavern, when the resolutions of the committee, since the last general meeting, were read and approved. The constitution which had been drawn up, and discussed at various times in the committee, was then approved, and ordered to be printed and engrossed; and the legislative council, for the first three years from the day of landing in the colony, was then elected, consisting of the following gentlemen— 1792 Feb. 2.

Mr. Dalrymple.
Mr. Young.
Sir Wm. Halton, Bart.
Mr. King.
Mr. Dobbin.
Mr. Beaver.
Mr. Upton.*

Mr. Paiba.
Mr. Ximenes.
Mr. Drake.
Mr. Hancorne.*
Mr. Clutterbuck, and
Mr. Brodie,

Who immediately elected Mr. Dalrymple for their governor, and Mr. Young for their lieutenant-governor:—although we were about sailing with the knowledge and approbation of ministers, yet, without any charter, or having any person among us appointed by government, the owners of the ships, which we had chartered, began to be apprehensive of their being liable to seizure by a foreign power, against which contingency, the council became sureties to their full value; and further to exonerate the purchasers of land, or absentee subscribers, from becoming liable to a joint responsibility with the settlers, on account of any debt they might contract; the following advertisement was published in the Gazette, and several newspapers, viz.

* Lieutenants in the R. Navy.—Mr. Upton did not go out, and was succeeded in the council by Mr. Bayly.

1792.
Feb. 9.

Bulam Settlement.

Notice is hereby given, that the *subscribing settlers* to the colony about to be established on the island of Bulam, on the coast of Africa, are alone responsible for any articles purchased, and expences incurred by the said association; and that all others having any concern in the business, are solely purchasers of land from the settlers, and in no way liable to any responsibility whatever. It is likewise hereby intimated that the said subscribing settlers to the aforesaid colony, do not intend to have any dealing upon credit, or any joint commercial concerns, beyond the amount of the first investment; and all parties whom it may concern, are hereby desired not to advance any goods, or to give any kind of credit to any persons whatever, in the name, and upon the faith of the said association.

J. Heriot, Secretary.

No. 103, *Hatton Garden, Feb.* 9, 1792.

22d. A surgeon was appointed with a salary of sixty pounds per annum, and a grant of 500 acres of land; and an assistant surgeon with a salary of thirty pounds and 250 acres;* instruments and medicines to be found by the colony.

29th. By this time almost all the stores, &c. were purchased, and most of them shipped; one thousand pounds worth of goods and provisions, were insured in each of the two ships, to the island of Bulama, or any other place on, or near the coast of Africa, with liberty to touch at different ports in the way,

---

* Encreased afterwards to 500 acres. The salary certainly very small, but as much as our funds were equal to.

for three months; and the cutter was insured to the amount of four hundred pounds for twelve months.

<small>1792. March 5.</small>

Subscribers of every description were permitted to carry out two servants, and one additional one, for every 500 acres of land subscribed for, after the first.

Some of the subscribers appearing to be turbulent, discontented people, the council returned them their subscription money, and erased their names from the list of subscribers.

<small>6th.</small>

The constitution was this day signed by every person who intended to become a settler.*

<small>9th</small>

The committee which had been appointed to examine, and finally accept, or reject those persons who had offered themselves to go out as labourers to the association, agreeable to the terms of the proposals, made their report, by which it appeared that they had accepted 28 men, 13 of whom had wives; and that they had altogether 29 children.

<small>10th</small>

A surveyor was appointed on the same terms as the surgeon, and an assistant surveyor† on the same terms as the assistant surgeon.

<small>12th.</small>

Every thing being now nearly on board, and the vessels reported ready to drop down the river, the labourers were embarked on the morn of the 21st but it was the eve of the 26th before the Hankey sailed for Gravesend, when those members of the council and subscribers, who had not already embarked were to meet there, and instantly proceed on the voyage.

<small>21st.</small>

<small>26th.</small>

The trustees having been originally appointed to receive the

---

* See Appendix, Nº II.

† Lieutenant Yates of the R. Navy who did not go out.—The surgeon and assistant surgeon engaged to remain two years on the island, (their health permitting it) or forfeit their land.

1792.
March 26

subscriptions, and to pay the tradesmen their bills, which being now finished, their office of course ceased; it was judged expedient therefore to give the same gentlemen,* who had been extremely active and zealous in forwarding the enterprize, full power and authority to manage our concerns and act for us in England.

The ships were now at Gravesend, almost every person on board, and all of them anxiously waiting the order for departure, which was expected every moment, when an event took place, which, as it was totally unexpected, threw a considerable gloom over all their minds.

As a respectful representation of the intentions of the society had been submitted to the prime minister, at an early period of our association, and received his sanction, it had been hoped that all our subsequent proceedings had been equally satisfactory to government, nor was any individual concerned, at all aware that they were otherwise; when, on our arrival at Gravesend, the ships were prohibited from proceeding by an order from the secretary of state.

The rainy season on the coast of Africa was fast approaching, the daily expences of the ships enormous, when compared with our funds,† and the cause of our detention unknown: a few days therefore were of the utmost importance to us, as the least delay of our sailing threatened ruin to the enterprize.

31st. Under these circumstances it was deemed expedient to present a memorial to government, and the following was immediately

---

* Messrs. Alderman Le Mesurier, Col. Kirkpatrick, Geo. Hartwell, and Moses Ximenes, to whom were afterwards added Sir John Riggs Millar, Bart. and David Scott, M. P.

† About twenty-five pounds a day.

presented to the Right Honourable Henry Dundas, one of his Majesty's principal secretaries of state.

1792.
March 31

The Memorial of the undersigned traders and others his Majesty's subjects:

Sheweth,

" That your Memorialists have received information that the coast of Africa adjacent to the river Grande is very healthy, the soil rich, and abundant in all tropical productions, and that the inhabitants are of a peaceable disposition, well inclined towards the English nation, and extremely desirous to open an amicable intercourse for the purchase of English merchandise, and the sale of their own commodities, and that for this purpose the said inhabitants are willing to sell to such British subjects as are disposed to settle in their neighbourhood, some of the islands situated at the mouth of the said river, and other lands on the coast which are uninhabited by themselves, and are not in the possession of any European power.

" That your Memorialists being persuaded that a colony may be established, and a trade carried on upon the said coast of Africa in a manner very beneficial to themselves and advantageous to the parent state; have, with the assistance of some voluntary subscriptions, fitted up two ships, the Calypso of 298 tons, and the Hankey of 260 tons; and the sloop Beggars Benison of 34 tons; which they have fully supplied with British merchandise to a very considerable amount, and that your memorialists are preparing to embark with their families in order to proceed to the said coast of Africa.

" That your memorialists have it in contemplation on their arrival upon the said coast of Africa, with a view to lay the foundation of a permanent settlement on the said coast, there to cultivate sugar, cotton, indigo, and other productions of the torrid zone, and to establish a commerce on honourable and advantageous terms for the British nation, to purchase of the native chiefs of Africa, the island Bulam or such other island, or lands on the coast, as the said natives shall be willing to sell, and which shall be found eligible for the intended settlement: the primary object in which being cultivation, not commerce, your memorialists, far from wishing any exclusive privilege in trade, declare it to be their desire that all British subjects may be free to trade thereto, as well as themselves.

" That your Memorialists promise and engage, that they will conduct themselves in making the intended purchase, and in their traffic with the natives, in a just and orderly manner, and as good subjects, and that they will strictly conform to the laws of Great Britain, and of his Majesty's government; and that all purchases of land which they may succeed in, shall be made for, and in the name of his Majesty, as sovereign thereof, but at their own expences and costs, and that as soon as any such purchase is made, your Memorialists will lay the same, and a full detail of their proceedings before his Majesty's ministers.

" That your Memorialists in order to carry the said plan into execution, have appointed Messrs. Henry Hew Dalrymple, John Young, Sir William Halton, bart., John King, Philip Beaver, Peter Clutterbuck, Nicholas Bayley, Francis Brodie, Charles Drake, John Paiba, Richard Hancorne, Robert Dobbin, and Isaac Ximenes, to conduct and manage their affairs, and they have also appointed Messrs. Paul Le Mesurier, James Kirkpatrick, George Hartwell and Moses Ximenes, of London, a committee to correspond with your memorialists and to be entrusted with their concerns in England. *1792. March 31*

"Your Memorialists humbly submit the above plan to your consideration, trusting that their conduct in carrying the same into execution, will merit the favour and protection of government; and at the same time pray, that as they are at a great daily expence with the ships, and the proper season for going on the coast of Africa is fast elapsing, you will be pleased to take this memorial into consideration."

On application we received permission to move the ships round to Portsmouth, which had been fixed upon as the place where we were all to rendezvous prior to our final departure from England, and there wait the issue of our memorial.

The Hankey therefore sailed from Gravesend on the evening of the 4th, and the following one anchored in the Downs, where having left a code of signals* to be delivered to the Calypso and Beggars Benison on their arrival there; we proceeded the next day on our way to Portsmouth. *April 4.*

The two days employed in this passage were usefully devoted to the arranging of the births, sleeping, and mess places of the colonists on board the Hankey, which was no very pleasant, nor easy task, as is well known to those who have witnessed the uneasiness, and consequent dissatisfaction, of those who for the first time have found themselves crowded into the narrow space, necessarily resulting from many persons being confined within the limits of a single ship. However, *6th.*

---

* The direction of every thing on board the Hankey was committed to my care:—on board the Calypso, to that of Lieutenant Hancorne, and on board the Beggars Benison to Lieutenant Dobbin, both of the Royal Navy.

1792.
April 6.

as justice and impartiality, had entirely governed my conduct, though few were satisfied, none could find out that he had less room than his neighbour, and therefore could not encrease it without the injustice of diminishing that of some other person, which at length reconciled every one to his lot.

7th. The morning after we had left the Downs, to our great surprize and mortification, we discovered that we had the small-pox on board, it had been brought into the ship by an infant child of one of the labourers, whose mother, unwilling to part from her husband, and knowing that she would not have been received if it had been known that her child was infected with that dangerous disorder, had carefully concealed it from our knowledge, till it this day made its appearance in the child of another labourer.

Every precaution was immediately taken to prevent its spreading; those infected were separated from the rest of the colonists, the number of those who had not had the small pox ascertained, and our surgeon ordered to inoculate all those who were willing to undergo that operation.

This woman and her child had now been embarked 19 days; it was therefore thought useless to turn them out of the ship, as it was supposed that in that time the seeds of all the danger to be apprehended had already taken root; and although her inconsiderate, and almost inhuman conduct, in knowingly and intentionally bringing such a contagious and dangerous malady into a crowded ship, might have sacrificed the lives of many on board it, and indeed have entirely frustrated the undertaking; although, I say, such conduct might have justified rather harsh measures towards her on the part of the council, yet, as the danger was irremediable, except by preventive and cautious measures, and as it arose from what had already, and not from what would hereafter take place, the feelings of an affectionate wife, about to be separated from a husband whom she fondly loved, and from children in whom she lived, were suffered to have due weight on their minds. It was seen that a knowledge of the child's having this disease would inevitably have separated its agonized mother from either it or her husband, both equally dreaded by her; to avoid then the anguish of such a separation, she had been induced, thus furtively, to introduce this disease. It was a crime committed by feeling; it was a crime that might be committed by a virtuous, but that could not have been committed by a completely vicious character; she therefore with her child, was permitted to remain on board.

On the 8th we arrived at the Motherbank, and the two following days were employed in regulating the internal discipline of the Hankey, and recommending to the colonists the observation of such rules and measures, as, it was conceived, would contribute to the safety of the ship, and the health of those on board it.*

The Beggar's Benison joined us on the 9th, and the following day the Calypso, when the anxiety, and state of uncertainty which we had all experienced for some days, was at length terminated by our obtaining permission to sail, in the following reply to our memorial.

* The surgeon was ordered to keep a journal of the diseases of the people under his care, and of their treatment; and to send to the council a daily report of the sick, both according to the forms observed by the surgeons in his Majesty's Royal Navy.

D

African Memoranda.

Whitehall, 6th April, 1792.

GENTLEMEN,

I am directed by Mr. Secretary Dundas to acquaint you that, under the circumstances stated in your memorial to him, dated the 31st March last, and your having disclaimed and set aside a certain printed memorandum of agreement, and constitution* of government for a colony about to be established on or near the island of Bulam, in Africa, as engrossed and signed on the 9th day of March, 1792; he has no further objection to the departure of the ships destined for the services stated in your memorial above-mentioned.

I am, Gentlemen,
Your most obedient humble servant,
JOHN KING.

*To the Trustees for the
Bulam Association.*

Although this reply relieved us from much anxiety, and left us at liberty to pursue our projected enterprize, yet it produced much uneasiness in the minds of the members of the council, who now, for the first time, learned what it was that had given offence to government: they were told that printing the constitution was a high misdemeanour, and that they thereby had rendered themselves liable to severe punishment; that wherever they should make their settlement, there the laws of England attached; and that without an act of parliament, they had no authority to make bye-laws. No

---

* See Appendix, No. II.

criminal intentions, however, were attributed to them; it _{1792.} was admitted, very truly, that they had erred through ignorance, _{April 10.} and had not wantonly or intentionally incurred the imputation of guilt.* They were sufficiently punished however for their ignorance, for they were reduced to the necessity of either giving up the enterprize, or sailing without having any legal restraint on a class of people who, from the very nature of things, peculiarly required it. Nine thousand pounds had already been expended in the equipment of the vessels, and the purchase of stores and provisions that were thought essential to the success of the undertaking. Had it now been given up, a great part of that money would be entirely lost, and the subscribers deceived, who had paid it on the faith at least of the settlement being attempted. Although it was much apprehended that we should not succeed from our want of legal power to impose any restraint upon the conduct of individuals, however necessary it might appear, yet there were not two opinions on the propriety of sailing; we had gone too far to recede; and, ever ready to seize the most favourable point of view in which their favourite object could be seen, all who were embarked seemed impatient of delay, and anxious for the moment of departure.

Orders were therefore given for taking up the anchor, and on 11th, the 11th we got under sail, but the wind soon after dying away we anchored again in the evening off Yarmouth, in the Isle of Wight.

* It must be remembered that this constitution which will probably now be viewed with an evil eye, was drawn up at the latter end of the year 1791, and before the revolutionary monster had begun to devour every thing that could claim kindred with virtue. Though the crimes of the next ten years make one shudder at every thing which tends to give power to a democratic rabble, yet, I believe, if this constitution had been printed three years sooner, or if a late revolution had not taken place, it would not have been found fault with.

1792.
April 11. At noon this day Mrs. Riches, the wife of one of the labourers, who had brought the small pox on board, was delivered of a girl, and at 11 at night the infant son of Hugh Meares, another labourer, died of that dreadful disorder.

Prior to our getting under sail this morning it was agreed that if either of the vessels should part company by stress of weather, or from any other cause, it should proceed to the bay of Santa Cruz, in the island of Teneriffe, and there await an indefinite time the arrival of the other vessels.

12th.
13th. Calms prevented the ships moving till late in the evening of the 12th, and early the next morning they were all safe through the Needles, and beating down channel with very fine weather, but adverse winds.

While at the Motherbank one person had deserted from the Calypso, four had been discharged from the Hankey at their own request, and four others it was found absolutely necessary to discharge from the same ship on account of their very turbulent and improper conduct, which leaves the whole number of colonists at present embarked 275, as follows:—

	Men.	Women.	Children.	Total.
In the Calypso	83	33	33	149
Hankey	65	24	31*	120
Beggar's Benison	5		1	6
	153	57	65	275†

* One had died and another had been born.   † See Appendix, No. III.

CHAPTER II.

Proceedings of the Colonists from their leaving England to their arrival in the Bijuga* Channel on the Coast of Africa.

THE wind, which had changed to the westward as soon as we had got through the Needles, became fair the next morn, and increasing gradually to a stiff breeze, enabled us to clear the Channel on the evening of the 15th, when Sophia Ford, a girl who had died the preceding day of a decline, was committed to the deep. The next day we lost sight of the Beggar's Benison in the morn, and although in every consideration it was highly desirable that the ships should continue together during their passage, yet, from a very unaccountable inattention on board the Calypso, that ship parted from us in the following night. {1792. April 13. 14th. 15th. 16th.}

As the weather was very fine, and the Calypso had the advantage of the Hankey in sailing, no blame whatever could be attached to the master of the latter ship, the Calypso was lost sight of indeed almost in the wind's eye, so that it was ever in her power to bear down upon, and close with the Hankey.

The wind had hitherto been very moderate, but on the 19th it increased so much as to produce a sea which was very inconvenient to those unaccustomed to it, and the consequence {19th. 20th.}

---

* This is called in our charts the Bissao's entrance, and the islands on the south side of it are called in them the Bissago's islands; but adhering to the native pronunciation I call the latter the Bijuga islands, and the former the Bijuga channel.

1792.
April 20.

was that most of the landmen, and all the women were sea sick; the latter, some of whom had infants at the breast, had been more than 24 hours without nourishment of any kind, and would have been so much longer if I had not undertaken to cook for them; for some, who would have relieved them if able, were labouring under the same disease; and the surgeon, whose more immediate duty it was to attend to them, was wholly destitute of feeling; he left to those, who had folly enough to feel, the charge of taking care of his patients; this certainly was not a very dignified employment, it was at least a useful one, and had I not undertaken it these poor women might have suffered much from hunger ere any other would have relieved them. I had already been employed since our sailing in functions equally low, and therefore was in some degree prepared for it; but at times I was compensated for the meanness of these employments by the exercise of authority pertaining to more dignified posts, for I verily believe that there is not an office or gradation of rank in naval service, from the admiral and commander in chief down to the jack of the bread room, which I had not already exercised in this ship. The fact is, that to govern and maintain order and regularity amongst a licentious rabble, without any legal power, was an exceedingly difficult task, and only to be accomplished by example. I soon perceived that I must either give up the point, which threatened ruin to the undertaking, or accomplish it by the constant exercise of unremitting exertions; the latter was most congenial to my mind, and therefore there was no employment however humble in the general opinion of the world which I hesitated to undertake; but, having once done this, I ordered whom I pleased afterwards to perform the same duty, and the consequence was, that from the sailing of the expedition to the final abandoning of the island, I was never more cheerfully, willingly, nor implicitly obeyed, when armed with the authority of martial power, than I was by the members who were embarked in this undertaking.

1792.
April 20.

We had now been long enough together to enable me to form some opinion of the probability of our success, from the general conduct and character of the colonists. I had from the first conceived that we had great exertions to make, and many difficulties to overcome before we could succeed in the establishment of a new colony; but at the same time thought that the exertions of every individual, being directed to the same end, would eventually insure our success; and not till I had been a week at sea, with this motley assemblage of unthinking mortals, was I convinced that those hopes which rested on the disinterested energy of individuals must be for ever given up: not that we had not any one on board the Hankey calculated for the expedition which we had undertaken; we certainly had some, but their number was small, very small indeed, when compared to all that were embarked.

Among some of those who had the direction of the enterprize, a constant attention to their own individual interest, and an entire neglect of that of the public; among others of them a total indifference to both; and a general apathy in all towards the adoption of such measures as would contribute to our success, left little ground for hope; added to which the general conduct of the subscribers was not such as to afford to the labourers an example of severe morality.

On Sunday morning prayers were read by a member of the council to the assembled colonists.

22d.

1792.
April 29.

The surgeon having reported every one well who had been infected with the small pox,* great care was taken to wash with vinegar, and then to smoke the cloaths worn, and places occupied by all who had been affected, or who had attended those that had been affected with it.

The public and private servants, accustomed to a life of labour, have had since their embarkation no employment to fill up their time; and this, the greatest misfortune that can happen to any one, produced in them such a rage for gaming, that many of them had really lost, not only all the land which they were to receive at a certain time, but even all their cloaths, except those which they wore. To put a stop to this eternal card playing, and arrest its pernicious effects, it was judged expedient to paste up the following notice in several of the most public places of the ship :—

" The members of the council on board the Hankey observe with much concern the prevalence of the idle practice of gaming, reprehensible in all cases, but in our situation eminently pernicious, as it has a direct tendency to the dissolution of all industry, frugality, good order, and good morals; without sedulous attention to the practice of which virtues, an infant colony cannot subsist, much less thrive.

" Those to whom the protection of others is confided would be wanting in their duty were they not to do all in their power to repress the progress of such an alarming evil, they therefore with this admonition give notice,

" That no play debts or wagers shall ever be recoverable either at the islands where we may stop in our passage, or at

---

* Six in number, besides the boy Meares who died in Yarmouth Road.

the place where we may finally settle: but on the contrary we promise full indemnity to the loser, and advise him to withhold payment."

Hankey, 29th April, 1792.

The next day land was discovered at a considerable distance to the westward, which was judged, from our reckoning, to be the island of Teneriffe; the wind, continuing to blow from it for the next three days, prevented our approaching very near to it before the 3d of May, when we discovered that an easterly current had carried us about 4 degrees to the eastward of our reckoning, and that the land which we had been in sight of for these four days was the island of Fuertaventura, not of Teneriffe as was at first imagined, so that we had in fact run between the former of those islands and the continent of Africa, instead of having gone to the westward, or outside of it.

All ships, I believe, in sailing from Great-Britain to the Canary Isles, are found to be to the eastward of their reckoning; this error in reckoning, being always the same way, may be easily and naturally accounted for by the constant influx of the waters of the Atlantic into the Mediterranean Sea; the effects of which must necessarily operate to a considerable extent beyond our tract.

The wind continuing westerly, the ship could not weather the island of Grand Canaria, which must necessarily be done before we could get to Teneriffe, where we expected to rejoin the Calypso; and making no progress in beating, it was thought advisable to anchor in the road of this island, where, during the continuance of the adverse winds, we might get refreshments for the colonists, many of whom, particularly the women

1792.
May 5.

and children of the labourers, stood in great need of them; and we should, at the same time, be completing our water, which would render it unnecessary for us to stay long at Teneriffe, whenever a favourable wind might enable us to get there. With this view then we brought too a fishing boat, hoping to procure a pilot from it, but were much surprized at all the persons in it refusing to pilot us to an anchorage; as we certainly were not gaining ground, and might be driven further off, if the wind increased, while the majority of the colonists were living on salt provisions only, which if continued would be doubtless very prejudicial to their healths, it was an object of magnitude to anchor where we could procure for them the necessary refreshments; it was therefore determined to stand well in with the land, and then send the jolly boat on shore to endeavour to procure a pilot. This task, like all others, devolved upon me.

I had witnessed in the West-Indies and in South America, in two remarkable instances, to what acts of injustice towards British seamen Spanish governors had been led by the narrow policy of their jealous government. I knew not whether the same rigorous policy was adopted in these islands towards foreigners, as in their more western colonies; but I certainly expected to be imprisoned if I landed, and said so before I left the ship. However, as it was absolutely requisite for the preservation of the healths of the colonists, that we should get into

---

* The labourers, having no fresh stock of their own, lived entirely upon salt provisions, of which they were allowed exactly the same quantity as seamen in his Majesty's navy. Women were allowed the half of a man's allowance—children under 7 years of age one fourth—those between the years of 7 and 12 the allowance of a woman, and above that age the allowance of a man.

port, I did not hesitate to go. Accordingly I left the ship in a little two-oared boat, and as we approached the shore observed a very heavy surf which seemed to bar all hopes of our landing. We however rowed up parallel to it for near an hour, in search of a place where we could with safety push in our little skiff, when seven priests, who had walked along the beach opposite to the boat, and whose curiosity seemed attracted by it, at length waved to us to pull in, which I accordingly did, though in great danger of being swamped, for the surf was high and irregular; but having foreseen the probability of such a circumstance I had selected two men who could swim as well as myself. On landing, about half a mile to the southward of the city of Palmas, these priests, whose astonishment seemed to be much excited by the smallness of the boat, thronged round me, and addressed me, first in Spanish, and afterwards in Latin, in either of which languages I was unable to reply. Having hauled the boat up on the beach, and left the two seamen to take care of it, I walked towards the city accompanied by the priests, and indeed every one we met on the road, for they all turned round and accompanied me, testifying their surprize at our being able to reach the shore. Another priest joined us who spoke French, with whom I entered into conversation. I told him that I had come from the ship in the offing, which was from London bound to the coast of Africa, having a great number of persons on board going to settle a colony there, with an intention of touching at Teneriffe, to join another vessel that had separated from us some days ago: but as the wind was unfavourable, and as we had many women and children on board who stood much in need of refreshment, I had landed to request that the gover-

1792.
May 5. nor would let me take off a pilot to bring the ship to a secure anchorage in this island.

We had by this time approached within a few yards of the city gate, when this priest advised me to stop till the governor had been apprized of my landing. I was going on, intending to go directly to the governor, but he entreated me to stop, observing that if I entered the city I should be put in prison, and not suffered to return to night. Unwilling to be a night from the ship, as those on board would be anxious about the safety of the boat, and unable to pursue their voyage if the wind should become fair without it, I took this good priest's advice, and sat down upon a stone seat by the road; but that the governor might be apprized as early as possible of my being there, I gave a drummer, who was among the crowd, an English half crown to go into the city, and tell the officer of the guard that there was an Englishman in waiting outside of the gate who wanted permission to see the governor.

Having waited more than an hour, and no notice whatever having been taken of my message, I determined to go into the city myself, as the evening was fast approaching, and the ship a considerable distance at sea; my friend the priest advised me not to attempt it; he said he could have no motive whatever in endeavouring to dissuade me from it but my own convenience, for that I should certainly be put in prison if I entered the city gate.

No good could possibly accrue from my remaining where I was; whatever therefore might be the consequence I determined on entering the city, and had just got to the gate when a corporal and four privates came out; and, without saying one word to me, the corporal took hold of my right shoulder, turned me round on my heel, and pointing to the boat marched me towards it. This conduct I thought somewhat rude, but as there was no arguing the point with these gentry, I walked slowly and sullenly on, waiting an occasion of seeing some officer to whom I might represent it. When we arrived at the boat I had expected to remain there with the guard, but they took the two seamen and marched us about a quarter of a mile further to a small square tower on the beach, when unlocking the door they made us enter, and mounting the steps we arrived at the top where there was a large jar of water and a twelve pounder: the door below was locked, and the guard remained on the outside. All this was done without exchanging a single word; indeed words would have been useless, as neither party could have understood the other.

Undeserving of the rank and authority of an officer must that man be who could treat three unarmed men in such a manner; and contemptible must be that nation which could justify or authorize such a conduct. Ignorant why we were confined, or how long we might be so, our attention, in about half an hour, was called towards the city by clouds of dust rising from its nearest gate, and we immediately afterwards perceived a great concourse of people coming towards us: they stopped nearly opposite to our boat, when an interpreter (the captain of the port who spoke very good English) was dispatched to the tower, and we were let out and marched towards this assemblage of persons, whom curiosity, he told us, had drawn from the city, as it was very uncommon for a foreign ship to have communication with this island.

The governor and principal officers formed a line across the

1792.
May 5.

road with the inhabitants in their rear. When we had arrived within about 20 yards of them we were ordered to stop, and the interpreter, placed half way between them and us, was ordered by the governor to ask whence I came, and what I wanted; to which having replied, he said that we should have every refreshment required, but that as the day was far spent I could not receive any thing to night except a pilot, whom he would send with me to bring the ship into port, and that on the morrow whatever I had ordered should be ready; he moreover begged that I would not consider myself as having been a prisoner during the time that I had been shut up in the tower, as that was a measure merely of precaution for my safety; which he otherwise could not have answered for as the inhabitants were unaccustomed to see strangers on the island.

It would have been very difficult for him to have convinced me that I had not been a prisoner, and very unjustly and unworthily treated; but as the great object of my landing was accomplished in his ready compliance with my demands, and as he seemed inclined to explain away the harshness of my reception, I said nothing more on the subject, satisfied with the prospect of receiving essential benefits, without entering into discussions which neither my situation nor circumstances demanded.

My boat was immediately launched by some fisherman, and three pilots were ordered into it, though one was all I asked, with whom I reached the ship about an hour after dark.

It appears singular that the island which gives name to the cluster called the Canaries, which alone of them all has a city, and which till very lately has been the residence of the governor-general, should have so little communication with Europeans, that the arrival of a single ship should produce surprize, and excite curiosity in its inhabitants: this arises from its want of a good anchorage for shipping, which deprives it of all direct commerce with Europe. Its produce and live stock, of which a great deal is reared on the island, is always sent to Santa Cruz in Teneriffe, by small vessels which pass daily between those two islands; so that the merchants of Santa Cruz purchase the whole exported produce of the Grand Canaria, and come in between the productors and the merchants of Europe to the great disadvantage of that island. To which may be added that the governor-general, who formerly resided at Palmas in Canaria, now makes his residence at Santa Cruz in Teneriffe, to the manifest prejudice of the former. A few small craft employed in fishing for their own consumption, on the neighbouring coast of Africa, is the only other trade, if such it can be called, carried on by the inhabitants of this island.

The next morning the wind became favourable, which, as the necessity of anchoring at Canaria was therefore done away, enabled us to sail directly for Teneriffe, and it became necessary to reland the pilots; at the same time it was thought advisable for me to go with them, and explain to the governor the cause of our not anchoring, to thank him for having sent them, and to bring off the refreshments which he had promised should be ready for me in the morning. In doing this no obstacle was foreseen, indeed it was almost impossible to conceive that any difficulties could arise from my going on shore merely to do an act of civility, and which my reception yesterday certainly did not absolutely demand; however I had many to encounter, which, with a little firmness and perseverance, I at last surmounted.

1792.
May 6.

In rowing towards the shore the pilots conducted us to a better place to land at than the one where we had landed yesterday; it was between an opening in a reef of rocks, that in some degree breaks the force of the outer surge before it reaches the beach, and was close to the town. When the boat had just entered this opening, probably twenty yards from the shore, I was much surprized by the sentinel calling to us to keep off, and presenting his piece at us; we instantly pulled short round, but were nearly swamped in so doing by the surfs breaking in upon the side of the boat. The captain of the port was present, and I asked why our landing was opposed? he said that no person could land without permission of the governor. I told him that I only wanted to land the pilots, and return to my ship, as we might lose the favourable wind by delay; but all to no purpose, refusal was persisted in, and we kept the boat's bow to the surf.

I had yesterday observed that the party of soldiers that marched me to the tower, had, instead of flints, only wood in the hammers of their locks, and this led me to examine that of the sentinel on the shore who opposed our landing, which I saw had only wood also, and therefore knew that he could not fire at us, which determined me to land in spite of him; therefore, watching for a good high surf, I took advantage of its almost irresistible force, pulled quickly in, and was left by it instantaneously high and dry upon the beach to the great terror of the astonished sentinel, who, when recovered from his surprize, requested that I would launch my boat again, otherwise he should be punished. I immediately requested the captain of the port to place my boat, myself, and the seamen, under the protection of this sentinel, until I could see the governor, which he readily did.

I had waited near two hours on the beach before the governor appeared, being told that he was at mass (it was Sunday) and would come to me when it was over; at length about noon he made his appearance; the whole town had long since been collected around us. I told him that the motive of my landing was to thank him for the pilots whom I had brought on shore again, no longer wanting them as the wind was favourable to our proceeding immediately to Teneriffe; and, at the same time, to avail myself of his permission to take off the refreshments, for the women and children, which he had yesterday promised I should have for that purpose this morning. He asked for our bill of health which I had not brought on shore, thinking it unnecessary as nothing had been said about it yesterday, and said that he could neither receive back the pilots, nor suffer me to purchase any thing until he had seen it. I assured him that we had not a sick person on board, which was really the case, and hoped he would therefore, in this instance, wave that piece of formality, and suffer me, on the score of humanity, to take off refreshments for the women under any precautions which he thought necessary, as it was easy for us to load the boat without coming in contact with any of the inhabitants; this he positively refused, and said that I should have nothing from the island, and should take back the pilots, for he would not suffer them to return to their families after having been on board our ship. Having for more than an hour endeavoured, without success, to prevail upon him to accede to my request by all the arguments and reasoning in my power, I changed the ground of my application, and said that what I had hitherto solicited as a favour I now demanded as a right; that the ship was in the same situation as one in distress; and that by the usage of all

1792.
May 6.

civilized people, and by the laws of nations, he was bound to relieve us, and that relief could only be administered in supplying us with fresh provisions; that if a ship of his nation, under similar circumstances, was to put into any English port, they would receive what they wanted by paying for it, and that was all I asked, subject to any restrictions he thought proper with respect to the mode of communication; as to the pilots, I would certainly carry them back if he chose. The Spanish governor still persisting in his refusal, I told him that it was immaterial to me whether I spent the next six months on the island of Grand Canaria, or on the coast of Africa, and most likely it would be on the former, for go from the island I certainly would not, unless carried off by force, till my boat was loaded with refreshments for the women, and that he would have to answer for the consequence. Here all argument ceased, and I sat down upon the beach near my boat.

At three o'clock the governor assented to my having whatever I wanted, and my little boat was loaded with fresh meat, vegetables, fruit, bread, milk, chocolate, and milch goats, which were put down on the beach, and the prices declared by the interpreter; the party then retired, and my sailors took the things up and placed them in the boat; the money I put into a basin of vinegar and retired; the interpreter then took it out, and gave it to the proper person, so that in no one time was I ever nearer to any of the natives than five or six yards. During this time one of the pilots had slipped away unperceived, and could not be found, so that I carried back only two of them, and reached the ship again about an hour after dark.

It was certainly an uncommon spectacle to see an unarmed foreigner, in a little boat which two men could carry, six or seven miles from his ship, and that a merchant ship, disputing with the governor of an island who had an armed force at his disposal, and obliging him to acquiesce in all his demands. The natives seemed to think them reasonable enough, and from the first appeared to favour my cause, and showed evident marks of satisfaction at my final success.

1792.
May 6.

The wind continuing fair we anchored in the road of Santa Cruz, in the island of Teneriffe, the following evening, and were much disappointed at not seeing the Calypso there, which we had all expected from our having been so long beating round the Grand Canaria.

7th.

The officers of health were pointed in their questions concerning the small-pox, and we, being happily enabled to say, with truth, that we had it not actually on board, readily obtained permission to land, but the people of the Calypso were not so fortunate.

We learned that she had arrived four days before us, and, on being questioned from the boat, had answered that the smallpox was not on board; Mr. Dalrymple, who was in his cabin at the time, probably from abhorrence of falsehood as well as of apprehensions of its consequences in this instance, took his boat and went on shore to contradict the report, and confess that the ship was actually infested with the small-pox. The event was that he was ordered immediately on board, there to wait the governor's determination, but he chose to weigh anchor, and made sail without further communication, and without leaving us intimation of a second rendezvous.

Had the Calypso remained at Santa Cruz, she would have certainly been made to perform quarantine, and not been suf-

1792.
May 7. fered to have had any communication with the inhabitants, but that would not have precluded the people on board from receiving fresh meat, vegetables, and fruit, or whatever might be conducive to the preservation of their healths, and it would have afforded us an opportunity of proceeding together to the island of Bulama; or even if any other rendezvous had been assigned before her sailing, that desirable event might have yet been accomplished: but this unaccountable and precipitate departure led to an event which had a lasting and serious effect on the minds of the colonists.

8th. The next day the Beggar's Benison arrived, and on the 11th a Liverpool vessel, whose master said that he had been on the island of Bulama, and professed being a pilot for that part of the coast. On questioning him on the subject we thought it highly expedient to engage him as a pilot. He agreed to precede us with his own vessel, and we were to give him thirty-four pounds sterling on our anchoring at Bulama.

It was judged eminently conducive to the preservation of the health of our people to serve out fresh meat to them alternate days, and to purchase acid vegetables to prevent a disposition to the scurvy, which might appear during the second stage of our voyage.

We bought also, for culture, seeds of most kinds of corn, and esculent plants, and scions of some frugiferous shrubs and trees, which could not be had in Europe.

12th.
13th. Our water being completed on the 12th, the next day we sailed in company with the Beggar's Benison, and the brig Friendship of Liverpool, which latter vessel was to lead the way into the Bulama channel.

During our stay at Teneriffe every caution had been observed to preserve the health of our people, and we sailed from Santa Cruz without a sick list. *1792. May 13.*

Some irregularities had however been committed by the people necessarily employed on shore, and two or three of them were very properly put in the guard-house, and sent on board the following day, but one of them had been cajoled to enter into a regiment on the island, who had left a wife with a young infant on board, a representation being made to the governor that we considered it as a violation of the laws of nations to entrap foreigners, who put into their ports in passing to their place of destination, he was given up, and sent back to his distressed wife.

Notwithstanding the hasty departure of the Calypso from Santa Cruz, we yet hoped to meet with her at the island of St. Jago, whither it was determined to proceed, not only on that account, but also to procure stock for the colony; and as the Liverpool brig was consigned to a merchant at St. Nicholas, an adjacent island in the same cluster, we consented to accompany it thither, on the condition that our vessels should not be detained there more than forty-eight hours, and that the same time should be waited for us afterwards at St. Jago.

On the 20th, the three vessels anchored in the road of Paraghuo, on the south side of St. Nicholas; where, learning that the brig would be detained three days instead of two as stipulated, the Hankey and cutter sailed the next morning for Port Praya, where we anchored on the 23d. *20th. 21st. 23d.*

On the 26th the Friendship arrived, but having unfortunately beat a hole in its bottom, by running on a sunken rock, was *26th.*

1792.
May 26.

disabled from proceeding farther, and the instruments of obligation were cancelled.*

The time that was judged necessary for the two vessels to wait for their consort at Port Praya, was occupied in filling the water casks and refreshing the people. The Hankey and cutter having waited for the Calypso five days, it was deemed expedient for them to proceed; but as the principal object of touching at St. Jago was to procure stock for the colony, the members of the council on board, fearing that the Calypso would not have an opportunity of doing so at any port between Praya and Bulama, thought proper to purchase twice the quantity that they would have done, had the Calypso had the same opportunity of supply.

This determination however could not be carried into effect without more room than they were hitherto possessed of, and the captain readily concurred with the proposed measure of rigging and sailing his long boat for the rest of the voyage, to accommodate the cattle on the ship's deck.

This was also a prudent step, as a measure of precaution, for we were about to enter an unknown channel of near fifty leagues in length, bordered in its whole southern extent by a long chain of sand banks, and of islands scarcely known by name; and on its northern side by islands better known it is true, but by shoals of whose position we were equally ignorant.

---

* This in the end was a favourable circumstance for us, for the master of this vessel, to compensate for his not being able to attend us, gave me written instructions for knowing the island of Bulama, and approaching it by soundings, by which I afterwards discovered that he had mistaken the Bullam shore on the north side of the entrance of the river Sierra Leone, for the island of Bulama at the mouth of the Rio Grande, very near three degrees to the northward of it.

It was determined therefore that the cutter and this long boat should precede us half a mile, on either bow, after our entrance into this channel, and make known their soundings by signal.

1792.
May 26.

The long boat was accordingly hoisted out and rigged, and we signed an obligation to indemnify the captain of the ship in case of her loss in this extra service. The command of her was given to Mr. J. W. Paiba, who applied for it, and four other volunteers, who were competent to this duty, assisted in navigating her.

Having bought for public labour, and for public stock, two bullocks, four asses, two goats, and two sheep, male and female, and two dozen of poultry; and after calculating the space in the ship, having allowed to subscribers, for their consumption, four fowls and one sheep among every four persons, and for breeding six fowls and one goat and kid, or one sheep, we weighed anchor, and proceeded on our voyage with the cutter and long boat, on the evening of the 28th. The remainder of the voyage was retarded by the circumstance of our being obliged to shorten sail, to enable the long boat to keep company with us, when it blew fresh; and, although we had a fair wind all the way, we did not make Cape Roxo till the 3d of June, and the same evening anchored in the Bijuga channel.

28th.

June 3.

We proceeded, having the small craft constantly a-head, and anchoring at dusk, until the morning of the 5th, when we at length anchored in sight of the three islands of Bissao, Arcas, and Bulama; judging it imprudent to proceed farther without some knowledge of the channel; the captain of the ship and myself left the Hankey and Beggar's Benison at an anchor, and went in the long boat to explore it.

June 5.

Having discovered two vessels at an anchor at Bissao, we were proceeding towards that place to endeavour to procure a pilot,

1792.
June 5.

when one of them, a brig, got under sail, and ran down to join us; it was an American, commanded by one Moore, endeavouring to procure a cargo of slaves; he advised us by all means to return with him to Bissao, where he said we should get a pilot, and whatever else we wanted. We learned from him that a strange ship, which had created some alarm in the Portuguese factory at Bissao, had been about ten days in the Bulama channel, apparently ignorant of it, and at a loss to know where she was; that he had endeavoured to speak her with his brig, and had got under weigh for that purpose some days ago, when, to his surprize, she made all sail, and he could not come up with her; that he had not seen any thing of her since, but on Sunday last had heard the report of a great many heavy guns in the direction of Bulama, which he doubted not proceeded from that ship.

We were well assured that this was really the Calypso, and were anxious not to lose time in rejoining her.

An hour before dark we landed with Mr. Moore at the Portuguese factory at Bissao, and were surprized to find a regular square fort with four bastions, and apparently, for we were not permitted to go round the works, about fifty guns mounted.

The strange conduct of the former ship in avoiding communication with this place, and our appearance so soon afterwards in a channel where they were not accustomed to see any square rigged vessels, except their own four annual ones, produced distrust, as well as surprize, in the minds of the Portuguese, and they actually took us for pirates. The consequence was that we were all made prisoners; and thus, though at peace with all the world, have I been once imprisoned by the Spaniards, and once by the Portuguese during this short voyage.

An appearance of embarrassment and mystery, on the part of the governor and Mr. Moore, so incompatible with the simple integrity of plain dealing, induced me, from the first, to suspect what would happen.

1792.
June 5.

The governor had readily promised us a pilot, but said that he could not procure one before the next morning, when I told him that we would then go away without one, as the people on board would be anxious for our safety; he refused to let us depart, the long boat was taken possession of, and we were lodged for the night in an empty room adjoining the guard: in vain I urged that this conduct of his was a violation of the laws of hospitality as well as of nations, and that to imprison the subjects of a power in amity with the queen his mistress, was a measure unknown to civilized nations. He replied that though he had detained us we were not prisoners, to which I answered that that was talking like a blockhead. However, if we are to be detained said I, we look to you for the security of our boat, and every thing which it contains, and we moreover expect of you two things. What are those, said he? "First, that you send us a good supper for we are hungry, and secondly, that you send us beds for we are weary and fatigued:" these he readily promised, and he did not deceive us. The next morning a soldier came for the captain of the ship; but none others were to attend him. This however was refused, and we declared that we would all go to the governor, or none; then sallying out together we were not opposed, and went in a body to a merchant's house where the governor was attending the arrival of the captain: here we had a violent altercation; he insisted that the captain of the Hankey should go back to the ship, accompa-

1792.
June 6.

nied by a Portuguese officer to examine his papers, and learn the object of our destination; to which I objected, as a measure which he had no authority to take, that I had already voluntarily made him acquainted with our views and our motives; that he could learn nothing more from our papers; and that I would not from compulsion, if I were captain of the ship, show him one of them. "Then, Sir, said he, if you were captain of the ship I would put both your legs in irons;" to which I replied " that he certainly had the power, but that he durst not exercise it;" "that as to myself, the expedition would go on just as well without me; and that it was perfectly immaterial to me whether I passed my time in the Brazils, which I had no objection to see, and where I supposed he might send me, or at Bulama; that he would not be able to keep me there much beyond a year, when a dreadful responsibility would await him." "How comes it, says he, that you who are not the captain of the ship talk so much, and give your opinion so freely while he is silent? Who are you that you thus assume so much?" "I am, in part, owner of that ship's cargo, and therefore authorized to advise the captain; but I am not a merchant, I never was, and never shall be one. Although in this jacket and trowsers, I am a British naval officer, accustomed to respect, and not to be intimidated by your unwarrantable and unjustifiable conduct. It was at length determined that I should be detained as a hostage, and the boat sent back to the ship with a Portuguese officer to examine her papers, which being complied with * they were promised every assistance.

---

* As there appeared no reason to refuse it, said the members of the council. Now

The half savage conduct of the governor was contrasted by that of Mr. de Sylva Cordoza, a principal merchant of Bissao, in whose house the preceding altercation had taken place; who, when the long boat was gone, begged I would consider his house as my own. He not only then, but ever after, treated me with great kindness and friendship, and to him I was indebted for many comforts during my residence on the island of Bulama.*

---

there was reason to refuse it, because the Portuguese had no right to demand it. We were pursuing our voyage whither we had a right to go, and not interfering nor intending to interfere with any settlement of theirs or of any other power; we had not committed any act of hostility against any nation whatever, and if we had, it was their business to prove it, and not ours; the onus lay with them, and not with us; therefore I would have refused shewing any papers. But, moreover, having sent a boat accidentally to their port to seek a pilot, and claim the privileges of hospitality, and of the laws of nations, did they not violate both by seizing the boat and imprisoning our people? therefore I would have refused. But is there nothing like national dignity? and had not this been wounded by their conduct? had any reparation been made? No. Therefore I would have refused—but it must be, though reluctantly, confessed that the majority of the members of the council had no idea of national dignity—and they at this time were less likely to make difficulties, as they had just received a piece of intelligence of which I was yet ignorant, which struck terror into the whole colony.

* The indolence and the ignorance of the Portuguese is astonishing. After supper Mr. Cordoza and another merchant had an argument about the position of Sierra Leone, that is whether it was on this side or the other of the Scarcies; which appearing not likely to be terminated, I asked for a bit of charcoal, and, being brought, traced with it upon the white washed wall the coast, with all its openings, from Cape Roxo to the Bananas; this decided the question but produced astonishment. " You have been much upon this coast," said they, " to have so intimate a knowledge of it?" " I never was here before," I replied. " But you must have very good pilots on board for this part." " We have not one individual in the ship that ever was on the coast of Africa before." " How then did you find the way up this channel? our own ships never attempt that without a pilot." " By means of our lead and constant attention to soundings." " Well," said they, " it must be admitted that you surpass all nations in naval skill."

1792.
June 6.
7th

The officer, who had been sent to the Hankey, returned in the night, the fears of the Portuguese governor were dissipated, and I was suffered to return to my ship early the next morning; I found that the Calypso had joined her consorts the preceding day, having experienced an event calamitous to the individuals immediately concerned, discouraging to their associates, and injurious though not fatal to the welfare of the colony. At this time there were not any sick on board the Hankey.

CHAPTER III.

Summary of the Calypso's Proceedings from the Time of her Separation to her rejoining the Hankey.

IT has been already related that the Calypso separated from us on the night between the 16th and 17th of April, and had arrived at Santa Cruz, the place of rendezvous, on the 4th day of May, from which latter place Mr. Dalrymple immediately sailed, on account of the small-pox being on board, without leaving for us any intimation of a second rendezvous, or his future intentions. At this time they had buried one man, David Cook, a labourer, who died of a consumption, and one child, Mary Williams, who died in convulsions.

1792.

Instead of proceeding to Port Praya, in St. Jago, and there waiting several days for the other vessels, as ought to have been done, the Calypso sailed directly for Goree, where they arrived on the evening of the 12th, a place ill calculated to supply the necessities of the colonists, Mr. Dalrymple had been induced to make this choice from an idea that he should there be able to procure a pilot for the Bijuga channel.

May 12.

Having been able to procure but little water, and less refreshments for the people, the Calypso sailed from Goree on the 19th, and on the 21st anchored in the Bijuga channel. On the 24th she got sight of the island of Bulama, and sent all the boats armed on shore. The next day one of the boats having

19th.

24th.

1792.
May 25. returned, the ship got under weigh, and proceeded towards that island, where she anchored in the evening.

26th. On the 26th a party of men was missing in the woods, and the
27th. next day another party was sent in search of them; some of
28th. the missing returned from the woods on the 28th, and the day
29th. following the remainder of them much fatigued. Some of them had, whether wantonly or not I am ignorant, set fire to the long dry grass, which spread with much rapidity to a great extent, and continued burning for many hours; in the mean time several of the colonists had erected small huts and tents on shore; parties wandered wherever they pleased in the day, and returned to the ship or not as they thought proper in the evening: in short, nothing could be more irregular or improper than their conduct. Whether the members of the council in the Calypso had now influence enough to controul or direct the colonists, I cannot positively say; but believe not: indeed their own conduct had been so thoughtless and ill-judged, that whatever influence they might have had at first was, I believe, now entirely lost. The colonists could not be ignorant that the ships were at first unnecessarily separated by the fault of those on board the Calypso, and they were much disappointed at not receiving the refreshments of which they stood in so much need, owing to the precipitate sailing of that ship from Teneriffe. This disappointment was still increased by their being carried to Goree, where refreshments were not to be procured. Dalrymple was a good man, but he had not firmness enough to check, and keep in awe the unruly and turbulent of the colonists; nor had he zeal and activity enough to lead and direct their restlessness to some useful end. Indeed nothing could surpass the anarchy and

confusion that reigned among that part of the colonists embarked on board the Calypso.

On the 30th a war canoe, of the neighbouring isles, was reconnoitring near the place where the ship was, but could not be prevailed upon to approach near her. One of the colonists was deputed to it for that purpose, but without succeeding: it contained between thirty and forty armed men. The cautious distance these people kept from the Calypso, induced the colonists to suppose that they had no friendly inclination towards them; and therefore those that had been accustomed to sleep on shore returned this night to their ship, leaving their tents, &c. standing. The next morning the tents, with several other things, were gone, which had been carried off by the natives in the night. If any thing could have convinced our people of the hostile disposition of the islanders towards them, this, one would suppose, had been sufficient; and it ought to have induced the council to re-embark every body till the island had been purchased, for they had doubtless no business on it. The landing, cutting down of timber, burning, and building, were in themselves acts of hostility on our part.

A sense of some degree of danger induced the colonists to unite their labour in erecting, what was ridiculously called, a block-house, but which was nothing more than a shed or hut inclosed with inch plank; and though no regular armed party was kept in it, or indeed on shore, this was the general receptacle of all their arms, for every man had been provided with a musquet, bayonet, and cartouch-box from the public store.

Till the 3d of June nothing particular occurred, every one did what he pleased, and nothing more. Some of the people again slept on shore, but no attempt had been made to recover

48 *African Memoranda.*

1792. June 3. them from their irregular conduct, or to direct the general strength to some useful end.

On Sunday the 3d of June, instead of assembling the colonists at prayers, and taking that opportunity of pointing out to them their precise situation, the difficulties they had to encounter, the necessity of order, regularity, sobriety, and industry; in short, the virtues that would ensure the prosperity, or the vices that would tend to the destruction of the colony; instead of doing this, which their situation imperiously called for, every one was wandering about the island in pursuit of some favourite amusement. Some were on the shore fishing among the rocks, or seeking crabs and muscles; others taking oysters from the Mangrove branches, while many were inland, botanizing or hunting after lizards; and others chasing, some—butterflies, and some—elephants; a few were sleeping by the hut where the arms were kept, and some of the women were sitting in its shade: thus were the colonists scattered at two o'clock when the Bijugas made an attack. They began by firing a volley into the hut; which rousing those who were asleep in it, as they rushed out they were shot. Those who were near the beach, and ran towards it on hearing the firing of musquetry, in order to get on board, were intercepted by another party, and met with the same fate. In short, all the men who were near the hut, at the time of attack, were either killed or wounded; and all the women and children taken prisoners. Some, at a little distance, hid themselves behind the rocks, till the firing had ceased, and by that means escaped to the ship; and all those who were distant in the woods, many of whom did not return until very late, escaped also. On board the Calypso, during this dreadful scene on shore, all was disorder, all confusion. They indeed

African Memoranda. 49

sent two armed boats on shore as soon as they could, to receive and protect those who had fled to the beach for assistance; but the work of death was done; the object of the savages accomplished. They had surprized and destroyed; and then, loaded with booty, had retreated to the bushes.

1792.
June 3.

When the boats reached the shore the firing had ceased, and a few colonists, who had been alarmed at it, having been near enough to hear, without seeing its effects till they passed the dead bodies, were standing up to their necks in water waiting to be taken on board.

Of those who were absent in the woods some heard, and some did not hear the firing, but they all returned, although late, in safety.

In this melancholy affair we had five men and one woman killed, four men wounded, and four women and three children taken prisoners.[a]

There can be no doubt that the Bijugas had watched the motions of our people for the two or three preceding days; and most likely from the 30th of May, when their war canoe first made its appearance, and they had observed them straggle into the woods in the morning by twos and threes, and return again in the evening, and that those who remained at the hut were

[a] *Killed.*   *Wounded.*   *Women taken.*   *Children taken.*
Aaron Baker,   * Mr. H. B. Gardiner,   † Mrs. Harley,   Two of Mrs. Baker's,
Step. Mollineaux,   * Richard Pool,   Mrs. Barnwell,   † One of Mrs. Harley's,
Edw. Williamson,   Dolphin Price,   Mrs. Mollineaux,
Wm. Howard,   Godfrey Norman.   Eliz. Thompson.
Constantine Long,
Mrs. Gardiner.

* Died of their wounds.   † Died at Canabac just after their redemption.

1792.
June 3.

generally asleep from one to three during the greatest heat of the day, and that no watch whatever was kept. They had therefore chosen the best time for commencing their attack, when those who were not absent were asleep. That they had watched us closely was evident from their firing at first at no individual person, but into the block house where the people were sleeping; and as they ran out they were killed or wounded one by one. The Bijugas immediately after rushed into the block house, where they found sixty stand of arms loaded and primed, which they instantly seized, and, turning against the colonists, killed them with their own weapons.

Not one Bijuga was either killed or wounded; indeed a single musquet had not been discharged at them; for those at a distance from the block house were unarmed; and those who were in it fell victims to their incautious conduct, ere their half-opened eyes could discover the cause of their alarm.

Kitchen utensils, wearing apparel, and other European articles, highly prized by the savages, besides sixty stand of arms, with a quantity of ammunition, was the rich booty obtained by them after their daring attack; and bad as that was it were well had that been all.

The Bijugas had foreseen that our people would endeavour to escape to the beach opposite the ship, in the moment of attack, and had therefore sent a party round to cut off their retreat, which they did effectually; and the poor women and children who had fled from the hut were all taken prisoners.

Some degree of humane consideration seems to have regulated the conduct of these savages, for they never attempted, in the attack, either to kill or wound any of the women or children; though after it was over, and they were retreating through the woods, they committed an act of cruelty on one of them, which is not to be reconciled even with the lowest possible degree of feeling.

1792.
June 3.

Among all who suffered on this occasion the fate of Mr. and Mrs. Gardiner was certainly the most cruel, and the most lamented.

He had been wounded by a musket ball, and was endeavouring to reach the beach, when he was intercepted by one of the party of the islanders that had been stationed for that purpose. To go back was certain death; to advance towards the ship it was necessary to pass this man. Unarmed, and weakened by loss of blood, Mr. G. advanced, bowing as he approached; but the savage regardless of his humiliation, made a stroke at him, with his well-tempered cutlass, which Mr. G. attempting to parry with his hand, it was severed from the arm at the wrist.* He passed on into the water, and was one of those standing up to his chin in it, when the boats from the Calypso arrived to carry them on board. He died a few days afterwards.

His wife, having witnessed the fate of her husband, was a prisoner in the hands of the savages; these, having rifled the block house, and stripped the dead,† began their retreat, with their

---

* Europeans can scarcely form an idea of the order in which these savages keep their arms. Their cutlasses I can compare only to razors. They try the edge of them on the back of the nail, as we do razors in Europe. They answer to them, very frequently, the purpose of a knife. I have seen one of them draw his sword, and cut off a steak of venison with as much ease as a butcher would with his long sharp knife in our markets. The blades are about four feet long, and Solingen is marked on them all.

† One of the slain had on a pair of what are called musquito trowsers, which buttoned at the ancle; these ignorant people not knowing how to unbutton them, and unable to strip them off without it, cut off both the feet for that purpose.

1792.
June 3.

prisoners and booty, across the island. Mrs. G. was unfortunately lame, and unable to keep pace with their rapid march, they therefore shot her.

To the numberless instances of the want of prudence on the part of the colonists, which have already appeared, one would suppose it scarcely possible to add another; yet, such was the total neglect of all measures which would contribute towards their safety, that four cannon, which had been shipped on board the Calypso, were not mounted; and when the terrified colonists fled to the water for protection not a single gun was out of the hold. Fortunately, however, the Bijugas did not pursue our people when in the water, for if they had, they might have put them all to death before any assistance could have been given from the ship

Armed boats, as was before observed, had been sent from the Calypso, as soon as the general confusion would permit, after our people were attacked. These did not land, but remained afloat, near the shore, to receive the colonists who were all embarked a little after dark. In the mean time the cannon had been mounted on board.

The irrational confidence of the colonists was now converted into the most groundless fears; and no attempt was made to recover either the dying, or the dead. Amongst those, who, in the morning, would have ridiculed, and laughed to scorn, the man who might apprize them of the danger of their straggling about unarmed, not one was to be found bold enough to propose going a hundred yards into the woods, to recover the bodies of their murdered relations and companions. Nay, they were afraid to go in a body, though they might have landed full seventy armed men: so equally absurd is the result of that conduct, which originates either in the madness of temerity, or the folly of fear.*

1792. June 4.

The next day a large party of armed men were landed (under a discharge of cannon from the ship to clear the woods) to bring off the water casks which had been left on shore; this being accomplished, the Calypso early the following morning got under sail to proceed to Bissao, and there wait the arrival of her consorts, without having attempted to revisit the block house, or recover the dead: the same day the Hankey and Beggar's Benison were discovered at anchor in the Bijuga channel, and the following morning the Calypso rejoined them, as related in the preceding chapter.

5th.

6th.

The Calypso had at this time many persons on board ill of a fever, but none had yet died of it.

* " For what is fear, but the betraying of the succours which wisdom offereth."
PROVERBS.

CHAPTER IV.

Proceedings from the Rejunction of the Ships, to the Abandonment of the Island of Bulama by the major Part of the Colonists, in the Ship Calypso.

1792.
June 7.

WHEN I quitted the Hankey on the morning of the 5th, I had left a quiet, clean, healthy, and orderly ship, the colonists contented and in good spirits; but when I returned on the 7th, I found a noisy, dirty, disorderly ship, the colonists dissatisfied and dispirited. That such a change could have been operated in so short a time was scarcely credible, but such was the effect of the Calypso's rejunction. The fever, from which the Hankey was still free, had already made its appearance in the former ship; and, instead of separating the infected from the well, and taking any steps to prevent the spreading of that dangerous disease, by prohibiting any unnecessary intercourse between the two ships, the whole time, since the arrival of the Calypso, had been taken up in the constant interchange of visits: nay, the affected themselves, the very persons who had the fever on them at the time, had been actually on board the Hankey; and the consequence was that many days did not elapse before the fever made its appearance in that ship also.

Nothing was heard but mutual reproaches from the people of the Calypso. The colonists accused the members of the council, in that ship, of a want of attention to their comfort and accommodation; they were tired with the length of the voyage, irritated with sickness, the loss of their associates, and the disappointment of their hopes; and became extremely dissatisfied with their situation. {1792. June 7.}

The members of the council, on the contrary, attributed their principal misfortune to the unruly and disobedient conduct of the colonists; these general and reciprocal complaints, produced, in the minds of a few, contempt; but in the majority of the colonists, despondency.

The first object after the junction of the ships was the redemption of our women and children. For this purpose I returned the same evening to Bissao, to negociate with Mr. de Sylva Cordoza, the mode of affecting their ransom; which he readily undertook to accomplish, by dispatching some of his grumetas* in a sloop, to the Isle of Canabac, (whither they had been carried) with a proper assortment of goods. On my offering to accompany his grumetas to that island, Mr. de Sylva observed, that it would be highly improper for any white man to appear in the business, as he was firmly of opinion that it would inevitably enhance the price of their ransom, if not defeat the very end of our endeavours; which, with little or no difficulty, he doubted not, his own grumetas would in a few days accomplish.

As nothing further could be done till the redemption of the captives, it was judged expedient to proceed with all the vessels to Bissao, and there wait their return, which would give us an opportunity of supplying the colonists with fresh provisions, fruit, and vegetables, which they stood much in need of, particularly

* Generally speaking, native servants, or those who work for hire; though sometimes applied to confidential slaves.

on board the Calypso; for most in that ship had not tasted either since their leaving England.

Accordingly at noon, on the 8th, we got under sail, and anchored the same evening in the road of Bissao, where were one Portuguese ship, an American brig, and an English sloop, all trading for slaves.

During our stay here, the king of the Papells sent a deputation to invite us to settle upon his territories; and the following curious composition, as the translation of the king's message, was given to us by one Birchall, who commanded the English slave sloop, and who on this occasion was our interpreter.

" The king of the Papells sent to me; he told me he was
" given to understand that you wanted to settle; but the Por-
" tuguese would not allow you to settle here. But it is not as
" they chuse.

" The king of the Papells wants to know, whether the coun-
" try belongs to them? the king wishes much you would settle
" here, though he doth not know what terms you have come
" upon. He wishes much you may settle here, though the
" Roman Catholics wish you to go elsewhere. The king wishes
" you would let him know any part you would like to pitch
" upon, provided you can agree; and come upon good terms,
" as at this time they wish some other government was here.
" He has sent his cane as a proof of his fidelity and attachment.
" Yesterday do not you recollect my hailing for a boat? There
" were then Papells on the shore from the king to settle this
" affair, as they say themselves, that the inhabitants of Bissao
" do not wish for any other company but themselves; but it is
" as I, the king of Papells chuse.

" You may depend on the king's word, as he declares he is

"ready to take up any cause against the Portuguese, that may
"hinder you from landing on any place you may wish to settle
"on. This is the business those Papells are upon, to know if
"you are willing to buy any ground, from the point as far down
"as you please. You may rely the king of Papells will protect
"you. If you do mean to purchase the ground, I will go on
"shore with you to the king's to-morrow, and show you the
"ground.

(Signed)   " T. BIRCHALL, Interpreter."

1792. June 10.

This offer the council declined for obvious reasons, and the next day the following answer was returned, accompanied by handsome presents, and signed by Mr. Dalrymple, on the part of the colonists.

" The British settlers, now at Bissao, gratefully return thanks
" to the king of the Papells, for his hospitable offer of a settle-
" ment in his dominions; but as they are desirous of avoiding
" all occasions of offence to their friends the Portuguese, that
" may tend to weaken the firm and faithful alliance which has
" long subsisted between their respective sovereigns; and, as the
" object of these settlers is to make an establishment elsewhere,
" that cannot interfere betwixt the claims or interests of any
" European power, they beg leave respectfully to decline the
" invitation, at the same time professing their wish to remain on
" terms of perpetual amity and alliance with the king of the
" Papells, and his subjects, and in peace and friendship with all
" men.

" Signed for myself and the rest of the settlers on board the
" ship Hankey, June 11, 1792.

" H. H. DALRYMPLE."

1792.
June 19.

On the 19th of June, the boat which Mr. de Sylva Cordoza had sent for our women and children, returned with three women and two children, who were purchased of king Bellchore, at the prices of slaves.* One woman and one child were still detained, by king Jalorem, another Canabac king, who resided at a different part of the island; and one woman had been killed in the woods, on account of her not being able to keep pace with the party, as before related.

These women had been very well treated by the Canabacs, for which they were probably indebted to the national prejudice of these people, who look upon white women rather as objects of disgust than desire. Their devil is white.

While our ships remained at Bissao, our people were employed in procuring wood, water, and fresh provisions; while the council was occupied in providing an agent and interpreters to assist in the negociation for the purchase of the island of Bulama, and in acquiring information relative to the surrounding islands and people.

If we were fortunate in meeting with Mr. Cordoza, the Portuguese merchant, we deemed ourselves not less so in finding the commander of an American vessel, who had come to Bissao, to procure slaves; and who, notwithstanding his nefarious occupation, appeared to us at that time an honest and disinterested man; and rendered us some essential services, though we were deceived in his real character as will appear in the sequel. This man, whose name is Moore, undertook to purchase for us the island of Bulama, leaving his reward to our own estimation of the value of the service, when it should be performed.

* Which amounted to 483¼ bars, equivalent to £80 11s. 8d. sterling.

Being assured that there was now no obstacle to our entering into a negociation with the Canabac kings, for the purchase of the island of Bulama, and having nothing to detain us longer at Bissao, the ships got under weigh on the 21st of June, and proceeded towards the west point of Bulama, where Mr. Dalrymple made his first landing.

Prior however to our quitting Bissao, it was necessary for us to do an act of justice to our good friend Mr. de Sylva Cordoza. The Portuguese, in general, of the factory were jealous of our arriving on the coast, and adverse to our settling in their neighbourhood; and they were not ignorant of the offer which the king of the Papells (with whom they are almost always at war) had made to us, of some land on the island of Bissao itself. With the governor and most of the merchants we had little communication, and received from them neither civilities nor supplies; but the hospitable door of Mr. Cordoza was ever open to us: he interested himself warmly in the redemption of our women, and by his exertions we were abundantly supplied with refreshments.

These kind offices gave rise to calumny, and he was accused of having prevailed upon the Papell king to invite us to settle in the vicinity of the Bissao factory; that he might continue to carry on the contraband trade, which it was asserted he had already done, to a considerable amount.

To obviate the effects of such a representation at the Court of Portugal, the following certificate was given by the council to Mr. Cordoza; and a copy of it transmitted to the Portuguese ambassador at London.

1792.
June 21.

"We, the undersigned, being a committee elected, with the approbation of the British ministry, for the purpose of conducting the affairs of a colony designed to be established on the island of Bulama, or elsewhere, on the coast of Africa, find it our duty to give this public testimony of the deep impression we perceive of the obligation we have incurred to Mr. Joseph de Sylva Cordoza, for his humane mediation, and assistance, in recovering to us the women and children of our association taken at the aforesaid island.

"Understanding that advice has been transmitted to the court of Portugal, that the said Mr. Joseph de Sylva Cordoza has been carrying on a trade with us, and has invited us to settle in the vicinity of the factory at Bissao, and that he has been made the subject of other calumnies.

"We do hereby solemnly declare, that he has not directly, nor indirectly, signified his wish for us to establish ourselves near any Portuguese settlement in Africa, and that he has not carried on any trade with us whatever; but that all our communications with the said Mr. Joseph de Sylva Cordoza, have been for the sole purpose of redeeming the captives of our association, and the procuring of necessary refreshments for our people: and that he has in all things reconciled his special duty as a loyal subject to his own sovereign, with the general duties of humanity and of hospitality to strangers."

The fever still continued in both ships, but only one person had yet fallen a victim to it in the Calypso, and none in the Hankey, the colony was notwithstanding diminished in number, several dissatisfied persons* having left the former ship at Bissao.

22d. In the evening of the 22d, we took up the anchorage formerly occupied by the Calypso in the bay at the west end of the island 1792. of Bulama; and at the dawn of the following day I went on June 23. shore, accompanied only by the mate of the Hankey, to see what remained of the block house, and the slaughtered carcases of its former inmates. Scattered planks and boughs were all that we saw, not a vestige of a human bone; we therefore returned on board, thinking that we had mistaken the place of attack, and not wishing to remain longer on shore than was necessary.

Unwilling however to quit this bay without making a further search, after breakfast a party of 30 armed men (15 from either ship) were landed, with the pious intention of burying the remains of those unfortunate people who were killed on the 3d of June: two skulls, and a few scattered bones, were all that we could collect, and these were carefully deposited in a deep grave, close by a large tree, on whose stem, that we might know the place hereafter, was deeply cut the figure of a cross. Having carried on board all the plank that lay scattered about, we again weighed anchor, to proceed to the eastern part of the island; but the Hankey having run aground, we were delayed until the morning after; when we proceeded with all the vessels to the 24th. entrance of the Rio Grande, and of the channel which separates the eastern side of Bulama from the Biafara shore; we anchored.

* Discharged from the Calypso at their own request while at Bissao—
        2 Subscribers.
        1 Subscriber's wife.
        1 Ditto, female servant.
        1 Public servant.
        4 Private servants.
        —
        9

These persons I believe expected to get a passage either to America or England, by Moore's brig or Birchall's sloop.

1792.
June 24. at 10 o'clock. This latter channel I immediately went to explore, and found it safe and commodious, having from 7 to 15 fathoms through its whole extent, within pistol shot of either shore.

25th. The day following I sailed in the Beggar's Benison for the island of Canabac, accompanied by Mr. Dobbin and Capt. Moore, to effect the object without which our enterprize were vain, as well as unjust.

We had put on board the cutter an assortment of goods which had been chosen in Europe, to make presents of to the native chiefs, and to purchase of them the island of Bulama; and two grumetas of Captain Moore's who were to be our interpreters to the Bijugas.*

26th. We anchored at Canabac late in the evening of the 26th, and had only day-light enough to land one of our interpreters,† to open the purpose of our coming, and deliver the customary presents for the king. He was joined on the beach by many of the natives.

Although we had learned through the Grumetas, who had redeemed our women, that the Bijugas were willing to treat with us for the sale of the island of Bulama, and had been told at Bissao, that we should find no difficulty in purchasing it, yet we were at the same time informed that these were a treacherous, and faithless people, in whose professions no confidence could be placed, and that we ought therefore to be always on our guard, for they would lose no opportunity of surprizing us if any thing was to be gained thereby. Gillion had therefore been directed

---

* The cluster of islands goes by the name of the Bijuga islands, Canabac is one of them; but all their inhabitants are called Bijugas.

† Whom I shall hereafter call Gillion, for that was his name, and an honest, good, and valuable man he was.

to tell the king, that no canoes would be suffered to approach us in the night, and that if any attempted it they would be fired into, and inevitably sunk.   1792. June 26.

Our cutter had been formerly a Gravesend boat, was of 34 tons burthen, armed with six swivels, and our numbers amounted to fourteen: if then we had suffered one of their war canoes, nearly twice as long as the cutter, and carrying from thirty to forty armed men to come along-side, though under the semblance of friendship, it would have been in their power to board, and possibly carry us; it was therefore deemed most prudent never to suffer one of their canoes to approach us, but if they persisted in the attempt, instantly to fire into, and sink it. These cautious measures were absolutely necessary to our safety. The swivels were constantly loaded and primed, matches kept burning all night, and half the company on watch calling "all's well" every five minutes; the other half lay down to sleep by their arms.

Early in the morning Gillion returned on board with the king's two sons:* he had been well received, and the king, he said, wished to see us on shore. There was no occasion for more than one person to go; therefore leaving the king's sons on board as hostages, accompanied by Gillion, and the necessary presents (for no one in this country appears the first time without them) I landed; the little two-oared boat lay off, upon her oars, to wait our return.   27th.

On board the cutter, where we were in force sufficient to protect ourselves, it was prudent to be armed, and on our guard; but alone, on shore, had treachery been intended, arms

* Jamber and Demiong.

1792.
June 27.

would have been useless, I therefore thought it most advisable to go unarmed, to show the natives that I placed confidence in them, had no dread, and put firm reliance in the laws of hospitality; which is certainly a virtue generally found among savages. I had consequently no weapon about me except a handsome hanger in my hand, which was intended as a present to the king.

Many natives on the beach waded into the water to meet the boat, and, accompanied by them, we walked to the town about a mile distant. Gillion had, in obedience to his orders, last night made inquiries after Mrs. Harley and her child, who were still in the hands of the Bijugas, having been detained by Jalorem the king of this town, when the rest had been redeemed of Bellchore the other king on this island. The first large house that we came to, Gillion pointed out as belonging to the king's women, and in it, he said, was the white woman; I determined therefore to go in, and apprize this poor woman of our having come to redeem her, and carry her back to her husband.

We entered the house, composed of three concentric circles, with six doors through one of its diameters; in the inner circle lay the poor woman; but it was so dark that one could not see, and she knew not of our arrival.

The natives however lighted many little parcels of long straws, which they held upright in their hands, and when burnt down nearly to their fingers, others stood by, with fresh ones, to replace them, so that we had abundance of light.

On a wicker frame, supported by half a dozen posts, about a foot from the ground, and covered with long grass, lay Mrs. Harley and her infant child. When the light enabled her to discover that there was a white man in the room, she stared upon me with such a look of hope, of doubt, of fear, and of madness, as I shall never forget; but which I cannot describe.

1792. June 27.

"Mrs. Harley," said I, " I am come to put an end to your sufferings, and to carry you back to your husband, whom I left well the day before yesterday."

" Who are you, Sir? how came you here? do I dream? are you a prisoner?" No—I am come here to redeem you and your child; to take you back to your family; and to purchase of the king the island of Bulama." " Will they let you go back? they won't let you go back; they will keep you here." " No danger of that," I replied; " we are now on friendly terms, and I trust shall hereafter live in peace and friendship.

A little more conversation passed; when I said, that I had not yet seen the king; that I must go to him, and enter on the business about which I had come; and that I would then return to her, and settle at what time I should take her on board. She instantly seized my hand, and said, " will you go away and leave me then?" No," said I, " you shall see me again in an hour." " I never shall see you again—you will go away and leave me—I won't part from you." " Be calm Mrs. Harley, and compose yourself, depend, upon my word, that the moment I have finished my business with the king I will return to you." " No—never—never—if you go away I never shall see you again—you will desert me—I see that you mean to forsake me— and I shall be left to die among these murderous savages."

" By the God that made me (I hope the expression may be forgiven) I will not quit the island without you." " But suppose they will not give me up?" " Then I will stay here and

1792.
June 27.

die with you." She believed me, and was appeased; and I proceeded to the king.

Surrounded by the natives, we at length arrived at his residence. How to act with respect to what had passed at Bulama in some degree puzzled me; to pass it over altogether in silence might not be thought right, and yet nothing could be said on the subject that would not recall the idea of our weakness, humiliation, and disgrace. The purport of my visit was, besides, to conciliate, and make friends for the future, and not to recriminate and demand satisfaction for the past.

I therefore said that it was the misfortune sometimes of the best friends to misunderstand each others intentions, and to quarrel; and that that had been the case with us; but as what had already happened could not be recalled, I should say nothing on that subject, but hoped that we should hereafter live like good friends and neighbours: for which purpose I had been deputed by the English at Bulama, with presents to him, and his brother king, Bellchore; to offer them our friendship; and to propose purchasing from them their hunting island of Bulama.*

Jalorem replied that what was done, was done; that he was sorry for what had happened; but that *then* they neither knew who we were, nor our intentions; *we were strangers, and we took their land;* however he knew *now* that we were good people; hoped we should always be good friends, and was glad, very glad, to see me at Canabac: as to what I had said about buying Bulama, he could not say any thing till Bellchore's arrival: he

* The island of Bulama was never inhabited by the Bijugas, but they used to hunt elephants, buffaloes, and deer upon it; and go over and cultivate, at the beginning of he rains, a few acres of rice at its western extremity.

had last night sent a person for him, and expected him this evening; and that then I should have an answer.

1792.
June 27.

I then told him that he had an English woman and her child; and that he must give them up to me, that I might carry them on board my vessel. To this he assented. The presents which had been brought on shore were then given to him, to which was added my hanger; and suitable presents were given to three or four of, what are here termed, his head men.

In return, the king gave me a bullock, a couple of goats, and a dozen of fowls; he then did me service,* and promised to come on board, and see me after dinner.

From the king I returned to Mrs. Harley to carry her on board; but that poor woman was in such a shocking state of dirt and filth, as is almost impossible to conceive, having never once been removed from the hurdle on which she was now lying, since her arrival on the island; and not having had her cloaths off for twenty-five days. Her little girl, about five years of age, was in the same situation; vermin had absolutely eaten little holes in her head and neck; and her shoulder-blade, lower part of the vertebræ, and hip bones, had made their way through the skin, and formed ulcers, from her emaciated body having lain so long with scarcely any flesh, on so hard a bed. It was impossible to remove them in their present condition, and as Mrs. H. was now fully convinced that there was no obstacle to her leaving the island, she assented to my going on board without her, and to return in the evening with soap, towels, &c. and some of my linen and cloaths for her to dress in.

*' Saluting is called, in this part of Africa, *doing service*, when Jalorem had given me his presents, he said he should now do me service; and seven very handsome brass blunderbusses were immediately discharged from close before his door.

1792.
June 27.

When we got down upon the beach, the natives crouded into the boat, as full as she could hold, and I could not get them out again, so that I was obliged to carry them on board, or stay altogether on shore. None of their canoes being suffered to go along-side, they had no means of getting on board but in our boat, hence their eagerness to get into her, for besides the gratification of their curiosity, they were each sure of receiving a glass of rum and a head of tobacco, which were presents of no inconsiderable value in the eyes of these people.

Soon after our return on board, Jamber and Demiong, the king's two sons, went on shore with these people, and the boat brought back Jalorem the king. While he was engaged by Mr. Dobbin on board, I returned to bring off Mrs. Harley and her child.

The king's women, on this occasion, behaved remarkably well, and exhibited that delicacy and feeling which, from either pole to the equator, will be generally found characteristic of their sex.

The repugnance which some Europeans feel to touch a black will give but a very faint notion of what these people feel at the idea of touching a white person; for besides the dislike of the colour, common to both, the Africans, couple with it, the notion of disease.* And after the women had cleansed, and clothed, Mrs. H. and her child, it was with difficulty that I could find a black man to touch the former, in supporting her to the boat.

Mrs. Harley was unable to walk, and her child could not even stand; it was therefore necessary that both should be carried;

---

* I speak of those only who have not been accustomed to see Europeans.

but how to effect that with the former we did not know, as there was neither chair, stool, nor plank upon the island.

1792.
June 27.

There was fortunately however a little Mandingo horse, as tame as a sheep, and not much larger, which had been given to Jalorem, and was quite a favourite. Upon this little animal we placed Mrs. H., but she required supporting by a man on either side, while we walked slowly down to the boat; and we were an hour endeavouring, in vain, to get one of the islanders to undertake that office, with Gillion our interpreter. At length a man, who was called the king's secretary, undertook it, but with evident disgust. Mrs. H. would not suffer me to do so, but most earnestly requested that I would walk by the side of one of the king's women, who was kindly carrying her child, and by no means lose sight of it.

The boat, as before, was completely in the possession of the natives, and no remonstrance of mine could induce one of them to quit it, though evidently so overloaded as to be in danger of sinking. The last person that got in was an ill-looking black, over the bow, when Mrs. H. who had been all along extremely frightened, and earnestly requesting me not to carry these men on board, gave a piercing shriek, and clung to me, as if she had been afraid of instant death, " For God's sake, Sir, do not receive that man," she exclaimed; " that is the man who murdered Mr. Mollineaux, and was the most active of the savages during the attack." I had no power whatever, and therefore could not get the man out of the boat, but assured her that there was no danger. She continued, notwithstanding, extremely agitated all the way, and could not even look at him, so great was her terror.

During the time that the king's women were preparing Mrs.

1792.
June 27.

H. to embark, I took an opportunity of walking through, and round, the town, accompanied by Gillion and the king's sons, with a view to obtain, by that means, a tolerable notion of its extent and population; and in this ramble I do not think that there was an individual from infancy just acquiring, to old age just losing, the faculty of walking, who did not accompany me. When I stopped they would form a circle round me, the boldest nearest, and the more timid further back. Those with the greatest curiosity would even venture to open, slowly and cautiously, the bosom of my shirt, and projecting one of their fingers, gently touch the skin, but as if it was the skin of a snake; they would also lift up my hat and touch my hair, and then clapping their hands together, express their astonishment by calling out Hoo-oo-oo-oo. If I suddenly moved in any direction, the people that I approached would fly as from an alligator, while all the rest would laugh at them.

I believe no white man (except Birchall, whom we met at Bissao, and who had been tied to a tree on this island, and narrowly escaped being put to death, which he richly deserved) had ever been on the island of Canabac before, at least not within the remembrance of any of its then living inhabitants. I was, therefore, a kind of animal that they had all heard of, but that few had seen. Notwithstanding their reluctance, particularly that of the women and children, to touch me, or let me approach them, yet none refused a pinch of snuff, but eagerly took it, when I held out my hand to offer it, and soon emptied my box.

From the ground which this walk would give me to form an opinion on, I judged that the town was about a mile in circuit, and computed its population at six hundred persons.

Jalorem remained on board till late in the evening; when he left us, having received many presents, and seeming well pleased. The next morning Bellchore arrived; when I went to see him, and give him similar presents to those which had been given to Jalorem. They both seemed as ready to sell, as we were willing to buy, the island of Bulama, and the following morning was fixed upon to hold the Palaver.* Accordingly after breakfast Mr. Dobbin, Captain Moore, and myself, with our interpreters, went on shore. The two kings, most of the old men of both their towns, several of the young ones, and many women and children were already assembled there.

{1792. June 27. 28th. 29th.}

We all squatted down together on the beach, under the shade of some large trees, the kings and ourselves surrounded by the elder, and those by the younger men, the women and children at a greater distance.

The palaver was begun by our stating the motives of our visit. When finished, Bellchore addressed for a considerable time, and with great fluency, his surrounding countrymen, who, with Jalorem, frequently nodded, and frequently vociferated assent. At length he addressed us, and said, that the Bijugas wished to live in peace and friendship with the English, and were willing to sell to us the island of Bulama.

We then spread out upon the beach the various goods which we had brought for that purpose, and which, they were told, was the price we were willing to give.

Bellchore made then another long oration to his countrymen; he was afterwards followed by Jalorem, and then three old men

---

* From the Portuguese word palabros, to talk; all meetings for the purpose of debate or discussion are therefore called Palavers, or talks.

successively spoke. The purport of all these addresses was to convince the persons assembled of the propriety of according to our request, to point out the value of the different things offered, and to assure them that as long as *White Man* lived near them, they should want nothing.

We were then informed that our price was accepted.

The deed of cession, four copies of which we had brought on shore, was then interpreted to them; and particular pains taken that they should fully comprehend every part of it. It was immediately afterwards signed by the parties, and witnessed by Captain Moore and Mr. Paiba. The palaver then broke up, and we separated; the natives to their town, and we to our vessel, mutually satisfied with each other.

Deed of Cession of the Island of Bulama, by the Kings Jalorem and Bellchore, to the British Colonists, for the King of Great Britain.

" Whereas certain persons, subjects of the king of Great Britain, conducted by H. H. Dalrymple, J. Young, Sir Wm. Halton, bart. I. King, Philip Beaver, Peter Clutterbuck, Fras. Brodie, Chas. Drake, John Paiba, Rich. Hancorne, Robt. Dobbin, Isaac Ximenes, and Nichs. Bayley, esqrs. as a committee to manage their affairs have arrived upon the windward coast of Africa, adjacent to the Rio Grande; and the said committee having invested P. Beaver and R. Dobbin, esqrs. two of their members, with full power to treat with, and purchase from us, our island of Bulama:

"We, the kings of Canabac, being fully convinced of the pacific and just disposition of the said persons, and of the great reciprocal benefits that will result from an European colony being established in our neighbourhood, and withal being desirous of manifesting our distinguished friendship and affection for the king of Great Britain and his subjects, do hereby, in consideration of the value of four hundred and seventy-three barrs* of goods, by us this day received, for ever cede and relinquish to the said king of Great Britain, all sovereignty over the island of Bulama, which sovereignty our ancestors have acquired by conquest, and have ever since maintained undisputed in peace.

1792.
June 29.

" We do further solemnly guarantee to the said persons, their heirs, and assigns, against all enemies whatever, the full and peaceable possession of the said island: and by these presents, do bind ourselves and our subjects to aid and assist them against all their enemies whatever; and the same shall have all the force of a firm and faithful treaty of defensive alliance between the king of Great Britain and ourselves: and, together with the island aforesaid, we do relinquish all claim to any future tribute, subsidy, or composition whatever.

" And all the premised conditions, we, the two parties, do bind ourselves to the mutual observance of, in the presence, and in the name of the omnipotent GOD of truth and justice, and the avenger of perfidy; and we have hereunto set our hands, this 29th day of June in the year of our LORD one thousand seven hundred and ninety-two."†

This treaty made and concluded at the island of Canabac in the presence of
WM. C. MOORE,
J. WM. PAIBA.

JALOREM ⋈ King,
his mark.

BELLCHORE ⋈ King,
his mark.

P. BEAVER, R. DOBBIN.

* £78 16 8 sterling; and £50 0 0 was given to Captain Moore for his agency.

1792.
June 29. In the evening it remained for us to perform the last friendly office to poor Mrs. Harley. She had departed this life early in the morning, before we went on shore, and her body was committed, this evening, to the deep. She had appeared better the night she went on board, and had taken some refreshment; but all the next day was exceedingly ill, and she had been able only to lie in one position all the time.

This unfortunate woman, when taken prisoner, was near the time of her lying-in, and had been forced a long march through the woods to the Bijugas Canoe, what effect this might have upon the infant in her womb, I am unable to say, but certain it is, that it was dead, and she not delivered of it, though far beyond her time; and this, I believe, was the cause of her death.

30th. The next day the infant Harley followed its mother, and was also buried in the sea.

July 1st. On the 1st of July the two Canabac kings came on board, and presented us with a couple of bullocks, and other stock, for which suitable presents were returned. A copy of the treaty was given to each of them, and an union-jack, which they were told must always accompany their boats when they came to Bulama, the latter to be always hoisted on their approach, and the former shewn to us, on their landing, that we might know their subjects from others. They soon afterwards left us, and we sailed to rejoin the Hankey and Calypso, which we did the

2nd. following morning in the channel between Bulama and the Biafara shore, whither they had moved the day after we left them.

While we were at Bissao, waiting the return of our captive

† This was an oversight; for these people, not being Christians, it ought to have run, in the year one thousand seven hundred and ninety-two of the Christian æra.

women, I had proposed* that the cutter and long boat should 1792. be employed in exploring the channels between the islands of July 2. Arcas, Gallinas, and Bulama, and the mouth of the Rio Grande, but this had been over-ruled. When, however, we had arrived at the mouth of that river, prior to our sailing for Canabac, I again proposed, and it was agreed to, that two boats should be daily employed in examining the shores of the island,† during our absence for its purchase; but that, to avoid the appearance of injustice or aggression, for which we had already so dearly paid, no person should be permitted to land until the purchase was completed.

On our return, however, we found that measures, the very reverse of these, had been pursued. No boats had been sent to explore; but a fishing party, under the protection of twenty armed men, had been daily landed to haul the Seine; it is true they procured a quantity of fish, but it was by an act of injustice; and they remained ignorant of what it behoved them most particularly to know—the best place for mooring the ships during the rains; and for building a town.

Having now a right to land, and cut down timber, and erect buildings, I had supposed that after our treaty had been publicly read to the colonists, which took place at 10 o'clock this morning, we should have gone seriously to work in clearing away the woods, and erecting our houses; and that the council had of course been prepared with some plan for carrying it into effect, with order and celerity. Accustomed as I had been to the weakness, folly, and absurdity of the measures hitherto pursued by the directors of this enterprise, yet I was astonished, I

---

* Minutes of the council, the 8th of June, 1792.   † Ibid, the 24th of June, 1792.

1792.
July 2.

must confess, at no intention being shewn, or even thought of, to avail ourselves of the right which we had now acquired; and which had been so imprudently and so eagerly seized, when we had it not. Not a word was mentioned, nor the least idea discovered of landing and commencing our labours; and the council and colonists separated, as if the written instrument itself was to create them a town.

I, however, took a party of twelve men from the Hankey, landed, and worked till sunset. When we returned on board, I proposed to the council:*

" That a working party consisting of two-thirds of the colonists in both ships should land every morning at day-light, under the direction of two or more members of the council, to clear the ground intended for the scite of the town.

" That a guard of six men, commanded by another member of the council, should attend them.

" That three parties of four men each, including the commanding officer, be employed daily to examine the shores of the island for the best water; one party to go along shore to the northward, another along shore to the southward, and the third inland; and that no other person be suffered to land armed.

" That the captains of the ships Calypso and Hankey be directed to moor their ships in their present situation, and that our carpenters be immediately employed in building a house over each ship to protect the colonists from the rains."

Before any thing effectual could be done, it was necessary to accede to these propositions, or something like them; but their discussion was postponed, and it was then determined that the

* Minutes of the council, the 2d of July, 1792.

question—"*Where* the ships shall be stationed during the rains" be discussed to morrow at 10 o'clock; and this was the first intimation I had of any design to abandon entirely the colony.

1792.
July 2.

Observing the discontent that so generally prevailed on board the Calypso, I had proposed, soon after her rejoining us,* that all the dissatisfied and discontented members of the colony should be informed that one of the ships should be ready to carry them back to England, as soon as we could clear it of its stores; but this was not agreed to; and now instead of letting the discontented only go, they wish to abandon the colony entirely.

In consequence of yesterday's resolution, the disposition of the ships during the rains, was this morning taken into consideration; when Mr. Beaver proposed, " that it is the opinion of the council that the present situation is the most proper place to moor the ships in, during the rainy season."

3d.

    Of which opinion there were 4
    Against it 9
            Majority 5

  It was then proposed and
Resolved,
  " That seeing that the rainy season has already commenced, and it appearing from the information of Captain Moore, as well as *from every information we can collect,* that we cannot land because of the rains and fogs at least for four months, and that with every precaution, there will probably be a considerable mortality among the settlers

---

* Minutes of the council, the 14th of June, 1792.

during that time; and considering withal, that a great proportion of the adventurers in each ship, are solicitous to return to Europe, it is the opinion of the council that the *two ships and the sloop* should be remove to Sierra Leone to water, and *there* the expediency of proceeding to England, or of returning hither after the rains, shall be taken into consideration."

What, in the name of common sense, did we come here for? Did we not know that the rains would commence when they did, before we left England? What information have we collected now, that we had not before? Mortality in some degree must be expected in such an enterprise; when was a colony settled without it? Not that of New Plymouth, Rhode Island, New Hampshire, nor Connecticut; not that of Maryland, Virginia, the Carolinas nor Georgia; and why are we to expect being exempt from what is the necessary and inevitable attendant in the clearing a new country? Many are solicitous to go: let them go in one of the ships; but why take both?—to go to Sierra Leone for water; is not water to be procured here? But *there* to consider of the expediency of returning to England or hither; and why not consider of that expediency here?—because *here* people would be ashamed to say that they would give up the enterprise, and return to England without even having made an attempt for its success; but *there*, sickness, vexation, and disappointment, would have so disheartened every body, that they would certainly acquiesce in the measure of returning to Europe.

Of all the individuals of which the colony was composed, I believe that I was the only one who had determined to return to Europe after the first rains, or at least who had avowed such an intention before leaving England. In one year I thought most of our difficulties would be over, and I had no idea of remaining longer. But to return in this shameful manner I could not. I did not come here to go back again directly; at least not without making some attempt to succeed.

1792. July 3.

Against this resolution of the council, therefore, with three others, I entered my protest; but two out those three thought proper to go away with the rest; and at the same time I informed the council that I should remain on the island with my servant, though every body else might leave it, and I expected, therefore, that one vessel would be left with me.

My determination being known, many persons came and voluntarily offered to remain with me, the next morning they amounted to between 80 and 90; it was therefore, on that day agreed, that the Hankey and Beggar's Benison should remain at Bulama with us, and the Calypso proceed with all convenient expedition to Sierra Leone, and thence to England, with those persons who were desirous to leave the island.

4th.

Of those who had volunteered to remain on the island with me, for I had not asked one of them, I advised the married ones to return in the Calypso, which they refusing to do, I endeavoured to prevail on them to send home their wives and children, as ill calculated to encounter the difficulties which I foresaw we should meet, but they persisted in keeping them with them.

Changing the persons and cargoes of the two ships was now undertaken, and occupied us till the evening of the 18th, as we could only work during the intervals of the rain, which was frequent and heavy during the greater part of that time.

Three new members of the council had been elected in the

1792.
July 19.

room of the same number that had resigned:* and on the 19th the Calypso sailed for Sierra Leone.

The fever had hitherto continued in both ships; the Calypso having buried three who had died of it since we left Bissao, and sailed with many sick. The Hankey had buried three persons also, and had now two colonists and three of the ship's company labouring under that disorder. Seven colonists† had besides been discharged from the Calypso at their own request, to go to Bissao, and thence seek a passage to Europe.

Thus vanished the schemes and plans which had been formed in England, and cherished during the voyage, by the major part of the colonists; and thus was abandoned an enterprise, so readily and eagerly entered into by all concerned, without making even an attempt to succeed. That the labourers and servants should instantly acquiesce in the measure of abandoning the island did not surprize me, for most of them had no other motive in coming hither than to avoid difficulties in their own country; but they found difficulties also here. To avoid, and not to encounter difficulties is their object, and therefore the same motives which induced them to undertake, will also induce them to abandon the enterprise—these are present—those at a distance. The same reasoning will, I believe, apply even to some of the subscribers.

But what shall we say for the council, for those who conduct the undertaking, in thus giving it up without making an attempt

---

* Messrs. Aberdein, Munden, and Reynolds, in the room of Sir Wm. Halton, and Messrs. Bayley and Dobbin.

† The assistant surgeon, his wife and child, and a labourer with his wife and two children.

even for its success? The truth is, that general discontent and dissatisfaction was the cause. The council were dissatisfied and disgusted with the conduct of the colonists in general, and the latter were equally displeased with the conduct of their directors. And there was too much reason, I fear, for discontent on both sides. {1792. July 19.}

Soon after sailing, the turbulent dispositions of some of the colonists began to be manifest on board the Calypso. In that ship there were three members of the council, including the governor, and unfortunately these did not act cordially together; the consequence was, that all the necessary measures were not taken by them, for the regulation and government of those embarked in their ship, which might have been expected; and those who required restriction, seeing division among their chiefs, carried further than they probably otherwise would have done, their licentious conduct.

In the Hankey there were nine members of the council, who, though not perfectly drawing together, seemed sufficiently sensible of their situation and duties, to adopt and forward such measures, as were proposed to them, which seemed conducive to the public good. In that ship things went on pretty well till her rejoining the Calypso.

But this event, instead of being matter for congratulation, produced universal discontent, which, in a very short time, led to the preceding resolution. On the rejunction of the ships an uninterrupted and general intercourse took place between the colonists of each ship. Those who came from the Calypso found that their fellow settlers in the Hankey had received supplies at Canaria, Teneriffe, and St. Jago, that the ship was loaded with stock, its inmates healthy, and in general con-

1792.
July 19.

tented. By contrasting this situation with their own, many of them not having eaten a fresh meal since their leaving England, their comrades slain and made captives, their ship infected with the fever and the scene of discontent, that irritation against their leaders which had too long since been conspicuous, could not fail to be increased. Those who went from the Hankey to the Calypso heard nothing but detailed complaints, and reciprocal accusations of insubordination and imbecility, from the governors and the governed. Their hopes, hitherto as sanguine as when they left England, thus suddenly checked, produced nearly as much discontent in the Hankey as in the Calypso. There was a settled gloom on the countenances of all, which it is difficult to convey an idea of, and which it was melancholy to behold.

In this situation it was difficult to procure acquiescence in the council to any public measure,—to rouse them to action and energy impossible. Two things however appeared to all absolutely necessary; and these were to redeem our captives, and to purchase from the natives the island of Bulama.

Dalrymple was a perfect gentleman, and a sensible, amiable, and well-informed man, yet in every thing relating to colonization, he was but a mere " dreamer of dreams;" he felt the difficulties which he had got into, was disgusted with most of the colonists, and had determined to return to Europe: any proposition, therefore, to measure back our steps, whether by Sierra Leone, or direct to England, was sure to meet with his hearty concurrence.

Young, the next to him in council, was a man in mind and information inferior to none whom I have ever had the happiness to know. I respected, I loved him; and never was in his company in my life, without leaving it, both wiser and better, from his knowledge and his virtues: but he also was disgusted, and therefore ready to sanction the same proposal.

1792.
July 19.

There were other members of the council whom I had also long known and esteemed—but their minds had all received the same unaccountable shock, and they were equally disposed to give up the enterprise.

Thus the council were of a mind readily to adopt any wish expressed on the part of the colonists to abandon the island; and the colonists, from causes above related, conceived every place better than the one before them; so that during the absence of the cutter *in negociating the purchase of the island, its relinquishment,* though not formally avowed, *was certainly determined on.*

In adopting this resolution I do not find fault with either the labourers or servants, or even the subscribers; they acted perhaps wisely, certainly not inconsistently; but I cannot concede so much to the council; at least to those who were its original members. For, although they had met with some unlooked for disappointments, and had cause for dissatisfaction, yet ought they not to have persevered? But what become of their avowed motives for having undertaken this expedition? To purchase land in Africa—to cultivate it by free natives—to induce in them habits of labour and industry—and to ameliorate their condition, by the introduction of religion and letters: these motives could not have been very strong.—Poor Africans!

However, as it is, in the present state of mind of those who are gone, I do not consider the colony weakened by their absence. I feel for my friends, because I think they have done wrong; but they are better absent than present, if discontented.

1792. July 19. *General View of the Dispersion of the Colonists since leaving England.*

Calypso.

Died on the Passage .. 2
Killed at Bulama and
   died of their wounds 8
Died at Bissao 1
     at Canabac 2
     at Bulama ..... 3—16
Deserted at Goree 1
Discharged at Bissao .. 9
     at Bulama 7—16
Sailed to Sierra Leone 85
Remained in the Han-
   key at Bulama 31
                   149

Hankey.

Died on the passage .. 1
   at Bulama ...... 3— 4
Discharged to the ship
   Hankey 1
Sailed to Sierra Leone
   in the Calypso 61
Remained in the Han-
   key at Bulama 54
                  120

Beggar's Benison.

Sailed in the Calypso
   to Sierra Leone 1
Remained at Bulama .. 5—6

                 126
                 149
        Total 275

CHAPTER V.

A JOURNAL

WRITTEN ON

THE ISLAND OF BULAMA:

FROM *THE SAILING OF THE CALYPSO*,

TO THE

FINAL EVACUATION OF THAT ISLAND.

BY LIEUTENANT PHILIP BEAVER,
OF HIS MAJESTY'S ROYAL NAVY.

La condition de ceux qui gouvernent, n'est pas autre que celle de ce Cacique a qui l'on demandait s'il avait des esclaves, et qui répondit: *Des esclaves, je n'en connais qu'un dans ma contrée, et cet esclave là, c'est moi.*

RAYNAL Hist. Phil. et Pol.
Prefixed to BARERE's "Pensée du Gouvernement, &c."

PREFACE

TO

LIEUTENANT BEAVER'S JOURNAL.

I HAD long doubted whether or not I should publish the Journal I had kept during my residence on the island of Bulama, or whether it would not have been better to make short extracts from it only; but, though the form of a Journal is tedious, and the matter, in that shape, generally uninteresting, yet on this occasion it was thought best to preserve it, because it was written at the time, and with the feelings which our situation then called forth. It were easy to have put it into a different form and language, but then it would not have been what it professes to be, a transcript of my Journal actually written on the island.

There are parts, very many perhaps, which require an apology, and which it may be said, should not have been published: for instance, my first day's Journal of the 19th of July, and the one following, and those of the 12th and 17th of August, with many others; but, as before observed, it was thought best to publish the Journal as it was written; because it is conceived that if it had any interest at all, it arose from laying before the reader, our precise situation and sentiments at the time; making him as it were, one of the colonists, without experiencing any of their difficulties.

As this Journal, therefore, was written without the most distant idea of publishing it, and with the greatest probability of never being carried off the island; as it was written amidst some danger, and great bodily, as well as mental exertions, it is confidently hoped that the liberal-minded will not too rigidly criticise it; about the opinions of others I am not very anxious.

Words have been sometimes, but not frequently, altered: the sense never.

CHAPTER V.—Continued.

Lieutenant Beaver's Journal, &c.

ABOUT one o'clock the Calypso sailed for Sierra Leone, with the major part of the colonists, and saluted us with three guns, which was returned with seven. In the evening the committee met and unanimously voted me their president, and Mr. Hancorne their vice-president. {Bulama, 1792. Thursday, July 19.}

Mustered the colonists whom I found to be in number 86, of whom ...... 48 are men.
13 women, and
25 children.
—
86 besides 4 seamen, and a boy in the cutter.*
—

Being elected president, not only by the committee, but the voice of the whole colony, and having the flattering distinction, (for I confess I am weak enough, if it be a weakness to think it such,) of being the only man to whom they look up for direction and protection, I have a fresh spur to continue that indefatigable labour, and unwearied attention to their good, which I feel confident I hitherto have done.

I am determined to do every thing in my power, attended with whatever exertion or danger it may be, for the success of

* See Appendix No. 4.

1792.
Thurs.
July 19.

this undertaking; and without consulting, or giving way to, the ever varying opinions of either the committee or the people, (which has already proved so injurious to this enterprise) pursue those measures, and those only, which I think conducive to their welfare, and the permanent establishment of this colony.

In justice to myself, to those who have elected me, and to my brothers in Europe, I have thought fit in this the first day's Journal of my direction, to write these my sentiments and determination, that if it should be so ordered that I to am die without having opportunity, or time, to carry either into effect, I may be distinguished, at least, from the common herd; and not ranked among those men, for the generality of whom I have the most sovereign contempt.

And I do most earnestly request those who may be appointed to look over my papers, in case of my death, to read this day's Journal in the presence of them all, that they may at least have the satisfaction of knowing that the confidence they placed in me, was in some degree merited; and that while I had lived, I had determined never to desert them.

P. BEAVER.

Friday, 20th.

As since our arrival on this island there has been, hitherto, little or no order; no work done; every one going whither he pleased, and returning when he chose, whence the idleness and licentiousness of every description of persons have arisen to an intolerable height, which, if not immediately and effectually curbed, will not only render of no avail the endeavours of that small portion of sober minded, useful, and industrious members of the community, who wish to be of service, but probably draw them from a proper sense of their duty, it is necessary that vigorous measures be pursued. The great diminution of our numbers also renders it necessary to their preservation, that immediate, and implicit obedience be given to those orders which I may think necessary to issue; and which, if I am to direct them, they must obey.

1792. Friday, July 20.

Therefore, however unpleasant the task, I shall begin with the severest discipline, which they, from the nature of things, can bear, that discipline I can always relax; but, should I begin otherwise, it will be difficult, if not impossible, to bring them from a state of too much indulgence to a severer regimen. It is high time that they should know whom they are to obey, and what they have to do.

I therefore, last night, drew up the following regulations, and read them this morning. Having first assembled the colonists, I asked if they agreed to be governed by that constitution which they had all signed in England; to which they immediately assented. Then, having pointed out, as well as I could, the necessity which I thought there was of adopting all these regulations, I requested that those who had any objection to any of them, or to any part of them, would then make their objections. They were unanimously approved of. I then sent four men on shore to clear ground for a garden, and the rest were employed on board in thoroughly cleansing the ship.

The regulations, above alluded to, were divided into five heads, as follows:

First—*Health of the Members of the Community.*

As the success of our colony will depend in a very great degree on the portion of health enjoyed by its members, it behoves us, independent of the principles of humanity, to pay the most sedulous attention to the preservation of that which

1792.
Friday,
July 20.

they now enjoy; this end, I conceive, will be best answered by the following regulations:—

1st. To knock down all the bulk heads* between decks and not to suffer the screens, which will be given in their stead, to be unfurled after the hour of of ten in the morning, except in the case of sickness; by which means we shall enjoy a free circulation of air.

2d. To sweep the Births between decks twice every day, the first time at 10 A. M. the second time at 2 P. M.

3d. To have the chests moved, and a thorough cleaning between decks, every other day.

4th. To fumigate the ship twice a week.

5th. To wash between decks with vinegar once every fort night.

6th. To prohibit washing cloaths between decks.

7th. To send all the animals out of the ship.

8th. To build a house over the ship.

9th. To supply the colonists as often as possible with fresh provisions.

Secondly—*Safety of those Members.*

As paying attention to the health of the members of this community will be of little use, unless they can enjoy it in safety, I propose the following means for that end:

1st. That all the men of the community be divided into four equal parts.

2d. That one division be at all times on deck, as a guard.

3d. That no individual of that division be allowed to leave

---

* Wooden partitions.

the deck until he be relieved by another, unless it be with the consent of his officer.

4th. That each individual be furnished with a musquet, bayonet, and proper accoutrements, which, it is expected, will be kept in proper order; that is to say, always fit for service.

Thirdly—*Discipline*.

As we shall not be safe, though armed, without discipline, the act of the British parliament, entitled, "An Act for punishing mutiny and desertion, and for the better payment of the army in their quarters" will be rigidly enforced while under arms.

Fourthly—*Religion*.

It is conceived that no man can object to public prayers being read, to the whole community every Sunday morning.

Fifthly—*General Regulations*.

For the sake of order and regularity, it is necessary that no one quit the ship, without my leave; that, when on shore, no private parties go into the woods without my permission; that every one work when, and where, I order him, and only as I order him; that the water, necessary for the days consumption, be hoisted up by the division that has the morning watch, at day light; that no one wash but with rain water, upon deck, and before the windlass; that all lights be extinguished between decks at 9 o'clock, and that there be no singing after that hour.

The first part of this day was fair, in the latter we had heavy rains and violent winds.

1792.
Friday, July 20.

	Men.	Wom.	Chil.	
Colonists { Well	44	10	24	—Total W. 78 } Grand Total 86
Sick	4	3	1	—— S. 8

Sick list of ship's crew, 3.*

Saturday, July 21. Unwilling to lose any time in endeavouring to procure fresh provisions, vegetables, and fruit for the colony, I this morning sent the cutter to Bissao for some; and took that opportunity of writing to Mr. de Sylva Cordoza, expressing a wish to enter into a contract with him for a regular supply of those articles, during the rains. And, as the filling of water, and getting it on board, would greatly impede our progress in building the house over the ship, and other important occupations, on shore; I put all the empty water casks into the cutter that they might be filled at Bissao, while she was waiting for the stock.

A party was employed on shore in extending the garden, and another cutting scantling for the house, intended to be built over the ship, to secure the people from the heat of the sun and the violence of the rains.

No rain in the early part of the day, but after 9 A. M. continual light rain with a southerly wind.† In the morning died Mrs. Rodell of atrophy, whom we immediately buried; and in the evening died Mr. Hancorne of the fever. Served out osnaburgs, for screens, in lieu of the bulk-heads which have been knocked down.

---

* The state of the health of the colonists is given at the end of every day's Journal, that the reader may trace the progress of disease and death, and the rapid reduction of our members; the sick of the Hankey's crew are noted separately.

† To give the reader some idea of the climate of Bulama, a general and connected account of the winds, weather, &c. from July 1792 to November 1793, is given in the Appendix, No. V.

Sick list of ship's crew 4.

1792. Saturday, July 21.

Colonists $\begin{cases} \text{Well } 44 .. 11 .. 24 \text{—Total W. } 79 \\ \text{Sick } 3 .. 1 . 1 \text{—} \phantom{\text{Total}} \text{ S. } 5 \end{cases}$ Grand Total 84.

(Men. Wom. Chil.)

Sunday, 22d.

At day-light buried Mr. Hancorne;—heavy rains prevented my reading prayers; wind southerly.

After dinner sent a party of observation (three subscribers whose wish it was to go) into the country. They returned a little before dark, frightened, almost to death, by a buffaloe! and brought with them seven young wild ducks, which they had taken out of a nest on the top of a very high Pullam, or cotton tree. They had met with nothing worthy of notice; unless it be a savannah, of which they speak highly; and which, they suppose, contains about 100 acres.

From their account of their journey, I conclude it must bear about W. by N. of the garden, distant two miles.

Sick list—ship's crew 4.

Colonists $\begin{cases} \text{Well } 43 .. 8 .. 25 \text{—Total W. } 76 \\ \text{Sick } 4 .. 4 .. 0 \text{—} \phantom{\text{Total}} \text{ S. } 8 \end{cases}$ Grand Total 84.

(Men. Wom. Chil.)

Monday, 23d.

One party employed on shore extending the garden, another cutting scantling for the house, and a third party making a stye to receive our pigs.

About noon I was surprized to see a schooner come round the S.W. point, and haul in for the harbour, but more so at her colours, which were those of the Isle of Man. I immediately went on board and found that it was called the Fisher, and belonged to a slave ship of that name, now lying in the Rio Nunez; that it was under the direction of a Mr. Bootle, a mulattoe man, who had formerly (as servant to a Mr. Ormond, a great English slave trader in the Rio Pungos,) kept a factory at Bulola,

1792.
Monday,
July 23.

a Biafara town, about 70 miles up the Rio Grande; which factory had been given up ever since Mr. Ormond's death.

Mr. Bootle was last at Bissao, where having seen the Calypso, and learning from her where we had fixed ourselves, called in, merely out of curiosity, in his way up the Rio Grande; whither he was going, to endeavour to re-establish his former factory at Bulola. With him was one Ashley, the third mate of the Fisher.

Bootle seemed an intelligent man. I asked him to stay and dine with me; and while dinner was preparing, that I might converse with him alone, which could not well be done on board, I took him on shore under the pretext of seeing what we were doing.

Entering at once on the subject for which I had brought him on shore, I told him that I wished much to become acquainted with our neighbours, the Biafaras, on the opposite shore; but, as I had never before been in this country, nor indeed any man in the colony, I found it a matter of some difficulty to get at them; for not knowing where their nearest town was, and having no pilot, I did not think it safe, in our situation, to hazard the cutter, the only vessel we had, up the Rio Grande to seek for it. I therefore begged he would remain with me, till my cutter returned from Bissao; and that then I would go up the river with him. He said that he could not possibly wait; but that he would leave me one of his men to pilot the cutter up when she returned; and that he should be happy to render me any service with the natives in his power. Having asked him if the Biafaras were a warlike people, likely to be dissatisfied with our being on this island, or likely to attack us, he answered, that they were a quiet, inoffensive people, that would never attack us; but that as this island belonged, in right, to them, and not to the Bijugas, of whom he had heard that we had bought it, they would expect to be paid for it. I then asked him if he thought they would sell to us the opposite island called Great Bulama: as I wished much to have possession of both sides of the harbour; and if they would sell it, what he thought would be the probable amount of its price. He was astonished at my calling it an island, was sure that it was not one, had not a doubt that the Biafaras would sell me what land I pleased on the opposite side; and that the sum they would ask would be trifling. I told him that if he would assist me in purchasing the opposite land, and I succeeded in the purchase, I would give him 100 bars for his trouble: he promised to do every thing in his power to that end, with the greatest readiness; and without wishing the least recompense. We then agreed that he should sail this evening, make presents in my name to the kings of Ghinala; open to them the business; and send down his boat to inform me of the issue. Requesting him to be silent on the subject, we returned to the ship. Having sent him some porter and wine, before he sailed this evening, he sent me back a couple of hogs; which will be serviceable to the sick. Fine weather the greatest part of this day, wind to the southward, sent all the dogs on shore.

1792. Monday, July 23.

Sick list of ship's company, 3.

Colonists
	Men.	Wom.	Chil.		
Well	41	12	23	—Total W.	76
Sick	6		2	—— S.	8

Grand Total 84.

Every body on shore cutting down the woods, except two carpenters, who are building the house over the ship; the sur-

Tuesday, July 24.

1792.
Tuesday, July 24.

veyor and myself marked those trees which are not to be cut down; put some seeds in the ground; gave the surgeon a keg of millet for the sick. As much time was lost in the working parties coming on board to dinner, a barrel of beef and another of pork was sent on shore, with the necessary cooking-utensils, that it might be dressed there.

Fine weather all day, if we except a tornado which lasted about an hour.

Sick list of ship's company, 3.

Colonists $\begin{cases} \text{Well } 43 .. 11 .. 22 \text{ —Total W. } 76 \\ \text{Sick } 4 .. 1 .. 3 \text{ —— S. } 8 \end{cases}$ Grand Total 84.

(Men. Wom. Chil.)

Wednes. 25th.

The carpenters employed on board as before; a party on shore making a poultry house, and enclosing it with a large yard; all the rest of the colony cutting down and burning the woods. Fixed a lightning conductor to the main topmast head of the Hankey, killed one of the hogs, which I got from Bootle, and desired the surgeon to dispose of it as he thought proper among the sick; the number in whose list are, ship's company, 3.

Colonists $\begin{cases} \text{Well } 42 .. 11 .. 23 \text{ —Total W. } 76 \\ \text{Sick } 5 .. 1 .. 2 \text{ —— S. } 8 \end{cases}$ Grand Total 84.

(Men. Wom. Chil.)

Very fine weather all day with a S.W. wind.

Thurs. 26th.

The Colonists employed as yesterday. Having now made a good broad opening from the high water mark, abreast of the ship, to the top of the hill where the garden and offices are, and where we intend to erect our buildings, I removed thither, from the landing place, my tent, and hoisted before it the English colours. Sent the pigs on shore. Have reason to believe that all our bullocks, asses, sheep, and goats, have been killed by wolves,* or other beasts of prey, as we have not seen any of them these three days. Very little rain all day. Wind S.S.W.

1792.
Thurs.
July 26.

Sick list of ship's company, 3.

Colonists $\begin{cases} \text{Well } 42 .. 11 .. 24 - \text{Total W. } 77 \\ \text{Sick } 5 .. 1 .. 1 ---- \text{S. } 7 \end{cases}$ Grand Total 84.
(Men. Wom. Chil.)

Carpenters still employed covering the ship, a party enclosing the poultry yard, the rest of the colony extending the opening that we have cut to the hill, and burning the felled wood.

Friday, 27th.

Received a letter from Mr. Bootle, assuring me that he had not a doubt of my effecting the purchase I had mentioned to him, if I came up in the cutter with a proper assortment of goods. I now communicated what I had done to the gentlemen of the committee, who had been puzzling themselves to guess the cause of this visit from a strange boat; and were all astonishment when they saw a letter addressed to me, not having the least idea that either the one or the other came from Bootle. —No rain all day.—Wind S. W. by S.

Sick list of ship's company, 4.

Colonists $\begin{cases} \text{Well } 41 .. 11 .. 24 - \text{Total W. } 76 \\ \text{Sick } 6 .. 1 .. 1 ---- \text{S. } 8 \end{cases}$ Grand Total 84.
(Men. Wom. Chil.)

Carpenters still covering the ship; the rest of the colonists cutting and burning wood. Sent Bootle's boat back with Wm. Meares, one of the labourers; having detained one man from the boat to pilot me up in the cutter. Weather remarkably fine, with a fresh S.S.W. breeze. Two seamen belonging to the Hankey, who had yesterday lost themselves in the woods, re-

Saturday, 28th.

---

* They were sent on shore in consequence of my regulations adopted on the 20th. There were landed 2 oxen, 4 asses, 7 or 8 sheep, and about a dozen goats.

1792.
Saturday, July 28.

turned this evening, having seen nothing of consequence, except an elephant which fled from them.

Sick list of ship's company, 4.

Colonists $\begin{cases} \text{Well } 42..11..24 \text{ —Total W. } 77 \\ \text{Sick } 5..1..1 \text{ ——— S. } 7 \end{cases}$ Grand Total 84.

Sunday, 29th.

Last night the cutter returned from Bissao with necessaries for the sick, and four bullocks, one of which was killed, and served out both to the colonists and ship's company; and a part reserved, at the disposal of the surgeon, to make soup for the sick. At ten o'clock read prayers, after which, for the first time, I had an opportunity of going a little way inland. Returned in about two hours, having seen four runs of water, one of which was a very good one, not far from my tent; that is, just above the high water mark, on the larboard shore of the first creek to the northward of it. The land which I walked over, as far as I am capable of judging, was good. I saw none which was so difficult to cultivate as that on, and round, the hill which we are now clearing. Sent three parties of observation into the woods; they discovered nothing except runs of water in abundance, and near.

As I intended to go up the Rio Grande to-morrow, I thought it necessary to appoint a vice-president in the room of the late Mr. Hancorne, and therefore proposed Mr. Munden, who was accordingly elected by the committee.

Sick list of ship's company, 4.

Colonists $\begin{cases} \text{Well } 40..11..24 \text{ —Total W. } 75 \\ \text{Sick } 7..1..1 \text{ ——— S. } 9 \end{cases}$ Grand Total 84.

Monday, 30th.

At day-light got the cutter alongside the Hankey, and having taken out the water and the bullocks, put those goods into her which were thought necessary for purchasing, from the Biafaras, the opposite shore, called by the natives Great Bulama. Requested Mr. Munden to employ three people in making a pen for the cattle; the rest in cutting down and burning timber between the landing place and my tent only; and to finish, as fast as possible, the house over the ship. At one o'clock taking Mr. John Paiba, one of the subscribers, with me in the cutter, we cast loose from the ship for Ghinala, with a fresh S. W. breeze; heavy rains and hazy weather. Just after we had left the ship, a boat, with the master of the Experiment schooner, that was up the Rio Grande, came alongside; he was very ill, and had come down for medical advice. Sent him on board the Hankey. In a short time we got round the point which forms the northern headland of the mouth of the river Grande, and in somewhat less than four hours arrived at the entrance of a creek which leads up to Ghinala, having sailed about thirty miles up the most beautiful river I ever saw, indented on either side the whole way, but more particularly on the northern shore, with deep and large bays, and many creeks; carrying all the way much more than sufficient water for the largest ships. In nearly a north direction we sailed up this creek about four miles, and anchored, a little after five, close by the Fisher and Experiment schooners, both of them tenders to English ships employed in the slave trade, the one in the Rio Nunez, and the other at the Isles de Loss.*

Matchore, one of the kings of Ghinala, a district of the Biafara country, who is also called king of the Rio Grande, was

---

* So corruptly called by our sailors, and chart makers, from Ilhas dos Idolos. The Islands of Idols.

1792.
Monday,
July 30.

on board the former vessel; I therefore went there, and was introduced to him by Mr. Bootle.

Mr. B. still assured me that the land called the Great Bulama, was not an island, and though the whole northern shore was a continued chain of bays and creeks, yet not one of them had the appearance of a channel separating a large island from the continent, I therefore agreed with him that it most probably was not an island. I have not time to satisfy myself on this head by examining it; and therefore mean, after making presents to the two kings, purchasing from them refreshments for the colonists, and assuring them of our friendship and inclination to live on amicable terms with them, to return to the ship without purchasing any land.

Tuesday,
31st.

Heavy showers at intervals all day; wind S.W. Went on board Bootle's vessel early in the morning, and there saw with Matchore, Niobana the other king of Ghinala. Mr. Bootle told me that both the kings were very angry when he had informed them that I meant to go away without purchasing any land. Requested them both to come, with Mr. B., on board my cutter; where we would talk the business over; which they promised, and I returned on board.

Mr. Bootle and Matchore came soon after; but Niobana, having had some little palaver with Bootle, and being offended in some degree with the part Matchore had taken in it, refused to come.

I sent my own boat for him. He still refused. Bootle told me that this was in consequence of his having told him, in the morning, that I intended sailing without making any purchase; that he quarrelled violently with him; and accused him of advising me to go away without paying for the island of Bulama, which he said belonged to the Biafaras and not to the Bijugas. I requested Mr. B. would tell Matchore, that any claims which they had to make to the island of Bulama I would willingly hear; and, if well grounded, readily satisfy: but for that purpose it was necessary that both kings should be present, as I would by no means listen to any claim made by one king only. This was carried to Niobana, who persisted in his refusal to come on board. Late in the day I sent to him again, saying that I came to him with presents, and to offer him my friendship; but, as he valued neither, I was about to return. This brought him on board. When seated, he said that he was glad to see me; " he always wished to see White Man in his country." I replied, that from his conduct I should have supposed otherwise; that I was glad to see him, but should have been more so had he come earlier.

1792. Tuesday, July 31.

I then saluted him, and, after the usual ceremony of giving drams, entered upon the palaver.

Niobana began by claiming the island on which we have settled; said that he heard that we had purchased it from the Canabacs, and were building there; that in so doing we had done wrong; that it belonged to the Biafaras, and not to the Bijugas, (here he appealed to Matchore, and all the people, who assented to what he had said;) that his father, when dying, had told him that Bulama had belonged to him, and that he had inherited it from his ancestors; that they had formerly lived upon that island, but as the Bijugas were always at war with them, they had quitted it, and the shores near the mouth of the Great River; and had retreated to the place where they now are, that they might live in peace; and that their living at a distance from, certainly could not do away their right to, those lands.

1792.
Tuesday, July 31.

I replied, that having accidentally heard that Bulama belonged not, in right, to the Canabacs, I was induced, on that account, to come hither, and to know if the Biafaras had any claim to it; and that I had never intended to take possession of another person's land without the free consent of its owner. He said I did right. It was now dark; both the kings were intoxicated, as were all their people, who were both noisy and troublesome. I therefore endeavoured to get them out of the vessel, which with some difficulty, was at length accomplished; for they wanted to remain with me all night, as I had promised to go up to their town the following morning. Hauled the seine, and caught as many fish as we could consume in the three vessels, most of them were mullet, but there were besides three pair of soles, two saw fish, some cat fish, and three or four other sorts of common fish.

Monthly state of the Colony.*

	Men.	Wom.	Chil.		
On the Calypso's departure the 19th of this month we had { Well	44	10	24	—Total W. 78 } 86.	
Sick	4	3	1	— S. 8	
Making altogether	48	13	25	= 86	
Since which time we have lost by .... { Death	1	1	0	—Total .... 2.	
Present state of Colony ...... { Well	41	11	23	—Total W. 75 } 84.	
Sick	6	1	2	— S. 9	
Making altogether	47	12	25	= 84	

Wednes. August 1.

Early this morning, having one of Mr. Bootle's men for an

* I have inserted this monthly state of the colony here, notwithstanding I was at this time absent, to shew the progress of sickness and mortality.

interpreter, I left the cutter, and having rowed about a mile 1792.
and a half up the creek, landed; then walking about a mile, the Wednes.
first half through swamps, and the latter up a gentle ascent, we August 1.
arrived at Niobana's town, where we found Matchore, whose
town was about a quarter of a mile distant on the left hand.
They seemed much pleased at my arrival, and saluted me by
firing five blunderbusses. They repeated their wish to have
White Man settle there. Having divided the greater part of
some rum and tobacco, which I had brought with me, between
the two kings, and given the rest to the surrounding natives, I
told the kings that I wanted to buy some of their land on the
continent, as well as the island of Bulama, and that if they
would return with me, in my boat, I would shew them what
goods I would give. They replied that I might buy what land I
wanted, but that they could not come on board to settle that
palaver till to-morrow. We returned to our vessel; in the
evening hauled the seine, and caught abundance of fish. Showery
all day. Wind S.W.

This morning the Experiment sailed for Bulama, and by it I Thursd.
wrote to the gentlemen of the committee.* At ten, a number of 2d.
the natives appearing opposite the vessel, we sent the boat for
them, when king Matchore, and about twenty men and women
came on board. Niobana, in consequence of illness, remained in
his town, but had sent *his head woman with his cane, to represent
him.* Bootle came on board and we began the palaver. As I
had observed that there was no doing any thing with these people, if they got much liquor, I determined not to give them

* Appendix, No. 6.

1792.
Thursd.
August 2.

any (except the dram which it is customary to give them on their first coming on board) until the business was settled.

Matchore having named the goods which he wanted, they were immediately laid before him, and I now thought every thing was finished; but he kept me from 11 o'clock, the time these things were produced, till sun-set, changing sometimes one thing and sometimes another. At one moment he would have six or eight guns, and the next I must take them back again, then he would re-demand them; and so on with every separate article, debating on each with his people whether it should be accepted or not, all of them talking at the same time and making a noise sufficient to stun one. At length, when going on shore, he said that he would take with him only half the goods, and leave the remainder on board. I thought this was a stratagem to keep me here, till they had drunk out all my spirits, knowing that I would not go away before they returned and signed the treaty, if they had in their possession half the goods at which the lands were valued; I therefore took every thing from him again, and told him that if Niobana and himself did not come early the next morning to finish the transaction, I should get under sail and leave them, as I cared little whether I purchased the land or not. They seemed not much pleased, and went on shore. Showery all day—wind S. W.

Friday 3. About nine a large canoe was coming alongside, with those people who were on board yesterday, except Matchore who had walked, and was on the beach opposite the cutter. The opposition of a strong S. W. wind to the ebb tide had raised a considerably short sea; as they came near us we threw to them the end of a rope, when all getting up together they overturned the canoe, and the man who had hold of the rope, letting it go, they were carried astern by the tide. All the men could swim, but three women could not; they were supported by three men each, till they were secured on the bottom of the canoe: our boat immediately went to their assistance, and was near meeting the same fate from their eagerness to get into her. As no lives were lost I was exceedingly rejoiced at the accident, for when they came on board they said that the palaver must be short, as they were all very cold and wanted to get home to dry what little clothes they wore. Matchore and Bootle, and Niobana's representative, the old woman and the cane, having come on board, in less than two hours the palaver was finished, and Matchore had signed the conveyance of the island of Bulama, and a much greater extent of land on the opposite shore, together with all the adjacent isles,* for goods, which they immediately carried on shore, to the amount of about twenty-six pounds sterling.† We hauled the seine again in the evening, and caught abundance of mullet; showery all day —wind S.W. Matchore in the morning made me a present of a bullock and half a dozen of fowls.

Early this morning I went up to Niobana's town, to get him to sign the conveyance of the land which I had yesterday purchased; and which Matchore had signed on board the cutter. He did so; and immediately afterwards taking hold of both my hands, and lifting them up near to his lips (I supposed with an intention of kissing) he spit in them, saying

* Appendix, No. 7. † Appendix, No. 8.

1792.
Saturday,
Aug. 4.

that now Bulama and the other lands, which I had been treating for, were mine; that his town, even where I stood, belonged to me; and that now we were brothers. To be called the brother of Niobana I had no objection, but would willingly have dispensed with the ceremony by which I was made so. Niobana was very solicitous for me to make an establishment at Ghinala, and endeavoured to prevail upon me to leave a white man there, for " if white man live here, said he, we shall want nothing, but if white man does not live here we shall want every thing." On my requesting to take with me some of their subjects to work on the island, as grumetas, for four barrs a month, both the kings promised to let them come hereafter; and Matchore said that his son should accompany them, but at present they declined sending any.

To prevent disputes hereafter, I had been very anxious that they should fully comprehend the direction of the boundary line, which separated the lands I had purchased from theirs; and in this, I believe, we succeeded. We had taken also great pains to ascertain of these people whether the land they inhabited was separated from the continent by an arm of the sea, that is by any narrow channel or creek: but to all our questions they returned such vague, and sometimes contradictory, answers, that we could put no reliance in any of them. For my own part I am almost convinced that the land called the Greater Bulama, is not an island,* and that the creek we are in extends very little farther. I have none but white men with

* The charts make it an island; see that numbered 8 in the African Pilot by Laurie and Whittle. Some of the Portuguese Grumetas told me that water went all round it, but I am very much inclined to doubt this.

me; it has rained almost the whole of the time that we have been here; and I do not like to expose them too much to weather that in all probability would lay them up, by examining this creek. Had I Grumetas, I would have gone myself.

1792.
Saturday, August 4.

About noon we sailed, Bootle for Bulola, ourselves for Bulama. At dark, the tide having made against us, we were obliged to anchor just within the mouth of the river; but anxious to get back to the Hankey, I took the boat for that purpose, and reached her in about three hours. The sick list had increased in my absence, four. Master Hancorne, an infant of a year old had been buried; the cutting down the trees had been continued; the covering over the ship finished; and a pen made for the cattle. The American brig commanded by Moore was in the harbour, having put in in distress, after losing two anchors off the isle, or rather rock, of Alcatras.*

---

* MEMORANDUM for those who have never been up the Rio Grande to find the creek which leads to Ghinala (pronounced by the natives Inala.)

The course, from the entrance, up the river, is E.N.E. for about 30 miles, when you come to the mouth of this creek on its northern shore; it may be known by the two following circumstances:

1st. That opposite to it there is a similar opening on the south side of the river.

2d. That the river here forms the first bend or elbow, running above it East and West, but below it E.N.E. and W.S.W.

Haul up this creek north about $2\frac{1}{2}$ miles, and then keep about N. by E. $\frac{1}{2}$ E. $1\frac{1}{2}$ mile more, when you may come too in four fathoms at high water, which will leave you two at low; the tide rising here about twelve feet. Should you prefer more water, you may anchor a little sooner, it shoaling gradually from 10 fathoms as you go up. You will not see either village or hut. Fire two guns as a signal for trade, and some natives will soon appear opposite your vessel. You may safely trust to your lead.

As far as I went, there is no danger in running up the river if you keep nearly mid-channel; but on the second point from the entrance, on the north side, there is a ledge of rocks which appeared to me to run off about a cable's length, and to show themselves at half tide.

1792.
Sunday,
August 5.

At eight in the morning the cutter came in.—Heavy rains all the forenoon prevented my reading prayers. Read to the

When going up the river we had a pilot, and a fair wind, and kept mid-channel. We saw no danger except the rocks above noticed on the second point, and we had no bottom all the way, till we entered the creek; but we were going pretty fast, and our hand line was only 16 fathoms in length.

In coming down the river we had no pilot and a contrary wind. In turning down we stood within pistol-shot of either shore, the lead always going, and got bottom only three times, each time in stays, and each time we had 13½ fathoms water. We saw many buffaloes on its banks.

All the charts which I have seen of this river place the island of Bissegos in the middle of it, and nearly half way from its mouth to Ghinala creek, but very erroneously; for the river, to that height, has not a single bend, and there the trifling one of two points only.

Now, as I before observed, there is a creek on the south side opposite to the one which leads to Ghinala: this creek, after running to the South and West, *may*, by inclining to the N.W. re-enter the Rio Grande in some of those bays which we passed on its southern shore; and this I take to be the case, for the pilot said that he had *heard* that a boat by going up that creek, might come out again at high water, in some place or other, but where, he did not know, never having been there himself. Thus, I imagine, the island of Bissegos is formed; whether upon good grounds or not, those who read this may judge; for they will then know as much on the subject as I do. Two things however, are certain; one, that there is *no island* where Bissegos is laid down by the chart makers; and the other, that *there is a place called Bissegos* on the south side of the Rio Grande, which I have always understood to be upon an island.

I never yet saw a good, nay a decent chart of this part of the world. If any man should attempt to run by them, I mean within the shoals of the Rio Grande, he will inevitably lose his vessel. As an instance, I will take the *Island of Mantere*, laid down to the southward of Bulama and nearly S.W. of that land which forms the south point of the mouth of the Rio Grande, between which and Mantere there is laid down a good *ship channel*, carrying from 20 to 10 fathoms all the way. Now, *there is no such island in that position—no such channel*; and he, who would run by his chart, would, where he expected 20 fathoms of water, find trees 20 feet high, probably in the midst of a Naloo village. The point, called Tombaly point, is on the continent, and not on an island; and the coast line on the East and N.E. of this imaginary island should be continued to it.

colonists the treaty which I had concluded with the kings of Ghinala; served out fresh beef, which had been issued once to the colonists, while I was up the Rio Grande. Just before dark I went to examine a canoe, that had landed about a mile above the ship, from Bissao bound to Tombaly, the people were getting wood. I asked them to come on board that I might have an opportunity of making them some little present, but they refused our offer.

1792. Sunday, Aug. 5th.

Sick list of ship's company, 3.

Colonists $\begin{cases} \text{Well } 32..11..21 \text{ —Total W. } 64 \\ \text{Sick } 15..1..3 \text{ —Total S. } 19 \end{cases}$ Grand Total 83.

(Men. Wom. Chil.)

No rain all day. At day-light a boy named Coggins, who had been ill of a fever some days, fell overboard; he could not swim, but the boat picked him up just as he was sinking. In two hours he died—buried him. Every body employed in cutting down and burning wood. Thermometer at noon 76—wind S.W.

Monday, 6th.

Sick list of ship's company, 3.

Colonists $\begin{cases} \text{Well } 37..11..22 \text{ —Total W. } 70 \\ \text{Sick } 10..1..1 \text{ — S. } 12 \end{cases}$ Grand Total 82.

(Men. Wom. Chil.)

Changeable weather. Employed on shore clearing the land. A schooner arrived from Bissao with an anchor and cable for the American brig. By this schooner Mr. De Sylva sent me four hogs and a dozen fowls.

Tuesday 7th.

As there were several sick in the Calypso when she sailed from this place, Mr. Ballard, our assistant surgeon, went in her to attend them as far as Sierra Leone, to which place I was to send the cutter to bring him back.*

* Mr. Ballard, one of the subscribers, who had put his name down with others to

1792.
Tuesday, Aug. 7th.

In order therefore that those, who wished to write to Europe, might have time to prepare their letters, I this day made it known that early to-morrow morning I should go in the cutter to Bissao, to endeavour to procure a regular supply of fruit, vegetables, and fresh provisions from that place, during the rains, and thence dispatch her to Sierra Leone to bring back our assistant urgeon.

In consequence of this notice, Messrs. Reynolds, Paiba, and Neild, subscribers, and Henry Rodell a labourer, wrote letters to me, requesting leave to go home. What a farce! Can any thing be more ridiculous? Is it not odd that these people could not have made up their minds sooner? It is only 19 days since the Calypso sailed, had they gone then it would have been better; for though I care not a farthing myself, if four fifths of them go, yet I see that it greatly dispirits those who remain; but by some fatality or other, the actions of almost every individual have been so *ill advised as to do no good, and so ill timed* as to do the *most possible harm*.

Sick list of ship's company, 2.

Colonists { Well 38 .. 11 .. 21 —Total W. 70 }
{ Sick 9 .. 1 .. 2 —Total S. 12 } Grand Total 82.

(Men. Wom. Chil.)

Wednes. 8th.

About seven this morning I sailed with the cutter, through the north channel, for Bissao, carrying with me three subscribers, one labourer, and his child, who were going home; Mr. Gandell the secretary who was to return with me; and Wm. Meares, a

---

remain on the island when the majority of the settlers had resolved to go away in the Calypso, was appointed our assistant surgeon, in the room of Mr. Williams previously discharged; but, as there was no surgeon in the Calypso, and many sick, he had permission to go in that vessel to Sierra Leone, however, as he never returned, as a Colonist, his name does not appear among those in appendix No. 4.

labourer, and Wm. Reeves a boy who was to assist in navigating the cutter to Sierra Leone and back again. We ran upon a sand bank, where we remained about an hour and anchored betwixt seven and eight in the evening, between the isles of Sorciere and Bourbon, having had fine weather and a S. W. breeze all day.

1792
Wednes.
Aug. 8th,

Ran up to Bissao and anchored opposite Mr. De Sylva's house; sent the master of the cutter to inform the governor of my arrival; and waited myself on De Sylva, who readily promised to supply me with what stock, vegetables, and fruit he could procure, once a fortnight; but feared he should not be able to supply me with the full quantity of either which I had demanded. Dined and slept at Mr. De Sylva's house—incessant rain.

Thursd.
9th.

A Mr. Williams who came out of England as our assistant surgeon, and quitted the Calypso at Bulama, is with Mr. De Sylva as his domestic surgeon; he has buried his wife here, and now wants to get home with his son, a little boy; he therefore requested me to order him a passage in the cutter to Sierra Leone, which I accordingly did, merely out of humanity, and on account of his little boy, for he is a miserable wretch, destitute of every good quality.

Rainy weather.—The great object of my coming hither being accomplished, and Mr. De Sylva having promised to let one of his vessels carry me back tomorrow morning, I this evening dispatched the cutter to Sierra Leone, with directions to wait there three days for Mr. Ballard the assistant surgeon; and foreseeing that those members of the council who had left the colony, and might yet be there, would probably interfere with, and detain, the cutter, to the great detriment of our undertaking, I gave the master directions not to obey any orders, but those which he had already received from me.

Friday,
10th,

1792.
Friday, August 10th.

I had requested Mr. De Sylva to ride out with me this evening, wishing to see something of the Papell country. In the morning I had walked out a little way with him, to see the natives make their rice Lugars;* but when the horses came to the door this evening, I found myself too ill to mount; feeling, for the first time in this country, a violent fever upon me.

The governor, with the collector, who by the bye manages him, came this evening to Mr. De Sylva's; where it was debated whether or not they should put me in prison; which, had it not been for the remonstrances of De Sylva, I believe would have been the case. They however wished to put a guard over the house to prevent my having any communication with the natives, but the owner of it answering for me on that score, they departed.

I knew that I had been the subject of their conversation; which, on the part of the collector, had been very violent. De Sylva spoke a little English; and I asked him if they did not want to send me to prison again: he said yes; but don't be afraid of that; I shall persuade them to the contrary. I told him that the only sensations which I could feel for such men were those of contempt, and not fear: and begged he would tell them so. This he however declined.

Saturday, 11th.

Being very ill all day Mr. De Sylva persuaded me not to go away as I had intended. Fine weather.

Sunday, 12th.

Finding myself no better, I resolved to go back while I was yet able. At day-light, therefore, this morning I left Mr. De Sylva's house; where I had experienced every civility and attention; and went on board the vessel, which he had prepared to carry me to Bulama; and which was filled with so many good things that he seemed determined that I should not have a wish unsatisfied.

* Plantations.

He had also sent on board a cow and a calf and three dozen fowls. 1792. As soon as I got on board, I was obliged to go to bed, where I Sunday, lay till noon; when crawling upon deck, I found that the Gru- Aug. 12. metas, instead of anchoring, had suffered a strong ebb tide to carry us down amidst the shoals between Arcas and Bulama, and that we were almost as far from home as when we sailed. The tide was now making in our favor, and as we could not well go wrong I again went to my bed; but with the assistance of the patron,* as I was unable to stand alone. At sun-set, the tide turning against us, we were obliged to anchor; and as it was impossible for the sloop, that I was in, to reach the Hankey before the next day, and as I found myself much better in the cool of the evening than in the middle of the day, I took the little boat and went in quest of our ship which I reached between nine and ten o'clock at night.

Mr. Ozanne who had left England in a deep consumption was dead; also that truly good and valuable man, Mr. Ben. Marston our surveyor. Mr. Marston was born in Marblehead, New England, where he was a respectable merchant, and had considerable property, at the commencement of those unfortunate troubles which terminated in the separation of that country from England In consequence of his loyalty he had not only lost a comfortable competency, but had undergone, for the last ten years, unheard of, and almost incredible difficulties. Sometimes he was whole days without bread; and weeks together his daily expenditure amounted only to three-halfpence—a penny worth of bread and a half-penny worth of figs. Too noble to beg, yet willing to work; but, unknown and friendless in England, no one would employ him. Thus did this good man struggle in poverty for ten years, in that country which he had fought for, in that coun-

---

* Master.

1792.
Sunday,
Aug. 12.

try, for whose interest he had quitted his friends, his relations, the lands of his ancestors, and every thing which is dear to man.

I never heard this good man rail at, nor say harsh things of that country, by which he had been so ill treated; he bore all patiently. He was about 60 years of age; had been educated in Havard College, New England; and was both learned and pious. Happy in having known such a man, I felt it a duty to endeavour to record his virtues. Should this Journal, by any accident, ever reach Marblehead, it may be a consolation to some of his friends and family to know what became of him, and at the same time to know, that, if he did not die a rich, he died a good man; for I cannot be suspected of flattering or overcharging the character of that man whom I never saw till in this expedition; and who, though it ought to have been otherwise, was in such a situation as would not be likely to procure an interested panegyrist. It may also be some consolation to them to learn that his virtues were not unknown, and that though we may have but little ourselves, we have at least sufficient to respect it in others; that this good man lived respected, and died regretted by all, and is now, we trust, receiving the reward of his virtues and sufferings in this world.

The sick list had increased one in number, and the colonists had been served with fresh beef once, during my absence. The secretary I left at Bissao.

	Men.	Wom.	Chil.		
Colonists { Well	32	10	17	— Total W. 59 }	Grand Total 72.
Sick	7	2	4	— — S. 13 }	

Sick list of ship's company, 4.

Monday, 13th.

Fine weather in the morning; rains the latter part of the day; wind S.W. People employed on shore in cutting and burning wood. The sloop which I had left last night came in this morning. As I found myself much better to day, I went on shore to see what progress we had made; and in truth I was much disappointed, for but little appeared to have been done. Conceiving that smoking might contribute towards the preservation of the healths of the colonists during the rains, I this day issued to each of them pipes and tobacco. At any rate, if smoked below, it will answer the purpose of fumigating the ship.

1792. Monday, Aug. 13.

Mr. Morse, one of the subscribers, who has been educated in the profession of a surgeon, hearing that Williams had left Mr. de Sylva at Bissao, wished to enter the same family in his stead; and requested that I would let him go to Bissao in the sloop which brought me thence. I have not yet asked any one to remain with me, and believe I never shall; for of the whole number I cannot select half a dozen that deserve their bread. As to asking my leave, it is ridiculous in the extreme; for, were I inclined to detain them, they all know that I have no power to do it.

		Men.	Wom.	Chil.		
Colonists	Well	31	10	17	—Total W. 58	Grand Total 72.
	Sick	8	2	4	—— S. 14	

Ship's company sick, 4.

Prevented doing any thing on shore by heavy rains, attended by strong S.W. winds; very ill in bed all day; desired Mr. Rowe, the surgeon, to send me a list, every morning, of those to whom fresh provisions were absolutely necessary, and I would order fowls to be killed for them. It blew hard all night, and *our only boat* broke adrift; fortunately, at day-light this morning, we discovered it just drifting round the point in the North Channel. Had it continued dark a quarter of an hour longer, we should have inevitably lost it: this, trifling as it may appear to people in Europe, would have been, to us, a very

Tuesday, 14th.

1792.
Tuesday,
Aug. 14.

serious and irreparable loss; we had no other; none could be purchased at Bissao; and Captain Cox, of the Hankey, had only one, which of course he would not leave behind him; neither would he like to lend it to a parcel of unthinking landsmen, who would want it on shore six times every day—three times to carry them to their work, and three times to bring them back to their meals.* I know not any one circumstance that would have retarded our work more than the loss of this boat; yet, when in England I proposed bringing out two more boats, our *wise men* smiled.

The Hankey's pinnace, however, recovered it, half way to Arcas, and returned in about eight hours.

The sloop that brought me from Bissao returned this day, and by it Mr. Morse left the colony.

Colonists $\begin{cases} \text{Well } 28 .. 10 .. 17 - \text{Total W. } 55 \\ \text{Sick } 10 .. 2 .. 4 - \text{—— S. } 16 \end{cases}$ Grand Total 71.

Sick, ship's company, 4.

Wednes. 15th.

Wind S.W.—weather hazy and showery. People on shore cutting and burning wood. Requested the surgeon would send me, every morning, a list of those persons to whom flour ought to be served, instead of salt provisions. Ill in bed all day.

Colonists $\begin{cases} \text{Well } 29 .. 10 .. 17 - \text{Total W. } 56 \\ \text{Sick } 9 . 2 .. 4 - \text{—— S. } 15 \end{cases}$ Grand Total 71.

Sick, ship's company, 4.

---

* As we had not yet any covering on shore, except a little tool house, it was impossible, from the rains, to cook for the people on shore. Therefore, at day-light they were carried on shore to their work, and at eight brought back to breakfast; at nine they were relanded, and at noon came on board to their dinners. At two P.M. they went to their work again, and were finally brought on board at sun-set.

African Memoranda. 1792.
Thurs.
Aug. 16.

Heavy rains prevented the people doing any thing on shore. Wind S. W. Ill in bed all day.

Colonists $\begin{cases} \text{Well } 28..9..17 - \text{Total W. } 54 \\ \text{Sick } 10..3..4 - \text{——— S. } 17 \end{cases}$ Grand Total 71.

Men. Wom. Chil.

Ship's company sick, 4.

Friday, 17th.

Strong S. W. wind all day, without rain. People at work on shore as usual. Able to sit up a little to day. Wm. Pullen died early this morning of a fever, and was interred.

The three days preceding this, I have not been out of my bed. On the 14th I was very ill, but not supposed to be in immediate danger; from the morning of the 15th I grew gradually worse, till about eight in the evening, when my recovery was absolutely despaired of.

I am aware that I shall be accused of consummate vanity for what I am now about to write: be it so—for I allow that even to the last moment of my recollection, when I absolutely thought that I was no longer for this world; when I was actually deprived of my speech, but not of my senses, I felt great consolation in what I heard every one say of me; for as no one conceived that I was sensible, or could possibly live an hour longer, they probably spoke only their real sentiments.

The people had crouded about the cabin door all day, inquiring after my health, and shewed great anxiety for my recovery. As the front of the cabin, from one side of the ship to the other, was one continued window, I could hear every thing that was said, but could not be seen, on account of a canvas screen round that part where my cot hung. Reader! if this should ever be seen by other eyes than my own, call me vain if you please, for I do assure you that I was exceedingly so, when I heard every

1792.
Friday,
Aug. 17.

individual speaking only my praise; the breath of slander itself could not accuse me of any one thing which I wished not the world to know: every one said that I had killed myself by my exertions for their good; that labouring and exposing myself so much as I had done no constitution could stand; that now they *must* go home, for, as they had lost me, there was no one left who could take care of them.

Between seven and eight in the evening I could no longer articulate; but was seized with a rattling in my throat, which I conceived to be a symptom of my no very distant dissolution. I was still sensible; and, indeed, for an hour after this rattling first seized me. It was now that I heard every one say that it was all over; and that Captain Cox, sitting by the sky light almost immediately over me, said that to-morrow he should have orders to get ready to sail for England. This, now that I am better, Mr. Munden and Mr. Aberdein, the only two members of the committee, have confirmed; as they had made up their minds to give such orders the moment that I was dead; for neither of them would take charge of the colony, and, indeed, if they would, nobody would have staid when I was gone.

I can with truth aver, that if in these moments I had the least wish to live, it was to preserve this colony. Death, if thou never comest clothed in greater terrors, I shall ne'er be afraid to meet thee; for the happiest moments of my existence were those, when I expected to cease to be. May my future life be such as to enable me always to meet thee thus!

About nine, I fell into a dose; and did not awake until late next morning, the 16th, when I was out of danger; and am this day well enough to sit up a little.

1792.
Friday, Aug. 17.

Colonists $\begin{cases} \text{Well } 28 .. 9 .. 18 \text{ —Total W. } 55 \\ \text{Sick } 9 .. 3 .. 3 \text{ ——— S. } 15 \end{cases}$ Grand Total 70.

Men. Wom. Chil.

Ship's company sick, 3.

Saturday, 18th. Fine clear weather, and fresh S.W. wind. People on shore clearing the ground as usual. Myself much better.*

Sunday, 19th. Tolerably fine weather; S.W. wind. Gain strength astonishingly. Requested Mr. Munden would read prayers to the colonists. Killed a couple of hogs for them. Therm. noon 81.

Monday, 20th. Very fine weather; S.W. wind. Strong enough to go on shore for a few minutes. People cutting and burning wood.

Tuesday, 21st. Same wind, weather, and employment. Therm. 81.

Men. Wom. Chil.

Colonists $\begin{cases} \text{Well } 30 .. 9 .. 18 \text{ —Total W. } 57 \\ \text{Sick } 7 .. 3 .. 3 \text{ ——— S. } 13 \end{cases}$ Grand Total 70.

Wednesday. 22d. Light rains all the morning; fine weather the remainder of the day; wind S.W. Sent the frame of the large boat, which we brought from England, on shore; and, having Captain Cox's permission, set the Hankey's carpenter, to whom I am to give five guineas for this job, and one of our own people, to set it up.

Mr. Aberdein and myself tracing the lines for a block-house, which I intend building on the top of the hill. Set three people about cutting and squaring timber for its erection: the remainder of the colony going on with the cutting and burning of wood.

Knowing the indolence of most of the colonists, and at the same time convinced of their interested dispositions, for they have no idea of doing any one thing, unless the whole good promised by it centers in SELF, I think the only, or at any rate

---

* Where no notice is taken of the sick, it must be understood, that they continue the same as in the last statement.

1792.
Wednes.
Aug. 22.

the surest, and readiest, way to get a covering, or a house, for every individual, is by making every individual interested in the same building. And, as a block-house is absolutely necessary for our defence, I think it best to make the same building answer the double purpose of defence and dwelling. By these means, too, I shall have every one under my own eye; and, being collected in one body, we shall, of course, be much stronger than if separated. I therefore intend to allot a single house, all of equal dimensions, to each subscriber, and one of another class of houses, also of equal dimensions, to each married labourer, the single ones to occupy them by fours; and these houses shall be drawn for by lot, that no one may complain of preference of situation, &c. But to encourage the industrious, those who work most shall have their houses covered first.

Was I, instead of building this block-house, to suffer every man to build a house for himself, the inconveniences would be many. For instance, should he chuse an improper place, I cannot interfere. If it is an unhealthy spot, he will say, I am to inhabit it and not you; if too distant, and I cannot protect him, he runs the risk and not me; if the house he is building be too small and too weak, he, only, will have thrown away his time in erecting it, the inconvenience will be his and not mine; if the house be too large and too strong, some time will have been thrown away—he will have lost that time and not me; should he work but little, and I reproach him with idleness, he will say, if my house is not finished in due time, I may be exposed to the inclemency of the weather, but not you: thus should I for ever be answered, were I ever to interfere with the building of their private houses. One man would be building a drawing-room, while a much better would be content with a kitchen. If it be objected that these people will not act so ridiculously, that they will see the necessity of building and living close together for their mutual defence, and that they will readily sacrifice many little conveniences for the PUBLIC GOOD, I answer to the former, that I have seen them, if possible, act more ridiculously; the latter they none of them comprehend. Another thing to be taken into the account is, that were they once to begin working for themselves, they would work when, and where, and how they pleased; they would always be straggling and scattered; and should I want any public work done, I should not be able, at any rate, to procure one of them, till he had finished his own house; probably not even while he could find a job, however trifling, to do for himself; if, indeed, I should be *ever* able to get them from their own, to the public work again.

1792.
Wednes.
Aug. 22.

Thus a block-house, if ever erected, would be the last. Is it not strange that these people so delicately alive to the sense of danger, are the last to think of erecting a building for their protection and defence. Man—what a contradictory animal thou art!

In order, therefore, to have a house of defence, and a house for each colonist, erected as early as possible; in order that our labour be concentered, and directed by one person, to one end; and that end be public security, and public good, I have determined that no private buildings be erected. I will neither give the materials for building, nor an inch of ground to build upon; and will, till we are reinforced, clear grounds, and erect buildings for the public only.

Five or six days after the departure of the Calypso, Mr. Cur-

1792.
Wednesd.
Aug. 22.

wood, one of the subscribers, was much offended, because I would not let him build a little house for himself on shore. Had I suffered him to do so, I could not have refused to others the same privilege, and instead of having what little ground we now have cleared, we should not have had, perhaps, the twentieth part of it, if any at all. Many subscribers are now dissatisfied that I will not give them a little spot for a garden; were I to do so, their whole labour would be *there;* rather than put their seeds in the *public garden,* they suffer them to rot. Noble minded men think what you please of my conduct; call it tyrannical if you please, but if I will not please you, though at the expence of *your good only,* you surely must not expect me to do so, at the expence of *my own understanding.* Ten years hence you may probably think that I have done right. Therm. 82.

Sick as before.

Thursday, 23d. The weather continues fine—with light S.W. winds—the different parties employed in setting up the large boat, cutting and squaring timber for the block house, and burning the branches of trees. Therm. 78.

Colonists { Well 28 .. 9 .. 18 —Total W. 55 } Grand Total 70.
{ Sick 9 .. 3 .. 3 —— S. 15 }

Ship's company sick, 2.

Friday 24. The same weather and employment. In the eve the Fisher schooner anchored here from Bulola.

Mrs. Ashworth died of a decline. Therm. 78.

Colonists { Well 26 .. 9 .. 17 —Total W. 52 } Grand Total 69.
{ Sick 11 .. 2 .. 4 —— S. 17 }

Ship's company sick, 2.

Satur. 25. Heavy rains and calm all the morning—latter part of the day fine weather and S.W. wind. Parties at work as usual, when the rain admitted of it. At day-light buried Mrs. Ashworth. Fumigated the ship. The Fisher sailed this evening, with many goods which Bootle had written to me for. I prevailed upon the pilot of this vessel to leave a little black boy, of Kacundy, who was under his care, with me to learn English. Therm. 80.

1792. Saturday, Aug. 26.

Colonists $\begin{cases} \text{Well } 26 \ldots 8 \ldots 16 \text{ —Total W. } 50 \\ \text{Sick } 11 \ldots 3 \ldots 5 \text{ — — S. } 19 \end{cases}$ Grand Total 69.

   Men. Wom. Chil.

Ship's company sick, 2.

Heavy rains, with a S.W. wind, prevented my reading prayers; at 4 P. M. a sloop belonging to Bissao, came alongside from Canabac with three natives of that island, who brought with them a copy of our treaty with their kings, which had been left with them for the express purpose of being sent on board our ship, before they should venture to approach with their canoes. They told us that Bellchore had come to pay us a visit; and had landed on the other side of the south point of the Harbour, where he was now waiting. Taking Mr. Aberdein in the boat with me, I immediately went to bid him welcome and to bring him on board. He and his people had quitted their canoes, and, sitting in three different parties, of nearly equal numbers, round as many different fires, were satisfying their hunger with some venison which they had this morning shot upon our island. The old king, who immediately knew me, having put on, over his goat-skin, his ceremonial dress, and changed a red woollen cap for a three corner'd hat, with as many buttons on each side as it had corners, and one on the crown, went with seven of his men in my boat on board the Hankey. His two canoes which followed with the rest of his men, in number 40, I desired he would order ashore, in

Sunday, 26th.

1792.
Sunday,
Aug. 26.

a small creek, about a quarter of a mile from the ship; which he immediately did; and thither I sent them provisions.

When the hour of sleep arrived, the old king, who had by no means spared the rum which had been placed before him on his arrival, would not go to bed, till a bottle and a glass were placed by his pillow; for, said he, "suppose I must wake in the night, that time I can drink rum too." I had spread a mat for him on one side of my cot and laid thereon a pillow, but having seen a dressing gown of mine he would not lay down without it; he must have that to keep him warm. Things being thus adjusted, he quietly took possession of his mat. Three of his men slept on the other side of me, and the remaining four under my cot. The four watches were this night, for safety, contracted to two. Killed a bullock for the colony. Therm. 78.

	Men.	Wom.	Chil.		
Colonists { Well	25	.. 9	.. 17	—Total W. 51	} Grand Total 69.
Sick	12	.. 2	.. 4	——— S. 18	

Ship's company sick, 2.

Monday, 27th.

Showery weather and S. W. wind. This morning I saluted Bellchore with six guns; and, afterwards, to shew him the distance to which I could throw a shot, fired a four pounder directly up the river, a squall prevented his seeing the shot fall and he supposed it went into the wood five or six miles distant.

As a formidable number of his people, considering our strength, were on the island, I judged it not prudent to send more of our men to work on shore, than those who were employed in preparing timber for the block-house, which from three were this day increased to six, being all in the colony that could be found useful for that purpose; the rest of our people being kept on board, properly prepared to protect, or support, those on shore, if any unfortunate circumstance should happen to produce a misunderstanding between them and the Bijugas.

1792. Monday, Aug. 27.

Bellchore had this morning given me a bullock, two goats, and nine fowls; the former, at his request, I ordered to be killed, and then went on shore, thinking that there would be less probability of any quarrels happening between the Bijugas and our people if I were there; and not conceiving it possible that any could take place on board. However when I returned to the ship to dinner, the expressive countenance of Bellchore immediately convinced me that all was not right. That surly and uncomplying disposition, that contempt and intolerance of other nations, manners and customs, that uncivil treatment of strangers, which characterise the illiberal of all nations, but more particularly of ours, had greatly offended our guest.

The Bijugas are particularly fond of the entrails of bullocks; and when that on board had been killed, one of them carried to Bellchore, in the cabin, some of them cooked after their own fashion; which, it must be allowed, was rather offensive to the sight, being scarcely at all cleaned, and but just warmed through on the coals; this so offended Mr. Munden that he indignantly turned the poor Bijuga and his food out of the cabin, and on the interference of Bellchore, he rudely turned him out also. This indignity he could not forgive, and though frequently afterwards invited into the cabin, would not enter it till I came on board.

There doubtless was enough to create disgust; but it was certainly as easy, and would have been much more civil, for Mr. M. to have turned himself out, instead of his guest; and that was a conduct which our situation, one would have supposed, would have led him to pursue, rather than give offence to a people

1792.
Tuesday, Aug. 18.

whose good opinion we were particularly interested in acquiring.

Bellchore however entered the cabin with me to dinner, and after it, we went together on shore. He was astonished at the quantity of ground which we had levelled for the foundation of the block-house, (being 180 feet by 115) and said that "plenty of time must pass before that house can be done." He admired much our English fowls; being in size nearly three times as large as those of the Bijugas; and I gave him a cock and a hen to improve his breed. We then returned on board, where the watches were kept as last night.

Colonists $\begin{cases} \text{Well } 25..9 . 18 \text{ —Total W. } 52 \\ \text{Sick } 12..2 .. 3 \text{ — } \text{—— S. } 17 \end{cases}$ Grand Total 69.

Men. Wom. Chil.

Ship's company sick, 3.

Tuesday, 28th.

Showery, squally weather. Varying winds. At seven this morning, Bellchore, to whom I had made many presents, took his leave, and we saluted him with six guns. Our parties employed as before, in setting up the large boat, squaring timber for the block-house, clearing the ground by fires, and felling trees.

Our number of men capable of working, being reduced from 44 to 24, I this day contracted the watches from four to three, and at the same time excused seven from watching at all, in order that they might begin their work every morning at day light; which I could not have expected had they kept either the first or middle watches. *viz.*

1 Man employed about the boat.
6 ——————— about the block-house. Therm. 80.

	Men.	Wom.	Chil.		
Colonists { Well	24	9	18	— Total W. 51 }	Grand Total 69.
Sick	13	2	3	— — S. 18	

1792. Tuesday, Aug. 28.

Ship's company sick, 3.

Wed. 29. Frequent, and heavy showers, which greatly retard the progress of our several parties on shore. Wind S. W. This evening died John Ashworth, of a mortification in his hand, the consequence of a wound which he had received from the fin of a cat fish, when hauling the seine.

I had intended building the block-house without any ground plates, by letting the large upright posts four or five feet into the ground, as I conceived that mode would be equally strong with the other, and that, by it, we should save much labour. But finding that among those four persons who know any thing on the subject, there are various opinions, as to the propriety of that mode of building, and as they are all, most undoubtedly, more competent judges than myself, I desired each to give me his opinion, in writing, this evening; requesting that they would take care to keep in mind a great, nay indispensable, requisite, that of uniting with just sufficient strength, the greatest possible celerity of building, as I did not care a farthing how the building looked, provided it was sufficiently strong, and quickly finished. They were all of different opinions with respect to the mode of *logging and tying together* the building, but were all, except Dolphin Price, for having *ground plates* which they said were absolutely necessary. As Mr. Curwood was most conversant in these things, and was a strenuous advocate for this mode of building, I gave up my opinion to his, and committed to his direction the building of the east store room.

1792.
Wednes.
Aug. 29.

Ship's company sick, 3.

Colonists $\begin{cases} \text{Well } 25 \ldots 9 \ldots 17 \text{—Total W. } 51 \\ \text{Sick } 11 \ldots 2 \ldots 4 \text{——— S. } 17 \end{cases}$ Grand Total 68

Thursd. 30th.

Heavy rains prevented our working on shore in the morning, when we fumigated the ship; in the evening we had fine weather, and the parties at work as usual. A small sloop from Tombaly, bound to Bissao, came along-side and asked for some meat; which was readily given to them, and they departed. Early in the morning John Ashworth was buried, and this evening died his son Thomas of the hooping cough and Mrs. Box of a fever. Therm. 78.

Ship's company sick, 2.

Colonists $\begin{cases} \text{Well } 25 \ldots 9 \ldots 17 \text{—Total W. } 51 \\ \text{Sick } 11 \ldots 1 \ldots 3 \text{——— S. } 15 \end{cases}$ Grand Total 66.

Friday, 31st.

At day-light buried Mrs. Box and Thomas Ashworth. Fine weather before, and heavy rains after noon The different parties employed on shore as usual. In the evening the Experiment, schooner, arrived. Therm. 78.

Sick, ship's company, 2.

Monthly state of the Colony.

On the 31st. of July we had $\begin{cases} \text{Well } 41 \ldots 11 \ldots 23 \text{—Total W. } 75 \\ \text{Sick } 6 \ldots 1 \ldots 1 \text{——— S. } 9 \end{cases}$ 84.

Since which time we have lost by $\begin{cases} \text{Death } 4 \ldots 2 \ldots 3 \text{——— } 9 \\ \text{Desertion } 5 \ldots 0 \ldots 1 \text{——— } 6 \\ \text{Absent on duty } 2 \ldots 0 \ldots 1 \text{——— } 3 \end{cases}$ 18.

Present state of the Colony $\begin{cases} \text{Well } 25 \ldots 9 \ldots 16 \text{— Total W. } 50 \\ \text{Sick } 11 \ldots 1 \ldots 4 \text{——— S. } 16 \end{cases}$ 66.

Showery weather. N. E. wind. Parties employed as before. Mr. Hood, who went on shore at day-light with the carpenters' party, had gone, in the morning, to pay his daily visit to a Guinea-hen's nest, which he had discovered about 200 yards distant from the tool-house. I had not seen him all the forenoon; but as he was unwell, having a dysentery, and a very bad ulcerated leg, and never idle when able to do any thing, I made no inquiries after him, or what he was about; and, when I went on shore with the parties after dinner, learned, for the first time, that he had not returned. From his very weak state of body, we supposed he had fainted on the way, and had not sufficient strength to return, though we were not entirely free from apprehensions for his life.

1792.
Saturday,
Sept. 1.

A gun was instantly fired from the ship, that if he had only lost his way, its report might direct him back; and we divided ourselves into three parties, and continued searching for him in the woods till it was quite dark, when we returned to the ship, never expecting to see him again. But, as it was possible for him to be within the report of a gun, at seven o'clock, when all was silent, except frogs and musquitos, we fired another gun, and kept a light (which perchance might direct him back) burning in the main rigging all night; leaving orders with the officer of the watch, to be particularly attentive to any noise or hailing from the shore. Therm. 79.

Sick, ship's company, 4.

	Men.	Wom.	Chil.		
Colonists { Well	21	9	15	— Total W. 45	} Grand Total 66.
Sick	15	1	5	— — S. 21	

A boat arrived this morning from Bissao with stock for the colonists, and in her returned Mr. Gandell, the secretary, very

Sunday,
2d.

1792.
Sunday, Sept. 2.

ill of a fever, which had been the cause of his having been so long absent. Mr. Arffwiedson died this morning at four o'clock, of a putrid fever, and was buried at six. Read prayers.

Finding the rains had so retarded our progress on shore, that we should with difficulty complete our block-house and fort, before the expiration of the Hankey's charter, when that ship would leave us; it was thought essential to our own safety to employ the colonists on shore, in the evening, as on other days. Chas. Robinson, one of the subscribers, refused to go with me, avowing that nothing should induce him to work on the sabbath-day. This measure had not been lightly adopted; the necessity of the case, in this instance,* justified it; as the health, safety, and very existence of the colonists, depended upon their having a place of strength and security, before the Hankey left us. My arguments with this gentleman were therefore very short. I told him that if he did not work, I should take care that he did not eat on a Sunday; this was a gratification which he had no inclination to forego, and all his scruples vanished.

On landing we were greatly rejoiced to find that Mr. Hood had returned, about two hours before, to the tool-house.

This man, who had lost himself in the woods yesterday morning, wandered about the remainder of the day, till within about two hours of dark; when the growling of an animal, which he took to be a wolf,† stopt him; a tree, and a small bush were between them, and as he had neither arms, nor any thing else that he could defend himself with, he very prudently mounted the former. Here he was annoyed by a different kind of enemy.

* The sabbath was made for man; not man for the sabbath. Mark ii. 27.
† I do not believe that there are any wolves on the island, but there are a great many Hyænas, and that this was one I have not the least doubt.

A family of monkeys inhabited this tree, and seemed inclined to dispute his right to occupy their habitation. Mr. H., however, had a knife, with which he cut off one of the branches, and having severely chastised the boldest of them, who had approached too near, he remained the peaceable possessor of the tree: in this situation he remained all night, having never heard either of our guns. In the morning he ventured to descend, and endeavoured to find his way back; with the miserable certainty of starving in the woods, if he should be unable to effect it. About 10 o'clock he came to a point whence he saw the ship at a distance; and here, on his knees, he returned thanks to GOD for his safe return. A creek of considerable length, was, however, between him and the ship, in getting round which he was near four hours, when he arrived at the tool-house, exceedingly fatigued, and, having lost one of his shoes, much cut in one of his feet: but, what is the most extraordinary, entirely cured of the dysentery; and the ulcer in his leg a great deal better.*

1792.
Sunday, Sept. 2.

Weather very fine. Wind S.W. Therm. 80.—Killed two hogs for the colonists.

Sick, ship's company, 5.

Colonists { Well 20 .. 8 .. 15 — Total W. 43 } Grand Total 66.
          { Sick 16 .. 2 .. 5 — ——   S. 23 }

Men. Wom. Chil.

---

* Mr. Hood had eaten nothing while in the woods, except a small, wild, yellow plum, the pulp of which was in a pleasant degree acid, and which grows in abundance on the island. This induced me, after the surgeon had left us, to recommend this plum to others, affected with the same disorder (that is, flux or dysentery, for by which name I should call it, I am ignorant,) and two persons were cured once, and Mr. Hood three different times of the flux, by eating these plums. I will not say that the plums absolutely cured them; they might have got well without eating them; I only mean to assert, that those who did eat them, always got rid of the flux

1792.
Monday, 3d.
Showery weather and S. W. wind. Employed about the block-house, building the boat, clearing the ground by fires, and felling trees; Mr. Aberdein with myself tracing the lines of the fort. The ship sighted her anchors, the cables were not rubbed, neither were the anchor-stocks worm-eaten.

Tuesday, 4th.
Similar wind, weather, and employment.

Wednes. 5th.
Having remarked lately that the sick lists never came to me till the morning after the day for which they were written, I this day requested Mr. Rowe would send them to me every evening at eight o'clock.

$$\text{Colonists} \begin{cases} \text{Well } 20 .. 8 .. 14 \text{ — Total W. } 42 \\ \text{Sick } 16 .. 2 .. 6 \text{ — S. } 24 \end{cases} \text{Grand Total } 66.$$

Men. Wom. Chil.

Ship's company sick, 3.

Thursday, 6th.
Very fine weather. S.W. wind. Parties employed as before, except about the boat, both the carpenters who were at work on it, having lamed themselves. Killed a hog for the sick. Mr. Aberdein, this evening, cautioned me to beware of Mr. Curwood, and told me that he was exceedingly dissatisfied, and took great pains to make every other person so, particularly Messrs. Fielder and Donnelly, two young men, subscribers; that he conceived his object was to make every one desirous to go away in the Hankey, and thus force me to leave the island, by which means they would get a free passage home. Therm. 82.

Friday, 7th.
Very heavy rains prevented our working in the morning; and in the evening, when we had fine weather, (every person who had been employed about the block-house, as well as those about the boat, being ill) nothing was done on shore but clearing the

two days afterwards. Whether or not the plums could be the only cause, I leave to the determination of more competent judges.

ground by fires, and on this business we could only muster six men. Therm. 77.

1792.
Friday, Sept. 7th.

Fine weather and S.W. wind. Observing a canoe on the Biafara shore, whose people were cutting timber, I sent Mr. Munden to inform them that no person had authority to cut wood on either side of this harbour, without having first obtained my permission. They belonged to the governor of Bissao, professed ignorance that they were acting wrong, and promised never to do so again: Mr. M. then gave them permission to load their boat. A party burning wood, and the ship's carpenter at work about our boat. Died of a fever, and was buried this evening, Mrs. Meares. Therm 81.

Saturday, 8th.

Fine weather, if we except one tornado. Read prayers. Employed in the evening burning wood. Therm. 71.

Sunday, 9th.

No rain all day. The ship's carpenter employed about our boat, every one else burning wood. Therm. 84.

Monday, 10th.

The captain of the Hankey finding that neither the shores of the island, nor the continent, afforded him stone ballast for his ship, determined to ballast her with wood, and for that purpose sent all the men he could spare, on shore, to cut it. Died, and was buried, an infant child of Riches, the labourer, who was born on board the Hankey, about five months ago.

Fine weather. Parties employed as yesterday; and one man well enough to work at the block-house. Erected a large shed, as a work shop for the people employed about it. Therm. 83. Mr. Rowe, the surgeon, a daring and turbulent man, difficult to be governed, takes every opportunity of sowing dissension, and creating disgust, among the colonists. What his end or aim be, I cannot divine, unless to force me to abandon the colony.

Tuesday, 11th.

Weather fine. Winds variable. Work as usual. Therm. 81.

Wednes. 12th.

1792.
Thurs.
Sept. 13.

Tornadoes. Calms. Thunder. Lightning. Rainy. Dry. Clear. Cloudy. Ever changing weather. This day we muster two men at work about the block-house; the others employed as before. Died last night, and was buried this morning, Mrs. Gandell. Therm. 78.

Friday, 14th.

No rain. Parties at their usual work. A sloop anchored here from Bissao, going to Tombaly. In a tornado last evening, this vessel had been struck with lightning; one man was killed, whom they had buried on the north end of the island; and another had been very much hurt; her mast was shivered to splinters, and they requested permission to cut a stick to make another; which was not only granted, but, when they had brought it to the beach, we made it for them; and afterwards gave them some beef and biscuit, when they departed.

I saw the man on shore, sitting on the beach, who had been burnt by the lightning. His left side, from a little above the hip, all the way down the outside of his thigh and leg, as far as the ancle, was perfectly raw, being burnt in a most shocking manner. I went for a bottle of sweet oil and a feather, with which I returned, and anointed with the gentlest hand, and greatest care, the burnt parts; all which time he appeared perfectly indifferent to my attention. When I had finished, I gave him the bottle and the feather, and by means of an interpreter, told him to do the same three times a day; that it would ease the pain, and soon heal the wound. He took the bottle and the feather with the greatest indifference, without altering a muscle in his countenance, without shewing the least symptom of being pleased, or of gratitude, and without uttering a word in reply: to what can such indifference be attributed?—This man was a Manjack.* He did not even look at me when I went away. {1792. Friday, Sept. 14.}

Fine weather, if we except a couple of tornados. Winds round the compass. Usual employment. Therm. 83. {Saturday, 15th.}

Winds variable and weather squally. People at work as usual from day-light till 9 in the morning, when I carried them on board and read prayers. At 3 P.M. went to work with them again. Killed a bullock for the colonists. Therm. 80. {Sunday, 16th.}

No rain. The people that have hitherto been employed in clearing the ground by fires, were this day set to dig up the roots of the trees on the ground which the block-house will cover. Every person who was employed about the house is ill, and unable to work. {Monday, 17th.}

It had been my intention to have surrounded the block-house with a square fort, having a bastion at either angle, the lines of which indeed I had traced; but I find that it is beyond our strength, and that with difficulty we shall be able to complete our block-house before the Hankey leaves us. Therm. 82.

Winds as before. No rain except in one tornado. One man employed on the block-house; other parties as before, that is, the ship's carpenter about the boat, the colonists digging up roots of trees, and the Hankey's ship's company cutting timber for ballast. {Tuesday, 18th}

Variable weather. Parties employed as yesterday. Died, and was buried this morning, Rich. Reeves, a boy. Therm. 83. {Wednes. 19th.}

No rain. Parties employed as usual, except that which was employed in digging up the roots, which was this day occupied in making a good, broad, public road, from the block-house to {Thurs. 20th.}

---

* A native of Jatt's Island.

1792.
Thurs.
Sept. 20. the beach, to facilitate our getting our goods up the hill. Died, and was buried, Dan. Sly, a labourer. A Spaniel dog that had been absent nine days, returned this evening to the tool house. Killed a bullock for the colony. Therm. 83.

Frid. 21.
Satur. 22. Fine weather, and usual employment, yesterday the Hannah schooner, Birchall, anchored here, from the Bananas.

Sunday, 23d. Read prayers to the colony. Prevented by a tornado from working in the evening. The Hannah sailed. Therm. 83.

Monday, 24th. No rain. Parties employed as usual, except the Hankey's ship's company, who left off cutting wood, in order to get their ship rigged. Therm. 83.

Tuesday, 25th. No rain. Similar employment; finished our new boat, which I named the Perseverance, she is about seven tons burthen. Therm. 83.

Wednes. 26th. Violent tornado with rains in the morning. Parties employed as before. Therm. 81.

Thurs. 27th. No rain. Usual employment; Spencer, the carpenter, who has been a long time ill, now able to do a little work at the block-house, in the mornings and evenings. Finished the road. Therm. 82.

Friday, 28th. No rain. Employed as usual, except those who had made the road; who are now clearing the ground, within the lines of our block-house. A canoe brought us bullocks from Bissao. Died, and was buried, Hugh Meares, one of the labourers, a good old soldier, and a valuable man.

From the 5th inst. to this day, the surgeon has never sent me one sick list, during which time there have died two men, two women, and two children.* The surgeon has pretended all this time to be ill—too ill to visit the sick, or make out for me a

* Mrs. Meares died on the 8th, and Mrs. Gandell on the 12th. The infant

list of their names; though he has been constantly walking about, and eating always with a good appetite. He is a monster of inhumanity. Therm. 84.

1792. Friday, Sept. 28.

Ship's company sick, 3.

Colonists $\begin{cases} \text{Well } 14..5..12 - \text{Total W. } 31 \\ \text{Sick } 20..3..6 - \quad\quad \text{S. } 29 \end{cases}$ Grand Total 60.

(Men. Wom. Chil.)

Clear weather and usual employment. From the great and unexpected mortality among us, I was this day reduced to the melancholy necessity of curtailing the intended dimensions of our block-house: that is, by reducing it nearly to a square, being now* 115 by 116¼ feet, and before intended to have been 180 by 115 feet. By thus reducing it we have not lost one hour's labour, as all our work has hitherto been confined to a public store-room, of 64 feet, on the east side. Died this evening, and were buried, James Box, and his son William, both of fevers. Therm. 81.

Saturday, 29th.

Ship's company sick, 3.

Colonists $\begin{cases} \text{Well } 13..5..11 - \text{Total W. } 29 \\ \text{Sick } 20..3..6 - \quad\quad \text{S. } 29 \end{cases}$ Grand Total 58.

(Men. Wom. Chil.)

Thick foggy weather. Two hands about the block-house from day-light till nine o'clock. Buried Box and his son, and read prayers. Prevented by a violent tornado, attended with much lightning and heavy rains, from doing any thing on shore in the evening. Therm. at noon and at the commencement of

Sunday, 30th.

Riches died on the 10th; the boy Reeves on the 19th; Dan. Sly on the 20th; and Hugh Meares on the 28th. Neither of the last four having ever appeared on a sick list.

* About the size of the Royal Exchange in London; that is, covering the same ground.

1792. Sunday, Sept. 30.

the tornado 83—one hour and a half after, which was near its termination, it was down to 75. Killed a bullock for the colony.

Sick of ship's company, 3.

Monthly state of the Colony.

	Men.	Wom.	Chil.		
On the 31st of August we had { Well	25	.. 9	.. 16	—Total W. 50 }	66.
Sick	11	.. 1	.. 4	—— S. 16 }	
Since which time we have lost by { Death	4	.. 2	.. 3	—Total	9.
Acquired by returning from Bissao {	1	.. 0	.. 0	—Total	1.
Present state of Colony { Well	12	.. 5	.. 11	—Total W. 28 }	58.
Sick	21	.. 3	.. 6	—— S. 30 }	

Monday, October 1st.

Employed about the block-house, cutting logs for it, and levelling the ground within the building; the sailors employed about their rigging. As we consider the rains as now almost, if not quite over, we took the house off the main deck of the Hankey, and sent it on shore. Launched the Perseverance, and began logging the east store-room.

Captain Cox, of the Hankey, gave notice, that he should sail on or before the 16th of next month.

We have hitherto kept a regular watch, at three watches, those only who could handle an axe being excused. Our numbers being so exceedingly weakened by death, and sickness, and having so much to do during the short stay that the Hankey will make here, I judge it expedient to discontinue the watching, that the whole strength of the colony may go to work every morning at day-light. Therm. 83.

Stuck up the following paper between decks:

Hankey, 1st October, 1792.

Monday, October 1st.

Finding myself obliged to curtail the space at first intended for the scite of our block-house, and consequently reduced to the necessity of contracting the dimensions of the different rooms whch it may contain; I wish that all those subscribers, agents, labourers, or servants, who intend returning to England in the Hankey, whose charter will expire on the 12th of November next, would be obliging enough to communicate their intentions to me by letter, before 11 o'clock to morrow; in order that I may avoid the unnecessary labour of building more houses than will be occupied, and of too much contracting those that will.

P. BEAVER.

Ship's company sick, 4.

Colonists $\begin{cases} \text{Well } 11 \ldots 3 \ldots 10 \text{—Total W. } 24 \\ \text{Sick } 22 \ldots 5 \ldots 7 \text{———— S. } 34 \end{cases}$ Grand Total 58.

Tuesday, 2nd.

Employed cutting wood for and logging the east store room and landing and rolling up the hill, beef, pork, &c. Messrs. Gandell and Smith subscribers, and Griffiths and Barret labourers wrote to me declaring their intention to return in the Hankey. Therm. 85.

Ship's company sick, 4.

Colonists $\begin{cases} \text{Well } 9 \ldots 3 \ldots 10 \text{—Total W. } 22 \\ \text{Sick } 24 \ldots 5 \ldots 7 \text{———— S. } 36 \end{cases}$ Grand Total 58.

Wednes. 3rd.

Not a Carpenter able to lift a tool; myself with a little assistance continue the logging; every body seems much depressed; not a soul among them capable of exertion. Compton the labourer told me that it was his intention to go home. Therm. 84.

1792.
Wednes.
October
3rd.

Ship's company sick, 3.

Colonists $\begin{cases} \text{Well } 10 \ .. \ 3 \ .. \ 10 \text{ —Total W. } 23 \\ \text{Sick } 23 \ .. \ 5 \ .. \ 7 \ \text{———} \ \text{S. } 35 \end{cases}$ Grand Total 58.

Tuesday, 4th. One carpenter at work with me; those who work at all employed rolling provisions up the hill. A cask of pork had been left in the tool-house with the head loose upon it; this morning we found that the head had been pushed off, and the chime of the cask was covered with a long brindled hair, rubbed from the belly of some animal that had endeavoured to get at the meat which was low down in the cask: left four people on shore to sleep in the tool-house, hoping they might shoot this animal, if it returned, in the night. Therm. 84.

Ship's company sick, 4.

Colonists $\begin{cases} \text{Well } 11 \ .. \ 3 \ .. \ 10 \text{ —Total W. } 24 \\ \text{Sick } 22 \ .. \ 5 \ . \ 7 \ \text{———} \ \text{S. } 34 \end{cases}$ Grand Total 58.

Friday, 5th. Two or three light showers in the course of the day. Employed in cutting timber for, and logging, the block-house; completeing the east store room, and getting provisions on shore. The party in the tool house without success. I therefore this evening carried every body on board, but left a shark hook, baited with a piece of salt pork, attached to a stump of a tree, by a small line, expecting to catch a hyæna, for that is the animal, we suppose, that got at the pork-cask. Therm. 84.

Ship's company sick, 5.

Colonists $\begin{cases} \text{Well } 12 \ .. \ 2 \ .. \ 10 \text{ —Total W. } 24 \\ \text{Sick } 21 \ .. \ 6 \ .. \ 7 \ \text{———} \ \text{S. } 34 \end{cases}$ Grand Total 58.

Saturday, 6th. Light rain all the morning, fine weather in the evening—wind westerly. No carpenter at work; employed cutting wood for, and logging, the store room, and landing provisions; at 1 P.M. our cutter returned from Sierra Leone without our assistant surgeon, which had been our only motive for sending her thither, having been absent ever since the tenth of August; and having been detained, in a most unwarrantable manner, by those members of the committee, at that place, who had abandoned the colony on the departure of the Calypso. She brought back Captain Paiba, one of the subscribers, with his wife and child, and a servant boy, and what was of infinitely more importance, from Bissao where she had touched, two Papel grumetas whom Mr. De Sylva Cordoza had procured for me.

1792.
Saturd.
October
6th.

I have been long endeavouring to procure natives to labour for me for hire, in the language of the country called grumetas,* for I have long since seen that not only from sickness, but from a kind of stupor, general depression of spirits, and a total unconcern even for their own safety, which has, in a most unaccountable manner, seized every person almost in the colony, we shall not be able to complete our block-house, or afterwards keep it, unless it be by means of the natives.

Wm. Meares and Wm. Reeves, two colonists who went to assist in navigating the cutter, were both dead. Richard Johnson, one of the seamen, had also died at Sierra Leone, and Mat. Beck,

---

* From the Portuguese word, grumete, I suppose, which signifies the meanest sort of sailor. It is particularly applied to those natives who Trade for Europeans in canoes; but is generally applicable to all those who labour, for others, for wages. Many Portuguese words are incorporated into all the African coast languages, indeed a kind of Portuguese patois is almost every where spoken in it. I conceive that the first Portuguese visitors might have hired natives as pilots, and interpreters to go in their small vessels, whom they would probably have called grumetes, whence the present word grumeta.

1792.
Sunday, October 7th. another, had deserted, and Joseph Glover, seaman, had entered. Therm. 83.

Fine weather. No carpenter capable of working. Employed in logging till nine, when we went on board, and I read prayers, went to work again at three in the afternoon. Therm. 86. Killed a bullock for the colony.

Monday, 8th. Hot sultry weather. Light westerly winds. Landed the last of our provisions. One carpenter at work, and our logging party strengthened to day by the two grumetas. Put in the first post for the row of houses on the north side of the block-house.

I have seen enough of Mr. Curwood's mode of building, and his ground plates, to determine to follow Dolphin Price's method with the remainder of the block-house. Therm. 84.

Tuesday, 9th. Weather as yesterday. Employed about the store-room and the north side of the block-house. Seeing that with our strength, and the greatest exertion of it, it is doubtful whether or not we shall be able to complete the *outside* of the block-house before the departure of the Hankey, I judged it expedient to hire the three sailors belonging to the cutter to work on shore with us, at the rate of one shilling a day, each; who, with the two blacks employed yesterday, increase our working party more than one third. Therm. 85. At 10 P. M. the ship's cook fell over board, and was drowned; we heard a great splash in the water, and ran instantly from the cabin on deck, but having examined all round the ship without either seeing or hearing any noise in the water, we returned again, and it was morning before the man was missed.

Wednesd. 10th. Weather as before, with a tornado, generally, once in 24 hours, whic increase in violence. With my blacks and sailors I get on rapidly at the block-house; scarcely a colonist at work. Visited at noon by a canoe from Tombaly; gave them provisions. The

Hankey's crew ballasting their ship with wood. Died and was buried, Sarah Reeves, aged 10. Therm. 84.

1792. Wednes. October 10th.

Sick list, (the last of which I received on the 5th) of ship's company, 5.

Colonists $\begin{cases} \text{Well } 10 .. 4 .. 11 \text{—Total W. } 25 \\ \text{Sick } 24 .. 5 .. 7 \text{—— S. } 36 \end{cases}$ Grand Total 61.

(Men. Wom. Chil.)

In the above statement is included Paiba's family, of four, which joined us on the 6th. We have, besides, three seamen and two grumetas well, at work, and the Master and cabin boy take care of the cutter.

This evening the following letter was sent by Mr. Rowe, the surgeon, into the cabin, addressed to Messrs. Paiba, Beaver Munden, and Aberdein.

GENTLEMEN,

From the declining state of my health, occasioned by diseases brought on me by the extreme fatigue I have gone through in the service of the association, joined to the perpetual anxiety of mind I have laboured under, from the constant and brutal ill treatment I have received from Lieut. Philip Beaver, and to the want of proper nourishment, I find it impossible for me to perform the functions of my duty in this debilitated state, but as I have engaged to stay till the 23rd of December, I therefore beg you will consider this as *a formal and official resignation* of my appointment, as surgeon to the Bulama assosiation, at that date—as after that period it is my intention to return to some climate more probable to restore me to my pristine health.

Gentlemen,
I have the honor to be,
Your's, &c.
J. ROWE.

1792. Wednes. October 10th.

What does this mean? As to his ill health, he, to all appearance, is as well as when he left England—he says he has the liver complaint—it may be so. As to the severe fatigue which he has undergone, he has never been out of the ship but once or twice, and then for his own amusement. And on board he had nothing to do, except attending the sick, and that he has never done. As to the brutal ill treatment which, he says, he has constantly received from me, I am not aware of ever having spoken to him, except about the health of some of the colonists. As to his nourishment it is the same as that of others.

I have, in truth, sometimes sent for him to visit particular patients, and have sometimes made a point of seeing myself that he visited them daily; but it was after I had found that some had died without his ever having seen them; that others almost dead had never been visited by him; and that some, though exceedingly ill, from his known inhumanity, would not suffer him to come near them.*

* John Ashworth, who died of a mortification which took place in consequence of a wound which he received from a cat fish, would not suffer this man to come near him for the last three weeks of his existence, though in great bodily pain, and requiring surgical attendance. The Evening on which he died he sent for me, recommended his children to my particular care and protection, and then requested me to pray with him, which I readily did. I asked him if he died in peace and charity with all mankind, and had sincerely forgiven all those who might at any time have offended him; his reply was, that he died in peace and charity with all mankind, except Doctor Rowe; and him he never would, and never could, forgive. "How then can you expect forgiveness for your enormous sins and wickedness if you refuse to forgive that man, who has, probably only inadvertently, offended you? how dare you call upon our Holy Father to forgive you *your trespasses* as *you forgive them* who trespass against you? Remember that you have not, in all human probability, many hours to remain in this world, and that you are now committing a great sin in persevering in this uncharitable conduct."

Mr. Rowe, I moreover observed, though probably rough in his manner and treatment of his patients, was a good man in his heart, though that was of no importance to him; it concerned his eternal happiness most sincerely and unfeignedly to forgive him: that

African Memoranda.

Sultry weather, employment as yesterday. Therm. 85 No sick list sent to me. At 8 P. M. the Hankey parted her cable in a violent tornado, and drove on shore at the landing place; the ebb tide, having made strong, rendered it impossible to get her off again before morning. *1792. Thurs. October 11th.*

Hazy, cloudy weather, with a fine S.E. breeze. Employed as before. Captain Cox finding that his ship would not receive any damage by remaining on the mud; and that it would be much easier in such a situation to get on board the wood with which he was ballasting the ship, as well as to land our goods, determined to let her remain where she was. Therm. 85. *Friday 12th.*

Ship's company sick, 6.

Colonists $\begin{cases} \text{Well } 10 \;..\; 4 \;..\; 10 \text{—Total W. } 24 \\ \text{Sick } 24 \;..\; 5 \;..\; 8 \text{———— S. } 37 \end{cases}$ Grand Total 61.

(Men. Wom. Chil.)

3 Seamen of the cutter } Well.
2 Grumetas ....

Three violent tornadoes last night. Cloudy, squally, showery weather all day. With the cutter's people and the grumetas, I continue my labours; every colonist seems deprived of his faculties. Therm. 85. Sick list the same as yesterday. *Saturday, 13th.*

Violent tornadoes, with strong winds and heavy rains. Pre- *Sunday, 14th.*

---

any way in which he had offended him, could, in comparison with his own offences against the Almighty, be considered as a drop of water only when compared with the ocean, and that he could not have the least hope of salvation if he died with this unchristianlike enmity towards any one. I succeeded at length, and he most sincerely and unfeignedly, I firmly believe, forgave this Mr. Rowe, and died in peace and good will towards all men. All this took place by the bed of Ashworth, between decks, about three hours before his death, in the hearing of the major part of the colonists, and I believe of this Mr. Rowe himself. If this be brutal treatment, then I am a brute.

1792. October, vented, by the weather, from reading prayers. Mr. Banfield, whom we lost last night on shore, was this morning found stowed away, in an empty arm-chest, on the beach. He has long since shewn symptoms of insanity. Died and was buried the infant Paiba, eight weeks old. Therm. 81.

Monday, 15th. Squally, with showers. Employed as usual. Therm. 83.

Tuesday, 16th. Cloudy weather. No rain. The cutters people and two or three colonists going on with the logging—myself and a black fellow making cement for it. Captain Cox hauled his ship off the mud to her old birth. Therm. 84.

Wednes. 17th. Clear weather and fine S. W. breeze. Began boarding the upper part of the block-house. Died this evening and was buried, Wm. Reeves, after a long illness; in whom we lost one of our most valuable labourers. Therm. 83.

Sick, ship's company, 6.

	Men.	Wom.	Chil.		
Colonists { Well	14	6	13	— Total W. 33 }	Grand Total 59.
Sick	19	3	4	— S. 26 }	

Cutter's sailors.. 2 well,... 1 sick.

Grumetas...... 2 ditto.

Thursd. 18th. Sultry weather. Little wind. Employed as before, that is, logging, boarding, and making mortar. Therm. 87. Mr. Banfield, who has been some time in a state of lunacy, attempted to destroy the ship's steward by laying his skull open with a three cornered scraper; and we have very strong grounds to believe that the ship's cook, who was drowned on the 2d inst. was rolled over board in his sleep by this Mr. B., at that time insane. We know that the cook was lying asleep in a tarpauling great coat, stretched along the rough-tree, just before the accident happened; and that Mr. B. was then on deck, and the only person there, and when asked what splashing that was in the water, replied, " nothing but one of the cook's old kettles:" for his own, as well as for our safety, I thought it necessary to keep him in irons.

1792. Thursd. Oct. 18.

Usual employment. No sick list given me since the 17th, though the surgeon is as well as any man in the colony: from him I this evening received the following letter:

Frid. 19. Sat. 20.

Sir,

It is a task as unpleasant to me as ineffectual, to use any verbal remonstrance to you.

On the written application of many unhappy sufferers I now address you by letter, as you have ever had the superintendance of the provisions and stores. It is now five days since any provisions (except bread) have been served out to the sick, who now, for want of proper nourishment, form the major part of the people, and who (from that circumstance) have declined in their health, and are now so visibly declining, that their fate is inevitable; the flour, for this long time past, which has been served out to the sick, has not been eatable, and when sharp necessity has urged its use, has occasioned sickness, and violent pains in the bowels.

You, sir, ought to be conscious that the lives of his majesty's subjects, and our fellow creatures, are not to be so frittered away. There can be no plea in vindication, when there is now plenty of rice in the ship, and it is a fortnight since fresh meat has been given to the people. In vain will medicine be administered, where hunger is making such cruel devastation, and,

1792.
Saturday,
Oct. 20.

from what I hear, the circumstances of the association are far from demanding such ill-timed parsimony.

I am, &c.

J. ROWE.

To Philip Beaver, Esq.

This man seems as mad as Banfield. Let us coolly examine his letter: he says, " on the written application, &c." It is strange that any colonist should apply to him, instead of to me, for the redress of any grievance, for he was held in such utter abhorrence, by every one of them, on the departure of the Calypso, that to a man, they wanted to make it a condition of *their staying*, that Mr. Rowe *should go*, that he should be absolutely turned out of the colony. And it was not from any regard to Mr. Rowe, for I then knew him to be a bold, daring, and unprincipled villain, but to convince the colonists, that they were not to govern, nor to dismiss public servants, that I made a point of keeping him; particularly, as it was his own wish to remain. I know not what he has since done to gain, or I to forfeit, their good opinion. He next says, " that it is five days, &c." Had it been five days, as advanced, since provisions were served out, no blame could attach to me, unless I had been made acquainted with the circumstance; for though I do almost every thing that is done, yet I have not been in the habit lately of seeing the provisions issued: but unfortunately for his assertion, Mr. Robinson, who has lately had that duty, was too ill on Wednesday last, that is *three days* ago, to serve out provisions, and I myself superintended the serving of flour, by James Watson, and that for two days, which brings us to *yesterday* the 19th; but moreover, Mr. Gandell, the secretary, and this very man, the writer of this very letter, this Mr. Rowe, the surgeon, (who can believe it?) received provision from *my hands*, both yesterday and the day before. " That the sick form the major part, &c." is a melancholy truth, which I most severely feel, and lament; but, without me, I believe, the number would have been greater; for I have procured them every refreshment in my power, which no other man in the colony, if he had the inclination, had the ability to do; have fed them from my own table; have even cooked for them myself, when they have been neglected by this very surgeon. " That the flour is bad," I also deplore; there is only one cask left, which I myself have never tasted, having ordered it to be served to the sick only; among whom, thank GOD, I am not. " That the lives of our fellow creatures are not to be frittered away," I allow; and I feel conscious that I have saved many of them. I alone, in the colony, keep up their spirits, and were I to withdraw, one half of them would die with fear. " There can be no plea in vindication:" this I do not understand. " There is plenty of rice:" true, there is rice; but not plenty. But no one has ever asked for any; and Mr. Rowe himself, this very complainant, has a *written authority from me*, to order whatever there is in the ship, for the sick, *when he thinks proper*. " From what I hear, the circumstances," &c. The association is in debt more than nine hundred pounds; and though I have not spared any expence, any labour, any trouble, in order to procure as much fresh provisions, vegetables, and fruit, as possible, which is impartially distributed to every individual in the colony, save only that the sick have a greater share reserved for

1792.
Saturday, Oct. 20.

them; yet this is all done at my own risk,* and the money may all go out of my own pocket. Is not this man mad? Who can be safe from such a villain?

Sunday, 21st.

Foggy weather all day. Employed, through necessity,† as usual. Served out rice to the colonists, not from Mr. Rowe's letter, but because I could not give them fresh beef, and they

---

* I do not claim any merit from this; for had not the common feelings of humanity dictated such conduct, common prudence would. At this time I had plenty of port, sherry, porter, coffee, tea, chocolate, sugar, portable soup, &c.; and few, very few indeed, of the colonists had either. Mr. Rowe had my authority, and my servant had orders, to issue them to whom he thought necessary. I say again, that I do not claim any merit from this; but if I am attacked, I must defend myself, and therefore I mention them; and though this man could not speak truth when living, I call his ghost to witness the truth of my assertion.

A strong constitution, with a mind not readily depressed, nor easily diverted from its purpose, had enabled me to make exertions which every individual was not equal to; and therefore, from an early period in the expedition, most of the colonists had looked up to me.

Now the major part of them, at least, were dissipated vicious characters, and some of them most infamous; who required the strong hand of the law to keep them within the bounds of decency and decorum. But we had no legal restraint whatever: How happened it then, if I merit the reproaches contained in Mr. Rowe's letter, that these lawless people have in every instance, followed my directions, obeyed my orders, and placed implicit confidence in all my proceedings? I never flattered one of them, and never will. How comes it then, I say, that of all these people, not one of whom I had ever seen or heard of before this expedition, no person has called in question any of my proceedings, nor hesitated an instant to obey any of my injunctions? It is because *they feel*—because *they are convinced*, that my conduct has been disinterested, and impartial, and all my exertions tending only to *their security*, and to *their comfort*. This, I trust, is of itself a sufficient answer to Mr. Rowe's letter. And I call upon the living, for some there are, to bear witness to the truth of these assertions. I repeat once more, that if I am attacked, I must defend myself;—which is my only justification for this note.

† Prayers on Sunday morning were from this day discontinued, till we conceived ourselves out of all danger from an attack by the natives.

had none last Sunday. In the evening, the Fisher, schooner, Bootle, arrived. Therm. 85.

1792. Sunday, Oct. 21.

Sick list of ship's company, 5.

Colonists $\begin{cases} \text{Well } 11 .. 6 .. 11 \text{ —Total W. } 28 \\ \text{Sick } 22 .. 3 .. 6 \text{ —— S. } 31 \end{cases}$ Grand Total 59.

Men. Wom. Chil.

The master and two seamen of the cutter ill besides.

Cloudy weather. Worked as usual till breakfast; after which I thought it necessary to assemble all the colonists, in order to read to them Mr. Rowe's letter, which I received on Saturday night.

Monday, 22d.

After having asked Mr. Rowe for the " written application" on which his letter was founded, and then for a copy of it, (both of which were denied, with a threat that it should be laid before the House of Commons, ridiculous!) I inquired of the people which of them had signed it? Here I was interrupted by Mr. Rowe, who desired them not to answer, telling them that they were not under military discipline, and that I had no authority to ask them that question. I assured them that my only motive in wishing to know who had signed it, was merely that I might address myself particularly to them, and to them only. That I knew not the contents of the paper, which, it was said, they had signed; but supposed it to be full of complaints and remonstrances on my conduct. I then asked *every man individually*, whether or not he had signed such a paper. *One subscriber* and *five labourers* said that they had, *at the request of Mr. Rowe,* signed a paper, stating it as their opinion that the *flour was bad,* but nothing more.

I then read Mr. Rowe's letter, and refuted, article by article, every accusation which it contained. I afterwards asked them

1792.
Monday,
Oct. 22.

collectively, and individually, which of them had been dissatisfied with any, and with what, part of my conduct? What reason any one of them had to complain? And if they had any, why they did not come to me, as they had always been accustomed to do, when they had any complaints to make, or any favors to ask? I also asked if I had not been very attentive to them all when sick? And if most of them had not been supplied, at some time or other, from my table when ill, even for three weeks at a time? To all of which they answered, that none of them were dissatisfied with any part of my conduct, and that they were sensible that I had done much for them. Those who had signed the paper, which Mr. Rowe threatens to produce against me in England, declared that, in signing that paper, nothing was farther from their intentions, than to throw any aspersions on my conduct; that they had signed it because the flour was bad; but that they had meant no harm by it.

From Mr. Rowe's refusing to shew me the original, and also, after having promised to let me have a copy, refusing permission to my servant to copy it, I have strong reason to suspect that he wrote the paper himself; that he had made the badness of the flour the original subject; and had afterwards either introduced something else, or given them a different paper to sign, and was afraid that my servant should know his hand writing, as he had been in the habit of receiving from him the sick lists. Mr. Rowe's whole conduct, since the departure of the Calypso, has been most perverse and insolent, ever aiming to create dissensions and animosities in the colony, and by every means in his power endeavouring to depress, their already too much depressed, spirits: but this day, by every means of provocation in his power, by every violence of language, and insolence of conduct, has he even exceeded himself. I therefore told him, in the presence of the whole colony; that if he did not quit the island before the 23d day of December, I should on that day stop his provisions and turn him out of the block-house; and if, before that day, he gave me any more trouble, by forming parties and cabals in the colony, I would put him in irons, and chain him, like a bear, to a tree. This measure, arbitrary as it may appear, is become absolutely necessary. He knows that I do not jest; and I trust that the threat will be sufficient.* In the evening went to work again as usual. Killed a bullock for the colonists, which I had purchased of Bootle. Therm. 84.

1792. Monday, Oct. 22.

Clear weather. At work as usual, but with a very diminished party, being only six in number: that is, two colonists, two

Tuesday, 23d.

* This language, and this conduct, may appear strange to an English reader; but it was absolutely necessary to the preservation of the Colony. Mr. R. was a bold, and daring man, who, like many others, had thought that, to establish a colony, nothing more was necessary than the mere act of taking possession, and now, discontented and depressed from our great sickness and mortality, had formed the project of *forcing me* to abandon it. Any body was at liberty to leave it; GOD knows I never asked one man to remain, but advised many to quit it; but this would not answer Mr. R.'s end. He had engaged to stay two years, except from ill health, or forfeit his land; now, if he could oblige me, he knew every body else would abandon the island, and then he could not have been said to have forfeited his grant: moreover, if I went away, I should have been obliged to prolong the charter of the Hankey, and so pay for every individual's passage home to England; but if I remained, he must not only forfeit his grant, but pay for his own passage back. Had I, therefore, on this occasion shewn the least symptom of indecision, or want of firmness, with respect to my conduct *towards him*, the colony was gone. I respect, I trust, as much as any man breathing, the feelings and the liberty of others, as well as the laws of my country. I had no legal authority; therefore, every act of force on my part, unless for self-preservation, must have been illegal. No man, probably, at present in existence, was ever placed in such a situation, and I rely with confidence that its peculiarity, and the necessity of the case will justify my conduct with respect to this, or any other, strong measure which I pursued.

1792.
Tuesday, Oct. 23. grumetas, one sailor belonging to the cutter, and myself. Mr. Birkhead, who commands the cutter, and who has been some days ill, gave me notice that, if he recovered, he should go home in the Hankey. The general despondency which the approaching departure of that ship has cast over the whole colony, has extended even to him. I regret it much, and am somewhat surprized; he is an old school-fellow, and I had an esteem for him. At noon, when there was not a cloud to be seen, it hailed for about three minutes. The hail-stones not much larger than pins-heads. Died, and was buried, Mr. Smith, a subscriber.

Wednes. 24th. Employed as yesterday, with the addition, to our numbers, of one colonist. Part of the east store-room being now covered, I slept therein, together with Mr. Aberdein, and three other colonists, for the first time; Mr. A. being ill, and the three latter my whole working party. We shall now save that time, which must necessarily have been lost, in going three times on shore to our labour, and as often returning to the ship.

Thursd. 25th. Two colonists and myself, with a sailor and two grumetas only at work. A boat from Bissao brought me eight bullocks, with a quantity of rice and limes. Died, and was buried this morning, John Hargrave, a seaman belonging to the cutter, and a child of Mrs. Reeves's, a little more than three months old. Therm. 86. The colonists seem all much dissatisfied: at what I cannot tell, but believe Mr. Rowe does all in his power to encourage it, and advises them to leave me.

Friday, 26th. Weather exceedingly hot; party at work, the same as yesterday; very little done the last three days, except putting in the posts on the south side of the block-house, which I got Bootle's men to do for me, as well as to bring in as many as will finish the west side, which will then complete the square. The Fisher sailed this evening for Bissao, in which vessel went Messrs. Paiba, Gandell, and Curwood, with a view to procure stock for their passage home in the Hankey. Hired George, a grumeta, from Mr. Bootle, who speaks pretty good English, at eight barrs a month; the other two grumetas are hired at four barrs each. Died, and was buried this evening, John Venus, a seaman belonging to the cutter, and Mrs. Reeves. *1792. Friday, Oct. 26.*

Myself with two men obliged to dig both graves, carry the bodies from the water side and inter them. I might, it is true, have ordered the grumetas to do so, but the disgust shewn yesterday by two of them, in touching a corpse, prevented my imposing that duty on them, by which I might lose their affections. Therm. 88.

Wind N.W. morning, S.E. evening. Finished the roof of the east store-room; employed in logging, putting up the western posts, and making cement, with two colonists, three grumetas, and one sailor belonging to the cutter. Died, and was buried, Mr. Banfield, who had been some time insane, and released from irons five days ago. Learn that Spencer means to leave the colony with Mr. Rowe, and go to Sierra Leone. Therm. 90. *Saturday, 27th.*

Note.—The thermometer, Farenheit's, has hitherto been exposed to the air, under the Hankey's poop: in future it will be placed under a double canvas tent on shore, and, when not otherwise expressed, noted always at its greatest height between noon and 2 P.M.

Same wind and weather. Employed as before, and planking down the inside of the east store-room. Killed a bullock for the colonists. Mr. Rowe, who has not given me a sick list *Sunday, 28th.*

1792.
Sunday, Oct. 28.

since the 21st, has positively refused to give me any more. Two colonists at work. Therm. 90.

Monday, 29th.

Wind and weather the same. Employed as before, and stowing away the provisions and goods in the east store-room, which was this day completed. It is exactly two months since I committed to Mr. Curwood's direction the building of this store-room; it is 53 feet by 14, and occupies, independent of the gateway in the centre, exactly one-half of the east front of the block-house. If we go on only at this rate, with the same strength, we shall be 16 months in completing it, but with our diminished number, years. I am no carpenter, but I will build the rest myself, better and quicker, or I'll lose my head. There have been constantly employed, when living and well, in cutting, squaring, planing, pinning, logging, and roofing this store-room,

Mr. Curwood,	John Reeves,
Price,	Daniel Sly, and
Hood,	James Watson;

and after the launching of the Perseverance, James Spencer. It is true Reeves and Spencer were only a kind of hedge carpenters; Curwood, a coach-maker; and the rest only just able to handle a tool; for we have not a real carpenter by trade, in the whole colony. Therm. 89.

Tuesday, 30th.

Same weather and employment. Got four carriage-guns on shore. Two boats arrived from Bissao, with Mr. De Sylva Cordoza, and those persons who went thither in the Fisher, on Friday last. Learn that Fraser means to leave the colony. Therm. 91.

Wednes. 31st.

Employed principally in logging. This evening Mr. De Sylva returned, and with him went away my two Papel gru-

metas, this is a great loss, for by the grumetas and Peter 1792.
Hayles, a seaman belonging to the cutter, almost every thing Wednes.
lately has been done. However, they wished to go; and I did Oct. 31.
not even ask them to remain; but paid them their wages, and
made them presents besides. A violent tornado, and the rain
came much into the store-room. All this day, by permission
of Captain Cox, the Hankey's crew have been stowing our
goods away in the store-room. Mr. Gandell, the secretary,
with his infant child, left the colony, and went to Bissao.

Monthly state of the Colony.

	Men.	Wom.	Chil.		
On the 30th of September we had	Well .. 12 .. 5 .. 11—Total W. 28				58.
	Sick .. 21 .. 3 .. 6—— S. 30				
Joined by the cutter on the 6th inst.	1 .. 1 .. 2—— ...... 4.				
Lost by	Death .. 3 .. 1 .. 3—— ... 7				9.
	Desertion 1 .. 0 .. 1—— ... 2				
Present state of the colony	Well .. 5 .. 3 .. 10—— W. 18				53.
	Sick .. 25 .. 5 .. 5—— S. 35				

Employed principally in logging; the Hankey's crew assisting Thurs.
us as yesterday; scarcely any of our own people at work. Novemb.
Therm. 90. 1st.

Same employment. Hankey's people still assisting us. Learn Friday,
that Sparks means to leave the colony. Therm. 91. 2d.

Muster six hands at work. Hankey's sailors still assisting us. Saturday,
Therm. 92. 3d.

Four of the Hankey's sailors came on shore to cut logs for us, Sunday,
with whom, I have two colonists, Peter Hayles, and a grumeta, 4th.
at work. Got four of our cannon up the hill. This day week

1792.
Sunday, Nov. 4. the Hankey's charter will expire, who would suppose it from the conduct of our people? Killed a bullock for the colony. Therm. 92.

Monday, 5th. Five colonists at work. Got the spirits on shore.

Tuesday, 6th. Employed as usual. Got two more cannon on shore. Died, and was buried this evening, Mr. Ward. Found that Smith's grave had been opened, and his body much torn: suppose by Hyænas. Therm. 84.

Wednes. 7th. Four colonists at work. Landed the last of our guns, making altogether four six-pounders, and four four-pounders. Therm. 92. A boat from the governor of Bissao came to request permission to cut timber, which was readily granted.

Thurs. 8th. Little wind. Excessively hot. At noon another boat arrived to cut timber. To each man of the two boats, about 20, I promised a shirt, if they would cut logs for me, and bring them in from the woods, this day and to-morrow. In the evening, most of the colonists landed from the Hankey with their baggage, but through their own indolence, there is no shelter for them. Riches and Lister scarcely alive, the former ill of a fever, the latter of fever and flux, I put into the store-room; the rest, like myself, weather it out as well as we can. This is all their own faults, for had they worked with common spirit and diligence, the block-house might, ere this, have been completed.

Placed a four-pounder before each of the store-room doors. One at the south, and one at the western, gate. And cut loup-holes in the front of the store-room for small arms, and close quarters. Fired an evening gun at sun-set, which it is my intention to continue. Four colonists at work. Therm. 93.

Friday, 9th. Weather as before. Therm. 96. The canoes' people cut.

and brought in, for me, as many logs as our whole strength could have effected in a fortnight. The colonists getting on shore their remaining baggage, and the sailors stowing away our goods. The canoes left us, and, by them, Spencer and Fraser deserted the colony. At gun fire assembled the colonists, and appointed to each a proper place to repair to, with his arms, in the case of alarm. Ill with a slight fever all day. *1792. Friday, Novem. 9th.*

Wind and weather as before. Getting on with our logging. Birchall's sloop arrived in the evening. Though ill with a fever, turned out three times in the night, from alarms given, through the fear and madness of Robinson. Made him at last go to sleep under my cot. Therm. 95. Died and was buried Thomas Lister. *Saturday, 10th.*

From the 10 inst. I have been too ill to keep a journal, and am now scarcely able to scribble a few lines to the trustees, before the Hankey sails,* whose charter expired the day after I was confined to my bed. *Friday, 23rd.*

* The letter which I wrote to the trustees by the Hankey, was, I think, dated the 23rd of November 1792. It was written during that and the two preceding days, in those intervals when I had the full possession of my senses, and was able to apply myself, for a short time, to writing, for long I could not; and each of the first two of those days, as well as for several before I was delirious generally from about 10 A.M. to 2 or 3 P.M.; and this was the case in almost all the severe attacks of the fever which I afterwards had. This was owing to the excessive heat between those hours, for I invariably got better as the sun declined, and never experienced the violent raging of the fever till the sun had again acquired power on the following day. This of all the numerous papers relative to the colony is the only one of which I have not a copy. Unable myself to write one, I had nobody to perform that task for me, and what is very singular this is almost the only paper that I know of, which is not to be found in the Bulama office, whether it be yet in existence I know not, Mr. Wadstrom had access to them all, when he was writing his essay on colonization, and it is probable that he might have mislaid it, or that it might have remained among his papers at his death. However if I could have procured it, I had intended to have given all the letters which I wrote from

1792.
Friday, Novem. 23rd.

On Friday last, the 16th, a canoe arrived from my friend Mr. De Sylva, at Bissao, with four bullocks, and, what was of infinitely more importance to us, in our present circumstances, four grumetas. One of them named Johnson, is a Nova Scotian, a good hand at an axe, and our interpreter; the three others are Papels:* the same day I desired that George, whom Bootle had left with me, might be sent to Bulola in the pinnace to endeavour to procure me some Biafara grumetas.

On Monday the 19th, a canoe arrived from Bissao to ask permission to cut timber.

Yesterday the 22nd, Birchall sailed, having left in my charge two Papel grumetas, and a pinnace, which I have sent to Bulola, till his return from the Bananas.

Since my illness there have died,
Monday the 12th, WM. COMPTON,
Thursday .. 15th, NAT. ASHWORTH, boy,
Saturday .. 17th, ELIZ. ROWE, a child,
Sunday . .. 18th, GEO. WINFIELD and } boys.
JAMES REEVES,
Wednesday.. 21st, WM. C. BARRET and
DOLPHIN PRICE,
Thursday .. 22nd, JOHN ASHWORTH, boy.

This morning the Hankey attempted to sail, but a calm obliged her to anchor again. She however got under sail about seven o'clock in the evening and left us.

Employed in logging and getting our effects up the hill from

Bulama to the trustees, in the appendix; as they would probably, give a more correct notion of our situation and ideas at the time than can be formed even from the perusal of a journal.

* Johnson, as a clever, and a head man, at 12 bars, the others at six bars a month.

the beach. Four Colonists well, the cutter's sailor, and six grumetas.

1792. Friday, Novem. 23rd.

Every body seems low and depressed; but the ship is gone and our own exertions must decide our fate.

Let us take a view of our numbers and situation.

State of the Colony, at the Hankey's departure.

	Men.	Wom.	Chil.		
On the 31st of Oct. we had { Well	5	3	10	—Total W. 18 } 53.
Sick	25	5	5	—— S. 35
Since which time we have { Death	4	0	6	—— 10 }
lost by .... { Desertion	2	0	0	—— 2 } 26.
Returned in the Hankey* {	6	4	4	—— 14 }
Present state of the Colony { Well	3	0	1	—Total W. 4 } 27.
Sick	15	4	4	—— S. 23
Peter Hayles a sailor belonging to the cutter, ...					1
					28

Besides six grumetas, and one absent in the pinnace.

The east store-room, fitted for close quarters, is complete, and the whole external logging will be so I expect in four or five days.† We have four four-pounders on the top of the hill, and

* Messrs. Munden,   Mrs. Hancorne,   Eliz. Curwood,
       Paiba,   Paiba,   Rich. Curwood,
       Curwood,   Curwood,   Thos. Blake,
       Robinson,   Rowe,   Edw. Pierce,
       Rowe,
Edw. Fowler,

together with Mr. Birkhead the master, and Joseph Glover the cabin-boy of the cutter.

† The perpendicular Posts of the block-house, have logs of not less than six nor more than eight inches diameter, horizontally spiked to them, from the ground to the height of seven feet. Above the logging are inch planks for seven feet more. The interstices of the logs are to be filled up with a mortar or cement. See the plan.

1792.
Friday, Novem. 23rd.

four six-pounders at the foot of it; a cutter of 34 tons, and six swivels, fitted with close quarters; the Perseverance which we have built of seven tons and two swivels; the Hankey's long-boat, which I have purchased, rather more than half that size; a pinnace which rows with eight oars, left me by Birchall; a six-oar'd yawl that we brought from England, and a two-oar'd dingy belonging to the cutter, together with about 200 stand of arms.

Thus,

On leaving England we were in number 275 persons.

On the Calypso's departure, ... 91.

On the Hankey's departure, ... 28.

In the evening I assembled the colonists, at least those who were capable of moving, and though not exactly fit for the task, as this is the first day, out of many, that I have been able to move myself, I endeavoured to cheer up their spirits, pointed out as well as I could, their precise situation, laid before them most of their difficulties, and the means by which they might be overcome.

For the information of him who may succeed, and for the good of those who may survive me, I think it necessary to say something here of Peter Hayles, the only seaman I have in the cutter.

Mr. Birkhead who commanded her, and is gone home in the Hankey, having in vain attempted to persuade me to abandon the colony, during my illness a few days ago, said that his conscience would not permit him to leave me, without making me acquainted with the character of the only man that I had left in this vessel. H was he said a most notorious villain; that he had always great difficulty in keeping him in any thing like order; that when at Sierra Leone he had quarrelled with his most intimate friend Johnson, one of the cutter's sailors, who had died there, and had threatened to kill him ; and that Johnson, extremely frighten- **1792.** ed, had claimed his protection, and made him acquainted with Friday, the following circumstances. Novem. 23rd.

That Peter Hayles had been a notorious pirate, in a small schooner, in the bay of Honduras; that he had also run away with one vessel, in which he had sailed, and sold her; and that he had set fire to another, and then plundered her, for which he had been tried, but escaped ; that he, Mr. Birkhead, had slept with a brace of pistols under his pillow, all the way up from Sierra Leone, fearing some attempt from this man, and that he verily thought he would one day or other run away with my cutter. I was sorry to learn all this, for he is certainly the most useful man in the colony. However knowing a man to be a villain is getting over every difficulty. I therefore requested Mr. Birkhead would go on board, unbend the sails, run in the bowsprit, and leave the rest to me. This happened I think eight days ago, and the same day I had promised to increase Peter's wages, from £1 15 0 to £3 per month.

The pinnace returned this evening from Bulola, without grumetas, but brought the queen's son, Tabangagay, with some trifling presents from his mother Woody Toorey, and a promise of grumetas hereafter.

Continue the logging with four men, including the sailor, and Saturday, exclusive of the grumetas, which hereafter must be understood. 24th.

Sent the pinnace to Bulola, which I named the Industry, with Tabangagay and presents for the queen his mother. Therm. 95.

Same employment. Killed a bullock for the colony. Sunday, Three men well. Therm. 91. 25th.

Began to put posts in the ground, for the erection of Tambours Monday, 26th.

1792.
Monday, Novem. 26th. round the gateways.* A boat from Bissao came to ask leave to cut timber, and in her came Spencer, whom I forbade to land. Hired the men of this boat to cut logs for me one day. By this boat I learn the melancholy fate of poor Mr. Bootle; his vessel is cut off † by the Manjacks; himself, Mr. Ashley, and all his grumetas killed, except two, who are made slaves.

Tuesday, 27th. Same employment.‡ The grumetas belonging to the Bissao canoe still cutting logs for us. Therm. 85. Four men well.

Wednes. 28th. Employed about the Tambours, fixing wall plates, and boarding up the north side of the block-house. The Industry returned from Bulola. Three men well. Finished the logging of the block-house, Tambours excepted.

Thursday, 29th. Employed logging the Tambours. Killed a hog for the colonists. Therm. 91. Two men well.

Friday, 30th. This day remarkable for every man, woman, and child, in the colony being ill, except myself. With the grumetas I continue logging the tambours.

Monthly state of the Colony.

In number the same as on the Hankey's departure, but every body ill except myself.

Saturday, Decem. 1st. Employed as yesterday. One man well. Died and was buried this evening, Mr. Donnelly. A canoe stopped in its way to Bissao; got its people to cut logs for me.

Sunday, 2nd. Employed as before. Killed a bullock for the colony. Died, and was buried Mr. Webster. Therm. 92. Three men well.

* See the plan.

† The country expression for seizing any vessel by stratagem, or surprize; and putting to death its people.

‡ No notice will hereafter be taken of the winds and weather till the commencement of the next rains; for some account of it, see Appendix No. 5.

Same employment. Four men well. Therm. 92.

Employed as before. Died and was buried, Alexander Thompson. Four men well. Therm. 91. In the evening a boat stopped in her way from Bissao for Tombaly.

Employed as before; the grumetas of the canoe cutting logs for us. At eleven o'clock, observed Bellchore, with two canoes, coming round the point, having the union-flag flying which I had given him at Canabac.

Beat to arms, saluted him; and then loaded the four-pounders with grape and cannister. By this time he had landed and marched up to the eastern gate with two and thirty well appointed men. Having placed two sentinels at each gateway, with orders not to admit any one within the square, and to put to instant death any who might attempt it by force, I went out and met him, and conducted him to my tent, pitched a few yards without the eastern gate. His people I put in possession of a hut, which had been built for my own grumetas.

The Portuguese canoe, about sailing as Bellchore came round the point, terrified at his approach, returned and anchored close under our guns, but sailed again about an hour afterwards.

Divided our whole force, consisting of four colonists, besides myself, whom I could not call well, but who were capable of bearing arms, and seven grumetas, into two equal watches, the command of one I gave to Johnson, having no subscriber well enough to take it. The other I kept myself.

Bellchore dined with me in my tent, having two of his chief men, squatting on their hams, one on either side of me, the whole time; to whom he occasionally gave large pieces of meat. It was thought, during this meal, that I run great risk of assassin-

1792.
Wednes.
Dec. 5.

ation. I believe I might: but though my friend Aberdein, who was very ill, and Johnson, the grumeta, endeavoured to dissuade me from it, yet I thought that our safety would have been more endangered from my shewing any symptom of fear, by keeping back, than by trusting my person unarmed among these three armed savages.

After dinner, Bellchore was particularly solicitous for me to take *him* into the square, and through the store-room, which I at length complied with; and he then returned to his own men. Not long afterwards one of the grumetas came and told me that he had over-heard Bellchore tell his people, " that most of the white men were dead, and that the living were all sick but the captain, (meaning me;) that he had put us here, and that he could send us away, *we were his chickens;*"* therefore, said the grumeta, he means to attack you.

This, I certainly thought very likely, and therefore, at sunset, assembled the four colonists and the grumetas; told them what Bellchore had said, and that I really believed they had come here with a view to attack us; that if they behaved with common firmness, there was no danger; for I doubted not that they would repulse them, if attacked; but that if they did not, there was no safety, for, rather than be taken by these people, I would blow them all up.

There was about a ton of gunpowder, a few feet only from my cot in the store-room; and I ordered Nash the cooper, to take the heads out of two of the barrels, one at either end, and by these were placed lighted matches. The north and west gate-

* This is an expression of contempt by which the Bijugas call the Biafaras, with whom they are always at war.

ways were blocked up, and there was a four-pounder in the east and south ones.

1792. Wednes. Dec. 5.

The Bijugas, as before mentioned, occupied a hut, about 30 yards from the block-house; and I made their king Bellchore, having first pointed out to him the powder and the matches, sleep in my cot. A few minutes afterwards, Nash, who had been accustomed to sleep on board the cutter, (where I had only one man, and who was now on board, with orders to fire directly into the hut if he heard *two* musquets discharged in the night,) came to me, and requested to go on board the cutter to sleep as usual—this I refused. He threatened to swim on board; and I promised to shoot him if he made the attempt. He had never yet known me break my promise, and therefore went to the post where I had ordered him. I laid down, wrapped up in a cloak in the middle of the east gateway, with a brace of pistols under my head. Five sentinels called all's well, every five minutes, and the night passed in peace.

The night was cold, and the wind was N.E. Two of the colonists are worse, and two of the grumetas are ill. All day taken up with Bellchore, endeavouring to get him away before night, without his perceiving that it arises from fear. Having made him and his people very handsome presents, I succeeded about an hour before dark, when he left us. Saluted him as he went out of the harbour. I attribute our safety to the powder; he certainly meant to attack us.

Thurs. 6th.

At day-light went to work again. Employed in logging the tambours, and boarding the upper part of the block-house. At noon, assembled our four men and the grumetas; then severely upbraided Nash for his base and cowardly conduct, during Bellchore's visit, and praised Peter Hayles for being the

Friday, 7th.

1792.
Friday,
Dec. 7. only white man in the colony, well, who appeared at that time destitute of fear. The former seemed much ashamed, and the latter highly pleased. Therm. 89. Five men well.

Saturday, 8th. Same employment. Very foggy. Therm. 88. Four men well.

Sunday, 9th. Same weather and employment. Died of a fever, and was buried, Mrs. Harwin. Killed a bullock for the colonists. Therm. 88. Three men well. Myself a little feverish.

Monday, 10th. Employed as before. Died of fevers, and were buried, Peter Box, Henrietta Fowler, and Hannah Riches. Therm. 90. Three men well. Myself ill of a fever.

Tuesday, 11th. Foggy weather. No wind. Same employment. When going to dinner, Peter Hayles told me that all the grumetas, except Johnson, were dissatisfied and meant to leave me. Greatly astonished, ill as I was, I sent for them all; told them that I had learned that they were not pleased with their situation, and begged that they would tell me the cause of their dissatisfaction: beginning with Emanuel, he said that he liked his situation very well, and was much pleased with my conduct till within these two days, when, at beat of drum in the morning, I looked angry at them all. It is true I did look angry, and was very angry, because for the last two days the grumetas have been very dilatory in going to their work. Antonio I next addressed: he said that there was a great deal of work, that he had never received a pair of trowsers, though he had been here a month, and that he wanted to go and pay a debt of rice, which he owed in his own country. That there was much work I allowed; but that no one worked harder than myself; the trowsers he might have had by asking for them, and his rice might be paid at any time. George had no complaint—" no more him want go see him shipmate." This man I procured from Bootle; he has learned that two of his shipmates escaped the melancholy end of that man, and were now at Bissao; these people, he said, he wanted to go and see. Liverpool, without assigning any reason, said that he wished to leave the place altogether. Lysander was sick, he said, and wanted one of his own country doctors.

1792.
Tuesday,
Dec. 11.

I told them all, that every man on this island was free to leave it whenever he pleased; that they had voluntarily come to work for me, and that I would not detain them a day longer than they wished, adding, that though I stood in need of a few grumetas, they were at liberty to depart by the first boat, if they did not like their situation. Johnson told me, in the evening, that the grumetas were by no means dissatisfied; but that they were afraid to remain on the island, in such a small number, for fear of Bellchore; that, not only they, but he, was also sure that he meant to attack us; and that if I would let him go to Bissao, he would return with many more grumetas. Therm. 92. Three men well. Myself very ill of the fever, which the palaver has augmented.

Employed as before. Therm. 89. Three men well. Delirious in the middle of the day. Much better in the morning and evening.

Wednes.
12th.

Very ill—delirious part of the day. In the evening, after having somewhat recovered my deranged senses, sent for Messrs. Fielder and Hood, the only subscribers able to move; made my will, and gave them advice how to act in case of my death.

Thurs.
13th.

Died of a fever, and were buried, both Mr. and Mrs. Freeman, this couple I married the 4th of last month. They were both taken ill about ten minutes after the ceremony was performed, and have been so ever since. They both died this

Friday,
14th.

1792.
Friday,
Dec. 14.

morning within ten minutes of each other, and were both buried in the same grave. Myself a great deal better in the morning, but delirious great part of the evening.

At night, Johnson came to me and told me that all the grumetas meant to leave me to-morrow, and go away in a canoe that had stopped here, from Tombaly, just before dark; he begged that I would speak to them, if I found myself well enough in the morning; the cause, as before observed, is the fear of Bellchore, which my illness now increases; as nothing would induce them to stay, were I to die.

Saturday, 15th.

Exceedingly ill. Johnson brought to the side of my bed, this morning, all the grumetas, who, to a man, said that they meant to go to Bissao in the canoe that was now here. I told them that if they would stay a week, to complete the gateways, I would then send them there in one of my boats: this they did not like, and seemed determined to go. I therefore directed Peter Hayles to pay them their wages, and they all went away, except George, whom Johnson had prevailed upon to remain till to-morrow, to assist him in navigating the Industry to Bissao, to endeavour to procure me some more grumetas.

Harwin, one of the only three men who are well, told me this evening, that he wished to leave the colony, and go to Bissao, which I readily acceded to, having never asked a man to remain, who shewed the least inclination to leave the island. Such dastardly wretches were never seen. Died, and was buried, this evening, Mr. Fielder. This is the man, who, two days ago, made my will, and whom I thought likely to be my successor. He was young and brave,—fit to draw a lion's tooth.

Sunday, 16th.

Still very ill. Sent Johnson and George with the Industry to Bissao; in her, Harwin and his son left the colony, leaving my servant, James Watson, the only colonist well on shore; and Peter Hayles in the cutter. Watson and myself slept in the east gateway, every other being barricadoed; and I collected the colonists, being seven sick men, into the adjoining birth, that we might be in a body, in case of an attack. Two sick men, with Peter, guard the cutter. Killed a goat for the colonists. *1792. Sunday, Dec. 16.*

A great deal better, which I in a great measure attribute to a cool, clear, strong N. E. wind. This is the first of many days that we have been without fog. Peter and my man do a little work. Arrived two boats from Bissao; one of which brought letters for me from Captain Cox, of the Hankey, which ship is now at that place, having run on shore, near the isle of Formosa, and having had a narrow escape from being lost. His ship, he says, is exceedingly sickly, having buried, since he left us, no less than six of his crew, Mr. BIRKHEAD, and the following Colonists: *Monday, 17th.*

  Mrs. HANCORNE,   Mr. MUNDEN,
    CURWOOD,   ROBINSON,
     EDWARD FOWLER,

which is somewhat astonishing, as there were only two of the crew slightly ill, when they left this port; and not one had been buried during the whole of their stay here.

Continue to get better. A fine breeze from the N. E. Peter and my man continue at work; but what is their work, to what we have to do? It is like a drop of water compared with the ocean. Peter is weak with a slight flux, and Watson is not very strong. Died, and was buried, Joseph Riches. Myself well enough to walk about a little; the N.E. wind continued to blow fresh all day, the therm. in the morning was 72, and has not risen higher than 77; in short, it has been the coolest and plea- *Tuesday 18th.*

1792.
Tuesday, 18th.

santest day that I have yet experienced on the island. Its bracing coolness has almost cured me, who have been from day-light till dark exposed to it, while our indolent sick have been pent up all day in their stinking eating house, which has scarcely been cleaned since they came on shore, rather than exert themselves so much as to go into this renovating air. In the evening, when we leave off work, Peter goes on board the cutter; and my man and myself remain to defend the block-house! 'tis well we are not attacked. Since the departure of the Hankey, I have had no one to speak to, no conversation. I do not think it safe to shew lights, and therefore cannot read in the evening; indeed, my head at present could not bear it; so that, after we leave off work, I sit about two hours alone in the dark, in sullen deliberation on what we are to do on the morrow, and then go to bed. How different this, from the life I have been accustomed to!

Wednes. 19th.

Getting about famously. Assist Peter and Watson a little at boarding; a strong N.E. wind all last night, and the thermometer, at day-light this morning, only 65. I never remember having seen it so low. At noon, 88.

Thurs. 20th.

Same weather and employment; an additional hand at work. This cold weather does wonders for me. Killed a goat for the colony. Therm. morning 67—noon 87.

Friday, 21st.

This morning a boat arrived from Bissao, and brought me a cargo more valuable than gold—5 grumetas. Died this day Mr. Aberdein, the last member of the council, who had been exceedingly ill ever since the departure of the Hankey, and has been for more than a fortnight removed to the cutter; where it was thought he would breathe a purer, and a cooler, air. He was a man of great virtues, and great misfortunes. Died also

Thomas Sparks, the last subscriber but one. With Peter and Watson, I finished boarding the outside of the block-house. My new grumetas do not seem to like their first employment, that of digging graves for, and burying, the dead. If they had not arrived I know not what we should have done. Have over-worked myself and feel very ill.

1792. Friday, Dec. 21.

Since the first of this month, of 19 men, 4 women, and 5 children, we have buried 9 men, 3 women, and 1 child, which is, except one, half of the whole colony. It is melancholy no doubt, but many have absolutely died through fear. More courage, and greater exertions, I firmly believe, would have saved many of them; but a lowness of spirits, a general des-pondency, seems to possess every body. When taken ill, they lie down and say that they know they shall die; and, what is very remarkable, I have never yet known one recover after having, in such a manner, given himself up.

Employed the men belonging to the Portuguese boat in cutting logs for us. Peter, Watson, and our grumetas, cutting and squaring rafters. Myself very ill—delirious great part of the day. The Portuguese boat sailed in the evening.

Saturday, 22d.

Same weather and employment. Three men well. Myself very ill.

Sunday, 23d.

The fine bracing weather continues. Rather better.

Monday, 24th.

Continue mending. Therm. morning 70; noon 90.

Tuesday, 25th.

Began roofing the *west store-room*. Employed cutting and squaring rafters. Three colonists well; myself almost so. Therm. 70, morning; 90 noon.

Wednes. 26th.

Same weather. Employed getting up rafters and roofing. At noon Johnson returned with the Industry from Bissao, and, to my inexpressible pleasure, brought with him 23 grumetas; 18

Thurs. 27th.

1792.
Thurs.
Dec. 27.

of whom are men, 3 women, and 2 boys, which, together with himself, and the five here before, make my grumeta men amount to four and twenty. All those who before had left me now returned, except one who had been detained on account of a rice debt; and Tomana, who had piloted me up the Rio Grande to Ghinala, and who was the only person on board the Fisher schooner that escaped with life when she was cut off by the Manjacks, was among my new grumetas.* Johnson tells me that the five who came here on the 21st were obliged to leave Bissao for murder. By him I received another letter from Captain Cox, who informs me that he is going to St. Jago, one of the Cape de Verd islands, to endeavour to get more men:

* This man was a Timaney, and was the person who left the little Kacundy boy with me, on the 25th of August last, to learn English, which he did very quickly. He narrated the circumstance as follows: In the morning the boat was sent on shore with two men to get water for the vessel. Mr. Bootle and Ashley were sitting down on the deck eating their breakfasts, and the crew were at their's below. A canoe came alongside with about a dozen Manjacks; they sat down on the quarter deck, and the head men were partaking of breakfast with Mr. Bootle. In a few minutes, Messrs. Bootle and Ashley were stabbed by the persons immediately next to them, when the people below, hearing cries, jumped upon deck armed, and as they got on deck were shot. Tomana jumped overboard and swam on shore, where, with the two others already there, he was seized and sold to the Portuguese merchants, at Bissao; but having property to a greater amount than what had been given for him, he had indemnified the merchant who had purchased him, and was again free. I asked Tomana what was the cause of this atrocious act. He said, he had learned, that some time ago, a white man had killed a native of that town where they were, and that they had killed Bootle in revenge; that they never forget nor forgive an injury; and that the first white man that fell into their power was sure to suffer for their countryman that had fallen; but that now, as it was all settled, " white man might go there again." How cautious ought people to be in their conduct towards these men. What inducement to load them with kindness! that if ever a poor miserable European be cast on their shore, he may experience at their hands, nothing but benevolence, and be lost in admiration of their officious civilities; not knowing that it resulted from an invariab e rule of their conduct, to return measure for measure.

he also says, that De Sylva, and all the Portuguese, advise my quitting the island, as they are convinced the Canabacs will attack us. Therm. 90. Four men well.

1792. Thurs. Dec. 27.

Employed cutting logs, and logging the tambours; cutting and squaring rafters; making mortar, and roofing the west store-room. Four men well. Therm. 88.

Friday, 28th.

In the evening, two or three of the grumetas came to me, and said that Fransisco, one of their party, was not a good man; that he wanted to eat one of them (John Basse) who had been this day taken very ill. As I could not comprehend what they meant by saying that one of them wanted to eat another, I sent for Johnson to explain. He said that the man accused of eating the other was a witch, and that he was the cause of John Basse's illness, by sucking his blood with his infernal witchcraft; and that these people had come to request that I would let them tie him to a tree, and flog him, after they had finished their work. I told them that there was no such thing as a witch; that it was impossible for this man to suck the blood of another, by any art which he could possibly possess; that he could not be the cause of another man's illness by such means; and that with respect to flogging, no one punished, on the island, but myself. Johnson, who is as bigotted, in this instance, as any of them, says that he is well known to be a witch; that he has killed many people with his infernal art, and that this is the cause of his leaving his own country, where, if he should ever be caught, he would be sold as a slave; and that he, with difficulty, had prevented the other grumetas from throwing him overboard, on their passage from Bissao hither. Johnson, moreover, told me that there was another witch among the grumetas, who had the power of changing himself into an alligator, and that he also

1792.
Friday,
Dec. 28.

had killed many people by his witchcraft, and was consequently obliged to run from his country. They therefore most earnestly entreated me to let them punish them, country fashion, and they promised not to kill either of them. Astonished at the assurance, that neither of them should be killed, if they were permitted to punish them; I told Johnson that if such a thing should occur, I would immediately hang all those concerned in it; and then endeavoured to reason them out of their foolish notions respecting these two poor men. Johnson replied that it was the custom of the country for "white man" never to interfere in these cases; and that at Bissao the governor never took notice of their thus punishing one another according to their own country fashion, and that they expected the same indulgence here; for that if these people were in their own country, they would either be killed or sold, as witchcraft was never forgiven, and its professors never suffered to remain in their own country when once found out. I had now all the grumetas round me, among whom were the accused themselves, and endeavoured again to convince them of the innocence of these people, by pointing out the impossibility of their hurting others by any magic or spell, or of transforming themselves into any other shape. When many of them said this man had often avowed his frequently turning himself into an alligator to devour people. "How say you Corasmo, said I, did you ever say so to any of these people?" Yes, was his reply. "What do you mean? Do you mean to say that you ever transformed yourself into any other shape than that which you now bear?" Yes, was the answer. "Now, Corasmo, you know that white man knows every thing; you cannot deceive me; therefore avow to those people that you never changed yourself into an alligator, and that these are all lyes." No, was his reply;

who can believe it? "*I can* change myself into an alligator, and *have often* done it!" This was such an incorrigible witch that I immediately gave him up to the grumetas, to punish him, but desired them to be merciful.

1792. Friday, Dec. 28.

It is scarcely credible that a man can so work upon his own weak imagination as to believe, which I doubt not this man did, its own fanciful creations to be realities.

Strong S. E. wind and hazy. After the grumetas had left me last night, 1 regretted having delivered up to them the two poor miserable wretches accused of witchcraft. From ten till twelve at night their cries were most piteous and loud, and though distant a full half-mile, were distinctly heard. This morning they cannot move. A little after we went to work, two Canabac canoes entered the harbour. Beat to arms; saluted them; got the grumetas within the block-house, and shotted our guns. Jamber and Demiong, Jalorem's two sons, landed with about forty armed men. They brought me two bullocks and two goats, as a present from their father, and six white cocks from his head wife. Jamber and his brother remained with me in the east gateway, and their people occupied our grumetas huts. A sentinel at each gate, a good look out, and Peter Hayles, with two grumetas on board the cutter, with the same orders which he had when Belchore was here. No work done. The grumetas quarrelling one with another all day long. Therm. 65 morning, 88 noon. Two men well.

Saturday, 29th.

The Bijugas entertained me this morning with a sham fight, and afterwards with a dance. Their quickness and agility is astonishing. I never saw the broad sword so well handled; and they throw their spear, or assagaye, with unerring certitude. In the evening, one of the Canabacs cleaning his gun, it accidently

Sunday, 30th.

1792.
Sunday, Decem. 30th.

went off; and its contents, a great number of slugs, were lodged in one of their own people's feet. The report of this gun caused an immediate alarm; both parties flew to arms, suspecting some treachery, but we soon discovered the cause, when all was quiet again.

After this, Jamber determined immediately to go away.* John-

* Had it not been for this accidental discharge of one of the Bijuga's guns, I should certainly have been attacked by them that night. Suspecting that they meditated an attack I had tried as much as possible, without suffering them to perceive my suspicions, to get them away that evening; but Jamber, the youngest of Jalorem's sons, would not go; he moreover said, that he should stay two or three days longer, as his father would not expect his return before that time. I was sitting between him and his brother when this musquet went off about five o'clock, and to shew that neither party trusted each other, every man of each instantly flew to his arms. Every one appearing ignorant of the cause of the firing, having placed all my men at the different gateways, I went to the hut where I saw one of the Bijugas wounded in the foot by the gun of another having accidentally gone off; he was extended on his back, and held in that situation by his countrymen, while one of them was employed in cutting the slugs out of his feet. About half an hour afterwards, Jamber came and told me that he should go away directly; astonished at such a determination, I asked why; but he could not, at least did not, give me any reason for it. Seeing him now resolved to go, I pressed him to stay, but in vain. They all left me about eight o'clock in a dark night, without a possibility of reaching Canabac, or even of making much progress before morning. Jamber was a fine intelligent lad, about twenty years of age, whom I had particularly distinguished at Canabac, by giving him extraordinary presents, as well as during this visit to me at Bulama. He had this evening asked me for many things which were all given to him, and he had been exceedingly lavish in professions of esteem and regard for me. Yet that very night was he to put me to death; at least to attempt it.

From many of the Portuguese grumetas, who were after this at Canabac, I had the following account of their intentions. Jamber and his brother, who were inside of the block-house, were to seize an opportunity of stabbing, and then firing at me; the report of this musquet was to be the signal for those outside to rush to the east gate, where these were to knock down the sentinel and let them in. The accident above related was considered by the Bijugas *as a bad omen*, as a certain prognostic of their not succeeding in the proposed attempt, and they did not think themselves safe while they remained so near us. These were the reasons that induced them to go away that

son tells me that the man who accidentally wounded the other will be sold for a slave on his return. Sent suitable presents by Jamber to Jalorem and his principal wife; and gave others to him, to Demiong, and to his people. The grumetas quarrelling all day. Killed a bullock for the colony. 1792. Monday, Decemb. 31st.

Same employment as on the 28th. No work having been done during the Canabacs visit. Jamber, in his hurry, left behind him the copy of the deed of conveyance of the Island, which had been left at Canabac with his father, to be always produced by his people when they came to this island. Therm. morning 64, noon 87.

Monthly state of the Colony.

		Men.	Wom.	Chil.		
On the 30th of November we had	Well	1	0	0	Total W. 1	28.
	Sick	18	4	5	S. 27	
Since which time we have lost by	Death	9	3	1	13	15.
	Desertion	1	0	1	2	
Present state of the colony	Well	2	0	2	W. 4	13.
	Sick	7	1	1	S. 9	

night. Of Belchore I had been exceedingly cautious; he was a notorious character; but of Jamber I had not the least suspicion, that is, of assassination. It is true that I expected to be attacked, but rather against, than with, his inclination; his authority I did not think sufficient to restrain his countrymen from making one, when they had any prospect of plunder; but keeping him and his brother inside of the block-house, I thought would tend to prevent, instead of to forward it. This conduct seems to confirm what we were told on our arrival at Bissao, that the Bijugas were most to be feared when you were loading them with kindness; that with one hand they would receive a present, and with the other stab you. Neither Jamber, his brother, nor any of Jalorem's men, ever returned to Bulama.

1793.
Tuesday, Jan. 1.

Grumetas.
24 Men,
3 Women,
2 Boys.
—
29.
—

Began plastering the block-house, and putting in the inner posts for the north row of houses. Began also taking up the roots of those trees, near the block-house, which had been felled in the rains. Therm. morning 63, noon 87.

N. B. The N. E. breeze, which has so regularly blown for these last three weeks, generally begins about nine or ten at night, increases till about midnight, when it is pretty strong; retains its vigour till about ten the next morning; from which time till noon it gradually dies away, and we have calms or light airs till it springs up again at nine in the evening.

Wednes. 2nd. Same employment. Shot a guana, two feet seven inches in length, and roasted it; very delicate food. Therm. morning 65, noon 92.

Thursd. 3rd. Same employment. This morning one of the grumetas drew his knife on me. Had I a pistol, I believe I should have shot him. This crime is common with them; they all carry knives in their girdles, and the instant they have any quarrel the knives are directly drawn. If this is not stopped, at least towards white men, I know not what may be the consequence. At noon I assembled all the grumetas, and endeavoured to convince them of the enormity of the crime which Domingo Swar had been guilty of, that his life was forfeited; and that he now only lived through my clemency. They seemed astonished at his boldness, sorry for his crime, and acknowledged that his punishment ought to be great. The man himself was half dead with fear. I told them that no punishment, short of death, could atone for his crime, and that if he had attempted to wound one of the colonists, that would have been his fate; but as the attempt was made upon me, whom twenty of them could not wound,* I should remit his punishment, from his excessive folly. I then ordered a block to be put on the branch of a large tree, and reeving a rope through it, declared that I would hang immediately, the first of them that should ever be guilty of a similar crime. Domingo was then ordered to the beach, there to wait the first boat's arrival to carry him off the Island, and was told, as he valued his life, never to appear again in my presence. In the evening, the James and William cutter arrived in her way from Sierra Leone to Bissao, where she was going for stock: Mr. Ballard, our former assistant surgeon, was in her. Three men well; grumetas constantly quarrelling among themselves. Therm. morning 67, noon 87, 3 P. M. 92.

1793. Thurs. January, 3d.

Employed as before. On the application of the Master of the James and William, I let him have ten barrels of pork, six tierces of beef, and two hogsheads of bread, for the use of the

Friday, 4th.

---

* Though the natives make slaves of, and put to death, their own countrymen, on whom witchcraft, in their manner, has been proved; yet they firmly believe, and always say, that " all white men are witches." They thought that I was a very great one, and that few things were impossible for me to do. This idea I of course was desirous to strengthen; and therefore wished them to think that I was invulnerable by any of their common arms. They themselves always wear gris-gris, or charms; which they purchase of the Mandingoes, to guard them against the effects of certain arms, or of poison, and which they put the utmost reliance on: they have one against poison; another against a musquet; another against a sword; and another against a knife; and, indeed, against almost every thing that they think can hurt them, and therefore would readily believe that their weapons could not wound me; but they all allow that there is no gris-gris (pronounce grigory) against " great gun."

1793.
Friday,
Jan. 4.

Sierra Leone colony. After dark we were much astonished by learning from a Bissao canoe, that an English ship " having too much white people" was at the back of this island, among the shoals between it and Arcas, and that there would be great difficulty in her getting out again. Therm. 89. Three men well.

Saturday, 5th.

Early this morning I went with the two-oared boat on board the James and William, just sailing, in order to ascertain what ship was at the back of the island, and to extricate it, as far as my knowledge would serve, from its present difficult situation. It was calm the greatest part of the day, we therefore made but little progress. The block-house I left in the charge of Mr. Hood; enjoining him to be very vigilant.

Sunday, 6th.

Little wind—the day was therefore well advanced before we got through the channel which separates this island from that of Galenas, soon after which we discovered the ship that I was in quest of, about seven miles distant, at an anchor between Arcas and Bulama. As she was directly to windward of us, surrounded by banks that are left dry at low water, and the ebb tide having just made, it was impossible for the cutter to get near her to-night; I therefore, a little before dark, quitted this vessel which had hitherto towed us, and rowed towards the ship which I reached a little after eight o'clock. It was the Scorpion sloop of war, commanded by Capt. Ferris, who had been ordered by Commodore Dod of the Charon, whom he left at an anchor off Cape Roxo, to visit the island of Bulama, and afford us such assistance as we might stand in need of, and as might be consistent with his Majesty's service. Captain Ferris had sent his boat to the block-house, through the eastern channel, since I had left it; which boat had returned a few hours before I got on board. The officer, who was in that boat, said that at day light this morning he counted twelve canoes close to the S. W. point of the harbour, and that they immediately retreated round it. As I had never seen more than two canoes at a time, and that very seldom, I was under considerable apprehensions for the safety of the colony, as I was convinced they could be no other than Bijuga canoes, and that nothing but an hostile intention could have carried them thither. Captain Ferris told me that, as he could not get with his ship up to Bulama, he should return to-morrow to his commodore off Cape Roxo. Having apprised him that he had been misled by bad charts, and that I would, if he would permit me, shew him a very good channel round the west end of the island, he assented to try it the next day.

<small>1793. Sunday, Jan. 6.</small>

In the morning, after the master had sounded, and buoyed off, the channel, the Scorpion got under sail; but from light and adverse winds it was late on Wednesday evening before we anchored off the block-house. In the Bulama channel a merchant ship under English colours passed us from the Isles de Loss bound to Bissao, commanded by Moore, who had been our pilot to Canabac. This I believe is the first English merchant *ship* except ourselves, that ever went through that channel.

<small>Monday, 7th. to Wednes. 9th.</small>

As soon as the Scorpion was at an anchor, I went on shore to the block-house, after an absence of five days, having never before been absent from it five minutes. Very little work had been done; and they had all been much frightened, having seen three canoes on Saturday night, which had been hailed from the cutter, without making any answer. They had been under arms every night since, and on Sunday a party of thirteen men went into the woods to see if they could discover any traces of people having been lately there. They reported that they had seen branches of trees quite green, that had evidently not been cut

1793.
Wednes.
Jan. 9.

many hours, and with which the people from the canoes had probably sheltered themselves the night before. Our own people had been very troublesome and insolent to Mr. Hood.

Thurs. 10th.

Captain Ferris visited the colony, of which I gave him a statement, according to a form which he produced. No work done to-day. The first holiday since we have been on the island.

Friday, 11th.

Employed digging up the stumps of trees, and squaring timber for wall plates and beams. Was this day obliged to discharge Tomana, one of my best grumetas, for having disobeyed my orders, a circumstance in my present situation not to be forgiven, for, on implicit obedience to them, depends the safety of us all. With him went also William, the Kacundy boy, a fine lad, who had learned to speak English very well. Four men well. Gave two bullocks to the Scorpion's crew.

Saturday, 12th.

Same employment. This evening the Scorpion sailed. From Capt. Ferris I received every civility; and from his saying that he had orders to render us any assistance in his power,* I requested permission of him to ask, among his crew, for six volunteers to strengthen the colony, as I had heard that there were men in his ship who would accept the offer; but he told me that was a point in which he could not assist me, as he had no authority to discharge any of his men. However, one of his midshipmen of the name of Scott, who was very anxious to remain, he at

* When the men of war, that annually visit the coast of Africa, were about to sail from England, our trustees in London, knowing that the Hankey must have left Bulama, and not having heard of those colonists who had remained on the island, since the melancholy accounts which they had received by the Calypso, requested the admiralty would be pleased to order them to touch at Bulama, and inquire into our situation, and render us what assistance they could. Captain Dod, of the Charon, not thinking it safe to risk his own large ship in a long unknown channel, containing many sand banks, had dispatched Captain Ferris in the Scorpion, for that purpose.

length discharged, and I gave him the command of the cutter. Therm. 86. Four men well, including Mr. Scott. Myself ill.

1793. Saturday, Jan. 12.

Employed rooting up stumps, putting up beams, and laying on cement. Received, by a Bissao canoe, three bullocks, three dozen of fowls, and 500 yams. Therm. 89. Four men well. Myself ill. Killed a bullock for the colony.

Sunday, 13th.

Same employment. Therm. 91. Four men well. Myself very ill.

Monday, 14th.

Employed about the tambours, plastering the logging, taking up stumps, cutting and squaring beams and rafters. Found that Nash and Griffiths had plundered the store-room of rum; stopped their allowance for a month, and threatened to flog them both. The grumetas, noisy, troublesome, and riotous, particularly old Fidalgo, whom I was obliged to put in irons. No man, I believe, was ever so plagued with such a set of rascals. Myself exceedingly ill with the fever all day. Four men well.

Tuesday, 15th.

Myself so ill that I did not get up till the people had finished their dinners, and then obliged to assemble all hands of them, black and white, and lecture and threaten them: turned Fidalgo off the island. Four men well.

Wednes. 16th.

Having given orders that the Industry, with three men, whom I had appointed for that service, should sail early in the morning for Bulola; and being much better in the morning than I had reason the night before to hope for, I got up as she was going away, and discovering a fourth man in her, called her back: this man was George, one of my most valuable men, who, the night before, had asked my leave to go in this boat, which I had refused. This barefaced contempt of my orders I immediately punished, in almost the only way I could, by turning him off the island; and the rest of the grumetas had latterly behaved so ill,

Thursd. 17th.

1793.
Thursd. Jan. 17.

that I told them all that they were a set of scoundrels and might go away too, if they chose: seven accepted my offer, and I immediately sent them in the same boat to Bissao. It is singular that I have been obliged to dismiss my two best grumetas for the same offence. Same employment. Four men well.

Friday, 18th.

Very thick fog till 10 A.M. Same employment. Began roofing my house. Four men well; and the rest getting better fast. Myself a great deal better.

Saturday, 19th.

Same employment. Therm 91. Four men well.

Sunday, 20th.

Same employment. Grumetas very well behaved since the 17th. Killed a bullock for the colony. Therm. 88. Six men well.

Monday, 21st.

Put up the first south gate. Therm. 86. Six men well. In the evening the Industry returned and brought us nine grumetas. They confirmed our suspicions of the Bijugas having been here with an intention of attacking us, on the night of the 5th; and, according to their account, (which is taken from a grumeta just returned from Canabac, where he had it from the Bijugas themselves,) the very fortunate circumstance of the Scorpion's being at the back of the island, and the providential arrival in the harbour of her boat on the evening of the 5th, which Captain Ferris had dispatched to find out the settlement, was the cause of our safety. They relate that twelve canoes, containing about 150 men, were assembled, seven from Formosa, and five from Canabac, the whole under the command of Bellchore. That they landed, and were within about 50 yards of the block-house at eight o'clock at night; the grumetas were singing and making much noise at play, as usual, at that time. Bellchore halted and said, " I hear too many tongues." While thus hesitating, by the greatest possible good fortune, the Scorpion's boat had reached the harbour; the officer in her seeing a light, and hearing a noise at the block-house, but ignorant whether it was the settlement he was in search of, or a native town, did not think proper to land till day-light, and therefore anchored in the river near the opposite shore: there he fired two musquets; this alarmed the man in the cutter, who discharged another, and this was answered by one from the block-house. Bellchore had known that a ship, " having too much white people," had been two days at the back of the island, and had twice heard her evening gun: he therefore thought that we had been reinforced, that he was discovered, and that this accidental firing was the communication of concerted signals. He immediately decamped, and those were his canoes that the Scorpion's officer saw the next morning.

<small>1793. Monday, Jan. 21.</small>

The colonists thus most miraculously escaped the greatest danger they have ever yet been in.

Same employment, and a party clearing the ground, by fires, of the branches of fallen trees, an operation which has been omitted for these last three months. Therm. 86. Six men well.

<small>Tuesday, 22d.</small>

Same employment; finished the south gates. Died in an epileptic fit Wm. Nash, a man who had never been of any use to us. Therm. 90. Six men well.

<small>Wednes. 23d.</small>

Same employment. Therm. 98. Five men well. Killed a bullock for the colony.

<small>Thurs. 24th.</small>

Same employment. Therm 96. Four men well. Grumetas drawing knives at one another.

<small>Friday. 25th.</small>

Same employment. Therm. 84. Three men well. At 11 at night heard a musquet fired far to the westward.

<small>Saturd. 26th.</small>

Same employment; blocked up the east and west gateways. At noon two Bissao, and one Bijuga, canoes arrived. The Bijuga canoe had been conducted hither by one of the Bissao boats, from an island which I had not hitherto heard of. It was called

<small>Sunday, 27th.</small>

1793.
Sunday, Jan. 27.

Suöga, and was said to be on the other side of Canabac. The king's son, with ten men were in it, in their way to Bissao; he said that his father had ordered him to call and see "the white man of Bulama," to offer him his friendship, and a present of two white capons. He told me that ever since Suöga had been inhabited, which I learn is about ten years only, they had never yet once cut off a boat; intending thereby to give me a great idea of their moderation, because they had never once seized on an unsuspicious crew, and either murdered them, or sold them for slaves. I accepted his present and proffered friendship, and made him suitable returns. On going out of the blockhouse, I was not sorry to hear him say, that " that man must have good heart who can come here to fight." By one of the Bissao canoes I turned away two grumetas, one for having drawn his knife on another grumeta; and the other for having fired his musquet, though without ball, at another; and discharged two more at their own request. Therm. 86. Four men well.

Monday, 28th.
Discharged ten grumetas at their own request, and sent them in the Industry to Bissao. Employed as usual. Therm. 85. Four men well.

Tues. 29.
Wed. 30.
Thurs. 31.
Employment, &c. as before; lost two watches out of my bureau. Therm. 85—86—85.

Monthly state of the Colony.

	Men.	Wom.	Chil.	
On the 31st December we had { Well	2	0	2	—Total W. 4 } 13.
{ Sick	7	1	1	—— S. 9
Since which time we have lost by { Death	1	0	0	—Total........ 1.
And acquired from the Scorpion {	1	0	0	—Total........ 1.
Present state of the Colony .. { Well	4	0	1	—Total W. 5 } 13.
{ Sick	5	1	2	—— S. 8

Grumetas.

  7 men,
  2 women,
  2 boys,
  ———
  11 total.

1793.
Thurs. Jan. 31.

February.
Frid. 1.
Satur. 2.
Sund. 3.

Same employment. Five men well. Therm. 93—94.

Finished plastering the block-house, otherwise employed as before. In the evening the Industry returned with three grumetas, Captain Moore, of the ship Nancy, who had been our pilot to Canabac, and Mr. Ballard, apothecary to the Sierra Leone company. Therm. 93. Five men well.

Monday, 4th.

Removed two six-pounders from the foot to the top of the hill. Therm. 96. Five men well. Captain Moore talked to me a great deal about a plan of his for establishing a factory among the Papells; and about redeeming Bootle's schooner.

Tuesday, 5th.

Same employment. Therm. 96. Five men well.

Wednesd. 6th.

Same employment. Sent the Industry to Bissao to endeavour to procure sailors for the cutter. Captain M. and Mr. B. returned by that conveyance. Therm. 95. Four men well.

Thursd. 7th.

Began again to fell trees, and extend the cleared ground, which has been omitted for these four months, except what was necessary to work up for use. Otherwise employed as before. Therm. 94. Three men well.

Frid. 8.
Satur. 9.

Same employment. Removed the last two six pounders from the bottom to the top of the hill, and fixed the north gates. Therm. 90. 94.

1793.
Sunday, Feb. 10.

Having fixed the north and south gates, and blocked up the east and west gateways, I conceive ourselves perfectly secure from any attack from the natives. We therefore this day ceased working on the Sabbath, which I had thought it unjustifiable to do, before our people could go to prayers in safety. Read prayers. Therm. 99. Five men well. In the evening exercised the people at great guns and small arms. Killed a goat for the colony.

Mon. 11.
Tues. 12.

Employed as before. Therm. 90. Six men well. The Industry returned this evening, with a supply of rum, and eight grumetas. Learned that the Hankey had arrived, after a passage of only six days, at St. Jago, but in such a sickly state, that only five men were alive out of the pasengers and crew.*

---

* This however was exaggerated. The Hankey did not arrive in England till the 2d of October 1793, when the enemies to the success of the Bulama undertaking raised a report that this ship had carried the plague from Bulama to Granada in the West Indies, and had thence brought it to England; this report was for a considerable time believed. The Hankey was sent to Stangate creek to perform quarantine, and orders were afterwards given for sinking the ship and her cargo; however, *on examination, the falsehood and malignity of this report being proved*, this order was confined to the Bulama baggage only.

When the Hankey left Bulama not one of her crew had been buried, although so many of the colonists had; however, a few days afterwards she became very sickly, and this was, most likely, increased by the extraordinary labour consequent on the ship's running a-ground on the 4th of December in the Bijuga channel, in which situation she remained to the 9th; and the boat having been sent, about ninety miles, to Bissao, for assistance, I find noted in the Hankey's log on the day of her return, which was the 8th, " *all the people which came from Bissao in the pinnace taken ill;*" this was in all probability owing to their great fatigue, and exposure to the sun in the day, and the dews in the night. Certain it is that there was a great mortality in the ship after leaving Bulama, during the time that she remained in the Bijuga channel, but very little afterwards. Messrs. Cox, the owners of the Hankey, having been good enough to lend me that ship's log from the time of our chartering her, to her return to Irongate, I have in the Appendix made such extracts from it, from the time of her quitting Bulama, till her release from quarantine, as will enable the reader to form his own opinion

Same employment. Therm. 88—92—90—90. Six men well. Sent the industry to Bulola.

1793.
Wednes.
Fe. 13, 16.

Read prayers to the colonists. At noon the English slave ship the Nancy, Moore, accompanied by the Fisher schooner, which, it may be remembered, was cut off some months since by the Manjacks, anchored in this harbour. Moore wrote me a letter, stating how he had acquired possession of the Fisher, and requesting me to take charge of her; this I however declined, but assured him that she would be safe under the protection of our guns.

Sunday, 17th.

After dinner some of the colonists and Johnson, the grumeta, were very riotous, particularly the latter; so much so, that it was necessary to beat to arms. James Watson I was obliged to knock down with the but end of my fusil, and was then going to seize Johnson, and put him in irons, when he presented a cocked pistol in each hand, and said that he would rather be killed at once than put in irons, as he knew that I should flog him severely. At this moment Peter Hayles, who was close by me, asked if he should fire at him, saying that, if I would give the orders he would shoot him dead on the spot. This sanguinary fellow I called a scoundrel, and, ordering his musquet to be taken from him, gave my own to Mr. Hood, and then went up to Johnson and seized him by the collar; he immediately burst into tears, and dropped both his pistols, saying that he could not fire upon an unarmed man. He was immediately confined, both legs in irons. In this affair Mr. Scott, and Hood, and indeed all

---

of the ground there was for reporting that ship infected with the plague, or Bulama fever, on her return to England. No one death is omitted that appears in the log. See Wadstrom on Colonization, second part, pages 159 and 160---and Appendix, No. 9.

1793. Sunday, Feb. 17th. the colonists, except Box, Watson and Dowlah, the two latter blacks, behaved very well. Watson and Johnson were both half drunk.

As this is a day on which we have ceased to work, it had been my intention this afternoon to have made a little excursion into the country, but the conduct of the rascally crew I have to deal with prevented it. Therm. 94. Six men well.

Monday, 18th. Fixed the west gates; learned from Moore that Demiong had cut off an English boat in Jalorem's Port. Therm. 96. Six men well.

Tuesday, 19th. Same employment. Therm. at 1 P.M. 100. Three men well. At the request of Moore, I this day took the affidavit of the three blacks who had saved their lives when the Fisher schooner was cut off by the Manjacks, and also of some of the Nancy's crew, relative to the people who were afterwards employed in this schooner, when she came into the hands of a Portuguese merchant. The object of these affidavits was to prove that Bootle had been killed, and his vessel seized, at the instigation of a merchant of Bissao, who wanted such a vessel, and who afterwards bought her, and then navigated her by the very people who had seized her; and that Moore, who was employed by the same owners, was therefore justified in taking her by force from this Portuguese merchant, which he did on the 14th instant, when every person that was in her jumped over board and swam on shore.*

* This is what is termed country law, and will doubtless astonish an European reader, who has been accustomed to make reason and justice the rule of his conduct. I have inserted, in the Appendix, Mr. Moore's letter, and the affidavits; as they will enable the reader to form some opinion of the morality, and manners, of those white people who are carrying on the slave trade on this part of the coast. It must be observed that the affidavits were drawn up by Mr. Moore, I had nothing to do but to swear the persons. See Appendix, No. 10. It will be seen by the affidavit that

Employed as before, the carpenter of the Nancy working for us. Therm. 98. Three men well. In the evening went to look at a spring which Mr. Scott had discovered in the morning in a creek to the northward. It was copious, and appeared sufficient to supply four thousand persons daily. *1793. Wednes. Febr. 20.*

Same employment, assisted by the carpenter of the Nancy. Therm. 96. Two men only well. All who are sick have fevers. The Nancy also very sickly. *Thursd. 21st.*

Johnson, who is, to a person in my situation, an invaluable man, has now been in irons for five days. He is very humble, very penitent, and I can but ill spare the loss of his very useful labour; therefore after I had well lectured him, and he had avowed that he considered he owed his life to my forbearance, I liberated him. This man was born in America, and brought up a blacksmith, he afterwards became a carpenter, and during the troubles in that country entered into the British army; he was a long time an officer's servant, and had travelled over the greatest part of Great Britain and Ireland. Besides the above trades, he understands caulking, is a tolerable sailor, a good servant, an excellent hair-dresser, and an admirable cook. He is moreover my chief interpreter, and a great means of procuring me grumetas. He found his way to Bissao, from Sierra Leone, about three years ago. At Bissao he has been often in prison, is much in debt there, and was obliged to fly from that place. Though I know that he is a great rascal, yet he is so exceedingly useful that I am unwilling to part with him. He can turn his hand to any thing.

Tomana has sworn to a very different motive for the Manjacks conduct, than that related by him to me on the 27th December last.

1793.
Friday
Feb. 22.

Same employment. Since Moore's arrival all my grumetas have been restless and uneasy, which is now increased to an extraordinary degree. Therm. 95. Three men well.

Saturday,
23d.

Employed as before. Therm. 95. Three men well. The Industry not having returned yet from Bulola, I this morning sent Mr. Scott to Bissao, in the Nancy's boat, with copies of the affidavits taken on the 19th instant, and a letter from myself to the governor, with a view of settling Moore's affairs. The grumetas are very uneasy, and have taken the strange notion into their head that Captain Moore and myself have been consulting for some days past how to carry them all off. In the evening I assembled, talked to, and reasoned with them on the absurdity of their conceiving it possible for me to harbour an idea of that kind, when they knew that I never dealt in slaves, nay never admitted a person to be one on this island; that they were at liberty at all times to come and to go when they thought proper, and that to every individual they knew that I had always paid the wages of his labour. They left me apparently satisfied.

Sunday,
24th.

The Industry returned this morning from Bulola, with two grumetas, and seven Biafara visitors " to make trade." Read prayers. Killed a bullock for the colony. In the evening, having requested Captain Moore to take charge of the blockhouse, I took the only two white men who were well, with a Biafara who came hither as a hunter, to make a little excursion into the interior, whither, from more urgent business which had kept me at the block-house, as well as from the danger of my being ever absent from it, I never yet had an opportunity of going. We found an excellent spring about a mile up the creek, to the southward of the block-house, and then went about four miles directly into the country, and after an absence of three hours returned to the block-house; having shot an owl, a brace of doves, a pigeon, a couple of Guinea hens, and a deer. We might have shot an elephant, having been within thirty yards of one; but from the account of the dreadful fury of these animals, when wounded, which I had read that very morning, in Bosman's Description of Guinea, I would not let the Biafara hunter fire at it, though he was exceedingly urgent to do so, and much chagrined at my refusal.

Having never before seen an elephant I was exceedingly anxious to get near it, and had approached to within about twenty yards, when it walked off; and though I immediately ran after it, it walked fast from me, and was soon out of sight, though we continued to hear it, as it walked through the underwood and young trees as a man would through a field of corn, for a considerable length of time after. When the hunter wanted to fire at this animal he drew his gun, which was loaded only with deer shot, and put in a piece of an iron rod about an inch long; he assured me that a musquet ball would not penetrate its skin, except immediately behind the ear, or in the flank, and that he always fired at elephants and buffaloes with iron. This animal was of a dark mouse colour, or rather approaching that of an iron grey, and appeared to me to be about eleven feet high. I knew that there were elephants on the island, from many of the colonists, on the first arrival of the Calypso, having seen them, and from the grumetas; but from this short excursion to-day I was quite astonished at the number which there must be upon this island, from the numerous tracks, and palpable vestiges of them, which we every where saw. We crossed two savannahs of I suppose from fifty to seventy acres each, and saw many

1793.
Sunday, Feb. 24.

deer and Guinea fowls, doves and pigeons beyond number, and monkey's in almost every tree; but although we saw many buffaloe tracks we did not meet with any of those animals. A more beautiful and luxuriant country I never saw.

Monday, 25th.

Employment as usual; finished the west store-room. Therm. 91. Three men well. The dissatisfaction which has so long been visible among the grumetas increases rather than diminishes, for which reason I mean to let all go that chuse to-morrow. They still think that I intend to sell them to Captain Moore. The Biafara hunter killed four Guinea fowls and a deer to-day.

Tuesday, 26th.

Sent the Industry to Bissao with the dissatisfied grumetas, all the last comers went, all the old standards remained, amounting to six. Fixed the east, and last gate. Employed in cutting rafters in the woods. At noon Mr. Scott returned with the Nancy's boat from Bissao, and to my utter astonishment informed me that Moore, since leaving that place, in his way to this island, had wantonly attacked a Portuguese boat, and had wounded some, and made slaves of others of its people, and would have taken the boat itself with all the crew, if it had not escaped by superior rowing. I asked Moore if this was true; he answered yes, but it was done by Pearce, his mate, in the Fisher schooner, that he was dissatisfied with his conduct, and that all the responsibility must rest with him. I immediately sent for the mate and for Frazer (who was formerly of this colony, but now in the Fisher) and examined them as to the circumstance of the attack upon the Portuguese canoe.

It appeared from them that Moore had sent the mate to bring the canoe to him, and that the people unwilling to get into the Fisher, probably suspecting some treachery, had been fired upon by Pearce; two were wounded, one of whom he had brought with him, as well as another black who had not been hurt, and these two people were now actually on board the Nancy as slaves. The other wounded man swam to his own canoe.* In this infamous transaction I thought Moore equally culpable with his mate; for though he did not order him to fire at, or wound these people, yet he kept them afterwards as slaves; and instead of endeavouring to make any reparation, or bring his officer to justice, had screened him, and kept the whole affair from me. I told Moore, that had I known of this act of piracy on his arrival, I should not at all have interfered with the Portuguese governor in his favour; that the act of seizing the Fisher was in itself bad enough, though attended with no shedding of blood, nor making of slaves, and that though here, by many, it might be regarded as a venial act, sanctioned by what is termed " Country Law," yet that was a law not admitted among civilized nations; and concluded by observing that I thought him equally guilty with those who had immediately committed the act. Henceforth he was not admitted to my table, where before he had been accustomed daily to dine. Therm. 94. Four men well. The hunter brought in a couple of Guinea fowls.

Employed cutting, and burning, and putting up rafters, my Biafara visitors working as hard as any of the grumetas. At noon a Portuguese boat from the Rio Grande, landed Matchore, the king, who, with his wife, and three attendants, had come to pay me a visit. In the evening the boat left us, and I took that opportunity of writing to the governor of Bissao, expressing my sentiments on the nefarious conduct of Moore, to whom I gave

---

* The depositions of Pearce and Frazer, the only two white men on board the schooner, will be found in the Appendix, No. 11.

1793.
Wednes.
Feb. 27.

a copy of my letter. The uneasiness and anxiety expressed by my grumetas a few days after Moore's arrival, is no longer a mystery, for they doubtless had known of the affair, though I was ignorant of it, and seeing that these people were kept, they certainly had some reason to be alarmed; though my general conduct might have convinced them there was no ground for suspecting such infamous procedure on my part. But " all white man rogue," as well as " all white man witch"* is an article of general belief among these people; and for the former, I am sorry to avow, they have, unfortunately, too much ground. The hunter, who had been out, said that he had shot an elephant in the head, and had followed it for some time, leaving it under a tree, ready to drop. Therm. 95. Five men well.

Thursd. 28th.

Employed in cutting, burning, rooting, and about the houses inside of the block-house. This morning went with the hunter in search of the elephant which the former had wounded last evening. After three hours tedious and useless search, we gave it up, though the hunter's sagacity in following its track was astonishing. Saw evident marks of elephants being near us, probably twenty times, one herd of buffaloes, and a few deer, but could not get a shot. With Matchore came a Mandingo priest, or gris-gris merchant—that is a seller of charms, which, carried about a person, secure the wearer from many evils—such as poison, murder, witchcraft, &c. To this priest I had made some handsome presents, and he this day, in return, gave me twelve gris-gris, and assured me that they would inevitably secure me from all danger, at the same time he gave me directions how to dispose of

---

* I am aware that to write correctly, I should have written wizard; but I am here only repeating the natives' manner of expression.

them. Some were to be carried about my person; one secretly placed over each gate-way; another kept under my pillow; and another under the floor of the house I was building, &c. I received them with as much gratitude as if I had implicit belief in their virtue, and promised to follow his directions in their disposal. I was the more astonished at this present, because in the morning when he boasted of the strength, or virtue, of his grisgris, I had ridiculed them, and desired him to put all that he thought proper, to protect against death from a musquet, on the neck of one of my fowls, and that if I did not immediately shoot it dead, I would give him ten bars. He asserted that if one of them was tied round the neck of the fowl, it was impossible for me to shoot it, and all the natives believed him; but he would not venture to put their virtue to the test of the proposed trial; and we said nothing more on the subject, as I was too much interested in keeping upon good terms with this man, to push the matter so far as to offend him. The Bijugas hold these people in great veneration, and say "that they talk with God."

1793.
Thursday
Feb. 28.

Captain Moore this evening came and informed me that one of his seamen had deserted, and seemed to think that I knew something about it, though I was totally ignorant of the fact. The hunter brought in a flintombeau.* Therm. 89. Four men well.

* A beautiful, small, species of deer.

1793.
Thurs.
Feb. 28.

Monthly state of the Colony.

	Men.	Wom.	Chil.		
On the 31st of Jan. we had { Well	4	0	1—Total W.	5 } 13.
Sick	5	1	2— —— S.	8
Present state of the Colony { Well	4	1	2—Total W.	7 } 13.
Sick	5	0	1— —— S.	6

Grumetas.

7 men,
2 women,
1 boy.

——

10 and 12 Biafara visitors.

——

Friday, March 1. Same employment. The hunter brought in five Guinea fowls. Therm. 87. Three men well.

Saturday, 2d. Employed as usual. The Nancy and Fisher sailed about two P.M., and had scarce got out of the harbour, when John Williams, the man whom Captain Moore told me had deserted from his ship on the 28th ult. made his appearance, and requested me to employ him in my cutter. Having asked him where he had been for these last three days, he replied in the woods, and that in the nights he had slept in a tree, fearful, that if he had come into the grumeta's huts, I should have suffered Moore to carry him on board again, where he had already suffered much cruel treatment from the mate, and that he would rather have perished than have gone back again.

Great and valuable as this acquisition was to our strength, I certainly knew nothing of his deserting, or of his hiding himself in the woods; and, had our strength been less, and want of men more urgent, would never have condescended to entice them away from their duty. But, had he come and sought my protection, from the cruel treatment of his employers, he certainly should have had, what, I trust, no human being will ever seek, of me, in vain. Therm. 84. Four men well. The hunter brought in, in the morning, six Guinea fowls; in the evening four Guinea fowls and a cabre de mat.* Caulking the Perseverance. Got from the Fisher this morning a Sierra Leone black for the cutter.

1793.
Saturday, March 2.

Read prayers. Therm. 94. Five men well. The hunter brought in a flintombeau in the morning, and said that he had shot another elephant. In the evening went with him in search of it; saw the blood at the place where it stood when he wounded it, traced it a long way, and then lost the track in a multitude of others. Returned in about three hours much disappointed; we saw many Guinea fowls, and a few deer, but did not get a shot.

Sunday, 3rd.

Employed in cutting, burning, rooting, squaring, and roofing; finished caulking the Perseverance. The hunter brought in two Guinea fowls. Therm. 94. Four men well.

Monday, 4th.

My Biafara friends, among whom was the hunter, left me this evening in the Perseverance. They had been very serviceable to us all the time that they were here, doing full as much work as any of our own grumetas. They are a quiet, peaceable, inoffensive people. Saluted Matchore with seven guns when he left us. Not one of his people departed without having re-

Tuesday, 5th.

* A species of deer, called by the grumetas, in the Portuguese Patois, cabre de mat, or goat of the woods. It resembles the deer in form, the goat in colour, and coat.

1793.
Tuesday, March 5.
ceived presents, among whom the hunter, and Mandingo priest, were, after himself, those who were distinguished by the most considerable ones; the former for his useful labour on the island, and the latter from the great importance that it was of, for me, to secure his favourable opinion. Just as Matchore left us, the Industry returned with 16 grumetas—11 new, and 5 old ones. Therm. 95. Four men well.

Wednes. 6th.
Employed as before; and began to make bricks, to build proper houses for the grumetas, that they may be sheltered before the commencement of the approaching rains. A canoe from De Sylva brought me four bullocks, six hogs, and thirty fowls. Therm. 92. Five men well.

Thurs. 7th.
Employed as yesterday. One of the grumetas left us in De Sylva's boat, because, he said, " there was too much work here." A boat stopped a short time from Bissao in her way to the Bijugas.

Friday, 8.
Satur. 9.
Same employment. Therm. 92—90. Men well, 5—6. Killed a hog for the colonists. The cook came and complained to me (who will believe it?) that Box and Griffiths, two of the colonists, were too idle to heat the water to scald it, though killed for their own eating. Do such miserable rascals deserve to have any care taken of them?

Sunday, 10th.
Read prayers. Therm. 92. Six men well. In the evening exercised the colonists at small arms, and fired at a target.

Monday, 11th.
Employed in cutting, burning, squaring, and putting up rafters, and making bricks. Therm. 95. Six men well.

Tuesday, 12th.
Same employment, Gustave Albus, who is ill, says that "one of the Grumetas is eating him." Therm. 86. Seven men well.

Wednes. 13th.
Light N.E. wind all day. Same employment. It was new moon yesterday morning, and high water this morning at 10

minutes past 11, which makes the tide flow full and change, 10ʰ 22′. It flowed this morning exactly 16 feet perpendicular height, which is seven inches less than it flowed last night with a fresh S.W. breeze. This is the equinoctial moon. Therm. 89. Seven men well. *{1793. Wednes. March 13.}*

Strong N.E. wind all day. Same employment. A boat arrived from Moore at Bissao, informing me that he had settled all his business, amicably, with the Portuguese; and offering to take home some of our people, who had applied to him when he was here, if I would give them provisions for the voyage, round by the West Indies; and to charge himself with any letters which I might have to send to Europe. The tide flowed to-day 16 feet 1 inch, being one inch more than yesterday. A boat stopped a short time in her way to Bissegos. Myself busy writing to the trustees. Therm. 89. Eight men well. *{Thurs. 14th.}*

Employed as before. Discharged this day at their own request, to go home in the Nancy, Thos. Box and Thos. Griffiths, two worthless and indolent vagabonds, who have never done any work, who have never been of the least use to us; also Mrs. Riches, the only surviving woman, widow of one of the labourers, and Mary Box, the only surviving girl, leaving the men of the colony five in number; the boys two, as follows: *{Friday, 15th.}*

    1 P. BEAVER,
    2 JOHN HOOD,
    3 WM. BENNET,
    4 JAS. WATSON, a black, born in America,
    5 THOS. DOWLAH, a lascar,
    1 THOS. HODGEKINSON, } boys.
    2 GEO. ASHWORTH,

1793.
Friday, March 15.

In the Cutter.

1 John Scott,
2 Peter Hayles,
3 John Williams,

not one of whom came out of England with us, the 1st came from the Scorpion; the 2d entered at Teneriffe, and the 3d deserted from the Nancy.

So that of 275 persons who sailed from England 11 months ago, to settle in this island, there remain only three white, and two black men, with two boys; which, together with the three sailors, is the whole strength of the colony. For such a power we have work enough before us. At eight o'clock this evening there was a fire of full two miles in extent on this island, to the N.W. and within, I suppose, about two miles of us.

Saturday, 16th. Same employment. Moore's boat left us with the persons discharged yesterday; sent with them for their provision on the voyage—one hogshead of bread, one tierce of beef, and two barrels of pork.

Sunday, 17th. Read prayers. Seven men well. Therm. 91. In the evening exercised the colonists at the great guns and small arms.

Monday, 18th. Employed as before, and about the north tower. Therm. 95. Five men well.

Tuesday, 19th. This morning saw two elephants in the water, on the opposite shore. Therm. 94. All hands well.

Wednes. 20th. Employed in cutting, burning; and about the west half of the north row of houses, the north tower, tambours; white-washing, and making bricks. Sick, Bennet. Therm. 88.

Thur. 21.
Frid. 22.
Sat. 23.
Same employment. Therm. 94—88—88. Bennet sick.

Read prayers. Sent the Industry, with Mr. Scott, to Bissao. Therm. 88. Bennet sick.

1793. Sunday, March 24.

Employed as usual till nine o'clock, when Bellchore, with two canoes, paid us another visit. Left off work, and collected the grumetas within the block-house, which Bellchore, and two attendants only, are permitted to enter, at the gate of which they deliver up their arms, and they are returned to them when they go out again. The rest of his people, in number 28, occupy the grumetas' huts. I am now strong enough not to care for these people, they can do nothing by open force. I had intended to have reproached Bellchore for his treacherous conduct in having been here with a large armed force, with a view of attacking us; to have assured him that nothing that he had done was unknown to me; then to have flogged him, and turned him unarmed from the island; but as we were now safe, and had nothing to fear from them hereafter, I thought it more advisable, on reconsideration, to receive him in a friendly manner, and pretend ignorance of what had passed.

Monday, 25th.

In the evening, at the request of Bellchore, we fired several six-pound shot in various directions, to the great admiration of the Bijugas, particularly one, which I had told them, before it was fired, should come out of the water four or five times. It did so in fact seven times, and they all exclaimed, clapping their hands, " all white man witch;" this, simple as it appears to us, they could by no means comprehend, and thought that nothing short of witchcraft could possibly foresee that a shot fired into the water, should come out of it again four or five times. Another shot they were told should go through a tree, distant I suppose not more than 200 yards. It went through its centre, and they were all astonishment: but what seemed to

1793.
Monday, 25th.

stupify them with wonder was the accidental circumstance of my sitting upon one of these six-pounders while it was fired.

It has ever been my custom, since the departure of the Hankey, to fire a morning and evening gun, that is, one at dawn of day, and one at sunset. When the latter is fired the drum is beat, the colonists retire to the block-house, which is then locked, and the key put under my pillow, and no one can, after that time, go in or out without my permission. We had for some time left off firing to amuse the Bijugas, when, it being just sunset, I was sitting upon the gun that was to be fired, talking to Bellchore: as the boy approached with the match, Bellchore ran away, for though they are highly delighted with the noise of a cannon, they keep at a very respectful distance, while it is fired; and notwithstanding they have so often seen my little boy, not more than twelve years of age, fire one, I suppose no consideration could induce one of these people to do so. As before observed, I was accidentally sitting upon the gun when the boy came to fire it: Bellchore immediately ran away—I remained—the boy fired, and I verily believe they expected to see me dead.

They had before a great idea of the power which I possessed in common with all white men, of performing miracles, or rather of being a magician, and they now believed me invulnerable—a belief that I was at no pains to undeceive them in. Therm. 86. Bennet sick.

Tuesday, 26th.

As we did no work while Bellchore was here, in the morning I amused him and his people, as well as myself, in shewing them many things which riveted their faith in my magic power, and which they at last believed to be unlimited.

I made them remark the north point of my circumferenter, and then, desiring them to turn it several times round, or put it in any other position, observe that they had not the power of moving that point, because I had ordered it to remain where it was. They saw that it was so, and could not comprehend why it was, unless by my power, fixed to that point. The bubble in the spirit level of my theodolite, they thought alive; and the distinctness with which they viewed distant objects, through a good telescope, encreased their belief in my magic. But there was one thing yet to shew them, which would fully convince them that nothing was to me impossible. It was near noon, and I was regulating my watch by the sun. The watch had for some time taken up their attention, which they thought, as well as the spirit level, was alive: particularly after, (for at first they would not believe that the minute hand had motion, which is too slow to be readily perceived by the eye) I had made one of them hold a pin, five minutes before the minute hand, and then explained to him, that in a certain time that hand would go to the pin, and then pass it; for instance, whilst another walked to a certain tree and back again. This they all perceived; but, wonderful as it was to them, it ceased instantly, as well as every thing else, to occupy any of their attention, when I played off my last trick. With my quadrant I brought the sun down upon the top of the block-house, and then desired Bellchore to look at it, which he did, and then, one after another, all his people; when, placing one of his men before me, I told him that I would put the sun upon his head. The poor Bijuga at first was frightened, and unwilling to stand where I desired him; but, on my repeated assurances that no harm should come to him, he consented, and I shewed to his astonished countrymen the sun upon his head.

1793.
Tuesday,
March 26.

In the evening Bellchore left me. He had been much struck

1793.
Tuesday, March 26.

with the strength and magnitude of our building, and will never, hereafter, I am confident, attempt any thing against us. Besides, what can he expect to atchieve against a man who can sit upon a cannon "against which there is no gris-gris" while it is fired; and can put the sun upon another man's head? The Industry returned this evening from Bissao with six new grumetas.

Wednes. 27th.

Employed about the tambours, east row of houses, burning wood, and making bricks. Therm. 94. Sick, Bennet. The boat returned from the Rio Grande, with a hunter from Bulola, four Biafara grumetas from Ghinala, and two of Matchore's sons as visitors. Undressed myself this night for the first time, except when I was ill, for eight months and nine days; for, though I trust that I have no improper fears, I have hitherto always thought it prudent to have arms within my reach, and to be ready to act in a moment, without losing the time necessary for dressing, in case of surprize; from open force we have now nothing to fear.

Thurs. 28th.

Same employment. Killed a bullock for the colony. Therm. 92. Sick, Bennet. The hunter brought in two Guinea fowls.

Friday, 29th.

Same employment—therm.—and sick. The hunter shot a buffaloe, but it got away.

Saturday, 30th.

Finished roofing the east row of houses. Therm. 93. Sick, Bennet. The hunter brought in an animal of the deer kind, the grumetas called it a gazelle. It was three feet three inches high, of a reddish brown on the head, back, and sides, from the lower part of which its colour grows gradually lighter, and is quite white under the belly; the hinder legs somewhat longer than the fore; the back gibbous or curved like that of a hog; the tail round, and seven inches long: it had four teats, no horns, when skinned, &c. it weighed 40lbs. without the head.

African Memoranda. 211

Read prayers. Therm. 91. Sick, Bennet. In the evening 1793. exercised great guns and small arms; served venison and Guinea Sunday, fowls to the colonists. The hunter brought in, in the morning, March 31. three Guinea fowls; in the evening one Guinea fowl and a flin-tombeau. This is a most beautiful species of the deer. It was 17 inches high from the fore feet to the shoulder; 17¼ inches from the hind feet to the rump; horns 1¼ inch long, annulated, (seven rings) which fall back and then curve forward, rather curving also to each other at their extremities; two feet two inches long; tail five inches, which appears flat from hair spreading out on either side of it; mouse coloured head and back, which gradually grows lighter, till under the belly it is quite white; back convex; its legs above the fetlock were one inch ⅞ in circumference: it had a young one, but that was not shot.

Monthly state of the Colony.

	Men.	Wom.	Chil.		
On the 28th of Feb. we had { Well	4	1	2 — Total W. ·7 } 13.
Sick	5	0	1 ——— S. 6
Since which time went home in the Nancy	2	1	1 — Total .... 4.
And joined us from the same ship	1	0	0 — Total .... 1.
Present state of the Colony .. { Well	7	0	2 — Total W. 9 } 10.
Sick	1	0	0 ——— S. 1

Grumetas.

28 men,
 3 women,
 2 boys,
 ——
33 and 2 Biafara visitors
 ——

1793.
Monday, April 1.

Employed about the tambours, east tower, burning wood, making bricks, cutting and squaring inner ground plates, rafters and door posts. Therm. 94. Sick, Bennet.

Tuesday, 2nd.

Employed as yesterday. Sick, Hood, Bennet, Watson, and Dowlah, that is, all in the block-house, except the two boys. At noon parted with my Biafara friends. As I could not send a boat to Ghinala, we landed them on the opposite shore, whence they were to walk home, at least, I should suppose, twenty miles through the woods. This, I hope, will be the means of establishing a frequent intercourse between us, as I begged that they would soon return the same way, and bring many of their countrymen with them, and promised, on their appearance, to send a boat and bring them over.

The hunter brought in, in the morning, a flintombeau; in the evening a cabre de mat, or goat of the woods. This animal is of the deer species also; and is much the size of the flintombeau, but not so delicately, nor so elegantly proportioned. Its hair is black along the vertebræ, reddish brown on the sides, which gradually lightens to a dirty looking white under the belly; it is very coarse and resembles that of a goat, whereas a flintombeau's coat is remarkably fine; its horns were an inch in length, but not seen, being hid by hair that grew entirely round them, quite erect, $1\frac{1}{4}$ inch long; and immediately between the horns there was a small tuft $2\frac{1}{4}$ inches long; the tail round, with a small black tuft at the end.

	Fore legs.	Hind legs.
The flintombeau killed to day was	$15\frac{1}{2}$ inches	$16\frac{1}{2}$ inches.
The cabre de mat	$14\frac{1}{2}$	$15\frac{1}{2}$

Wednes. 3rd.

Same employment. Therm. 89. Sick, Hood, Bennet, and Dowlah. The hunter shot a buffaloe in the South Creek which the boat brought to me. It was a female: dun colour, five feet two inches long from the rump to the inside of the horns; the horns 3¾ inches at their base, and 9¼ long, gradually diminishing from the base to a very sharp point in which they terminated, inclining a little backwards, and curving much towards each other: 14 inches from the outside of the base of the horns to the tip of the nose, from which the eyes were 10½ inches distant. Ears 9¾ inches long, 6½ broad, pendant from which was black hair 5 inches long, as well as from the shoulders half way the length of the back. Fore legs 2 feet long, hind ones 2 feet, 8¼ inches; hoofs 3¼ inches broad, 4¼ long; eyes very small; long hair on the upper and lower lip resembling a beard; coat, fine and shining; tail 22½ inches long, with a tuft of black hair 4 inches at the end, 8 inches circumference at its insertion, 2 at the end; a hind quarter weighed 68lbs.* {1793. Wednes. 3d.}

Same employment. Therm. 95. Sick, Bennet, Watson, and Dowlah. By a boat from Bissao I received a letter from Moore, informing me that a Portuguese ship had arrived there with the intelligence of the war in Europe. Hunter not out. Sold Johnson the Hankey's long boat. {Thurs. 4th.}

Finished the east tower, employment as before. Sick, Bennet and Dowlah. The hunter brought in a deer and two pigeons. {Friday, 5th.}

---

* It probably might have been as well to have omitted these uninteresting, and unscientific, descriptions of the various quadrupeds that were shot on the island; but, without it, many probably would not believe that these animals were on it, so questionable has the lying of some, made the relations of other voyagers. Even Bruce himself, the persevering, the courageous, the immortal Bruce, has not been believed. I first saw his work in the garrison library at Gibraltar, in the year 1799; none did I ever read with more attention: and none ever published, carried with it more internal conviction of the truth of his transactions in the countries which he describes; yet, for a long time it was denied that he had ever been in Abyssinia.

1793.
Friday,
April 5.

This deer was of a different kind from any hitherto shot. The hunter called it a gazelle pintado, or spotted gazelle. It was three feet nine inches long, fore legs two feet two inches, hind ones two feet four inches, brown neck, and a very fine thin coat on it, black along the vertebræ, red coloured body, with a longitudinal white stripe on its sides from the hind part of the shoulder to the fore part of the hind leg, with four parallel equidistant stripes of the same colour going from the longitudinal one, at right angles with it, immediately across the back till they joined the one on the other side. White irregular spots on each haunch, white inside the legs, four teats, ears long and broad, with little coat on them, eyes large and black, tail eight inches long with a black tuft of two inches at its extremity; it had an opening like a scent bag, an inch and a half deep, inside of each hind quarter. Of the two pigeons, one was a common one, but I could not say whether the other resembled most a pigeon or a parrot. Its colour was that of a pigeon, mixed with green, its legs were exactly those of a parrot, and the bill between both, not so much hooked as the latter, but much more so than the former.

Saturday, 6th.

Same employment. Therm. 90. Sick, Watson. At nine observed an elephant, about midway across the harbour, swimming from the opposite shore to this island. The ebb tide was bringing it every moment nearer to the block-house, which gave us an opportunity of firing about twenty cannon shot at it, but without effect. We then lost sight of it in the northern creek, when I sent the hunter in the two oared boat to get between it and the shore, and by firing at it to turn it towards the block-house again, while I marched a party round on the beach to oppose its landing. The boat succeeded in turning the animal, having lodged four or five iron slugs in its head from the distance of about twelve yards, it then attempted to land immediately opposite our party, but the mud was so exceedingly soft, our people sinking in it up to their knees, that it was obliged to swim down along shore, in water just sufficient to let its legs feel the bottom, till it found a hard place to land upon. The two oared boat keeping up a constant fire upon it, as well as ourselves from the beach, it always turned suddenly upon the boat at each discharge of a musquet from it, as if to attack it, and immediately afterwards resumed its course. At length it arrived at our landing place, which is very hard, it stumbled on landing, or rather fell upon its knees, but immediately recovered and galloped into the woods. Its head was cut all to pieces; and it received a volley of at least fifteen musquet balls on landing, but I do not believe tht either pierced its hide.

1793. Saturday, April 6.

From over exertion, and fatigue, in the elephant-hunting on the 6th, I went to bed immediately after it, ill of a fever, and did not get up again till yesterday the 13th, all which time the people have been employed as usual. To-day too ill to read prayers, though able to walk about a little. Sent the Perseverance to Bissao with fourteen discharged grumetas. Johnson left me also to-day with his boat, on a kind of trading voyage, he is to return in a fortnight. Therm. 88. Sick, Dowlah and Hodgekinson.

Sunday, 14th.

Employed burning, and fitting up the west store-room. Just before sun-set we saw seven elephants take the water together, on the opposite shore, and immediately afterwards one more; they swam directly across. Sent the two oared boat to attack them; they came immediately over to the block-house, and three cannon shot were fired at them, but it was so very dark

Monday, 15th.

1793.
Monday, April 15. that the boat could scarcely be distinguished from the animals, on which account the firing was discontinued. They were most of them wounded by the people in the boat, and received a volley as they landed at our landing place, whence they escaped into the woods, making a tremendous crash among the trees. Had it been day light some of them must have been killed, as they kept close together and passed quite under our cannon.

Tuesday, 16th. Employed as yesterday, and squaring rafters to finish the eastern half of the north row of houses and the north corner of the east store-room. Therm. 92. Same sick.

Wednes. 17th. Employed burning, putting up rafters, making doors to the west store-room, and removing goods from the east to the west store. Lightning in the evening, the first since the last rains. Therm. 86. Sick, Bennet, Williams, Dowlah and Hodgekinson.

Thursd. 18th. Employed as yesterday. This day the sun vertical. Therm. 90. Sick, Bennet, Williams, and Dowlah.

Frid. 19. Same employment and sick. Therm, 89—87.
Satur. 20.
Sund. 21. Read prayers. Therm. 86. Sick as before.

Monday, 22. Employed burning, finishing the outside and top of the roof, and the fronts of the houses inside. Therm. 86. Sick, Williams, Dowlah and Hodgekinson.

Tuesday, 23d. Same employment. Therm. 89. Sick, Williams and Dowlah. The hunter shot a bull buffaloe, which the whole colony were four hours in bringing about a mile, after its entrails had been taken out, and its head cut off.

Wednes. 24th. Same employment. Therm. 86. Sick as before. Discharged my Biafara grumetas at their own request, among whom is the hunter, and landed them on the opposite shore, whence they are to walk home. The hunter, who is now gone, supplied the colonists with abundance of fresh provisions all the time he was here, at the trifling expence of six barrs a month, and my finding powder and shot. 1793.
Wednesd.
April 24.

Same employment. Therm. 90—90—85. Sick, Williams and Dowlah. Thurs. 25.
Frid. 26.
Satur. 27.

Read prayers, broke my thermometer. Sick, Hayles, Bennet and Dowlah. The Perseverance returned with 14 grumetas, and one woman, and a cask of wine. Killed a hog for the colonists. Sunday,
28th.

Employed finishing the block-house, clearing a spot of ground on which to build houses for the grumetas, clearing grounds to be inclosed, and cutting posts and rails for inclosing them. Sent the Perseverance to the Papel country for grass to thatch with; and measured off exactly half an acre of ground adjoining to the western front of the block-house, to be inclosed for a garden. Sick as before. Monday.
29th.

Employment and sick as yesterday. Tuesday,
30th.

Monthly state of the Colony.

		Men.	Wom.	Boys.		
On the 31st of March we had	Well	7	0	2	Total W. 9	10.
	Sick	1	0	0	S. 1	
At present	Well	5	0	2	W. 7	10.
	Sick	3	0	0	S. 3	

Present Number of Grumetas.

22 men,
1 woman.
───
23
───

1793.
Wednes.
May 1.
Employed inclosing grounds, clearing them of stumps, and finishing the inside of the block-house. Sick, Bennet and Dowlah.

Thurs. 2d.
Employed as yesterday and inclosing the garden. Began to build the grumetas' houses, with the bricks that have been some time since made.* The Perseverance returned with grass for thatching. Sick as yesterday.

Friday, 3d.
Employment and sick as yesterday.

Saturday, 4th.
Wind at S. E. morning, W. and N. W. evening; indeed it has blown from every point of the compass, not only to-day but for the two preceding ones. About eight o'clock this morning some of the people saw several whirlwinds; and about twelve o'clock, when at work in the north tower, I observed eight or nine in the course of about twenty minutes—the nearest about forty, and the farthest about one hundred, yards distant. At this time the air on shore, except only the space occupied by the whirlwinds, was perfectly still, not a leaf to be seen in motion, though on the water there appeared to be light currents of air in different directions, or, what is termed by seamen, cats' paws. These whirlwinds lasted not more than two or three minutes, some progressive, others fixed as it were to a point, carrying up ashes, dust, and leaves spirally, while others from a point went in a gradually increasing circle, the diameter of the greatest of which never, I think, exceeded fifty yards, after, I suppose, a dozen revolutions. The force of these whirlwinds was not very great, for

---

* These bricks were not the size of those of Europe, it would never have answered our purpose to make them so small; though the smaller, the better baked they would doubtless have been. An English brick is, I believe, generally 9 by 4½ inches and 2½ inches thick. Ours were on the contrary, 2 feet 6 inches in length, one foot wide, and 10 inches thick.

when they were immediately over the shoots that had sprung from the roots of the trees, which we had cut down last year, they broke not their tender branches, but tore off, and carried up many of their leaves. This I thought might be owing to the great pliability of the young branches; but they had the same effect only on the old and large trees, taking up the leaves, but leaving their more stubborn and brittle branches unbroken. The force of these whirls I conceive to have about equalled that which seamen call a strong breeze; that is to say, a little less than that which constitutes a gale. It may probably be thought that I had little curiosity in not going out and endeavouring to get into one of them, which I certainly might have done; but I was so exceedingly fatigued from hard labour, and the power of the sun at that time was so great (for we felt not, as I before observed, the least air) that I did not think it would sufficiently recompense my trouble. These reasons may appear trifling; but let those judge who have experienced the lassitude occasioned by excessive labour, in a calm day, under a vertical sun. The sun is now frequently obscured by passing clouds, to which we have been strangers since the latter end of October; it indicates, I believe, the approach of tornadoes, and the commencement of the rainy season. Employment and sick as before.

1793. Saturday, May 4.

Read prayers. Sent the Perseverance to Bissao with seven grumetas; two went without leave, and stole a gun from me. In the evening exercised the colonists at great guns and small arms. Killed a goat for the colony. Sick, Bennet and Williams.

Sunday, 5th.

Employed in inclosing fields and the garden, taking up stumps, building the grumetas' houses, and finishing the inside of the block-house. Sick, Bennet, Williams, and Watson. Saw four

Mon. 6, to Thurs. 9.

1793.
Thursd.
May 9.
large, and three young, elephants in the water on the opposite shore, where they remained about an hour, and then went back into the woods again.

Friday, 10th.
This morning an old and a young elephant took the water about two hundred yards from the block-house—fired four six pound shot at them without effect. The two oared boat wounded the young one, about the size of a jack ass, when the mother turned upon the boat. They however both got into the woods and were traced by their blood about half-a-mile. In the evening I went in search of them, but without success. Peter Hayles accompanied me; and, firing at a deer, burst my buccaneer,* fortunately without hurting himself. We found in two different places the bones of elephants, which had the appearance of being exposed for a long time to the air. Among these bones were many teeth, that is grinders, in their sockets of the jaw-bone; but we searched in vain for their tusks.

About one o'clock two musquets were fired, and a white cloth displayed on the opposite shore, the signal between my Biafara friends and me. The boat was sent for them, and returned with twelve, including Matchore's son, who with two more came from Ghinala; the others had requested Matchore's permission to accompany them, and were from a place which they called *Jim*; not far they said from *Geba*. Employment and sick as before.

For some time past a wonderful stupidity seems to have possessed all the colonists, except Mr. Scott. Whether it arises from sickness, or from fear, or from both, I cannot tell, but the fact is evident: their minds, if ever they had any, are annihi-

* A gun so called, from having been formerly principally used by the buccaneers. Mine was about eight feet long, and intended to shoot elephants and buffaloes only.

lated. It is very strange, but not the less true, that the memory of every individual, Mr. Scott excepted, is exceedingly impaired, in some to such a degree as to render them almost idiots. The boy Hodgekinson, who was a sharp lad, can with difficulty remember any thing he has been ordered to do, more than ten minutes—Bennet is little better—Dowlah is a fool—Mr. Hood is half stupid, and Watson much the same: Hayles and Williams are by far the best, but neither of their memories, particularly the latter, is as retentive as it was; the boy Ashworth is as sharp as ever. <small>1793. Friday, May 10</small>

Employment and sick as before. <small>Saturday, 11th.</small>

Read prayers. Served fowls to the colonists. In the evening exercised great guns and small arms; and played the conjuror to my Biafara friends. Williams sick. <small>Sunday, 12th.</small>

This evening a circumstance happened which proves, I think, that there is much truth in Lavater's notions of physiognomy.

After dark, I had several of the Biafaras in my room, showing them prints, by candle-light. It was some time before they comprehended that they were intended to represent objects in nature, whether living or inanimate; and I am not sure whether they would have comprehended it at all, if I had not luckily hit upon a view of Sierra Leone, in which was introduced an elephant and a monkey: these they understood immediately, and were highly delighted; and afterwards quickly understood whatever was shewn to them. I was turning over Lavater's Essay on Physiognomy, and at length opened upon "the angry wicked man." The instant they beheld it, they all screamed, and fled out of the room: and this I take to be as convincing a proof of the truth of Lavater's idea of this character, as can well be obtained.

1793.
Monday,
May 13.

Same employment. My Biafara friends left me this morning, and were landed on the opposite shore. About high water (2 o'clock) we observed thirteen elephants, about two miles distant, swimming across the channel from the opposite shore. Sent the two oared boat to endeavour to prevent their landing till they were driven under our guns. Mr. Scott fired at and wounded one of them much advanced before the rest; but it got into the woods having landed on a hard beach; but the rest, a little higher up, had got into a kind of bay, where the mud is left dry at low water, about three quarters of a mile from the shore. The water by this time had ebbed considerably, and left a great portion of this mud dry. The elephants, unable to proceed through the mud on shore, were prevented by the firing of Mr. Scott in the boat, from returning to the river. In this situation, unable to advance, and unwilling to swim back into the fire, they remained till the water had entirely left them, and they were unable to move. Mr. Scott, observing that they could not turn round, landed, hauled his boat on the mud, and, distant only a few yards, kept up a constant fire upon them.

Observing, with my glass, that the elephants were incapable of motion, I beat to arms, and leaving the block-house locked up, in charge of a sailor belonging to the cutter, marched the men, to the number of fifteen, along the shore, with the hope of killing them all. We had, I suppose, about two miles to walk in the mud, every step we took sinking up to our knees, and sometimes deeper, which so fatigued us, that when we came up with these animals, we were scarcely able to stand and load and fire at them. The elephants themselves, from their ponderous bulk, sunk till the broad surface of their carcases came in contact with the mud; when they were suspended, but incapable of motion, with their greatest exertions, as, in this situation, they had no firm substance on which to place their feet. During upwards of three hours that we were firing at them, not one of them altered its situation a yard; the firing, when I arrived, had been chiefly directed at two, a mother and its young one, though several of the others were wounded by a ball or two; the young one, though still alive, had its proboscis and tail cut off, and made most piteous moans; indeed it was such a spectacle that, from its sufferings, I was sorry that we had attacked them: however I forbid every person firing at any other than this young one, and its mother, which was also sadly galled.

1793. Monday, May 13.

We all stood on one side of the mother, at the distance of from four to twelve yards, and expended 250 shot; 150 of which, I suppose, were lodged in and about its head, before it expired; besides latterly, when it was weak, it received ten or a dozen wounds in the flank, from a bayonet, quite up to the hilt. In short the intestines of the largest were coming out before it died. There was one much larger than the rest, the only male among them. The animal that we killed, when we levelled a musquet at it, would throw about its proboscis, toss up the mud with its tusks, and make most lamentable cries, as if sensible of our murderous intention. As I fired most of the shot latterly, having the colonists to load for me, I could perfectly ascertain that the animal was sensible that its pain arose from the weapons in our hands; for the moment I presented the gun it would make those cries, and throw about its snout and head; if I withdrew my piece the animal was quiet, and the moment I presented again, it would renew its lamentations. The young one, which was about the size of a buffaloe, died a little before

1793.
Monday, May 13.

its mother. It was impossible to move these animals, therefore cutting off their tails, ears, and proboscis, we returned to the block-house by the boats, where we arrived about seven o'clock. Some of the proboscis was dressed for supper, and is I think excellent food: much like calves' palates.

From this evening's experience I am determined never again to attack any of these poor animals, not even were I to see them again in the same situation, unless provided with iron slugs; for it exceeds in cruelty almost any thing to fire leaden balls at them, seeing their little effect, when even so very close. Had I this day been provided with iron slugs, I might have killed these twelve elephants in as many minutes. The female we killed had, unlike all other quadrupeds, two breasts, resembling those of a woman, and placed immediately between the *fore legs*.

Tuesday, 14th.

Same employment. Williams sick. After breakfast I went for the dead elephants in order to get their tusks. The tide had flowed nearly over the large one, so that I could do nothing till the ebb; the little one I did not see, and suppose that it floated out of the harbour by the night tide: the living ones of course had gone on shore the moment they floated. As nothing could be done at present, I sent the large boat back and determined to avail myself of this opportunity of going through the narrow channel, which separates a small island from the N. E. end of Bulama. We were not more than a mile from its entrance, and with the favour of the tide, I conceived we might row round the little isle in about two hours. This channel, I had been told, is almost dry at low water. When I entered it we perceived four animals in the water; their heads and rumps protruding out of it like two little black rocks. We have frequently seen, from the block-house, animals lying basking in the sun on the shores up the harbour; but never nearer than three or four miles, and never on their legs, so that I knew not what they were, nor had any idea of their form, and could never spare time from our more necessary occupations at the block-house, to go and attack them. One of the grumetas, who had picked up a few English words down the coast, told me that they were sea-cos, meaning sea-cows; and all the rest of the grumetas called them, in their Portuguese Patois, pesc-cavallos, or fish-horses.

1793.
Thursday,
May 14.

I had never seen either, but supposed that it might be the former, called at Jamaica Manatee, and there reckoned very delicate food, which the grumetas affirmed these to be.

I had never before quitted the block-house without carrying with me three or four of my own guns, but our elephant shooting yesterday had, with mud and salt water, rendered most of them useless, till they were again cleaned. Among these was my rifle; and my buccaneer was burst four days ago, so that I had with me now only a common fowling piece.

The first three of these animals, as we rowed towards them, disappeared under water, when we had got within 200 or 250 yards of them, frightened, I suppose, by the noise of the oars. As the tide was carrying us towards the fourth, we ceased rowing, to let the current gently drop us down upon it without noise. The animal was not swimming, but standing in the channel, in, I suppose, about five feet water: the body immerged, and the head just above it. It looked steadfastly at the boat till we were within about 20 yards of it, when I lodged a ball half way between its eyes and nostrils: it immediately tumbled down, but instantly rose again, snorted, and walked into shallower water, where I had an opportunity of seeing its whole body, and then discovered that it was an hippopotamos, and not a sea-cow. It

1793.
Thurs.
May 14.

afterwards advanced a little towards the boat, then towards the shore, and turned entirely round once or twice, as if at a loss what to do, plunging violently the whole time. At last it walked into deeper water, and then dived: we watched its rising, and then pursued it; and this we did for near three hours, when, at length, it landed on a narrow neck of sand, which separates this channel from the large one, and walked over it into 15 or 16 fathoms water. We then gave up the pursuit, having never been able to get a second shot at it. The longest time it was under water during the pursuit, was 20 minutes, but immediately after being wounded it rose every three or four minutes. Its body appeared to be somewhat larger than that of the largest buffaloe, with shorter, but much thicker legs; a head much resembling a horse's, but longer; large projecting eyes; open, and wide distended, nostrils; short erect ears, like a cropt horse when it pricks them up, or those of a well cropped terrier. I perceived nothing like a mane, and the skin appeared to be without hair; but of this I am not certain, for being totally ignorant whether the animal was ferocious or not, immediately after I fired, we rowed from it, expecting it would attack us, for our little crazy boat was scarcely bigger than a washing tub, and a boy was constantly obliged to keep bailing it to prevent its sinking; so that if it had attacked the boat it would instantly have shook it to pieces; and we were never afterwards so near to it again. When it walked over the sandy point, we were distant about 100 yards.

I had never before seen an hippopotamos, nor did I ever suppose that there were any in the neighbourhood; but the moment I saw its body out of the water, I knew it to be one, from prints which I have seen of that animal in books of Natural History, particularly Buffon's: and I cannot help remarking that that animal, and the elephant, with many others, are always well delineated, while in others we cannot trace the least resemblance. Any person who has once seen a print of an elephant or an hippopotamos, would, if he met them in a desert, immediately recognise them for those animals, from the accuracy of representation; but, if he saw a dolphin, and referred to the general representation of that fish to give it a name, he would be puzzled, as it no more resembles the painting of one, than that painting does a lion.

1793.
Thurs.
May 14.

Returning, without having gone through the channel as intended, we saw the other boat towing the elephant, which had floated towards the block-house. In the evening, we, with some difficulty, got out the tusks, which were very small, weighing both together only fourteen pounds. The tusks of the females are always, I understand, small; and the hollow at the root goes much farther up than in the males, which of course diminishes their weight. These hollows are filled with a substance somewhat resembling marrow, but of a greenish hue, and I should have dressed the tusks, like marrow bones, to have tasted it, had not the animal been killed 24 hours, and begun to stink abominably. The legs too, I had intended to have dressed *a la Vaillant*, but the sharks had so torn them while lying in the water, that they were very offensive also. For the same reason I did not taste the milk, which came from the animal stringy and ropy, was also of a greenish hue, and very tenacious and glutinous. The elephant grounded in about three feet water, on its side, and while Peter Hayles was cutting out its tusks with a broad axe, I sat on its upper side with a long pike to prick the sharks on the nose, which surrounded it, and keep

1793.
Tuesday, May 14;

them from him, during which time there were never less than seven or eight trying to nibble at it.

Wednes. 15th.

Employed as before. A boat stopped in her way from Bissegos to Bissao. Learning that a new governor had just arrived from Lisbon to Bissao, and having strong reason to believe that the Portuguese merchants there are, in general, hostile to the success of this colony, and may endeavour to prejudice him against us on his first arrival, I took this opportunity of writing to him a congratulatory letter on his safe arrival at his new government; assuring him at the same time, that it would ever be with me a great object to live in the most perfect harmony with our neighbours the Portuguese.

The elephant carcase stinking most abominably, we towed it into the middle of the river, whence, with the ebb tide, it floated out to sea, surrounded by sharks and vultures.

Thursd. 16th.

Same employment, no sick. Every night for this last week we have had a few pallid flashes of lightning, accompanied by distant peals of thunder. This evening we have had much thunder and lightning.

Friday, 17th.

Same employment. Hayles sick. About nine o'clock last night we had a tornado, the first this season, at S.E. with much thunder, lightning, and rain; it lasted about two hours.

Saturday, 18th.

Same employment. Sick, Hayles and Bennet.

Sunday, 19th.

Read prayers. Sick, Hayles, Bennet, Williams, and Hodgekinson. Killed a hog for the colony.

Monday, 20th.

Employed as before, making more bricks and cutting pales for the fences. Sick, Hayles, Williams, and Bennet. We have stood still for some time for want of bark-rope to begin thatching; I therefore sent the Industry, this evening, to Bissao to buy some; obliged to seize up one of the grumetas, who refused to go in her; but did not punish him, as his comrades answered for his future good behaviour. Peter Hayles's agreement expired yesterday, and he this day informed me that he wished to leave the colony. This man, on the Hankey's departure, I had engaged for six months, at increased wages; conceiving that at the expiration of that time, and indeed long before, we should be strengthened by new colonists. I can ill spare him now, for he is, by far, the most useful man in the colony. {1792. Monday, May 20.}

A little after dark the Perseverance returned with fourteen grumetas and some rice. In her came a Portuguese soldier, his wife, and child, who had deserted from the garrison at Bissao. In the middle of the night the Industry returned, as she leaked so much that with difficulty the people in her kept her from sinking.

Employed about the grumetas houses, and clearing ground for the erection of another similar nest of buildings. Cutting posts, rails, and pales, bringing up bricks, and repairing the Industry: finishing the inside, and clearing the block-house square. Sick, Williams and Bennet. This evening Mr. Hood informed me that near six months ago, Peter Hayles offered to another man on this island, to run away with the Beggars' Benison cutter; and at last he told me that this man was my own black servant, James Watson, an American, who, however, opposed Peter's views; and that Johnson, another American black, was concerned with Hayles also. I was much displeased with Mr. Hood for having kept me so long ignorant of this circumstance, particularly as I have trusted Johnson with a great many goods in the boat, which I sold, or rather gave, to {Tuesday, 21st.}

1793.
Tuesday, May 21.

him, with which he left me the 14th of last month, and was to have returned in a fortnight; but I am now convinced that he has left me altogether, and I am lucky in not having been more plundered.* What vagabonds have I to deal with?

This accounts for what I then thought a most unaccountable eagerness in Peter Hayles to have my orders to shoot Johnson, on the 17th of February last; which he doubtless would have instantly done, had I ordered him, and thereby have got rid of one of those two, to whom he had proposed his intended treachery.

Wednes. 22d.

Employed clearing ground for the erection of another nest of houses; cutting posts, rails, and pales, bringing up bricks, repairing the Industry, finishing the inside of the block-house, rooting up stumps, levelling the ground, paling the garden, white-washing, painting, and tarring. Am prevented from proceeding fast with the first nest of grumetas' houses, from the want of thatching rope. Distant thunder in the evening almost all this month.

Thurs. 23. to Satur. 25.

Same employment. Sick, Williams. A boat arrived from the governor of Bissao requesting permission to cut timber.

* Johnson told me that his wife's relations owed him a great deal of money on the island of Bissao, and that if I would let him go and collect his debts he would return in a fortnight and settle altogether on this island. I had purchased the Hankey's long-boat when that ship left us, had hauled her up on the beach, and never since made use of her. This boat, Johnson told me, would make his fortune, by trading, if I would sell it to him. He was a most useful and valuable man, and I was inclined to do every thing that could attach him to me: the boat was therefore caulked, painted, launched and rigged, and he was hereafter to give me 60 barrs for it; and to assist him in his first little trading voyage I lent him 200 barrs worth of goods. He left me to return, himself, in a fortnight, but I never saw him more, and the last that I heard of him was that he was in prison at Bissao. A proper reward for his ingratitude.

African Memoranda.

Sunday, May 26. 1793. Read prayers. Sick, Williams. Sent the Perseverance and Industry to Bissao for grass and thatch-rope, and with discharged grumetas.

Mon. 27. Tues. 28. Same employment, and building the south nest of grumetas' houses. Sick, Williams.

Wednes 29th. Finished inclosing the garden. About nine, we had a gentle rain, without wind, which lasted about an hour. Same employment. No sick.

Thurs. 30th. Employed building and inclosing. The Industry returned with six grumetas, grass, bark-rope, rum, wine, sugar, garden seeds, and yams.

Friday, 31st. A heavy tornado, with a great deal of rain. Employed solely in covering the north nest of grumetas' houses with rafters.

Monthly state of the Colony.

In number 10, as on the last day of the last month; and not one person sick.

Grumetas.

19 men,
3 women,
———
22.
———

Besides the Portuguese soldier who deserted from the garrison at Bissao, with his wife and child.

Saturday, June 1. Covering the grumetas' houses. Sick, Hayles, Williams, Bennet, and Hodgekinson. Lame, Watson.

Sunday, 2nd. Read prayers. Put up what thatch we had ready, as without such precaution, another tornado, if attended by heavy rain,

1793.
Sunday, June 2.

might wash down the walls of the house. The bricks, only sun-baked, are hard enough, if sheltered from the rain, but if not, they would soon crumble to pieces.

The country mode of thatching is the best and most expeditious I ever saw; far excelling that of Europe.

Monday, 3d.

Employed about the grumetas' houses, taking up stumps, and hoeing the garden. Sick and lame as before.

Tuesday, 4th.

Saluted in honour of his Majesty's birth-day.

Wednes. 5th.

Employment, sick, and lame, as before. The Perseverance returned with 16 grumetas, grass, yams, and cassava roots. A schooner came from Bissao for timber.

Thursd. 6th.

Employed about the grumetas' houses, taking up stumps, finishing the inside of the block-house, fixing new axle-trees to the gun-carriages, and hoeing the garden. Sick, Williams, and Hodgekinson. Sent the Industry to Bissao for grass and rope for thatching. Finished the north nest of the grumetas' houses.* Killed a hog for the colonists.

Friday, 7th.

Pulled down the temporary huts that had been erected for the grumetas. Tornado this evening. Sick, Williams, Bennet, and Hodgekinson.

Saturday, 8th.

Heavy showers the greatest part of the day. Employed as before, and planting cassada,† yams, maize or Indian corn, and

---

* These nests were 34 feet in front by 21 in depth, divided into three equal sized houses, and each house into two rooms 10 feet square each; they were built of sun-baked bricks, and covered with thatch.

† Sweet cassada or manioc, (by which latter name only it is called by the Portuguese,) I do not remember ever to have heard before of this most excellent and valuable root. The manioc, or bitter cassada, common in our West India islands, I know perfectly; its poisonous juice requires purification by fire, before it can be used as food. The sweet manioc, on the contrary, is just as wholesome when raw as boiled, and is by no means unpleasant to the taste in its crude state. Neither does it at all resemble

pine apples. Obliged to punish Gaspar Lombe, one of the grumetas, for improper behaviour. The schooner sailed loaded with timber, having left ten men behind to cut more. Sick, Williams and Dowlah. The rains I consider as now completely set in. *[1793. Saturday, June 8.]*

Read prayers. Served out fowls to the colonists. Same sick. *[Sunday, 9th.]*

Employed about the south nest of the grumetas' houses, taking up stumps, and clearing the ground of them, cutting and squaring posts for the west row of houses, inclosing grounds, *[Monday, 10th.]*

the jamipha, or sweet cassada, nor any other species of the jatropha which I have ever yet seen described. It was planted from cuttings; each cutting strikes down from three to seven roots, which, when arrived at maturity, are dug up and eaten either boiled with meat, or alone: and constitutes a principal article of the natives' food. This root resembles more in size, conformation, and taste, the English parsnip, than any other vegetable production that I am acquainted with; but is, I think, superior to it, being not quite so sweet, and more farinaceous; it resembles also, in taste, the chesnut. If this manioc is really unknown in our West India islands, I know not a more valuable present that could be sent there: as it is very nutritious, grows quickly, requires little trouble in the cultivation, and is very productive; and I think might withstand those dreadful, and destructive, hurricanes, which have so frequently destroyed the plantain walks, and ground provisions, in those islands, whence the negroes derive their principal food.

In the Appendix, No. 12, I have inserted a copy of my garden book while on the island. This little book, which I kept because I knew that no other person would if I did not, was kept merely that the experience of one rainy season might not be lost to those colonists who might come out hereafter to settle on the island; and is inserted in the Appendix, not to give information on any proper mode of culture, for my profession has been adverse to such acquirements. Acknowledging then my ignorance of gardening, or cultivation, of which I do not even profess to have a common knowledge, it is inserted only, because, like the Journal, it was written at the time, without any view to system, arrangement, or publication, and may probably enable those, who are capable of judging, to form some idea of the climate and fertility of the soil; and possibly to deduce, from my ignorance of the mode of treating the plants, that under more skilful management, many might have succeeded which failed with me, and that all of them might have thriven better.

1793.
Monday, June 10.

making axle-trees for the gun-carriages, and in the garden. In the evening the Industry returned from Bissao with grass, but without rope: as the Papels and Portuguese are at war, they could not go into the country. Four grumetas came by this boat. Sick, Williams and Dowlah. Began the west row of houses inside the block-house. We do not build these houses because we want them ourselves, having already more than we can occupy, the north and east rows being complete, besides the two store-rooms; but they are built to be ready to receive the first reinforcement, and as the colonists never do any field work, their labour being always confined within the square, we should have nothing for them to do, unless we go on with these houses.

Tuesday, 11th.

Finished the south nest of grumetas' houses. Sent the Perseverance to the Papel country, for cattle, goats, fowls, &c. Same sick.

Wednes. 12th.
Thurs. 13th.

Same employment. Finished the axle-trees. Last night the Perseverance returned on account of contrary winds. Sent her away again to-day with two additional hands.

Friday, 14th.

Heavy rains. Employed as before, and putting seeds and roots in the ground. Sick, Williams and Bennet.

Saturd. 15th.

Many showers. Employed as before, and in the gardens. The garden is properly inclosed, and adjoining the west side of the block-house; but we have besides a clear spot just without the N.W. field, of about a quarter of an acre; this we are planting with manioc and yams, and is called the Grumetas' Garden. Sick as before.

Sunday, 16th.

Sometimes cloudy, and sometimes fair. Winds in all directions, and calms. Read prayers. In the evening exercised great guns and small arms. About four o'clock two musquets were discharged on the opposite shore by the Biafaras. Sent the boat for them—10 in number, among whom were king Matchore's brother and son; they brought ivory, cloths, and fowls for sale, together with a wild boar which they had shot in the woods.

1793. Sunday, June 16.

In the evening, some of the grumetas who had been in the woods brought me two elephant's tusks, which they had found in the interior of the island. They both together weighed 153lbs. that is, one weighed 75 and the other 78lbs. and had the appearance of having been long separated from the living animal, probably very many years, as the surface of them was quite spoiled and decayed. Sick, Williams, and Bennet.

Winds and weather variable. Employment and sick as before. The king's brother made a demand upon me to-day of one of the elephant's tusks which the grumetas had yesterday found in the woods. On my refusal, he made a very long speech to convince me of the justice of his demand. Every thing found, he said, in the king's country, belonged to the king; but that to reward those who found things, and carried them to him, he always gave one half to the finder, as a reward for his trouble and honesty; that if I had killed the animal and expended my powder and shot, and time, to procure these tusks, the king in that case would have had no claim, but as they were accidentally found, the king had certainly a right to half. All his countrymen said that he was right, and that, that was country law. I answered that his claim was contrary to my treaty with the king, and therefore I could not accede to it, and there the matter ended.

Monday, 17th.

Cloudy weather, and variable winds with thunder. A heavy tornado with much rain. Employed taking up stumps, clearing

Tuesday, 18th.

1793.
Tuesday, June 18. the ground of them, roofing the west row of houses, inclosing the N.W. field, and in the garden. Sick, Williams, Bennet, and Hodgekinson.

Wednes. 19th. Wind and weather very variable. Same employment. Discharged nine grumetas by a Bissao boat. Sick, Williams.

Thurs. 20. Frid. 21. Variable weather. Same employment. Sick, Williams, Bennet, and Hodgekinson. Killed a goat for the colony.

Saturday, 22d. Employed as before, and burning rubbish off the cleared ground. Same sick.

Sunday, 23d. Read prayers. In the evening exercised great guns and small arms. Sick, Williams and Hodgekinson.

Monday, 24th. Very unsettled weather; taking up stumps, and inclosing the N.W. field. Sick as before.

Tuesday, 25th. Sometimes cloudy and sometimes clear. Employed as yesterday. Sowed clover and lucern in those places of the E. and N.W. fields, where the stumps of the trees had been taken up, and the soil replaced.

Wednes. 26th. Obliged to send a boat on the Biafara side to cut posts, rails, and pales for the inclosures, as we have used all those on the island that are tolerably near to us. Sick, Williams.

Thursd. 27th. Calms and light airs, showers, thunder and lightning. Employed taking up stumps, and ant hills;* and cutting and fixing posts, rails, and pales. Finished the N.W. inclosure.† Sick, Williams.

Friday, 28th. Able to do very little on account of heavy rains. Sick, Williams and Bennet. Hayles lamed in the hand by a cat-fish.

Saturday, 29th. Same employment, sick, and lame.

* Bug-a-bug Hills. The Termites. See Smellie's Philosophy of Natural History.
† This field is rectangular, and is 6 chains 76 links, by 5 chains 39 links, and consequently contains 3 acres, 2 roods, and 22 poles.

Read prayers. The Perseverance having been absent 18 days I am rather uneasy about her, and fear that she may have been cut off; I therefore sent the pinnace this evening to Bissao to make inquiries concerning her. Hauled the seine, and served out mullet. Sick, Bennet, Williams, and Hodgekinson; lame Hayles.

1793. Sunday, June 30.

Monthly state of the Colony.

In number as on the last day of the last month.

Men. Boys.
Well 6 .. 1—Total W. 7 } 10.
Sick 2 .. 1—— S. 3

Grumetas.

26 men,
3 women,
2 boys.
——
31 besides the Portuguese soldier, &c. and Biafara visitors.

Incessant rains prevent our working. Same sick.

Monday, July 1.

Rain all the morning; in the evening taking up stumps. The Industry returned without having seen or heard any thing of the Perseverance. Peter Onsfield,* an American black, who came here on the 10th of last month, has the charge of this boat, which I gave to him the day after his arrival; he appeared to me to be an intelligent man, but whether he be a rascal and has run away with her, or an honest man, and cut off in the Papel country, I cannot tell: but one or the other, I doubt not, is the

Tuesday, 2d.

---

* The person mentioned by the name of Peter, in the declaration of Moore's men, as employed by Mr. Gavine, of Bissao. Appendix, No. 10.

1793.
Tuesday, July 2.

case. I am obliged to employ such men as chance throws in my way. Had I any choice, few that are here should remain.

In the morning an hippopotamos, in the river, was close under the block-house. Chaced it with two boats, when we found two more, which we hunted for six hours, having very severely wounded one of them, but as we never could drive them out of the water, we at length gave up the fruitless pursuit. Sick as before.

Wednes. 3rd.

In the morning little rain. Employed taking up stumps, building a poultry house, inclosing a poultry yard, and paling the north side of the east field. In the evening the heaviest rain I have yet seen. It penetrated every part of the block-house, though not a drop entered the grumetas' houses. I am determined therefore to thatch the block-house; and as the north nest of houses is sufficiently large for the grumetas, I shall send my books and those things which may be damaged by the rain, to one of the houses in the south nest, and the other two shall be appropriated as an hospital. Sick as before.

Thursd. 4th.

Clear morning, rain in the evening. Employed taking up stumps, cutting and fixing posts, rails, and pales, inclosing the poultry yard and thatching the poultry house. Removed my books and stationary to one of the houses in the south nest. Sent the Industry to Ghinala, with Janjan the young Biafara prince, his uncle, and the rest of the party. Punished one of the young grumeta boys for theft. Sick as before.

Friday, 5th.

A few showers in the course of the day. A canoe arrived from Bissao for timber, and in her came two soldiers from the governor of that place, with a letter from him requesting me to give up to them the deserter who came here on the 20th of May last.

Employed as before and making a goat and calf house. In the evening to my great joy and surprise the Perseverance returned, though with damaged rice, dead fowls, and ruined arms; and without cattle of any kind. Peter excused his long absence by saying that the Papels had daily promised to bring him bullocks, goats, &c. but that he was always deceived, and at length came away without them. The rice was damaged, the fowls drowned, and the arms spoiled by the heavy and almost incessant rains which they had on their passage back, having no cover to the boat. Sick as before. *1793. Friday, July 5.*

Showers. Last night the Industry returned, and to-day I sent her and the Perseverance, both under the direction of Peter Onsfield, to the Balantee country for grass to thatch the blockhouse, having built over the stern-sheets of the latter a booby hatch to shelter the crew from the weather. Employed as yesterday. Sick, Bennet, Hayles, Williams, and Hodgekinson. Lame, Hood. Punished a grumeta for disobeying my orders. *Saturday 6th.*

Read prayers. Killed a hog for the colony. The boat that arrived on the 5th went away with the Portuguese deserter. *Sunday, 7th.*

I did not feel myself justified in keeping this man after he had been claimed by the Portuguese governor, neither did I like to give him up to that punishment which would necessarily be inflicted upon him when he returned: I therefore made the best terms I could for him with the Portuguese governor. I would not suffer his men to take forcibly away the man who had claimed my protection; but I advised him voluntarily to return, and promised to use every exertion in soliciting the remission of his punishment, in which I succeeded. This man, on his arrival at this island, told me that twenty more soldiers would follow his example, and come here, if I would promise to keep

1793.
Sunday, July 7. them, and he verily believed that every man in the Portuguese garrison would come over to me if I kept those twenty. I knew this before: I have long known it from Johnson, and indeed from all the grumetas, that every one of them would desert to me if I chose to receive them. But much as I want men, and valuable as their acquisition would be, I would rather lose those which I now have, than receive others who, by coming, must commit a crime. Sick, Hayles, Williams, Bennet, Watson, Dowlah, and Hodgekinson.

Monday, 8th. Variable weather. Same employment. Sick, Williams, Hayles, Bennet, Dowlah, Hodgekinson, and Hood.

Tuesday, 9th. Finished the poultry house and yard, and put into it fifty-seven laying hens and five cocks; twenty-three female goats, and one male. Served out fowls. Sick as before.

Wednes. 10th. Employed taking up stumps, and inclosing a spot of ground intended to shelter large cattle; that is a farm yard. Sick as before.

Thur. 11.
Frid. 12. Same employment and sick. Finished inclosing the farm yard.

Saturday, 13th. Heavy rains all last night. Wind from all points, and weather of all kinds. Little work done. The Perseverance and Industry returned with thatching grass, fowls, goats, and rum. Sick as before.

Sunday, 14th. Very heavy rains all last night, insomuch that every one in the block-house was wet. This day fine. Employed in thatching the block-house. Sick, Hood, Hayles, Williams, Bennet, Dowlah, Hodgekinson, and Ashworth; drunk, Watson. Served out fowls.

Monday, 15th. Wind and weather continually altering. Sent the Perseverance to Ghinala for cattle and goats. In the morning employed in thatching, in the evening prevented from doing any thing by the arrival of Bellchore with thirty men in two canoes. Called in the grumetas, and gave Bellchore's men the north nest of houses; the king and two of his people remaining with me in the blockhouse. Sick as before.

1793.
Monday, July 15.

Wind and weather as yesterday. Traded with Bellchore. This king saw yesterday the Perseverance go up the Rio Grande, at which he was not much pleased; and this day at noon some Biafaras appeared on the opposite shore, shewed the accustomed signal, and discharged several musquets. The old man immediately told me that there were Biafaras on the opposite side come to see me, and asked if I meant to send my boat for them. I replied that they were Portuguese cutting timber for the governor of Bissao, who wanted me to send for them; but neither he nor his people seemed satisfied.* Put up a little thatch. Sick as before. I was this day obliged to put John Lopez, one of the grumetas, in irons, for drawing his knife on James Watson, when sentinel at the east gateway.

Tuesday, 16th,

At day light Bellchore left us. He was exceedingly importunate to make me promise to come and see him at Canabac; he was labouring that point the whole of yesterday; "his women do nothing but cry to see me;" I must come and satisfy them, " or they will die." The cunning old rascal! he forgets that " all white man witch" He plainly sees that he can do nothing by force, and now he wants to get my person into his power; were I to go, that would be safe, but he would never let me return till he had got all the goods in the block-house as the price of my ransom. He wants rum, powder, tobacco, and arms; and

Wednes. 17th.

* The Bijugas and Biafaras are irreconcileable enemies, and always at war.

1793.
Wednes.
July 17.

he believes the block-house is full of them. Half an hour after he left us, sent the boat to the opposite shore for my Biafara friends: they are eight in number, from King Niobana. Put up some thatch. Sick as before. Served out fowls.

Thurs. 18th.

Rain great part of the day, with intervals of clear weather. At noon the Biafaras left me. Employed thatching and cutting pales. Sick as before.

Friday, 19th.

Variable weather. Same employment. Sick, Hood, Hayles, Bennet, Williams, Watson, Dowlah, Ashworth, and Hodgekinson, that is, every body but Mr. Scott and myself. This day twelve months the Calypso and discontented colonists left us. At nine o'clock last night I had written my journal, and was sitting down to a broiled fowl for supper, when the mate of the cutter knocked at the block-house gate and was let in. My door was opened, and two Europeans, two Englishmen, appeared before me. It is impossible to express my astonishment, my joy, my feelings, at the sight. Their florid complexions, their appearance of health and vigour, were such a contrast to the yellow skins, and shrivelled carcases, which I had for a long time been accustomed only to see, that I gazed upon them the whole evening. I thought them the handsomest mortals I had ever beheld. But how came they here? One of them, asking if my name was Beaver, said that he commanded a vessel in the service of the Sierra Leone company, and was from London bound to that place, but that he had been ordered to stop at Bulama with letters for me, and some provisions for the colony; that he had anchored his vessel at the back of the island, and had come in his boat to search out the harbour, and had fortunately discovered the cutter just before dark, to which he had been pulling ever since, against a strong flood tide, for information. This is the first time we have received letters from England since our leaving it: the report we had received from Bissao of our being at war with France is confirmed. Numerous questions kept us up till two o'clock; and this day Mr. Scott returned with them to pilot their vessel into this harbour.

1793. Friday, July 19.

Rain all day. No work done. Every one of the colonists sick, except myself and Mr. Scott, who is gone to pilot the Felicity schooner in. A boat arrived from the governor of Bissao to ask if a strange vessel which he had seen, off the isle of Arcas, was English.

Saturday, 20th.

Clear weather. I had this day to inflict a very severe punishment, and, as it was for a crime which, if suffered to pass unpunished, might eventually be the cause of the destruction of us all, I early in the morning sent for all the grumetas, and held a palaver: The crime was that for which the man was put in irons on the 16th, where he had been ever since.

Sunday, 21st.

My grumetas occupy houses built on purpose for them, and never, except their cook who comes for provisions, enter the block-house but when sent for; but, on the arrival of Bellchore, or any of the Bijugas, they all come within it, and mount guard day and night, during the time that they remain on the island; all the gates at those times are shut and secured, except the eastern one, where the wicket only is left open, at which there are constantly two sentinels, one of whom is always a colonist, if their healths permit it, with orders never to admit a Bijuga within the gate, unless I am there in person to sanction it, always to keep their posts clear from a crowd, and if any one should endeavour to force his way in, to put him to instant death. These orders are absolutely necessary to our preservation; they are thoroughly understood both by the colonists and

1793.
Sunday,
July 21.

the grumetas; and if they had not been implicitly obeyed on Bellchore's first visit, after the departure of the Hankey, we should at that time, most probably, have been every one killed. From open force, it is true, I have now nothing to fear, while the colonists are well; but on the 16th, when Bellchore was here with thirty men, all well armed, Mr. Scott and my black servant, at that time sentinel, were the only colonists well, and the former was actually on board the cutter; so that, though I had three sick colonists in the block-house, I was the only person in it, besides Watson, capable of exertion, and I had three Bijugas, the king and two others, in my room, who, though unarmed, had each their long knives in their girdles. Thus situated, John Lopez wanted, in the morning, to introduce a Bijuga at the eastern gate, whom Watson refused to admit, and pushed Lopez away: high words ensued, and Lopez drew his knife, when their noise brought me to the gate and I put him in irons, which probably saved his life, as Watson had brought his musquet to the charge, and might have run him through the body.

I endeavoured to convince the grumetas of the enormity of this man's crime, and of the danger they all run, as well as ourselves, from his conduct, as they knew that if any thing had happened to ourselves they would all have been made slaves; and assured them that if any man hereafter should be guilty of the like offence, I would hang him up on one of the trees before their houses; but for this time I should let this man off by inflicting corporal punishment only. They all seemed perfectly satisfied that he deserved punishment, and said that they would flog him if I would give him up to them. I said no, that I only could punish on this island, and the dismissing them all from the block-house except two, one of each nation (Manjacks and Papels) who were kept to witness the punishment, I ordered him to be tied up, and in their presence he received twelve dozen lashes with a cat-o'-nine-tails. Sick, Hood, Hayles, Bennet, Watson, Hodgekinson, and Ashworth. As there were no signs of the Felicity, and as I was exceedingly anxious to get my letters, at nine o'clock I went in the pinnace to find her out, taking with me the man whom I had punished, to prevent his endeavouring to stir up the rest of the grumetas to any act of violence during my absence; for although they had all acquiesced in the necessity of punishing him, I know not that they did so as to the measure; and a man smarting under his correction is moreover likely to be stirred up to acts of violence and revenge, which in his cooler moments he never would have thought of. Indeed as I had twenty-one of them to deal with in the morning, and Williams only well,* I had held the palaver with a brace of pistols on the table, as they are very apt to draw their knives when they can do it with impunity.

Williams had charge of the block-house, and thirteen grumetas were left in their houses; the other eight went with me in the pinnace, and we reached the schooner, in the channel between this island and Galenas, about three P. M. It being calm we could not move this evening.†

---

* This expression of being well must be understood in a very different sense from that in which it is taken in Europe. There Williams would be thought not only ill, but very ill. My distinction between well and ill is simply this, that all those who are incapable of moving about, or doing any work, are included in the list of the latter, and all those who are capable of doing any work, though far from enjoying any thing like health, are included in the former list; and in this sense the summary of the sick and well is always to be taken in this Journal.

† By this vessel I received many letters; and, among the rest, one from the trustees,

1793. Monday, July 22.	Fine weather. At six P. M. anchored the Felicity in this harbour. The Perseverance returned last night, with fowls only. Sick as before.
Tuesday, 23rd.	Employed cutting pales and inclosing. Received from the Felicity ten barrels of pork and a box of shoes. Sick, Hood, Hayles, Williams, Bennet, Watson, Hodgekinson, and Ashworth. Arrived a canoe from Bissao, and in her came a Mr. Ginioux, a merchant of that place, with a view, I believe, to purchase things from the Felicity.
Wednes. 24th.	Weather variable. Employment and sick as before. Wrote to the trustees. Although no earthly consideration would have induced me to have placed myself in my present situation, could I have foreseen, on our leaving England, that we were so near a war, or even that there was a distant probability of one; yet being here, I cannot leave it. Had, I say, war been foreseen, I had never been here: and although I have every thing to expect—promotion—wealth—honour—by immediately joining my profession; nay, though by the condition of my leave of absence by the Admiralty, I am obliged so to do within six months after being so required by the Gazette, which time is now elapsed, yet I cannot do it.* How can I go? If I take every body with me I abandon the colony when there is no necessity for so doing; I deceive those who placed themselves under my care; I betray the subscribers at home; I betray the interests of humanity.

expressing a confidence in obtaining a charter, a promise to send out more settlers in about two months, an exhortation not to leave the island, an approbation of our conduct, and an opinion that the war would not last beyond the current year. See Appendix, No. 13.

* My half-pay was consequently stopped, not for the time that I was in Africa only, but for the six months preceding, which I have never since received.

It is true I am under no written obligation; I receive no pay; I receive no support; I have no master—true—but I feel that I ought to stay, and therefore, be the consequences what they may, here will I remain. Should I go, and leave the colonists, they would all be killed; they could not exist without me. Should I not in that case, besides desertion, be guilty of murder? What do I get by remaining here? nothing. Yes I do: the satisfaction of feeling that I act as I ought to do. I have therefore written to the Admiralty the following letter;

Island of Bulama, 24th July, 1793.

Sir,

I have to request that you will be pleased to inform their Lordships, that, by a vessel which arrived here on the 22d inst., I was informed that all half-pay officers have been ordered, through the medium of the Gazette, to return to England: also to inform them that I have here the direction of a small colony whose very existence depends upon my presence. If I disobey their Lordships orders in the Gazette, I know that I am liable to lose my commission: and if I obey it, I never deserved one.

I hope their Lordships will observe the peculiar difficulty of my situation, and give me credit when I aver that the King has not an officer more attached to him, his country, and constitution, than myself; that it is with the greatest regret I find myself obliged to be absent from the fleet in the time of War; and that I shall embrace the first opportunity of joining my profession.

I have the honour to be, Sir,
your most obedient and very humble servant,
P. Beaver.

To Philip Stephens, Esq.
Secretary to the Admiralty.

1793.
Thurs. July 25. Rainy, changeable weather. Employment and sick as before. The cutter parted her small bower. The boy Hodgekinson, who has been long ill, and who from having been a sprightly, sharp boy, is become almost stupid, has applied to me to let him go away in the Felicity, to which I immediately assented, and accordingly discharged him this day.

Friday, 26th. Rain all day. No work done. Sick as before. The Felicity made an unsuccessful attempt to sail.

Saturday, 27th. Sometimes rain, at others clear. Employed cutting pales. The Felicity sailed. We this morning discovered that the small two oared boat was gone. This is to us a very great loss: We suppose she broke adrift in the night. Dragged for the cutter's anchor without success. Sick as before. The grumetas are all dissatisfied, and have indeed appeared so for many days; they all want to go.

Sunday, 28th. No rain all day. Made another fruitless attempt to sweep the cutter's anchor. Sent the Perseverance and Industry to the Balantee country for grass. As the grumetas wanted to go away, I promised to let *half* go in these boats, and the other half the moment they returned. Just as the boats were departing I was informed that all the grumetas had got into them and were determined to go. I have never yet kept any man a moment after he had told me that he wished to go away, and by giving them this liberty I have never wanted grumetas; for the boats have generally returned with more new ones to the island than equalled the number of those who had departed. But I was derermined to convince these people that I had hired *grumetas* and not *masters*, and therefore would not suffer one of them to depart, except those necessary for the navigation of the boats; and those I did not pay their wages. I afterwards found that eighteen white cloths

Sunday, July 28. had been stolen out of the store-room; that many of my fowls were killed, and their feathers hid in the grass; and that the cow had got out of the N.W. inclosure, which she could not possibly break through. It is I believe ordained that I am always to be surrounded by villains. In the evening I found that four men out of the eleven whom I had detained, had hid themselves in the wood. Killed a hog for the colony. Well, Scott and myself. A canoe came from Bissao to cut timber.

Monday, 29th. Began again, after two months omission, to take up the remaining stumps in the N.W. field. Sick as before. Three of the grumetas returned from the woods.

Tuesday, 30th. Rain all day. Little or no work done. By a canoe that stopped in her way from Tombaly for Bissao, one of the grumetas deserted. Same sick.

Wednes. 31st. Employed as on Monday. Sick, Hayles, Bennet, Williams, Watson, Dowlah, and Ashworth.

Monthly state of the Colony.

                                                 Men. Wom. Boys.

On the 30th of June we had { Well 6 .. 0 .. 1—Total W. 7 } 10.
                                      { Sick 2 .. 0 .. 1—   S. 3 }

Since when we have discharged { ...... 0 .. 0 .. 1—Total .... 1.

Present state of the colony .. { Well 3 .. 0 .. 0—Total W. 3 } 9.
                                      { Sick 5 .. 0 .. 1—   S. 6 }

Grumetas.

17 men,

2 boys,

——

19, of which 7 are away in the boats.

1793.
Thurs. Aug. 1.
Few intervals from rain in the course of this day. Employed taking up the roots of trees. Sick as before.

Friday, 2nd.
Remarkably fine weather all day. Employed as before. Finished a couple of gates; one to go across the road, in the north fence of the east field; and the other to communicate from the same road, with the N.W. field. This is the first day for some weeks that any one of the colonists has been able to do any work.

Saturday, 3d.
Fine morning; rainy evening. Employment, and sick as before.

Sunday, 4th.
Alternate showers, and fine weather. Read prayers. Same sick.

Monday, 5th.
Clear morning; rainy evening. Taking up stumps and paling. Sick as before.

Tuesday, 6th.
Rainy weather. Same employment. In the evening the Perseverance and Industry returned with 13 grumetas and grass. They brought back many stolen goods, which the last grumetas (or rather those who went in the boats, every one of whom, except Peter, deserted) had carried off, which were recovered through the means of the governor, from whom I received a very handsome message. Mr. Scott added to the list of sick.

Wednes. 7th.
Variable weather. Employed as before, and thatching. Sick, Scott, Hayles, Bennet, Watson, Dowlah, and Ashworth. Killed a hog for the colony.

Thurs. 8th.
Showery all day. Employed as before, and repairing boats. Finished thatching the block-house. Sick as before, and myself.

Friday, 9th.
Showery all day. Same employment and sick. Myself very unwell. The cow which I had lost was seen in the woods, but so wild that we were obliged to shoot her.

1793. Saturday, Aug. 10. Rainy weather. Same sick and employment. Myself very unwell indeed.

Friday, 23rd. From the 10th to this day I have been too ill to keep my Journal, and now scarcely well, this being the first day of my getting out; every body else is sick. During my illness the grumetas had been entirely employed in taking up the stumps of trees; and having finished the N.W. and E. meadows, began this day on the S.W. field. Showery all day. A sloop came from Bissao for timber.

Sat. 24. to Thur. 29. Heavy rains generally. Grumetas, when the weather will admit of it, taking up stumps. Every one of the colonists, except myself, ill; insomuch that I am obliged to send for a black man from the cutter to cook, no one being able to undergo that business.

Friday, 30th. Rainy weather. Learn by a boat from Bissao, that an English vessel from Sierra Leone has been there seven days. Robbed of all my shirts and silk handkerchiefs, they were in the south nest of houses. All hands sick.

Saturday, 31st. Rain all morning; fair evening. Employed as before. Punished a grumeta for breaking into the south nest of houses, and robbing them, with 202 lashes. Every colonist being ill, was obliged to make the grumetas punish their own countryman, which they, however, allowed that he merited. Recovered only two shirts; the rest I suppose carried away by the canoes.

Monthly state of the Colony.

Nine in number, the same as on the last day of the last month, but all sick except myself.

1793.

Saturday, Aug. 31.

Grumetas.

19 men,
2 boys,
——
21

Sunday, Sept. 1.
Mond. 2. Fine weather. Taking up stumps. All hands sick.

Tuesday, 3rd. Tolerable weather. Same employment. Died of a fever and was buried, Mr. Scott: he had been ill since the 6th of last month, and always very low spirited from the time of his being taken ill. All the rest sick, but mending for these last three or four days.

Wed. 4.
Thurs. 5. Tolerably clear weather, with now and then a few light showers; a tornado last night, which we conceive indicates the approach of the cessation of the rains. A boat from Bissao landed a grumeta. Same employment. Watson well.

Friday, 6th. Showers. A sloop came from Bissao for timber. Watson and Dowlah well. Myself ill.

Satur. 7.
to
Mon. 16. In general showery. Grumetas at their usual employment. Myself too ill to read prayers the last two Sundays; but now getting a little better. Hood, Watson, and Dowlah well. The rest sick.

Tuesday, 17th. Heavy tornado in the morning. Myself tolerably well, but all the rest sick again, except Hood.

Wednes. 18th. Alternate showers, and fine intervals. Mr. Hood added to the sick. Bennet complained that the grumeta whom I had punished wanted to stab him, but could not prove it.

Thursday, 19th. A few drops of rain. Grumetas at their usual work. Sick as before. Served out fowls.

Clear weather. Last night arrived a Boat from the Sierra Leone vessel at Bissao, with tea and sugar for the colony. Also the Perseverance, having been detained by some of my former grumetas at *Biaume*, and having had goods to the value of nine bars taken from her. The grumetas that went hence in this boat, left her at Bissao, when more were hired, who also left her at *Biaume*, in consequence of the boats having been put in their gris-gris house; others were hired at *Biaume*, who left her at Bissao, and at length others, after an absence of 40 days, brought her to Bulama from the latter place. No grumetas would come from Bissao to Bulama, as the governor there, they said, not only punished his grumetas severely, but gave them low wages, and starved them. To unravel the cause of this sudden change in the opinions of these people, who have hitherto been so anxious to come here, because they have been well fed, well paid, and well treated, that we could with difficulty keep them out of our boats, it must be remembered that many things were stolen out of one of the store-rooms, the latter end of July. I had on that occasion sent to the governor of Bissao, requesting that he would stop my people on landing, order them to be examined and if any of the missing goods were found upon them, to seize them for me; part of which he did recover for me. These grumetas, to palliate the villainy, spread a report, which was quickly communicated to all others, that I not only flogged them all most severely, but almost starved them, and withheld their wages; and therefore they had paid themselves. Most of these rascals lived at *Biaume*, from which place the Perseverance is just returned, and there one of them named Joze de Noone, avowed the theft, and said that he, with seven more, had made a ladder, scaled the house in the night,

1793.
Friday,
Sept. 20.
and had taken away the clothes formerly mentioned, a piece of blue cloth, and six musquets; and then desired Peter (the man who had command of the boat) to pay him four bullocks' money for the ivory which he had found upon the island, formerly mentioned, and which, he said, I had taken from him. This Peter refused; and the boat was put into their gris-gris house; which is much the same thing as being taboo'd in the language of the South-sea Islanders, or in plain English, an embargo was laid on her. At length, after more than a month's detention, for nine bars the boat was released. This voyage has cost me 80 bars, for which I have only a milch cow and a calf.

These vagabonds say I flogged them severely. I punished the thieves, and the man who was going to stab a sentinel; and so I always will; but none others have I punished. They say they were starved. A hogshead of biscuit, a cask of rice, a barrel of beef, and another of pork, were always open for their cook to take what he chose. They say I withhold their wages. I sent a boat for grumetas the latter end of July, and those who went in her did not receive their wages, because they ought to have returned with the boat, when they would have been paid and discharged as they desired. But they had robbed me, were afraid to return, deserted therefore from the boat, and consequently lost their wages as they never came back for them. They say that what wages I give are low. They are the same that I have always given, and much higher than they can get elsewhere. It is true that the articles I now pay them with are not so various as they formerly were, many of them being all expended; but they have the same value, though their choice is confined to fewer things. The truth is, that the major part of my latter grumetas were Manjacks, whom I formerly had not;

and they are a deceitful, lying, thieving, lazy, treacherous people—full as bad as the Bijugas. Served out tea, sugar, and molasses. Sick all except myself. By Peter I received a kind message from the governor of Bissao, begging me not to punish any of my grumetas, but send them away if they behaved ill; and to have regard for my life, which would be in much danger from their thirst of vengeance. A Manjack, he says, never forgives an injury while the man lives who inflicted it. I have never injured one of them, I have only given them what they deserved. _{1793. Friday, Sept. 20.}

Tornado in the morning, rest of the day fine. Employed as before, and paling. Watson and myself well. _{Saturday, 21st.}

At three in the morning the heaviest tornado I ever experienced with violent rain, thunder and lightning. Several trees were blown down, and one near the S. E. corner of the blockhouse was shivered with lightning. Read prayers to three of the colonists who were able to attend. The grumetas are dissatisfied and want to go away. Bennet, who is frightened out of his senses, thinks that they have some hostile intention, and wishes a watch to be kept in the night. Poor fool! Weak and emaciated as every one is, a week's watching would kill us all. _{Sunday, 22d.}

Clear weather. Began to take up the stumps in the farm yard; still paling. Assembled the grumetas, and held a palaver, to find out, if possible, their cause of discontent: they had nothing to complain of, and left me, seemingly, perfectly contented. _{Monday, 23rd.}

Fine weather. Employment and sick as before. Killed a calf for the colonists. _{Tuesday, 24th.}

Sent the Perseverance in the morning to Bissao for grumetas. _{Wednes. 25th.}

1793.
Thurs.
Sept. 26. After dinner all the grumetas laid down their tools, retired to their houses, and said that they would not work, which they did not, till I pointed a four pounder into their house, when they went to work again. Sprained my back, in my exertions to get the gun ready, forgetting how weak I was.

Friday, 27th. Fine weather. Same employment. Sick, Hayles, Williams, Bennet, Dowlah, and Ashworth. My wine key has been taken away, and wine stolen, which makes me suspect that I have thieves *inside* as well as *outside* of the block-house. Grumetas idle and insolent.

Satur. 28 to Mon. 30. Same weather and employment. Read prayers on Sunday. Sick, Hood, Bennet, Dowlah and Ashworth.

Monthly State of the Colony.

On the last day of August we were nine in number, all of whom were sick except myself; since which time we have buried Mr. Scott.

	Men.	Boys.		
At present we are { Well	4	0	Total W.	4 } 8.
Sick	3	1	S.	4

Grumetas.

15 men,

1 woman.

——

16

Tuesday, Oct. 1. Showery, with thunder and lightning. Finished taking up stumps in the farm yard.

Wednes. Oct. 2. 1793. Windy, calm, cloudy, clear, rainy, dry, ever-changing weather. In the evening my Biafara friends made their appearance on the opposite shore. Sent the boat for them, which returned with Janjan, the king's son, and nine others.

Thursd. 3d. Winds and weather variable. Same employment. Janjan says that the Portuguese are continually " telling his father bad of *me ;*" and he supposes that they " tell me bad *of him :*" " but his father pays no attention to what they say, and I must do the same: his father wishes I would build a house at his town, as till then he is obliged, though against his inclination, to trade with the people of Bissao, as a refusal to do so would bring on him war. He could not send me cattle when my boat was last at Ghinala, because, at that time, *he was ill and bewitched,* and *his cattle were bewitched and died.*"

Friday, 4th. The Perseverance returned last night with ten grumetas. My Biafara friends left me this morning. Employed in taking up stumps, and paling. Began this day to dig a well in the centre of the square, when, if we find water, we shall have every necessary of life, *within the block-house,* for at least a year to come.

Saturday, 5th. Clear weather. Same employment.

Sunday, 6th. Read prayers to three of the colonists who were well enough to attend. Sent the Perseverance to Bissao with grumetas. Sick, Hood, Hayles, Bennet, Williams, Dowlah, and Ashworth.

Mon. 7, to Wedn. 9. Fine weather. Employed paling, and making the well in the square. A boat from Bissao came for timber.

Thurs. 10th The Perseverance returned, and brought me three grumetas. By her I learned that the Ocean, the Sierra Leone vessel at Bissao, was to sail this evening, and not to pass this island as I had been taught to expect, but to sail back through the western chan-

1793.
Thursd.
Oct. 10.

Friday,
11th.

nel as she had come. Wrote immediately to the trustees, and sent back the Perseverance with my letters.

Same employment. It has before been observed that sickness, fear, and despondency, have had strange effects upon the minds of the colonists: Indeed they are at this moment, every one of them, almost ideots; their mental faculties seem entirely worn out; loss of memory, or difficulty of recollection, with which they are all more or less affected, I have been accustomed to think they had in some degree really feigned; and had attributed to indolence, in a great measure, their frequent omission of doing things which they had been ordered to do, and which was always excused by " I really forgot, sir:" But to-day I have had two remarkable instances of the total failure of memory in Mr. Hood and Peter Hayles. The former thought he was well enough to do a little work, and begged I would give him something to do. I accordingly lined a post for him to square, part of which he did square, and then eat his dinner; went to work again on the post, left off, laid down and took a nap, awoke and came into the square about an hour afterwards, that is, about five o'clock. I asked him how he proceeded with the post, and if he felt himself at all fatigued? He asked what post? " The post I lined for you to square in the morning," I replied. " I do not recollect your lining any post," said he. " Who then lined the post that you have been squaring to-day?" I asked. " I have not been squaring any post to-day," was his reply. " Why what have you been working at then?" I asked. " I have not been at any work to-day," was the answer. I took this man to the post where he had squared it, and yet could not convince him that it had been done by him this very day: he remembered nothing at all of the matter. This seems almost incredible, but it is every word true; and I am thoroughly convinced that the want of recollection was not feigned, for Mr. Hood is a man of veracity, and a good, quiet, hard working man, always willing to do whatever is in his power.

1793. Friday, Oct. 11.

The other instance was in Peter Hayles: A new canoe, just finished, stopped here in her way from the Rio Grande to Bissao. I thought it was the largest I had seen in this country, and therefore after dinner gave Peter Hayles my rule, and desired him to go down on the beach and measure this boat, that is to bring to me its length, breadth, and depth. He left me about three o'clock, and had to walk about three minutes to the boat. I saw nothing of him again till near sunset: he had been wandering along the beach all that time, his mind totally unoccupied. " Well Peter, where are the dimensions of the boat, and why did you not bring them to me sooner?" said I. " What boat, sir? what dimensions?" said he, " The canoe that I sent you down to measure," I replied. " You never sent me to measure any canoe," he answered. " What, have you then not measured the canoe?" I asked. " No," was the answer. " For what purpose then did I give you my rule?" " You never gave me any rule, sir." Feel in your pocket," said I. The rule was there, but Hayles had no idea how it came there, nor the most distant recollection of my having given it to him.

I fear that what I have written will not be believed; for even to me it appears incredible; it is nevertheless every word true. How is it to be accounted for? I have had sickness as well as others, more bodily exertion than any other individual, and more mental exertion than all of them put together; and yet I am the only person in the colony whose memory is totally unimpaired. It is

1793.
Friday, Oct. 11.

true I have never been afraid, while every other person has lived in fear and trembling for these last eleven months. Whether or not fear can produce such effects I shall leave to the physician and the philosopher to determine. The fact is as I state it.

Before the boy Hodgekinson left me, he has frequently, when sent with a message across the square, returned more than once to ask what he was sent for, incapable of retaining what had been committed to his memory for that short distance.

Saturday, 12th

Foggy and hazy weather. Same employment.

Sunday, 13th.

Myself not well enough to read prayers. Assembled the colonists and asked them if they were not all villains?*

Monday, 14th.

Employed cutting, paling, and making the well; disrated Hayles before the assembled colonists. Killed a goat for the colony.

Tuesday, 15th to Thur. 17.

Same employment and sick. In digging in the well this morning, something yellow and shining was dug up and immediately given to me. "Suppose we should find gold, sir?" said Williams. "I had rather find water," said I. He thought I was a fool.†

---

* I have forgotten the immediate occasion of this; but, as it stands on my Journal, and as the reader will have seen reasons sufficient for the question, I have not erased it. Perhaps it may be an act of justice, to make an exception of Mr. Hood.

† If the Bijugas, with a view of getting possession of what they consider our immense wealth in the block-house, should ever entertain serious thoughts of attacking us, which I very much doubt, their surest mode of proceeding would be by blockade, and though such a measure would indicate a degree of knowledge and foresight which they do not seem to possess, yet it is possible, and might even be suggested to them by some more enlightened neighbours. Such a measure would not

Friday, Oct. 18. Last night the Perseverance returned, not having been able to deliver my letters, as the Ocean had sailed. The man who commands her, might, I think, have given me notice of his departure time enough to have written home, considering how unfrequent opportunities occur of my doing so. Tommy Albus* sent me word that I must arm my grumetas, and beware of the Bijugas. Found water in the well at the depth of 21 feet 4 inches.

Saturday, 19th. Fine weather. Same employment and sick. Finished the well.

Sunday, 20th. Read prayers. Killed a goat for the colony.

Monday, 21st. Employed taking up stumps, and inclosing: began making a pond, in the east meadow, for the cattle.

Tuesday, 22d. Same employment and sick.

Wednes. 23d. At day-light this morning I found that Peter Hayles had taken the boat from the cutter in the night, and had deserted, leaving the boat aground upon the mud; and that Bennet had left the block-house, having taken all his own things, and some of mine: he escaped by the west gate, as we found the key in it this morning. He had access to all keys, being at this time my servant; the keys hung in my room, the doors of which

---

be likely to be undertaken in the rainy season, when the heavens would supply us, for a longer time than they would have patience to keep the field, with sufficient water for our support; but, without water in the block-house, a blockade of a week, in the dry season, must be fatal to us; for though the water which we consume is brought from a spring at the foot of the hill, not many yards distant, yet the hill is so steep just above that spring, that I could not protect those who went to it, either by cannon or musquestry, and the natives with their long guns would have it in their power to pick every man off as he went for water, for the want of which we must surrender, or die with thirst; to avoid which alternative, though I did not think either probable, was my motive for digging the well in the block-house.

* A friendly Papel trader residing at Bissao.

1793. Wednes. Oct. 23.	were never shut; the key of the east gate, the only one we have been accustomed to use, was always, after sun set, placed under my pillow. We have now two mouths less to feed; Bennet has never done any thing but crawl about the block-house; Hayles has been my most useful man, but of late not worth his salt. They are no loss; whether they are yet got off the island or not, I cannot tell, as I have made no inquiries after them. Employed as before. Sick, Williams, Dowlah, and Ashworth.
Thursd. 24th.	Rain morning, fine the rest of the day. Employment and sick as before. This morning a letter was found in the locker on board the cutter, from Peter Hayles, addressed to me, asking my leave to go, after he had run away!* The south nest of houses, where the stationary is kept, I find has been plundered of paper, pens, 15 ink stands, all the wax and wafers, and one trunk: this is the work of my grumetas.
Friday, 25th.	This morning arrived the William, schooner, and Jane, pinnace, from the Rio Nunez, bound up the Rio Grande, David James Laurence, a mulattoe, owner and commander. Same employment and sick.
Saturday, 26th.	The above vessels sailed for Bulola. Usual employment.

* From the date of his letter, unless he had mistaken the month of October for September, it appears that he had for more than a month intended to desert. As a curious specimen of letter-writing I insert it below.

To Mr. Beaver.

Sept. the 20

Sir I hope that you wil parden me for riteing to you, which I know I am not worthy of, but I hope you will forgive me for all things past, for I am going to try to get a passage to the Cape deverds and then for Amarica, Sir If you will be so good as to let me go I shall be grately ab bleaght to you, Sir I hope you will parden me for runing away, Sir I am your most obedient umld Servent

PETER HAYLES.

Sir I do rite with Tears in my eyes.

1793.

Sunday, Oct. 27.
Read prayers. Killed a goat for the colony.

Monday, 28th.
Foggy weather. Served out tea and molasses; found that much tea had been stolen, and that the grumetas had again broken open the out-houses. Set a man trap there, warning the grumetas of what would happen to any man who endeavoured to enter any place I had forbidden him.

Tuesday, 29th.
Last night, in conversation, Mr. Hood told me that he did not like to desert me, but that he thought it not safe to remain any longer upon the island; and that he therefore had made up his mind to go away; that it could not be called deserting me, as he had remained, and would remain with me so long as there were any hopes of our remaining here being of any use; but that, from our present weakness, our own grumetas had it, at all times, in their power to put us to death, and which he had no doubt they would readily do for a little rum and tobacco; that I had lately been twice advised that the Bijugas meant to attack us, and that to attack, was to destroy us; that their safety on this island depended not only upon my life, but my health even; and that if any thing should happen to me, their retreat would be cut off as they had no one to navigate a vessel; that every night, when he laid down, he expected it would be his last, and that our longer remaining here was only braving the Bijugas to kill us; that Peter Onsfield had told him that my life was in imminent danger, and that on it depended their safety; that he thought it a duty which he owed, not only to his wife and children, but to himself, not to throw away his life, which must be the consequence of his remaining here; that we were now in great danger, without a chance of being serviceable either to ourselves or others, by continuing in it; besides, what had absolutely determined him, was a confession from Williams

1793.
Tuesday,
Oct. 29.

and Dowlah, who had made him their confidant, of their intention of deserting me: the latter told him that he should leave me, and go to Bissao the first opportunity, the former said that he would not run away, as by that means he should forfeit his wages, and that he could not afford to lose so much money; but said he, I have my box already packed up, ready to put in the boat, and I listen with attention to hear any noise or riot on shore in the night; and then, he observed, he should put his box in the boat and scull over to the opposite shore, not only with his own things, but that he should take something else as an equivalent to his wages; and why should he not, he asked, " for you must all be killed, and I may as well get something by it as any body else." Mr. Hood further told me that Peter meant to leave me in about six weeks and go to Geba. Thus have two resolved shortly to leave me, and a third, (the only sailor I have, and who of course commands the cutter) at the very moment when I should stand most in need of his assistance, in the very moment that I should be attacked. This is an unheard of piece of cowardice and treachery. He will not desert me when it would not be of much importance—in a moment of peace; no; he will remain so long as we are all quiet, and time his desertion at a moment which will give spirits to our adversaries, and depress those of the remaining people. He will not only avoid assisting me, but inspire my enemies with confidence, and contribute all in his power to their success. This conversation took place about eight o'clock, and a few hours afterwards, that is, about midnight, we were alarmed by the man in the cutter, who said that he heard the Bijugas on shore. The grumetas corroborated his assertion, and we were under arms all night, but saw nothing of them to day. Peter tells me that had the Bijugas attacked us, most of the grumetas would have run into the bush* at the first fire. Was ever mortal surrounded by such miserable wretches? Employment and sick as before. Discovered the thief. The grumetas all armed. 1793. Tuesday, Oct. 29.

At noon this day my servant delivered me a letter, in the form of a petition, signed by all the colonists, which contained an avowal of every person's intention to leave the island when the William returns from Bulola,† which I expect every hour. I immediately assembled them and asked their various reasons; and they all replied that it was solely on account of their personal safety; that they were all satisfied with my conduct to- Wednes. 30th.

---

* The term of the natives for a *wood*.

† *To Philip Beaver, Esq. the Governor of Bulama.*

The humble petition of John Hood, John Williams, James Watson, and Thomas Dowlah,

    Sheweth,

That we are at all times ready and willing to do every thing in our power under our worthy governor's direction for the establishing the colony, but Peter Hayles and William Bennet, a few nights since, on hearing that we were to be attacked by the Bijugas in a short time, ran away and left us two short of our number, which, with the death of Mr. Scott, made nearly half our strength; and not having any reinforcement from England, which was expected, find ourselves in a very dangerous situation, not only from fear of the Bijugas, but of our own grumetas, and as a small vessel will be here in a few days, we think it our duty to make this public declaration, in order that you may be prepared for our departure, by the first vessel that comes; it is not out of disrespect to you, sir, far from it, we are all sorry to leave you; but we hope that you will value your life as we do ours, and leave a place which you cannot hold without risking your life every moment, both night and day; we therefore beg you will value your own life for the sake of ours, and embrace this opportunity to leave the place before it is too late. If it is once known how weak we are, by the Bijugas, you, and all of us, shall have our throats cut in a short time, and as you, sir, are the only person here capable of navigating the cutter, we most earnestly pray you will hear our prayers, as our only reason is to preserve our lives. And your petitioners, as in duty bound, shall ever pray, &c.

1793.
Wednes.
Oct. 30.

wards them, and would stay by me if there were any hopes of its being of any use; but not having received the expected succours, and having been lately weakened by the death of one, and the desertion of two other colonists; expecting daily to be attacked by the Bijugas; and not conceiving themselves safe even from our own grumetas, it appeared to them to be madness any longer to remain. They therefore conjured me to yield to their request, to go with them, and carry them away in the cutter to Sierra Leone, or wherever else I thought proper. I told them that I would not go; that I could not prevent their deserting me; but that I would keep the place with some Portuguese soldiers, whom I should be able to procure at Bissao. I then made them all promise me, that they would not suffer, by any means, our grumetas to know their intentions, nor speak on the subject to Mr. Lawrence, the owner of the William, till I had received an answer from Bissao, respecting the assistance which I meant to ask; and that I would then call them together again, and give them a final answer.

In the evening I took an opportunity of speaking to every one of them separately, to try if I could not by reasoning and promises shake their resolution, but to no purpose; I had always the same answer, " we are too few, and shall certainly be killed." Mr. Hood even told me that fear had so completely possessed him, that he never got any sleep in the night for some time past, always expecting after dark to have his throat cut; and that he was not ashamed to avow, that a few evenings ago, when putting on a dry shirt at dusk, just after he had finished his work, in the work-shop, it accidentally got entangled with the vice, it was over his head, and he could not see, and that, in that situation he remained motionless for near a quarter of an hour, fully convinced that a Bijuga had got hold of him. He endeavoured to reason with himself, he said, upon the absurdity of his fear; but he had not the power to move. Punished Domingo, one of the grumetas, with 100 lashes for robbery. A little rain in the evening. *1793. Wednes. Oct. 30.*

Thunder, lightning, and rain, great part of last night. Employed taking up stumps, making a pond in the east meadow, paling, and repairing boats. Sick, Ashworth. Lame, Williams. *Thursd. 31st.*

Monthly state of the Colony.

	Men.	Boys.		
On the 30th of September we had { Well	4	0	— Total Well 4	} 8.
{ Sick	3	1	— — Sick 4	
Since which time we have lost by { Desertion	2	0	— — .... 2.	
At present we are { Well	5	0	— — Well 5	} 6.
{ Sick	0	1	— — Sick 1	

Grumetas.

19 men,
1 women,
1 boy.
———
21
———

Fine weather. Same employment. Sick and lame as before. Finished inclosing S.W. field.* *Novem. Frid. 1.*

Read Prayers. Killed a goat for the colony. Sick and lame as before. *Saturday, 2d. Sunday, 3d.*

* The same size as the N.W. field: that is, 3 acres, 2 roods, 22 poles.

1793.
Novem.
Mon. 4,
to
Thurs. 7.

Employed taking up stumps, digging the pond, and finishing the south paling of the east meadow. Sick, Dowlah and Ashworth; lame Williams. Found water in the pond at the depth of eight feet.

Friday, 8th.

This morning a boat arrived here from Tombaly, and a canoe towing an English, copper bottomed, schooner, which they were taking to Bissao to sell, that had been cut off by the Naloos, when aground at *Comanterra*; one Englishman they said had been killed, but the rest escaped in their boat. *Comanterra* is situated on the other side of Tombaly; how far the man knew not, but it had taken him five tides to go from the latter place to the former. They left us in the evening. This is the second English schooner that has been cut off by the natives since my residence on this island. The one by the Manjacks, the other by the Naloos. Which of these nations is the worst I cannot tell, they are both bad enough, and neither of them to be trusted.

Saturday 9th.

Same employment; sick, and lame as before. Went this morning in the small boat to examine the N. E. creek of the harbour. In rowing up it I saw a kind of deer, which I had never seen before, nor do I remember ever having seen it described. It was a female, and had a young one grazing with it on the border of the shore, distant from us, I suppose, about seventy yards. As I was anxious to examine it I did not fire. It had no horns, but its head and crest were exactly those of a deer; the rest of its body, except only the tail, exactly that of a horse. Its height appeared about that of a buffaloe; colour dark brown; the ears seemed round at the top. Had I seen only the head neck and forehand of this animal, I should, without any hesitation, have called it a deer; but had I only seen the body I should as readily have pronounced it to be a horse. It was very full and round about the buttocks, and its legs appeared to have all the strength of that animal; but the tail resembled the deer's, only apparently a little longer. <small>1793. Saturd. Nov. 9.</small>

We saw also in this creek, five hippopotamoses, but so shy that we could not get a shot at them. We landed at the upper part of it, and observed much cleared ground on four adjoining eminences, from twenty to thirty acres each; the greatest part of this creek is dry at low water.

Read prayers. Sick, Dowlah, Watson, and Ashworth; lame, Williams. Held a palaver with the grumetas; they as usual allowed *"that I had got the reason."* <small>Sunday, 10th.</small>

Same employment. All sick and lame but Hood and myself. Served out fowls to the colonists. <small>Monday, 11th. Tuesday, 12th.</small>

Mr. Hood informed me to-night that James Watson meant to run away by the first boat, and that he would not have been here now, had he been well; that they were all astonished that I had taken no further notice of their request to go away; that they thought I was devising some plan for keeping them here; and that they meant to speak to me to-morrow on the subject, as they were determined to go, and that immediately, for by delay they might stop a day too long; and that the grumetas meant to leave me on Sunday next, whether I paid them their wages or not. <small>Wednes. 13th.</small>

From the 29th of last month, when we were alarmed at the idea of the Bijugas being near us, the grumetas have all been armed; and not one of them will even go to work in the day, though in sight of the block-house, without having his musquet, loaded and primed, lying by him: so panic struck are these people at the idea of being attacked by those treacherous

1793.
Wednes.
Nov. 13.

islanders. At them I am not surprised, but that the colonists should betray the same pusillanimous mind is astonishing.

Thurs.
14th.

Employed as before. Sick, Dowlah, and Ashworth; lame, Williams. At breakfast this morning I received a second paper from the colonists expressive of their determination to leave me as soon as possible.* Assembled them again. They all averred that fear was their sole motive to such a step. After having said every thing in my power to convince them that their fears were groundless, and exhausted every argument that occurred to me to induce them to remain, they still told me that they were determined to go, and that if I would not go with them in the cutter, they would run away and leave me to my fate. Mr. Hood said that nothing could induce him to remain upon the island; that he and the rest had, he conceived, done their duty by remaining with me so long; that he was sorry to leave the island, and more so to leave me alone on it, but go he would. As nothing could alter the determination of either individual, I was obliged to consent; but I told them that I would not

---

* This paper ridiculously called a petition, as well as the former, is as follows:

The humble petition of John Hood, John Williams, James Watson, and Thomas Dowlah,

Sheweth,

That your petitioners have informed you in a former petition, the dangerous situation we conceive ourselves to be in; we therefore beg leave to remind you for your own sake, as well as our ownselves, to consider of the danger which so alarms us, and if you are determined to risk your life, and endeavour to keep possession of the island, which we are sure you cannot do, if we were all to stay with you, for which reason we hope you will excuse our declaring we are determined to seek our safety by quitting the island as soon as possible, for the preservation of our lives only.

To Philip Beaver, Esq.

Bulama, 14th November, 1793.

leave any thing behind, and therefore could not go for some time, as I must send up the Rio Grande to endeavour to hire Mr. Lawrence's schooner, to carry some of our goods, as the cutter would not contain them all. Before we are loaded it is yet possible that some assistance may arrive. Who knows? Thus, after all my labour, fatigue, and exertions, am I obliged to leave this island, and go to sea with a vessel, not provided with any thing which she ought to have, not even with anchors, and only one sailor, and that one lame. Sent the Industry up the Rio Grande to Mr. Lawrence, to propose hiring his vessel, and to get his pinnace to carry my grumetas to Bissao. Thus, abandoned by my own people, and the grumetas leaving me, what can I do? Of what use would it be for me to remain here alone? with grumetas I could keep the island, but I should only be hiring so many masters, without a prospect of doing any good: but of this others must judge.

1793.
Thurs.
Nov. 14.

Employment, sick, and lame, as before. Served out fowls to the colonists. Finished the inclosures.*

Friday, 15th.

Read prayers. The pinnace returned from Bulola. Mr. Lawrence wrote that he should sail the following tide for this place, and that he would render me every assistance in his power. Assembled the colonists again, told them that their

Saturday, 16th.
Sunday, 17th.

	A.	R.	P.
* The east field	5	2	7
The N. W. field	3	2	22
The S. W. field	3	2	22
The cattle and poultry inclosures	1	0	30
The garden	0	2	0
Grumetas' garden	0	1	0
	14	3	1

1793.
Sunday,
Nov. 17.

fears were groundless, and urged their remaining on the island. They said that nothing could alter their determination. I told them that, from imaginary, they were running into real, danger. By going to sea in the cutter in her present situation, without rope, without sails, without anchors and cables, without a chart of the channel on which any dependance could be placed, without a pilot, and even without an individual who knew any thing of the place; to which was to be added without sailors, as we had only one, and he was not only lame, but had a fever every day in which he was at all exposed to the sun; that since I had been on this island only three vessels had attempted to go through this dangerous and intricate channel, and they were all well equipped, and well manned; that one of them had returned hither in distress, having lost her anchors and cables; and that the two others had arrived at Sierra Leone, but with the loss of an anchor each; that as I had neither men to make nor shorten sail, to work the vessel, nor to bring it to an anchor, in case of necessity, it was most probable that we should be cast away; and that they then would, too late, see their folly in flying, from imaginary, into real danger: besides, that if I should be taken ill, which was not unlikely, from being obliged to be much exposed to the sun, they had no one capable of navigating the vessel, and that by steering a random course, on the one hand they might be wrecked on the coast; and on the other, run into the Western Ocean, where they might be becalmed, expend all their water, of which they had not many casks, and miserably perish; that though I might keep my health, which was now but in a precarious state, yet, the only seaman I had, who was never many days together well on the island, might be laid up. He might die; in that case I could not always keep the deck, I could not for ever be at the helm, 1792. I must at times be refreshed with repose and with sleep, or Sunday, nature would be exhausted. Who then, I asked, was to take Nov. 17. charge of the vessel? who could steer? or who could tell me which way it had drifted? or, supposing we are in anchoring ground, and on those occasions come to an anchor; where is our strength to take it up again? In short, if either Williams the sailor, or myself, were rendered incapable of exerting ourselves, what would become of them and the vessel? Their answer was, " If we remain death is certain, if we go we have a chance."

Same employment. Sick, Dowlah, and Ashworth; lame, Monday, Williams. In the evening the William, schooner, and Jane, pin- 18th. nace, arrived with Mr. Lawrence.

Having done every thing in my power to prevail upon the co- Tuesday, lonists to alter their resolution, and to remain on the island; 19th. having offered to each individual one hundred acres of my own land, if they would remain only till succours arrived; and having endeavoured, on Sunday last, to prevail upon them through their ruling passion, fear, to remain on the island, by pointing out the danger of leaving it, but all to no effect, I this morning finally determined to quit it; and therefore ceased clearing the ground of stumps, and sent Mr. Hood to Bissao in the Jane pinnace,* with all the grumetas whom I discharged, except Peter Onsfield and six others, with a letter to the governor, informing him of my intention, and at the same time offering him any thing which I had upon the island, which he might wish to purchase.† Employed shipping provisions and stores on board

* His instructions will be seen Appendix, No. 14.
† He at the same time carried presents of twenty bars each, for Mr. de Sylva to transmit to Jalorem and Bellchore, kings of Canabac, and Matchore and Niobana,

1793.
Tuesday, Nov. 19.

the cutter, and getting her ready for sea. Sick and lame as before.

Wednes. 20th.

Employed as yesterday, making rope for the cutter, and overhauling and mending her sails. Same sick and lame.

Thursd. 21st.

Same employment, sick and lame. A canoe arrived from Bissao to cut timber. An instance occurred to-day of imbecility of mind, in one of the colonists, that, accustomed as I have been to observe repeated proofs of it in them all, perfectly astonished me. We have many half, and quarter, minute sand glasses, by which to heave the log, for the purpose of keeping the vessel's way, and ascertaining its position. Most of these are damaged by the rain and will not run. I was therefore obliged to open them, dry the sand, and, when replaced, ascertain the number of seconds that each would run. My watch had no second hand, neither had any other on the island, but I thought this might be done by means of the vibration of a pendulum, which, when fixed, Dowlah was desired to count out loud, while I watched the running of the sand. He went on to eleven, and there stopped. I was surprised, but desired him to begin again. He again counted to eleven, and stopped. I asked him why he did not go on? He said he could not count any farther: "Try," said I, "after eleven comes twelve, then thirteen, fourteen and fifteen, which is as far as I want you to go, as it is only a quarter of a minute glass that I am trying." He began again, and again, but never could get beyond eleven. Count then to ten, said I, and then begin at one, and count up again:

kings of Ghinala, and to inform them that I was about leaving the island, but should return after the next rains. Also a letter addressed to the master of any English vessel which might arrive after our departure with succours; informing him of our having quitted the island.

Thursday, Nov. 21. 1793. this I could not get the idiot to do, he could not comprehend it, and all that I could get from him was, "that he once, in Scotland, got a little learning, but that he had forgot it all again, he did not know how it was, but so it was, that he had forgot it all again." Incredible as this may appear, every person on the island can vouch for it, and I was obliged to get another person to count the vibrations. This man is a Lascar, but has been, since his youth, in England.

Friday, 22d. This evening two boats arrived from Bissao, with a person called Capitano Fransisco Corea, deputed by the governor and Mr. de Sylva Cardoza, to purchase what goods he thinks proper, on their account. This capitano is a Mandingo, born in the neighbourhood of Geba, has been to Lisbon, frequently to the Cape de Verd Islands, and has for years commanded a small vessel on this coast; he speaks very good Portuguese, is dressed in the European fashion, has considerable property, reads and writes, can ascertain the latitude by the sun's altitude, and appears to be a very intelligent man.

Saturday, 23d. Employed loading the cutter, and selling goods to Corea. Sick as before. Last night Mr. Hood returned, and to-day the Jane pinnace went to Bulola. Sent presents by her to Woody Toorey the queen, informing her that I was going to leave the island now, but should return after the next rains. This day twelve months the Hankey left us.

Sunday, 24th. Sick and lame as before. Myself too ill to read prayers.

Monday, 25th. Employed shipping plantation tools of various kinds. The Portuguese grumetas stealing and hiding as many of them as they can, in the bushes. Watson and Peter stole my rum and got drunk. What rascals!

1793.
Tuesday, Nov. 26.
Getting the cutter ready for sea. Sick, Hood, Dowlah, Ashworth, and Watson, the latter in consequence of his drunkenness; lame Williams.

Wednes. 27th.
Same employment. Sick, Hood, Dowlah, and Ashworth; lame Williams.

Thursd. 28th.
Ready for sea. The Jane returned this evening, Sick, myself, Dowlah, and Ashworth; lame, Williams. As of our number (six), three are ill and one lame, Mr. Lawrence has lent me two grumetas to assist in navigating the cutter.

Friday, 29th.
Having sold to Corea all that he wanted, and shipped every thing else, except the eight cannon, two ploughs, and a great number of small leaden bars, which I was obliged to leave behind, I this morning at nine o'clock got under sail and quitted the island, leaving Corea with his grumetas and mine, unroofing the block-house, which I had sold him for £100 sterling. The large boat, the Perseverance, loaded with barrels of beef and pork, which the cutter could not contain, is towed a-stern; in her are also twenty goats; we have seven more in the cutter, some pigs, and some poultry; and Mr. Lawrence, with the William schooner, and Jane pinnace, accompany us. Mr. L. tells me that I may get rid of my plantation tools to advantage in the Rio Nunez, by exchanging them for ivory. I mean therefore to touch there, on my way to Sierra Leone, for that purpose.

I must confess that in going out of the harbour I feel a great reluctance at being obliged to abandon a spot which I have certainly very much improved; and to see all my exertions, my cares, and anxieties for the success of this infant colony entirely thrown away. But, at the same time, I do feel an honest consciousness that every thing that could be reasonably expected from me has been done, to secure, though without success, its establishment. Little wind. In the evening anchored off Tombaly point in thirteen fathoms. Sick, Dowlah, and Ashworth; lame Willams. Myself very far from well. *(1793. Friday, Nov. 29.)*

N.E. breeze morning. Calm evening; when we anchored off Canabac in 20 fathoms. Same sick and lame. Myself very unwell. *(Saturday, 30th.)*

N.E. breeze morning. Calm evening; when we anchored in seven fathoms, between the isles of Jamber and Mayo. Same sick, &c. *(Sunday, Dec. 1.)*

N.E. wind morning. Calm at noon. Anchored half a mile to the southward of Honey Isle. In the evening a S.W. wind, got under sail, and at dark anchored about 12 miles S.E. by E. of Honey Isle, in five fathoms. Sick, &c. as before. *(Monday, 2d.)*

Morning, light N.E. air. Weighed about high water, and stood to the S.E.; Myself too ill to stand in the sun to take an observation. At dark anchored in seven fathoms. No land in sight. Sick, &c. as before. *(Tuesday, 3rd.)*

Light N.E. breeze morning. S.W. air evening. At dark anchored in six fathoms, having just seen land bearing E.N.E.; breakers to the eastward and northward of us. Sick, &c. as before. The goats begin to die pretty fast, as they have but a scanty allowance of very poor grass. *(Wednes. 4th.)*

In the morning weighed with a light air; reefs, sand banks, and breakers, in almost every direction. Sometimes at anchor, and at others under weigh. Just before dark anchored in five fathoms, the rock of Alcatras being W. by N. five or six leagues. Sick, &c. as before. Myself much better. *(Thurs. 5th.)*

In the morning light airs. Got under weigh, and about two P.M. were obliged to anchor in three fathoms water, as there *(Friday, 6th.)*

1793.
Friday, Dec. 6.

was no wind, and the tide was setting us fast directly on breakers. An old rotten cable, by no means trust worthy, is the only thing now between us and perdition. It is true that if the cutter should be lost, we have a good stout boat, the Perseverance, by which we may reach the continent, but I doubt much whether any of us, in our present debilitated state, would survive the necessary exertions and exposure to the sun before we could reach it; yet these blockheads, so feelingly alive to a sense of danger on the island, seem perfectly contented with their present situation. Our security is in the gentleness of the winds, the smoothness of the waters, and the clearness of the weather, which is uncommonly fine. Alcatras N.W. Northerly about seven leagues. Sick, Hood, Dowlah, Ashworth. Lame, Williams. Myself getting better. Goats dying fast.

Saturday, 7th.

At seven in the morning got under weigh, which was as soon as the tide would permit us. A light northerly wind; run out south, and then steered S. E.; breakers on the larboard beam and bow as far as we can see. At nine P.M. anchored in ten fathoms. Sick, &c. as before.

Sunday, 8th.

At day-light got under weigh with a N. E. breeze, and at ten made the land about the mouth of the Rio Nunez. At dark anchored off its entrance.

Monday, 9th.

Calm. Taking advantage of the tide in the evening we anchored off the town of Kelibantoo in the Rio Nunez.

Tues. 10.
Wed. 11.

Tiding it up the river. In the evening of the 11th anchored off Mr. Walker's factory at Kacundy about 72 miles from the mouth of the river. The factory, as well as a slave ship, called the Sandown, saluted me with seven guns each: returned an equal number.

Thurs. 19th.

Having procured what ivory I could, and sold my large boat,

the Perseverance, to Mr. Walker, I quitted Kacundy on the 1793. evening of the 17th. Yesterday got aground and was left dry a Thurs. tide, and this evening cleared the mouth of the river in our Dec. 19. way to Sierra Leone. I never in my life saw any thing equal to the dew at Kacundy. In the night it penetrated two blankets under a canvas awning spread over my cot; and the foggy vapours were so thick in the morning that they were never dispersed, during my stay in the river, before 11 o'clock.

Fine weather, at sunset, Cape Verga E. by N. ¼ N. seven or Friday, eight leagues. 20th.

Light S. E. wind all day. At noon passed the Nancy from the Saturday, Isles de Loss bound to Barbadoes, Captain Moore was dead.* 21st.

---

* It may not be amiss to state here this man's conduct relative to me and my dispatches with which he was entrusted on the 15th of March last. The principal fact was related to me, soon after my arrival in England, by Mrs. Rowe, (the widow of the late Mr. Rowe, our surgeon) who was present at the time of the conversation in Moore's cabin, very ill of a fever, and not expected to live.

By those who have had perseverance enough to read this Journal through, it may be remembered that Mr. Rowe left the island of Bulama in the Hankey; from that ship he was landed at Bissao, where he shortly after died, and his widow was there, ill, on Moore's arrival. Moore, very humanely offered to give her a passage home in his cabin, if she had no objection to the going round by the West Indies; it was her only prospect of getting soon to Europe, she gratefully accepted his offer, and was embarked, very ill, just before he seized the schooner in Bissao Road, which brought him again to Bulama.

It is afterwards related that on my discovering his infamous proceedings towards some blacks, in a Portuguese canoe, whom he had seized and wounded, on his way from Bissao to Bulama, I had thought it necessary to examine, on oath, his mate and another white man, as to the mode in which those people were taken; Moore was present during the examination, and I assured him that I should transmit those affidavits to England: he seemed not to mind that, and observed that his mate had acted without his orders, and all the responsibility was therefore with him. Moore was never afterwards asked to my table.

The next day he sent for Peter Hayles and Johnson on board his ship, and had

1793. Saturday, Dec. 21. At sunset the north end of the Isle of Tamara, one of the Isles de Loss, S.E. four leagues.

them in his cabin, drinking grog, on one side of which Mrs. Rowe was lying in a cot, not expected to live. He led the conversation towards the colony, and said that Mr. Beaver was mad and would sacrifice them all; that if we were not cut off by the natives, which he was sure we shortly should be, we never could do any thing with our small number; and that by remaining with me they were only sacrificing themselves to my obstinacy. "Now," said he, "you might easily run away with his cutter, and leave him by himself, for I tell you he is a madman. You are both Americans, are you not?" "Yes." "And you can navigate a vessel, Hayles?" "Yes." "Well then, you have only to get some of his grumetas on board the cutter, and then run away with her. The grumetas you may sell to any slave ship down along the coast; you may then go to America and sell the cutter, nobody will know any thing about it, and your fortunes will be made." These men seemed to lend such an ear to his advice, that Mrs. Rowe had given me up for lost. She endeavoured by all the means in her power to make me acquainted with what was plotting against me; but Moore took care that she should not, for he would not suffer any person to go near her but himself, and though she frequently desired that a message might be sent to me, to say that she wanted to speak with me about her deceased husband's effects, yet this was always refused, though Moore said that he would take any message which she might have to send. She asked for a scrap of paper, that she might write me a line. This also was refused, and she says that she was so closely watched, unable to move, that no person on board was permitted to go near her, that could either give her paper, or ink, or deliver a message from her to me.

At the time of the above conversation Mrs. R. was so ill that it was thought impossible for her to recover, and probably they thought her insensible at the time: they however, notwithstanding, conversed in a kind of whisper. Moore never knew that she had heard a word; but that he thought it possible, is evident from his great care to prevent, on her getting a little better, any communication between her and myself. The above are, as nearly as I can relate, Mrs. Rowe's words, after having expressed her astonishment at seeing me in London, in June 1794. She is still living; and though an adherence to truth has obliged me to speak evil of her husband, yet justice requires that I should say she is as amiable as he was the reverse of it. So much for what immediately concerned me. Now for the dispatches. On my arrival in England I was astonished to learn that the trustees had never received those sent by Moore, which he had promised me to deliver to them in person; they contained, among other papers, copies of the above-mentioned affidavits, and a statement of

Light airs. At sun set saw the Bullam shore, the north side of the river Sierra Leone; and at 11 P.M. anchored in 6¼ fathoms of water. 1793. Sunday, Dec. 22.

At day-light got under weigh. Saw Cape Sierra Leone about 10, and at noon, it being calm, anchored off it. At 3 P.M. a light sea breeze springing up, we again got under sail, and soon after, a boat came alongside from Free Town, with the captain of the company's ship the Harpy, whom Governor Dawes, understanding from the William, which vessel had got in before me, that I was off, had kindly sent out, with refreshments for the sick, and seamen to assist us in getting to an anchorage, which we did just after sun set, in St. George's bay, in six fathoms water. I immediately went on shore to the Government-house, where I met with a most friendly and hospitable reception. Here I saw half a dozen white men, neat, clean, and well dressed, who had the appearance of English gentlemen, a sight that my eyes had not been accustomed to, for much more than a year. Monday, 23rd.

---

the case in the body of the letter. Now, I do not think it very uncharitable in me to suppose such a man capable of opening my packet, and, finding those statements, determining never to deliver it. And this I doubt not was the case, for after his death, and after my return to Europe, my packet made its appearance. It was delivered to Mr. Alderman Le Mesurier, at that time Lord Mayor, to whom it was addressed, *but without the affidavits*, with the following superscription in red ink:

" Captain Moore left this Packet at his lodgings in Liverpool, since which he died, and this was opened and forwarded to Mr. Higgin, 18, London-street."

Whether Moore thought that the advice he gave to Hayles and Johnson would inevitably insure my destruction, and so, by his keeping back my dispatches prevent his infamous conduct towards the Portuguese blacks from being known, it is impossible for me to say: he is now dead, and may he as readily receive from the Father of all mercies the forgiveness of his injuries towards them, as I most readily and sincerely forgive all his injuries towards me.

When hauling aft the main sheet, in coming to an anchor, though there was very little wind, the boom was carried away, and a stick of a proper size to make another was not to be procured here. I had only one seaman, and no chance of procuring more to navigate the cutter to England; besides, she wanted caulking, sails, and rigging, which, if to be had at all, would have cost nearly as much, at this place, as the cutter would be worth if she arrived in England; to which being added the risk of her being captured if we fell in with any of the enemy's cruizers on our passage, (for she was only a Gravesend boat of 34 tons, and six swivels,) the war having now been commenced nearly a year. These considerations united, determined me to sell the cutter and accept the very kind offer of Mr. Dawes, the governor, to take a passage with those persons who were with me, in the company's ship the Harpy, which he assured me would sail on the 1st of March next.

Although this delay of two months, before I could sail for Europe, was matter of much regret, yet, as some compensation, it gave me an opportunity of looking about me, and afforded me leisure to recruit my greatly exhausted strength, which indeed, I stood much in need of. A fever with which I was attacked, and the jaundice which I afterwards had, were soon got the better of by the care and attention of Dr. Winterbottom; and the kindness of every one was such as to demand my grateful acknowledgements.

It was the 20th, instead of the 1st of March, before the Harpy was ready to sail, when, having sold the cutter and her cargo for somewhat more than a thousand pounds, and having discharged Watson and Dowlah, who preferred remaining at Sierra Leone to returning to Europe, as well as Williams and the boy Ashworth, the former having entered on board one of the Sierra Leone Company's vessels, and the latter choosing to remain with Mr. Lawrence; Mr. Hood and myself embarked on board the Harpy, and arrived at Plymouth on the 17th of May, 1794; after an absence of little more than two years.

CHAPTER VI.

Apology for those parts of the preceding Journal which may appear either illegal, or harsh.—Objections foreseen and answered.—Difficulties which we had to overcome stated.—Natives' opinion of the European character.—Advantages resulting from our having remained upon the island.

HAVING brought my Journal to a conclusion, it may be necessary to say a few words on two or three points which might appear to require explanation, and to anticipate some objections which it is probable may be made to some of the transactions related therein.

<small>Motives for requiring the colonists' assent to be governed by that constitution which we had promised to set aside previous to our leaving England.</small> Had I foreseen the exact situation in which I was to be placed, on the departure of the Calypso from the island of Bulama, I am not sure that I should have sailed on the expedition; not that the prospect of the difficulties to be encountered would have deterred me; but, the persuasion that, if I remained behind after the sailing of that ship, the law had armed me with no power to act with energy, would, I trust, have deterred persons less scrupulously obedient to the laws of their country than myself, from voluntarily placing themselves in such a situation.

To begin by avowing that the first act of mine, in the direction of the reduced colony, was an illegal one, seems to argue a degree of moral turpitude, inconsistent with the virtues which such a situation required. But when it is proved that such a situation could not possibly have been foreseen, and that such an act arose from absolute and unconditional necessity, it will not, it is hoped, be condemned.

It has already been related that we were ignorant of having committed any misdemeanour, in drawing up our constitution of government, previous to the arrival of the ships at Gravesend; and, that in consequence of our memorial to government, we were permitted to proceed, on condition only of our "*having disclaimed and set aside a certain printed memorandum of agreement, and constitution of government, for a colony about to be established on or near the island of Bulam, &c.*" Now this was taking from us every semblance of command over the colonists; however, having gone so far, it was deemed, even under that disadvantage, better to proceed than to abandon the undertaking.

The subsequent events, which led to the abandoning of the island by the majority of the settlers, no one could possibly have foreseen; but they were all such as rendered a coercive power, on the part of the governor, more necessary than ever.

In this state of things, I had declared my resolution to remain on the island, which induced others to do the same; and although the form of electing me President of those members of the council who remained, was not yet gone through; yet, it was sufficiently understood that I was to direct, and that those who remained, did so on the faith of that opinion.

Now, before I had expressed my determination to remain on the island, I had well weighed the propriety of such a measure. I saw the dishonour of retreating, and the difficulties of remaining: and putting private considerations out of the question, which, if they had been suffered to have any influence at all, would have induced me to go away, I reasoned in a national point of view, thus:

In thus early and precipitately giving up the enterprise, do we not prove that we were not sincere in our professed motives for undertaking it, viz. to ascertain whether or not the tropical productions could be here raised by the hands of *free natives;* and whether by means of *culture* and *commerce* we might not introduce *civilization* among them? And would not such conduct be dishonourable to us as a body; and *therefore* dishonourable to the nation?

Did we not undertake this expedition by means of subscriptions, the greatest amount of which was from absentees, for which each subscriber was to receive a number of acres of land, proportionate to their several subscriptions; and did not this imply in them a confidence that we should at least make an attempt to secure to them the land for which they had so subscribed? and in resolving in a body not to make that attempt do we not deceive them and dishonour the nation?

Have we not had, by a handful of natives, our men slain, and women made captives; which must degrade us in the eyes, not only of the neighbouring African nations, but also in those of the Portuguese; and have we done any thing since to retrieve our character, to convince them both of our integrity and firmness, of our moderation and fortitude? and will not our determining in a body to quit the island, with the present impressions against us, bring dishonour on the nation?

Have we yet met with more than *one* serious misfortune? and although some difficulties stare us in the face, is it not disgraceful to us, as Englishmen, to turn our heads from them and fly? and will not such conduct bring dishonour on the nation?

To all these questions there could be but one answer—Yes.

I therefore determined to stay; but how? To be the nominal chief of a colony, without power, without authority? No.

To return I thought dishonourable to my country, to remain I thought essential to that honour. But I had no power from government; and it had declared that the settlers had no authority to invest me with any. What was to be done? I did what I thought that government would have authorised me to do, if it could possibly have foreseen my situation; and what my peculiar situation will, I hope, justify me in declaring.

I refused to take charge of the colony, until the assembled colonists had *agreed to be governed by that constitution which we had disclaimed previous to our sailing from England*; and which they did on the morning of the 20th July, 1792, before I read to them my new regulations.

This previous condition, in my then situation, was absolutely necessary; for although I knew that the people whom I had undertaken to direct were to be managed more by example than power, yet there were some among them, though few, who could be kept in order only from an idea of my possessing the latter: and though it was in idea only, for I certainly had none *legally*, I had, however the name of it, and the *name* only goes much farther than many people are aware of.

Trivial as such an assent, on the part of the colonists, may appear to those who were never placed in similar circumstances, it was to me of the utmost importance, as it invested me with very great authority; which probably will produce a smile, our numbers and situation being considered; when I say that by the third article in the chapter on the executive power, it made me " *commander in chief of the military force by sea and land; and invested me with all the powers incident to a captain general and commander in chief, and high admiral;*" and by the eighth article of the same chapter, authorised me "*to act without the consent of the other members of the council, taking the responsibility upon myself;*" and by the third article of the fifth chapter on the public defence, authorised me " by beating to arms" *to proclaim martial law.** Now although this authority was in name only, yet, as before observed, there is a great deal in the *name* without the *thing*.

I trust that, every thing considered, what I have already advanced will justify me in the first step which I took. Confident that that power was never used but for the benefit of the community, and the honour of my country, I have endeavoured not to justify its exercise, but its assumption.

Measures apparently harsh justified. From Mr. Rowe's two letters, which appear in the body of my Journal, it may be supposed that my conduct towards him was harsh and severe; however, I consider my observations on them at the time, and the notes accompanying them, as a sufficient justification of myself; I shall only here observe that it is scarcely possible for one man to have shown towards another more forbearance than I did towards him. With respect to the punishment of the grumetas, which, when necessary, was never trifling, I shall say a few words. These did not take place till after we had been long upon the island, when most of our numbers had been swept away by death; the few survivors whom they were accustomed to see near, were not of that description, nor in that situation in which they had been accustomed to see white men; and their frequent intercourse and individual characters, tended

---

* Appendix, No. 2.

much to lessen that idea of superiority with which they had hitherto been accustomed to behold Europeans; to keep up that superiority was of the utmost importance, in which indeed we succeeded beyond what could have been expected.

Banishment was, for some time, the only punishment for their offences, and this was to them a serious one; as it cut off from them all chance of procuring those European articles which had been the chief inducement of their coming to the island. To this punishment I could have wished at all times to adhere; but when, from mortality and sickness, we were so reduced, as to embolden them to lift a hand against a sentinel, and to plunder my store-rooms, corporal punishment became necessary; further forbearance had been weakness, and might have led to the most fatal consequences; and this punishment, to be useful, must be severe. Yet on no one occasion whatever did I punish a grumeta *without having first held a palaver* with the rest of them*; who on every occasion acknowledged that " *I had got the reason,*" and acquiesced in the propriety of the punishment; and this acknowledgment would not have been made, if it had not really been their opinion. If too it be considered that the men of the various tribes whom I employed upon the island were, many of them, the most vicious of their country, it is, I think, rather matter of astonishment that they were punished so seldom, than matter of blame, that they were punished at all.

* A palaver in this case, is something like a trial. Every body being assembled, the complainant states his case, to which the accused replies, and every one present, that chuses so to do, may speak on the merits of the case; after which they consult among themselves, and then declare their opinion, by saying who " *has got the reason,*" which, if in favour of the defendant, is a complete acquittal.

Be that as it may, they were never punished but for crimes which, if passed unnoticed, threatened our very existence.

The best proof, however, of their opinion is, that most of them returned to me several times, and that to the last day of my remaining upon the island of Bulama, I possessed the good will of all the neighbouring nations. "*The white man of Bulama can't do bad,*" was to the last acknowledged by them all; and they at all times came to me without suspicion or fear. Indeed, the good opinion of the natives was so essential, not only to our security now, but to the success of the undertaking hereafter, that I would have borne any thing consistent with dignity and prudence, rather than take those measures which might tend to estrange their good will; but here, as elsewhere, respect will not attach to indecision and weakness: to secure that, required conduct prompt, decisive, and bold, provided only that it were just.

Reasons for building the block-house on a hill which was difficult to be cleared;

The hill, on which the block-house was built, was, as it is remarked in the Journal, more difficult to clear, from the uncommon quantity and size of the timber which grew on it, than the adjoining lands; and this observation may induce some to suppose that we should have acted more wisely, if we had placed it on that ground which was least difficult to be cleared. Had we had in view solely the construction of a house of residence, this supposition would have been unquestionably true; but as we were to consider security, convenience for commerce, and, above all, health, the spot we fixed upon united in an eminent degree all these requisites, although it was the most difficult to clear of any land, which we had seen; but we had difficulties to encounter, and if we once began to give way to them, there was no saying where we should stop.

It may be thought too, perhaps, that the scale of this building was too great for our strength, and that much time was thrown away, and much labour lost, in constructing an edifice so disproportionate to our numbers. To this I reply, that the plan was not disproportionate to our numbers when first it was adopted, and that in consequence of the great diminution of our numbers by death, I did reduce the front of the building 64 feet, that is more than one third; as it was intended at first to have been 180 feet in front, which was afterwards reduced to 116. If it appear, thus diminished, larger than was necessary, it must be recollected that it was of the utmost importance to have it as large as we had strength to make it, on account of the health of those who were to inhabit it; which it was thought more likely for them to enjoy in a large open space, than in a very contracted one; and the outer logging being once finished, we were safe from any attack from the natives, and might finish the inside at our leisure. Moreover, I clearly saw that we could not spread and occupy the country before we had a reinforcement of our numbers; and it was conceived to be of the utmost importance that they, on their arrival, should find shelter ready for them, from the want of which we had already suffered so severely. The block-house therefore was not built as a mere temporary habitation, to answer our purpose for one rainy season only; but as a permanent building, which I hoped to see surrounded by a fort, and which might afterwards have been converted into very useful store-houses. The labour was our's, and I saw not how to give it a more beneficial direction than to the comfort and protection of those who might hereafter arrive.

Another objection may be made to our building at all, since it appears that when speaking of the Bijugas they are always

The Bijugas though spoken of always as enemies, in the Journal, not to be considered so absolutely, but relatively.

considered as enemies. This may appear strange after we had purchased the island from, and entered into a treaty with, them; and may lead to a conclusion that it will never be safe to make an establishment in such a neighbourhood. This would, however, be a mistake. Although the Bijugas were our friends by treaty, yet they are never to be trusted when they can gain any thing by hostility. They supposed our wealth immense; and would therefore never have hesitated at the means, if they had seen any probability, of getting possession of it. This nation, besides, is always at war with its neighbours, that is, they are at all times armed; and they always seize persons and goods which they may accidentally meet with, whenever they conceive themselves to be the strongest party. They are the *Algerines* of that country—robbers by profession.

After our treaty with them, they would not, I dare say, have ever viewed us with hostile eyes, unless for the sake of plunder. Had we not been possessed of wealth, great in their imagination, an attack need not have been dreaded from them; but, as it was, an attack was certain, whenever they saw the probability of its being successful.

Suppose half a dozen strangers should encamp on a plain in any nation in Europe, and it was generally known that these strangers had a great number of casks and bales filled with money; would they not run a great risk of being attacked in the night by robbers, with a view to plunder them of their wealth. The desire of killing these strangers would not produce the attack? but the desire of possessing their wealth would, and the consequence necessarily must be that the attackers kill those who stand in their way. Thus it was with us. We were the strangers possessing the wealth, and surrounded by robbers. But as we were enabled, with such a small number, to convince them that such an attempt would have been fruitless, there can be no difficulty in a larger number of settlers being always able, with common prudence, to cause themselves to be held in respect; and therefore there can be no objection, on that score, to the making the establishment.

I think it will be granted that I undertook the direction of the colony under peculiar disadvantages: *Peculiar disadvantages under which the direction of the colony was assumed.*

1st. In the only act of hostility which had taken place between the natives and settlers, the advantage remained with the former. They had the courage to attack them, when, in spirits, healthy and vigorous, their numbers doubled those who now remained on the island; and in this attack they not only killed, wounded, or made prisoners, all whom they saw, amounting to no less than seventeen; but carried in triumph to their island sixty stand of our arms. Their success, on this occasion, would have somewhat staggered their faith, one would suppose, in one article of their creed, that is, "*that all white man witch.*" However, be that as it may, it must have greatly lowered us in their eyes, with respect both to courage and prudence. And this disadvantageous impression was made upon the most savage, restless, and warlike, of all the surrounding nations. But it was not of importance only, inasmuch as it affected the opinions of the native nations with respect to *us,* but also as it affected our opinion with respect to *them:* and it had such an effect on the minds of the colonists, that they never recovered from their terror of the Bijugas. *Advantage obtained over us by the natives in arms.*

The next disadvantage was the complete setting in of the rains by that time. The crown of a hill, opposite to the ship, was fixed upon for the place of our destined habitation, this was *Rains set in.*

covered with a thick forest, which must be levelled with the ground, and then shaped into a fortress, ere we could hope for either shelter or security. This, even in the dry season, would have been a task; in the wet season, it was a severe one.

Diminution of our number. The third disadvantage was the great subtraction of our strength, which, from what has just been said, required increase, instead of diminution, to make us respected; it had also the effect of increasing our labour in the same proportion as it diminished our number.

Fever. The fourth was the fever having made its appearance among us; and the

Despondency. Fifth was the general depression and despondency produced by their united effects.

All these merely accidental. Now all these disadvantages were merely accidental, and by no means necessarily connected with our undertaking, which, though not *then*, certainly *hereafter*, may be easily avoided. If therefore, we surmount these, does it not afford rational ground to suppose that our undertaking was practicable? I think it does.

The Africans' opinion of the character of white men. It has frequently been remarked that the Africans consider " *all white man witch*," they also believe that " *all white man rogue.*" There is no species of cheating, of deceit, or of treachery, of which they did not think a white man capable, nay, they even thought those the predominant traits of his character; and, when we consider that those Europeans with whom they had hitherto had any intercourse, were probably among the lowest and basest of their colour, this ought not so much to surprize us. Whether the English had any reasonable hope to be excluded from these unfavourable impressions, the reader will be enabled to judge from the following circumstances:

The only Englishman, that is, the only white man of that nation, who appears to have been among these islands, and known to the surrounding nations, was one Birchall, who undertook to be the interpreter between the Papels and us on our arrival at Bissao; and this was the only white man who had ever been, prior to myself, on the island of Canabac. It is not probable, nay, it is not possible, that a man in his situation and employment could have very correct notions of moral rectitude, nor any of those feelings which soften down and humanize the character. This man was the master of a small trading sloop, belonging to the Bananas, and was employed among the neighbouring rivers and islands in procuring slaves for his owner. He had just knowledge enough to write and keep his own accounts; and this degree of knowledge, so low among us, as scarcely to raise a man above the brute creation, was here sufficient to make him pass for "a witch." However, it is not likely that such a man would be very nice or delicate in his trading with the natives; on the contrary, it is more probable that in all his dealings with them he would display much cunning and little probity: that he was not over burthened with the latter, will, I think, appear from what follows:

At Bissao he had been entrusted by a merchant with a certain slave, whom he was to deliver to Jalorem, one of the kings of Canabac. He went to Canabac to trade, but said not a word about the slave, and carried him away with him to the Bananas, where he turned his value to his own account: returning to this neighbourhood he touched again at Jalorem's port. The Bijuga king had by this time been made acquainted with the trick which Birchall had played him; and, when he had him in his power, on shore, he asked him for the slave which he had undertaken to bring from Bissao for him; Birchall denied having received one; but the king persisted that he had, and told him that if he did not immediately pay him, in goods, the value of a prime slave, he would seize his vessel. Birchall sent orders on board not to send the goods on shore, but to get under sail and proceed to Bissao, trusting to the Portuguese merchants to procure his release. However Jalorem, observing the vessel preparing to quit his port, tied Birchall to a tree, and told him that the moment his vessel quitted the port, without having paid him his goods, that moment should be the last of his life. Birchall was therefore glad to stop his vessel and comply with the king's demands.

Birchall's conduct, on this occasion, would have justified Jalorem, (I mean by what is termed " *country law,*") in " *cutting off*" his vessel; that is, *in seizing it by force, putting to death all those who oppose, and selling as slaves all those who surrender.* Such was my worthy predecessor on the island of Canabac.

Now, I have not related this story with a view of hurting this Birchall, nor of ruining his character; neither the one nor the other will take place; and if he should ever see this account, he will probably laugh, and think me an ignorant fellow, for expressing either indignation or astonishment at it; and say that there is nothing more common in that part of the world. All this I know to be the truth; and therefore have related it, not, I again say, to hurt the feelings of this man, that is impossible; but to convey, to the mere European, some idea of what is there called " *country fashion,*" and " *country law;*" and to enable him to form some notion of the kind of opinion which the Africans must form of us, when conduct, like that described above, is common among most of those white people who visit them. I need not mention the various modes which Europeans also take to over-reach them in trade, by light weights, short measure, and diminished capacity, &c. all of which are now as well known to the natives as to us; and therefore, as before observed, they consider us as a compound of treachery and deceit. There is nothing degrading, nothing base, nothing infamous, but what they consider to form part of the white character.

Let us, however, now inquire what advantages have been derived from our efforts to keep possession of the island. If all which were expected, have not resulted therefrom, the fault is not with me; neither is it with the trustees who remained in England: the failure must be attributed, in some measure, to a variety of untoward circumstances, many of which were beyond the power of human controul; and though we did not succeed to the utmost extent of our wishes, yet, in my humble opinion, we so far did succeed as *to establish the practicability of our plan*; and this, of itself, is of so much importance, as to induce me to hope that our labour has not been uselessly employed; nor our time altogether thrown away.* Another im-

_{Advantages derived from our remaining on the island.}

---

* Although I am not an advocate for Rousseau's mode of educating his Emilius, yet I cannot help thinking that the more practical knowledge one can acquire, the better: it makes a man acquainted with his own resources, and a less dependent being. I therefore, so far as relates to myself only, consider my time on the island of Bulama, (independent of the motives which led me to, or kept me there,) instead of being thrown away, as the best spent period of my life; for I was so completely thrown upon myself, as to be obliged to rely more upon my own individual resources and exertions, than I otherwise, probably, ever should have done.

For one year of that time I had not an individual to converse with; and lived almost as much the life of a hermit, as if there had not been another human being upon the island. It is true that I set every body to work, and directed them what to do, but there our intercourse ceased: their work done, the grumetas retired to their houses, the settlers to their rooms, except at the latter part of my stay upon the island, when, in

Unfavourable opinion of the natives changed in our favour.

portant point gained was the favourable alteration which we were enabled to make in the minds of the natives relative to the character of white people.

order to keep up for Mr. Hood, the only surviving subscriber, some degree of respect, which he appeared to me to be fast losing, I always had him to dinner with me, which occupied the hour between one and two.

Besides, during the seventeen months that I remained on the island, I had occasion, and indeed was obliged, to practise more occupations and professions, (though I never before had a tool of any kind in my hand,) than would otherwise have ever been the case, in the whole course of my life. To wit:

1st. Carpenter.—In all its branches, from that of making a broom-stick, to that of building a house.

2d. Joiner.—In such works as making chairs, tables, stools, shelves, and cupboards, &c.

3d. Sawyer.—Which I found the most difficult of the whole.

4th. Brick-maker.

5th. Tanner.—When I left the island I had just finished tanning a number of goat skins, for the bottoms of a set of chairs.

6th. Thatcher.

7th. Chandler.—I made candles, both dips and moulds.

8th. Rope-maker.—I was obliged to make a great deal of rope before I could leave the island with the cutter.

9th. Sail-maker.

10th. Caulker.

11th. Plasterer.

12th. Carcase butcher.—It more than once fell to my lot to skin and cut up a bullock, which had been killed for the colonists.

Among those which are dignified by the name of professions may be reckoned,

1st. Engineer.—If the fixing upon the ground, and tracing the lines of a square fort, with a bastion at each angle, will confer it.

2d. Architect.—Insomuch as the drawing the plan, elevation, and section of the block-house, ere it was commenced, can entitle me to it.

3d. Surveyor.

4th. Apothecary.—With this difference, in practice, that I never *made a bill*. Indeed that practice was confined to one disease only, fever. To each man that came to me with it, I gave four grains of tartar emetic, or fifteen of ipecacuanha, which having operated, he had as much bark

By a conduct dissimilar, I trust, in every respect from that of the white men with whom the neighbouring natives had hitherto held any communication, we soon shook this unfavourable opinion; and by a continuance of the same conduct converted it, ere long, into confidence, esteem, and respect; and left them at last with such favourable impressions towards Europeans in general, *but towards Englishmen in particular,* as will I doubt not, be long remembered; and greatly tend to facilitate any future attempt to make an establishment in their country.

The first great dissimilarity between our conduct, and those of the Europeans whom they had been accustomed to see, and which could not fail to strike them with astonishment, was our refusal to purchase slaves. This they could not account for; neither were they altogether pleased with it at first; for, when negociating with Niobana for the purchase of the Biafara territory, he said that "*it was very hard that we would not buy his slaves.*" Having made him comprehend that our intention was rather to cultivate the earth, than to trade; but that we should,

in Port wine, as he could swallow, while the fit was not on him; to women and children the dose was less, in proportion to their strength and constitution. This must be understood as being done after the surgeon had left us only, and this was the usmost extent of my sins in this profession.

I might greatly increase both lists were it necessary. Some of the employments were not, certainly, very dignified; however, to make amends, I was honoured with very fine, nay magnificent, titles. The Portuguese always called me governor; the Bijugas capitano; but all the other nations king, (rey.) If, therefore, I felt humbled by the low employment of stripping a bullock of its hide, I might the next hour not only recover my importance, but feel more exalted than I had before felt humbled, by being accosted with the title of rey. And again, if the title of king should turn my head with vanity and pride, I might the next day be brought to a more just estimation of my consequence by being obliged to cook for the colonists.

notwithstanding, at all times trade with him for wax, ivory, cloths, &c.; in short, that we would buy every thing which he had to sell, except only slaves, whom he could always dispose of as he had been accustomed to do heretofore, he appeared satisfied; although he could not comprehend why we would not purchase the one, nor why we cultivated the other.

However, in all our dealings with the Bijugas and Biafaras, (and they never paid us a visit without bringing something to dispose of,) as well as with the numerous canoes which stopped at Bulama, which they never did but with a view to trade, and which were navigated by grumetas of all the various surrounding tribes, our conduct was so open, so honest, so totally destitute of fraud and chicane, such a contrast to what they expected, as to make an immediate and strong impression, in our favour, on the minds of them all; which they failed not to communicate to their countrymen, who considered us as most extraordinary characters, being the first white men they had ever heard of "*who could not do bad.*" Instead of going in search of trade, like other whites, and displaying an eagerness to purchase every thing within our reach, we remained quietly on our island; where, at the same time we always bought whatever they brought us for sale, but without shewing the least inclination to over-reach them in the exchange.

The beneficial effects of this conduct were very soon felt, without the aid of which, indeed, we should not have been able to have kept possession of the island for the last twelve months; but from no circumstance did we derive so much benefit as from our not dealing in slaves. The African tribes put no more faith in one another, than they do in Europeans, where a power over their persons is in question; the temptation to abuse it by selling them for slaves, is too great ever to be risked. Hence they go always armed, and never voluntarily place themselves in the power of a neighbouring, though friendly, tribe.

But we purchased not slaves, neither sold we any, nor was any man permitted to be considered in that light on the island. Here then was removed, at once, all cause of fear and distrust, relative to their personal security, by coming to Bulama. Such new doctrine, such novel conduct, required however some little time firmly to establish its truth and sincerity; and it was more than two months before I could get a single grumeta to trust himself among so many white strangers. By that time however Mr. De Sylva Cordoza had procured me a couple, who remained with me a little more than three weeks, when taking the opportunity of that gentleman's coming to Bulama, they both left me when he returned. Their labour was never more wanted than at that time. The Hankey was about to depart; the colonists exceedingly dispirited; some of them leaving us; and most of the remainder sick. However, I did not hesitate an instant in assenting to their departure; and, paying them their wages, I made to each of them at the same time a present: and by pursuing this conduct I never (from a short time after the Hankey's departure) wanted grumetas. These two had remained with us long enough to be able to give to their countrymen a more detailed account of us and our conduct, than they had hitherto received; and this was so favourable as to induce others to put the same trust in us which they had done; when at length, from repeated trials of this kind, being convinced that we neither bought nor sold slaves, that every man was paid for the full value of his labour, and suffered to depart whenever he chose,* they placed in me such faith as, I believe, they never did before in any white man. They came to me *unarmed*, and remained weeks and months at a time on the island, without the least suspicion† of my ever intending them evil: and this confidence was not placed in me by one nation only, but by every one that had heard of "*the white man of Bulama;*" for that was the name by which I was generally known among them, whether Manjack, Mandingo, or Papel, Bijuga, Biafara, or Naloo. They all put implicit confidence in me, and all equally acknowledged that "*the white man of Bulama can't do bad.*" Thus, by the negative merit of treating these people with common integrity, was I not only able to acquire their confidence, and by their labour to do almost all that was done upon the island, but also to overturn one of their strongest prejudices against us; and to convert their well-grounded suspicion of fraud and deceit in all Europeans, into esteem and respect for the character of a white man.

When I was obliged to abandon the island, we had cut down and burnt the trees of about fifty acres of ground, thirteen of which had the roots taken up, and were inclosed in three separate inclosures: we had a garden of half an acre, and a cattle and poultry yard of twice as much more, all inclosed with pales, each having a gate and a stile: we had a block-house of 115 feet square; two nests of grumetas' houses, each 34 feet by 21, and a good broad road leading to each; a well dug in the block-house, and a pond for fresh water dug in the field. Now by

* Except on one occasion (the 28th of July, 1793) for the reasons given in that day's Journal.

† Except that produced by Moore's conduct, mentioned in the Journal of the 23d, 25th, and 27th of February, 1793.

whose labour was all this done? Except the block-house, almost all by the grumetas; they alone at least cleared the ground, which was the most difficult and the hardest work. We had at that time in the garden many tropical fruits, esculent vegetables, and cotton trees; all of which appeared to be in their native soil, and thriving admirably. Now what is the result of all this? The result is that I HAVE PROVED THE PRACTICABILITY OF OUR PLAN.

What did we propose to ascertain?

First—Whether we could cultivate the tropical productions on the Island of Bulama and the adjacent shores?

Second—Whether we could do so by the means of *free natives?*

Third—Whether by *cultivation* and *commerce* we might not introduce among them *civilization?*

The first of these queries is proved beyond a doubt, not only by what I cultivated on the island; but from all tropical productions growing wild on it, or in its vicinity.

Now then for the second, which is by far the most important. It will appear by the list of grumetas in the Appendix * that in about one year I employed on the island 196 of them. These grumetas were not all of one nation; neither were they only of two; but they were of three, of four, of five, and even of six,†

---

* No. 15.

† I regret much that I did not, when on the island, keep an account of the nations to which my several grumetas belonged, as, besides being more satisfactory to the reader, it would have enabled us to form some little notion of their national character. However, by far the greatest number were Papels and Manjacks; about a dozen of the whole number were Biafaras, a few Balantees, four or five were Naloos, but only two Bijugas. I had Biafara visitors frequently, and with them sometimes came Mandingos, but I never had a Mandingo grumeta, though they have frequently come to the

and they were all free. Had it been prudent, with my reduced force, to have employed more, I could easily at all times have doubled or trebled their numbers. These grumetas cleared all the ground that was cleared, they made the inclosures, and worked hard and willingly, generally speaking, at whatever task was assigned to them. I have no hesitation therefore in declaring *that the second also is proved:* and *the third will necessarily follow*—for COMMERCE will follow CULTIVATION, and CIVILIZATION will result from them both.

Conclusion. When the peculiar disadvantages enumerated in the former part of this chapter, are added to those arising from the general character of the settlers, and of some of the grumetas, as well as from the smallness of our force for the last year, our having been able to command respect, and to accomplish what we did, must remove from the mind, I think, of all unbiassed persons, every doubt as to the practicability of accomplishing all which we had promised ourselves, had the expedition been planned with more wisdom, or executed with more energy. And although we were obliged to quit the island at the moment when we had shelter and protection for more settlers, and fields ready for the plough, yet I trust that our labour has not been altogether fruitless, but that we have been paving the way for some more fortunate enterprize. And though in this undertaking our mortality has been great, nay dreadful indeed, yet have we the satisfaction to

island in that situation, in canoes belonging to Bissao. I sometimes also had visits from Bulola, a place about 70 miles up the Rio Grande, but in what nation to place its inhabitants I know not. They are I think a mixture of Biafaras, Naloos, and Mandingos; at least people of each of those nations reside at Bulola, and there is frequent intercourse by land between Kacundy on the Nunez, and Bulola on the Grande. Woody Toorey was at this time queen of Bulola; she often pressed me to come to her town, but I never was able to accomplish it.

say that no one ever fell by the hand of an enemy;* that we never had any quarrel with the natives; and that the English character which we found considered by them as sordid, base and cowardly, we left beloved, respected, and admired; yet its enmity was feared as much as its friendship was courted. And although we have not been hitherto able to reap the fruit of our labour, I hope that the day is not far distant, when some enlarged and liberal plan will be adopted to cultivate the western coast of Africa, without interfering with the freedom of its natives. Such a plan, pursued with a wise policy,† is the surest way of intro-

---

* The reader will remember that we had not arrived when the Calypso's people were attacked by the natives.

† Perhaps it may be said that the Sierra Leone company's establishment is such a one as I seem here to require; but I say No. I deny its liberality, and I deny the wisdom of its policy. I have a very great respect for those gentlemen who have been the most active in establishing and directing the concerns of that company; their conduct has been exceedingly disinterested, and the object of it most praiseworthy and noble; but I cannot say as much for the wisdom of their measures; and if I were asked what, more than any thing else, has retarded the making establishments for the purpose of cultivation on the western coast of Africa, I should, without any hesitation, say the Bulama expedition, and the Sierra Leone company. But the mischief done by the former is nothing to that of the latter. The former was a little insignificant attempt, by a few individuals, with very confined funds; which from excessive folly, was soon given up, and which would not have proved prejudicial to the Africans, in whose favour it was undertaken, had it not been for the great mortality which took place in that island, and on board the Hankey after her departure from it; and which was in this country, by those who were inimical to the success of our enterprise, called the plague, or Bulama fever; and such serious representations were made on the subject as produced an order from the Privy Council to sink that ship, though, on further inquiry, it was not carried into effect, and the ship was restored to its owners, after their having sustained very considerable loss by the industry with which certain interested people kept up the report of the malignity of the distemper, which, it was said, that ship brought home, and for which there was not a shadow of foundation. But this report was not easily forgotten; and if one talked of settlements on the western coast of Africa, he was immediately put in mind of the Bulama fever

ducing civilization, and at the same time of abolishing slavery; and if the preceding account shall in the smallest degree lead to

and the ship Hankey. Thus what was really intended to benefit the Africans, has hitherto only been of disservice to them: so much for Bulama. But how shall we estimate the extent of the mischief done to the African cause by the Sierra Leone company? Here is a great company, with a very large capital, directed by members of the legislature, and persons of great commercial concerns and influence, from whom much might be expected: for, with their wealth, their knowledge, and their means, what might not be hoped, if the thing attempted be practicable? But if, with all these advantages, they completely fail, who can expect hereafter to succeed? Nay, who will make the attempt? It is in this point of view that I consider the Sierra Leone company as having done infinitely more mischief than good to the cause which they have so disinterestedly undertaken.

Their whole conduct has been so absurd, as to strike every person, except those concerned, at first sight; nay I could not have believed it, if I had not been a witness to it myself: and I said in the year 1794, (when I believe they had expended about £80,000, if I am wrong in this sum, there are many able, and I dare say willing, to put me right) that as long as they pursued their then system, every farthing which they expended was completely thrown away. I know not whether the same system be still pursued; but this I know, that if it is, every shilling laid out by them might as well have been thrown into the sea; and I boldly aver that if they ever do succeed, it will be by means quite different from those, at that time, adopted. I consider the abolition of slavery, and the introduction of letters and religion to the Africans, to be the chief objects of that company; without, at the same time, losing sight of the advantages to be derived from cultivation and commerce. The objects are amiable and interesting, and deserve the attention of all great and good men. How lamentable then must it be, to see such advantages, as this company has possessed for more than ten years, made not the least use of, nay, rather tending to retard, than hasten, the objects of their wishes. I hesitate not to say that they might by this time, by pursuing proper measures, have had as much fertile land in Africa as they could possibly occupy; that they might have had almost innumerable, populous, and well cultivated plantations; on all of which the people should have been much further advanced towards civilization than they are at present; and that they should have had better notions of religion; (as to letters, as far as mere reading and writing goes, probably much more could not have been done) and they should now have annually imported into this kingdom, African produce, to the full amount of one million sterling. I say all this might have been done, and I think I should have no difficulty in proving it. Now,

such a measure, I shall be amply repaid for all the time and trouble I have expended, and all the difficulties I have encountered.

instead of all this what is the present situation of the company? Having spent an immense capital, they possess a steril territory; to keep possession of which they are obliged to have recourse to parliament for pecuniary aid; and they are neither beloved nor respected by the natives. But what could they ever have expected from cultivation? I will not say that they have fixed upon *as bad* a spot for that purpose as could have been found for 100 leagues on either side of them, but I say that they have fixed upon *the worst*. On the Bullam shore the soil is very poor, but on the Sierra Leone side there is scarcely any soil at all; and when they make a hogshead of sugar there, I will engage to do the same at Charing Cross. If commerce were one of their principal objects, they have chosen a tolerable good situation, with an excellent port.

I trust that from the foregoing observations I shall not be considered as an enemy to the Sierra Leone company, or the cause which they have espoused. So far as the sacrifice of my own individual comforts, and even interest, may tend to prove me in earnest, in any undertaking, so far I hope that my conduct at Bulama will entitle me to be credited, when I say that no person in the world more sincerely wishes them success than myself; but it is the very sincerity of that wish which has induced me to write this note. More than two years ago I expressed the same sentiment to Lord Hobart and to Mr. Sullivan, and it cannot be conceived that I should so far commit myself, as to state what I have done above, unless I felt a perfect conviction of its truth. I may be wrong, for who is free from misconception and error? If so, it is very easy to set me right; and I shall rejoice to see that my opinions are ill founded. But until that is done I must be permitted to consider the *system pursued by the Sierra Leone company, as tending rather to retard, than advance, the civilization of the Africans, or their emancipation from slavery.

* See this subject pursued, Chap. XI.

CHAPTER VII.

Recapitulation of the principal causes of our failure—none of which can be attributed either to the difficulty or impracticability of the Enterprise itself.

To a person who has perused the foregoing pages much need not be said upon this subject; for, after such a series of error, of folly, and of imbecility, success, rather than failure, must have produced astonishment.

I shall however endeavour to collect into one point of view the principal causes of our miscarriage, and this with a view of proving that our want of success was *not owing to the impracticability, or difficulty, of the enterprise*, but to the measures pursued by its proposers and conductors.

<small>Causes of failure originating in Europe.</small>

<small>The season too far advanced when the enterprise was first determined upon.</small>

In the 1st place the season was too far advanced when our proposals were first published; (the 9th of Nov. 1791) for if none of those unforeseen delays, which afterwards took place, had happened, we should not have been able to have taken possession of the island more than two months earlier than we actually did; which would not have been many days prior to the commencement of the rainy season; whereas the best time to have arrived at the island would have been about the middle of November, when we should have had certainly more than six months dry weather, in which to have erected habitations and cleared ground.

The next wrong step was the increasing of the number of the members of the committee, or council, to conduct the enterprize; for though I do not mean to say that any individual who was afterwards added to it was the principal cause of our failure, and much less do I mean to aver that any one of the six original proposers of the undertaking discovered either energy or talents sufficient to secure its success, yet, increasing their numbers, without adding any thing to their ability, was increasing the means, and the probability of weak measures and disunited counsels. Moreover, those who were afterwards added to it did not carry with them exactly the same views and intentions which governed the first proposers. I think therefore that it would have been much better to have left the management of the undertaking to the latter only; and the probability of succeeding would have been increased had they been reduced to three; and much more so, had one person only had the direction: for, I am fully convinced that in enterprizes of this kind the direction should be left to one. He should have full power; and should be responsible for the use of it. *Increasing the number of the council.*

The next wrong measure was the sailing without a charter. It has been seen that unless we had waited another year, there was not time to procure one; and as a respectful representation of our views and intentions had been made to his Majesty's ministers, it was thought that no objection would have been taken to our framing certain rules and regulations for our own governance, until that desirable object could be obtained; neither did we know, until the ships were detained at Gravesend, by an order from the secretary of state, that our conduct had been reprehensible in so doing. However, *Sailing without a charter.*

our disclaiming and setting aside that agreement, which contained those rules and regulations, was made the condition of our being permitted to sail. We were, therefore, reduced to the necessity of entirely giving up the enterprise, when ready to depart; or of undertaking it without having any legal authority over a class of men who certainly required some legal restraint. We had gone too far to recede, and therefore, under those disadvantages, sailed.

Not carrying out the frames of houses for shelter. The not carrying out with us the frame of one or more large houses, to shelter the people immediately on their arrival, was a fatal error. Had we arrived in the middle of the dry season, this, though at all times proper, would not have been so absolutely necessary; because, in a thickly wooded country, it is not very difficult to find shelter from the sun. To this omission I attribute much of our mortality. Had the frame of a house been carried out, it might have immediately been erected on a clear spot near the beach; and might in two or three days have been rendered sufficiently secure from any attack of the natives, by means of pallisadoes, and we should not in that case have been reduced to the necessity of constant and hard labour in the rains to erect a house, not only for shelter, but absolutely for our very existence; and the whole rainy season might have passed away, without our having been obliged to do more than, in the fine intervals, to clear some little plots of ground for plants and seeds: whereas the necessity of our labouring in the erection of a house for shelter and defence, lost to us the whole of that season for the purposes of cultivation.

General character of the colonists. Another cause of our failure must be sought for in the characters of the colonists, the conductors and the conducted. We had not been sufficiently scrupulous in the acceptation of those who offered themselves as public servants, or labourers; and who were after a certain time, to receive a grant of land and become settlers. In this case people are always liable to deception; for it is impossible to divine how men will turn out, before they have been tried; and though some of them did turn out very bad, yet there were others that proved themselves to be good, honest, and industrious men. Although the selection of public servants, therefore, might have been better, yet, it was by no means so prejudicial to the undertaking *as the general character of the majority of the subscribers themselves.*

Among them there were certainly some very respectable persons, some whose correct principles, and honourable sentiments, are not to be exceeded by any. But these were but a small portion when compared with the whole: and it must be kept in mind that something more than mere passive virtue, than mere negative merit, is required in those who are to direct such undertakings. It requires the constant exercise, and active exertion, of many manly virtues: and I fear that indolence was too predominant in the, otherwise, best regulated minds among us. On the contrary, those who were not so well disposed were ever restless and active, and the members of the council, particularly on board the Calypso, instead of at once boldly opposing this restless activity, or wisely turning, training, leading and directing it to some useful end, shrunk back with disgust from what appeared to them an Herculean task. They were seized with a kind of lethargy; and left to a few turbulent demagogues the power of ruining the colony.*

* When the terms of subscription were so very moderate, it is not to be wondered at, that in such a great city as London, some profligate and worthless characters were

Carrying out women and children. Women and children are ill calculated to struggle against the difficulties, which must necessarily be encountered, in first settling a new country: but, independent of every other consideration, the mere room which they occupied in the two ships operated perniciously towards our enterprize. Nothing is more necessary in a hot country, towards the preservation of health on board a ship, than plenty of room and the free circulation of air; now of the 269 persons which the two ships contained, 122 were women and children, who occupied full half the space, and whose useful labour could be considered as nothing. To this crowded state of the ships I think much sickness, and consequent mortality must be attributed.

The expenditure of the public money. The expenditure of the public money had been very injudicious: at least fifteen hundred pounds more than was necessary, had been expended in the first outfit. This sum would have been sufficient to have either purchased, or chartered, a small vessel that might have brought out a reinforcement, and some necessary articles, at the end of the second rainy season; and had such a vessel arrived before the latter end of November 1793, it would certainly have prevented the evacuation of the island at that time,* though it might

to be found among the subscribers; but I think we had more than one would have expected. One of those who remained after the Calypso's departure (I have nothing to do with names, the mentioning of which I have generally avoided, and he is now dead) had been guilty of wilfully setting fire to a house, of robbery, of murder, of forgery, and of incest—of all which I had full proofs after his death.

* A brig had been chartered by the trustees in London, early in the year, to bring out to us both settlers, and those articles which were most immediately wanted, but the war breaking out, this vessel was first detained for a convoy, afterwards obliged to put back from stormy and adverse winds, and then had a very tedious passage to Bissao, where she arrived, but without any settlers, about a fortnight after I had quitted the island of Bulama.

only have protracted it for a short period. The war, also, in which we were at that time engaged, must be considered from various reasons, which are too evident to require enumeration, as another cause of our failure. *War in Europe.*

The foregoing may be considered as the chief obstacles to our success, which originated in Europe; but these would not have entirely produced it, had not weakness unexampled, and absurdity unparalleled, directed the proceedings of that part of the community which was embarked on board of the Calypso— for to that ship only must be attributed most of our misfortunes. *After leaving England. Ill conduct of the Calypso.*

The separation of that ship from us, at an early period of the voyage, under circumstances peculiarly favourable for our keeping together, argued no very great attention to the general interest of our proceedings. This however would have had no other ill effect, than the anxiety it produced in our minds for the time, had that ship waited for us, according to agreement, at Teneriffe; but its sudden, abrupt, and unaccountable departure from that island, without having left for us a second rendezvous, or any intimation of their intended future proceedings, was the first of a series of inconsiderate, and almost incredibly absurd, measures, which terminated in the landing on, and taking possession of, the island of Bulama, without first having purchased it, or acquired even the consent or approbation of its owners; and which finally led to the slaughter of our men, and the leading captive our women and children by a savage people. *Separation of that ship. Its sudden departure from Teneriffe. Taking possession of the island, before it was purchased. Attack from the natives.*

The fatal measures which led to this event have already been related, its immediate operation towards the failure of the enterprise was by the delay which it created before we could commence our labours, ere which, the fever had made some havock; and the rains had completely set in; which produced the resolu- *Fever. Rains* tion of immediately abandoning the enterprise, by the major part of a disgusted, disappointed, and dispirited people.

<small>After the Calypso's departure.</small>
It remains now to point out the causes of the failure of that portion of the colonists who yet remained upon the island: and here it will be sufficient to mention that dreadful, that <small>Mortality.</small> melancholy mortality, which so soon swept away our numbers, and rendered us incapable of doing much more than merely keeping possession of the island, till the arrival of support from Europe: but there, a war was waging, which threatened to drive back, with rapid step, its astonished nations, to a state of barbarism worse than even that of the people by whom we were surrounded; and which, from its extent, and importance, left little room for us to expect either notice or succour; <small>And not receiving any succours.</small> and that little was frustrated by the person to whom I had committed the charge of my letters to the trustees, stating our situation; as he had thought proper never to deliver them.

Thus have I briefly recapitulated the principal causes of our failure,* none of which can be traced back either to the difficulty, or impracticability, of the undertaking itself; but are all discernible either in the errors committed in Europe, prior to our sailing, and which may hereafter be avoided, or to those committed by the people on board the Calypso, which cannot be exceeded. If, however, the survivors had received any assistance from Europe after the second rains, the colony would, notwithstanding these errors, have been preserved; and, I think I can confidently assert, that, had every person, who sailed in this expedition, carried with him only the same mind, and same

---

* Soon after my return to England in 1794, at the request of a general meeting, at the Mansion-house, I stated, for their information, my opinion of the causes of our failure; which is inserted, Appendix No. 16.

zeal for its success with myself, we should in the end have triumphed over them all; and that at this moment Great Britain would have been possessed of a rich, fertile, valuable, and extensive colony, on the western coast of Africa.

To endeavour to prove that such a colony may yet be acquired will be the object of the following pages.

CHAPTER VIII.

Geographical outline of that part of the African Coast and Continent which is comprised between the Rivers Gambia and Grande; with a brief notice of its southern Inhabitants, its Soil, and principal Animal and Vegetable Productions.

THAT part of the western coast of Africa, lying between the rivers Grande and Gambia, and comprized within the 11th and 13th degrees and 20th minute of north latitude, is not formed by the main land or continent, but by a long chain of low, and fertile, islands, separated from each other, and from the continent, by narrow, navigable, branches of the sea.*

On the northernmost of these islands is the Cape of St. Mary, which forms the southern headland to the entrance of the river Gambia; hence the coast runs nearly south, along five islands, for about 24 leagues, to Cape Roxo, whence it takes nearly an E.S.E. direction along four other islands, for about 45 leagues, when we arrive at the island of Bulama, situated at the mouth of the river Grande. Thus between the mouths of these two

* See a large map of Africa published by Arrowsmith in November 1802; but more particularly the large map at the end of Wadstrom's Essay on Colonization, and the Chart numbered 8 in the African Pilot published by Laurie and Whittle. As I have mentioned Mr. Wadstrom's map, I will take this opportunity of observing that he has, among other authorities, quoted me in that map, for some information relative to the Foulahs and Mandingoes. Now, whether what is there stated relative to them, be true or not, I am totally ignorant. He, therefore, must have acquired that information from some other person; and my name has been placed there by mistake.

rivers the sea coast is formed by ten islands in an extent of 69 leagues, or rather more than 200 geographical miles.

The continent between these two latitudes, is bounded on the north by the river Gambia, which is navigable by large vessels for near 80 leagues, and by small ones, to the falls of Barraconda, more than 300 miles from its mouth; the river Grande is its southern boundary, which is navigable by ships to Bulola 72 miles from its entrance; how much higher, by boats, is not exactly known:* the Gambia and high mountains are its eastern, and the islands before-mentioned its western, limit. Few countries of equal extent seem better adapted for commerce and for defence; three sides, and the largest part of the fourth, being embraced by the sea and two great rivers, and the remainder guarded by high mountains. Numerous rivers, rivulets, and creeks, dividing, intersecting, and watering its western part, and thus facilitating its communication and commerce, seem to point it out as a most eligible spot for European colonization.

To the southward of those *continental islands,* if I may be allowed the expression, there is a cluster of other islands, running in nearly a parallel direction, and separated from them by a channel, generally speaking, about five leagues in breadth: these last are called the Bijuga islands; and form, with the former, one immense harbour, from Cape Roxo to Bulama, of nearly 150 miles in length; but as I shall speak of the Bijuga islands, as well as of Bulama, under separate and distinct heads, I shall

* The Abbé Demanet, and the African Pilot, asserts that this river is navigable for 150 leagues, which I am very much inclined to doubt; because the tide, as I was informed when at Bulama, flows no higher than Bulola, only 24 leagues up the river; which at that place, at low water, is only three fathoms deep.

now confine my observations to the before described territories, nearly surrounded by two great rivers, and the sea.

Inhabitants.

The northern part of this territory is inhabited by various tribes, or nations, who are chiefly fixed near the winding shores of the Gambia; the western chiefly by Feloops; the southern and eastern by many nations, of whom, as I have some little personal knowledge, I shall separately speak.

Feloops. The nameless island whose S.W. point is known by the appellation of Cape Roxo, which forms the salient angle of the two coast-lines leading to the Gambia and the Grande, is inhabited by a people called Feloops, with whom we had no communication. They have the reputation of being a brave, and an independent people. This island is formed by the rivers Casamanza and Cacheo, both navigable for decked vessels; it is about 50 miles in length; the Portuguese had formerly a factory upon it; but what trade they now carry on there, is by means of canoes, and small craft, navigated by grumetas from Bissao. It has internal communication with the Gambia, by the Pasqua river, a little above James fort, and again by the Casamanza, 100 miles above it.

Papels. Cacheo is the next island to the S.E. which is formed by the river of that name, and Jatts' river. On this island the Portuguese had also formerly a very considerable factory; they now carry on some trade there, by means of small vessels from Bissao; but no native Portuguese reside upon it. It is about 45 miles in length, and inhabited by Papels.

Banyans. North of this island are a people called Banyans, inhabiting the continent and several little islands formed by various branches of internal rivers and creeks.

South of Cacheo is Jatts' Island, embraced by arms of the sea; a beautiful little island about seven leagues in length, and inhabited by a people called Manjacks. *Manjacks.*

To the S.E. of Jatts' Island are the islands of Bassis and Bissao; both together are about 60 miles long; they are fertile and populous, and inhabited by Papels; on the latter, the Portuguese have a considerable factory and a strong fort. *Papels.*

North of these islands is a large one, near a hundred miles in length, inhabited principally by Balantes, but its eastern extremity is occupied by Mandingoes, and its western by Papels. *Balantes.*

N.E. of Bissao is another island, on whose eastern side the river Geba loses itself in the sea, occupied also by Balantes; and to the east of this island is a large peninsula, part of the continent* occupied by the Biafaras. *Biafaras.*

Geba lake, part of that river, and the bordering territories in the north and the east, are occupied by the Mandingoes. *Mandingoes.*

One is astonished at the great variety of tribes, or nations, which are to be met with on the sea coast of Africa. Almost every island is inhabited by a different nation, almost every rivulet separates distinct tribes. During our residence on the island of Bulama we had communication, by our open boats, which never went more than 70 miles from us, with seven distinct nations. That is, the Manjacks, Papels, Balantes, Mandingoes, Biafaras, Naloos,† and Bijugas.

* The chart before referred to in the African Pilot, makes an island of this land, by water communication between Ghinala and Courbaly, which puzzled me when we first occupied Bulama, but my visit to the first named of those places convinced me that there is no such communication by water.

* The Naloos occupy the sea coast, between the mouths of the rivers Grande and

Languages.

Ignorant myself of all the native languages, it is impossible for me to say whether these people each speak really different languages, or only different dialects of the same, but my grumeta interpreters always declared to me that their languages were essentially different. There is a kind of Portuguese patois, which may be called the commercial language of the sea coast, current with them all.

General resemblance.

These various tribes or people have a general resemblance; but a little observation will readily enable one to discriminate the people of one tribe, from that of another.

Characters of the tribes.

The Manjacks are of middling stature, generally ill-featured, and exceedingly revengeful.

The Papels, of which nation were the greatest number of my grumetas, are of common stature, tolerably good looking, and are an industrious, faithful, people; but the Portuguese, who for near two centuries have had an establishment upon their island of Bissao, contrive always to sow dissension among them, and so keep them ever at war with each other.

Some account of the Portuguese settlement on the island of Bissao.

As I have frequently had occasion to mention this establishment of the Portuguese, I will here give a short account of it.

On the east side of this island, nearly opposite to the isle of Sorcieres, the Portuguese have built a large, regular, square fort, with four bastions, on which are mounted near 50 guns; the garrison always consists of about 300 soldiers, who are generally, if not always, convicts. When they first established themselves here is not, I believe, exactly known; for, in some

---

Nunez, and carry on a great deal of trade with the Portuguese at Bissao, from their principal town of Tombaly. The Nunez is navigable for large ships to Kacundy, about 70 miles from its mouth, between which place and Bulola on the Grande, there is frequent land communication, as those rivers approach each other very near at those places. Bulola is inhabited by a mixed race, though chiefly Biafaras.

disputes which one of their governors had with Mons. Brue, the director-general of the French Senegal Company, in the year 1700, neither party seemed able to fix the date of their earliest possessions here. That of the Portuguese, I have no doubt, was prior in point of time to that of the French; and took place, most likely, very early in the 17th century. Even the time when the present fort was built, I do not exactly know;* and could not learn, either from the Portuguese or the natives, when I was at Bissao; but it has certainly been built since the year 1703, because in that year, on account of the decline of their commerce, and the establishment which the French had made upon the same island, they found their profits so unequal to the maintenance of their establishments, that they demolished their fort and abandoned the island to their more active and enterprizing rivals in commerce.†

Though we do not know the precise time when the Portuguese re-established themselves on this island; yet we know that, with little intermission, they have been fixed here for near 200 years, possibly more. Of their formerly numerous fortifications, this is now the only one they have left in this neighbourhood; and their trade and consequence is greatly diminished. The present trade is confined to four annual ships which arrive from Lisbon, (having in their way stopped at St. Jago, one of the Cape de Verd islands, to procure certain cotton cloths, the manufacture of that island, and which are here in great estim-

* The Abbé Demanet might probably have settled this point, but I have not been able to procure in London a copy of his work. Nouv. Hist. de l'Afrique Franc. published in Paris, in 1767.

† Relat. de l'Afrique Occident. Par Labat, vol. v. p. 198 to 208, and p. 229. Paris edit, 1728.

ation as an article of trade,) with cargoes adapted to the purchase of slaves; and they carry hence, besides ivory, wax, and hides, about 2000 of them every year to Brazil, whence they return to Portugal with sugar, tobacco, rice, and other productions of that colony.

The merchants at Bissao procure this number of slaves by means of a class of natives called grumetas, who have generally been brought up from infancy in their houses, and who are in general an honest, industrious, and faithful class. They navigate all their small craft, whether canoes, or decked schooners and sloops; and carry on, for their principals, all the commerce of the country. The merchant, who seldom quits his own habitation, sends them with goods to the value of a certain number of slaves, either to Zinghicor, Cacheo, Geba, or any other place; where they make their purchases, and then return to their employers, who are seldom cheated, or deceived, by them; never, I believe, if their own conduct has been to them upright and just. Most of these slaves are procured from the Mandingoes at Geba; some from the Cacheo and Casamanza rivers; very few from the Biafaras, or Bijugas, but many from the Naloos. All these, however, would not supply their demand, if they had not found out means of procuring a great number from the Papels, on whose island they are fixed.

This island, though little more than 40 miles long is, unfortunately for its inhabitants, governed by no less than 13 kings, who are seldom, if ever, altogether at peace. These petty wars, instigated and cherished by the Portuguese, furnish them with a considerable number of slaves; but so hateful has the conduct of that nation been, that none of it ever venture to visit the interior of the island, and indeed are not safe out of the reach of their own cannon.

To return, however, to the native nations:—of the Balantes I cannot say much of my own knowledge; they did not appear to me to have any perceptible difference from their neighbours the Papels.

Characteristics of the tribes resumed.

The Mandingoes are a good looking, well proportioned, and warlike people, extremely quick, and very mercantile; from the neighbourhood of Geba, they communicate with the Mediterranean and the Gold Coast. I do not mean to insinuate by this, that as a nation they carry on any extensive trade with places so far north or south of them; on the contrary, it is very confined; not more than a dozen, probably, in the neighbourhood of Geba, having made those journeys; and these are called priests, or in other words Mahometans; hence, though very erroneously, the whole nation has been called Mahometan: whereas, the profession of that religion is confined, almost solely, to these wandering, religious, merchants, who acquire considerable wealth, by selling to their own countrymen, as well as to the nations through which they travel, sentences of the Koran; which, by those infatuated people, are considered as having the power of preserving them from any particular evil which they dread.

These priests are considered as very holy men, and are held in great veneration by all the people among whom they travel; and, according to the expression of the Bijugas, are said " to talk with GOD." Wherever they go they are the king's guests, and are every where welcome to remain as long as they please; their merchandise consists of some paper, a reed to write with, and some ink, with which they manufacture their charms, or spells; and they generally continue their residence at each place, so long as there is any demand for the sale of their *gris-gris*. These, as before observed, are nothing more than sentences of the Koran neatly sewed up in leather, or cloth, and attached to the neck, arms, wrist, or ancles of the people; who firmly believe in the efficacy of their virtue. If, by good fortune, any one wearing these charms should accidentally escape any misfortune, or evil, which seemed almost inevitable, it would be attributed to the virtue of his gris-gris; and not only the reputation, but the fortune, of the person who made them, would receive a considerable increase, from his being ever after considered as selling " strong gris-gris," which would insure him a preference, and an increased price, over every other competitor whose gris-gris had not undergone the same ordeal.

This gris-gris trade is so lucrative that it will not be wondered at if some impostors, if indeed all may not be considered as such, are found carrying it on; that is, men who, though they can speak, yet cannot write, Arabic, and are therefore incapable of giving to their gris-gris that form in which alone consists their virtue; that is, the form of some sentence from the Koran. That this is the case I have no doubt, for I have now in my possession half a dozen gris-gris purchased of a Mandingo priest, which are not written in any language whatever: the papers are indeed covered all over with odd scrolls and figures, but there is not an Arabic word, nor even letter, upon them.

Had this impostor professed himself to have been initiated in the traditionary doctrine of the ancient priests of Memphis, instead of a disciple of the prophet of Mecca, I should not so readily have found out the deceit; as his whimsical figures, though totally unlike the Arabic character, had some resemblance to the Egyptian hieroglyphics.

The Mandingoes dye leather of a very beautiful red colour, and are not to be excelled in the neatness of their working it by any nation in Europe.

Of all the people that we had communication with on the coast of Africa, the Biafaras are, by far, the most mild, peaceable, and inoffensive. In their persons they are rather tall, but at the same time of a slender, or feminine, make, and, (which has been ill-naturedly termed a female quality) they have a wonderful propensity to talking. Instead of the robust, compact, bodies, of their neighbours, the Bijugas, they exhibit in their persons, what would probably be termed by our damsels in London, the genteel figure of Africa.

The Naloos are a middle sized, well proportioned, people, more ugly, in general, than any of those of whom I have hitherto spoken: that is, the flat nose and thick lip, which are frequent with them all, preponderates, more with this people than the others. They are said to be a treacherous race.

Advances made by these people from absolute barbarism.*

These various tribes seem pretty much upon a par with respect to civilization, or rather, in the small progress which they have made from the savage state.

It has generally been customary, in estimating the degree of civilization to which a people have attained in emerging from

---

* I must be here understood as speaking only of the tribes before mentioned, occupying the southern boundary, as I know that there is some difference between those on the borders of the Gambia and these; the former, for instance, milk their cattle, catch fish with lines, and have horses and sheep, &c.

barbarism, to describe them either as hunters and fishers trusting to the chase and the waters for their precarious subsistence, or, removed one degree from that lowest state of society, depending, like the Tartars, upon pasturage for their support; or, lastly, by their industry, cultivating the earth, and drawing from it all the riches produced by agriculture; but these people cannot be classed in either of those stages of the progressive improvement of society, though they partake of them all.

They lead so much of a hunter's life that most of the animal food which they consume is procured by the chase, yet, they are so far pastoral that every village has always herds of tame cattle, and flocks of goats, grazing in its neighbourhood; and they are agricultural, inasmuch as that every tribe so far cultivates the earth as annually to sow rice and maize, and plant yams and cassada, sufficient for the year's consumption of the whole community; and this, from what I could learn, is done by general labour; and, when gathered, is lodged in public buildings in the village: but by what authority, and in what proportion, distributed, I cannot take upon me to say.

Make cloth.

Dress.

They all manufacture a narrow cloth from the cotton which grows abundantly in their country; these cloths are about two yards long and four inches broad: ten of them, sewed together, makes one of a very good size, which the women wrap round their hips, and it then reaches half way between the knee and ancle; another of the same size is carelessly, but not inelegantly, thrown over one of the shoulders and brought round under the other arm; and these, together with beads, bracelets, and ear rings,* the common ornaments of all savages, form their whole

* It is astonishing that these barbarous ornaments are still so generally worn by the belles of Europe; which, with the no less savage customs of dancing and painting

dress. Their heads are sometimes covered with the cloth which goes over the shoulder, at others it is left bare. The dress of the men is exactly the same as that of the women, substituting only, for their ornaments, others as trifling, called gris-gris, with which their arms, ancles, and necks, are sometimes loaded. These cloths are generally very coarse, but I have seen some, that came from the Gambia, very fine, and dyed at the edges with either a beautiful blue or scarlet colour. They understand forging into heads, for their spears or assagayes, the iron which they procure from Europeans, which, with the making of mats, baskets, and earthen jars, spoons and combs, seem to be the only manufactures on which their industry has hitherto been exerted; except that the Mandingoes, as before observed, are famed for the art of tanning and working that leather which we term Morocco. Manufactures.

These people are always armed either with a gun, a sword, or an assagaye or spear, or all of them together, according to the wealth of the individual; but as we recede from the sea, the bow and arrow is more generally used. They all invariably wear a long knife stuck in the cloth which goes round their middle, to which they are too apt to appeal on any occasional differences arising among themselves. Their arrows I was told were poisoned; but though I lacerated the thighs of many fowls with them, nothing further resulted from these wounds than what would necessarily occur from a simple scratch. Arms.

A mans wealth is calculated from the number of his wives: these have each separate houses, in the same inclosure, there- Wealth.

(I mean of their persons) seem as prevalent as ever. Powdering the hair is only painting it white, and I see no rational difference between that, and the Bijugas filling theirs with red ochre, except, that red ochre best becomes a black countenance.

Houses.
Furniture.

fore the extent of one of these inclosures and the number of houses which it contains, are sufficient indications of the consequence of the owner. Their houses are either made of clay, or sun baked bricks, and are thatched; the furniture consists of a few mats, earthen jars to cool their water, and calabashes. Their manner of thatching is simple, ingenious, and expeditious, far superior to ours, and no houses are better secured from the rain than theirs, not a drop ever penetrating them.

Government.

The government of these Tribes, if they can be said to have any government at all, is monarchical; at least they have each of them a king, or kings, for almost every large village appears to have one; but their authority seems limited indeed, not exceeding that of a father, or master of a family, in this country.

Religion.

They may be said to have as little religion as government. They believe that a particular spirit does all the good in the world, but that a much more active one does all the evil; and this latter is the only object to which they address either prayers, sacrifices, or offerings. They believe in a future life, and that the good will there enjoy much happiness: the punishment of the wicked, as far as I could learn their opinion, is entirely negative, and consists rather in the privation of that happiness, then in the suffering of any positive pain. These notions engender but a loose morality; and theft, and murder, are not held by them in that abhorrence with which they are viewed in Europe.

Soil.

Of the above described territories, my own personal knowledge is confined to that part of the southern boundary comprized between Cape Roxo and Ghinala, an extent of about 180 miles, and I do not believe that in the whole world there can be found one more rich and fertile. My pursuits, however, have been such, as by no means to render me a competent judge of the qualities of soil; I shall, therefore, only observe that a fine black mould richly covered with wood, where the natives have not cleared the land to make their lugars, every where appears. The southern bank of the Gambia, and the shores between the Capes St. Mary and Roxo, we learn from those who have described, or visited, them, are thickly wooded, and highly fertile and productive.

Produce.

The natives of these countries are abundantly supplied with animal and vegetable food, which they procure with little trouble, and scarcely any culture.

The land affords them great plenty and some variety, of both tame and wild animals. The former are cattle, goats, and poultry; and, among the Mandingoes, horses. Their domesticated animals are seldom slaughtered for their own consumption; except on occasions of palavers, the arrival of guests, &c.; but are kept chiefly with a view of making, what in that country is called, "small trade," in contradistinction to that carried on for slaves, ivory, wax, &c., and may be said to procure them the luxuries of life, such as, to the men, tobacco, pipes, powder, knives, &c., and to the women, beads of various kinds, small looking glasses, &c. *Principal animals. Domestic.*

Their cattle are small, somewhat less than our Alderney breed, but fat and well flavoured, so also is the flesh of their goats: they have not yet learned to make use of their milk, either by drinking it, as it comes from the female, or by making it into butter and cheese.*

Wild. These people rely chiefly on their guns for their supply of animal food, which the woods afford in abundance, of the wild kind; of which, elephants, buffaloes, deer, and hogs are the most valuable and the most common.

Of the elephant I shall have occasion to say much, when we come to Bulama; and shall therefore say nothing of that animal here.

Buffaloes are in great plenty in the woods: their hide is remarkably thick; a musket ball will scarcely penetrate it, except in a particular place or two, unless the hunter is very near to them; their flesh is strong and unpleasant.

Of deer there are two or three kinds, but the flesh of each is dry and unsavoury, and, in my opinion, much inferior to that of their goats.

But nothing can be more sweet, nor more excellent food, than the wild hog, which is frequently met with in the woods. These also afford many birds, such as guinea fowls, pigeons, doves, parrots, and others; while the sea shore is covered with those of the aquatic kind, which are found in other countries of the same latitude.

The sea abounds with fish of various kinds, which the natives have not yet learned the art of entrapping by the hook and line; they notwithstanding catch a great number by means of nets, weirs, and fish-pots, turtle are sometimes caught among the islands, not that which is called the green, but the hawk's-bill

* It must be kept in mind that I am speaking only of the people between Cape Roxo and Ghinala; when at Kacundy, on the Rio Nunez, I tasted very good butter, made by the Foolahs, which had been brought a journey of ten days.

kind, which the natives will not eat; besides fish, the sea, not unfrequently, affords them a delicious repast in the flesh of the hippopotamos, of which they are extremely fond.

Having thus noticed the principal animal, it remains to speak of the vegetable productions of these countries; and those of either not now taken notice of, will be found under the head Bulama.

Of those which are cultivated, rice, yams, manioc, Indian corn or maize, ground nuts, plantains, bananas, pumkins, water melons, oranges, limes, pine apples, papaws, &c. &c. are the chief; and of those which are wild, the sugar cane, cotton shrub, and indigo plant seem the most valuable: besides which there are trees of almost every size and texture. In short, no country in the world is more amply enriched than this is, with the chief productions of the animal and vegetable kingdoms.

CHAPTER IX.

Of the Bijuga Islands and Inhabitants.

IT has been observed in the preceding chapter that to the southward of the Continental Islands, forming the coast line between Cape Roxo and Bissao, there was a cluster of other islands, making an immense harbour to the island of Bulama.

Their situation,

This groupe of islands is called in our charts the Bissagos islands, and are placed on shoals, called the shoals of the Rio Grande; these are the Bijuga Islands.

S. S. W. of Cape Roxo, at the distance of about twelve leagues, and in the latitude of 11. 40. north, is the N. W. edge of what are called, by seamen, the shoals of the Rio Grande. These shoals, or sand banks, extend thence in a S. E. direction full forty leagues, and are interspersed with many marshy and half-drowned, and many inhabited, islands. The north and the eastern edges of this bank are terminated by them, but the south and the western limits of it are not exactly known; at least we are so ignorant of them, that, to my knowledge, several ships have lately struck upon them, out of sight of land; and more vessels have been lost upon these shoals, I verily believe, than on all the rest of Africa. We can scarcely be said to be better acquainted with them than with the Yellow Sea.

The northern edge of these islands and shoals forms the southern limit of the great channel leading to the island of Bulama, and the mouth of the Rio Grande: although there are some shoals in this channel, yet it is every where abundantly wide, with a sufficient depth of water for the largest vessels; and in every part of it ships may anchor in perfect safety at any season of the year.

The eastern edge is formed by the islands of Galenas, Porcos, Canabac, Mayo, Honey and Poison; along which there is a deep, though narrow, and somewhat dangerous and intricate channel. The isle of Jamber, (though belonging to the Bijugas,) and the shoals between it and the Naloo shore, I consider as forming the eastern boundary of this passage.

Of the south and west limits I have not any knowledge.

Of the islands which lie scattered over this immense bank, scarcely more than the names of some of the principal ones is known to Europeans. Whether or not there be any channel for ships between them, we are yet in the dark; but I am inclined to think that there is not. None of them are more than half a dozen leagues in length; they rise gradually from the shore and appearance. towards the interior, and never appear to be more than forty feet above the level of the sea; they are extremely fertile, that is the inhabited ones; and are richly clothed with wood; they are evidently alluvial, having in the course of time been formed by the deposit of the Rio Grande, and the neighbouring streams,* on the large sand-bank which forms their base.

---

* Monsieur Golberry calls these island volcanic, and says that " the whole coast of Africa, from Cape Blanco to Cape Palmas, offers every where traces of their former volcanic state, but more particularly between the Capes of St. Mary and Verga;" now (although he is in general pretty correct) nothing can more strongly point out his total ignorance of these islands, and the coast between the two last-named capes, than the above observation; for I suppose that it is not possible in the whole world to name an extent of country more totally free from any volcanic appearance than this is. The islands, as well as the continent, being composed of a fine dark rich mould, without either rock, stone, lava, or scoriæ; and scarcely any where more

Number inhabited.

Thirteen of these islands, it is said, are inhabited. Bellchore, one of the Canabac kings, is my authority, though I know not, nor could I procure, their names; all that I know is, that Warang, Carashe, Cazegoot, Canabac, and Suoga (this last not named even in our charts) certainly are inhabited. I have no doubt that more than the five islands here named are so, but I do not believe that they amount to thirteen in number.

Of the Bijugas.

The nations and tribes, of whom we have hitherto spoken, resemble each other, not only in their general manners and customs, but also in the degree of progress they have made from absolute barbarism; but the Bijugas, of whom I am about to speak, have not the smallest resemblance imaginable, except in colour, to any of the African nations, by which they are semi-surrounded.

Exceedingly uncivilized.

These, of all the Africans, on this part of the coast are the most uncivilized, faithless, and warlike; and are distinguished among the neighbouring nations by the appellation of wild men.

Described.

The Bijugas are above the middle size, muscular, bony, and well-proportioned; they have the appearance of great strength and activity; their noses are more elevated, and their lips less

---

than sixty feet above the level of the sea. At Cape Verga the high land begins upon the sea coast, and thence continues to the southward, and at Sierra Leone is very high, which with the Isles de Loss probably may have a volcanic origin; but that is certainly not the case with the land to the northward of it; for on the Nunez even, the high land approaches not the sea nearer than Kacundy, which is seventy miles from it. It would be an undertaking worthy of the English government to order a survey to be taken of the Bijuga islands, and the coast line between Cape Roxo, and the mouth of the Rio Nunez.

thick, than their neighbours; their teeth good, which are sometimes filed to a sharp point like the teeth of a saw; their hair woolly, and shaved into every fanciful form, or shape, which can be imagined, from wearing the whole of it to none; what they do wear is generally dressed with red ochre and palm oil, as ours is with powder and pomatum.

Every Bijuga is a warrior; his amusement the chace, his delight war. Not so far advanced in civilization as their neighbours, they are yet ignorant of weaving the cotton into cloth; a deer, or a goat skin, is therefore the only dress of the men. In their arms they are more splendid: A long buccaneer gun, kept in the most perfect order, is carried in the right hand; a solingen sword, about four feet long, and as sharp as a razor, not figuratively speaking, for it is sometimes employed as one, is slung on the left shoulder; the hilt of it coming close under his arm. In his left hand he holds a round convex shield, formed of interlaced witheys, covered with buffaloe's hide. The same hand grasps a spear. *A nation of wariors. Dress. Arms.*

Except a few days in the year, when he prepares the ground for, and sows, rice, war and the chace is his sole occupation; and he is never without his arms; to keep which in the most perfect order is his greatest pride. No people understand the use of them better than they do; with their gun they seldom miss their object; and with their spear, or assagaye, I have seen them strike a reed, about ten inches long, and not thicker than a tobacco pipe, at the distance of twenty yards; and in the use of the broad sword they are more active and expert than any people whom I have ever seen.

When they attack, they first discharge their guns, kneeling and supporting the left elbow on the left knee, they then throw *Mode of attack.*

it down, and advancing to a proper distance, covering themselves with their shield, they launch their assagaye, and then have recourse to their sword. They approach squatting, with their shield nearly covering their whole body, its convex form is admirably adapted to turn off the enemy's shot, indeed a musquet ball will not penetrate it.*

<small>General plunderers.</small>

Unconnected by any ties with the neighbouring nations, whom they generally hold in contempt, they consider the world as their own; and that what it contains they have a right to plunder. If they can be compared to any state known in Europe, it must be to the Algerines; they war with every body, and always plunder the weak; but there is one nation against which they are particularly inveterate, no living person in either remembering even traditionary peace between them; this nation, mild and inoffensive, as the Bijugas are the reverse, is held in such sovereign contempt by them, that, regardless of numbers, wherever they meet, they attack them.

This nation is the Biafara. Bulama was for a long time the chief object of contention between these hostile nations, till at length the Biafaras, tired and worn out with the continual attacks of their martial neighbours, evacuated the island, and re-

---

* During the time that I was in Jalorem's village on the island of Canabac, waiting for poor Mrs. Harley to get ready to embark, one of these Bijugas, probably with a view of amusing me, went through all these motions, and I was the object of his attack; having first snapped his unloaded piece at me, he threw it down, and approaching a little nearer, launched his assagaye close by my ear, and then coming within the length of his sword, he made with it such quick and rapid flourishes round my head, as seemed highly to delight the spectators, making at the same time the most hideous faces, with a countenance that he had previously rubbed all over with white ashes, probably to make himself look like their devil. I thought it prudent to smile, and look pleased at these tricks; but was very glad when they were over.

tired to Ghinala, up the Rio Grande. Here, however, they would not be safe, if, happily for them, the Bijugas were not far behind all their neighbours, in their knowledge of the adjacent shores, and the management of boats. This is the more extraordinary, as an insular situation has always been supposed favourable to early improvement in the navigation and management of boats and small vessels; yet these people, although all their predatory incursions are made on the water, have not yet learned to use a sail, notwithstanding all the boats, that visit their islands, or are navigated by the neighbouring nations, use sails as well as oars; and they have never yet ventured so far up the Rio Grande as Ghinala. This one fact is, I think, sufficient to shew how far they are behind their neighbours in their progress from absolute barbarism.

The nearest of the inhabited Bijuga islands to us at Bulama was that of Canabac, the inhabitants of which had, (besides Bulama till we purchased it from them) the islands of Galenas, so named from the quantity of Guinea fowls upon it, Ilhos dos Porcos, or Hogs Island, and those of Mayo, Jamber, and Honey, all uninhabited, for hunting islands; on the last two they annually cultivate rice. *Certain islands kept by them for the purpose of hunting.*

It did not appear to me that the Bijugas of Canabac had any slaves in their island; those of their own nation are probably never reduced to that state, unless for the crimes of witchcraft and adultery; and then, most likely, instantly sold to the Portuguese, as well as all those who might have fallen into their hands by the chance of war.

Their women, who seemed to perform all the menial domestic duties, are as simple in their dress as the men; a thick fringe *Dress of the women.*

made of the shred of palm leaves, about six inches long, tied round their waist, formed their only covering.

Government. Their government, like all others on the coast that I know any thing about, is monarchical, but the power of the sovereign seems trifling; he cannot be known from his subjects by any external mark of dress, or respect shown to him; and he eats out of the same calabash with any of his people.

Religion. As to their confined notions of relgion I believe that they are the same as those of their neighbours; but they have one peculiarity; and that is, of sacrificing a cock, prior to their undertaking any thing serious, or sanctioning any weighty measure: such as the undertaking an expedition for plunder, selling one of their islands, or even entering into trade with a person whom they have not known. Should a white stranger go to their island, with a view to make a treaty or the forming of any connexion with them, they would previously sacrifice one or more cocks; and from the examination of the gizzard (I was given to understand) they pretend to ascertain whether the motives of his visit are good or evil. When in Jalorem's house, I observed a little round place made of clay, somewhat resembling an oven, in one corner, and I asked Gillion, my interpreter, what it was, and said that I should like to look inside of it. He desired me *not to look at it too much,* for Jalorem's people would not like it, it was " *his gris-gris house:*" now in this place, I believe, but am not certain their sacrifices take place.

It is singular that the presents which I received from the women of Bellchore, Jalorem, and the king of Suoga, were always cocks, and generally perfectly white ones.

On Canabac there are two towns or villages, each governed by a separate king, who, when I was at Bulama, were named Bellchore, and Jalorem.

Bellchore is the dread of the neighbouring people, and is reckoned the greatest warrior the Bijuga nation ever produced. He still boasts of having set fire to the town of Bissao, notwithstanding its strong fort and numerous garrison; and, to others, he will probably boast of his triumph over us on the western point of Bulama. He is old, but upright and active, and stands full six feet high; his large black eyes, the fire of which seventy rains have not yet extinguished,* are the most penetrating I ever saw; his nose is long, large, and projecting; his teeth regular and white; his limbs well proportioned; his understanding clear and acute; and in both body and mind he stands pre-eminent among his countrymen. But his courage, his policy, his restless activity, his daring enterprizes, and his love of war, which have rendered him the admiration of his own countrymen, have procured him, at the same time, the hatred and detestation of all those nations that lie within the reach of his lawless expeditions. *Character of two of their kings.*

Jalorem, on the contrary, is distinguished from the rest of his countrymen, by his mildness and peaceable dispotition.

These people, like those before mentioned, have their poultry, goats, and cattle; cultivate rice, yams, &c.; and have all the common fruits of the country. Fish, which surround, in numerous shoals, their fertile little island, they have no idea of catching, but with their spears; and these they throw with such unerring certitude, as abundantly to supply their wants. *Produce. Mode of catching fish.*

Warang, or Formosa, is the most western, the most populous,

---

* The year is divided into the dry and rainy reason.

and the largest of these islands. Canabac is the easternmost, and that which is best known; with the inhabitants of none of the other islands had we any communication, except by one boat from Suoga, which lies to the N.W of it. There has not, it is said, been any known instance of these islanders having warred with each other.

<small>Never go to war with each other.</small>

CHAPTER X.

Of the Island of Bulama; its Produce—Animals—Climate.

AT the bottom, or east end, of that immense harbour formed by continental islands on the north, and the Bijuga Archipelago* on the south, and at the mouth of the Rio Grande, in the 11th degree of north latitude, is the island of Bulama. A small island, at its north-east point, is separated from the Biafara shore, by a narrow branch of the sea, not exceeding 200 yards, and the channel between this small island and Bulama affords a passage for boats at half tide, but not at low water; the whole east side of the island forms, with the Biafara shore, a remarkably fine harbour of about two miles in width, with water in every part of it for the largest ships, within a cable's length of the beach; and in all places a good clear bottom; its S.E. side confines the waters of the Rio Grande, whose embouchure is considered to be between the south point of this island, and Tombaly point on the Naloo coast; the west side of the island is separated from that of Galenas on the eastern edge of the Bijuga cluster, by a good broad channel with very deep water; the north side is bordered by extensive shoals which extend all the way to the island of Arcas. This island, I conceive† to be Extent.

Bulama; its situation.

---

* I am aware of the real etymology of this word, but custom will justify my making use of it in its present acceptation.

† Having been 17 months on the island of Bulama it may appear strange that I do not speak more positively as to the extent of this island, but the truth is, that except

342   *African Memoranda.*

Appearance.
about seven leagues in length, its breadth various, from five to two leagues; the land rises gradually, generally speaking, from the shore, to the moderate height of about 50 feet above the level of the sea, and appears to be covered with wood, though there are some natural savannahs in it, and some places cleared by its former inhabitants, or late Bijuga lords; the soil is every where rich and prolific, and affords ample pasturage to innumerable elephants, buffaloes, deer, and other wild animals which graze on its surface; the sea, which surrounds it, is sheltered from violent agitation in every direction, and abounds with excellent fish of various kinds; in short here reigns abundance of every thing requisite to the comforts of savage life.

Its general appearance is that of the most luxuriant vegetation. It seems to have been produced in one of nature's happiest moods.

Concise account of.
An island, thus advantageously gifted, was not likely to remain uninhabited, and we accordingly find it, in the earliest times that we are acquainted with it, in the possession of the Biafara nation, who had then a town on its N. E. end; its proximity to the Biafara peninsula enabled cattle to pass with ease

---

from eye measurement, I have no ground to go upon, for when we first went there in the Hankey, I left that ship for Canabac ere she had entered the eastern harbour, which I had previously explored in a boat. I afterwards went through the east channel to Bissao, and returned the same way; I once also went nearly round the island, by going from the block-house along the south side, and round the west point, to join the Scorpion sloop of war, at an anchor on the S. E. side of Arcas; and at another time I went in a boat to join the Felicity at an anchor between Bulama and Galenas; now, from these excursions I may have a tolerable notion of the size of the island, but not such a correct one as to enable me to speak positively as to its extent, never having had any means of measuring it; for after we once really took possession of it, I was never, except as before observed, five miles from the scite of the block-house, and could scarcely ever indeed, with prudence, leave it at all.

from the continent to this island, and the consequence was that it abounded with elephants, buffaloes, and deer, of all which animals the Bijuga islands are entirely destitute. To a people, such as I have described these, here then was an inducement to hostility which could not be resisted at any rate. It was an important object to them, to acquire the right of hunting on it. The facility of passing from Canabac to its western point probably suggested to the warlike inhabitants of the former the idea of expelling their Biafara neighbours: not content therefore with the privilege of hunting, they commenced and carried on such a constant and cruel war with them, that they at length succeeded, a little before the close of the 17th century, in driving them from it; when, to live at peace, and out of the reach of these turbulent islanders, they retired up the Rio Grande, and fixed the royal residence at the town of Ghinala. The precise time of the Biafara retreat is not exactly known; it however had taken place previous to the year 1699, when the French visited Bulama for the first time, with a view of establishing a factory on it; which was at that time given up, because they found the island much larger than they had expected, and they had not numbers sufficient to maintain themselves.*

The Bijugas have never attempted to settle upon this island, it having remained, since the Biafara expulsion, the uninhabited boundary of the two hostile nations. They however, annually cultivated, before we purchased it of them, a few acres of rice on its western end; and hither they frequently resorted to amuse themselves in the manly exercise of the chase, as well as to obtain food, which the flesh of the animals, so procured, afforded

* Labat. vol. 5. p. 88.

them. The tusks of the elephant enabled them to purchase guns, powder, and shot; and those two sovereign remedies against all African complaints, rum and tobacco. From the hide of the Buffalo they covered their well-formed shields, and the skin of the deer supplied them with their only dress.

French plans for settling it. The advantageous position of this island for commerce has not been unnoticed by our neighbours the French; for we learn " that it was recommended to the French government, as a proper spot for a colony, by M. de la Brue, director-general of the French Senegal Company, who visited the island, in the year 1700, and described it minutely;"* and afterwards " by the Abbé Demanet, who resided for some time on the adjacent coast, and has given a map of Bulama and Rio Grande, in his Nouv. Hist. de l'Afr. Franc. 2 vol. 12mo. published in 1767." † This book I have never seen, but from Wadstrom's account of his description of the island I am inclined to believe that the Abbé never visited it himself; but has described it from the relation of De la Brue, as given by Labat. Be this, however, as it may, I shall here only observe that though the account of both Labat and Demanet are pretty accurate as to the fertility of the island, and the excellence of its harbour; yet in some other things they are exceedingly erroneous, as in their account of the great irregularity and violence of the tides, and the force with which the sea breaks on its shores; but more particularly Demanet, who, so late as 1767, says that its black inhabitants are partly Christians, partly Idolaters, and partly Mahometans; when it is pretty well known that it had not then been inhabited since the 17th century, and certainly never by either Christians

* Wadstrom's Essay on Colonization, part II. p. 130.   † Ibid.

or Mahometans. For the third time this island was proposed to the French government as proper for a colony in 1787, by a Mr. Barber, an Englishman then residing at Havre de Grace, and had not the French revolution taken place, a colonial expedition to Bulama would certainly have been undertaken, by order of the government of that nation.*

The first attempt however to cultivate this island was reserved for us. Of the failure of this attempt enough has already been said. It has, however, again been lately recommended to the French government, in a work † of which I shall have occasion to speak more particularly hereafter. I shall here just remark that the Bijuga islands, and the shores between Cape Roxo and the Rio Grande, seem to have been much more frequented, and much better known in the early part of the last century than they are at present. *First attempts by the English.* *Better known formerly than now.*

The soil of this island, it has before been observed, is remarkably rich and prolific. I will endeavour to enumerate its principal vegetable productions, all of which if not now actually on the island, where there is at present no cultivator, either have been, or may be there cultivated, as they are all in abundance in the neighbourhood. These are *Soil.* *Vegetable productions.*

RICE, of which there are two kinds: one called upland, which is sowed on dry and elevated ground, from which the rain runs off after it has fallen; the other is sowed in low marshy places, or in trenches made to retain the water, and is called the lowland rice. The former is the least productive, but is reckoned most nutritious, and always bears the highest price. *Rice.*

I had an opportunity when at Bissao, of once seeing the Papels

* Wadstrom's Essay on Colonization, p. 132.
† Fragmens d'un voyage en Afrique, par M. Golberry, vol. II. p. 225, Paris, 1802.

prepare their ground for the lowland rice, in the beginning of August. With an instrument, something like that with which we cut turf, thrust about three inches under the soil, they first turned it up to the right, and then to the left; the soil thus turned up formed a little ridge on each side of the trench whence it was taken, and the trench was about a foot wide; when it rained, the water was retained in these trenches, and the rice sown in them; when the plants had attained a proper height, they were taken out, and transplanted in rows on the adjoining low lands. Whether African rice be more nutritious than American, I will not pretend to say; but Moore, who was a native of the latter country, told me that it was; his observation was " that slaves would absolutely starve on Carolina rice, whilst they would look well and grow fat on that of Africa." There is certainly a difference in the flavour of the two.

Yams.

YAMS are the next principal article of food with the natives, these grow wild on the island, but are not so good as those which are cultivated; for which purpose the ground is hoed, and then formed into little hillocks, in rows about three feet asunder; the yam is first cut into slices of about two inches thick; those slices are then quartered, and two quarters put into each hillock; the eyes, which are most numerous at each end, are not selected, as those of the potatoe, with us; but are generally thrown away; they are planted at the beginning of the rains, and are fit for use by the latter end of November.

Manioc.

The sweet CASSADA, or MANIOC,* is the next chief article of

---

* Labat mentions the Manioc as growing in Africa, vol. V. p. 81, but from the plate which accompanies it, as descriptive of the manner of preparing it, he evidently alludes to the bitter, or poisonous, cassada of the West Indies. Now, that cassada I know very well, and have often eaten of it in the West Indies, but I never

their consumption, but as so much has been said about it in a note, pp. 232,3, I shall only observe here that it is planted in hillocks like the yam, but arrives much earlier at maturity.

MAIZE, or INDIAN CORN, and ground nuts, are also consumed in considerable quantities, though the latter is more particularly confined to the Bijuga islands, where there is also a ground pea, peculiar to that cluster, which forms a considerable portion of the nourishment of its natives. Besides these, there are plantains, bananas, calalue, ochra, pumkins, guavas, papaws, oranges, limes, water melons, pine apples, &c. Indigo grows wild on the island, and the sugar cane and cotton shrub, on the adjoining continent, and some of the neighbouring isles. There are also in Bulama an immense quantity of *annual* vines, which produce a purple grape that is exceedingly sour.

Maize and ground nuts.
Various others.

Except some natural savannahs, and those spots cleared by its former inhabitants, or since by the Bijugas, the island is covered with wood of various sizes and grain; from that of the majestic oak to the most diminutive shrub, and from the close texture of the iron-wood, to the soft, porous, grain of the pullam, or cotton tree.† Most of the woods are fit for house building, and some of them for the turner, and cabinet maker; particularly one, which in colour, but not in scent, resembles the cedar; but is much closer and harder grained. Small vessels fit for the trade of the country might be built of the timber which grows

Woods.

saw it in Africa, neither did I ever see the sweet cassada in the West Indies, though each may possibly be found in both these regions. However, I am inclined to think that this latter is unknown in our West India islands; if so, its introduction there would be a very valuable acquisition to the food of the blacks.

† I never knew that the silky kind of cotton which this tree produces was of any value, but Labat says, p. 27, vol. V, that he has seen very beautiful stockings made of it.

on the banks of the rivers; but I think that it is in general too heavy for ship building, except for beams and knees.

<small>Animals. The elephant.</small>

Of the animals on this island the principal one is the elephant. The ridiculous accounts given by many authors of this animal, and of the danger of attacking or wounding it, or of even meeting with a troop of them, though they should not be attacked, are so exceedingly remote from truth, that I will speak somewhat at large of it. Bosman in his account of Guinea,[*] gives a most dreadful detail of the rage of one of these animals, that had been wounded, at one of the factories on that coast; this account I had unfortunately read on the morning of the day on which I first saw one of these animals. We were quite near enough to have killed it, and had plenty of time so to do, for which my hunter was exceedingly anxious; but Bosman's account was so fresh on my mind, that I would not suffer him to fire; and at length the animal walked away from us. Labat gives a similar account of the fury of the elephant when wounded, and of the danger there is in attacking[†] it; and then gravely gives an account of the manner in which the Africans kill them with their assagayes. He says that " the negroes never undertake this dangerous chace in less numbers than twenty-five or thirty; the boldest and the fleetest approaches the animal as near as possible under cover of the trees, and, when near enough, strikes with all his force his assagaye into its flank, because there the skin is most easily penetrated; the elephant immediately turns towards him who had given the stroke and pursues him with all its force; but he retreats to the places where his companions are hid behind trees; and

[*] I quote from memory, and therefore cannot refer to the page.
[†] Labat, vol. III, p. 274.

those near whom it passes fail not to pierce it with their assagayes. These new wounds encrease its fury; it ceases sometimes to pursue him who had given the first wound, to follow some one of those by whom it had since been struck; and while it pursues him, others approach, and give it fresh wounds, which, producing loss of blood, diminish its strength, and its ardour in the pursuit of its enemies; at length it falls, and the hunters surrounding it on all sides, accomplish its death." Now, nothing can be more ridiculous than this account. If it be true, the elephant cannot be a furious animal; and if the elephant be a furious animal, the account cannot be true.

We know that, except in the flank and behind the ear, a musket ball will scarcely penetrate the skin of the elephant; can an African arm launch with more force an assagaye, than powder will project a ball? An elephant into which I had previously put more than two hundred balls, when weakened from its numerous wounds and loss of blood, I was enabled to penetrate in the flank with an European bayonet, but I question very much whether an African assagaye would have pierced its skin: this however is certain, that an elephant cannot be killed by assagayes, however numerous its foes. But if the elephant be the enraged animal described by Labat, when wounded, what prevents its killing all its enemies? It will walk as fast, if not faster than a man can run; and if it pursued the person who gave the first wound, it would be impossible for him to get a dozen yards, before the enraged animal would have him within reach of its trunk; as to those placed in ambush behind the trees, it is impossible for them to wound the elephant unperceived; when the "furious animal" would have nothing to do but to throw its proboscis, like the lash of a whip, round the tree and the man, to reduce in an instant his pigmy bones to dust. My hunter drove a wounded elephant to our landing place at Bulama, where I opposed it with a party of men; it immediately galloped into the woods, passing some of us on the right, and some of us on the left, within at least a dozen yards, without any attempt to annoy us, but, on the contrary, seeking its safety by flight. This elephant, on landing, fell upon its fore knees, but immediately recovered itself, with great activity, and galloped into the woods. I mention this circumstance only because some people believe that the elephant cannot get up if it once lies down; it was the only time I ever saw an elephant gallop.

From what has been here said concerning this animal, the Bulama elephants must either be very unlike the rest of their species in Africa, or Bosman and Labat must be erroneous in their account of its fury when wounded. Now as I am inclined to believe that elephants are much the same in their disposition, whatever part of Africa they may be found in I put to the account of fable all that those two writers have said concerning the danger of attacking this animal.

The truth is that if an elephant be attacked, it will endeavour to escape by any opening that it can perceive; but if it be entirely surrounded, its rage and its strength must be felt in some part of the surrounding barrier, ere it can be broken. When our little boat attacked the elephant on the river, finding that it could not escape, it turned upon it every time that the hunter fired, and immediately afterwards pursued its course; but when we fired at it on shore, it turned not upon any of us, because there were many openings by which it might escape into the woods.

The Bijugas and Biafaras have both the same mode of attacking the elephant; for which purpose they carry a very long gun, called a buccaneer; which, instead of being charged with a leaden ball, which would be of no use, is loaded with a piece of an iron rod, nearly fitting the bore of the gun, of about two inches in length. When they perceive the elephant, one person creeps through the underwood, to approach the animal unperceived to within about forty yards, or nearer if possible; and then resting his left elbow on his left knee he takes aim, either at the flank or behind the ear, whichever may be the fairest mark; but if the animal should be in such a position as not to admit of the hunter's seeing either, he would not fire, knowing that if wounded in any other place, the animal would walk off with his charge, and then he would lose all chance of killing it. The wounded animal immediately retreats; for I believe there is no instance of an elephant being directly killed at one shot. In a few minutes the hunter leisurely follows, tracing it by the blood trickling from the wound for about one hundred yards; and then marking the trees, he returns home. No consideration would induce one of those hunters afterwards to go in sight of an elephant on the day in which he wounded it; for he supposes that it would instantly destroy him. Here we see the origin of Bosman's and Labat's accounts. However, the next day he sets out with a party for the spot to which he had traced it the preceding one, expecting the animal to have died of its wound, and thence resumes the pursuit; if the blood should have ceased to flow, and they are no longer able to follow the animal by that guide, they examine the grass, and observe whether it has been trodden down, and has afterwards erected itself again; and the branches of trees and underwood, lately bruised and broken off;

and they are so exceedingly discriminating in these things, as to be able to say, with tolerable precision, how much time has elapsed since the grass was trodden down, or the branch broken off by any animal, from the mere inspection of the bend or bruise. If by these means they again get sight of the wounded elephant, and it should not be dead, they get another shot, and repeat the same precautions; but if it should be dead, they take with them as much of the flesh as they can carry, leaving the rest to ants, vultures, and hyænas, who quickly devour it. When they suppose that it has been long enough exposed to the air for the tusks to be loosened from their sockets, for they have no means of getting them out by any instrument, they return for them. One of these goes to the king, and the other remains to the party.

In a country where elephants are numerous it must be evident that this mode of tracing them cannot be often successful, as the frequent crosses of the tracts of others may lead from that of the one which was wounded; so that the natives generally procure their ivory more by chance than any thing else, by accidentally finding in the woods the tusks of some of those animals which had died of their wounds. Of all those which my hunter wounded on the island I never got one. It is true that we ourselves could not well leave the block-house for any length of time; and he, being a Biafara, was afraid to go far, lest he might fall in with some Bijugas, who would inevitably capture him; we therefore had not altogether a fair opportunity of seeking for them; and had it not been for the two which we had the good fortune to kill, should have left the island without having had an opportunity of closely examining one.

This animal certainly is not to be found on any of the Bijuga islands; and I believe not on any of those between Cape Roxo and Bissao; but of this I am not quite sure. The length of time however that factories have been established, and commerce carried on by the Portuguese from the river Casamanza to the last named island, renders it exceedingly probable, that their avidity for ivory had either destroyed or, driven from those islands the elephants that might formerly have occupied them.

That district of the Biafara country which is comprized between the river issuing from the Geba lake (which empties itself into the sea a little below Courbaly to the eastward of Bissao) and the Rio Grande, together with the island of Bulama, abounds with elephants. The number of these animals on this little island almost exceeds belief; it was nearly impossible for us to proceed fifty yards inland without meeting recent and palpable vestiges of them; and the skeletons of old ones that had died in the woods were frequently found. It has been related in my journal that they often swam across that arm of the sea, which separates Bulama from the Biafara peninsula, which is about two miles in breadth; but, which is very extraordinary, I never once saw an elephant attempt to swim from the island back to the continent; it was generally at the latter end of the dry season that they came over; whether it arose from fresh water being more abundant on the former than the latter, or a greater quantity of plums, which at that time constitutes the greatest part of their food, I cannot pretend to say, but the fact is as I state it. We saw them come from, but never saw them return to the continent.

This gigantic animal is extremely harmless and inoffensive; its food consists of grass, the leaves of trees, and a certain farinaceous plum, which is produced in great quantities, on the island of Bulama, by very large trees, whose wood resembles cedar in colour but not in odour. At the latter end of the dry season, when the grass is burnt up, and the trees, for want of moisture, put not forth so quickly their luxuriant and rapid growing leaves, the elephant principally subsists upon these plums, until the annual return of rain again supplies it with a sufficient quantity of grass.

The general height of those full grown elephants which I saw upon the island I guess to be about ten feet. I guess only, for unluckily I suffered the full grown female, which we killed, to float out to sea, without having taken her dimensions;* in that herd of elephants, of which we killed two, there was only one male, and it was of a size much superior to any which I had either before, or have since, seen; it appeared to be at least twelve feet high. The largest elephant's tusk which I ever saw weighed exactly a hundred weight, or 112 pounds, but I am told that they are found much larger, these enormous tusks I

---

* I fear that it will be sometimes thought that I have been idle and inattentive, or at least that I have not made the most of the opportunity afforded me during my residence on the island of acquiring all the information within my reach. I do not pretend that I have so done, for which various apologies might be made; such for instance as the constant expectation of relief, support, and succour, which would then have left one at liberty to procure such information without neglecting the more urgent concerns, and almost immediate safety, of the colonists; but, when it is considered that from dawn of day when I rose, to sun set when we left off work, I had never, except when placing others to work, or giving directions, a tool out of my hands of some kind or other, save only at the hours of meal; and that besides, I kept ten different books, with copies of each, for the information of him or those who might succeed me, besides my own Journal, and had during that time seven separate attacks of the fever; I say all these things considered, I trust that, though there may have been on my part some omission, I have not been altogether idle.

should suppose are produced only by the males, as those of the female which we killed, though full grown, weighed only seven pounds each.

Buffaloes in numerous herds are every where to be met with upon the island. These animals are dangerous, if met with on a large clear tract of ground, or in a savannah; for, though they will sometimes take fright and run away; at others they will run directly at you; when those who are not acquainted with the spanish mode of bull fighting on foot, run great risque of being killed. However, as extensive tracts of clear ground are not here to be met with, one is generally safe from them; for wherever there is a tree, there is security: but in the centre of a clear spot of 100 acres I had rather meet with as many elephants, than one buffaloe. These animals are generally found during the greatest heat of the day, in the dry season, in the creeks and on the shores of the island, almost totally immerged in water, little more than their heads appearing above it: in the cooler hours they are met with grazing on the island. Their flesh is coarse and rank: the natives approach them as they do the elephant, and shoot them with iron instead of lead. Their hide is exceedingly thick, and body large, with rather short legs. The beautiful little domesticated breed of cattle, of the neighbouring isles, and adjacent continent, is not on this island.

There is an animal of great bulk that frequents the waters and the shores of this island, of which I cannot say much, never having been able to kill one: this is the hippopotamos. Its bulk exceeds that of a buffaloe; but its legs are shorter and thicker, the flesh is said to be excellent food, and its teeth are reckoned the most valuable of ivory.

Deer. Of deer there are four kinds on the island, the common gazelle, the gazelle pintado, the flintombeau, and the cabre de mat: these, at least, are their names in the Portuguese patois of the country. As they have all been described in the journal, I shall here say nothing more of them, than that their numbers exceed almost belief; and, that, if I did not hope that ere long some attempt will be made to repossess ourselves of this island, which will give an opportunity of confuting any thing which I may advance if ill-founded, I would not say, what I now advance, and that is, that on the island of Bulama there are more elephants, buffaloes and deer, than one could suppose the soil capable of nourishing.

Wild hog. The wild hog has been killed on this island, though I never met with one, it is common on the Biafara peninsula.

Monkey. Of other animals, not yet mentioned, the monkey is most common; they are every where in great plenty; and are most excellent food; particularly in what seamen call a sea-pye. They are so numerous on the island of Bulama, that I have seen on a calm evening when there was not an air sufficiently strong to agitate a leaf, the whole surrounding wood in as much motion, from their playful gambols among its branches, as if it had blown a strong wind.

Guana. The guana is frequently met with and is very good food either roasted or fricasseed.

Lizards. Lizards, as in all similar climes, are numerous and harmless.

Snakes. Of snakes we killed about a dozen, neither of which was more than two feet long, though one of very great dimension was found, I understood, by some of the colonists in the Calypso prior to our arrival; the grumetas were afraid of them, but whether they are venomous or not I cannot pretend to say, as none of our people were bit by them. I should think that they would be very good stewed, but did not try, as I foolishly suffered the grumetas to dissuade me from eating them, after I had ordered a couple to be so dressed.

Of birds that are useful for food the most common is the guinea fowl, which are exceedingly numerous. There are, besides, plenty of doves, pigeons, and parrots, with many smaller birds of beautiful plumage; but none, that I ever heard, of harmonious song. Great flocks of vultures are every where seen; those which we shot generally measured seven feet from the tip of one wing to that of the other. They are very useful in speedily devouring those animals that die in the woods; without which, the exhalation from the putrid carcases of dead elephants, buffaloes, and deer, would be almost insupportable. The bird called in the West Indies the carrion-crow is also useful here for the same purpose. Eagles of the sun, somewhat larger than the vultures, with jet black bodies and white heads, are also common; but I never saw more than two of them together. There are wild ducks and geese; but they flew so high that we were never able to shoot any; we however got a nest of the former, full of young, from the top of a very high pullam, or cotton tree. *Birds.*

The only beast of prey, near the sea coast, that infested the country, was the hyæna, and this was scarcely known on the populous islands; but on Bulama we certainly had a great number of them, which was owing, I am inclined to think, not only to its being uninhabited, but to the small island at the N. E. end of it being not more then 200 yards from the continent. On our first arrival, they made great havock among our goats and sheep; but after we had made inclosures for them we *Hyæna.*

never lost one; indeed they never attempted to leap over the paling, yet we heard them, almost every night, prowling round the enclosures, and making a most hideous noise—a noise, which it is both difficult to imagine or describe. We never heard nor saw one in the day; they then retire, we suppose, either into holes in the earth, or to the thickest part of the forest. I frequently measured the impression of their feet round the blockhouse, which, during the rains, was often left as distinct as that of a seal on wax; and found it almost invariably to be four inches by three. This gives one an idea of a large animal; and I should suppose that they are somewhat larger than a large Newfoundland dog. My grumetas told me that they would never attack a man, and they called them loup; whence, on my first arrival, I thought that they were really wolves: but from the noise which they make, and the hair which is mentioned in the journal, as having been got from one of those animals, I have no doubt in my own mind that they are really hyænas.

The grumetas seemed to have some knowledge of the leopard. They said that it was spotted and would " eat a man ;" but it did not appear to me that it inhabited any of the islands, or sea coast of which I have spoken; it may probably be found to the northward and eastward of Geba, where there are certainly lions.

In the enumeration of the animals and vegetables to be found on the island of Bulama, or those countries with which we had communication, it will probably appear extraordinary that, among the former, horses (except only the Mandingoes) sheep, geese and ducks are not mentioned as domesticated: and among the latter that the cocoa-nut tree is omitted. I believe that all these are in abundance on the borders of the Gambia, and probably half way, and more between that river and the Grande, as they certainly are a little to the southward of it; but they are not to be found on any of the islands between Cape Roxo and Bulama, not that they are difficult to be procured, but they are not yet among the *wants* of these people; and the Portuguese, the only European power established in this neighbourhood, have been either too much occupied by their trade, or too indolent, to introduce them.

The horse, as before observed, is common at Geba; but thence (except at Bissao, where the Portuguese merchants may each have one or two for their own riding) to Cape Roxo and Bulola unknown. The natives, ignorant of his value both for agriculture and for war; have no notion of riding for amusement or pleasure; and therefore are not at the trouble of rearing this noble animal, of whose useful qualities they have not the least notion.

Although sheep are in great plenty on the Gambia, to the north, and on the south shore of the Nunez, yet have they never been introduced into those countries bordering on the sea between that river and Cape Roxo. The natives have as many cattle and goats as they can rear, and therefore think it folly to domesticate another animal, for which they have not any occasion: for the same reason they have neither tame ducks nor geese; there are numerous wild ones, but the common fowl they think alone worth taming.

The same indifference, to what they consider as useless or superfluous articles of consumption, deprives these people likewise of the delicious beverage contained in the cocoa nut; for although the useful tree which bears that fruit is very common a little to the southward of them, yet it is not to be found among these people; although the palm tree, of which the cocoa-nut is a variety, is here very common.*

<small>Ants.</small>

The greatest plague which we felt on our first arrival was the immense quantity of ants upon the island. There are on Bulama five different sorts, but not all equally troublesome or destructive; those that were most so, however, fortunately for us, as otherwise the island would have been uninhabitable, retired as we built upon, and occupied, the ground. The different sorts are :

First, The TERMITES, called in that country bug-a-bugs. These ants build their nests in an irregular conical form, from six to eight feet high, and from ten to fifteen feet in circumference at their base; they are of the colour, and about the hardness, of a half-burnt brick, and are frequently so close and so numerous† as to be easily mistaken, at first sight, for native towns; and which I really thought those were, that I first saw upon the S.W. end of the island of Bissao : no wood, unless I believe, strong scented, such as cedar, sandal wood, &c., is free from their depredations; and I have known an oak plank, three inches thick, lying upon the ground, completely hollowed out by them in one night. They begin their devastation from the ground underneath, and touch not the outer surface; so that the plank has all the appearance of its former solidity until it is moved; when there does not appear to be more than the thickness of a sheet of paper left of

---

* I planted two cocoa nuts at Bulama, which had been given to me from a Sierra Leone vessel, but they had not come up when we left the island; I fear that they were too old.

† Our inclosed garden contained exactly half an acre, and in it we had to knock down twenty of these bug-a-bug hills; it is said that they always build their nests on the best soil.

its former substance, all the internal part being entirely eaten away. Wood appears to be the chief substance against which they direct their rage; and this will never be hurt by them if it does not come in contact with the ground. Those posts which I placed in it were covered with either tar or paint under the ground, and for a few inches above it, for the purpose of repelling these destructive insects; but whether it was attended with the desired effect, we do not know, as they were not examined when we came away. The nests which we destroyed were not attempted to be rebuilt, and these destructive ants retired from our habitations; so that I should think that were the island well peopled they would quickly be destroyed. Exposure to the sun will kill them. The internal structure of their nests is very curious; whence there are innumerable channels or passages which lead deep under ground. We never destroyed one of them without finding at the bottom of it, what is called by the grumetas the queen (rainha) bug-a-bug; it was generally about three inches long; its head, which was perfectly that of a bug-a-bug, being the only resemblance it bore to the rest of the community; its body was annulated, and of a white, gelatinous, matter, resembling what is called the pith in the vertebræ of animals; but what appeared to me to be the most extraordinary was its being, apparently, incapable of progressive motion; for though its body was in a constant undulating motion, it never moved forward. These queens were always found placed between two pieces of thin, well worked, smooth, clay, laid one over the other, and their internal surfaces exactly fitting, in about the centre of which there was a concavity formed in each, to fit exactly the body of the insect, which was always sure to be found there. The bite of this insect is very severe.*

2dly. The BLACK ANT. It is difficult to stop the progress of these formidable, and innumerable, insects. If a brook be in their way they will go under it; if a house or a wall, they will either go under or over it. It is said that they will kill any animal, not excepting even the elephant itself, if they surprise it asleep; many astonishing things are told of them; and some, so wondrous, have we seen ourselves, that I almost fear to relate them; neither would I, if there were not persons living who could vouch for the correctness of the account. Shall I be believed when I say that I have seen them destroy living, full-grown, rats? I did not see the beginning of the attack, but one day, with several other persons, we stumbled upon an immense number of these ants, which occupied a space of, I suppose, about twenty feet in circumference, in the midst of them were two full grown rats, twisting about in the greatest agony, covered entirely with these ants. I do not believe that they had been long attacked by them, for their hair was pretty entire, in less than half an hour there was not a bit of it left upon either of their backs, and they appeared as if they had been scalded; their ears and eyes were full of them; and in somewhat more than an hour one of them was motionless, or dead, the other nearly so: with a long pole we killed it, to put it out of its misery. The rats though covered with ants when we first saw them, had quite strength enough to have run away, instead of which they did nothing but writhe and twist about, until their strength was entirely exhausted. Upon our first landing we were greatly an-

* Those who wish to know more of this kind of ant will find it well described in Smellie's Philosophy of Natural History.

noyed by these ants; several of the colonists being at different times awakened in the night, from their getting about them; and one woman I thought would have absolutely gone mad, before she could be disengaged of a great number that entirely covered her body, and had so got into her long, and thick, head of hair, that it was an operation of some time, entirely to clear her of them. These insects, one would suppose, must have a very acute sense of smelling; for if a piece of meat be dropped on the ground, and not one of them is to be seen, it would in a very short time be surrounded by them, and quickly devoured and carried away. We therefore used to place pieces about as traps, and when a great number were collected about them, they were destroyed by throwing hot coals upon them. At first we attempted it by pouring on them boiling water; but after lying, to all appearance dead, for about half an hour, they would get up and run away. They generally march in countless millions, and I have frequently watched their progress, like a stream of black ink, about two inches broad, for many hundred yards together. Sometimes they would go under ground, without any apparent necessity for so doing, and appear above it again at a short distance; and this would sometimes be frequently repeated, but always with uniform pace and in the most perfect order; at others they would continue the whole time that I watched them above ground; and at others again, after they had once entered the ground I was not able to trace their quitting it again. What struck me as the most remarkable circumstance in the march of these ants was, that at certain intervals, probably four or five inches on either side, in their line, there were larger ants always stationary, always with their heads towards the line of march, and always with their forceps wide open: these sentinels, like two rows of posts, always preserved the parallelism of the two sides of the column, as much so as it is in the two edges of a roll of black ribbon, to which they may, not inaptly, be compared. All the large black ants were not thus stationary, but many were in the lines with the smaller ones, and probably occasionally relieved the others; but I never saw a small one thus standing sentinel. The small ants were in length rather more than the fifth of an inch, and the larger one about four-tenths of an inch, and were in point of numbers compared with the former, probably, as about one to one hundred. When these ants have bitten, if pulled from the part, they generally leave their forceps behind them, which makes two small punctures that are easily perceived. Like the other sort described, these (or there would be no living for them,) always quit the habitations of men; and from three weeks after our landing, to the time of our quitting the island, we were not in the least annoyed by them. They trouble not the Portuguese inhabitants of Bissao; and I am told by the natives that they never enter their towns. These ants destroyed in one night, soon after our arrival, a whole litter of pigs, and more than a dozen fowls. The two kinds of ants above noticed have not the least similarity in their conformation, and not less dissimilar is their mode of living; the one subsisting chiefly on wood, the other on animal food; these latter, like the vultures, are of use in devouring dead carcases.

3dly. A smaller black ant, whose nests are sometimes on the ground, and sometimes on the branches of trees. These are not troublesome, except when disturbed; their bite is not very severe.

4thly, A common sized red ant, these are found only on, and about trees; I never saw any of their nests; their bite is pretty sharp. When we killed a bullock, it generally remained all night suspended by a rope to the arm of a large tree, on which these red ants used to make great havock, until we learned an easy mode of securing it from their depredations; and this was by simply drawing a circle of chalk all round the rope, over which those insects would never venture.

5thly, A large black ant, about three-fourths of an inch in length. These are seldom met with in greater numbers than six or eight together, generally singly, or by two's and three's. They are frequently found in the bottom of holes or pits, and live chiefly under ground; their bite is painful, and when killed, they emit an intolerable stench.

There are numerous swarms of bees in all these countries, which make their combs and deposit their honey in the hollows of trees; to get at which the natives cut them down. We had no better mode, on the Island of Bulama, to get at their honey, of which I have sometimes had three large pails-full brought to me in one morning. *Bees.*

There is also on the island a fly, called the honey fly, which lodges its sweets in the hollows of trees, but the quantity is so trifling as scarcely to deserve notice. *Honey fly.*

Climate.

This may be thought rather a delicate subject. It may be asked, what can you say good of the climate of that island, where almost all the Europeans died? To which I reply, that the mortality of those Europeans, though in some measure certainly to be attributed to the climate, was much more to the adventitious circumstances which have been already noticed; and I am inclined to think that, independent of its having really been the most unhealthy season of the year; independent of our hard labour, and great exposure during that inclement season; independent I say of all these, I am inclined to think that much of our very great mortality may be attributed to the uncommon depression of spirits which our situation produced on the minds of most of the colonists; and I verily believe that I should have died too, if I had ever suffered my mind to have been so subdued. But how far this despondency might have contributed to our mortality must be left to the decision of physicians.

One thing I will readily concede, and that is, that newly cleared, and newly settled countries never were, and never can be so healthy as those which have long been cultivated. The history of the settlement of every province in North America confirms this. But this unhealthiness, attendant, more or less, on all newly settled countries, is not to be attributed to the climate. It is a necessary consequence of the thing itself; and never was, and never can be, separated from it. This, however, is an evil which the labour of every day will diminish. I will now endeavour to give an idea of the climate of Bulama.

The temperature of the climate here, like that of all countries between the tropics, must be hot; but the degree of heat does not depend, in so low a latitude, on its absolute proximity to, or distance from, the equator; the heat of all countries situated so near it depending much more on local circumstances than on latitude; such, for instance, as the nature of the country over which the prevalent winds blow before their arrival, or the nature of the soil on which the sun shines.

If on, or near, the equator, the wind reaches you over a large extent of water, or previously traverses very high mountains, and the sun shines upon a soil either green or dark, the temperature of the air under such circumstances will, there, be much cooler than it will be on a spot twenty degrees either north or south of it, if to get thither the wind passes over low, sandy, or rocky ground, and if the sun's rays be reflected from either sand or white stone. Thus islands are cooler in hot countries, and warmer in cold ones, than places in the same latitude on a continent. But if those islands should be of a sandy or rocky nature, the heat arising from the reflected rays of the sun would more than counterbalance the coolness arising from their insular situation. Hence the almost insupportable heat, at times, on the islands of Malta and Minorca; though one be 36 and the other 40 degrees from the equator; hence the insufferable heat of the Bocca-chica of Carthagena, in South America; and of Madras beach, in India.

Bulama is in the eleventh degree of north latitude; if we travel on that parallel east, it will conduct us near to Calicut on the Malabar coast, and between Tranquebar and Pondicherry on the coast of Coromandel, in India; the same parallel, traced the other way, will lead us between the islands of Trinidada and Tobago, in the West Indies; the latter of these islands may serve to give a notion of the temperature of the air at Bulama.

The east is subject to those periodical winds called monsoons, whose changes are attended by exceedingly bad weather, and very heavy squalls, called tiphoons; and the west is very frequently visited by those dreadfully destructive tempests, called hurricanes. But the same latitudes on the coast of Africa, are happily exempt from each of those dangerous and tremendous gales. However, as thunder, lightning, and violent winds are essential, sometimes, to the purification of the air, Africa, in this latitude, has its tornados.

A tornado, though very violent, is never dangerous; it always gives sufficient warning of its approach, and lasts not long. Dark, heavy, and black clouds, are generally first seen rising from the South to the S. E., and, as they rise, forming a large black arch in the heavens, which moves slowly to the eastward, and, when it arrives between S.E. and East, the tornado generally comes on. I particularly observed every tornado at Bulama for two-thirds of one season, and the whole of another, from their first appearance, till their rage was entirely spent: and I never knew one give less than an hour's notice, but generally two, and sometimes four hours; and, except seven, out of seventy, they were all between the East and S.E. points of the compass, generally attended with much thunder, lightning, and rain; and they usually lasted from one to three hours.

To secure themselves from their violence, those seamen who are conversant with them, furl their sails, and thus wait their approach; for if a ship be caught by one of them with much sail set, she will probably lose her sails or masts, if even the ship itself be not in danger; for as to taking in sail, it is entirely out of the question. Their duration is so short, that the sea has not time to get up, if the violence of the wind, indeed, would permit it; and no lee shore is to be dreaded, as here, they almost always blow from the land. So little dangerous are they, that of the seventy that I witnessed, in two years, no accident occurred, except from lightning, and two vessels were struck by it in that time. Of these tornados two were at N.W. a very uncommon thing, three at N.E., and two at E.N.E., the other sixty-three between East and S.E. At the commencement and the latter end of the rainy season, they are sometimes, but not frequently, without rain; they begin about the middle of May, and indicate the approach of the rains; they are most frequent in the months of September and October, and cease about the beginning of November. I have been thus particular about tornados, because I have heard much of the signs by which their approach may be known; that is, a small black speck, or cloud, in the heavens, called the ox-eye. Now I declare that I never yet saw such a *small* black cloud in the heavens prior to their coming on; but invariably saw a *large* black cloud rising above the horizon, to the southward or S.E., which, as invariably, gradually lengthened into a long black arch, from which the wind generally came between an East and S.E. direction. The idea of their coming on, only at high or low water, is probably too absurd to merit confutation; however, having found such an opinion prevalent on the coast, I noticed the time of tide when they began, during the season of 1793, (see Appendix, No. 5,) which sufficiently proves that opinion to be ill-founded.

The rainy season begins with the month of June, and ends about the middle, or latter end of October:* what are termed the smoky, or foggy, months follow; after which, fine clear weather, with pretty regular land and sea breezes, prevails, until the beginning of the ensuing rains.

To give a more clear and connected notion of the climate we will briefly note the prevailing weather in each month of the year, beginning with June, when the rains commence.

* I speak here of Bulama; to the southward I believe that it begins earlier and ends later. In 1792 our first rain was on the 4th of June, the last on the 15th of October. In 1793 the first rain, except with a tornado on the last of May, was on the 7th of June; it rained five times after the 15th in October, and on the 3d and the 11th of November; but I think that the rainy season might be said to be over in the middle of October.

June—Thunder, lightning, and rain, about fifteen days out of the thirty—frequent tornados—winds variable, but the N.W. most prevalent.

July—Thunder and lightning four or five days in the month, rain about twenty-five—three or four tornados—S.W. winds principally.

August—Thunder and lightning seven or eight days—rain about twenty-five—tornados seldom—thermometer from 74 to 82—wind generally S.W.

September—Rain about fourteen days—frequent tornados—thunder and lightning seven or eight days—wind generally S.W. the first half of the month, and variable the latter half—thermometer from 77 to 85.

October—Rain about seven days—tornados frequent—thunder and lightning about six days—winds variable, but more from the S.W. than any other point—towards the latter end of the month sometimes from the N.E. particularly in the morning—foggy four or five days—thermometer from 81 to 91.

November—Rain once or twice—wind generally N.E. in the morning; calm or S.W. winds in the evening—clear weather the greatest part of the month—thermometer from 84 to 96—thunder and lightning four or five evenings.

December—N.E. wind and fog most days of this month—thermometer from 64 to 92; generally about 66 at day-light, with the N.E. wind, and 90 at noon.

January—A N.E. wind almost every morning this month, and generally calm afternoon—fogs frequent—thermometer from 63 to 98.

February—Clear weather—wind generally N.E. before, and S.W. after, noon—thermometer from 88 to 96; one day, when calm, it rose to 100.

March—Generally clear, with calm, or N.E. wind morning, and S.W. or sea breeze evening—thermometer from 86 to 95.

April—Clear, with N.E. winds in the early, and S.W. winds in the latter part of the day—thermometer from 85 to 94.

May—Winds variable—in the latter part of the month mostly from the N.W.—passing clouds begin to obscure the sky and warn us of the approaching rains—and lightning and distant thunder, generally in the evening, announce to us the speedy arrival of tornados, three or four of which may be expected in the last half of this month, sometimes with, and sometimes without rain.

From the above short statement it appears that variable winds, though the N.W. is the most prevalent, blow on the approach, and at the commencement of the rains, during the months of May and June.

That during the rainy months of July, August, September, and the rainy half of October, the wind generally blows from the S.W. quarter; after which time until the month of May, N.E. or land winds are pretty general in the mornings, and S.W. or sea breezes as general in the evenings.

NOTE FOR SEAMEN.

The erroneous position of the islands of Bissegos and Mantere (as placed in the African Pilot) have already been noticed in my Journal when I went to Ghinala, though I knew not where to place them myself; being able to affirm only *where they are not*, but *not where they are*. It is impossible, therefore, for me to give any directions for sailing up the Bijuga channel; but I have collected in Appendix, No. 17, all those extracts from the Hankey's log, from that ship's making the land until her anchoring at the mouth of the Grande, which can be of the least possible use to any person bound up the same channel hereafter.

CHAPTER XI.

Advantageous position of the Country sketched in Chapter VIII for the purposes of Cultivation and Commerce—its Colonization proposed—Commodities intended to be there produced—how these might affect our West Indian possessions—what effect the Colonization of this Country might have on the African character, particularly with respect to Slavery—and how far it may conduce towards the introduction of Letters and Religion into that Country, as well as to a more accurate knowledge of its interior. Reasons for fixing upon the territory between the Gambia and the Grande, and for beginning the Plantations on the latter, instead of on the former River. Conclusion.

FROM looking over the map of that part of Africa whose outline is traced in the beginning of Chapter VIII, and from what is there said, it will appear that on the western coast of Africa there is a fertile country, inhabited by various tribes, or nations; bounded by high mountains, two large navigable rivers, and the sea; intersected with many small rivers, with more than 500 miles of navigable coasts for ships of burthen, and many more than a thousand navigable for boats; having on its southern side, one vast, continued, safe, and commodious harbour, of more than 100 miles in length, from Jatt's island to the mouth of the Rio Grande.

Advantageous position of the country between the Gambia and Grande for cultivation.

In this great extent of fertile and navigable country, comprized between the rivers Gambia and Grande, there is only one European factory, and that indeed not upon the continent, but upon the island of Bissao, and no attempt has hitherto been made, except our fruitless one, by any European power, to settle any of these countries, for the purposes of cultivation; and no European power has certainly any claim to the soil, which belongs to its present possessors, the native Africans, except only so much as we have already purchased from them.

<small>Property of the soil in the native Africans.</small>

Admirably adapted as this country is to facilitate its own internal commerce, by means of its large rivers, and the numerous small ones, which, in a very great portion of it, admit the approach of small vessels to carry off its produce by water; yet it is not less eligibly situated for external commerce, its distance from this country being scarcely more than half that to the West Indies; and communication with it, at all seasons, practicable, and easy; without the dread of tiphoons and hurricanes; or being cramped, and retarded, by trade winds and monsoons.

<small>Equally adapted for commerce as for cultivation.</small>

This country then I should propose to colonize. I am well aware that this proposition will be opposed by a very respectable, and weighty, body of men, the West India planters; as well as by all those concerned in carrying on the slave trade: but even though it might be hostile to their interests, which I by no means concede, yet if it will be beneficial to the country at large, it is a measure that ought to be adopted.

<small>Its colonization proposed.</small>

<small>Opposition expected to it.</small>

Many people doubt whether it be the interest of this country to extend her colonies or not; probably not—generally speaking; but so long as we continue to consume the same quantity of sugar and coffee, and to use in our manufactures as much cotton and indigo as we do at present, the one proposed will be to the advantage of the mother country, particularly in the two

<small>Whether it be the interest of this country to extend her colonies.</small>

last mentioned articles, for which a considerable sum of money is annually paid to foreigners.

In this colony I should propose the culture of cotton, coffee, tobacco, and indigo, as the staple commodities, but chiefly the first; and in the course of time, when the planters may have cleared a sufficient quantity of ground, and have capital enough to undertake it, the culture of the sugar cane. And these should be cultivated by free natives; no person in a state of slavery being permitted to be kept, in any part of the colony. *[Articles intended to be cultivated.]*

We are informed, by respectable authority,* that the British colonies do not furnish more than one sixth part of the cotton necessary to supply the demand of this Country. Having given an account of the first cost and settlement of a cotton plantation, his words are " with every disadvantage, however, the demand for cotton-wool, for the British manufactories, encreases with such rapidity, *that it cannot be doubted the cultivation of it*, with the cautions recommended, *will be found highly profitable*; the British dominions *not supplying*, at present, *more than one sixth part of the home demand.*"—Here, then, we have authority, and that West-Indian authority, that the cultivation of cotton would be beneficial to this country, and that its culture would not interfere with the produce of our West Indian colonies. Now cotton is the chief article that I should recommend to be cultivated; all others, when compared with that, being only secondary objects.

It appears from the same author that in 1787, cotton-wool was imported into Great Britain from all parts, to the amount of 22,600,000lbs. Now let us suppose that the present annual

* Edwards' History of the West Indies, Vol. II. p. 272, 2d edition.

demand of that commodity amounts to 24,000,000lbs.; of which our own colonies supply one sixth part, here then is a deficit of 20,000,000lbs., for which we have to pay foreigners; if then these 20,000,000lbs. could be produced in the projected colony, there would be a clear saving, to this country, of the amount of its value; and reckoning that at only one shilling per pound, it would amount per annum to one million pounds sterling. That this quantity might be easily produced in the country proposed to be cultivated, would not be difficult to be proved; nor even that it might be produced on the small territories which we have already purchased.

<small>Estimate of the expences attending the establishment of a cotton plantation in the West Indies.</small> Mr. Edwards, after having given an account of the various kinds of cotton, its mode of cultivation, and the risques attending it, proceeds to give an estimate of the expences attending the establishment of a cotton plantation in the West Indies; his words are, "*I shall now bring into one point of view
" the several particulars attending the first cost and settlement
" of a plantation in this sort of husbandry, and the returns
" which may reasonably be expected from a small capital
" thus employed. I fix on a small capital, because I conceive
" that a cotton plantation may be established on a more
" moderate fund than any other; and it is for the interest of the
" community that men of small fortunes should be instructed
" how to employ their time and labours to the best ad-
" vantage."

" I will allot fifty acres for the first purchase, in order
" that the planter may have room for that purpose. Sup-
" posing therefore that one half only is planted in cotton at
" the same time, the capital will be invested as follows:

---

* Edwards' History of the West Indies, Vol. II. p. 269, 2d edit.

African Memoranda.

Cost of fifty acres of land, at £5 currency *per* acre.............................	£250	0	0
Expence of clearing, fencing, and planting 25 acres, at £7 *per* acre....................	175	0	0
Purchase of twelve negroes, at £70 each....	840	0	0
	1265	0	0
One year's interest, at 6 *per cent*............	75	18	0
One year's maintenance, clothing, and medical care of the negroes.....................	120	0	0
Total expenditure in Jamaica currency (equal to £1040 sterling).....................	1460	18	0

"The returns are now to be considered:—In Jamaica it *Returns of the same.* is commonly reckoned that one acre of cotton will yield annually 150 pounds weight, and in some years nearly twice as much; but I am afraid that, on an average of any considerable number of successive crops, even the former is too great an allowance. By accounts which I have procured from the Bahama Islands, it appears, that in 1785, 1786, and 1787 (all of which years were considered as favourable), the produce of the cotton lands, on an average, did not exceed one hundred and twelve pounds *per* acre.

"The price in the Bahamas and Jamaica was the same, viz. 1*s*. 3*d*. sterling *per* pound. Allowing therefore average produce *per* acre to be one hundred weight, the returns are these: viz.

	Sterling.		
"25 cwt. at 1*s*. 3*d*. sterling *per* pound	£175	0	0
"Deduct incidental expences, as materials for bagging, colonial taxes, &c.............	25	0	0
"Remains in sterling money...............	150	0	0

"Which gives an interest of upwards of fourteen *per cent.* on the capital; arising too from the lowest priced cotton."

<small>Estimate of the expences attending the establishment of a cotton plantation in Africa.</small>

Now let us give an estimate of the expences attending the establishment of a cotton plantation of the same number of acres as the above, on the island of Bulama; and then see what the returns may reasonably be expected to be.

Cost of fifty acres of land, at 10 shillings *per* acre........	£25	0	0
Expence of clearing, fencing, and planting 25 acres, in the wear and tear of tools, at 5s. *per* acre............	6	5	0
Hire of twelve grumetas, at six bars* each a month, for one year............	72	0	0
	103	5	0
One year's interest, at 6 *per cent*............	6	3	6
One year's maintenance, clothing, and medical care of the grumetas§............	60	0	0
Total expenditure............	169	8	6

* The bar is a nominal sum; it was reckoned at 3s. 4d. when I was at Bulama; six of those bars therefore make a pound sterling. Supposing each grumeta to have six bars a month, that would amount nominally to 144 pounds; but they are paid their wages in such goods, though valued at six bars, as do not cost in England more than half that sum; indeed generally not quite so much. I reckon therefore the wages of each grumeta at 10s. a month, which is more than sufficient, as the common wages given by the Portuguese are 4 bars only, or the value of 6s. 8d. per month, but as there are some, more trusty, or head men, who have 8, and even 12, bars a month, I reckon the average at six.

This sixty pounds is much more than sufficient, and is allowed only for maintenance; the grumetas, not being slaves, clothe themselves; indeed most of their wages generally go to that purpose; as to medical care, when they are ill, they always apply *to their own country doctor.*

Now let us consider the returns. Reckoning the produce per acre, at one hundred weight, as in the preceding calculation, and estimating the value of the cotton, at 20 per cent. *under that of Jamaica, which is the lowest priced;* that is, reckoning it to be worth 1*s.* only *per* pound, the return will be for

25 cwt. at 1*s. per* pound £140

Deduct incidental expences, as materials for bagging, colonial taxes, &c.................... 25
———
Remains in sterling money   115

Returns of the same.

Which gives an interest of more than 70 *per cent.* on the capital; though the produce be sold 20 per cent. *under the lowest priced cotton at present.**

The land already purchased in Africa, that is, the island of Bulama, and part of the Biafara peninsula, cannot contain less than 400,000 acres of land. Now, allowing as in Mr. Edwards's estimate, each acre to produce one hundred weight of cotton, the half of the above purchased land would produce 20,000,000lbs. (setting aside the 12 over every hundred,) which if sold at 20 *per cent.* under the present lowest priced cottons,

Quantity of land already purchased.

What it is capable of producing.

---

* When at Kacundy in 1793, a Mr. Walker, called Doctor Walker, from his having formerly been surgeon to a slave ship, was owner of the principal factory there, he was a very intelligent man, and had then planned a cotton plantation of 100 acres, an estimate of the expence of which he gave to me, but which is locked up among other African papers, at present out of my reach. He told me that his motive for so doing was because he foresaw the ruin of the slave trade, and that he chose to be prepared to employ those whom he had when he could no longer export them, he seemed to have no doubt of its success. The trade carried on from this place with the Foulahs is extensive and profitable, and might easily be continued to Bulola on the Grande. The mountainous slopes at Kacundy I should think admirably calculated for the production of coffee.

would be worth one million sterling; and, when manufactured, full six times that sum.

However, as it would require some years to bring into cultivation such a quantity of land, and as the proportion of one half of the whole is too much to be cultivated in cotton, we must wait until we have purchased more land in that country, to enable us to make such a large return of cotton to Europe.

But, to make a beginning; suppose, that 100 different persons should undertake the establishment of as many cotton plantations on the island of Bulama, and that each plantation should consist of 100 acres, of which the half only, or 50 acres, should be planted with cotton at one time; here then would be 5000 acres employed in the cultivation of cotton: and let us reckon the first year as nothing, and consider the second year of cultivation, as the first year of return; that first year of return, according to the above calculated produce and price, will amount to £25,000 sterling. And if a similar number of adventurers had gone out the second year, to put in cultivation the Biafara peninsula, the produce of the second year of return would amount to £50,000 sterling; and I think there can be no doubt, that if the colony be properly attended to, and wisely regulated, the value of its exported produce to this country would in less than 20 years amount to one million per annum; while of British manufactures imported into it the amount might be nearly as much more.

If it be asked, why then have we not had more returns from Sierra Leone; and how comes it that, after having spent such immense sums, that company is obliged to have recourse to parliament for support; I answer because that colony has neither been properly attended to, nor wisely regulated; and has been, from beginning to end, one of the most uncommon, and almost incredible, instances of colonial folly, in its regulation and management, that the world ever witnessed; and, as before observed, I consider it as having tended rather to retard than accelerate the civilization and the freedom of Africa.

But, to return to our subject; independent of the profit on cotton, the colonists might derive a very considerable one from trading with the natives in the articles of rice, pepper, ivory, wax, gum, and hides: all of which would be readily bartered for English goods, with a very considerable profit to the settlers. To carry on this trade to advantage, they should have small decked vessels of from 10 to 20 tons, (about one to every ten plantations) to sail up the various creeks and branches of the sea; there to collect the produce of the country, and transport it to Bulama. *Profits on trade with the natives.*

As to *Rice* I know not whether it would be worth the planter's while to send it to England; except in seasons of scarcity: all that I know is, that he may buy it, in almost any quantity, on the coast of Africa, exceedingly cheap, and that if he can find a market for it in Europe, it will answer very well.

Pepper is not to be procured in the neighbourhood of Bulama; but, as an article of commerce, it may be procured to leeward; as also dying woods.

Ivory, in great abundance, may be procured in almost every creek that a boat can enter.

Wax is also very plentiful; and

Hides of buffaloes and deer may not only be purchased for almost nothing, but may be obtained by taking only the trouble to shoot and skin the animal.

Gum I saw but little of, but it is to be procured in the Gambia.

These articles, taken one with another, would yield to the settler a neat profit of at least 50 *per cent*, and would keep his small vessel in constant employment, while he was encreasing his plantation; by these means also we should become intimately acquainted with all the approachable parts of Africa by water, and greatly add to our geographical knowledge.

Indigo.

Indigo is another article which I should propose cultivating on Bulama. It grows wild all over the island. The profits on the cultivation of this plant are immense: but it requires constant attention, during its fermentation, or the produce of the whole plantation may be lost; the vapour arising from it in that state is said to be exceedingly unhealthy: these are the two objections to its cultivation. The quantity of indigo annually imported into Great Britain amounts, it is said,* " to one million and a half of pounds, of which five parts in seven are purchased, with ready money, from strangers and rivals."

This money might be saved to the country, by the cultivation of that plant on the island of Bulama, or neighbouring coast of Africa.

Coffee.

Coffee is the third article of cultivation which I should propose. It does not appear that the island of Bulama is particularly calculated for the cultivation of the tree which produces this berry, as its soil may in general be too rich, and not sufficiently elevated; however, in the extent of country proposed to be cultivated, many spots will, I doubt not, be found, proper for its culture.

* Edwards's West Indies, vol. II, p. 284.

Mr. Edwards in his estimate of the expence and return of a coffee plantation of 300 acres in Jamaica, makes the total expence amount to £15,059,* in the currency of that island, which is 40 *per cent.* worse than sterling. And the return on the 4th year (there being none the first three) amounts to about 7¼ *per cent.* on the whole; the 5th and subsequent years produce a clear profit of 24¼ *per cent.* Now a similar plantation cultivated by free natives, on the coast of Africa, would make much greater returns for the capital so employed, because one of the chief articles of expence in the West Indian statement is that of purchasing 100 negro slaves, and the compound interest thereon for three years; amounting, both together, to more than one half of the whole expence; therefore, a coffee plantation of equal extent with this of Jamaica, might be put in cultivation, on the coast of Africa, for £7500, which there requires £15,000; and the African returns would be, instead of 24¼, rather more than 50 per cent; for there are other items which might be diminished if it were necessary so to do.

Expence and returns of a plantation of coffee in the West Indies.

Double what it would be in Africa.

Considering that the French part of the island of St. Domingo in the year 1792, exported nearly 80 millions† of pounds of coffee, which I should suppose was now reduced to less than one-eighth of that quantity, it is reasonable to suppose that the cultivation of this berry, on the coast of Africa, notwithstanding the increased quantity raised at Jamaica, since that period, would find a ready market in Europe, and add largely to the revenues of this country.

Tobacco is the 4th staple of the proposed colony; but what quantity, and to what value, this country might take of it, I

Tobacco.

---

* Edwards's West Indies, vol. II, p. 296. † Idem, p. 299.

am totally ignorant, but should suppose that the culture of this plant would produce the greatest sum, next after that of cotton. At Kacundy I saw it growing.

The sugar cane. The 5th and last article proposed to be cultivated is the sugar cane, but this I should not recommend until the colony had been established 10 or 15 years. Even then it might be thought proper to prohibit its culture, as interfering with the prosperity of our West Indian colonies.

Fruit. I say nothing here about the exportation of fruit, but I am well convinced that this part of Africa might supply the English market with a number of oranges equal to those which are now sent to it from Portugal and the Western Isles; and there are many other articles of inferior consequence that would well repay its cultivators.

How this cultivation might affect our West Indian colonies. One great objection to the colonizing the proposed country, for the purposes of cultivation, will probably be that it will interfere with our islands in the West Indies. Now, of the articles proposed to be cultivated, the first two, and the most important, (except tobacco which is here out of the question, that plant not being cultivated in our West Indian colonies,) it has been proved from West Indian authority, cannot be fully supplied to us by our West Indian settlements. Inasmuch, therefore, as the cultivation of these two articles are concerned, it cannot affect our West Indian islands; but their cultivation will save to this country more than a million of money annually, now paid to foreigners for them.

The cultivation of coffee would not, I should suppose, on account of the demand for it beyond the produce, be very prejudicial to our West Indian plantations.

It remains now to speak of sugar. I conceive that the culture of the sugar cane on the coast of Africa would tend considerably to lessen the value of sugar, and consequently injure our West Indian islands; if so, the culture of that plant, and even coffee, might be prohibited, in the proposed colony on that coast; but I see no reason why it might not be undertaken for the purposes of producing cotton, tobacco and indigo.

Without the gift of prophecy one may conceive it possible, that, ere the close of this century, we may not have an island left in the West Indies.* Much more extraordinary things have passed under our own eyes. Now, if ever that should be the case, the colony proposed, under the restriction of not making sugar, so long as we possessed those islands, would be in a state soon to supply us with that article, if ever such a calamity should befal us.

But there are other objections. It will, in all probability, be said, that free Africans will not labour, and that if they would, their numbers are not sufficient to cultivate so much soil, as will enable us to make the returns I expect; and probably after all, that they will not sell us their land. Objections answered.

As to the first objection, I know that those who chuse always to see the African character in its worst light will probably say that they never will be induced voluntarily to labour; and that The Africans not averse from labour.

* The report of the Bulama trustees was shewn by a friend of mine, in January 1793, to Mr. Bryan Edwards, who stated that, if the accuracy of that report could be relied upon, the success of the Bulama establishment could not be a matter of doubt; and added, that if he were not already possessed of a great number of uncultivated acres in Jamaica, he would himself embark in it. He entered with great minuteness into the subject, and besides the fitness of the soil and climate for all the produce of the West Indies, he calculated also on the difference of freightage between Bulama and our West Indian colonies; as also on the certainty that the latter cannot long remain in our possession.

I betray a total ignorance of it, in supposing that they can ever be brought to cultivate the earth for wages. That assertion may be made; but my answer is, put it to the test. And I moreover say that, as far as my little knowledge of the Africans will enable me to judge, I have no doubt of their readily cultivating the earth for hire, whenever Europeans will take the trouble so to employ them. I never saw men work harder, more willingly, or regularly, generally speaking, than those free natives whom I employed upon the island of Bulama. What induced them to do so? Their desire of European commodities in my possession, of which they knew that they would have the value of one bar at the end of a week, or four at the end of a month. Some of them remained at labour for months, ere they left me; others, after having left me, returned; they knew that the labour was constant, but they also knew that their reward was certain: which reward they could not by other means acquire. Most of these men came from the island of Bissao, where there was a Portuguese factory, possessing much more, and a greater variety, of European commodities than I had; but they had no means of acquiring them; for, if they had not a slave, ivory, wax, or any other merchandise to barter, how could they procure them of the Portuguese, who were traders and not cultivators? Therefore, if a Papel wanted a hat, a shirt, a bandana, a fathom of blue baft, or a Romall, he came to Bulama to work for it. Here it may not be amiss to observe, that these grumetas had seldom any portion of spirits, as the wages of their labour. I had it not; they therefore laboured for articles of clothing, dress, or finery; something to make them, or their wives, look more gay. I think, therefore, that, as far as my experience goes, I am warranted in saying that the Africans are not averse to labour, unless those in the neighbourhood of Bulama are unlike the rest of their species. So much as to the question of labour.

As to their numbers, this I allow to be small; exceedingly so, when compared to the extent of their territory. But though this will operate against our cultivating as much, and as speedily, as we could wish; yet it will greatly facilitate our purchasing their territory; for were it more populous less would be sold, as a greater quantity of land would be required for their own support. I consider, therefore, this scanty population, when compared to the extent of territory, as exceedingly favourable to the projected colony; because, if their number be few, there is less danger of insult or attack, if we should ever unfortunately be for any short time upon bad terms with them. And if the colony be wisely conducted, the population will rapidly increase; and, in twenty years there will be a numerous band of youths, brought up under English government, attached to their landlords, and conversant with their language; whose manners will partake more of the English than the African; and whose labour would be employed chiefly on the soil. This population would continue to increase as fast as the territory could be cleared; and I have no doubt that the province between the Gambia and the Grande would, under a wise government, in 50 years be the most populous district in Africa. *Their scanty population not detrimental in the outset.*

As to any supposed difficulty in the purchasing of land from the natives, and erecting houses, I know that there will be none on the southern border of the above territory; almost all those tribes with whom I had connexion solicited me to come and build a house and reside among them. As to the quantity of disposable land, I have no other ground upon which to form an estimate of it, than from what I saw in two nations, *Their land easily purchased.*

the Bijugas and the Biafaras. Among the former my instance must be taken from Canabac. That island has two towns only; and the one I visited was reckoned the chief. We will, however, suppose Belchore's town of equal extent and population; this will give us (from the grounds on which I estimated the population of Jalorem's town, as stated in my Journal June 27, 1792) 1200 souls as the whole population of the island of Canabac. This island we will consider as about 16 miles long and 10 broad, which will give us more than 100,000 acres for its whole contents; of which, I am confident that I speak far within bounds when I say that, not 100 acres are cultivated by the natives; or in other words not one acre in a thousand; and as the land uncultivated by the natives is of little or no use, or value to them, it would be readily parted with for a trifle. We see then that on the Island of Canabac alone, more than 99,000 acres of such disposable land may be purchased. In the same proportion land may be purchased in every island in the cluster. But these are mere trifles when compared to what may be purchased on the continent; as the towns there, at least on its southern side, are neither so numerous, nor so populous, as on the islands; for instance in 72 miles up the Rio Grande there are only three towns, so that I think we may fairly assume that not one acre, in two thousand, is cultivated on that part of the continent between the rivers Grande and Gambia; of which full 300,000 acres between Ghinala and Bulama have been already purchased; and the latter contains above 100,000 more, making altogether more than 400,000 acres.

The banks of the Gambia, which I have never visited, are, on the contrary, I believe, thickly sprinkled with populous towns; but the intermediate space between that river and the Grande,

Of which they do not cultivate above one acre in a thousand on the Bijuga islands.

And not more than 1 acre in 2 thousand on the northern borders of the rivers.

has scarcely any; so that upon the whole I consider myself as having over-rated the proportion of cultivated to uncultivated land, when I say that it is as one to two thousand.

Supposing the colonization of the country between the Gambia and the Grande, as well as the uninhabited Bijuga isles, to be undertaken by individuals sanctioned by government, or else by government* itself, I should recommend the repossessing ourselves of Bulama immediately; and, upon the fertile soil of that beautiful little island I should commence such a plan of cultivation, which, with common prudence and common success, would, I doubt not, in less than twenty years export to the parent country produce to the value of more than a million sterling; and, it requires no great share of credulity to believe, might soon after take from Great Britain her manufactured goods to more than that amount; for which the colony would make its chief returns in raw materials, for British industry to work up; and these would be returned to it at an amazingly encreased price; which is, of all others, the most advantageous commerce that one country can carry on with another. *[Hints for commencing the colonization of this country.]*

We will therefore suppose the colonization of these countries seriously intended; and that a certain number of persons are arrived, at the proper season of the year, that is to say, just after the rains, on the island of Bulama; those persons will find an uninhabited and fertile soil; and grumetas, or labourers, may be readily procured in the neighbourhood. Six months

---

* It would be better undertaken by government, on whose account all the land should be purchased, which I think might be done for less than 5000 pounds; and grants of certain portions of it should be made to individuals at 10s. an acre. Now supposing the above territory to contain only 18,000,000 of acres the whole when granted away, would produce to government 9,000,000 sterling.

dry weather may be certainly reckoned upon, if they arrive at the proper time; in which they may clear their grounds for cultivation; and cotton, as the least difficult and least expensive, and making the best return, all things considered, I should recommend to be first cultivated. During the dry season the colonists would also erect their houses and make a public road &c.; while the governor should be making purchases of land on the continent and among the Bijuga islands for future settlers; and in doing this he would meet with no great difficulty, as all the ground uncultivated by them is of no use, any further than as affording them the means of the chace. And indeed they are ever anxious to have white people settled in their neighbourhood, as when that is the case they always expect a constant supply of European goods. In the mean time, while the cotton is growing, some small returns might be made to the mother country in the native produce enumerated in page 381.

Having, in the first year, made two establishments on the island of Bulama, one at the east, and the other at the west, end of it; the former of which is to be considered the capital of the colony; I should the next year form one on the Biafara shore opposite to it; and another just to the westward of that branch of the Grande which runs up to Ghinala. These would be both on land already purchased of the natives; but, if the government at Bulama has been at all active, other territories will have been purchased in the first year; in which case I should form a third establishment at Bulola,* and a fourth in

* Although Bulola is without the boundary line of the territory proposed to be colonized, being on the Naloo peninsula on the south side of the Grande, yet, from the character of its inhabitants, and their desire to have us established among them, I should there form a settlement, probably it might be thought wise to extend the

the isle of Galenas; so that at the beginning of the dry season of the second year, we should have six distinct establishments on this part of the coast. At the beginning of the third year, three, four, five or six other establishments might be formed on some of the Bijuga islands, or on some of those close to the continent, or, on the continent itself, north of the Rio Grande; and I should now consider the colony as sufficiently strong and permanent to require no further assistance from government.

In the above outline, I have confined myself to the southern shore, but I think it would be as well, nay better, to begin the first year at both ends. In which case I should recommend the taking possession of James's island in the Gambia, and constructing on it a considerable fort; and the second year an establishment should be made on the Pasqua river.

In establishing this colony there are certain points which must not be swerved from; whenever they are, the colony, if not ruined, will be retarded; these are: *In which certain points must be rigidly adhered to.*

First, that no land be ever taken from the natives by force; and that we do not ever make a settlement without their consent. We should even re-purchase the land already bought rather than our right to it be disputed. *Land never to be occupied but with the free consent of its owners.*

The second is, that no person can be employed as a slave in any of our settlements, nor on board any ship or vessel belonging to the colonists. At the same time that the employment of slaves is prohibited to the European colonists, these must also be forbidden to interfere in the smallest degree whatever, with southern boundary of the colony and carry it to the Rio Nunez, which is navigable for ships of 300 tons burthen, though with two or three bars, up to Kacundy about 70 miles from its mouth, between which place and Bulola on the Grande, there is frequent communication. *No slaves are to be employed by a colonist either on shore or afloat. But the government of the colony not to be suffered to interfere with the traffic of slaves by the native princes.*

the employment of them by the native kings or chiefs, in their own towns or territories. Nothing must be done against their independence. The abolition of that execrable trade must be left to the gradual, but sure, operation of reason, and example. Should we endeavour to prevent the native chiefs from selling slaves; so sudden, and so violent, a check to one of their immemorial customs; the reason, the policy, or the justice of which, it is impossible for them at first to comprehend, would ill dispose them towards us; and make them either treacherous friends or open enemies to the success of our undertaking; at the same time that not one slave less would be annually sold, notwithstanding our ill-advised and absurd attempts to prevent it; and by such means the slave trade never will be abolished. Whereas if these people are left to themselves, and to the operation of reason and example, without the smallest shock to any of their customs or prejudices, I question very much if a slave will ever be seen in any native town of the colony at the expiration of fifteen or twenty years. But if a misguided zeal for the abolition of slavery be manifested, it will tend to prolong its continuance, and the colony never can, and never will flourish. The absurdity of very well meaning persons, in thinking that they can overcome vices, customs, or prejudices, immemorially rooted in an unenlightened people, by shocking, instead of gradually enlightening their understandings, has done a great deal of mischief already. To begin by telling a native chief, the instant you have got into his country, that of his six wives he must put away five, because it is a great sin, and forbidden by the laws of God, to have more than one, will certainly astonish the chief, but will not induce him to part from his wives. As to the word sin, it is impossible that it can convey any idea to him; it is not within the limits of possibility for him to comprehend the idea which it is meant to convey; and of the laws of God he will have as little knowledge. But he will know that it is the custom, and ever has been, in his country, for every man to keep as many wives as he can afford; and that he is respected in proportion to the number of them which he maintains. Now to insist upon his parting from the cause of his respect, without assigning any comprehensible reason for his so doing, betrays a more barbarous mind than the one intended to be enlightened. If, after this, the same person goes on, and tells the chief, that drunkenness is also a sin, and that he must give up drinking spirits; in short, that he will not sell him any, nor suffer any to be sold to him for the future; the chief, who has been accustomed to drink spirits, and to see every one else do the same, when it was to be procured, will begin to think this European a little unreasonable; and will not be desirous of having him for a neighbour. But if the European goes on, and tells him that he must change his religion and become a Christian, or else when he dies that he will be roasted like a yam, always in torment but never thoroughly done; this chief will probably inquire what he means by being a Christian, that he may avoid this roasting. When his European instructor goes on from one dogma to another, all alike unintelligible in the present intellectual state of the chief, till he finishes with the doctrine of the Trinity, the belief in which, he tells this chief, is essential to his salvation: the latter, who thought him unreasonable at first, now thinks him * outrageously so; and that

---

* If I may be thought to have spoken too lightly on subjects so serious, my apology will be found in the contempt and indignation I feel at the ill-directed efforts of those

he is either a mad man, a fool, or an impostor; and to get rid of people professing such doctrines, will be his constant endeavour. Absurd as such conduct must appear, I have seen conduct towards a native chief yet more so; and much mischief has already been done by the fanatical zeal of some misguided people. I could give instances, but they are so incredibly extravagant, that they would scarcely find credit among sober minded people. If conduct like this be pursued in the intended colony, it will never succeed, and the condition of the natives will never be improved.

<small>Virtuous, sober, and religious example in Europeans, productive of more good towards the Africans, than overcharged zeal for their reformation and conversion.</small>

If those Europeans who settle there are of industrious habits, and confine themselves to one wife, whose offspring they bring up with care and affection, the very habit even of imitation, (more particularly as it would be an imitation of people acknowledged their superiors in every thing) will in time, and that not very distant, introduce the same custom among the native chiefs, and from them it will descend to all others; and thus what the furious zeal of a bigot would have endeavoured to bring about in a day, a week, a month, or a year, at the expence of rudely attacking all their prejudices, but which he would never have accomplished, might gently and gradually be effected, and made to appear their own work, without our having in any instance wounded any of their feelings.

As to drinking; if Europeans set them the example of sobriety, if they will not employ a drunkard, and always consider a man who has been seen in that state, as having dishonoured,

---

misguided and self-appointed missionaries. The language I use is such as must naturally suggest itself to their ignorant *catechists*. And the great truths of Christianity will be more exposed to ridicule than veneration, by the exercise of this " zeal without knowledge." Romans x. 2.

and debased himself, they will soon confine that vice to a few of the lowest and most thoughtless of the people; who, by the bye, if they have the propensity, will not have the means of gratifying it.

As to Religion; there is much more danger of doing evil, than probability of doing good, by an excessive zeal for its introduction. In this, as in other points, example is much; if we are constant in our attendance at divine worship, and conduct ourselves there with decorum and reverence, this will have more effect on the minds of the Africans, towards converting them to Christianity, than any thing that could be said by any fanatical zealot; and if we leave its operation to the slow workings of time, we shall certainly attain our object; which the folly of an enthusiast might only place farther from us.

So of Slavery. Interfere not with the natives buying or selling slaves; but let no European employ one. His grumetas, who till the ground for hire, must be reasonably paid, well fed, comfortably lodged, and have a little piece of ground to raise vegetables, and to keep poultry. These grumetas, unless they have a very unreasonable master, will be generally contented and happy; and if they have a good master they will never quit him; and generally speaking would risk their lives on his account. It would be seen in a very short time that these grumetas would annually produce more profit to their master, than if they *had been all sold* for slaves; nay, than if they *could be all sold* EVERY YEAR, whereas they can be sold *but once*.

One great motive of the Africans in making slaves, indeed I may say the only one,* is to procure European goods; slaves are the Principal motive of the natives for making and selling slaves.

* This is to be understood of those who are made so by force and treachery; some crimes, as for instance, witchcraft, and adultery are, I believe, in every part of

money, the circulating medium, with which great African commerce is carried on; they have no other. If therefore we could substitute another, and at the same time that other be more certain and more abundant, the great object in trading in slaves will be done away. This may be done by the produce of the earth. Let the native chiefs be once convinced that the labour of a free native in cultivating the earth, may produce him more European goods in one year, than he could have purchased if he had sold him for a slave, and he will no longer seek to make slaves to procure European commodities, but will cultivate the earth for that purpose; and he would be a gainer, even if the labour of one man should procure, annually, goods only to the amount of one half, or one fourth, of the value of a slave; because these he will have *every year*, the former he could have only *once*.

Marginal note: How these may be done away.

The third point is, that convicts be not sent to the colony, and the fourth is, that black troops be not employed there, unless they are absolutely natives of the colony, of whom it might be advisable to have about a dozen, but not more, from each town, to serve as soldiers.*

Marginal note: Neither convicts nor black troops to be employed in the colony.

Africa, punished with either slavery or death. But the desire to acquire these European commodities frequently produces the unfounded accusation of both; and as the value of the accused person, if convicted, goes to the accuser, the king, and the judges of the cause, he has little chance, unless he be of a powerful family, of escaping condemnation. The art of the Africans, on the sea coast, in laying snares for the accusation of a person, particularly of an European unacquainted with their manners, of the latter crime, equals that of some of our most notorious swindlers.

* When I say black troops, I mean native Africans, who have been either in Europe or in the West Indies. I should have no objection to carry to the new settlement one hundred Lascars that might be found in London, the climate would be natural to them, and they would be useful, but not so much so as the native grumetas;

If we do not give cause for quarrels with the natives, if our conduct be just and upright towards them, they will forward our views with all their strength. But on the contrary, if our conduct be unjust and oppressive, though they might not openly attack any of the establishments, yet would they cut off any white as he straggled in the woods, or traded in their creeks; unless they were ever on their guard and well armed; and there would be no security but in strength. However, as it is possible, though highly improbable, that some native tribe may act unjustly and hostilely towards us, I should in that case, recommend at first a palaver, in which I should endeavour to procure redress, and if I failed, my next step should be to convince every other tribe, or nation, of the injury which we had received, and the necessity we were reduced to, by the refusal of the aggressors to give us satisfaction, to punish them for their conduct. And this punishment, when at length obliged to have recourse to it, should be severe, should be dreadful. In short, the just vengeance of the colony should be dreaded, as much as its impartial justice should be loved, admired and respected. *If our conduct be just so will be that of the natives*

If their's be otherwise, how we ought to act.

To endeavour to lessen the misery, and consequently to increase the happiness of mankind, cannot, one would hope, draw excessive censure on the person, however mistaken he may be, or however ill digested his plans, who strives to accomplish so desirable an end. With great deference therefore, but without fear, I shall say a few words on the subject of African slavery.

Slavery, I think, may generally be said to be that state which makes death preferable to life. Instances innumerable, in both *Idea of slavery.*

---

but I would not take with me a single African who had ever been in London. I would rather carry thither a rattlesnake.

refined and savage societies, might be adduced to prove not only that it has been so thought, but that those so thinking, among whom may be reckoned the most noble characters, have proved their sincerity in such profession, by preferring the former to the latter. A man who, in a state of slavery, does any thing mean, base, or pusillanimous, is immediately excused by the world, by the general exclamation of *what could be expected from a slave?* This universal excuse for the infamy of any man's conduct in such a state, is sufficient to prove, if any proof be required, the *general opinion* of the debasement of mind, and of the abject state, to which persons so situated are reduced. Nothing more is requisite to prove *that a state of slavery is a state of misery and of infamy.* It has however frequently, and justly, been observed, that to all general rules there are exceptions. So, slaves have been known, sometimes to be happy, and sometimes to be great; but the former only proves the absence of intellect, and the latter its presence, joined in all likelihood to an uncommonly noble and magnanimous spirit. These exceptions, therefore, do not away the generally miserable situation of those who are reduced to slavery.

Number of slaves carried annually from Africa. From Africa there are annually carried, to cultivate the West Indian Islands, from seventy to eighty thousand of its natives, who are destined to drag out the remainder of their lives in hard labour and captivity. Of the mode in which these people are made slaves, much has been said, and I believe, by those who are advocates for the abolition of slavery, made for the most part to appear worse than general custom will *European mode of procuring them exaggerated.* sanction. However there can be no doubt but that many of them are frequently *caught* by means which nothing on earth can justify; but the majority are generally, by Europeans, fairly purchased.

On their arrival at the island where they are destined to remain, they are generally treated by their new masters with kindness and humanity; for, whatever may be said to the contrary, humanity is a prominent trait in the British character. Their labour is however hard, their condition slavery: and this last is sufficient to embitter all their thoughts, and render them miserable. Though, as I said before, and do not doubt, many of them may be comfortable, nay happy, yet how few these to the general aggregate? And upon what a slender tenure does that comfort or happiness depend?

If then some means could be traced out, which would have a tendency to abolish this slavery, without affecting the commercial interests of the country, or the property of individuals, I should think that there could be no reasonable objection to the adoption of them.

However, before we proceed to state them, it may be as well to observe that they tend not to the direct abolition of the slave trade; and that they have nothing to do with the general emancipation of those already in that state. This, by the bye, is a notion which has commonly been attributed to those who have been the advocates for the abolition of the slave trade, but I believe very unmeritedly. Be that, however, as it may, I shall say only this for myself, that no man is a greater enemy to slavery than I am; and I shall rejoice at every measure which wisely tends to its abolition; but that more is to be dreaded from too much accelerating than from slowly attempting to accomplish that object. As to general emancipation, no one can think of it even without horror; for instead of improving the

<small>The immediate abolition of the slave trade not desirable.</small>

<small>Idea of general emancipation.</small>

condition of the blacks in our West India islands, it **would** add to their present misery, rebellion, murder, rapine, and cruelty; and would at once sweep from the face of the earth all the white population of our western possessions, by the hands of assassins.

And of partial emancipation. There is however one mode of emancipation which seems unobjectionable, and which is, I understand, practised by the Spaniards.

That is to suffer a slave to work out his freedom by days. This is done when, from habits of industry, he has acquired so much property as will amount to the value of the sixth part of his annual labour, (Sunday not being reckoned) with which he buys his freedom for Monday; having this day to his own use, the exercise of the same industry will afterwards enable him to buy Tuesday; and these two days will sooner enable him, by the same means, to purchase Wednesday; and so on till he has completely emancipated himself. From this mode of emancipation I cannot see any danger, as it can be effected only by the industrious, and habits of industry once taken up are not likely to be laid by. Blacks who have so freed themselves would in all probability prove good subjects. If it be said that, freedom once acquired, there is no motive for the continuance of those industrious habits, I say that, freedom once acquired, there are other motives which will operate almost as strongly; and those are, in his new situation, to acquire respect; and this will generally be done by the acquisition of wealth, which will require the exercise of similar industry. Whether this be ever practised in our own colonies I do not know. The above mode might possibly be improved by admitting the purchase of half a day, or even one working hour, at a time.

To return to my subject. As one of the means that would inevitably tend to the gradual abolition of the slave trade, I would recommend the cultivation of Africa, by its free natives; in which cultivation none but freemen should be employed. This would, in the first place, tend to diminish the mart of slaves in that place; and it would also tend to lessen the desire of procuring them, at least by force, by fraud, and premeditated and unprovoked attacks. For what generally is the motive which induces those tribes upon the coast, so barbarously and so frequently to *catch* and sell each other to Europeans? The desire of being able to procure rum, tobacco, powder, and other European articles, which they have no other means of acquiring. But if, by labouring for a week, a month, or a year, they may have it in their power to procure them as the wages of their labour, their minds will be turned from the precarious means of theft and murder, for that purpose, to those of labour and industry, which, in a very few years, would make a wonderful alteration in these people's notions of the iniquity of the former procedure: besides, they would feel the good effects of such a change of conduct in their own security; for where depredations of that kind are common, every tribe is liable to them; but when they no longer *catch* slaves, they will no longer themselves, be liable to be *caught*.

The cultivation of Africa would tend to the gradual abolition of slavery.

Now what effect would the cultivation of Africa have upon its inhabitants? The cultivation of the soil, must necessarily induce commerce, and the intercourse resulting from this exchange, this barter, this trade, will, and must, soften and civilize the most barbarous of the two parties, carrying it on; and will, by degrees, introduce letters, and, in the end, the christian religion, to that, at present, ill-fated people.

To the civilization of its natives and to the introduction of letters and religion.

But how will this affect the slave trade, seeing that christians carry it on at present? The people from whom they procure slaves, being more civilized than they are at present, and finding a safer and surer mode of acquiring wealth, than by plunder and rapine, will no longer pursue those nefarious practices by which they formerly supplied us with slaves; and the difficulty of procuring them will insure more care in the possessors of our West Indian colonies, to keep up the stock which they already have. This keeping up of the stock naturally leads one to ask a question, which is, " what part of the habitable globe, except our West Indian islands, can be pointed out, where the population (except in cases of tyranny, cruelty, intolerance, or some other oppression) does not increase?" I believe none. However if it does not increase, it does not (except in the above cases) decrease. How comes it then that in the West Indian Islands a constant fresh supply is required? Does not this argue some radical evil? It certainly does. And what is this evil? Slavery!

Population in well governed countries always encrease.

Slavery adverse to it.

I do not mean, in the most distant manner, to insinuate here that this arises from ill treatment; I will allow it to be as good, and as humane as possible; yet, such is the effect of slavery that it cannot, nay, it should not, keep up in population its own numbers.

The cultivation of Africa will moreover facilitate our means of acquiring a knowledge of its interior.

Besides the good effects, already mentioned, which, it is conceived, will attend the cultivation of that portion of Africa above proposed, it is also thought that it will afford us more frequent, safe, and beneficial means of exploring, and becoming acquainted with, the interior of that country, than can ever result from the laborious, the perilous, the indefatigable exertions of a few European individuals; who, at times, with unshaken fortitude, have attempted, and may yet attempt, the difficult task of acquiring a knowledge of it.

Though the zeal, the patience, the fortitude and the intelligence, of a Bruce,* a Ledyard, a Lucas, a Houghton, a Park, a Browne, and a Horneman, may make us acquainted with the route to, and position of, many towns and kingdoms, together with the trade and manners of their inhabitants, in the interior of Africa; yet, with their journeys cease also their use. They lead not, at least they have not hitherto led, to any useful establishments; but leave us satisfied with marking on a map, with tolerable precision, another spot for the scite of a town, or kingdom, in the interior of that quarter of the globe, which, to us, is at present, almost a blank.

Requisites for an European who intends exploring the interior of Africa.

I will here just note that there appears to me to be some requisites in an European, who intends exploring the interior of Africa with much probability of success, which seem to have escaped the attention of some of our countrymen. These are, a complexion not differing much from that of a Moor, and a residence of from three to four years on the northern part of Africa, between Morocco, Tangier, Tetuan, Algiers, Tunis and Tripoli, which would give a tolerable knowledge of the language,

---

* I do not by any means intend to class Mr. Bruce with any other traveller, his labours are above all praise, he is a sun amidst a few twinkling stars. It is somewhat extraordinary that this illustrious traveller, who, in almost every page of his book, will convince an attentive reader, that *he had really visited the country and the people which he describes,* found difficulty in being credited in his own country; while another book, which in almost every page (except in the description of the Cape of Good Hope, where the account of persons and their employment, and occurrences is true) will convince a person, at all acquainted with savage life, that *he had not visited the people whom he described,* found faith in the same country, and was for some time really believed. It is perhaps needless to say that these are the fictitious travels of Damberger.

commerce, and manners of these people; the Mandingo language should also be acquired, especially by those who explore from the west. Thus qualified, one might always pass for a Moor. In making these observations I do not intend, in the smallest degree, to detract from the merit of those who have already made such attempts; the least meritorious of whom, I will readily concede, did much more than I, under similar circumstances, could have done. They are made only, because they struck me forcibly when on the island of Bulama, at a time when my thoughts were frequently occupied by the subject; and, if attended to, may be of use to some person, who may hereafter wish to make discoveries in that quarter.

Cultivation would alter the route of interior trade by drawing it to its neighbourhood. To return, however, to our subject: in cultivating a portion of the western part of Africa it is conceived that some degree of civilization, as well as commerce, will follow. The first may, for some time, be confined to the territory colonized; but the second will begin immediately to extend, by little and little, into the interior; the inhabitants whereof finding always a supply of European commodities, for whatever they might bring to barter, except slaves, on the territory between the Gambia and the head of the Grande, will certainly prefer that to the more distant situation to which they would be obliged to carry them, were they to drop down the course of the former river to the neighbourhood of James Fort; and this, so long as slaves were to be purchased in the Gambia, would produce two annual caravans, or companies of traders, from the interior of Africa; the one pursuing the old route to the Gambia, with slaves only; but the new one, which would arise from our being able to purchase their merchandise, would stop at the nearest settlement, where they would barter all other commodities, except slaves, for European goods. For, it is not probable that people, having either elephants' teeth, wax, gum, or any thing else, to barter, would go two or three hundred miles farther than was necessary, unless a better price might induce them so to do, which is not probable; for, in the first place, we should consider, probably, the navigation of the Gambia as exclusively our own; but, were it not so, no Europeans would be able there to undersell us.

The convenience of this mart being once established, and the certainty of European articles being always there, might induce the interior traders to come, instead of annually, whenever they had commodities to sell, which would keep up, except in the rains, a constant communication with the interior. This constant communication would tend to civilize all those people through whose territories it was carried on; and this increased civilization would produce additional security, which would tend also to augment that communication. *Would render communication with the interior more frequent,*

But while these Africans come to us from the interior, I see no reason why we should not also visit them with caravans, which would carry the place of mart continually to the eastward, till at length we had a trade, through the interior, from the mouth of the Grande, to Darfur, Abyssinia, and the shores of the Red Sea. Now, these caravans that I should propose to establish in the West are not to be hastily undertaken, nor undertaken by white men. It would require some time to make ourselves acquainted with their route, the names, and the nature, of the people among whom it lay; and perhaps a knowledge of one or two languages. This I should endeavour to acquire, by at first confiding to one of the most intelligent of the interior African merchants, whom I should make my friend, *And open the way for Europeans to appear there.*

one or two of the most acute natives, whom I could find in the extent of the colony, with the consent of their relatives of course; by these means, which I would increase as often as prudent, we should acquire a slow, but accurate, knowledge of the general route, manners, &c.; and when a sufficient knowledge of these was acquired, I should endeavour to set forward a caravan, or number of traders from the West towards the East; but no white man should accompany it. Much caution and prudence are required in the mode of introducing this new course of trade: however, I do not foresee any obstacles which may not be surmounted.

It may be objected that the interior African merchants would oppose this innovation, or direct retrograde motion of the course of commerce. By whom will this objection be made? If by those who are advocates for the abolition of slavery, I say only that it is worth trying If by those who are advocates for its continuance, I say, that you characterise the Africans as a stupid and indolent people. If they are the former they will not object to our carrying them goods, on the score of its being contrary to their interests; and if the latter, they will rather have merchandise, which they want, put down at their own doors, than have to perform a long and tedious journey in order to procure them; and to both I will say, that it is worth endeavouring, by this mode, to open a more extensive market for the produce of British industry.

These western caravans, once established, will make the white character better known, and more justly appreciated in the interior of Africa, than it is at present; and will pave the way for the appearance of the white trader there himself; which, once acomplished, with security to his person and property, will secure a market for English manufactures, beyond what most persons conceive.

It may also be objected that if the goods, in the first caravans that are to trade to the East, are entrusted to the natives only, they will cheat their employers, and make small profit. This I by no means allow: but, for the sake of argument, be it so. Profit, though small, will certainly accrue; but, it is not profit, it is information which we want at first. Information! what, get information from an African? Yes, and more than you will be enabled to procure from an European if your measures are wisely taken. *The best way of beginning to explore Africa is by the natives themselves.*

When we were obliged to leave the island of Bulama, a Mandingo of the name of Corea, was deputed by the merchants at Bissao to purchase, for them, whatever he thought proper. This Capitano Corea, for so he was called, was a merchant himself; he was the owner of many small vessels; and, in person, commanded one, which he had navigated from Bissao to Lisbon and back; and he, of course, could ascertain the latitude of his place. Who then so fit as such a man to explore the interior of Africa? I would have preferred him to Bruce himself. Because his colour, his country, and his language, would not only preclude prejudice and suspicion, but would give him facilities of making observations which a white could not possibly have. And why should we not bring up some young Coreas in our African colony? There is no difficulty in so doing; and by these young Coreas I should begin to explore Africa. Let them understand the Arabic and Mandingo tongues; let them understand the English, and know how to read and write in that language, which, with a little arithmetical knowledge, and being *Degree of knowledge necessary for them to undertake it.*

able to ascertain the latitude of a place, would qualify them sufficiently to impart to us most useful information.

<small>Why the Grande is fixed upon in preference to the Senegal and Gambia.</small> It may, however, be asked why, instead of the Senegal and the Gambia, I prefer the borders of the Grande to begin a cultivation, one professed object of which is to open a commercial communication with the interior of Africa; seeing that the two former rivers are not only of much greater extent, but their sources far inland, or to the eastward of any part of the Grande; and that it must appear to every one more rational to begin on the borders of that river whose navigable course is the longest, and stretches farthest into that country which is the object of our researches. This would be true if the object were merely to push an individual into Africa for the purpose only of exploring it, without any view to permanency of residence, or extent of cultivation. But as these latter must be taken into consideration, I prefer the northern border of the Grande for the following reasons:

First, Because the soil is better, and more thinly peopled than on either of the two other rivers; and because those who inhabit it are friendly to, and anxious to have, Europeans established among them. Whereas, the Senegal borders on the desert of Saara, and its northern shore, as well as part of its southern, is occupied by Moors, who are the greatest obstacle to the establishment of Christians in Africa. The Gambia, also, is too near the Moors, and both these rivers have more numerous and populous towns on their banks than the Grande, every one of which, there is reason to believe, has had its quarrels and wars with Europeans; and can, either from memory or tradition give, each, an account of its inhabitants having, at some time or other, been lawlessly plundered, murdered, or made slaves, by a vessel of some European nation; also from the constant trade that has, almost always, been carried on with them, and which must render them less friendly, other considerations out of the question, than those of the Grande, who have had much less European intercourse.

Secondly, Because with the before-mentioned advantages, I conceive that the Grande, notwithstanding the shortness of its course, when compared with the other two, is equally advantageously situated for carrying on commerce, on an extensive scale, with the interior of Africa; for which purpose it is necessary to get as near as we can, with prudence, to the source of the Joliba, or Niger. The sources of the three great African streams which run to the Westward, as well as the one which runs East, it is very remarkable, are all to be found in nearly the same parallel, that is, in about the eleventh degree of North latitude,* and not far from each other; and the navigable parts of the two Southern ones, are nearly equi-distant from the source of the Niger; the navigable part of the Senegal is certainly a little nearer to it, but its being bounded by Moorish territories is a difficulty much outweighing the advantage of its proximity to that river; we therefore put *it* out of the question. Now, for the purpose of carrying on inland commerce, a river is of no use, unless it be navigable. We, therefore, must take the navigable parts of the Gambia and the Grande from the head of the Niger, and we shall find in that case, that the distance will

* The source of the Grande, but without sufficient Authority, is by some placed very far to the South, as that river is made to run very considerably to the North, before it takes its western direction. But this assists not the argument, as it will be no longer useful to us, when it is not navigable eastward.

not be greater to carry thither goods from the latter, than from the former. I have taken the head, instead of the navigable part of the Niger, which I do not know; but which, it is conceived, from its known course, cannot make any material difference in favour of either.

Having thus with a light and unskilful hand traced the outline of what I think might be done on the coast of Africa, I must leave to some more able person, who may have applied his mind to the cause of its natives, the task of completing the picture, and placing in the strongest light all the real advantages that would result to this country from acting upon the system here recommended. But, before I conclude, I will again observe, that whenever in our intercourse with the natives, we depart from justice, whenever we introduce convicts, or black troops, into that country, we may then give up the colonization: for, in either of those cases, instead of its being beneficial, either to the natives or to us, it will to *them*, be a constant source of distrust, quarrels, disaffection and murder, and, to *us*, an expensive, perilous, and fruitless undertaking. But if on the contrary, our measures are justly taken, and wisely executed, the enterprize recommended will prove of great importance to the trade and commerce of this kingdom; not merely by the productions proposed to be there raised, and for which we now pay enormous sums to foreign countries, but by the opening of new and extensive channels to the introduction of our manufactures to the very heart of Africa. And it will, at the same time, in my opinion, be the safest and surest way of abolishing the slavery of the Africans, of usefully exploring the interior of their country, and of introducing among that people, religion, letters, and civilization.

NOTE.

IT was observed, in the preface, that these Memoranda would probably never have been published, had not a book which had lately made its appearance at Paris, been accidentally put into my hands. This book is intitled " Fragmens d'un Voyage en Afrique, fait pendant les années 1785, 1786, et 1787, &c.," and is written by a Mons. Golberry, who appears perfectly to understand the interest of his country in that quarter. It had been my intention, at first, to have dwelt at great length on its contents, and to have given a translation of its most important parts; but I shall content myself with just noticing the book, and its object, in the hope that those, whose province it is, will give it that consideration which it deserves; and prevent France from beginning to act upon this gentleman's plan, which would, beyond all doubt, be very beneficial to that country, and exceedingly detrimental to this.

This book was published at Paris in 1802, apparently with the sanction and approbation of the government of that country, and the system it recommends would doubtless have been immediately acted upon, had not the commencement of hostilities with this country put a stop to it. However, on the return of peace, it will probably be again taken up, unless anticipated by this country, which at this time may be easily done.

Mons. Golberry recommends to his government to turn its attention towards Africa, where he proposes to establish a government called that of Senegal, and which is to extend from Cape Blanco, on the coast of Barbary, in the latitude of 20. 47. N., to Cape Palmas in the fourth degree and thirtieth minute of the same latitude. This government is to be divided into three districts, of which Senegal is the chief, comprising the territory between that river and Cape Blanco; and the Isle St. Louis, in that river, is to be the seat of its government. The second district extends from the Senegal to Cape Verga, and Goree is to be the seat of its government. The third district extends from Cape Verga to Cape Palmas, and the seat of its government is Sierra Leone. Every settlement in each district is subordinate to that which is the seat of the government of that district, and these are subordinate to the one in the Senegal.

Commerce, cultivation, the exploring of Africa, and the civilizing its natives, are the professed objects of Mons. Golberry, as well as myself; with this difference between us, that the most important part of his commerce arises from the traffic of slaves, which I would not by any means admit; and he does not seem particularly nice as to the mode in which the sovereignty of the soil is to be acquired, for he speaks of conquering Bambouk, for the sake of its gold mines, with as much deliberation as if it were perfectly right and just for the French to march a small army into the country of Bambouk, (without any provocation, any quarrel, or any thing to justify hostilities) and say to its inhabitants, " Your country possesses gold which we want, and must have. Now if you will give us all your gold, you may remain quiet possessors of your country, but if not, we are come here either to expatriate you, or put you all to death." Conduct like this may accord with French notions of right, but I trust it will ever be held in detestation in this country. Mons. G. it is true, afterwards gives up this plan of conquering; not from its injustice, but from its infeasibility, and because he conceives that it would be more politic to endeavour to procure their gold by more pacific means.

Now one of the many advantages possessed by those countries, which I propose to cultivate, is that there are no gold mines in them, nor any expectation of them. All the riches which it can be hoped to derive from the earth, will depend upon its culture; which to its inhabitants may be productive of happiness and wealth. But gold mines to them would produce neither; on the contrary, they would cause only poverty and misery; and I should consider it as a great obstacle to cultivation, nay an insuperable objection to the undertaking it, in the proposed country, if mines of any precious metal were there expected to be found.

Besides this traffic in slaves, and taking possession of the natives territory without any ceremony, there are other differences between Mons. G's. system and mine. With him commerce is the primary object; cultivation, the civilizing the Africans, and exploring the country, being only secondary considerations, and encouraged only insomuch as they tend to promote and increase the former. Now these latter, with me, are the primary objects; as I conceive that they will each have a tendency towards the abolition of slavery, and commerce is left to take care of itself; which, it is supposed, must follow the cultivation of valuable produce.

Mons. G. although an advocate for carrying on the slave trade at present, thinks that, if his system were acted upon, it would have a tendency towards the abolition of that odious traffic; on which, he makes some unobjectionable observations at the conclusion of his work: in the whole course of which, where he takes frequent occasion to speak of this country, he always mentions the English with a degree of moderation, justice, and respect, exceedingly uncommon in modern French writers; and which, in these days of acrimonious temper, is highly creditable to him, and a proof of the liberality of his mind.

However, notwithstanding all this, we must not let Mons. Golberry run away with all western Africa. To the vast extent of his gripe, my proposed little colony is a mere speck, and would not, if attempted, interfere with his views. But, if ever his views are seriously taken up, and acted upon, by the French government, adieu, not only to the proposed colony, but also to all views, interests, and concerns whatever, of the English, on the western coast of Africa, north of Cape Palmas.

At present we have, I think, the means of for ever frustrating, at little expence, these views of the French. This may be done by taking possession of the isle St. Louis in the Senegal, not with any view of carrying on an extensive commerce, or even of exploring from the upper part of that tortuous river; and much less with a view of getting the gold mines of Bambouk, which country is embraced by two of its arms; but solely with a view of excluding the French; and if when peace shall again take place between the two countries, France be prohibited from trading to Arguin and the two Portendicks, all the gum of the three forest, bordering on the Senegal must be brought for sale to the possessors of the isle St. Louis. It is impossible that it can be carried any where else. We learn from Golberry that this will amount to two millions of pounds per annum, the profit on which would much more than maintain the establishment of that little island. Besides which one, two, three, or even half a dozen, of the fertile islands close to it might be planted with cotton, Indigo, and tobacco, so that without being obliged to go far up that unhealthy river, which indeed can only be done in the most unhealthy season, that of the rains, a very active and beneficial trade might be carried on close to its mouth; while, at the same time it would afford us the means of excluding our rivals.

A conviction that, to this country, a colony as important in every point of view, as any one which we now possess, is to be acquired on the western coast of Africa, which this work of Mons. Golberry directly tends to frustrate, is my motive and apology for noticing it, in this very long note.

APPENDIX.

APPENDIX.

No. 1.

A number of Gentlemen having formed themselves into a Society, and opened a Subscription for the purpose of making a Settlement, on an eligible spot on the Coast of Africa, offer the following Proposals:

I. EVERY settler subscribing thirty pounds, shall have five hundred acres of land. Every settler subscribing fifteen pounds, shall have two hundred and fifty acres. And every settler subscribing seven pounds ten shillings, shall have one hundred and twenty-five acres.

II. Every subscriber remaining in Europe, paying double the sum of the settlers respectively, shall have the same portion of land.

III. Every married yeoman or labourer, who shall become a settler, shall have forty acres of land for himself, twenty for his wife, and ten for each of his children; provided the whole does not amount to more than one hundred acres.

IV. Every unmarried yeoman or labourer, becoming a settler, shall have forty acres of land.

V. Every apprentice or indented servant, shall receive, at the expiration of his indenture, forty acres of land. If a premium be given, he shall receive sixty acres.

VI. Every female servant shall receive, on her marriage, twenty acres of land.

VII. The whole of the land will be equitably allotted.

VIII. No subscriber shall at any time possess more than five hundred acres,* either by subscription or by purchase.

IX. Every settler shall have a free passage to the said settlement, and an ample allowance of salutary provisions for six months, from the day of landing.

X. Every unmarried settler will be allowed one ton for his baggage; and every man with a family, one ton and a half—they must pay at the rate of sixpence per foot for all the baggage which they may carry out exceeding these quantities.

XI. Every person, on landing, must assist to clear the spot of ground, on which the town is intended to be built, or find a substitute.

XII. It is expected every person will produce a certificate of their sobriety and industry, before they are received as settlers.

XIII. No member of the colony shall, on any pretence whatsoever, have any concern, directly or indirectly, in buying, selling, or employing any slave or slaves.

XIV. It is the intention of the settlers, that no taxes shall be levied, other than may be sufficient to liquidate whatever debt it may be necessary to incur for the establishment of the colony, and to defray the necessary expences of government.

XV. Every male having attained the age of twenty-one, and possessing land, shall have a vote in the election of the legislative council.

XVI. No subscriber can be called upon for a second subscription.

XVII. Those only who subscribe on or before the twentieth of December next, will be entitled to the aforementioned advantages. It is expected, that the settlers of every denomination, will take with them necessary clothing, beds, and bedding—A list of which may be had at the committee-room.

N. B. Subscriptions are received at Messrs. Biddulph, Cocks, Cocks, and Ridge, Charing-cross, where a list of the subscribers may be seen.

* Increased afterwards to two thousand.

*** The Committee meets every Monday, Wednesday, and Friday, for the dispatch of business, at seven o'clock in the evening, No. 103, Hatton-garden, Holborn.

Signed by order of the Committee,

H. H. DALRYMPLE.

Nov. 9, 1791,
No. 103, *Hatton-Garden.*

No. 2.

Memorandum of Agreement, and Constitution of Government, for a Colony about to be established on or near the Island of Bulam, in Africa, as engrossed and signed on the ninth day of March, 1792.

MEMORANDUM OF AGREEMENT made this ninth day of March, in the thirty-third year of the reign of our Sovereign Lord George the Third, by the grace of God of Great Britain, France, and Ireland King, Defender of the Faith; and in the year of our Lord One Thousand Seven Hundred and Ninety-two, between us the subscribers about to settle a colony on the island of Bulam, or on some other part on the coast of Africa, on the one part; and the settlers or purchasers of lands in the said colony, on the other part; that is to say, that we having for certain considerations granted to persons remaining in England, allotments of land in our said colony, who thereby become purchasers of the same from us, do hereby covenant, promise and agree to and with each other, and bind and oblige ourselves to the performance of all the covenants hereinafter contained. And we hereby further agree, that we, by our governor and council, viz. Henry Hew Dalrymple, Esquire, Governor; John Young, Esquire, Lieutenant-governor; Sir William Halton, Baronet, John King, Philip Beaver, Peter Clutterbuck, Clotworthy Upton, Francis Brodie, Charles Drake, John Paiba, Richard Hancorne, Robert Dobbin, and Isaac Ximenes, Esquires, Members of

Margin notes: Preamble. Governor and council

to sign grants. our said council, shall and will sign memoranda and grants of land within the said colony or settlement, upon the terms and in the proportions as herein after expressed; that is to say, a grant of land, in the proportion of five hundred acres within the said colony or settlement, wherever it may be made by us, for the sum of sixty pounds sterling, paid by every purchaser of land to him, his heirs and assigns, for ever; and a further grant of two hundred and fifty acres of land for every thirty pounds sterling so paid by every purchaser of land to him, his heirs and assigns, for ever; and a further grant of one hundred and twenty-five acres, for every fifteen pounds sterling so paid by every purchaser of land, as aforesaid, to him, his heirs and assigns, for ever; and in the proportion of five hundred acres more for every additional sum of sixty pounds; and in the same proportion for every less additional sum so paid by every purchaser of land as aforesaid, to him, his heirs and assigns, for ever. And we do hereby covenant and agree, that our said governor and council before named, shall sign grants of land to each of themselves and the subscribing settlers, in the following proportions; that is to say, a grant of land for ever, in the proportion of five hundred acres for every thirty pounds paid by every subscribing settler, to him, his heirs and assigns; and a further grant of two hundred and fifty acres of land for every fifteen pounds so paid by every subscribing settler, to him, his heirs and assigns; and a further grant of one hundred and twenty-five acres for every seven pounds ten shillings so paid by every subscribing settler as aforesaid, to him, his heirs and assigns; and in the further proportion of five hundred acres for every additional sum of thirty pounds; and in the same proportion for every less additional sum so paid as aforesaid by every subscribing settler, to him, his heirs and assigns, for ever. And whereas certain settlers have paid the sum of twenty pounds sterling, after the twentieth day of February, such subscribing settlers shall receive a grant of two hundred and fifty acres of land, as aforesaid, to them, their heirs and assigns, for ever. And it is hereby covenanted and agreed, that every married yeoman or labourer who shall become a settler within the said colony, shall receive a grant of forty acres of land for himself. twenty for his wife, and ten for each of his children, to them, their heirs and assigns, for ever: provided the whole of such grants do not exceed one hundred acres. And it is hereby further covenanted and agreed, that every unmarried yeoman or labourer becoming a settler within the said colony, shall be entitled to a grant of forty acres of land, to him, his heirs and assigns, for ever. And it is hereby further covenanted and agreed, that every apprentice or indented servant shall receive, at the expiration of his indenture, the same benefits as yeomen and labourers, being original settlers of the same description respectively. And it is hereby further covenanted and agreed, that every female servant shall receive, on her marriage, a grant of twenty acres of land, for her, her heirs and assigns, for ever: provided, nevertheless, and it is hereby declared, that this distribution shall extend only to the colonists of the first embarkation. And it is hereby solemnly covenanted and agreed, that the grants of land to purchasers shall be divided and alloted in the same manner and at the same times as the lots of the settlers; the scite of the town, and the town lots to settlers and purchasers, excepted. And it is hereby further covenanted and agreed, that the said purchasers of lots of land within the said colony or settlement, shall be entitled, in their grant of land, to an allotment of one acre of land within the limits of the said town, to be considered as a town lot, for the purpose of erecting stores and other buildings. And it is hereby further covenanted and agreed, that all lands taken possession of by us the subscribers, that shall not be subscribed for, or granted to purchasers, or given to yeomen, on the day of the sailing of this expedition from England, shall be considered to belong to the purchasers of land, as well as to the original subscribers, in just proportions, according to the proportion of shares subscribed for or granted to Purchasers; provided that such purchasers shall not, at the time of receiving their grants, have signified their intentions of renouncing all right in any future sale or division thereof, and to be so expressed in their grant respectively: and whatever arises from the sale or division of all or any part of the said lands, to be considered as an appendage to the respective shares of land of the said settlers, and of such purchasers as have not signified their intention of renouncing such right, and in no other light whatever. And it is hereby further covenanted and agreed, that such land shall not be cultivated as a joint concern, but be left as taken possession of, until sold or divided, save and except the quantity of thirty-five thousand acres of the said sursplus lands, which are hereby declared to be exempted from such sale and division, for the purpose of making grants to settlers that

Marginalia: Grants to apprentices and servants; to maid servants, on their marriage. These terms to be extended no further than to the original settlers. All grants to be made at the same times, excepting the scite of the town, and town lots. One acre for a town lot. Property of the island in whom vested. Not to be cultivated as a joint concern. Reserved quantity of land 35,000 acres.

may hereafter go out to the said colony. And it is hereby further agreed, that every person entitled to possess one hundred and twenty-five acres and upwards, having contributed towards defraying the original expences of the settlement, shall have the right or privilege to demand and obtain a grant of thirty acres for a settler, on the reserved quantity of land, in the proportion of thirty acres to each individual, for every hundred acres so subscribed for by him. It is likewise hereby covenanted and agreed, that every purchaser of a grant shall have a right to demand and obtain a grant of thirty acres of land to each individual for every settler that he may send out, such number of settlers not exceeding one for every hundred acres so purchased by him: provided always that no expence from such measure be incurred by the colony. And it is further hereby covenanted and agreed, that the remaining quantity of land so reserved as above, shall be in the disposal of the governor and council for the time being, for the benefit of the colony. And it is hereby covenanted and declared to be a right in every purchaser of land in the said colony, at the commencement as well as at any future period of the undertaking, to send out at his own expence, any person or persons to superintend his interests; and every such person shall have full liberty, through his agent, to cultivate or not cultivate, traffic or not traffic, as he finds or conceives it most conducive to his interest, and shall be legally competent to do any act or thing which a settler on his own account may do, excepting only that he may not be permitted to draw goods from the public store for the purchase of labour. And it is hereby solemnly covenanted and agreed, that no power in the colony shall ever be competent to levying fine or tax on the uncultivated property of absentees, or any tax on the cultivated property of absentees, which shall not in equal proportion affect the property of the settlers. And we do hereby moreover covenant and agree, that if from any unforeseen event, a settlement on the island of Bulam, at present intended, should be found impracticable, or if the settlers should, after having attempted, or formed a temporary settlement, think proper to abandon it, this covenant and agreement are to be understood to extend to any other spot on or near the coast of Africa, whereunto the settlers may resort; and all the concern, advantages and engagements of the purchasers of lands, as well as of such settlers, to be thereto transferred. And all and every of the aforesaid covenants, engagements, and provision between us the subscribers and purchasers of lands, we the subscribers faithfully bind and oblige ourselves to perform and strictly observe; and each of us who shall fail herein; shall pay to the parties performing and observing the premises, the sum of ten pounds sterling in the name of liquidate penalty, over and above performance. Liquidate penalty.

CONSTITUTION OF GOVERNMENT.

CHAP. I.—Religion.

We do hereby declare and ordain, that in our colony no man shall be deemed responsible to another for his particular mode of faith or worship, but shall be equally eligible to any post or office, whether legislative or executive in our colony. Freedom of Religion.

CHAP. II.—Property, legislation and commerce.

ARTICLE I. All male settlers, having attained the age of twenty-one years, not being indented servants or domestics receiving wages, or mendicants, shall have a vote in the election of the legislative council, which election shall be determined by a majority of such votes. Qualification of electors.

ART. II. The legislative council shall consist of thirteen members, who shall have authority to make municipal or bye-laws, not contravening this constitution, or the fundamental laws of England, which we hereby adopt as the basis of our jurisprudence; and such bye-laws, we hereby bind ourselves to obey as implicitly as the common law of England. Number and power of the legislative council.

ART. III. The legislative council shall assemble in one month from the day of their adjournment, whether they be called by the governor or not, or whether the public business requires their meeting or not. They shall be an open court in the making or amending a law, of which public notice shall be given. To assemble in one month from the day of their adjournment. An open court.

ART. IV. The first legislative council being guarantee of the covenant The first between the settlers and the absent purchasers of land, as well as the commercial engagements of the colony, it becomes expedient that the members of it continue their functions until the lands be divided, and until the commercial association be dissolved; it is therefore ordained, that the first legislative council continue in office for the term of three years from the day of landing; at the expiration of the term of three years there shall be an annual election of the council; and the necessary qualifications of its members are hereby declared to be actual possession of one hundred and twenty-five acres of land, or personal property on the island or settlement, equivalent to three hundred pounds sterling.

council to remain for three years.
After which there shall be an annual election.
Qualifications of its members.

ART. V. The first act of every legislative council must be to chuse out of their own body a president or governor, who in case of equal numbers, shall have a casting vote in the enacting of laws; and the second act must be the election of a vice president, or deputy governor, who, in the absence of the president or governor, shall be invested with his authority, and execute all the functions of his office.

The first act of the council.

ART. VI. Upon enacting any law, seven of the council must be present, and those seven must be unanimous; if a smaller number be assembled, they shall not have the power of passing any law, although unanimous; but in cases of exigency, they may enact temporary regulations.

Number competent to make laws, or temporary regulations.

ART. VII. In cases of the misconduct of any member of the council, a general assembly of the people shall be convened, before which the allegations against him shall be stated; and, if there be found by them sufficient cause, he shall be expelled, and declared ineligible for a certain term, or for ever, according to the degree of his offence.

Provision for the misconduct of its members.

ART. VIII. In case of a vacancy, or vacancies in the legislative council, a meeting of the settlers shall be called to elect another member or members, within the space of one month, or as soon as convenient to the governor and council within that period.

In cases of vacancies.

ART. IX. No member of the council shall directly or indirectly hold an office of trust or profit.

No member to hold an office.

ART. X. As a fund must be raised for defraying the expences of the government, we hereby declare, that every settler or purchaser of land, by his agent, shall be permitted to carry or send out, on his own private account, an investment for the purposes of trade; and for the liberty of such

Liberty of

trade, every merchant or person so trading, hereby subjects and binds him-　*trade, on paying 7½ per cent.*
self to pay into the public treasury of the colony, a duty of seven and
a half per cent. upon such investment, for the term of one year only,
from the first settlement of the colony, the amount of the same to be
ascertained by the invoice: and we hereby further consent and agree, for　*Impost on exports, 5 per cent.*
the above purpose of defraying the expences of the government, to sub-
ject ourselves to an impost or duty not exceeding five per cent. on the
value of all exported produce. And we hereby further covenant and　*Appropriation of the public fund.*
agree, that the fund accumulated by traffic, if any there shall be, and
by the payment of private debts to the community, shall be appropriated
only to the purposes herein before specified.

ART. XI. To enable the colonists to cultivate their lands, we agree　*Labourers to be paid out of the public store:*
that the labourers, every one we employ, shall be paid from the public
store, by his employer giving him a ticket, specifying the time employed,
or the quantity of service performed, which ticket the agent or store-
keeper shall pay at sight, at a rate to be hereafter fixed by the governor　*rate to be fixed by the governor and council.*
and council, filing the same, and charging the value, including freight
and charges, to the settler's private account.

ART. XII. There shall be an agent or storekeeper appointed, to whose　*Agent or storekeeper.*
care the public investment shall be committed, and who shall keep a regular account of receipts and disbursements, and shall post his books
monthly, and submit the same to the inspection of the council.

ART. XIII. There shall be a treasurer appointed, who shall also act as　*Treasurer and collector.*
a collector of duties and taxes, and who shall at the same time submit his
books to the inspection of the council.

ART. XIV. All goods furnished from the public store to individuals　*Goods furnished from the public store, how to be paid for.*
(expect arms and implements, which are to be gratuitously given) shall
be paid for either in money or produce, within eighteen months from the
first establishment of the colony.

ART. XV. No public debt shall be contracted on any account, nor shall　*No public debt.*
any arrears to public officers, for public works or establishments, be
allowed to exceed the sum actually in the common fund; and commercial　*Joint commercial concern, when to cease.*
joint concerns shall cease and determine in eighteen months from the
first establishment of the colony.

ART. XVI. To prevent the undue influence of Property, we engage that　*Regulation* for labourers. no cultivator shall employ more than one native labourer to every forty acres, till all others are supplied in the same proportion.

Individual debt to the public.
ART. XVII. No individual shall be permitted to contract a debt to the public, exceeding the sum of one pound sterling for every acre that he shall have cleared.

No traffic in slaves.
ART. XVIII. No settler shall directly or indirectly be concerned in buying or selling of a slave or slaves.

Elementary right of the people.
ART. XIX. It is hereby declared, that the people have a right to assemble in a peaceable manner, to consult for the common good, to instruct their representatives, and to apply to the legislature for redress of grievances, by address, petition, or remonstrance.

CHAP. III.—OF THE JUDICIAL POWER, AND GENERAL LAWS.

Courts of justice.
ARTICLE I. All crimes against the public peace, all accusations against officers for misconduct, as well as all litigations between individuals, shall be tried by a jury of twelve freeholders, assisted by three members of the legislative council, as judges, who shall take this duty by rotation. The

Accusers. people shall appoint one accuser, by ballot, and the legislative council another, in the same manner.

ART. II. It being of the utmost importance to the safety and well-being of the colony, that a cordial intercourse be at all times maintained between the individuals thereof and the natives, we promise to be just in all transactions with them, and candid and hospitable in our

Disputes between the colonists and the natives, how adjudged.
deportment towards them, to the end that we may inspire them with confidence and respect. But as casual discord must be expected, from the nature of human passions, we hereby declare and ordain, that all disputes between the colonists and the natives shall be adjudged in the same manner as between the individuals of the colony.

Injury or insult to the natives to be atoned for.
ART. III. Every injury or insult offered by a colonist to any of the natives, shall be satisfactorily atoned for.

Injury or insult by the natives to the colonists how to be redressed.
ART. IV. If any injury or insult be offered by a native to any of the settlers, proper representation shall be made thereof to his prince or chief, and the individual so offending may be further punished by expulsion.

Penalty of wantonly killing of a native.
ART. V. If any colonist wantonly kill a native, he shall, upon conviction thereof, be delivered up to the prince of the country.

False testimony.
ART. VI. False testimony shall be punished with public infamy.

ART. VII. Theft shall be punished with public infamy, and restitution four-fold. *Theft.*

ART. VIII. The receiver of stolen goods, knowing them to be such, shall incur the same punishment as the thief. *Receiver of stolen goods.*

ART. IX. Crimes of greater turpitude shall be punished by banishment. *Crimes of greater turpitude.*

CHAP. IV.—OF THE EXECUTIVE POWER.

ARTICLE I. It is hereby ordained, that there shall be an executive council, consisting of the lieutenant-governor and two other members of the legislative body, to assist the governor in the execution of the laws; and these shall be chosen, one by the legislative body, and the other by the governor. *Executive council.*

ART. II. The governor, with the advice and consent of this council, or without it, shall have full power and authority, during the sessions of the legislative council, to adjourn and prorogue it to any term the said legislative council shall desire, provided the same do not exceed one month; and during the recess of the said council, to re-assemble it sooner than the term to which it may be adjourned or prorogued, if the welfare of the colony shall by him be judged to require it. *Governor's power to prorogue the council to any time within one month, and to re-assemble it sooner.*

ART. III. The governor of this colony shall be the commander in chief of the military force of the colony by sea and land; and shall have full power, by himself, or by any commander or other officer or officers, from time to time to exercise and discipline the militia and armed vessels, and to lead and conduct them to conquest, pursuit, and expulsion, as well by sea as by land, within or without the limits of this colony, of all and every such person or persons as shall, at any time hereafter, in an hostile manner attempt the invasion, detriment, or annoyance of this colony; and to take and surprize, by all means whatsoever, all and every such person or persons, with their arms, ammunition, and other goods, as shall attempt any species of violence on the safety or tranquillity thereof: and the governor shall be intrusted with all these, and other powers incident to the offices of captain general and commander in chief, and high admiral, to be exercised agreeably to the rules and regulations of this constitution, and not otherwise: provided that the said governor shall not transport *Commander in chief of the militia and armed vessels. Military power of the governor; limited by this constitution. Not to trans-*

any of the members of this colony, or oblige them to march out of the limits of the same, without their free will and accord, and without the consent of the legislative council.

ART. IV. He shall have power to remit fines and punishments, until the sense of the legislative council can be obtained.

ART. V. The governor, with the advice of the executive council, or without it, shall at all times appoint and commmission all officers of the colony who shall receive salaries, both civil and military; but when salaries are given, the legislative council shall fix such salaries.

ART. VI. No money shall be issued from the the public treasury, but by virtue of a warrant under the hand of the governor, with the advice and consent of the executive council, or without it.

ART. VII. All public boards, all superintending officers of public magazines and stores belonging to the colony, and all commanding officers of forts and armed vessels, shall once in every three months, officially, and without requisition, and at other times when required by the governor, deliver to him returns of all goods, stores, provisions, ammunition, cannon with their appendages, and small arms with their accoutrements, and all other public property whatever, under their care respectively, distinguishing the quantity, number, quality, and kind of each as particularly as may be, together with the condition of such forts and vessels.

ART. VIII. The governor shall have a casting vote in the executive council; if all the members dissent, he shall nevertheless have power to take efficient measures without them, taking the responsibility upon himself: the dissenting members, or any of them, shall have in all cases the privilege of entering his or their protest, with the reasons thereof, on the minutes of the executive council.

ART. IX. The lieutenant-governor for the time being shall, in the presence of the governor, be second in military command; and whenever the office of governor shall be vacant, by reason of his death or absence from the colony, or otherwise, the lieutenant-governor for the time being shall, during such vacancy, perform all duties incumbent on the governor; and shall have, and exercise all the powers and authorities which, by this constitution, the governor is vested withal when personally present.

ART. X. It being necessary for the safety and well-being of this community, that the chief magistrate thereof be enabled to act with freedom of mind and dignity in his high office, we hereby secure to him full protection and indemnity in the exercise of all constitutional powers, and promise him at all times the same implicit obedience therein, that we have promised to the future municipal laws of the legislative council. But as the sovereignty resides in the people, all their magistrates, whether legislative or executive, are responsible to them for their administration. It is therefore provided, that if the governor and executive council, or any members of it, in co-operation with the governor, transgress the limits which by this constitution are assigned to the executive power, he or they shall be amenable to the law as follows: *The governor protected in constitutional measures. Sovereignty of the people recognized. Governor amenable to the law.*

Art. XI. If any member of this community shall at any time think that the governor, or members of the executive council, has or have exceeded the power vested in him or them by this constitution; he may accuse the said governor, and members of the executive council who have concurred with him in the supposed illegal measure, before the legislative council, and in his or their presence, that they may have an opportunity of replying; and if it be the opinion of the majority of the council, (except the governor and executive council, who shall have no votes upon this occasion), that there be sufficient cause of impeachment, then a high court shall be formed by the following means, viz. The people, who are not members of the council, if they be the accusing party, shall elect from their own body, by ballot, five judges, of characters most remarkable for candour and intelligence; and the legislative council shall elect from their body, and by ballot also, seven Judges, provided none of these be members of the executive council (who are hereby all declared incapable of being chosen, as well as to choose); but if the council be the accusing party, they shall elect five judges, and the people seven. These twelve judges shall sit in open court, to hear the allegations against the governor, or members of the executive council, to examine all witnesses that he or they may adduce in his or their behalf, and impartially to award judgment, according to the best of their understandings. But the said court shall not be competent to censure him or them, for any act that he or they may have done by virtue of this constitution. Before this tribunal is assembled, each member is to take a solemn oath *Process of impeachment. High court for his trial, how formed. Open court, members of*

the same to take an oath or affirmation.
Witnesses to be examined on oath, written process.

(or affirmation, if he be one of the people called quakers) impartially to assist to try and determine, to the best of his understanding, the case that shall be brought before him. In this court, all the witnesses shall be examined on oath, the whole process shall be written, and not fewer than eight of its members shall be a majority competent to award judgment.

CHAP. V.—OF THE PUBLIC DEFENCE.

Militia.

ARTICLE I. As public safety is no less necessary than public order, we find it expedient to institute a militia, in which every male between the ages of sixteen and sixty, not having religious scruples to the contrary, shall be enrolled.

How armed and exercised.

ART. II. They shall each be furnished with a musket, bayonet, and proper accoutrements, and shall assemble once a week on the public parade, to learn the use of arms.

Subject, while under arms, to military law.

ART. III. Sensible that an armed force cannot be maintained without discipline, we hereby subject ourselves, while under arms, to an annual act of the British parliament, entitled, " An act for punishing " mutiny and desertion, and for the better payment of the army and " their quarters;" provided the punishment do not extend to death.

Officers how elected.

ART. IV. The officers of this militia (except the governor and lieutenant-governor) shall be elected by ballot from the heads of families.

Testing clause.

In witness of all, and the several clauses and agreements herein-before contained, we the said settlers have each of us hereunto severally set our hands and seals, the day and year first above written.

No. 3.

A list of those people who sailed from Gravesend, on the 4th of April 1792, on board the ships Calypso and Hankey, and the cutter Beggar's Bennison, with an intention of forming a settlement on the Island of Bulama on the western coast of Africa; together with the names of those who were born, or joined the community on their passage to, or after their arrival on, the coast, and the times of their several discharges, desertions, or deaths.

EMBARKED ON BOARD THE CALYPSO.

SUBSCRIBERS.

Council.

No. Henry Hew Dalrymple, governor, returned in the Calypso, 19th July, 1792.
Richard Hancorne, died on board the Hankey, 21st July, 1792, of fever.
Francis Brodie, returned in the Calypso, 19th July, 1792.

John Munden, returned in the Hankey, 23d November, 1792, and died on his passage to Bissao.
5 Richard Samuel Ward, died on board the Hankey at Bulama, 6th Nov. 1792, complication of diseases.
John Morse, discharged at his own request at Bulama, 14th August, 1792; he went to Bissao to practise as a surgeon, and died there 8th Sept. 1792.
J. Montifiore, discharged at his request at Bissao, 18th June, 1792.
Henry Burdett, returned in the Calypso, 19th July, 1792, and died at Sierra Leone.
William Bant, ditto, ditto.
10 Robert Seaton, returned in the Calypso the 19th July, 1792.
B. Thos. Longbothom, ditto.
Adulph Ahlelund, ditto.
George Keyburn, ditto, and died on his passage to Sierra Leone.

No. Willam Smith, died on board the Hankey at Bulama, 23d October, 1792, complication of disorders.

15 Richard C. Neild, went to Sierra Leone in the Beggar's Bennison, 8th August, 1792.

Thomas Flynn, returned in the Calypso, 19th July, 1792, and died at Sierra Leone.

Daniel Wightman, returned in the Calypso, 19th July, 1792.

John Lawless, died on board the Calypso, at Bissao, of fever, 20th June, 1792.

Robert Bostock, returned in the Calypso, 19th July, 1792, and died at Sierra Leone.

20 John Reynolds, went to Sierra Leone in the Beggar's Bennison, 8th August, 1792.

Thomas Ozanne, died on board the Hankey, at Bulama, 9th August, 1792, consumption.

Charles E. Aberdein, died at Bulama 21st Dec. 1792, mortified face.

George Fielder, died at Bulama 15th December, 1792, of fever.

John Harley, returned in the Calypso, 19th July, 1792.

25 John Hood, remained with Mr. Beaver on the Island of Bulama, and was the only subscriber who survived to come away with him.

Wm. Metcalf, returned in the Calypso the 19th July, 1792.

Hicks Metcalf, ditto.

John Squires, discharged at his request, at Bissao, 20th June, 1792.

Wm. Edward Ballard, returned in the Calypso 19th July, 1792.

30 Wm. Pullen, died on board the Hankey, at Bulama, 17th of August, 1792, of fever.

Abraham Curry, returned in the Calypso, 19th July, 1792, and died at Sierra Leone.

Dolphin Price, died at Bulama, 21st November, 1792, of fever.

H. Bland Gardener, died on board the Calypso, on the 10th, of wounds received on the Island of Bulama, in an attack of the Bijugas, on the 3d June, 1792.

Official Servants.

Owen Williams, assistant surgeon, discharged at his request, at Bulama, 6th July, 1792,

35 George Winter, clerk, died on board the Calypso at Bulama, 4th July, 1792, of fever.

Public Servants, or Labourers.

No. Wm. Thomas Dawes, discharged at his request, at Bulama, 6th July, 1792.
Henry Baker, returned in the Calypso the 19th July, 1792.
Aaron Baker, killed in an attack of the Bijugas on the Island of Bulama, the 3d June, 1792.
James Brickill, returned in the Calypso 19th July, 1792, and died at Sierra Leone.
40 Stephen Molineux, killed in the attack of the Bijugas on the Island of Bulama, the 3d June, 1792.
Thomas Saunders, returned in the Calypso the 19th July, 1792, and died on the passage to Sierra Leone.
William Foot, died on board the Calypso at Bulama, 24th June, 1792, of fever.
Edward Maynard, returned in the Calypso the 19th July, 1792.
Robert Harwin, left the Bulama colony 16th December, 1792, and went to Bissao.
45 James Box,* died on board the Hankey, at Bulama, 29th September, 1792, of fever.
Thomas Box,* left the Bulama colony, 15th March, 1793, and went to Bissao, to return to England by the English ship Nancy.
Peter Box, died at Bulama 10th December, 1792, of fever and flux.
Ambrose Harman, returned in the Calypso, 19th July, 1792.
Samuel Griffin, ditto, and died at Sierra Leone.
50 John Frazer, left the Bulama colony the 9th November, 1792, and went to Bissao.
Edward Williamson, killed in an attack of the Bijugas on the Island of Bulama, the 3d of June, 1792.
Constantine Long, ditto.
Thomas Griffiths, left the Bulama colony the 15th March, 1793, and went to Bissao, to return to England by the English ship Nancy.
William King, discharged at his request, at Bissao, 18th June, 1792.
55 James Bimrose, returned in the Calypso the 19th July, 1792.
Charles Edley, ditto.
David Cook, died on the passage out, the 15th April, 1792, consumption.
William Nash, died at Bulama 23d January, 1793, epileptic fit.
George Selwyn, deserted 18th May, 1792, at Goree.

* Discharged from the Calypso into the Hankey the 11th April, 1792, in order to make a more equal distribution of the colonists in each ship.

Subscribers' Servants.

No. Edward Fowler, returned in the Hankey, 23d November, 1792, and died on the passage.
61 R. Stafford, returned in the Calypso the 19th July, 1792.
   J. Robinson, ditto.
   George Winfield, ditto, and died on the passage to Sierra Leone.
   Thomas Blake,* returned in the Hankey, 23d November, 1792.
65 Joseph Nelson, discharged at his request, at Bissao, the 18th June, 1792.
   ——— Thompson, returned in the Calypso the 19th July, 1792.
   Lawrence Beaty, ditto.
   P. Devaynes, discharged at his request, at Bissao, the 18th June, 1792.
   Richard Smith, returned in the Calypso the 19th July, 1792.
70 Godfrey Norman, ditto.
   Benjamin Kauffman, ditto.
   David Gray, discharged at his request, at Bissao, 18th June, 1792.
   A. Nailor, returned in the Calypso, the 19th July, 1792.
   Wm. Howard, killed in an attack of Bijugas on the Island of Bulama, the 3d June, 1792.
75 J. Talbot, returned in the Calypso the 19th July, 1792.
   Wm. Johnson, ditto.
   Richard Pool, died on the 5th in consequence of wounds he had received in an attack of the Bijugas on the 3d of June, 1792.
   H. Wilson, returned in the Calypso on the 19th of July, 1792.
   John Cruikshanks, ditto.
80 Thomas Nomen, ditto.
   Andrew Garraway, discharged at his request, at Bissao, 18th June, 1792.
   John Coggins,* died on board the Hankey at Bulama, 6th August, 1792, of fever.
   John Winfield,* died at Bulama the 18th of November 1792, of worms.
   James Watson, one of two black men that remained with Mr. Beaver to the last, and was left by him at Sierra Leone, at his request.
85 S. Arfwiedson, died on board the Hankey at Bulama the 2d September, 1792, o fever.
   Wm. Smith, deserted 11th April, 1792, at Ryde in the Isle of Wight.
   Wm. Bennet, run from the Island of Bulama the 23d October, 1793.

* Boy.

[APP. NO. 3.] *African Memoranda.* 437

No. —— Harris, returned in the Calypso the 19th July, 1792.
    Thomas Lister,* died at Bulama the 10th November, 1792, of fever.
90 Joseph Watson, retnrned in the Calypso the 19th July, 1792.

Subscribers' Wives.

Mrs. Hancorne, returned in the Hankey the 23d November, 1792, and died on the passage to Bissao.
—— Curry returned in the Calypso, the 19th July, 1792.
—— Hood, ditto.
—— Harley, died at, Canabac, on board the Beggar's Bennison, on the 29th June, 1792, two days after she had been redeemed from the natives.
95 —— Flynn, returned in the Calypso the 19th July, 1792.
—— Smith, ditto.
—— Ahlelund, ditto.
—— Bant. ditto.
—— Montifiore, discharged with her husband, at Bissao, the 18th June, 1792.
100 —— Gardener, killed in an attack of the Bijugas on the Island of Bulama, the 3d June, 1792.

Asssistant Surgeon's Wife.

Mrs. Williams, discharged with her husband at Bulama, the 6th July, 1792.

Labourers' Wives.

Ann Baker, returned in the Calypso the 19th July, 1792.
Julia Baker, ditto.
—— Brickill, ditto.
105 Eliz. Mollineaux, do.
—— Saunders, do.
Sarah Foot, do.
—— Maynard, do. and died at Sierra Leone.
Jane Harwin, died at Bulama the 9th of December, 1792, of fever.
110 —— Harman, returned in the Calypso the 19th July, 1792, and died at Sierra Leone.
—— Box,† died on board the Hankey at Bulama, 30th August, 1792, of fever.

* Boy.
† Discharged from the Calypso into the Hankey, the 11th April, 1792, at the Motherbank, in order to make a more equal distribution of the colonists in each ship.

No. —— Griffin, returned in the Calypso the 19th July, 1792.
—— Edley, do.
—— Dawes, discharged with her husband at Bulama, the 6th July, 1792.

Subscribers' Servants.

115 Mary Watson, returned in the Calypso the 19th July, 1792.
Sarah Lowe, do. and died at Sierra Leone,
Amy Smith, returned in the Calypso the 19th July, 1792.
Catherine Barnwell, do.
Susan Evans, do.
120 —— Ellison, discharged at her request, at Bissao, 18th June, 1792.
Eliz. Thompson, returned in the Calypso the 19th July, 1792.
Eliz. Johnson, do.
Mary Hoskins, do.
Harrietta Fowler, died at Bulama, the 10th December, 1792, of fever.

Subscribers' Children.

125 Nancy Bant, returned in the Calypso the 19th July, 1792.
Betsey Bant, do.
Amelia Bant, do.
Jane Curry, do.
Sarah Hood, do.
130 Harriet Hood, do. and died at Sierra Leone.
—— Harley, died at Canabac, on board the Beggar's Bennison, on the 30th June, 1792, three days after her redemption from captivity.
—— Smith, returned in the Calypso the 19th July, 1792.
Jane Smith, do. and died at Sierra Leone.
Thomas Hancorne, died on board the Hankey at Bulama, 3d August, 1792,

Official Servants' Children.

135 —— Williams, discharged with his father, at Bulama, the 6th July, 1792.
Mary Williams, died on board the Calypso, on the passage out, convulsions

Labourers' Children.

No. —— Dawes,
—— Dawes, } discharged with their father at Bulama, the 6th July, 1792.

William Baker, returned in the Calypso the 19th July, 1792.
140 Julia Baker, do.
—— Saunders, do.
—— Saunders, do.
—— Saunders, do.
—— Foot, do.
145 —— Foot, do.
—— Maynard, do.
—— Maynard, do.
—— Maynard, died on board Calypso at Bulama 7th July, 1792, fever.
Robert Harwin, discharged with his father the 16th December, 1792.
150 Mary Box,* discharged with her brother Thomas, the 15th March, 1793.
William Box,* died on board the Hankey at Bulama, 29th September, 1792, fever.
—— Griffin, returned in the Calypso the 19th July, 1792.
Thomas Baker, do.
Susan Baker, do.
155 Sarah Baker, do.

EMBARKED ON BOARD THE HANKEY.

SUBSCRIBERS.

Council.

John Young, lieutenant-governor, returned in the Calypso, the 19th July, 1792.
Sir William Halton, bart, do.
John King, do.
Nicholas Bayley, do.
5 John Paiba, do.

* Discharged from the Calypso into the Hankey the 11th of April 1792, at the Motherbank, in order to make a more equal distribution of the colonists in each ship.

No. Charles Drake, returned in the Calypso the 19th July, 1792.
Peter Clutterbuck, do.
Isaac Ximenes, do.
Philip Beaver, remained on the island till the 29th November, 1793, when, all the labourers being either dead or gone, all the subscribers except one, and all the servants except two blacks, he was obliged to evacuate the island.

10 John Curwood, returned in the Hankey, the 23d November, 1792.
Benjamin Peirara, returned in the Calypso the 19th July, 1792.
Mordet Peirara, do.
Robert Webster, died at Bulama the 2d December, 1792, of fever and flux.
John Marsac, returned in the Calypso the 19th July, 1792.
15 John Piaba (second), went to Sierra Leone in the Beggar's Bennison, 8th August, 1792.
Francis Donnelly, died at Bulama the 1st December, 1792, of fever.
John Mallison, returned in the Calypso the 19th July, 1792.
Timothy Farrer, do.
Henry Perney, do.
20 Jos. Freeman, died at Bulama, the 14th December, 1792, of fever.
Charles Robinson, returned in the Hankey the 23d November, 1792, and died on the passage to Bissao.
Richard Ford, returned in the Calypso the 19th July, 1792.
William Banfield, died on board the Hankey at Bulama, 27th October, 1792, lunatic.
Thomas Sparks, died at Bulama the 21st December, 1792, of fever.

Official Servants.

25 J. S. Gandell, secretary, discharged at his request the 21st October, 1792, and went to Bissao; died in passage home on board the Hankey,
John Rowe, surgeon, returned in the Hankey, 23d Nov. 1793, and died at Bissao.
Benjamin Marston, surveyor, died on board the Hankey, at Bulama, 10th August, 1792, of fever.
John Borton, clerk, returned in the Calypso, the 19th July, 1792, and died at Sierra Leone.

Public Servants, or Labourers.

Thomas Atkinson, died on board the Hankey at Bulama, the 5th July, 1792, of fever.

No. Hugh Meare, died at Bulama the 28th September, 1792, of fever.
31 Wm. Meare, died on board the Beggar's Benison, at Sierra Leone, 29th August, 1792, of fever.

Daniel Sly, died on board the Hankey, at Bulama 20th September, 1792, of fever.

Joseph Riches, died at Bulama the 18th December, 1792, of fever.

Henry Rodell, discharged at his request, and went to Sierra Leone in the Beggar's Benison, 8th Aug. 1792.

35 John Ashworth, died on board the Hankey at Bulama, 30th August, 1792, mortified hand.

Thomas Bell, died on board the Hankey, at Bulama, the 5th July, 1792, of fever.

Wm. C. Barret, died at Bulama the 21st November, 1792, of fever.

John Hodgekinson, returned in the Calypso the 19th July, 1792.

William Reeves, died on board the Hankey, at Bulama, 17th October, 1792, of fever.

40 William Collins, discharged at his request, at the Motherbank, 11th April, 1792.

Subscribers' Servants.

Alexander Mason, returned in the Calypso the 19th July, 1792.

Cornelius Craig, ditto, and died at Sierra Leone.

David Bullock, returned in the Calypso the 19th July, 1792.

John Harpham, do. and died at Sierra Leone.

45 Thomas Mooney, returned in the Calypso the 19th July, 1792.

Robert Davis, do. and died at Sierra Leone.

John Avison, do. do.

James Ayleward, do. do.

James Spencer, deserted from Bulama, the 9th November, 1792.

50 Alexander Thompson, died at Bulama, the 4th December, 1792, fever.

Joseph Burgess, returned in the Calypso the 19th July, 1792, and died at Sierra Leone.

Edward Pearce,* returned in the Calypso the 19th July, 1792.

John Evans, do.

Robert Still, do. and died at Sierra Leone.

55 Thomas Dowlah, a lascar, who remained with Mr. Beaver to the last, and was left by him at Sierra Leone at his own request.

Thomas Mellin, returned in the Calypso the 19th July, 1792.

Richard Winslow, do.

*Boy.

No. Thomas Winslow, returned in the Calypso, the 19th July, 1792.

Thomas Collins, discharged at the Motherbank, 10th April, 1792, for turbulent conduct.

60 William Murrell, do. his own request.

Charles O'Neil,* returned in the Calypso the 19th July, 1792, and died at Sierra Leone.

James Richardson, returned in the Calypso the 19th July, 1792.

George Humphreys, discharged at the Motherbank, the 11th April, 1792, turbulent conduct.

John Hill, returned in the Calypso the 19th July, 1792.

65 Wm. Compton, jumped from the Hankey into the river and was drowned, 12th November, 1792.

Peter Campbell, discharged at the Motherbank the 10th April, 1792, turbulent conduct.

Wm. Wright, returned in the Calypso the 19th July, 1792.

Nathaniel Ashworth,* died at Bulama the 15th November, 1792, of fever.

Edward Cowley, returned in the Calypso the 19th July, 1792.

70 James Moore, do. and died on the passage.

John Broughton, do. do.

John Harpur, discharged at the Motherbank the 10th April, 1792, turbulent conduct.

Subscribers' Wives.

Mrs. King, returned in the Calypso the 19th July, 1792.

—— Young, do.

75 —— Paiba, do.

—— Drake, do.

—— Perney, do.

—— Ford, do. and died at Sierra Leone.

—— Curwood, returned in the Hankey the 23d November, 1792, and died on the passage.

Official Servants' Wives.

80 —— Gandell, died on board the Hankey at Bulama, 13th September, 1792, of fever.

—— Rowe, returned in the Hankey the 23d November, 1792.

* Boys.

Labourers' Wives.

No. Eliz. Bell, died on board the Hankey, at Bulama, the 5th July, 1792, of fever.
—— Atkinson, returned in the Calypso the 19th July, 1792.
Eliz. Meares, died on board the Hankey at Bulama, the 8th September, 1792, of fever.
85 Hannah Riches, discharged the 15th March 1793, at her request, to get a passage to England, at that time the only surviving woman on the island.
Mary Ashworth, died on board the Hankey, at Bulama, 23d August, 1792, consumption.
—— Hodgekinson, returned in the Calypso the 19th July, 1792.
Alice Reeves, died on board the Hankey at Bulama, 26th October, 1792, fever.
—— Barrett, returned in the Calypso the 19th July, 1792.
90 —— Rodell, died on board the Hankey, at Bulama, 21st July, 1792, of fever.

Subscribers' Servants.

Mary Salisbury, discharged to the ship Hankey, 19th July, 1792, and returned in that ship.
Martha Marshall, returned in the Calypso the 19th July, 1792.
Eliz. Harpur,   do.
Eliz. Eynott, died at Bulama the 14th December, 1792, of fever.
95 Patience Bates, discharged to the ship Hankey, the 11th April, 1792, and died returning in that ship.
Sarah Williams, discharged at the Motherbank, 10th April, 1792.
Sarah Walker, returned in the Calypso, the 19th July, 1792,

Subscribers' Children.

Mary Perney, returned in the Calypso the 19th July, 1792.
Eliz. Curwood, returned in the Hankey the 23d November, 1792, and died on the passage.
100 Richard Curwood, do.   do.
Mary Ford, returned in the Calypso the 19th July, 1792, and died at Sierra Leone.
Eliz. Ford, returned in the Calypso the 19th July, 1792

No. Rachael Ford, returned on board the Calypso, 19th July, 1792.
Susan Ford, do. and died at Sierra Leone.
105 Sophia Ford, died on board the Hankey at sea, the 14th April, 1792.

Official Servants' Children.

Eliz. Gandell, discharged with her father, 31st October, 1792, and died at Bissao.
Eliz. Rowe, died on board the Hankey at Bulama, 17th November, 1792, fever.

Labourers' Children.

George Ashworth, the only surviving child when the island was evacuated, left with Mr. Lawrence in the Rio Nunez, at his own request.
John Ashworth, died at Bulama the 22d November, 1792, fever.
110 Thomas Ashworth, died on board the Hankey, at Bulama, 30th August, 1792, hooping cough.
Lucy Bell, returned in the Calypso the 19th July, 1792, and died at Sierra Leone.
Sally Barrett, returned in the Calypso the 19th July, 1792.
Thomas Hodgekinson, discharged at his request to the Felicity schooner, 25th July, 1793.
Ann Hodgekinson, returned in the Calypso the 19th July, 1792.
115 Eliz. Hodgekinson, do.
John Hodgekinson, do.
John Meare, died the 11th April, 1792, at Yarmouth, Isle of Wight, of small pox.
Hannah Riches, died at Bulama the 10th December, 1792, fever.
Henry Rodell, discharged with his father, 8th August, 1792.
120 Wm. Reeves, died on board the cutter Beggar's Benison, at Bance Island, the 21st August 1792, of fever and flux.
Sarah Reeves, died on board the Hankey, at Bulama, 10th October, 1792, fever.
James Reeves, died at Bulama the 18th November, 1792, fever.
123 Richard Reeves, died at Bulama the 19th September, 1792, fever.

EMBARKED ON BOARD THE BEGGAR'S BENISON.

Council.

Robert Dobbin, returned in the Calypso the 19th July, 1792.

Master.

No. Geo. Birkhead, returned in the Hankey the 23d November, 1792, and died on the passage.

Seamen.

Richard Johnson, died at Sierra Leone, 25th Aug. 1792, fever.
John Venus, died at Bulama the 26th October, 1792, fever.
John Hargrave, died at Bulama the 25th October, 1792, fever.

Boy.

6 Matthew Beck, deserted at Sierra Leone, the 29th Aug. 1792.

Born.

April 11th, 1792, an infant of Mrs. Riches, which died on board the Hankey, at Bulama, 10th September, 1792, fever.
July 12th, 1792, an infant of Mrs. Reeves, which died on board the Hankey, at Bulama, 25th October, 1792, fever,
October 30th, 1792, an infant of Mrs. Rowe, which died the same day.

Entered on board the Cutter, after leaving England.

At Teneriffe, 9th May, 1792, Peter Hayles, seaman, deserted 23d October, 1793, from Bulama.
At Sierra Leone, 16th September, 1792, Joseph Glover, seaman, discharged at his request, the 12th November, 1792, to return in the Hankey.
At Bulama, 12th January, 1793, John Scott, master, died at Bulama the 3d September, 1793, of fever.
At Bulama, 2d March, 1793, John Williams, seaman, remained with Mr. Beaver to the last, and was left by him at Sierra Leone at his own request.

No. 4.

A list of those persons who remained, with Lieutenant Beaver, on the Island of Bulama, when the discontented colonists left that island with the ship Calypso, noting the time of their death, desertion, &c.

SUBSCRIBERS.

Council.

No. Philip Beaver, president, returned to Europe the 17th of May, 1792.

Richard Hancorne, vice president, died at Bulama the 21st of July, 1792, fever.

John Munden, left Bulama in the Hankey, the 23d November, 1792, and died in that ship three days afterwards.

Charles E. Aberdein, died at Bulama the 21st December, 1792, mortified face.

5 John Reynolds, left the colony and went to Sierra Leone the 8th August, 1792.

John Curwood, left Bulama in the Hankey the 23d November, 1792.

Robert Webster, died at Bulama the 2d of December, 1792, fever.

John Paiba, left the colony, and went to Sierra Leone, the 8th August, 1792.

Francis Donnelly, died at Bulama the 1st December, 1792, fever.

10 Joseph Freeman, died at Bulama, the 14th December, 1792, fever.

Charles Robinson, left Bulama in the Hankey, the 23d November, 1792, and died in that ship eight days after.

Wm. Banfield, died at Bulama the 27th of October, 1792, insane.

Thomas Sparks, died at Bulama the 21st December, 1792, fever.

Richard S. Ward, died at Bulama 6th November 1792, complication of diseases.

15 John Morse, left Bulama the 14th August, 1792, and died at Bissao the 8th of September following.

Wm. Smith, died at Bulama the 23d October, 1792, complicated diseases.

Richard C. Neild, left the colony, and went to Sierra Leone, the 8th August, 1792.

No. Thomas Ozanne, died at Bulama the 9th August, 1792, consumption.
George Feilder, died at Bulama the 15th December, 1792, fever.
20 John Hood, returned to Europe the 17th of May, 1794.
Wm. Pullen, died at Bulama, the 17th August, 1792.
Dolphin Price, died at Bulama, the 21st November, 1792.

Official Servants.

J. S. Gandell, secretary, left Bulama, and went to Bissao 31st October, 1792, died on board the Hankey 30th December following.
John Rowe, surgeon, left Bulama in the Hankey the 23d November, 1792, and died at Bissao the 13th of December following.
25 Benjamin Marston, surveyor, died at Bulama, the 10th August, 1792, fever.

Public Servants, or Labourers.

Robert Harwin, left Bulama and went to Bissao the 16th December, 1792.
James Box, died at Bulama the 29th September, 1792, fever.
Thomas Box, left Bulama 15th March, 1793, to return to Europe by the Nancy, then at Bissao.
Peter Box, died at Bulama 10th December, 1792, fever and flux.
30 John Frazer, left Bulama the 9th November, 1792, and went to Bissao.
Thomas Griffiths, left Bulama 15th March, 1793, to return to Europe by the Nancy, then at Bissao.
William Nash, died at Bulama 23d January, 1793, epileptic fit.
Hugh Meare, died at Bulama the 28th September, 1792, fever.
Wm. Meare, died on board the Beggar's Benison at Sierra Leone, the 29th August, 1792, fever.
35 Daniel Sly, died at Bulama the 20th September, 1792, fever.
Joseph Riches, died at Bulama the 18th December, 1792, fever.
Henry Rodell, left the colony and went to Sierra Leone the 8th August, 1792.
John Ashworth, died at Bulama the 30th August, 1792, mortified hand.
Wm. C. Barrett, died at Bulama the 21st November, 1792, fever.
40 Wm. Reeves, died at Bulama the 17th October, 1792, fever.

Subscribers' Servants.

Edward Fowler, left Bulama in the Hankey the 23d November, 1792, and died five days afterwards.
James Watson left at Sierra Leone in March 1794, at his own request.

No. S. Arfwiedson, died at Bulama, the 2d September, 1792, fever.
William Bennet, deserted from the Isle of Bulama, the 23d of October, 1793.
45 James Spencer, left Bulama the 9th November, 1792.
Alexander Thompson, died at Bulama, the 4th December, 1792, fever.
Thomas Dowlah, left at Sierra Leone in March, 1794, at his own request.
William Compton, jumped from the Hankey into the river and was drowned the 12th November, 1792.

Boys.

Nathaniel Ashworth, died at Bulama the 15th November, 1792, fever.
50 Thomas Blake, left Bulama in the Hankey, the 23d November, 1792.
John Coggins, died at Bulama, the 6th August, 1792, fever.
John Winfield, died at Bulama, 18th November, 1792, worms.
Thomas Lister, died at Bulama, the 10th November, 1792, fever.

Women.

Mrs. Hancorne, left Bulama in the Hankey, the 23d November, 1792; and died three days afterwards.
55 —— Harwin, died at Bulama, the 9th December, 1792, fever.
—— Box, died at Bulama, the 30th August, 1792, fever.
—— Curwood, left Bulama in the Hankey, the 23d November, 1792; and died two days afterwards.
—— Gandell, died at Bulama, the 13th September, 1792, fever.
—— Rowe, left Bulama in the Hankey, the 23d November, 1792; and returned to Europe in the Nancy.
60 —— Reeves, died at Bulama, the 26th October, 1792, fever.
—— Riches, left Bulama 15th March, 1793, to return to Europe by the Nancy, then at Bissao.
—— Ashworth, died at Bulama, the 23d August, 1792, consumption.
—— Meares, died at Bulama, the 8th September, 1792, fever.
—— Rodell, died at Bulama, the 21st July, 1792, fever.
65 Eliz. Eynot, died at Bulama, the 14th December, 1792, fever.
Henrietta Fowler, died at Bulama, the 10th December, 1792, fever.

CHILDREN.

Boys.

No. Thomas Hancorne, died at Bulama, the 3d August, 1792, teething.

Robert Harwin, left Bulama with his father, the 16th December, 1792.

William Box, died at Bulama, the 29th September, 1792, fever.

70 Richard Curwood, left Bulama with his father, the 23d November, 1792, and died on board the Hankey, the 19th December following.

George Ashworth, left with Mr. Lawrence, Rio Nunez, at his own request, in December, 1793.

John Ashworth, died at Bulama, the 22d November, 1792, fever.

Thomas Ashworth, died at Bulama, the 30th August, 1792, hooping cough.

Thomas Hodgekinson, left Bulama in the Felicity, the 25th July, 1793.

75 Henry Rodell, left Bulama with his father, the 8th August, 1792.

William Reeves, died on board the Beggars' Benison at Sierra Leone, the 21st August, 1792.

James Reeves, died at Bulama, the 18th November, 1792, fever.

Richard Reeves, died at Bulama, the 19th September, 1792, fever.

Girls.

Mary Box, left Bulama with her brother, the 15th March, 1793, to return to Europe by the Nancy.

80 Elizabeth Curwood, left Bulama with her father, the 23d November, 1792; and died on board the Hankey 13th January following.

Elizabeth Gandell, left Bulama with her father the 31st October, 1792; and died at Bissao.

Elizabeth Rowe, died at Bulama, the 17th November, 1792, fever.

Hannah Riches, died at Bulama, the 10th December, 1792, fever.

Sarah Reeves, died at Bulama, the 10th October, 1792, fever.

Infants.

85 Riches, born on board the Hankey, 11th of April, 1792; died at Bulama, the 10th September following, fever.

Reeves, born on board the Hankey, 12th of July, 1792; died at Bulama, the 25th October following, fever.

SEAMEN ON BOARD THE BEGGARS' BENISON CUTTER.

No. Peter Hayles, deserted from Bulama, the 23d October, 1793.
Richard Johnson, died at Sierra Leone, the 25th August, 1792, fever.
John Venus, died at Bulama, the 26th October, 1792, fever.
John Hargrave, died at Bulama, the 25th October, 1792, fever.
5. Matthew Beck, boy, deserted at Sierra Leone, the 29th August, 1792.

No. 5.

Some account of the weather on the island of Bulama, from the 20th July, 1792, to the 28th November, 1793.

Note. The thermometer, Farenheit's, was kept in the shade exposed to the air, under the Hankey's poop, till the 28th of October, 1792: from that day, under a double canvass tent on shore, till the 8th of December; and afterwards in the shade under the block-house roof. It is always noted, when not otherwise expressed, at its greatest height between noon and 2 P. M.

BULAMA, JULY 1792.

Day of Month	Height Therm.	
20	—	Clear weather till 3 P.M., when we had a violent tornado at N.W. with heavy rains; and another tornado from the same quarter about an hour afterwards. The rain continued till midnight.
21	75	No rain from four till nine A.M.; small rain with southerly wind the rest of the day.
22	—	Heavy rains all last night, which continued till noon, then light showers at the interval of an hour, or an hour and a half; a fresh southerly wind.
23	—	Light showers in morning, then fine weather till dusk, from which time it rained till 10 P.M. Light southerly winds.
24	—	No rain all day; just after day-light a violent tornado with much thunder, lightning, and heavy rain: it continued an hour.
25	—	No rain except between four and five P.M. Wind S.W.
26	—	No rain except between two and five P.M. Wind S.S.W.
27	—	Clear weather. Wind S.W. by S.
28	—	Small rain last night; none all day. Wind S.S.W.

Days of Month. Height Therm.

29 — Clear except a light shower or two about the middle of the day.
30* — Clear till 10 A.M., then rain all day. Fresh S.W. wind.
31* — Clear all the morning; rain all the afternoon.

AUGUST 1792.

1   75*   Heavy showers at intervals through the day.
2   74*   Morning clear; heavy rains the latter part of the day.
3   —*   Showery all day.
4   80*   No rain all day.
5   —   Heavy rain all the forenoon; fine the remainder of the day. Wind S.W.
6   76   No rain. Wind S.W.
7   78   Clear weather and wind W.S.W. till 4 P.M. when the wind shifted to the N.N.E. and it rained violently,
8   —*   Showery all day.
9   —*   Heavy rains through the day.
10   —*
11   —*
12   —   Violent tornado from one to four A.M. Fine weather all day.
13   —   Fine weather morning; rain latter part of the day. Wind S.W.
14   —*   Strong S.W. wind, and heavy rain all day.
15   —*   Showery, hazy weather. Wind S.W.
16   —*   Heavy rain all day. Wind S.W.
17   —*   Strong S.W. wind without rain all day.
18   —   Clear weather, fresh S.W. wind
19   81   A light shower or two in the morning; fine the rest of the day. Wind S.W.
20   —   Clear weather with a light S.W. wind.
21   81   Clear weather. Wind S.W.
22   82   Light rain all the morning; fine weather the rest of the day. Wind S.W.
23   78   Clear weather. Light S.W. wind.
24   78   Do.   do.
25   80   Heavy rain and calm all the morning. Fine weather and S.W. wind P.M.
26   78   Heavy rain and S.W. wind till one P.M.; then calm and cloudy without rain.
27   —   Showery. S.W. wind.
28   80   Showery morning with S.W. wind. P.M. squalls from the N.W. with rain.

* Those days thus marked, I was either absent or ill, and the account of the weather is taken from either Messrs. Aberdein, Hood, or Scott.

Day of month.	Height Ther.	
29	80	Frequent and heavy showers. Wind S.W.
30	78	Heavy rain all last night and this forenoon. Wind S.W. No rain P.M.
31	78	Clear forenoon; heavy showers P.M. Wind N.E. all day.

SEPTEMBER 1792.

1	79	Showery weather, N.E. wind.
2	80	Clear, wind S.W.
3		Showery, wind S.W.
4		Showery, light S.W. airs.
5	80	Fine weather, light S.W. winds.
6	82	Clear, wind S.W.
7	77	Heavy rain A.M., clear P.M.
8	81	Heavy rain all last night, clear all day with light S.W. wind.
9	79	Calm morning, and fine weather all day, except a tornado at east, which began at half past 9 A.M. and continued an hour, when the wind changed to the N.W. for the rest of the day.
10	84	Clear.
11	83	Clear, wind S.W. Evening a tornado from the eastward, from which quarter we have generally had one every 24 hours for this last week.
12	8 A.M. 77, noon 81, 8 P.M. 84	Clear, winds variable, last night in first watch, heavy tornado with much thunder lightning and rain.
13	78	Clear moring, rain P.M. winds variable, last night in the first watch a heavy tornado and one this evening.
14	82	Clear.
15	83	Clear, winds variable, two tornados these 24 hours.
16	80	Squally, winds from all points.
17	82	Clear, winds round the compass.
18	85	do. do. one tornado.
19	83	do. do. a great deal of rain, thunder and lightning last night.
20	83	do. winds variable.
21	83	do. do.
22	82	do. do.
23	83	Clear morning, tornado with rain evening.
24	83	Clear.
25	83	do.
26	81	Violent tornado with heavy rain morning, hazy, cloudy weather with a light S.W. wind the rest of the day, during which we saw not the sun.

APP. NO. 5.] *African Memoranda.* 459

Day of month.	Height Ther.	
27	82	Clear.
28	84	do.
29	81	do. winds variable.
30	83	Hazy weather, strong N.W. wind morning, afterwards variable, heavy tornado evening.

OCTOBER 1792.

1	83	Rain morning, clear and west wind P.M.
2	85	Clear, morning calm, P.M. westerly wind.
3	84	do. do. do.
4	84	do. variable winds.
5	84	Two or three light showers in the course of the day, hazy A.M., clear P.M.
6	83	Light rain A.M. clear P.M. with westerly wind.
7	86	Clear, calm or light westerly airs.
8	84	do. do.
9	85	do. do.
10	84	do. one tornado very violent.
11	85	Clear, calm morning, light westerly wind P.M. Tornado at 8 P.M. S.E.
12	85	Hazy, cloudy weather, a fine S.E. breeze.
13	85	Cloudy weather and fresh breeze morning, squally with showers P.M. three tornados last night.
14	81	Heavy rain morning, clear evening, one tornado, with strong winds and much rain the greatest part of last night.
15	83	Squally, with showers at times.
16	84	Cloudy, S.W. wind.
17	83	Clear, fine breeze from the S.W.
18	87	do. little wind.
19	86	Cloudy.
20	85	Cloudy and hazy, wind S.W.
21	85	Foggy.
22	85	Cloudy, wind N.E. morning, S.W. evening.
23	85	Clear. do. do. hail for two minutes the size of a pinshead, not a cloud to be seen.
24	85	Clear, light winds N.E. morning, S.W. evening.
25	86	do. do. do.
26	88	do. do. do.
27	90	do. wind N.W. morning, S.E. evening, exposed the thermometer to the sun at noon, it rose, in 20 minutes, to 126.
28	90	do. wind N.W. morning, S.E. evening.

Day of Month	Height Therm.	
29	89	Clear, wind N.W. morning, S.E. evening.
30	91	do. do. do.
31	90	do. at eight p.m. tornado.

NOVEMBER 1792.

1	90	Clear, N.W. wind morn. S.W. evening.
2	91	do. do. do.
3	92	do. do. do.
4	92	do. do. do.
5	92	do. do. do.
6	84	do. fresh S.E. wind morning, calm evening.
7	92	do. S.E. wind morning, do.
8	93	do. little or no wind all day.
9	96	do. do.
10	95	do. do.
11		Clear fine N.E. breeze all day.
12 to 19		Too ill to write.
20	—	Clear, N.E. wind morning.
21, 22		Too ill to write.
23	—	Clear, calms and light N.W. airs alternately.
24	95	do. N.E. wind morning, calm evening.
25	91	do. do. do.
26	89	Cloudy, wind N.E.
27	85	do. do.
28	91	Clear, light N.E. wind.
29	91	do. almost calm.
30	94	do. little or no wind.

DECEMBER 1792.

1	92	Clear, litle or no wind.
2	92	do. fine N.E breeze
3	92	do. light N.E. wind.
4	91	do. fresh N.E. wind.
5	—	Ill.
6	—	do.
7	89	Clear, wind N.E. morning, S.W. evening.
8	88	Foggy, N.E. wind all day.
9	88	do. do.
10	90	do. little wind.

Day of Month	Height Therm.		
11	92	Foggy, calm.	
12	89	do. N.E wind.	
13	—	Ill.	
14	92	Foggy, calm.	
15	—	Ill.	
16	—	do.	
17	—	Clear, N.E. wind, the first day without fog for some time.	
18	77	Very hazy and foggy indeed, with a fresh N.E. wind all day.	
19	{65 at day light, 88 at noon,}	Foggy, fresh N.E. wind till noon, then calm.	
20	{67 at day light, 87 at noon,}	do. do. all day.	
21	—	Foggy weather. fresh N.E. breeze.	
22	—	do. do.	
23	—	do. do.	
24	—	do. do.	
25	{70 morn. 90 noon,}	do. do.	
26	{70 morn. 90 noon,}	do. do.	
27	90	do. do.	
28	88	do. do.	
29	{65 morn. 88 noon,}	do. do.	
30	{64 morn. 88 noon.}	do. do.	
31	{64 morn. 87 noon,}	do. do.	

JANUARY 1793.

1 {63 morn. 87 noon,} Foggy, N.E. wind.

2 {65 morn. 92 noon,} Hazy, N.E. breeze died early, calm the rest of the day.

3 {67 morn. 87 noon, 92 3 p.m.} Hazy, light N.E. breeze, morning, calm from 11 a.m.

4 to 11 No observation.

12 {66 morn. 86 noon,} Hazy, N.E. wind.

13 89 do. light N.E. wind morning, calm evening

Day of Month	Height Therm.	
14	91	Light N.E. wind.
15	—	do.
16	91	Light N.E. air morning, wind W.S.W. evening, at one p.m. exposed the thermometer to the sun, it rose in twenty minutes from 91 to 125.
17	—	Ill.
18	92	Very thick fog, calm.
19	91	Little or no wind.
20	88	Clear, and fine N.E. breeze.
21	86	N.E. wind.
22	88	do.
23	90	Foggy, and N.E. wind.
24	98	do. do. till noon, and then calm.
25	96	Foggy, and N.E. breeze morning, calm evening.
26	84	do. and N.E. wind all day.
27	86	Foggy.
28	85	Very foggy all day,
29	85	do. drops of rain twice this day.
30	86	Foggy.
31	85	do. N.E. wind, drops of rain thrice this day.

FEBRUARY 1793.

1	93	Hazy, light Northerly winds.
2	94	Clear, N.E. wind till noon, then calm.
3	93	Clear and N.E wind all day.
4	96	do. till noon, and then calm.
5	96	do. do.
6	95	do. wind N.E. morning, S.W. evening.
7	94	do. calm morning. do.
8	90	do. light air morning do.
9	94	do. do. do.
10	99	do. little or no wind all day.
11	90	Little wind morning, fresh S.W. evening.
12	90	Calm morning, do.
13	88	Fresh S.W. wind all day.
14	92	S.W. breeze all day.
15	90	do.
16	90	do.

Day of Month	Height Therm.	
17	94	Easterly wind morning, calm evening.
18	96	Light S.W. wind.
19	100	Fresh N.E. wind morning, and fresh S.W. wind evening, from 1 to 2 p.m. when the thermometer rose so high it was calm.
20	98	Wind N.E. morning, S.W. evening.
21	96	do. do.
22	95	Strong N.E. wind morning, light S.W. evening.
23	95	N.E. breeze morning, do.
24	94	do. do.
25	91	Strong do. do.
26	94	do. do.
27	95	Light N.E. wind.
28	89	Foggy and strong N.E. breeze all day.

MARCH 1793.

1	87	Calm and hazy morning, S.W. breeze evening.
2	88	Light N.E. breeze morning, calm and S.W. airs evening
3	94	Clear, strong N.E. wind morning, strong S.W. do.
4	94	N.E. wind, and foggy all day.
5	94	N.E. wind morning, S.W. evening, foggy all day.
6	92	do. do.
7	87	do. do.
8	92	do. do.
9	90	do. do.
10	92	do. do.
11	95	do. do.
12	86	do. strong do.
13	89	Foggy and light N.E. wind all day.
14	89	Strong N.E. wind and hazy all day.
15	90	do. do.
16	89	do. do.
17	91	do. morning, calm evening.
18	95	do. do.
19	94	Light N.E. wind morn. fresh varying wind evening.
20	88	Calm morning, fresh S.E. wind evening.
21	94	do. do.
22	88	do. fresh S.W. wind evening.
23	88	do. do.

Day of Month	Height Therm.	
24	88	Calm morning, fresh S.W. wind evening.
25	86	do. do.
26	94	Calm till 2 p.m. and then a light S.W. breeze.
27	94	do. morning, strong S.W. wind evening.
28	92	do. till noon, p.m. it blew fresh from every point between North (round by the East) and S.W.
29	92	Calm morning, variable winds which settled in the S.W. evening.
30	90	do. evening S.W. wind, hazy all day.
31	91	Fresh wind all day between the N.E. and East.

APRIL 1793.

1	94	Wind between N.E. and East, morning, then calm, and S.W. breeze in the evening.
2	88	Light Easterly wind morning, strong S.W. evening.
3	89	Winds as yesterday.
4	95	do.
5	88	do.
6	90	do.
7	89	do. fresh S.S.W. evening——From Mr. Scott, being too ill to write.
8	90	Light N.E. morn. do. do.
9	89	do. do. do.
10	88	Calm morning, do. do.
11	93	Light N. morning, do. do.
12	89	do. E. do. do. do.
13	88	do. do. do.
14	88	Light Northerly wind morning, do.
15	94	do. do.
16	92	Light N.E. wind morning, fresh wind at West evening.
17	86	Calm till 11 a.m. fresh S.W. wind the rest of the day, lightning in the evening, the first since the last rains.
18	90	Calm noon, light S.W. airs evening, sun vertical to-day.
19	89	S.W. wind all day.
20	87	S.S.W. wind all day.
21	86	Hazy all day, S.S.W. wind till three p.m. and then calm.
22	86	S.W. wind and hazy weather all day.
23	89	do.
24	86	Calm all the morning, at day light we had a heavy shower of rain which continued twenty minutes, very large drops, fresh S.W. wind, evening.

Days of Month.	eight Ther.	
25	90	Light S.W. morning, fresh S.W. evening.
26	90	do. N.E. morning. do
27	85	Calm morning, do.
28	—	Broke my thermometer, S.W. breeze all day.
29	—	S.W. wind morning, West evening.
30	—	Easterly wind morning, S.W. afternoon.

MAY 1793.

1 South and S.W. winds all day.
2 Wind S.E. morning. S.W. evening,
3 Light south wind morning. Fresh wind at west evening.
4 Wind S.E. morning. West and N.W. evening.
5 Alternate calms and fresh winds from every point of the compass.
6 do. do. do.
7 do. do. do.
8 This morning had much the appearance of rain; indeed we have had heavy black clouds for these last three or four nights; winds very variable.
9 Strong north wind and hazy morning. Strong west wind and cloudy evening.
10 Hazy cloudy weather; fresh winds round the compass, lightning in the evening.
11 do. do. do. with dist. thunder.
12 do. do. lightning in the evening.
13 Winds variable, with hazy morning and cloudy evening, do. with dist. thunder.
14 Fresh north wind morning, and fresh west wind evening, hazy, lightning in the evening.
15 Calm and hazy morning, strong S.W. wind evening, do.
16 Winds variable; at nine p.m. near low water,* we had a tornado at S.E., the first this season, with much thunder, lightning, and rain.
17 Variable light winds and hazy weather.
18 do. do.
19 Winds strong and variable.
20 Winds as before, with thunder and lightning in the evening.
21 do. winds, at 10 p.m. we had a heavy dry tornado with lightning.
22 Strong N.N.W. wind morning, fresh S.W. evening.
23 North wind morning, strong west wind evening.

* From Moore and Bootle I learned, that it is a prevailing notion with masters of ships, on this coast, that tornados happen only at high or low water: to overturn which ridiculous opinion, the time of tide will be noted every tornado during this season.

Days.
24 North wind morning, fresh S.W. evening.
25 Fresh N. wind morning, do.
26 do.   do.
27 Fresh wind all day from N.N.W. to W.S.W. thunder and lightning in the evening.
28 Winds from north to west and strong, evening cloudy, thunder and lightning.
29 do. winds, at 7 p.m. a moderate dry tornado,   do.
30 Strong winds from north to west.
31 Northerly wind and cloudy morning, at 9 a.m. (near low water) a heavy tornado, with much rain, calm latter part of the day.

JUNE 1793.

1 Winds: light north morning, west noon, fresh S.W. evening, clear, thunder and lightning evening.
2 Clear weather, winds as yesterday.
3 do.   do.
4 Fresh wind from north to west all day, weather clear.
5 do.   do.   cloudy morning, clear rest of day.
6 do.   do.   do.   do.
7 do. winds, morning cloudy, then clear weather till 4 p.m. when we had thunder, lightning, and rain; one tornado 4h. 30m. p.m. low water.
8 Alternate calms and fresh winds from every point of the compass, with some thunder and lightning, and frequent heavy showers, and dark cloudy weather, rain great part of last night.
9 Calms and variable winds, cloudy till noon, clear after, evening thunder and lightning, one tornado 10 p.m. dry, near high water.
10 Clear weather and light variable winds all day, lightning in the evening.
11 do.   moderate breezes from N.N.W. to W.
12 Fresh winds from N.N.W to W.S.W. weather cloudy.
13 Calm and variable light airs, cloudy weather, two light showers, some thunder, one tornado 9 p.m. one-third flood.
14 Calm and variable light airs, cloudy weather, heavy rain p.m. much thunder and lightning, rain last night.
15 Dark cloudy weather, winds from all points, many squalls between south and east, and many showers with thunder in the course of the day.
16 Sometimes cloudy and sometimes clear, winds round the compass and sometimes calm, a shower in the morning.
17 Weather very variable, as well as the winds.
18 Cloudy weather, variable winds with thunder, much rain with the tornado; one tornado 2 p.m. very heavy, young flood.

Days.

19 Variable winds and cloudy weather, thunder in the evening, heavy rain with thunder and lightning all night.

20 Fresh east wind and cloudy till 2 p.m. then fresh south wind and cloudy the rest of the day, tornado at 2 p.m. much rain, low water.

21 Winds round the compass and light, weather cloudy, light rain from 5 p.m. till half past 6, with much thunder and lightning.

22 Winds between south and west, weather cloudy.

23 Calm at times, at others light winds between south and west, rain from 2 till 5, with thunder and lightning.

24 Cloudy weather, calms, and winds round the southern half of the compass, p.m. thunder and lightning.

25 Fresh N.W. wind morning, light S.W. evening, often cloudy and as often clear.

26 Moderate breezes from N.W. to S. weather as yesterday,

27 Calms, and light winds from S.E. to W. weather cloudy all day, with many showers, and thunder and lightning.

28 Calms, and variable winds, heavy rain last night and almost all this day, with much thunder and lightning.

29 Fresh N.N.E. wind till 2 p.m. then calm, weather sometimes cloudy and sometimes clear.

30 East wind and clear weather morning, S.W. wind, cloudy, thunder, lightning, and rain evening, tornado 2 a.m. near high water.

JULY 1793.

1 Calm and south wind, incessant rain from 7 p.m. yesterday to 6 p.m. to day.

2 South wind and rain all last night, and till noon to-day, p.m. south wind and cloudy weather.

3 N.N.E. wind and cloudy morning, with one or two showers, p.m. S.W. wind with thunder, lightning, and exceedingly heavy rain.

4 Morning N.N.E. wind and clear, one or two light showers, p.m. wind round the compass, thunder, lightning, and rain.

5 West and S.W. winds, a few light showers, weather cloudy.

6 Same winds, cloudy, many showers, heavy rain last night, tornado 3 a.m. very heavy, low water.

7 Sometimes calm, at others light S.W. and west airs, several showers.

8 Part of the day calm and clear, rest of it light winds from all points, and cloudy, from half past three p.m. till sunset, thunder, lightning, and rain, tornado 3h. 30m. p.m. near low water.

9 Winds and weather variable, few drops of rain in the middle of the day.

Days.
10 Winds from N.N.E. to S.W. weather cloudy and clear, thunder, lightning and rain evening.
11 Winds as before, cloudy all day, and rain great part of the morning.
12 Winds and weather variable, many showers.
13 Winds from all points, and weather, except blowing, of all kinds, rain the greatest part of the day, and all last night.
14 Calm, clear weather till 5 p.m. then light showers, heavy rain all last night.
15 Wind and weather continually altering, many showers.
16 do.   do. One tornado 3 a.m. near high water.
17 do.   do.
18 Wind principally from the S.W. rain great part of the day, with clear intervals.
19 Sometimes calm at others S.W. rain till 2 p.m. and great part of last night.
20 Rain all day, calm or S.W. airs.
21 Clear weather and light S.W. winds all day.
22 do.   do.
23 Clear weather with the exception of a few showers, wind S.W.
24 Alternate showers and clear weather, S.W. wind.
25 Rain and light S.W. airs morning, strong S.S.E. wind and rain p.m.
26 Hazy, rainy weather with S.W. wind.
27 Weather variable, wind from S.W. to west.
28 Fresh N.N.E. wind morning, from 8 a.m. light west and S.W. airs, cloudy, no rain.
29 Till 8 a.m. fresh north wind, afterwards N.W. and west winds, clear, no rain.
30 Light N.E. and east winds a.m. west and S.W. winds p.m. rain all day.
31 Fresh S.E. wind a.m. fresh S.W. wind p.m. no rain.

AUGUST 1793.

1 Rain the greater part of last night and this day.
2 Very fine weather, wind west to ten a.m. then S.W. to two p.m. after that N.W.
3 Fine a.m. rain p.m. sometimes calm at others light S.W. wind, rain all last night.
4 Alternate showers and fine weather, light winds from W.N.W. to S.W.
5 No rain a.m. much rain p.m. light westerly winds.
6 light rains a.m. heavy rain with thunder and lightning p.m.
7 A.M. showery, p.m. cloudy without rain, wind from west to south, evening thunder and lightning.
8 Showery all day, wind from east to S.W. a.m. thunder.
9 do.   wind from W.N.W. to S.W.
10 do.   wind from west to S.W.

Days.
11 Showery all day, wind from W. to S.W.
12 Rain greatest part of the day.
13 Rain all day and last night.
14 Fine day.
15 Rain till 8 a.m. The remainder of the day fine.
16 No rain.
17 Showery all day.
18 Fine day if we except a few showers.
19 Rain a.m. fine weather p.m.
20 Fine weather.
21 Strong S.W. wind, showery all day.   [Mr. Hood.
22 Showery all day, S.W. wind.——Being too ill to write, the above is taken from
23 S.W. wind, showery, hazy weather all day.
24 Showery all day, sometimes calm, at others light S.W. winds, distant thunder.
25 Incessant rain these last 24 hours, winds variable.
26 Few showers, fresh S.W. breeze, distant thunder.
27 Heavy rain all day, light S.W. airs.
28 No rain a.m. a couple of showers p.m. fresh wind from W.S.W. to S.W. much thunder.
29 No rain a.m. heavy rain p.m. wind S.W.   do.
30 Light rain a.m. heavy rain p.m. wind S.W.
31 Rain till 2 p.m. then clear,   do.   distant thunder.
Note—There has been incessant rain almost the whole of every night of this month.

SEPTEMBER 1793.

1 Fine clear weather all day, S.W. wind, evening much thunder and lightning.
2 Generally clear, but sometimes cloudy, no rain, wind N.N.E. a.m. S.W. p.m. thunder and lightning in the evening.
3 A.M. calm clear, p.m. light S.W. wind and rain, evening distant thunder.
4 Little rain, calm and cloudy morning, S.W. wind p.m.
5 Tolerably clear with a few showers, wind from N.W. to W.S.W. evening thunder and lightning, one tornado 9 p.m. S.E. half flood.
6 cloudy morning, strong E.N.E. wind and rain from 9 a.m. till 2 p.m. clear the rest of the day.
7 Rain last night and early this morning, rest of the day none, calm.
8 Clear, calm morning, fresh S.W. wind p.m.
9 Calm, cloudy, showery morning, constant rain and fresh S.W. wind p.m.
10 Cloudy and showery all day, calm morning, S.W. wind evening.
11 do.   do.   do.
12 Wind north morning, S.W. evening, cloudy all day, a few showers.

Days.

13 Showery, with fresh winds from most points of the compass, thunder and lightning evening.

14 Fresh southerly wind and cloudy all day, few showers, much thunder and lightning.

15 A.M. clear with S.W. wind, p.m. winds variable, weather cloudy, much rain, thunder and lightning.

16 Clear, calm morning, west wind evening.

17 In the morning a heavy tornado, with thunder, lightning and rain, rest of the day cloudy and calm, one tornado 7h. 30m. high water.

18 Alternate showers and fine intervals, wind S.S.E.

19 Little or no wind from the southward, weather cloudy.

20 Calm, or almost, weather clear.

21 Wind from east to N.E. morning, p.m. calm, one tornado 9 a.m. east, half flood.

22 S.E. wind morning, calm evening, one tornado 3 a.m. half ebb.

23 Clear, wind S.E. morning S.W. evening.

24 Clear, wind from north to west, one tornado 7 p.m. E.S.E. near low water, one tornado, p.m. 11h. E.S.E. two thirds flood.

25 Fresh S.E. wind and cloudy.

26 Winds variable, weather cloudy, rain from 11 a.m. till 3 p.m. one tornado 11 a.m. S.E. half flood.

27 Fresh N.E. wind morning, calm and clear the rest of the day.

28 Clear, N.E. wind morning, calm or S.W. airs p.m. one tornado 8h. 30m. p.m. half ebb.

29 Ever changing light airs, clear, one tornado 9h 30m p.m. half ebb.

30 Winds as before, with now and then a few drops of rain, one tornado* 12h. p.m. N.E. near low water.

OCTOBER 1793.

1 Cloudy, showery, N.E. windy day, with thunder and lightning, one tornado 4 p.m. E.N.E. half flood.

2 Windy, calm, cloudy, clear, rainy, dry, ever changing weather

3 Early in morning N.N.E. wind, then, calm, S.W. wind evening, one tornado 8h. p.m. E. by S. three quarters flood.

4 Calm or light variable winds, weather cloudy, one tornado 9h. p.m. E.N.E. three quarters flood.

5 Clear, variable light airs.

6 do. calm a.m. S.W. wind p.m. one dry tornado 9h. p.m. S.E. half flood.

7 do. calm or light varying airs.

* All these tornados have been attended with much thunder, lightning and rain.

Days.

8 Hazy, foggy weather, with a fresh N.N.E. wind morning, p. m. calm, (note first fog this season) one dry tornado 12 p. m. E. S. E. near high water.
9 Calm morning, fresh S.W. wind evening.
10 Wind N.E. morning, S.W. evening, foggy all day.
11 Light N.E. wind and foggy morning, calm and foggy rest of the day.
12 Foggy, south and S.W. winds.
3 Hazy, various winds, one tornado 4 p.m. N.E. near high water, one tornado 7h 30m p.m. S.E half ebb.
14 Cloudy, winds do. a few drops of rain, one tornado 8 p.m. E.S.E. one third ebb.
15 East wind, strong a.m. light p.m. weather cloudy, rain all last night, a little to day.
16 Clear, E. by S. wind, one tornado 9 p.m. N.E. near high water.
17 do. light varying airs, p.m. thunder and lightning, one dry tornado 9h 30m p.m. east, high water.
18 do. morning calm, p.m. fresh west wind.
19 do. winds various.
20 Morn calm, fresh west wind p.m. Thunder lightning evening.
21 Light varying airs and calms, a few drops of rain, weather cloudy.
22 Light northerly wind, a.m. cloudy, p.m. clear, evening thunder and lightning one dry tornado 9 p.m. east, quarter flood.
23 Clear, light varying winds.
24 Rain in the morning, rest of the day calm and cloudy, one tornado 2 a.m. E.S.E. about high water, one dry tornado 9 p.m. S.E. young flood.
25 Fresh S.E. wind till morning, then light varying airs.
26 Clear, calm in the morning, remainder of the day westerly wind.
27 Foggy, light N.N.E. wind morning, fresh W.S.W. p.m. evening lightning.
28 do. light northerly wind early, rest of the day S.W. and west winds, do. one tornado 11h 30m p.m. low water.
29 Variable winds morning, p.m. S.W. wind with a little rain, thunder and lightning.
30 Light variable winds and cloudy weather, an hour's rain p.m.
31 Fresh N.E. wind morning, light westerly wind p.m. much thunder, lightning and rain last night.

NOVEMBER 1793.

1 Clear weather, wind N.E. morning, S.W. evening, distant thunder.
2 Hazy do. do. lightning evening.
3 Variable light winds and hazy, thunder, lightning and rain from 8 to 9 p.m.

Days.
4 N.E. breeze morning, variable winds evening, one tornado 5 p.m. low water.
5 Clear, N.E. wind morning, calm p.m.
6 do.   do.   do.   evening lightning.
7 do.   do.   S.W. wind p.m.   do. one tornado 9 p.m.
8 do.   light variable winds   do.
9 do.   calm morning, S.W. wind evening.
10 do.   light varying airs.
11 Calm cloudy weather, except from 7 to 10 a.m. when we had a fresh E.S.E. wind, and heavy rain with thunder and lightning, one tornado 7 a.m. half ebb.
12 Cloudy, light N.E. wind morning, calm evening.
13 Hazy,   do.   do.
14 do.   light varying airs.
15 do.   do.
16 do.   do.
17 do.   do.
18 Clear, N.E. wind morning, calm evening.
19 do.   do.   do.
20 do.   do.   do.
21 do.   do.   do.
22 Light N.E. wind all day and clear weather.
23 Clear, light N.E. wind morning, calm p.m.
24 do.   do.   do.
25 do.   do.   do.
26 do.   do.   do.
27 do.   do.   do.
28 N.E. wind all day, clear weather.

No. 6.

Gentlemen, *Ghinala, 2d August,* 1792.

Finding the shore, called the Greater Bulama, not an island, it was my intention to return without purchasing it: but, at my first interview with the two kings of this country, they claimed Bulama, having, as they said, inherited it from their ancestors.

As I know there is some justice in their claim, I thought it absolutely necessary to stop to satisfy them, and I expect them on board every minute to talk the palaver.

Now conceiving it to be a favourable opportunity, when purchasing Bulama, to purchase also the adjacent shore, which I think may be done for very little more value, I shall endeavour to buy all the uninhabited land which lies between them and us; that is, all the territory south of a line drawn from this place to Goly, which territory you will see is bounded to the east by Ghinala Creek, to the south by the Rio Grande, and to the west by a branch of the sea, which separates it from Bissao. The sides, bounded by Ghinala Creek, and the Rio Grande, are elevated and cleared in many places, forming a chain of fine bays and creeks, with deep water, through their whole extent. Should our colony flourish, which I have no reason to doubt, this will be found an invaluable acquisition, as there is no one part of its banks where a town may not be built with every advantage for commerce.

I hope to leave this place in two days, and to bring with me refreshments for the sick.

I am, Gentlemen,
your most obedient humble servant,
P. BEAVER.

To
The Gentlemen of the Committee,
on board the Hankey,
Bulama.

No. 7.

Deed of cession of the Island of Bulama, together with other islands and territories, by the kings of Ghinala and the Rio Grande, to the British Colonists, for the king of Great Britain.

" Whereas certain persons, subjects of the king of Great Britain, conducted by Philip Beaver, John Munden, Charles E. Aberdein, and John Reynolds, Esqrs. as a committee to manage their affairs, having arrived upon the windward coast of Africa, adjacent to the Rio Grande, and the said committee having invested Mr. Philip Beaver with full power to treat with and purchase from us certain lands adjacent to the said river, we, the kings of Ghinala, and the Rio Grande, being fully convinced of the pacific and just dispositions of the said persons, and of the great reciprocal benefits that will result from an European colony established in our neighbourhood; and withal being desirous of manifesting our distinguished friendship and affection for the king of Great Britain and his subjects; do hereby, in consideration of the value of three hundred bars of goods, by us this day received, for ever cede and relinquish to the king of Great Britain, all sovereignty over our territories lying to the southward or westward of a line extended from Ghinala west-north-west, until it reach the sea, together with the Island of Bulama, and all other islands whatever, adjacent to the aforesaid territories, which sovereignty our ancestors have enjoyed from time immemorial. We do further solemnly guarantee to the said persons, their heirs, and assigns, against all enemies whatever; the full and peaceable possession of the said territories and islands aforementioned; and by these presents, do bind ourselves and our subjects to aid and assist them against all their enemies whatever; and the same shall have all the force of a firm and faithful treaty of defensive alliance between the king of Great Britain and ourselves; and together with the territories and islands aforesaid, we do relinquish all claim to any future tribute, subsidy, or composition whatever; and of all the premised conditions, we the two parties do bind ourselves to the mutual observance, in the presence, and in the name of, the Omnipotent God of truth and justice, and the avenger of perfidy. In witness whereof we have hereunto set our hands this 3d day of August, in the year of our Lord,* one thousand seven hundred and ninety-two."

his
NIOBANA, ⋈ King,
mark.
his
MATCHORE, ⋈ King,
mark.

This treaty made and concluded at Ghinala,
   in the presence of
    JOHN WILLIAM PAIBA.   P. BEAVER.

* This was an oversight, for as neither Niobana nor Matchore were Christians, it ought to have been written, in the year one thousand seven hundred and ninety-two of the Christian Æra. P. B.

No. 8.

A list of goods given to Niobana and Matchore for the purchase of the Island of Bulama, &c.

		Bars.	Prime Cost.
10	Danish guns,	60	£7 15 10
30	Flasks of powder,	60	4 10 0
1	Eighteen gallon cask of brandy	36	2 5 9
20	Flasks of brandy	20	1 5 6
30	lbs. of tobacco	15	0 15 0
15	Knives	3	0 1 6
			£16 13 7

The prime cost of the following articles cannot be exactly ascertained, not having the invoices.

2	Fathoms of scarlet cloth	16
1	ditto, of blue ditto	
6	Common hats	6
3	Large pewter basins	3
3	Smaller ditto	2
2	Bunches of Burdoe beads	2
2	ditto of Harlequin ditto	2
1	ditto of Muffaties ditto	1

The following articles were procured from Mr. Bootle.

5	Handkerchefs	5	
8	Cutlasses	8	
8	Iron bars	8	
1	Barrel of powder	50	£3 15 6
		300	

Recaptulation.

Amount of those goods the prime cost of which is ascertained	£16	13	7
Probable amount of those goods the prime cost of which we could not ascertain .... }	3	0	6
Probable amount of those articles which I received from Mr. Bootle....	5	19	0
	£25	13	1

No. 9.

Extract from the log of the ship Hankey, from the time of her leaving the Island of Bulama to her release from quarantine, noting all the deaths on board that ship.

1792.
Nov. 23d, Sailed from Bulama.

24th, Observed latitude 11. 26. N. The west end of Bulama bearing N. by W. one half, W. 4 leagues, and the east end of Galenas N.N.W three quarters, W. three and a half leagues.

25th, Died Mrs. Curwood, colonist, and George Wilkinson, seaman,

26th, Anchored at Bissao; died Mr. Munden, and Mrs. Hancorne, colonists, and John Mitchell, the ship's carpenter.

28th, Died, Edward Fowler.

Dec. 1st, Died, Charles Robinson, colonist.

3d, Sailed from Bissao; three of the crew taken ill of the fever.

4th, Ship run a-ground.

5th, In the afternoon sent a boat to Bissao to procure assistance; the ship beat a great deal all night, but did not make any water.

6th, Ship continues aground, and beats very hard.

7th, Ship labours a great deal, but continues tight; all hands on board sick.

8th, At noon the pinnace returned with a schooner and long boat which carried out an anchor and cable; at 5 got the ship off and made sail, but stuck fast again; died Mr. Woody, the third mate, and boy Dick, the apprentice; all the people who came from Bissao in the pinnace taken ill.

	9th,	Got the ship afloat again; died Patience Bates, and Joseph ——, boy.
	10th,	Charles Wood, seaman, died.
	11th,	Mr. Birkhead, colonist, died.
	12th,	John High, seaman, died.
	13th,	Anchored again at Bissao; Mr. Rowe, colonist, died; his death is noticed as if he had not been on board the Hankey, but had died in the town of Bissao.
	19th,	Richard Curwood, boy, colonist, died.
	21st.	Sailed from Bissao with the assistance of some men, who left them in the evening.
	26th,	At noon anchored in St. Francis's Bay, St. Jago, having mistaken it for Port Praya.
	30th,	Mr. Gandell, colonist, died.

1793.

Jan.	4th,	Anchored in Port Praya.
	13th,	The Charon, Commodore Dod, arrived; died Elizabeth Curwood, girl, colonist.
	23d.	The Charon sailed, having sent two seamen to the Hankey.
	24th,	The Scorpion arrived.
	26th,	The Scorpion sailed, having sent two seamen to the Hankey.
	27th,	The Hankey sailed from Port Praya.
Feb.	4th,	Died, Samuel Hodge, seaman, one of those who came from the Charon.
	14th,	Arrived at Barbadoes.
	15th,	Sailed.
	16th,	Anchored at St. Vincent's
	17th,	Sailed.
	19th,	Anchored at Granada.
March	27th,	Wm. Moseley, seaman, deserted.
May	31st,	The carpenter drowned.
July	23d,	Received six men from the commodore, and sailed with the convoy from Granada.
	28th,	Anchored at St. Kitts.
Aug.	1st,	Sailed.
Oct.	2d,	Anchored in the Downs, and ordered to perform quarantine.
	5th,	Sailed for Stangate Creek.
	8th,	Anchored in Stangate Creek.
	18th,	Delivered up the Bulama baggage.
	24th,	Released from quarantine.
	29th,	Moored at Iron Gate.

No. 10.

To Philip Beaver, Esq. Governor of the British Colony of Bulama.

Ship Nancy, Feb. 17*th,* 1793.

Mr. Beaver,
   Sir,

      Finding my business in the vicinity of Bassaw in a most disagreeable manner, and greatly at a loss how to conduct with that propriety that may hereafter appear legal and just; I shall in as explicit a manner as in my power make you acquainted with every circumstance relative to the same, praying your advice and assistance.

At the time of my arriving at Bassaw in the ship Nancy, under my command, I heard of a schooner belonging to the employ I now serve being cut off, and upon the best authority I could collect, found the facts to be as follows:

The schooner being on a trading voyage adjacent the Isle of Bassaw, a settlement of the Portuguese, who very well knew the situation of said schooner and crew; proceeded to cut her off, by the evidence I have taken care to procure, who are ready to declare upon oath before you. It appears that Mr. Gavine, one of the merchants of Bassaw, privately sent to the natives, where the said vessel was, to cut her off, bribing them to perpetrate the base action. It was accordingly done, and at the expence of the life of Mr. John Bootle, a Mr. Ashley, and several black men belonging to said schooner. The vessel was immediately put into the hands of said Mr. Gavine, upon what terms I know not; for it was my first business to demand the vessel, in behalf of my owners, of both the governor of Bassaw and himself, and all to no purpose. After many such applications, and consulting my officers on board my ship, it was thought most adviseable to take said vessel by force, as force had been made use of by Mr. Gavine in obtaining her. Accordingly I sent my boat to Bassaw on the 14th inst. and brought her out to the place my ship lay at. On the 15th I got under way with both ship and schooner, and proceeded to your colony. And as the vessel is now before your garrison, it is my wish that you take her into your own possession, and send some dispatch to Bassaw, to inform the governor of that establishment that my greatest wish is to come to a settlement respecting said business, as well as the debts due to me in that place. This done in a fair and candid manner. I can say no more.

I cannot point out any thing more that interferes in this business, but submit every other part to yourself,

And am Sir,
your most obedient,
humble servant,
WM. C. MOORE.

Sir,

I will just observe that there are many debts due to me in Bassaw, as trustee to the estate of John Ormond, deceased, for which I have made three fruitless attempts to recover, with no little expence and trouble; likewise many of my own private debts, the whole of which cannot be less than two thousand pounds sterling; and I flatter myself there can be no objection to adjust and liquidate them also.

WM. C. M.

From Mr. Beaver to Capt. Moore.

Sir,

In compliance with your request of yesterday I will, when my pinnace returns from Bulola, dispatch her to the Portuguese establishment at Bissao, and use all my influence and authority in endeavouring to procure you justice: I must decline taking possession of the schooner; but, while she remains here, she will be perfectly secure under the protection of my guns.

I am, Sir,
your most obedient,
humble servant,
P. BEAVER.

Hespereleusis,
18th February, 1793.

To Capt. Moore,
Ship Nancy.

Declaration respecting the seizure of the Fisher Schooner, at Jatts Island.

WE, the subscribers, late residents of the Isles de Los, on the windward coast of Africa, being duly called on by Philip Beaver, Esq. governor of the British colony at the Isle of Bulama, on the coast aforesaid, for our declaration and affidavit respecting the schooner Fisher, of Liverpool, late cut off on said coast of Africa, do, in the presence of Almighty God, most solemnly declare, that we late belonged to the aforesaid schooner, Fisher, commanded by a Mr. John Bootle, on a trading voyage to the Rio Grande and its adjacent parts. That we were up the Rio Grande, at the settlement of Bulola, formerly occupied by said Bootle, there pursuing our trade in a quiet peaceable manner; that whilst in this beforementioned situation we were informed that a certain Mr. Gavine, a resident of Bissao, a Portuguese settlement, did in a private and injurious manner write to the natives of Bulola, to cut off and seize the said schooner, Fisher, cargo, and crew, but that the natives of Bulola did decline every such malicious attempt and request, and did give us every information of his the said Mr. Gavine's treacherous design.

We also further declare, that some time after these serious matters had taken place, that our commander, or captain, thought proper to remove the said schooner, Fisher, to a certain part of the coast of Africa, known by the name of Jatts Island, inhabited by natives distinguished also by the name of Manjacks; that while lying there in the manner and form as at other parts of the said coast, that then and there, being in the month of Nov. 1792, they the aforesaid Manjacks did attack and surprise us by force of arms. and in a few moments put to death our commander, Mr. John Bootle, aforesaid, likewise a certain Mr. Ashley, two free black men, and three slaves. And we the survivors do also declare that at sundry different times afterwards we heard the aforesaid natives (Manjacks) say that it was never their intention to have cut off the said vessel, had they not been employed to do it by the before mentioned Mr. Gavine, who a few days previous to the cuting off the vessel had sent to them, the said Manjacks, to bribe and urge them to the seizing the said schooner.

And we do hereby also declare, that at the time Capt. W. C. Moore, of the ship Nancy, coming to Bissao, and there claiming the said schooner Fisher, and property, that he the said Mr. Gavine did at that time, as well as ever after, employ as grumetas, or hired servants, for defence of said vessel, the before-mentioned Manjacks, who were accessary to cutting off both schooner and men, and at the time that Capt. Wm. C. Moore did take the aforesaid schooner from the port of Bissao, that the said schooner was then manned and defended by the self-same tribe of natives that were the executors of cutting off said schooner.

SAMUEL TOMANA, ⋈ his mark.

SANCHO, ⋈ his mark.

TOM, ⋈ his mark.

Sworn before me this 19th of February, 1793, at Hespereleusis on the Island of Bulama,

(Signed)   P. BEAVER.

In the presence of J. SCOTT.

(A true Copy.)

N.B. Samuel Tomana was the only person on board the schooner that was left alive when she was cut off. Sancho, and Tom were on shore getting water at that time. They were bought, with the vessel, by Mr. Gavine, and remained in her till the time that Capt. Moore gained the possession of her.

(A true Copy.)

Declaration concerning the seizure of the Fisher schooner at Bissao.

WE, the subscribers, being duly called on by Philip Beaver, Esquire, Governor of the British colony at the Island of Bulama, on the windward coast of Africa, for our declaration and affidavit respecting the schooner Fisher, late taken out of the port of Bissao, by Captain Wm. C. Moore, of the ship Nancy, of Liverpool, do most solemnly swear in the presence of Almighty God, that on Thursday the fourteenth day of February, one thousand seven hundred and ninety-three; that we then belonged to the aforesaid ship Nancy, laying to anchor near the port of Bissao.

That on said day before-mentioned, we received orders from our commander, that night to go with our boat, and bring to the said ship Nancy the aforesaid schooner Fisher; in pursuance to the said order the ship Nancy's boat was accordingly manned for that purpose, and went to Bissao; that, previous to our going on board said schooner, a certain man named Peter, a hired servant to Mr. Gavine, the person that did withhold the said schooner from Captain William C. Moore, did, on Friday morning, the fifteenth day of February, 1793, come to us at our boat at Bissao, at about five o'clock; and by pointing out to us the difficulty of taking the said schooner Fisher from Bissao, saying, that Mr. Gavine had put ten grumetas or servants on board the said schooner to defend her, that they were of the tribe of Manjacks, those men that before had cut off said schooner Fisher, and desired us to make no attempt until the ensuing Sunday, at which time he, the said Peter, would see that those grumetas or servants were taken or sent on shore, and at that time he would give every assistance towards placing said vessel in the hands of Captain Moore.

THOMAS PEARCE, chief mate.

WILLIAM MOORE, ⋈ his mark, second mate.

HUGH MILLS, ⋈ his mark, seaman.

JOHN OWENS, ⋈ his mark, carpenter.

JOSEPH DE SANT, ⋈ his mark, seaman and a Portuguese.

Sworn before me this 19th day of February, 1793, at Hespereleusis, on the Island of Bulama.

       (Signed)   P. BEAVER.

In the presence of JOHN SCOTT.

      (A true Copy.)

No. 11.

Depositions of Thomas Pearce and John Frazer, relative to an attack made upon a Portuguese canoe, near the west end of the Island of Bulama, on the 16th of February, 1793.

Thomas Pearce deposes, that on the 16th of February, 1793, he was first mate of the ship Nancy, commanded by Captain William C. Moore, but at that time actually on board the Fisher schooner, of which he had the command; that the ship Nancy was at an anchor near the west point of the island of Bulama, and the schooner which he commanded laying alongside of her, when a canoe was discovered coming through the channel between the islands of Bulama and Galenas; he, the deponent, then received orders from Captain Moore to chase the said canoe, and bring her alongside his ship, if it proved to belong to the Portuguese; the deponent, having come very near to her, sent two black men in the schooner's yawl on board the said canoe, with orders to bring as many of her crew on board the schooner as they could, they were sent without arms, and were only to endeavour to get them on board the schooner for the purposes of trade.—On my asking the deponent what he would have done had not any of the men from the afore-mentioned canoe returned in his yawl? He replied, that he would have gone in her himself, and have brought them by force, but that he would not have hurt any of them unless they had opposed him.—The deponent states, that the yawl came back bringing three men belonging to the said canoe, having two fowls and some plantains to make trade with; that he, the deponent, then asked them to come into his schooner, which they refused to do; that he, the deponent, then took up a musket and presented it at them, upon which one of the three said people belonging to the afore-mentioned canoe, took hold of the muzzle of the musket, and endeavoured to wrench it from him, when he fired and wounded him in the act of jumping overboard; he, the deponent, then took another musket, fired at, and wounded, another of the said three men belonging to the afore-mentioned canoe, whereupon the third jumped overboard; he, the deponent, then went in the yawl and picked up two of these people, one of the wounded men swam to his own boat, then distant about 50 yards or thereabouts; the canoe then pulled in shore, the wounded man who swam away refused to be taken up by the schooner's yawl, for, when they offered so to do, he held up a knife, and they desisted; he, the deponent, then returned to the ship Nancy with the two men, one wounded, the other not. Again asking the deponent what he would have done if they, the blacks of the canoe, had not come in his yawl? he answered that he would have used all his endeavours to have taken the canoe.

> The above is the declaration of Mr. Thomas Pearce, first mate of the ship Nancy, and at that time commanding the Fisher schooner. Taken on the island of Bulama, on the 26th day of February, 1793, by me
>
> P. BEAVER.

John Frazer deposes, that on the 16th day of February, 1793, he belonged to the ship Nancy, commanded by Captain William C. Moore, but was at that time actually on board the Fisher schooner lying in the situation described by Mr. Thomas Pearce; he further deposes that they went in chase of a canoe coming through the channel between the islands of Bulama and Galenas, that when pretty near to her two men were sent in the yawl to bring on board the schooner what people they could out of the above canoe, for the purposes of trade; that when they came alongside, Mr. Pearce took up a musquet on their refusing to come on board his vessel, and that one of them endeavoured to wrench it from him; that he, Mr. Pearce, then fired and wounded the black man who jumped overboard, wounding him in the act of jumping overboard; that he, Mr. Pearce, then took up another musket, and fired at, and wounded another black man who was then in the water, and that the third jumped overboard also: that Mr. Pearce, this deponent, and others, went in the yawl, and took up one of them, and brought him on board the said schooner; the deponent with three other men were then ordered to go in chase of the aforementioned canoe, and bring it, if possible, on board the said schooner;

that the afore-mentioned canoe had then pulled to a great distance from them; when in pursuit they discovered a man in the water holding up his hand, and calling out loudly, and in his, the deponent's opinion, near sinking; they then rowed to, and took up, this man, one of the wounded, and then gave over chase and returned to the schooner.

The above is the declaration of John Frazer, belonging to the ship Nancy, but at that time actually on board the Fisher, schooner; taken on the island of Bulama, on the 26th day of February, 1793, before me.

P. BEAVER.

No. 12.

Garden Book.

1793.
May 21, Planted a pepper bush* which came the preceding night from Bissao, it put forth leaves the 30th, and was in full blossom the 10th of July, gathered ripe peppers from it on the 1st of September; from which day, till the time we quitted the island (29th November,) it supplied all the colonists, and would have done so for three months more.

Planted some mint which I received with the above; it throve much, and I left abundance of it on the island.

31, Sowed in tubs the following English seeds, which not only looked, but smelled very musty; they were the remains of some which we brought from England, and of course must have been two, probably three, or more, years old.

No. 1, Cucumbers.
No. 2, Rosemary.
No. 3, Thyme.
No. 4, Cabbages.
No. 5, Onions.
No. 6, Garlic.

* The bird pepper of Jamaica.

May 31, I did not expect that any of these seeds would grow, and I was not mistaken.

At the same time I sowed in tubs the following Portuguese seeds, which I had received from Bissao.

No. 7, Parsley.

No. 8, Cabbages.

No. 9, Lettuces.

No. 10, The seed of a sallad, to us unknown, which the Portuguese pronounced, as an Englishman would the following word, " quintre."

No. 11, Papaw.

At the same time were sowed in the tub,

No. 12, The seeds of some oranges which I had procured from Tombaly, a place of considerable trade in the Naloo country. And in the tub,

No. 13, The seeds of some limes, which I had received from Canabac, one of the Bijuga Islands.

No. 14, English balm.

Observations on the tubs numbered from 1 to 14.

The first six numbers being old, and musty seed, never came up.

No. 7 came up the 11th of June, was transplanted into rows the 25th of June, and looked well when I left the island.

No. 8 came up the 2d of June, forty of these plants were transplanted the 15th of June, and fourteen more the 17th of June; they were all destroyed by the caterpillars; on the 18th of June I transplanted the rest, in number 151, all of which were destroyed by the caterpillars, except seven, which were cut the 12th of October; none of them had any heart, nothing more than a few straggling leaves, scarcely worth boiling. Whether this was owing to their having been eaten off when young, and then shooting out again, which was the case with these, I know not, but think it probable, as at Bissao they raise tolerable cabbages, and at Sierra Leone, I was informed very good ones; from this time, that is the 18th of June, it was sufficient employment for one boy to kill the caterpillars. The number of these insects in the garden, this season, were much greater than would ever happen again, from the following circumstances: The western boundary of the garden was overhung by the branches of two very large plum trees, from which, these enemies to vegetation, were continually dropping in vast numbers; and as, of necessity, great part of the garden was laid in paths, the quick and luxuriant vegetation of the weeds and grass, which shot up in these, required the continual use of the scythe, which Mr. Hood and myself, (the only two who were suffered to do any thing in it) were either from more important occupations, or sickness, prevented from using, as often as necessary; hence they found shelter in the long grass in which they were to be seen in almost incredible numbers.

N. B. The above cabbage plants were as healthy and vigorous, when transplanted as any that I ever saw.

No. 9, Came up the 4th of June; transplanted 21st, answered very well.

No. 10, Came up the 18th of June, throve admirably, and was cut the 28th of June; its leaf, and manner of growing greatly resembles that of chervil; it has a rank oily taste, and makes but a sorry sallad.

No. 11, Came up in twenty-two days, were transplanted the 19th of August, and were fine little trees when I left the island.

No. 12, Came up the 5th of July, and were transplanted into beds young vigorous plants, the 15th of August.

No. 13, Came up the 21st of June, and were transplanted at the same time with the above-mentioned oranges.

No. 14, Which Mr. Hood had very carefully preserved, came up the 3d of June; transplanted the 15th; succeeded very well.

June 5th, Planted 22 banana roots, which I had procured from Bissao; four of them died; some of the rest began to shoot by the 10th, and all of them by the 20th of June, were very healthy when I left the island, and will doubtless bear the next rains.

Planted also two plantain roots, received at the same time, and which throve equally well.

6th, Sowed in tubs the following English seeds:

No. 15, Celery.

16, Hyssop.

17, Garlic, neither of which came up.

8th, Planted cassada* which put forth leaves the 15th of June, blossomed the 8th of October, and was dug up and boiled the 21st of October; from which day till I left the island, all the colonists had it, as often as they pleased, when about one-sixth only was consumed.

Note, This cassada I received from Bissao, with the plantain and banana roots on the 5th instant, a hole was then dug, about eighteen inches deep, in which their roots were placed, and then covered with the soil, whence they were taken up and transplanted, as ocsasion required.

* See note, p. 69.

June 8th, Planted yams, the earliest of which made their appearance on the 24th of June, and continued coming up till the 10th of July.

Note, Many people think that the eyes only of this useful root will grow; but all parts of it will re-produce. The yams which I planted were cut into slices of about two inches thick, these slices were then quartered, and one quarter was put into every hillock, every one of which came up; they were not quite come to perfection when I left the island; however I dug up about five hundred, and found them very good.

This day I transplanted some pine apples which some of the deceased colonists had planted in the woods, where they had remained, without any attention, all the last dry season; they were strong and healthy when I left the island, and thirty-two in number.

Sowed Indian corn, or maize, which came up the 10th of June, blossomed the 22d of July, and was cut the 15th of August. I sowed all the grains contained in three ears (being all that I had) but know not their exact number, suppose about 360, that is allowing 120 for each ear, two of these grains were put into each cassada hillock, they all came up very well, many, when four or five inches high, were eaten off by the caterpillars, and a great many more when full ear'd were destroyed by maggots, so that we only gathered 40 ears, the largest of which contained 3 or 4 large white maggots some of them a dozen.

9, Sowed seed of English cabbages, lettuces, onions and parsley, none of which came up.

Quentre (see tub No. 10, sowed the 31st May) which came up the 18th of June, blossomed the 8th of August, gathered the seed the 10th of September.

10, Planted yams, which began coming up the 26th of June, see yams the 8th of June.

11, Sowed English dwarf kidney beans, which never came up.

13, Sowed English cabbages in tub No. 18, two only came up on the 21st of June, I have no account of the time they were transplanted, they turned out like those which we cut, of the sowing of the 31st of May in tub No. 8.

14, Planted cassada, some of that which I received the 5th inst. from Bissao (see cassada 8th June) it put forth leaves the 18th June, blossomed the 10th of Oct. and was dug up and dressed the 28th of Oct.

Sowed English pease and beans, neither of which came up.

June 14, Transplanted 2 banana trees which some of the deceased colonists had planted in the woods, they did well.

Transplanted 7 roots of banana trees, which had been planted in our last year's garden, built over and trod upon ever since, and which now made their appearance in the square, within the block-house, five died, two succeeded.

Planted the west garden, quarter of an acre, entirely with cassada, which put forth leaves the 16th of June, was dug up and dressed the 22d of October,

15, Transplanted 13 wild vines from the woods into the garden, many of them had 4 or 5 small bunches of grapes, but scarcely any leaves, they all died.

Sowed the seeds of some oranges which I received from Lisbon, 8 only came up, on the 12th of July, out of about 100, they were transplanted the 6th of Sept. I left them healthy plants.

Planted cassada and yams

Sowed Tombaly orange seeds which came up the 7th of July and were transplanted the 27th and 28th of August.

Sowed Tombaly lime seeds which came up the 6th of July and were transplanted the 24th of August, which, with the above orange plants, throve admirably.

Sowed English celery—turnips—carrots and horned carrots, neither of which came up.

17, Transplanted some mint, which I received this day from Bissao, it spread amazingly and I left plenty of it on the island.

18, Sowed Tombaly ground nuts, which came up the 23d of June and blossomed the 16th of July—began digging them up the 18th of November.

20, Sowed English radishes—long red do.—cucumbers—lavender—parsley—roman lettuces—rosemary—thyme—onions—cardoons—brocoli and cauliflowers—none of which came up.

Sowed English artichokes which came up the 6th of July, were transplanted, 24 in number, fine strong plants the 10th of September, they all died in 4 or 5 five days ; and to please Mr. Hood

I sowed lupins, mignionette, sweet peas, china astor, ten-week stocks and summer savory, neither of which came up.

Tombaly ground nuts which succeeded as those planted the 18th instant.

Sowed cotton seeds taken out of some Biafara cotton, which I had purchased of a Mandingo priest who lives at Bulola, which came up the 3d day, I transplanted 21 plants the 15th of August, 60 plants the 10th of September, and 50 the 11th of September, they began to blossom the 17th of November, and were all in full blossom the 27th, fine strong plants.

June 22, Sowed the following English seeds, cress, roman lettuce, anise, cardoons and parsley, neither of which came up.

Sowed some Portuguese beans, calavances, which came up the 27th of June, blossomed the 4th of October, and were in great abundance, just fit for use, when we left the island.

Sowed papaws which came up the 7th of July, and were transplanted the 19th August.

25, Tombaly ground nuts, which came up in 4 days and succeeded as the former ones, also the following English seeds: cabbages, minster do., spinach, minster lettuces, turnep, Turkey rhubarb, mustard and cress, neither of which came up.

Country peas, these peas resemble those of Europe in shape and colour, but are about twice the size, they grow not in pods, but in the ground, and are propagated in the same manner as potatoes and ground nuts, indeed these are called the ground nuts (mancara) of the Bijugas, as those I procured from Tombaly are called the ground nuts (mancara) of the Mandingos and Naloos; these country pease are dressed in the manner of calavances, but are, in my opinion, much better, they came up the 5th of July and were fit to be taken up when I came away, those which I had dressed came from Canabac, where they are to be had in abundance.

26, Seed, brought from England, of clare, it never came up.

25, Sowed part of the N.W. and east fields with clover and lucerne, the clover seed looked bad and never came up, the lucerne was all up in three days, it grew kindly and looked well for the first fortnight, but never looked well afterwards, the stalks run up very long and slender, and there was very little green about the tops of them; in short, it all looked very sickly, much worse than any which I ever saw in England, the cause I pretend not to know, but think a great deal might be owing to my ignorance in these things, and that there is a great probability of its doing well if managed by a person at all acquainted with its cultivation. Mr. Hood is of a different opinion, and thinks it will not answer at all here, and he is certainly a much better judge than myself.

29, Sowed English cabbage seed, it never came up.

Biafara cotton seed, it came up the 4th of July, was transplanted the 13th of September, and was in full blossom the 27th of November.

Tombaly oranges, came up the 23d of July.

July 14, Planted 11 cucumber plants which I received from Bissao, 7 died, the other 4 bore an astonishing number, also 3 pepper trees, 10 guava trees, 1 lime tree, which I received at the same time, the first three were loaded with peppers. Seven of the guavas, three having died, and the lime tree were in a very thriving condition when I left the island.

30, English cabbage and parsley, neither of which came up.

August 26, 100 Tombaly limes, which came up in 15 days.

30, 100 do. do. do.

Sept. 6, 100 do. do. which came up in 19 days, about nine tenths of each of these last three sowings came up, and were all very fine young plants when we came away.

No. 13.

Extracts from the Trustees' Letter, received by the Felicity schooner, the 21st of July, 1793; and dated London the 23d May, 1793.

" SIR,

" We have the pleasure to acknowledge the receipt of your dispatches by the ships Calypso and Hankey, together with the extracts from your public Journals, and other papers which accompany them.

" Want of opportunity has been the sole reason of our not writing before, and in order to convey to you the present letter with the packets and parcels which accompany it, we have felt ourselves under the necessity of applying to the Court of Directors of the Sierra Leone Company, to request that they would order one of their ships to touch at Bulama in her way to Sierra Leone, which they have with great readiness and generosity granted.

" As the Sierra Leone company have acted with such liberality towards us, it is our intention to take the advantage of another vessel they propose to dispatch in about six weeks or two months, to send you by her some six, eight, or ten settlers, together with a fresh supply of such articles as shall appear likely that you may be in want of, and if in the interval we receive favourable accounts from you, or should meet with that encouragement from Government which we expect, we shall probably make the shipment very considerable, and send you a greater number of settlers and labourers, taking care that they be of the description you point out, and such as from their habits of life and dispositions, shall appear likely to benefit the colony.

" We, therefore think, that in about two months after you receive this, you may expect a vessel with a reinforcement of settlers, together with stores, provisions, and other necessary articles for your colony.

" Under these circumstances we cannot but express our most earnest wish that you will continue your endeavours for, and attention to, the prosperity of the colony, and that you will not think of quitting it, at least during the present season; but that you will exert yourself and keep up the settlement, and prevail on your associates to stand by you, so that your hard labours may not be rendered fruitless.

" With this you will receive a copy of all our minutes since you left this country, and you will see by those of the last meeting, that the members of our association are fully impressed with a due sense of your exertions,* and we can only add our earnest assurance that, as far as we are able, in our capacity of trustees to the association, you and the gentlemen with you, may depend on all the support and remuneration which it may be in our power to give you.

" We certainly consider you, and the brave fellows who have had the courage and perseverance to stand by you, as entitled to the protection and gratitude not of ourselves only, but of the public, and whenever the settlement of Bulam shall have arisen to a respectable height, your conduct under your present difficulties will make a shining figure in its history.

---

* At a general meeting of the Bulam association, 26th April, 1793,

" Resolved,

" That the conduct of Mr. Philip Beaver, at the island of Bulam, has been such as to merit the approbation, and to entitle him to the support of this association, and that it is equally our duty, as our interest, to send immediately such supplies to Bulam, as may enable Mr. Beaver and the settlers there, to continue in their endeavours for the prosperity of the settlement, until the association shall be enabled to undertake the colonization of the island on a more extensive plan."

"We send you several of our printed reports of last December, to which we have only to add briefly, that owing to the war in which this country is involved, his Majesty's Ministers have not had leisure to take under consideration the incorporation of our association, but we verily believe them to be extremely well inclined to us, and we hope and trust that our next will convey to you a very flattering report of the intention of Government towards our association.

"It remains only for us to request that you will send us by the earliest, and every other opportunity which shall offer, the most particular account you can of your situation, and of your wants, that we may provide for them in the best manner we possibly can, and we also repeat our earnest entreaty, that you will not think of quitting the settlement, more particularly as we have a strong opinion that the war will not last beyond the present year.

"We are, &c. &c.

"By order, and on behalf of the trustees of the Bulam association.

(Signed) "PAUL LE MESURIER.

"To Philip Beaver, Esq.
"Chief of the settlement of Bulam."

No. 14.

Memoranda given to Mr. Hood, the 18th of November, 1793.

You are to go in the pinnace, to-morrow morning, with all possible expedition to Bissao, and inform the governor of that place, that, from a vessel which was coming to this island, with some assistance, having fallen into the hands of the enemy, and other reasons, it is my intention to quit this island, and go to Sierra Leone till after the next rains, or such time as the wished for assistance may arrive; when I, or some other of my countrymen, will again re-occupy our present possession. That I shall proceed to sea this day week, with all my goods, shipped on board the cutter, and two other small vessels which I have hired, unless he or any of the merchants of Bissao may wish to purchase some of them, for whose answer, I shall postpone the beginning loading either of the vessels. Should they wish to purchase any of the stores, you will inform them, that I expect they will bring all the wax and ivory which they can collect in 24 hours—longer, you are not on any consideration to wait; nor they, if they expect to become purchasers, as I shall immediately on your return begin loading the vessels; and goods once shipped, will not again be taken out of the vessel.

Those goods that they cannot pay for in wax or ivory, I will take bills for, payable either in London or Lisbon; but, should it not be convenient for them to give me such bills, I will let them have the goods for a promissary note payable to me or bearer, which on my, or any other persons, returning hither, is to be discharged at the current coast price, in wax and ivory.

You may inform the governor that I have four long six, and four long four-pounders, together with grape, canister and round shot, cartridges, worms, sponges, ladles, rammers, powder-horns, priming-wires, and bitts; in short, every thing complete for each gun, which are at his service for the prime cost in England. I must have his positive answer on the subject by you, as they must be the first things shipped if I am to carry them away. He may also have a few army muskets, with bayonets, cartouch-boxes, &c. complete. Remember that he must have all or none. The eight cannon complete will amount to about 800 bars, a little more or less as the invoice will direct.

If the merchants mean to become large purchasers, they had better bring a couple of sloops or schooners, besides boats and canoes, as I can load them all. Request that, if the governor sends for the guns, a proper officer may attend the grumetas, to keep order and good discipline among them, and that the merchants pay the same attention to their grumetas, for it will be very unpleasant for me to be obliged to punish any of the subjects of Portugal.

You will herewith receive a list of those goods which I have to dispose of, which you will shew the merchants, and suffer them to copy; strictly enjoin them not to lose time in coming, as I cannot on any account wait.

I shall be glad to see all the merchants of Bissao at my house, except Mr. Joaquin Pedro Ginioux, who, when here last, committed a gross breach of the laws of hospitality, in seducing one of my two seamen to run away from the cutter.* This man I will not suffer to land upon the island, much less to come into my house. But you will tell him, though he has injured us, that we will do him all the good in our power, by informing him that the man, he so seduced, is a pirate—that he narrowly escaped with his life, for burning a vessel in the bay of Honduras—that he formed a plot of running away with my cutter to leeward, and there selling her—and that he most likely will run away with his vessel, if entrusted with the command of it to the Cape de Verds, and go to America, where he was born.

After you have explained yourself to Mr. de Sylva, on whom you are to wait, and the governor, of the purport of your visit, you are to request that they will, within twelve hours, supply you with one hundred fathoms of three-inch rope; fifty fathoms of two-inch; and fifty fathoms of one-inch. You are not unacquainted with the dilatory way of proceeding of the Portuguese. You will therefore demand a positive answer, whether they can supply you or not; and are by no means to suffer their promises, of procuring you those things if you will wait a little longer, to detain you a minute after your proper time.

P. BEAVER.

Bulama, 18*th* November 1793.

---

* I had learned that when here in July last, on the arrival of the Felicity, he tampered with Hayles to leave me, and had offered him, if he would do so, the command of a small vessel to trade between Bissao and the Cape de Verd islands, and that he has actually given him the command of one since he left me.

No. 15.

A list of the grumetas, or free natives, in number one hundred and ninety-six, employed, as labourers, on the Island of Bulama; with the several dates of their entry and discharge.

1792.

Oct. 6, Entered Jack, Tombaly; discharged 31st October, at their own request.

26, George; discharged 15th December, request.

Nov. 16, James Johnson; left me on a trading voyage, 14th April 1793; but never returned.

Lysander, Emanuel Drago, Antonio Lopez; discharged 15th December, request.

22, Liverpool, Lawrence; ditto.

Dec. 21, Emanuel Fidalgo, John Basse, Corasmo, Francisco, Joze; discharged 17th Jan. 1793, request.

27, Tomana, discharged 11th January, 1793, for disobedience of orders.

George, do. 17th do. for do.

Liverpool; do. 24th April, 1793, request.

Lawrence; do. 27th Jan. do. do.

Manuel Drago; do. do. for firing at another grumeta.

Antonio; do. do. request.

Paschal; do. 26th February 1793, request.

Domingo Swar; do. 5th January 1793, for drawing his knife on Mr. Beaver.

Gustine; do. 27th January 1793, request.

Girghola; do. 17th January 1793, request.

Antonio Lopez; do. 26th Feb. 1793, request.

Gustove Albus; do. 6th July, 1793, breach of trust.

Bastion Lopez; do. 27th January, 1793, drawing his knife on another grumeta.

Antonio de Goyez; do. 17th January, 1793, request.

Patrice; do. 5th January 1793, drawing his knife on another grumeta.

Domingo Lopez; do. 17th January 1793, request.

Manuel Lopez; deserted 27th January—returned the 3d February, and discharged 26th Feb. 1793, request.

Gillion; discharged 13th April 1793, request.

William, (boy); discharged 11th January, 1793, request.

1792.
- Simon, (boy); do. 14th April 1793, request.
- Christiana, (woman); do.   do.   do.
- Esperanza, (woman); do.   27th January, 1793, with her husband.
- Maria, do. 14th April, 1793, request.

1793.
Jan. 21, Lys, Esperean, Lucente, Emanuel Bear; discharged 27th January, 1793, request.
- Emanuel Tomboy; deserted 27th January, returned the 3d Feb. and discharged the 26th Feb. request.
- Domingo Lopez, Jockey, Commomoya; discharged 27th January, request.
- John Basse; discharged 13th April, request.
- Dominga, (girl); do. 27th Jan. do.
- Joze, (boy); do. 26th Feb. request.

Feb. 3, John;   do.   do.
- Domingo, Nichola; do.   do.
12, Francisco Fernandez, Francisco Lopez, Gustine Gomez, Lys Corea, Gaspar Moore, Domingo Albus, Antonio de Goyez, John de Goyez, Lucente; discharged 26th Feb. request.
24, Tonga, Francisco; do. 24th April, request.

March 5, Peter, Mark, Albert, Francisco Lopez, Antonio Fernandez; discharged 13th April, request.
- Antonio Verra; discharged 7th March, because he found his work too hard.
- Francisco Albus, do. 15th March, request.
- Domingo Noone, Gaspar Lombe, Joe Albus, (boy), John Lopez, Jockey, Lys Corea, Domingo Albus; do. 13th April, request.
26, Lysander, Joachin de Goyez, Joze Noone, Patron Lopez, Antonio Lopez, Florentine Mender; discharged 5th May, request.
27, Mathias, Desafora, Mara (woman), Bastion, Zarante, discharged 24th April, request.

April 5, Pedro de Costa, Joachin de Goyez, discharged 5th April, request.
14, Gasper Lombe do. 26th May, do.
29, Albert, Mark; deserted 5th May.
- Domingo Noone, Domingo Lopez, Joze, John de Goyez, John Lopez, Tomez, Manuel, Bulama,* Joze de Noone, Theobald, Pharos; discharged 26th May, request.

* This man was a Manjack, and said that he had not any name, so I called him Bulama

1793.

Emanuel Fidalgo, Catherine, (woman); discharged 19th May, request.

May 21, Lawrence, left the boat at Bissao 29th May.

Florentine Mender, discharged the 6th June, having finished his work.

John Beek, John Primado; discharged 19th June, request.

John Basse, discharged 30th May, idleness.

Tomez, do. 19th June, request.

John Lopez, do. 28th July, do.

Albert, Mark, do. 19th June, do.

Emanuel Fernandez; do. 6th June, sick.

Antonio; do. 19th June, request.

Patron Lopez; do. 27th July, do.

John, Patro Terre; do. 19th June, do.

Antonia, Dominga, (women); do. 28th July, do.

Josepha, (woman); do. 19th June, do.

31, Joyez de Noone; run from Perseverance at Bissao, 6th August.

Tomez; discharged 9th July, lame.

Joze; run from Perseverance at Bissao, 6th August.

Bulama, Domingo; discharged 7th July, lame.

Francisco; do. 11th August, request.

June 5, Gasper Lombe; run from the Perseverance at Bissao, 6th August.

John de Goyez; do.   20th Sept.

Tomez Lopez; discharged 11th August, request.

Barnave Albus; run from Perseverance at Bissao, 6th August.

Capitan de Goyez; discharged 11th August, request.

Antonio Fernandez; run from Perseverance at Bissao, 20th September.

Domingo Noone; discharged 11th August, request.

Theobald; run from Perseverance 13th July.

Tomez Pierara; discharged 11th August, request.

Portous Lopez; run from Perseverance at Bissao, 6th August.

Antonio Corea; run 30th July.

Antonio Morell; run away from Perseverance at Bissao, 6th August.

John de Goyez, Francisco, (boys); run away 7th July.

John Lopez; run from Perseverance at Bissao, 20th September.

Rosa Noone, (woman); discharged 28th July, request.

10, Joachinson, Paul Jones; do. 11th August, do.

Emanuel Tomboy; do. 19th June, lame.

Lucea Lopez, do. 28th July, request.

18, Peter Onsfield.

July 3, Thomas Rodrigue; run from Perseverance at Bissao, 20th September.

African Memoranda.

    Pedro Rodrigue; run from Perseverance, 13th July.
    Pharos, (boy); discharged 25th September, request.
  5, John Lopez, 3d; do. 25th July, for mutinous behaviour.
    Domingo, (boy); do. 25th September, request.
    Maria, (woman); discharged 28th July, request.

Aug. 6, Pedro Lopez, Joachin Lopez; discharged 6th October, request.
    Manuel Lopez, Magia Lopez; discharged 25th September, request, ulcerated legs.
    Domingo, Bastion Lopez; do. 6th October, request.
    Nase; do. 27th August, request, ulcerated leg.
    Portous, Supera Fuego; do. 6th October, request.
    John Primado; run away 30th September, breaking open house and theft.
    Manuel, Antonio, Antonio Lopez, Formosa, discharged 6th October, request.
  30, Portous; do.   do.

Sept. 5, Fuego; do.   do.
  20, Manuel Lopez.
    Lucea Lopez; run away 23d October.
    Maria Lopez; discharged 6th October, for theft, though a king's daughter.

Oct. 4, Domingo Albus; do 19th Nov. request.
    Lys Corea.
    Lawrence.
    John Beck discharged 19th November, request.
    Manuel Joze.
    Louis Lopez; do. 6th October, request.
    Hegebla; run away 8th November.
    Domingo, Gaspar, John Lucas; discharged 19th November, request.
  7, John Barigua;   do.   do.
  10, Barnave Albus, Joze Fernandez, do.   do.
    Francisco; left at Bissau the 18th October.
  18, Domingo, Pedro, Joachin, John, Formosa, Gouvern, Joan, (woman), Emanuel, (boy); discharged 19th November, request.

No. 16

London, 24th June, 1794.

Sir,

As a wish was expressed at our last general meeting, that previous to any new steps being taken, I should give my opinion to those concerned in the late attempts to colonize the isle of Bulama, on the coast of Africa, of the probability there might be of future success, if fresh subscriptions were raised for that purpose; and, at the same time, point out the causes of the failure of the first: I here send you in as consise a manner as I can my opinion of both.

To answer, as fully and satisfactorily as may be, the above questions, would, from the number of others which they involve, take up much more of my time than I can at present spare; therefore though many, nay most of them, admit a degree of proof, amounting almost to mathematical demonstration, I shall confine myself, at present, merely to assertions, the truth or fallacy of the grounds of which, will be left to the opinion of each individual; reserving to some future period, when I may have more leisure, a more minute detail of the various causes which have hitherto baffled our endeavours, as also of those which produce a well grounded hope of future success.

1st *Of the Causes of the failure of the late Expedition.*

Many might be enumerated:—but as I mean to be as brief as possible, I shall confine myself to three, which appear to me to have been the principal ones.

1st The carrying out men of the most infamous character and vicious habits.

2d The arriving on the coast of Africa at the most improper season of the year.

3d The omitting to carry out the frame and materials of a house, or houses, sufficient to secure the whole of the colony, immediately on their arrival, from the rains, and from the sun.

On the first of these I need not say much. It cannot be expected, that, in a situation, where authority, however necessary, could not be legally enforced, those men could be kept in any kind of order, who, under an old, established, and well regulated government, had been in the habit of living in open violation of it. Among the virtues peculiarly requisite in those who undertake to settle, or as it were to create, a colony, I should reckon sobriety, industry, honesty, patience, and fortitude. The major part of our people were drunken, lazy, dishonest, impatient, cowards.

On the second of these causes, I shall only observe, that the rainy season at Bulama begins the latter end of May, or the beginning of June. We arrived on the 5th of the last mentioned month, and had consequently the whole of the rains before us. With respect to the third, had we carried out the frame and materials necessary for the erection of a large house, it might have been finished in, at most, one month: but as all the timber, which I built with, was growing at the time of our arrival, it was the month of February in the following year, before I had a room to put my head in. The being exposed, during the whole of that time, to either the rains or the sun, must have certainly been a great cause of our great mortality. The three errors above noticed, namely, those of carrying out bad subjects, at the worst season, without means of shelter, are in themselves sufficient to prove, that we did not act on a well digested plan. The first of these can never be entirely avoided; the second arose from the danger which, it was thought, there was of others purchasing the island, if we delayed sailing; and the third from the ignorance, I believe, of those who directed the undertaking: as one of those, for these three errors, I beg leave to take to myself a great portion of the blame. But, though these were difficulties that might, and ought to have been avoided, they would not have entirely ruined the colony if there had been a sufficient firmness and decision in the conduct and characters of the members of the council. Among other causes of the failure may be reckoned the sailing without a charter; the having two many members in the council; the two ships not keeping together; and the unfortunate circumstance of losing some men by an attack from the natives. The very injudicious mode of the expenditure of the money might be reckoned another, as, from the sum subscribed, a sufficient portion might have been retained in the hands of the trustees, to fit out a small vessel, both with refreshments and men, at the end of the first rains. In three articles this was particularly conspicuous. The purchase of the plantation tools, the purchase of the salt provisions, and the chartering of ships; the carrying out women and children was, though it may not appear so at first sight, a great cause of expence, and a principal one of failure.

I have now enumerated what appear to me to have been among the principal causes of our miscarriage; if they appear not in the same light to others, I could wish that they would reconsider them. They are almost all of them demonstrably true; but, as I before observed, I shall only assert, and leave others to trace, how, and in what manner, they operated perniciously towards our enterprise. We come now to the other question.

2dly. *Of the Probability of future Success.*—Our first failure will here be of great service to us, if we consider our former errors as so many beacons, put up to warn us of danger. The first three which I enumerated, seem to have been the most essential, and, except the first, are easily avoided, as well as all the rest. May I be permitted, without the imputation of vanity, to say, that after all our former difficulties, my having been able with only four Europeans, and without the smallest succour or assistance, to keep possession of the island for the last year, to cut down 50 acres of timber, 16 of which were enclosed, and the roots taken up, to erect three large buildings, and to raise with ease, vegetables enough for more than 50 times our number, is a sufficient proof of the certainty of future success? But as it may here be expected that I should enter a little into particulars, I shall more fully state the grounds of my opinion. The end, I believe, proposed by the major part of the subscribers, was the cultivation of cotton; others proposed growing sugar, coffee, tobacco, and Indigo, while a few hoped to drive an advantageous commerce with the natives, for ivory, wax, and other productions of that part of Africa. The prospects of those whose views are confined to cultivation, must depend entirely upon soil; and this I am warranted to say, from the universal concurrence of those who have seen it, whether natives or Europeans, is remarkably fertile. It is deep, that is one foot and a half to two feet. I never saw a rock or stone upon the island, except one small space close under the block-house, and never saw a foot of bad soil; every thing which I planted throve admirably, and among those plants about 300 were cotton. They were only in blossom when I came away, I therefore had no opportunity of bringing home a specimen of it. But, supposing the cotton on that part of the coast to be of the very worst quality, it could not at all affect the value of the island, or the probability of success in its cultivation, as nothing can be more easy than to carry thither the seeds of either the Bourbon, or Parnambuco cotton. The former, I believe, is reckoned the best in the world, and the latter the next to it. The first place is about twenty and the latter nine degrees south of the equator. Bulama is eleven degrees distant from it on the north; so that there cannot be any great difference in the climate of those three places, but more particularly the two last; from which I should infer, that equally good cotton, planted in equally good soil, either at Bulama or Parnambuco, would be of equal value. Supposing the Bulama soil to be equally good with that of the other countries, in the same climate, whether north or south of the equator, I see no reason why, with equal cultivation, equally good sugar, coffee, and tobacco might not be produced on that island, as that which we know is produced, in the same degree of both north and south latitude. An advantageous commerce, I know, may be carried on with the natives in the two articles of ivory and wax. The central situation of Bulama, its harbour being a great thoroughfare for the Portuguese trade; its proximity to the three great rivers of Gambia, Grande, and Nunez, and the innumerable inlets, or small branches of the sea, navigable far inland with small vessels, between the first and last of those rivers, render it a most eligible situation for such trade. Its distance from Europe is not so great as that of the West Indies; the navigation to it is safe and secure; it contains one of the finest harbours I ever saw; the sea abounds with fish; and the number of animals, but more particularly elephants, buffaloes, and deer, on the island is almost incredible. The teeth of the former, and the hides, I should suppose, of the latter, are articles of some commercial consideration. With such advantages of soil and situation, a trifling sum, expended in a judicious manner, for the equipment of a small number of good men, embarked on board two or three little vessels, and directed by a man of common sense and great power, would, in my opinion, preclude a doubt of success. It might be commanded; but, when I say it might be commanded, I presuppose a greater firmness in those who go out, and more zeal and activity in those who remain at home, than has hitherto been evinced by either.

I am, Sir,
Your very humble servant,
P. BEAVER.

To
The Rt. Hon. Paul Le Mesurier, Esq.
　Lord Mayor of London.

At this meeting the following resolutions were agreed to.

BULAMA ASSOCIATION.

" At a general meeting of the subscribers to this Association, convened by public advertisement at the Mansion House, London, the 25th June, 1794."

The Right Honourable Paul Le Mesurier, Esq. M. P. Lord Mayor,
　　　　　in the Chair.

" Resolved unanimously,

" That the thanks of this meeting be given to Philip Beaver, Esq. lieutenant in the Royal Navy, late chief of the settlement on the island of Bulama, for the ability, zeal, activity, and perseverance, with which, under many difficulties, he conducted the affairs of that settlement, and for his constant attention to the interests of the Association; and to assure Mr. Beaver that the members of this association will ever hold his services in grateful remembrance.

" That a gold medal be presented to Mr. Beaver, expressive of the sense entertained by the Association, of his very meritorious services.

" That the thanks of this meeting be given to Mr. John Hood, for the spirit and resolution with which he supported Mr. Beaver, during the whole of his stay at Bulama, and that he be assured the Association will ever gratefully remember his services.

" That these resolutions be fairly transcribed, signed by the Chairman, and respectively delivered to Mr. Beaver, and Mr. Hood, and that they be published in some of the daily papers."

A true extract from the minutes.

J. K. MALLESON, Sec.

APP. NO. 17.] **African Memoranda.** 499

No. 17.

Extracts from the ship Hankey's log, from London towards Bulama; from that ship's getting soundings on the coast of Africa, to her anchoring in the east channel of Bulama.

H	K	H K.	Courses.	Winds.	Remarks, &c. Saturday 2d June 1792.
2	5	..	E.byS.	N.byE.	Fresh breezes and hazy weather.
4	4	1			
6	5	..	Up E.N.E.	Off E S.E.	Hove to and sounded, no ground at 100 fathoms; bore up again under the topsails.
8	..	..	E.byS.		
10	3	1			
10	4	..			Hove to and sounded in 25 fathoms, dark brown sand; fired a gun and altered the course to starboard.
12	3	1			
		1		East.	Variable light airs.
2	2	1	S.byE.	E.byS.	
	1	..	South.	E.S.E.	At 4 a breeze sprung up from the northward.
4	..	1		Calm.	
6	2	1	S.byE.	N.byW.	
8	2	..			
	..	1	Up East.	Off S.E.	Hove to, to speak the long boat, and then bore up again.
10	3	1	S.byE.	N.N.W.	
12	6	1			Beggar's Benison and long boat in company. Lat. observed, 13. 44. N

Sunday 3d June 1792.

H	K	H K.	Courses.	Winds.	Remarks, &c.
2	3	1	S.byE.	N.N.W.	Moderate breezes and hazy weather.
4	4	..			
6	4	..	South.		At 5 saw breakers on the larboard bow: at half past 6 abreast of the south break head of the shoal of Cape St. Mary's, which we passed in 4 fathoms, at half a mile distance; at the same time the westernmost land bore S.byE. 6 leagues; hauled to the westward. At 10 the soundings 15 fathoms, fired a gun and altered the course to port; carried the same water to half past 2 a.m. then 12 fathoms to 4; half past 4, 10 fathoms; at 5, 8 fathoms; half past 5, 7 fathoms, when we hauled in and made the trees on the land;
8	4	..	W.byS.		
10	3	1			
12	3	..	S.byW.		
2	4	1			
4	4	..			
6	4	..			At half past 6, bore up, carrying the same water.
	1	..	E.S.E.		
8	1	..			At 8 the southernmost land bore S.S.E.
	3	1	S.S.E.		
10	3	1	S.byW.		From 9 to 11 the water 5 fathoms, the southernmost land S.byE. half E.
12	3	1	S.S.W.		At noon Cape Roxo E. half S. 3 leagues, water 8 fathoms. Latitude observed, 12. 19. N

Monday 4th June 1792.

H	K	H K.	Courses.	Winds.	Remarks, &c.
	4	..	E.S.E.	N.N.W.	Moderate breezes and fine weather. At half past 1 Cape Roxo N.E.byE. half E. 5 miles, at the same time altered the course to S.byW. a quarter before 4 had 4 fathoms for three or four casts, and then 7 fathoms
2	2	..	S.E.	N.W.	
	2	..	S.byW.		
4	5	..		14 miles from the departure.	
6	4	..	S.S.W.		
	3	1	S.half E.		
	3	1	S.E.		At 8 anchored in 7 fathoms.
8	4	1	E.S.E.		
10					
12				N.W.	The tide (ebb) running by log 2 knots per hour.
2					
4					
6					At day light saw the three islands from the deck, bearing E.byS and from the tops Formosa in the S.E. quarter.
8	4	..	E.S.E.		At 7 weighed carrying from 7 to 11 fathoms.
10	3	1			At 9 the southernmost of the three islands N.byW. 4 or 5 miles, 13 fathoms abreast of Jatt's island.
12	2	1			At noon the southern point of Jatt's island N E.byE. 3 or 4 miles.

(Marked wholly.)

Tuesday the 5th June. Nautical time.—Remarkable fine weather. At four p.m. abreast of the east point of Jatt's Island, a mile and a half from the shore, water seven fathoms; between Jatt's and Bassis island ten fathoms. Half past five the S.W. end of Bassis Island N.E. four miles, at this time a strong flood tide. At seven anchored in seven fathoms; the S.W. end of Bissao island bearing E. one-half, N. two and a half miles. A.m. at six weighed, and at eight anchored again in ten fathoms, Bow (Arcas) island, S.E. three or four miles. The long boat went to discover and sound the channel leading to the island of Bulama.

Thursday the 7th June. Common or civil time.—At six in the morning weighed, to work up to Bissao, but a heavy tornado obliged us to anchor again at eight o'clock, in eight fathoms.

Friday the 8th of June.—At noon a light westerly wind sprung up, weighed and run up to Bissao, where we anchored in the evening, having gone *between* that island and the islet of Bourbon.

Thursday the 21st of June.—At eleven a.m. weighed with a light southerly air, and worked down towards Bulama. At six p.m. anchored in the Bulama channel, in seven fathoms at low water, the west end of Bulama bearing south, and Bow (Arcas) island E. by S.

Friday the 22d June.—At noon weighed, and at half past five anchored in a bay at the west end of the island of Bulama in sixteen fathoms.

Saturday the 23d June.—At one p.m. weighed, with light airs, and at five run upon a spit of sand that extends three or four miles to the southward of the west end of the Island of Bulama. At nine hove off and anchored in six fathoms.

Sunday the 24th June.—At eight a.m. weighed, run up, and anchored off the mouth of the Rio Grande, and the east channel of Bulama, in fifteen fathoms.

Wednesday the 27th June.—At ten a.m. weighed and worked up the east channel of Bulama, in which we anchored at four p.m. in fifteen fathoms.

From the foregoing extracts it will be seen that we had never less than six fathoms in the Bijuga channel, except for three or four casts of the lead, when we had borrowed too closely upon the western edge of the Cacheo bank. As to the ship's running upon the bank that runs south about four miles from the S.W. point of Bulama, I had pointed it out to Moore, who had undertaken to be our pilot, but he said that the rippling was occasioned by deep, instead of shoal, water, till the moment that we struck, there was six fathoms close to its edge. Till this channel is better known, caution certainly is required in going up or down it, but there is abundance of water in it for the largest ships in the world.

THE END.

MODERN SMALL ARMS

MODERN SMALL ARMS

IAN V. HOGG

97-337

Published by
Book Sales, Inc.
114 Northfield Avenue
Raritan Center
Edison, N.J. 08818

Produced by
Brompton Books Corp.
15 Sherwood Place
Greenwich, CT 06830

Copyright © 1994 Brompton Books Corp.

All rights reserved. No part of this publication may be reproduced, stored in a retrieval system or transmitted in any form by any means, electronic, mechanical, photocopying or otherwise, without first obtaining the written permission of the copyright owner.

ISBN 0-7858-0018-2

Printed in Slovenia

Over
UD
380
H582
1983

Page 1: A pair of counter-revolutionary warfare specialists armed with automatic weapons.

Pages 2-3: A group of U.S. Navy Seals. The man in the foreground is armed with an M16A1 rifle with an underslung M203 grenade-launcher.

Right: Hunting with a Beretta automatic shotgun.

CONTENTS

INTRODUCTION 6

PISTOLS 14

RIFLES 50

MACHINE GUNS 96

SHOTGUNS 132

Acknowledgments 160

INTRODUCTION

INTRODUCTION

In the 12 years which have passed since the first edition of this book was published many new small arms designs have appeared, as might be expected. However, if a graph was drawn showing the number of designs against the passage of time, a downward trend would be revealed. The conclusion seems to be that small arms design has reached a level of technology which will be difficult to improve upon, both mechanically and economically. As will be seen in the text, the United States has spent several years in an attempt to find an Advanced Combat Rifle which would show a significant performance improvement over the current M16A2. The best brains in the firearms business were applied, the results were technically outstanding, but the desired improvement was not achieved, which indicates the size of the technical barrier standing in the way of significant design advances. The economic factor can also be seen in the cost of the program – some $350 million.

So far as military weapons go, the point has been reached at which any major improvement can only be achieved at a grossly disproportionate cost; a hunter might be persuaded to pay a 50 per cent increase for his next rifle, and $10,000 for a shotgun is not considered outrageous, but an army contemplating buying rifles by the hundred thousand is likely to balk at such a premium on excellence. The simple fact is that the current military rifle is generally more accurate than the man firing it, and it is as efficient as it needs to be, given a reasonable amount of training in its use. There is no point in laying out vast sums of money for a percentage increase in the probability of hitting the target with the first shot, which is what rifle improvement really means. And bear in mind that half the world is running round with Kalashnikovs, a 50-year-old design, not exactly at the cutting edge of technology, but one which, nevertheless, is killing very effectively.

On the commercial market, too, economics have made their impact. Since 1982 many long-established gunmakers have vanished; from the 1982 edition we have removed Harrington & Richardson, Iver Johnson, Renato Gamba, Benelli, High Standard, BSA, Stirling, Midland, Parker-Hale . . . all names which, in 1982, we thought would last for ever. Some have been absorbed into other companies, others have simply died, all victims of the economic climate of the 1980s. Fabrique National of Herstal and Heckler & Koch of Oberndorf, two pillars of the industry, have both been sold, the former to Giat Industries of France, the latter to Royal Ordnance of Britain. Other companies are in financial straits and may not see the century out. Small wonder, then, that new ideas and bold commercial ventures are thin on the ground.

One of the more interesting aspects of the past decade has been to see several ideas from the past being resurrected and the benefits of modern technology applied to them. The practice of using a revolving barrel to lock the breech of a pistol had vanished by 1982, the principal reason being the difficulty and expense of machining the necessary curved lugs on the barrel and corresponding grooves in the frame and slide; but the rapid growth in the

INTRODUCTION

Previous pages: A Yugoslavian variant of a Kalashnikov.
Left: An Italian sniper with the Beretta M1 sniping rifle.
Top: Syrian special forces with AKM variants.
Right: The Spectre submachine gun.

use of computer-controled machinery, capable of automatically working to a level of accuracy which surpasses the best hand-worker, has allowed this system to make a return in the Colt 2000 and the Steyr TMP pistols. The 1950s and 1960s saw many attempts to produce effective fléchette rounds, cartridges in which the "bullet" was actually a finned dart capable of high velocity and hence flat trajectory and a better chance of a hit. The accuracy left a great deal to be desired, largely due to problems with the "sabot", the plastic collar which mated the thin dart with the much larger bore of the rifle, and as a result the fléchette fell from favor. It returned, however, in the American Advanced Combat Rifle program, vastly improved by the use of new materials, though still unable to unseat the traditional jacketed bullet from its place of dominance. Similarly, the Duplex bullet, tried in Vietnam and abandoned, also returned in improved form, while Heckler & Koch carried the caseless cartridge to its peak

INTRODUCTION

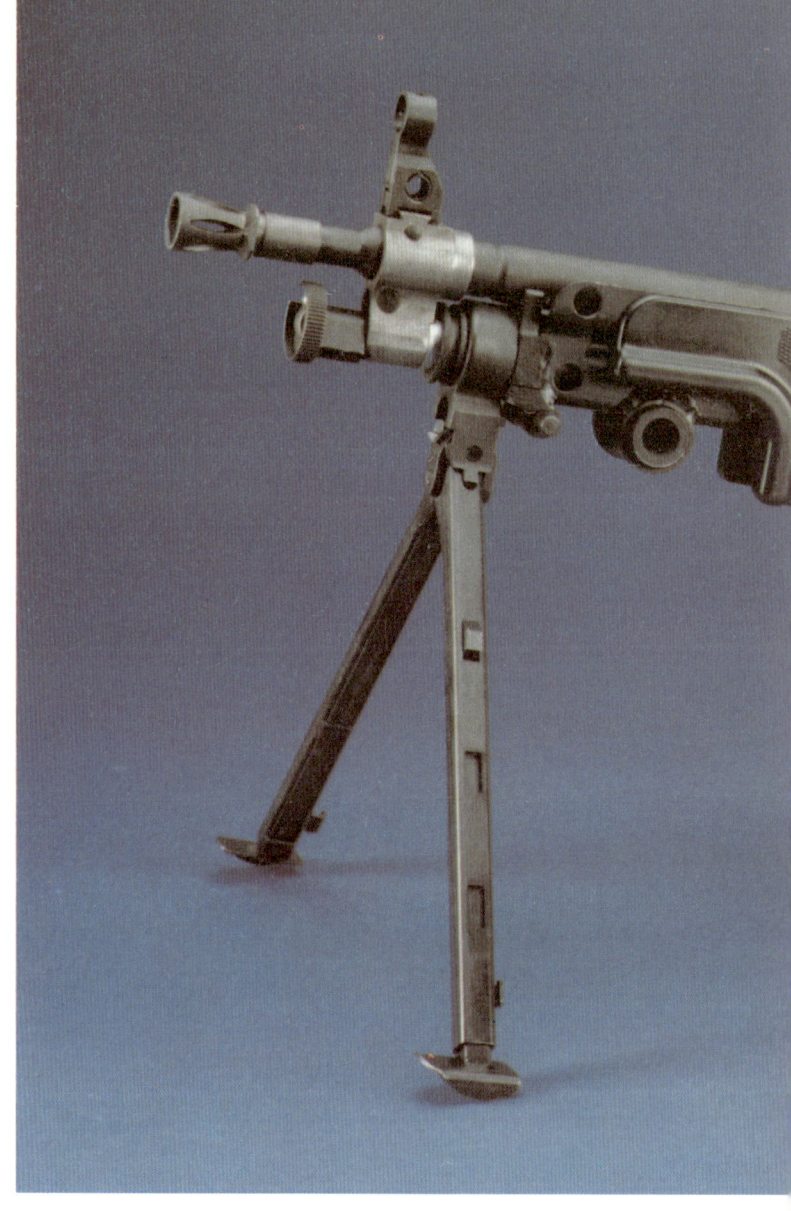

Above: Shiny new SA-80s undergoing trials with British paras.
Top: The Bushman Individual Defense Weapon.
Right: The FN Minimi machine gun.

INTRODUCTION

by designing a machine gun to suit it.

There is, therefore, no shortage of designing talent in the world; unfortunately, all their designs are evolutionary rather than revolutionary, making marginal improvements upon existing foundations, rather than striking out in some totally new dimension. And since major firearms development is invariably military-stimulated, the stagnation in military circles makes itself felt in the commercial arena as well.

As and when the military designs make a quantum leap into the next generation (and it is unlikely to be in this century) it will still leave the commercial gun unaffected, because current military thinking is towards such things as directed-energy weapons – lethal lasers, electric propulsion systems, liquid propellants, plasma weapons – which are unlikely ever to become acceptable as sporting weapons; I find it difficult to visualize trap shooting with a laser beam. Another military aim is the "non-lethal" weapon (a contradiction in terms if ever there was one) which will render an opponent incapable of retaliation for sufficient time to move him to a conventional prisoner-of-war compound.

This brings us back to where we began; firearms have reached a peak from which it is going to take a long time to move, largely because moving is not going to be cost-effective. Nevertheless, there is still room for small improvements and fine-tuning; new cartridges will continue to be developed, usually by hand-loaders in the first instance, but soon taken up by commercial manufacturers if they show any promise. Experience shows that innovation does not necessarily sell guns; quality and reliability, accuracy and, of course, price sells guns, and as the following pages show, there is still sufficient diversity in the gun-making business to satisfy just about every demand of either the soldier, the hunter, or the target enthusiast.

In the sections which follow I have adhered to a standard format, and the facts presented are based upon the manufacturers' information wherever possible; otherwise, they are based on reliable reports or upon actual examination of the weapon. I have attempted to handle and fire as many of the presented weapons as possible. Opinions are my own, presented as constructive analysis.

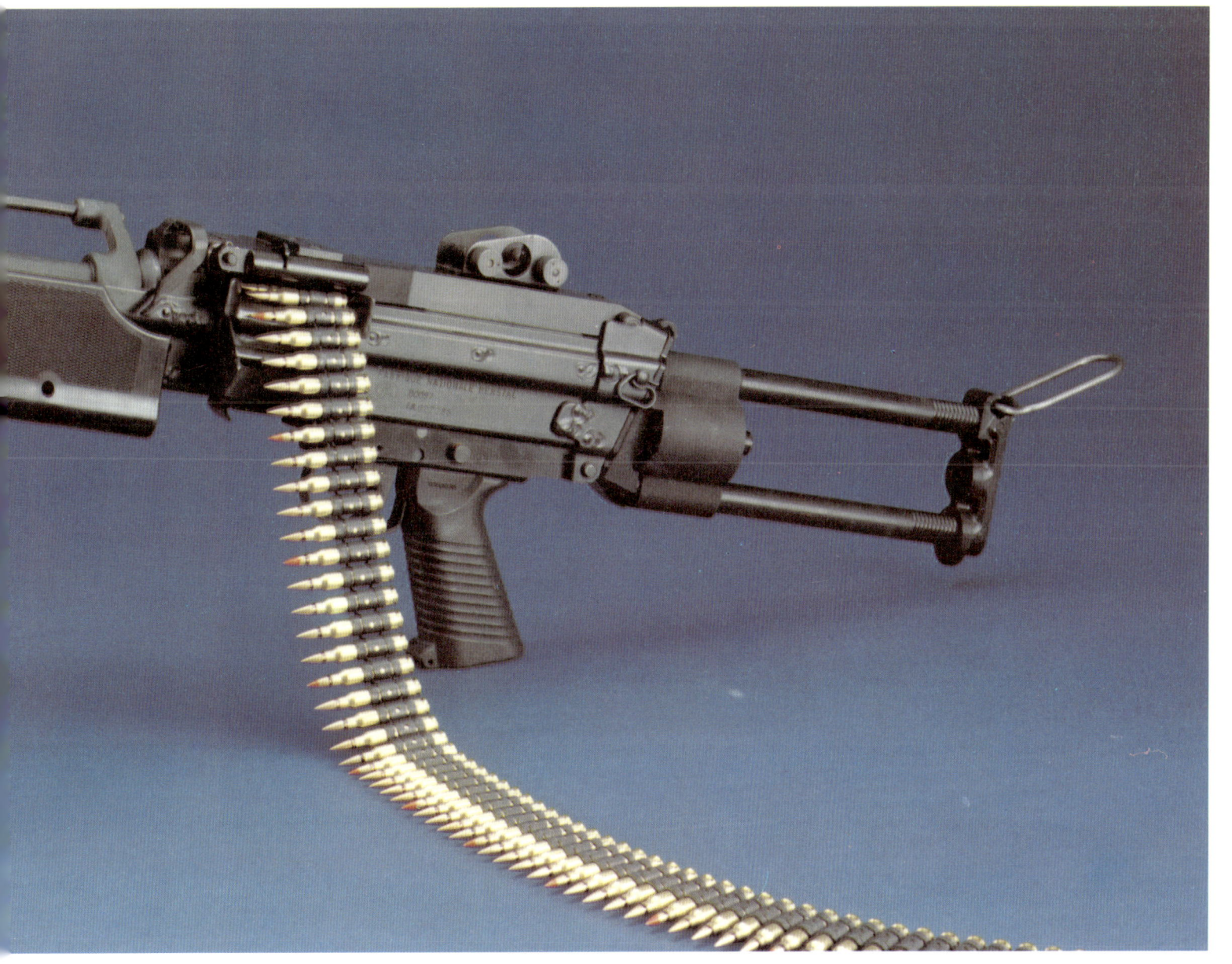

INTRODUCTION

INTRODUCTION

Left: A Browning .50 M2 machine gun with blank firing attachment and laser simulator.
Right: A Spanish Ameli 5.56mm machine gun.
Below: British troops armed with the Enfield L85A1 rifle.

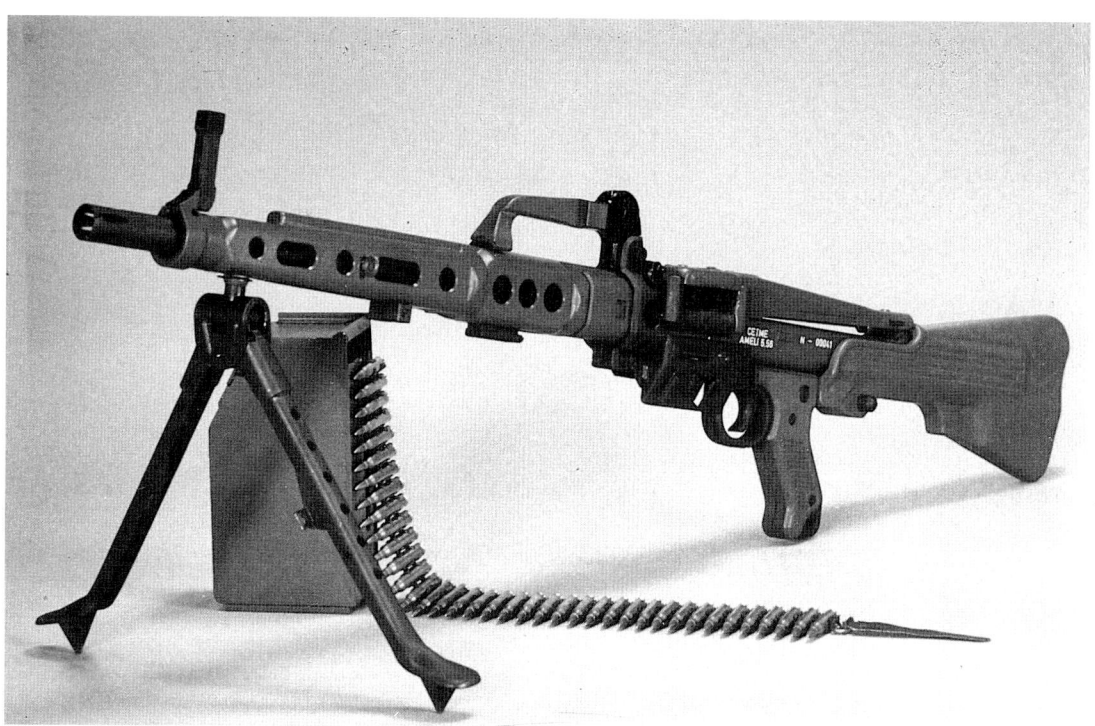

PISTOLS

ASP 9mm Auto Pistol

Manufacturer Armament Systems and Procedures, Appleton, WI 54911, U.S.A.
Type Semi-auto, locked breech, double-action
Caliber 9mm Parabellum
Barrel 3.25in (82.5mm)
Weight 24oz (680gm)
Magazine Capacity 7 rounds

Almost 20 years ago the clandestine services of the U.S. Government stated a requirement for a concealable but powerful automatic pistol, and the first response was a cut-down .45 M1911A1 Colt developed by the C.I.A. While this worked, it could hardly be said to be an elegant solution. It was noisy, had excessive muzzle flash, a magazine capacity of only four shots, and less target effect than the average .38 Special revolver. Another solution was sought, which was to be based on the 9mm Parabellum cartridge, and this led to the design which is now commercially available as the 'ASP', named for the company who make it.

The ASP is actually a re-manufacture. It begins life as a standard Smith & Wesson Model 39 which is then severely cut about. The butt, slide, slide stop and safety catch are all dimensionally reduced and lightening cuts are made in the slide so as to distribute the balance correctly. The barrel is shortened, throated and polished, the feed ramp smoothed and polished, and a custom-built barrel bushing pressed into the slide. New recoil spring and guide are fitted, every edge of the weapon hand-smoothed, and the entire surface coated with 'Teflon' to give a smooth, black, resistant finish. The butt plates are replaced with special models, with that on the left side having a transparent panel which allows the contents of the magazine to be checked. The trigger-guard is given a forward hook and the magazine floor given a finger rest, both aiding the holding of the pistol in combat mode. Finally a 'Guttersnipe' combat sight unit is fitted to the slide. This is a trough with the interior walls colored yellow, and if the sight picture is correct, the target can be seen within three equally-proportioned walls. If the aim is off, then the walls of the sight display an unbalanced picture which indicates the sighting error.

The resulting weapon is not cheap; it is necessary to buy the Model 39 first and then add $350 for the conversion. But for those whose life could depend upon quick and accurate firepower, the price is immaterial and the ASP promises to be the right answer.

Previous pages: A pair of Beretta 92 SB Compact pistols.

Right: The ASP 9mm combat pistol, displaying the visible magazine facility.

Above: The Spanish A-80 double-action pistol.

Astra Model A-80 Auto Pistol

Manufacturer Astra, Unceta y Cia, Guernica, Spain
Type Locked breech double-action semi-automatic
Caliber 9mm Parabellum
Barrel 3.75in (95mm)
Weight 34.2oz (970gm)
Magazine Capacity 15 rounds

The Astra company has been manufacturing automatic pistols since 1908. It has been providing Spanish military and police pistols since 1913 and has thus gained valuable knowledge of practical requirements as opposed to theoretical desires, and this shows in their latest pistol the A-80.

The A-80 is very much in the modern idiom – a double-action weapon with a large magazine. It is compact, simply built and easy to disassemble, yet it is also of a respectable weight so that it points well and balances nicely in the hand. The breech is locked by the normal Browning swinging link, though, as in most of today's models, the link is actually a shaped cam which withdraws the barrel downwards from engagement with the slide. Safety is attended to by having the firing pin positively locked by a sprung plunger except for the actual moment that the hammer is released by trigger action, at which time a portion of the trigger linkage lifts the plunger out of engagement and frees the firing pin. There is a de-cocking lever on the left side of the frame, its thumb catch just behind the trigger guard. Depressing this drops the hammer to be caught on the rebound notch, after which pulling the trigger will double-action the hammer to full cock and then drop it. An interesting point is that this de-cocking lever can be moved across to the right side for left-handed shooters.

The foresight is a blade with whitened rear face, and the backsight has a white line below the ample notch, so that they can easily be picked up and aligned in poor light. But the rear sight is fixed, except that it could possibly be drifted sideways for zeroing. Even so, the sights appear to be well aligned from the factory and the range performance with a stock model was satisfactory.

The A-80 is also manufactured in .38 Super and .45 ACP chambering; in the latter case the magazine holds nine rounds.

Astra .357 Revolver

Manufacturer Astra, Unceta y Cia, Guernica, Spain
Type Six-shot, solid frame, double-action
Caliber .357 Magnum
Barrel 3, 4, 6 and 8.5in (76, 102, 152 and 216mm)
Weight 40oz (1134gm) (6in barrel)

Astra Unceta have a long history of automatic-pistol manufacture, having made the Spanish Army's service sidearm since World War One, but they did not enter the revolver field until the late 1950s, and then with a relatively cheap line under the name of 'Cadix.' About ten years later, having gained some practical experience, they then produced this .357 Magnum model, an excellent revolver which will stand comparison with anyone's.

Like most Spanish guns, it has a

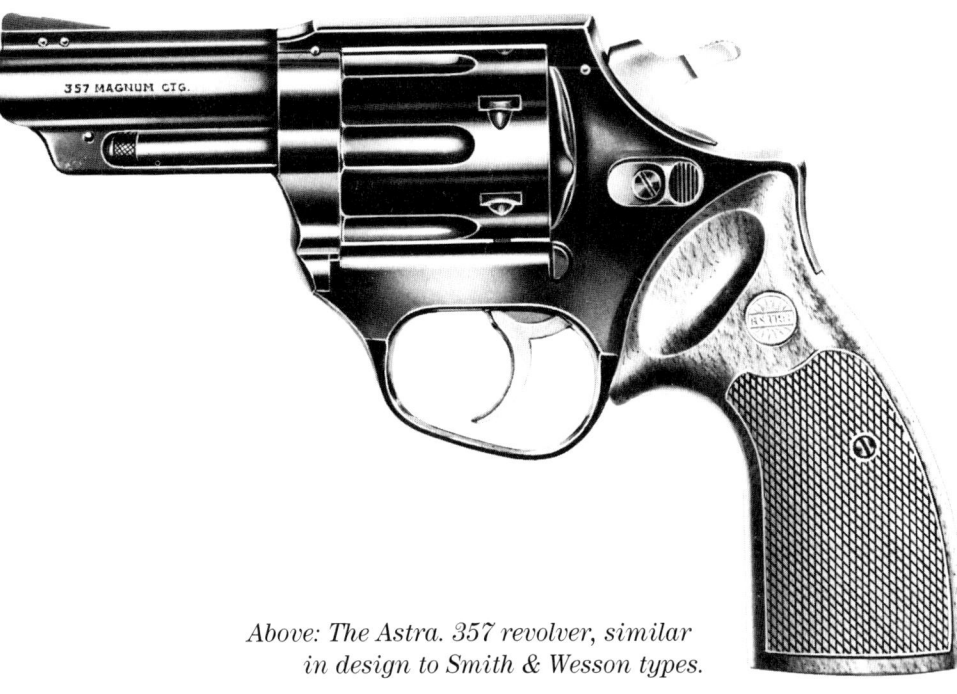

Above: The Astra. 357 revolver, similar in design to Smith & Wesson types.

ASTRA .44 MAGNUM REVOLVER

striking resemblance to the Smith & Wesson family. It is a conventional solid-frame weapon with swing-out cylinder, floating firing pin, and with a safety bar included in the lockwork. An unusual point is that the shorter (3 and 4 inch) barreled models have smaller grips than the longer-barreled models; it seems that their theory is that those who buy the short guns want a handy defensive weapon, while those who buy the longer barrel are looking for target guns and deserve target-style grips. All have fully-adjustable Patridge-style rear sights and ramp foresights.

The fit and finish is first-class; all have fully recessed chambers which enclose the cartridge heads, the walnut grips are neatly checkered, and the metal is well blued and polished to a deep luster. Both hammer spur and trigger are deeply grooved to give them non-slip properties.

The accuracy and reliability of these Astra revolvers is in keeping with their quality of finish. They can be expected to group as tightly as the shooter is capable of holding, and they show no signs of loosening after long wear. Though not inexpensive, they are good value and cost less than many comparable pistols.

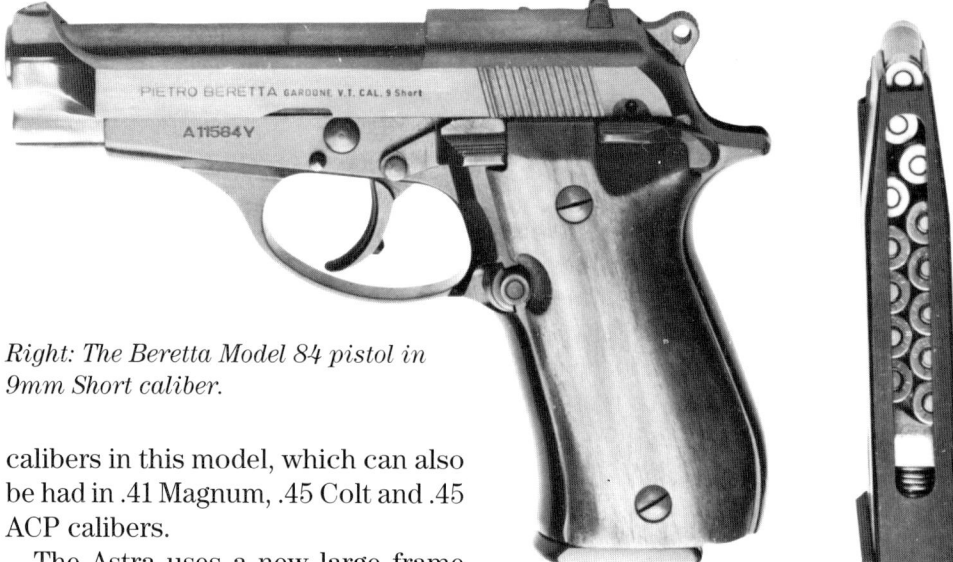

Right: The Beretta Model 84 pistol in 9mm Short caliber.

calibers in this model, which can also be had in .41 Magnum, .45 Colt and .45 ACP calibers.

The Astra uses a new large frame and, in basic features, follows the Smith & Wesson pattern; a shrouder ejector rod, left side push-forward catch for releasing the cylinder crane and double-action lockwork. The grip is somewhat large, though this may be felt desirable with such powerful cartridges, but it appears not to be everyone's taste as far as the shape goes, being too broad at the foot.

The foresight is a blade set on a ramp, while the rear sight is an open notch adjustable for elevation and

Below: The Astra .44 Magnum revolver.

Astra .44 Magnum Revolver

Manufacturer Astra, Unceta y Cia, Guernica, Spain
Type Six-shot, double-action, solid frame
Caliber .44 Magnum
Barrel 5.93in (150mm)
Weight 45oz (1275gm)

As stated the Astra Unceta company have a long record of manufacturing automatic pistols but they did not go into the revolver business until 1958, and it was several years before they went as far as a .357 Magnum. They have now gone to the limit in revolver

windage. With walnut grips and well-blued metal, it is an impressive revolver and is finished to a high standard. It shoots well, has a smooth trigger action, and is capable of making regular two to three inch groups at 25 yards.

Beretta Models 81 and 84

Manufacturer Armi Beretta SpA, I-25063, Gardone Val Trompia, Italy
Type Blowback double-action semi-automatic
Caliber 7.65mm ACP (Model 81); .380/9mm Short (Model 84)
Barrel 3.81in (97mm)
Weight (empty) 23.5oz (665gm) (Mod 81); 22.5oz (640gm) (Mod 84)
Magazine Capacity 12 rounds (Mod 81); 13 rounds (Mod 84)

These two pistols are members of the double-action family which appeared in 1976. They have met with considerable success both in adoption by many police and security forces and in commercial sales.

In many respects they are updated versions of the well-known Model 1934 Beretta which armed the Italian forces until 1945, robust blowback weapons with fixed barrels and with the unique Beretta configuration of cut-away slide over the barrel. However, bringing them up to date has added double-action lockwork and magazines of much greater capacity, with a better-shaped butt frame and walnut grips. The magazine release is in the forward edge of the butt beneath the trigger guard and can be located on the left or right side, as preferred. The safety catch is at the rear of the slide and can be operated from either side. When the chamber contains a cartridge the extractor protrudes on the right-hand side of the slide and shows a red indication; it can also be checked by feel in the dark.

The two models are identical except for their caliber and magazine capacity; due to changes in the magazine follower, the 9mm Model 84 actually manages to take one more round in the magazine than does the 7.65mm Model 81; the 84 is also slightly lighter, due to the barrel having similar external dimensions but a larger bore.

Beretta Model 92 Auto Pistol

Manufacturer Armi Beretta SpA, I-25063, Gardone Val Trompia, Italy
Type Locked breech, double-action, semi-automatic
Caliber 9mm Parabellum
Barrel 4.92in (125mm)
Weight (empty) 33.5oz (950gm)
Magazine Capacity 15 rounds

This appeared in 1976 as the third member of the new double-action family, and it has since been adopted by the Italian forces and by several other armies as their service pistol.

Breech locking is performed by a dropping block beneath the barrel, very similar in operation to that familiar to most people on the Walther P-38. It is a shaped block which is connected at its front to the underside of the barrel and, by lugs at the rear, to the slide, so locking the two together. A shaped heel rests on a transom in the frame, so that the block cannot unlock from the slide. After firing, recoil forces the slide to pull back, but it is restrained by the fact that the block cannot move down; as the entire barrel and slide unit moves rearward, against the recoil spring, so the locking block moves off the transom and is then free to fall, releasing the slide while the barrel stops. There is ample delay time to permit the bullet to leave the barrel. The return of the slide, reloading the breech, forces the barrel forwards and so lifts the block back on to its transom and also into locking engagement with the slide once more.

The extractor is mounted laterally, on the right side, and when the weapon is loaded it protrudes, revealing a red 'chamber-loaded' indication; this can also be felt in the dark, so that there is always a positive indication available. The safety is on the left side and locks both trigger and slide, and there is a half-cock notch on the hammer. The front sight is a simple blade, integral with the slide, while the rear sight is a square notch unit riding in a dovetail slot so that it can be laterally shifted for zeroing.

The Beretta 92 is a well-made, robust and functional military or police weapon. It is also sold in North and South America as the 'Taurus PT-92' marketed, accordingly, by Taurus S.A. of Sao Paulo, Brazil.

A variant model is the Model 92S which has a slide-mounted safety which, when applied, deflects the firing pin from alignment with the hammer, releases the hammer and breaks the connection between trigger bar and sear. A further variant is the Model 92SB which has the safety lever on both sides of the slide and moves the magazine release from its usual European position at the bottom of the butt to the American position in the front of the butt, just below the trigger-guard; this is normally on the left side, but can be switched to the right if required.

Beretta Model 93R Machine Pistol

Manufacturer Armi Beretta SpA, I-25063, Gardone Val Trompia, Italy
Type Locked breech, double-action, semi-automatic with burst-fire facility.
Caliber 9mm Parabellum
Barrel 6.14in (156mm) including muzzle brake
Weight (empty) 41.2oz (1170gm)
Magazine Capacity 20 rounds

This is an advanced weapon based on the Model 92 but with several additional features which place it in the 'machine pistol' category. It has been adopted by Italian Special Forces and security police, and interest has been expressed in several other countries.

Basically, the pistol is similar to the Model 92 in that it uses a dropping-block locked breech. The principal visible change is the use of a longer barrel which protrudes in front of the slide and has a prominent muzzle brake; there is also a folding front grip, hinged to the frame so that it lies beneath the frame front when not in

Below: The Beretta Model 93R machine pistol.

BERNARDELLI P-018 PISTOL

use or can be folded down to act as a grip for the left (or disengaged) hand. This proves to be more practical than one might think, giving a steadier hold than the more common two-handed butt grip. In addition there is a light metal folding stock unit which can be clipped to the bottom of the butt, and which then converts the pistol into something approaching a light carbine. Finally, the magazine has been lengthened to hold 20 rounds, so that it extends below the bottom of the butt. For those preferring a more elegant shape, the normal Model 92 15-shot magazine can be used.

The reason for all these changes is that under the right butt-plate is a three-round burst controller. The frame-mounted safety catch offers three positions: safe, single shot, and 3-round burst; placing the catch in this last position permits the firing of three rapid shots for one pressure on the trigger, the cyclic rate of fire being about 110 rounds per minute. This is low by machine pistol standards and therefore there is less disturbance of the aim; moreover the forward hand grip and shoulder stock, used either separately or together, and the damping effect of the muzzle brake, allow the firer firm control of the weapon, and high-speed photography shows that there is relatively little 'climb' during the firing of a burst.

Bernardelli P-018 Pistol

Manufacturer Vincenzo Bernardelli SpA, Gardone Val Trompia, Italy
Type Locked breech, double-action, semi-automatic
Caliber 9mm Parabellum
Barrel 4.80in (122mm)
Weight (empty) 35.2oz (998gm)
Magazine Capacity 15 rounds

Originating in 1865 as gun barrel makers, Bernardelli manufactured service revolvers for the Italian Army, 1929-33, and entered the commercial pistol market in 1945. The P-018 was first produced in 1982.

Intended originally as a military and police pistol, the P-018 is most usually found in 9mm caliber, though it has

Right: The Bernardelli P-018 pistol.

also been produced in 7.65mm Parabellum and 9mm Largo chambering in small numbers. The breech is locked by the familiar Browning dropping barrel, controlled by a shaped cam slot beneath the chamber which engages with the slide stop lever pin. There is an automatic firing pin lock, whereby the hammer cannot drive the pin forward unless the trigger is pulled completely through, the final movement before release of the hammer raising the safety device and freeing the firing pin. The pistol can be fired in either single or double-action modes, but there is no hammer-drop function on the safety catch and lowering the hammer on to the loaded chamber must be done manually.

Shortly after the introduction of the P-018, requests for something more easily concealed led to the development of the P-018 Compact. This is mechanically the same, but smaller in all dimensions (the barrel is 102mm, the overall length 198mm and the weight 950 grammes) and with a magazine holding 14 rounds.

A third model is the P-020, which is intended for competition shooting. It is chambered for the 7.65mm Parabellum round. It is generally the same as the P-018 but has a somewhat more luxurious standard of finish, with checkered walnut grips instead of plastic, and a micro-adjustable rear sight.

Unlike many of today's weapons, the Bernardelli maintains the tradition of building from steel forgings by machining. As a result they are strong and reliable weapons and are available in a variety of finishes from highly-polished blue to dull black Parkerised.

Browning BDA Auto Pistol

Manufacturer Armi Beretta SpA, I-25063, Gardone Val Trompia, Italy
Marketed by Browning Arms, Rt #1, Morgan, UT 84050, U. S. A.
Type Blowback double-action semi-automatic
Caliber .380/9mm Short
Barrel 3.8in (97mm)
Weight (empty) 23oz (652gm)
Magazine Capacity 13 rounds

This pistol resembles the Beretta Model 84 in most respects, and is actually made by Beretta in Italy, but there have been one or two modifications to bring it to the specification demanded by Browning. Another plus feature is that, in the U.S.A., it costs considerably less than an imported Model 84.

The BDA is a conventional blowback automatic pistol, perhaps unusual in having a larger magazine capacity than is common in American pistols. The principal difference between this and the Beretta 84 is the use of an enveloping slide and the addition of a slide-mounted safety and decocking lever which operates from both sides of the slide. Depressing this lever lowers the hammer from full- to half-cock position and locks it; once the safety is down the pistol cannot be cocked by thumbing the hammer back. Pulling the trigger allows the hammer to fall from the half-cock to the fired position, without touching the firing pin. Releasing the safety allows both thumb-cocking and double-action cock-and-fire action with a single pull on the trigger.

Sights consist of a fixed front sight and a non-adjustable rear sight which is held in a dovetail groove and can be laterally shifted for zeroing. Accuracy is satisfactory, the pistol grouping within a five-inch circle at 50 yards. Finish is excellent, with walnut grips inlaid with the Browning medallion.

Centrum Free Pistol

Manufacturer Centrum, Germany
Type Competition free pistol, single-shot
Caliber .22 Long RF
Barrel 10in (254mm)

Free pistols are principally a European avocation, being specialized single shot .22 weapons designed solely for national and international competition shooting. It is specifically intended for the UIT .22 free pistol contest in which the 10-ring of the target is two inches in diameter and the range is 50 meters. In short, it is the ultimate test of shooting ability, and the rules permit virtually any sort of pistol in order to evade any mechanical restriction and concentrate entirely on the shooter's skill. Hence the phrase 'free pistol,' which refers to the lack of restriction on style or type. In general these are hand-built and expensive weapons, vehicles for their owners' and designers' pet theories, but there are a few European gunsmithing firms who make 'stock' free pistols which can be the basis for individual modification.

One of the most recent is the Centrum made in Germany. It is a single shot weapon using a falling block breech operated by the trigger guard. The breech is opened and the cartridge loaded until it touches the extractor; the block is then closed and seats the cartridge firmly in the chamber. After firing the block is lowered, which ejects the empty case about one-tenth of an inch, after

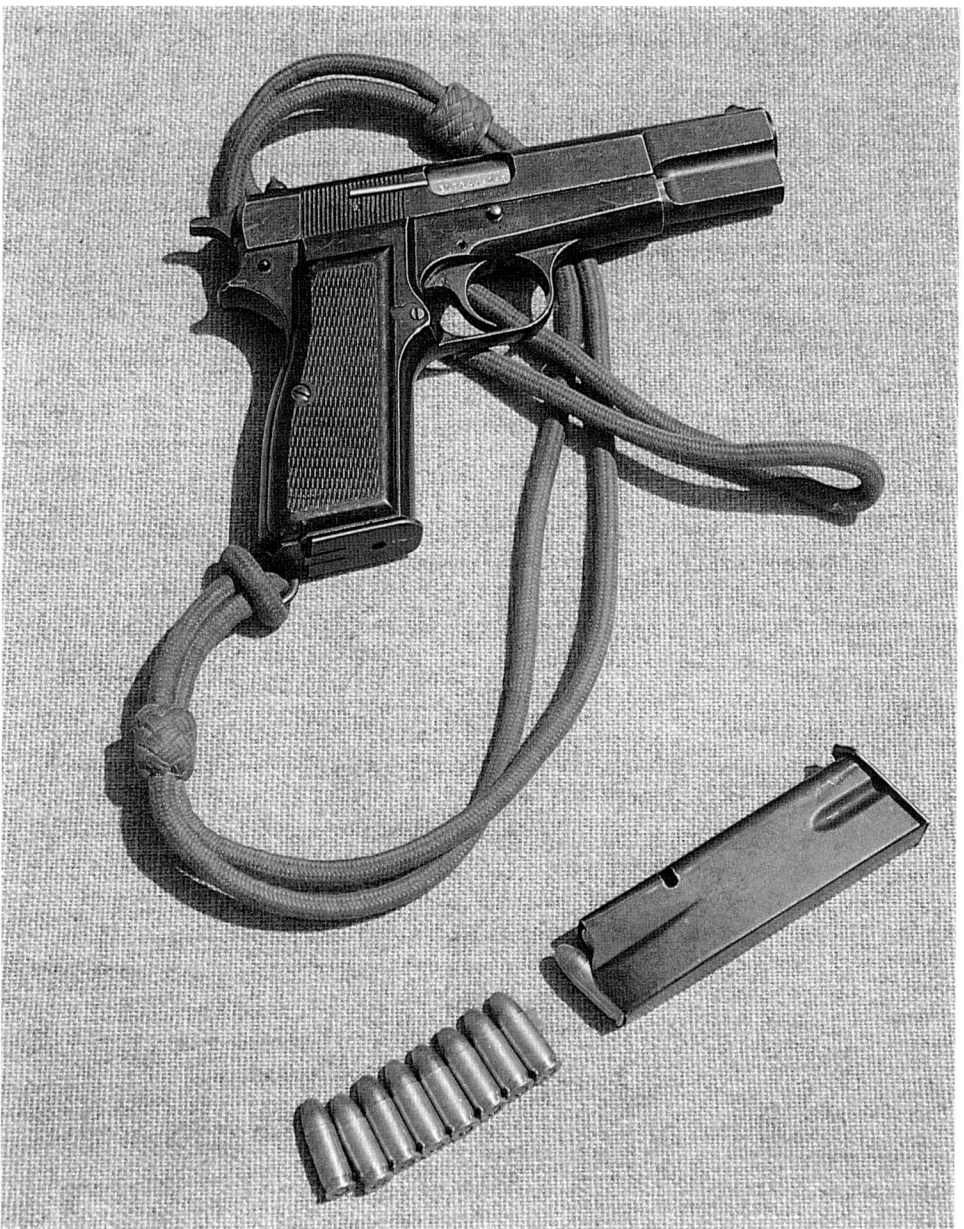

Above: The legendary 9mm Browning.

which a separate extractor, on the left of the chamber, allows the case to be pulled a further quarter of an inch from the chamber; it can be flicked out with the finger-nail. Rapid fire is, obviously, not a requirement in this type of contest.

The pistol has a set trigger which is set by a lever on the left side; the trigger itself can be adjusted for reach, travel, backlash and slack without having to dismantle anything. The foresight is mounted on a large ramp, and the blade is secured in place by a screw so that it can easily be changed. The rearsight is fitted on a dovetail extension over the grip; its location can be altered to suit the individual, and it is capable of adjustment for elevation and windage by click-stopped knobs.

The grip is anatomically shaped so that the barrel is low to the hand and thus there is practically no jump or recoil effect. There is also a wooden fore end, though this is for balance and appearance.

Practical firing shows that this weapon, which is a precision machine, needs to be fed with the best ammunition; it appears sensitive to the ammunition used and does not perform well with cheap cartridges. Each gun is supplied with a test target and a five-year guarantee, the target usually showing four or five shots in the 10-ring. These pistols are capable of doing whatever the shooter is capable of.

CHARTER ARMS PATHFINDER REVOLVER

Left: The Charter Arms .44 Target Bulldog.

Charter Arms 'Pathfinder' Revolver

Manufacturer Charter Arms Corp,. 430 Sniffens Lane, Stratford, CT 06497, U.S.A.
Type Six-shot, solid-frame, double-action revolver.
Caliber .22 Long Rifle RF, or .22 Winchester Magnum RF.
Barrel 6in (152mm)
Weight 22.5oz (638gm)

This is an enlarged version of the .22 Pathfinder introduced in 1972; the earlier weapon had a 3-inch barrel and proved popular as a pack gun. Now with the adoption of a 6-in barrel the gun becomes even more versatile.

The pistol uses a steel solid frame and an attractive point is that the walnut grips are of a good size to allow a firm grip, a feature frequently overlooked in this caliber. The swing-out cylinder is released by a catch on the left side of the frame or by pulling the ejector rod forward. The six chambers are individually counterbored and the ejector rod is long enough to push the empty cases well clear of the cylinder face. The foresight is a broad blade and the rear a wide slot; the rear sight is fully adjustable for elevation and windage, though demanding a small screwdriver to make the adjustment. The double-action trigger pull is light and smooth, while the single-action release is sharp, requiring 3-4lbs pressure to let off. Firing is by a floating firing pin and transfer bar system, by means of which the hammer cannot possibly contact the firing pin unless the trigger has been correctly pulled.

The pistol is available in either .22LR or .22WMRF chambering, though the cylinders are not interchangeable. The .22RF version will, of course, shoot .22 Long and .22 Short equally well. Either chambering gives perfectly good accuracy: 1½-inch groups at 25 yards.

Charter Arms .44 Target Bulldog

Manufacturer Charter Arms Inc., Stratford, CT06497, U.S. A.
Type Five-shot, solid frame, double-action
Caliber .44 Special
Barrel 4in (102mm)
Weight 20oz (567gm)

Charter Arms started their career by producing robust no-frills revolvers for lawmen and others, and one of their notable innovations was the .44 Bulldog, a short-barreled but powerful pistol which revived the .44 Special cartridge. This is a highly serviceable round which has tended to be overlooked in recent years, being edged out by the .44 Magnum, and it had a good reputation for accuracy. In response to various enquiries and requests, Charter have now redesigned the Bulldog to take maximum advantage of the cartridge's capabilities.

The Target Bulldog differs from the original Bulldog in having a one-inch longer barrel, complete with shroud for the ejector rod, and in having a fully adjustable rear sight. It is also slightly heavier, and the net result of the extra length and weight is a revolver which is rather more controllable than the original and which is sufficiently accurate to shoot two-inch groups at 25 yards all day. Lengthening the barrel has improved the velocity and consistency and has also cut down slightly on the muzzle blast, making the pistol more comfortable to shoot.

For those who consider the .44 Special a little too much, the Target Bulldog is also available in .357 Magnum caliber.

Chinese Type 64 Silenced

Manufacturer Chinese State Arsenals
Type Selective semi-automatic or single shot, blowback, with integral silencer
Caliber 7.65mm (.32, special chambering)
Barrel 4.88in (124mm)
Weight 44.8oz (1270gm)
Magazine Capacity 8 rounds

This remarkable weapon appears to have only one function in life, that of assassination. It is chambered for a special 7.65 × 17mm rimless cartridge with a low-velocity loading; it cannot be used with commercial .32 ACP semi-rimmed ammunition.

The Type 64 can be used either as a manually-loaded single shot pistol or as a blowback semi-automatic. For the utmost silence a selector bar in the upper part of the slide is pushed to the left and this rotates the bolt, locking it into lugs in the breech. When the pistol is fired the breech remains closed and can be opened only by pushing the selector across and manually retracting the slide. If the selector is left in its right-hand position, then the bolt does not rotate, nor does it lock, and when the pistol is fired the slide blows back in the conventional manner.

Silence is achieved partly by the special ammunition, which ensures subsonic velocity of the bullet, and partly by the built-in silencer. The casing which surrounds the barrel extends in front of the muzzle; the gases escaping from the muzzle behind the bullet are expanded into a wire-mesh cylinder surrounded by an expanded metal sleeve, while the bullet passes through a number of rubber discs which prevent the following gas escaping to the outside. When the breech is locked, the pistol is extremely quiet; with the breech unlocked the noise is somewhat greater due to the clatter of the slide moving backwards, but the report is still silenced.

Colt Double Eagle

Manufacturer Colt's Manufacturing Co. Inc., Hartford, CT.
Type Recoil operated semi-automatic, double-action
Caliber .45 ACP, 10mm Auto, .40 S&W, 9mm Parabellum or .38 Super
Barrel 5.0in (127mm)
Weight 39oz (1105gm)
Magazine Capacity 8-round box magazine (9in .38 Super and 9mm calibers)

The Double Eagle is the logical development of the well-known Government Model M1911A1 insofar as it uses the same basic mechanism, but allies it to a double-action trigger mechanism and a choice of modern calibers.

The pistol uses a forged stainless steel receiver and slide, and the traditional Browning method of locking the barrel by means of a link pivoting on the slide locking pin axis. As the slide and barrel recoil, so the link draws the rear end of the barrel down in an arc, withdrawing the lugs on top of the barrel from recesses in the slide top. By the time this withdrawal is complete, the bullet has left the muzzle and the chamber pressure is well within safe limits; the barrel stops and the slide continues to the rear to eject the spent case and then return to load a fresh cartridge.

This, of course, leaves the hammer cocked ready to fire the next shot in single-action mode. But once the pistol is loaded, pressure on a decocking lever beneath the left butt grip allows the hammer to be lowered safely on to the loaded chamber. From that position, simply pulling through on the trigger in double-action mode will raise the hammer to full cock and then release it to fire.

The Double Eagle originally appeared in .45 ACP and 10mm Auto calibers, with a 5-inch barrel. In 1991 these were augmented by 9mm and .38 Super calibers with the same barrel length, and then by new models: the Double Eagle Combat Commander was a .45 ACP pistol with 4.25-inch (108mm) barrel and a weight of 36 ounces (1020 grams); the Double Eagle Officer's ACP was in .45 or .40 S&W chambering with a 3.5-inch (89mm) barrel, weighing 35 ounces (992 grams); and the Double Eagle Officer's Lightweight was in .45 ACP chambering with 3.5-inch barrel and a blued finish, weighing only 25 ounces (708 grams).

All models have a high-profile three-dot sighting system, and an adjustable rearsight may be fitted. Finish is matt stainless steel or, in the case of the Officer's Lightweight, polished blue, while the grips are of impact-resistant synthetic Xenoy material.

Colt 2000

Manufacturer Colt's Manufacturing Co. Inc., Hartford, CT.
Type Locked breech, semi-automatic, self-cocking
Caliber 9mm Parabellum
Barrel 4.49in (114mm)
Weight 29oz (822gm)
Magazine Capacity 15 rounds

Introduced in January 1991, this pistol was originally designed by C. Reed Knight and Eugene Stoner and then adopted by Colt. It is probably the only modern pistol to use barrel rotation to lock and unlock the breech, a system used by comparatively few designs during this century.

The pistol, as originally produced, had a steel slide and polymer frame, though latterly the frame has also been made of steel. The barrel fits

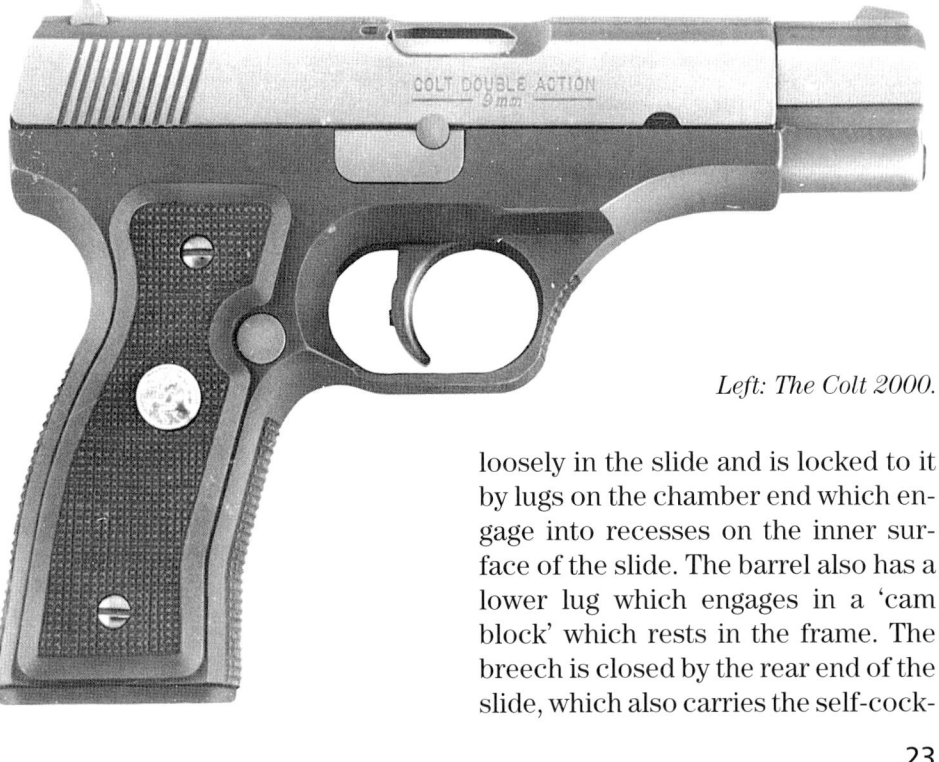

Left: The Colt 2000.

loosely in the slide and is locked to it by lugs on the chamber end which engage into recesses on the inner surface of the slide. The barrel also has a lower lug which engages in a 'cam block' which rests in the frame. The breech is closed by the rear end of the slide, which also carries the self-cocking firing pin mechanism. There is no manual safety catch, and the only external control is the slide stop release; it was the declared intention of the designers to produce an automatic pistol which was as simple and straight-forward to use as a double-action revolver.

Loading is done in the usual manner, by inserting a magazine in the butt and then pulling back and releasing the slide. Thereafter, firing is simply a matter of pulling the trigger; this presses back the striker and then releases it to fly forward and fire the cartridge. Barrel and slide then recoil, locked together, but as they move, so the bottom lug on the barrel is drawn along a curved path in the cam block, turning the barrel through an angle of about 30 degrees so as to free the upper lugs from their engagement with the slide. Once these are free the barrel stops, having come to the end of the cam path, and the slide, continues rearwards to extract the empty case, eject it, and then return under the pressure of its return spring. The next cartridge is loaded and the pistol is again already to fire. The striker is not cocked but is engaged with the trigger set ready for the next shot.

One of the advantages of this design is that a proportion of the recoil force is passed, via the bottom lug, to the cam block and then spread over a much greater area of the frame than is usually the case. This produces a much smaller amount of 'felt recoil' for the firer, and consequently the pistol is more easily brought back to the aim after a shot.

Czech CZ-75 Auto Pistol

Manufacturer Ceskoslovenska Zbrojovka a.s., Uhersky Brod, Czechoslovakia
Type Locked breech, double-action semi-automatic
Caliber 9mm Parabellum
Barrel 4.72in (120mm)
Weight (empty) 34.5oz (980gm)
Magazine Capacity 15 rounds

The CZ-75 is a military-style pistol produced for commercial sale throughout the world. It uses the familiar Browning action of locked breech in which the barrel has lugs above the chamber which engage in recesses in the slide; a shaped cam in a lump beneath the chamber moves across the slide stop pin during recoil, thus pulling the barrel down and withdrawing the lugs from the recesses, so freeing the slide to move to the rear and complete the extraction and reloading cycle. The pistol differs slightly from the usual Browning design by having a deep-waisted frame and the slide guide rails on the inside of this section, so that the shallow rear portion of the slide moves within the frame.

The external hammer is cocked during the recoil stroke in the usual manner, but there is a double-action lock which permits firing the first round from a hammer-down condition. The safety is on the frame and merely locks trigger and hammer; there is no hammer-drop facility. The sights are fixed military pattern, and the foresight is rather small, making deliberate shooting rather difficult. Nevertheless, the CZ-75 is accurate and consistent, and with adjustable sights fitted would make a reasonable competition weapon. The fit and finish are good and the double-action trigger movement is particularly effective. The pistol will accept practically any military or commercial ammunition without malfunction.

Dan Wesson Pistol-Pac

Manufacturer Dan Wesson Arms, Monson, MA 01057, U.S.A.
Type Six-shot, solid frame, double-action
Caliber .357 Magnum
Barrel 2, 4, 6 and 8in (See text) (51, 102, 152 and 203mm)
Weight 36oz (1020gm) (4in barrel)

Dan Wesson revolvers are not new, but the Pistol-Pac concept is so different that it deserves a place in any listing.

The Dan Wesson Company began in 1968 and rapidly made a name for its unique revolvers. The unusual feature was that the barrels were removeable and could be changed for others of different length, so that, for example, one could have an 8-inch barrel for target shooting and a 2-inch barrel for home defense, changing them around as required. The basic action is a solid framed double-action revolver; the barrel screws into the front of the frame in conventional manner, but it is then concealed by a jacket, carrying foresight and ejector rod shroud, which slips over the barrel and is then secured by a retaining nut screwed on to the muzzle of the barrel so as to hold the jacket firmly in place and place the barrel under tension. The jacket is automatically aligned with the foresight upright, and slight placement remains constant when barrels

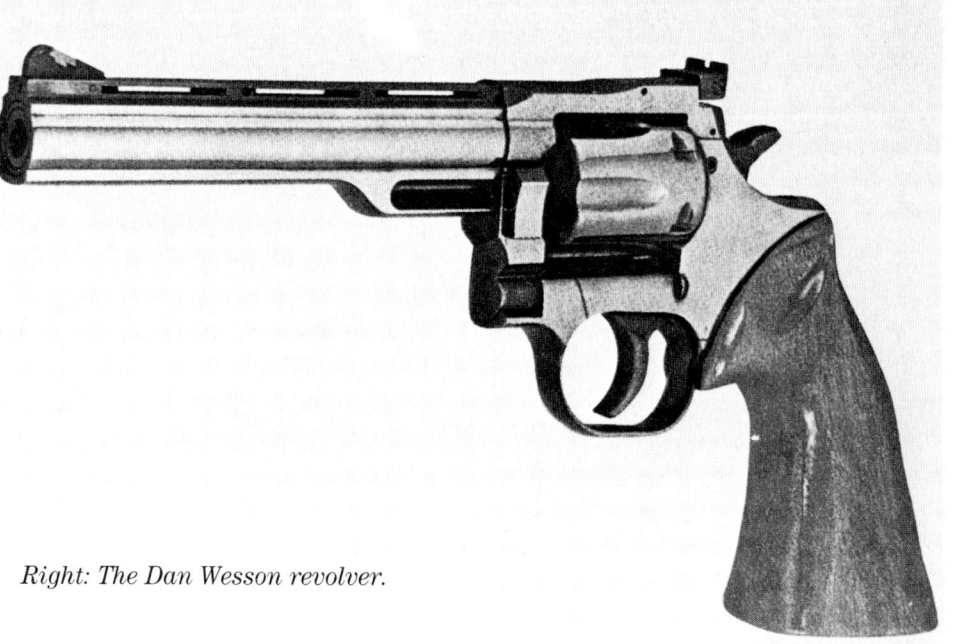

Right: The Dan Wesson revolver.

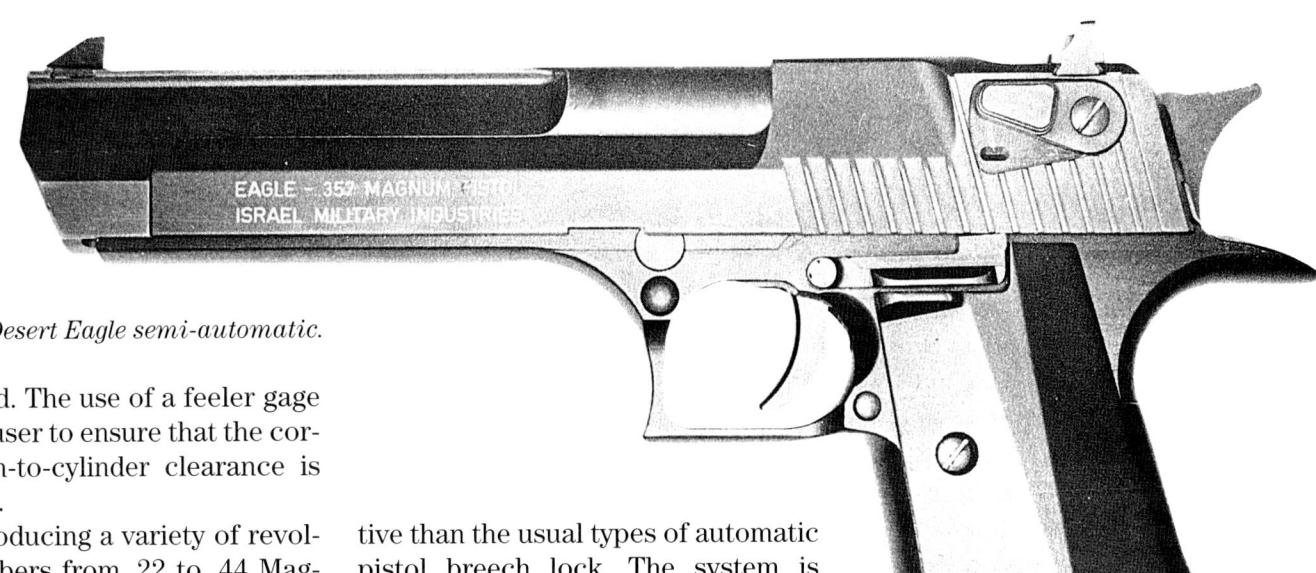

Right: The Desert Eagle semi-automatic.

are changed. The use of a feeler gage allows the user to ensure that the correct breech-to-cylinder clearance is maintained.

While producing a variety of revolvers in calibers from .22 to .44 Magnum, the Wesson system is best seen in their unique Pistol-Pac, a package in which the basic revolver is supplied complete with four barrels, two sets of grips (service and target) plus a block of wood for carving a third set to your own specification, and a stripping tool for removing the jacket and barrel. All this is neatly packed into a hand case lined with sponge rubber. The barrels provided are 2, 4, 6 and 8 inches in length. In .357 Magnum chambering the Model 15-2 is standard and it is supplemented by the 15-2 VH which has heavier barrels and jackets with ventilated ribs.

Dan Wesson revolvers have a high reputation for accuracy and reliability. The Pistol-Pac idea allows the shooter to have the best of several choices at his fingertips at all times.

Desert Eagle

Manufacturer Ta'as Israel Industries, Ramat Hasharon, Israel
Type Gas-operated semi-automatic
Caliber .357 Magnum, .44 Magnum, .41 Action Express or .50 Action Express
Barrel 6.0in (152mm) (A 14-in (355mm) barrel is also available)
Weight 3.88lb (1.76kg) (steel frame)
Magazine Capacity 9 rounds

The Desert Eagle is unusual in being a gas-operated pistol using a rotating bolt breech mechanism, a system more usually expected in rifles than pistols. This is due to the high power of the cartridges selected for use, which demand something more positive than the usual types of automatic pistol breech lock. The system is actually descended from a Swedish design some 50 years old, but this is its first practical application.

The barrel is fixed to the frame and has a gas vent in front of the chamber; this connects with a drilling in the frame which runs forward to a point just beneath the muzzle, then turns down to enter a gas cylinder. Inside this cylinder is a short-stroke piston. The slide has a solid rear section containing the bolt, and two long arms which stretch forward under the barrel.

On firing, gas passes from the barrel, through the drilling, into the gas cylinder and drives the piston backwards. It strikes the front end of the slide and imparts momentum to it, driving it backwards against a spring. As the slide moves, so it first rotates the bolt by means of a cam, unlocking the bolt from the barrel, and then withdrawing the bolt and extracting the spent case. The spring then drives the slide forward, collecting a fresh round and driving it into the chamber, and the final movement of the slide rotates the bolt to lock it to the barrel. The rearward movement also cocks the external hammer.

The pistol was designed to fire the .357 Magnum revolver cartridge, a rimmed round and one not usually found in automatic pistols. This was followed by a larger version to fire the .44 Magnum cartridge, another rimmed round, and a modified version of the original chambered for the .41 Action Express cartridge. In 1992 the ultimate appears to have been reached with a version chambered for the .50 Action Express round, an extremely potent cartridge. It might be added that the original intention for this weapon was long range silhouette shooting, but it has also found favor as a hunting gun. For this purpose the top of the barrel is grooved to accept telescope mounts; the standard sights are fixed, but an adjustable rear sight may be had as an option.

FN BDA9

Manufacturer FN Herstal SA, Liège, Belgium
Type Recoil-operated semi-automatic, double-action
Caliber 9mm Parabellum
Barrel 4.65 inches (118mm)
Weight 32oz (915gm) with empty magazine
Magazine Capacity 14 rounds

The Browning High-Power, or Model 35, became one of the most widely used military pistols in history, being adopted by over 55 armies, and it remains in production to this day, for demand has far from ended. But Fabrique Nationale moved with the times, and responding to more modern specifications they have developed the design into the 'BDA9' (for Browning Double Action 9mm) pistol.

FN 140DA AUTO PISTOL

FN140DA Auto Pistol

Manufacturer Fabrique Nationale d'Armes de Guerre, Herstal, Belgium
Type Blowback, double-action, semi-automatic
Caliber .380 Auto/9mm Short; .32 ACP/7.65mm
Barrel 3.81in (97mm)
Weight 22.5oz (640gm)
Magazine Capacity 13 rounds (9mm/.380) 12 rounds (7.65mm/.32)

The FN 140DA is intended as a general purpose defense weapon or for use by police and security forces. It uses a steel slide and alloy frame to keep the weight low and has a large magazine capacity, of the sort more commonly found in major-caliber military weapons. An impressive and popular weapon, it is in widespread use, having been adopted by the Belgian and several other European police forces.

The pistol is a simple fixed-barrel blowback in general form, though of extremely high-grade workmanship and reliability. It has a double-action lock and the trigger-guard is particularly large, permitting use in gloved hands. There is a complex safety system; the safety catch is mounted on the slide and has operating levers on both sides. On depressing the catch the firing pin is retracted into a safety system which locks the firing pin except during the final few degrees of trigger movement just before the hammer is released.

As with other pistols of this type, loading is done by inserting a magazine and pulling back and releasing the slide to chamber a round. This leaves the hammer cocked and the pistol can be fired in single-action mode; alternatively the de-cocking lever allows the hammer to be safely lowered on to the loaded chamber. From this position it is only necessary to pull through on the trigger to cock and release the hammer; there is no safety device to be manipulated. After the first shot, subsequent shots are in single-action mode until the hammer is again de-cocked.

The general appearance shows a definite 'family resemblance' to the older model, and the mechanism is broadly the same, using the FN-designed shaped cam beneath the chamber which, acting against the slide stop pin, causes the rear end of the barrel to be drawn down to disconnect from the slide during recoil. It is interesting to see that FN still adhere to the use of locking lugs machined in the upper surface of the barrel and mating in recesses in the slide, rather than simply forging a square block around the chamber and locking this into the ejection aperture as do many other modern designs. The fitting of the two lugs to their recesses is a precision task, but FN obviously think it worth the effort.

Above and right: The FN BDA9 pistol.

The principal change is the adoption of a double-action trigger mechanism and a de-cocking lever in place of the safety catch; this de-cocking lever is duplicated on both sides of the frame, so that the pistol can be used equally easily in the right or left hand. The magazine release is fitted for right-handed use, but can be easily removed and replaced on the right side of the butt for left-handed users. There is also an automatic firing pin

THE GLOCK PISTOL

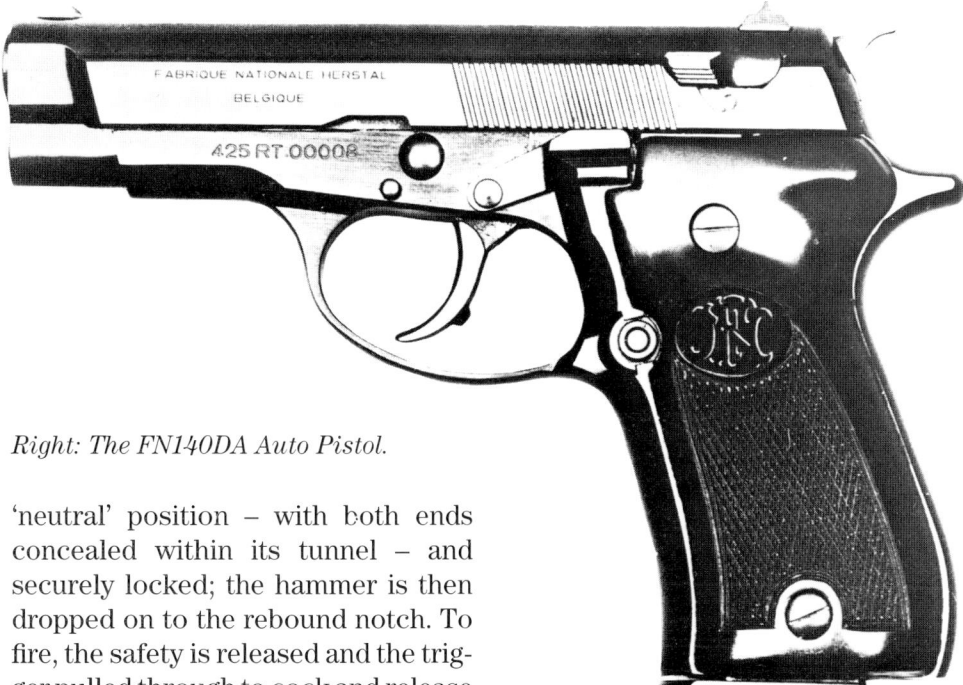

Right: The FN140DA Auto Pistol.

'neutral' position – with both ends concealed within its tunnel – and securely locked; the hammer is then dropped on to the rebound notch. To fire, the safety is released and the trigger pulled through to cock and release the hammer.

Any resemblance between this and the Beretta 84 is far from coincidental, since this is basically the Beretta 84 with some slight changes, notably the use of an all-enveloping slide instead of the open-topped slide which is virtually a Beretta trademark. There are also strong similarities between this and the Browning BDA sold in the U.S.A.

The Glock Pistol

Manufacturer Glock GmbH, Deutsch-Wagram, Austria
Type Recoil-operated semi-automatic, self-cocking
Caliber 9mm Parabellum, 10mm Auto, .40 S&W, .45 ACP
Barrel 4.49 inches (114mm)
Weight 23.8oz (676gm) with empty magazine
Magazine Capacity 17 rounds (19 rounds optional)
(Data refers to Model 17)

In 1980 the Austrian Army needed a new pistol, and for reasons connected with its rather complicated neutrality treaties, found importing one almost impossible. An Austrian manufacturer was therefore necessary, and the Glock company, which had previously been concerned with spades and knives, produced this modern design and obtained the contract. In 1984 the Glock pistol passed all NATO trials and was selected by the Norwegian Army. Now the pistol is in service with armies and police forces worldwide.

The Glock pistol is a product of modern technology, incorporating many innovative design features which provide ease and safety of operation, reliability, simplicity and light weight. The most prominent feature is the use of high-resistant polymer material for the frame; this led to scare stories when the pistol was first introduced, suggesting that it could be smuggled past airport security devices. But steel is still used for the stressed components, and the pistol can be easily detected by any airport security device.

The firing mechanism is also unique to the Glock. There are no safety or decocking levers; the safety devices are internal and consist of a trigger safety lever protruding from the trigger itself; a firing pin safety which prevents forward movement of the pin except when the trigger is pulled, and a drop safety catch which prevents accidental discharge should the pistol be dropped. As the trigger is pulled, these devices disengage in succession and the striker is cocked and released to fire the round. As soon as the shot has been fired the safety devices all revert to their safe condition and remain there until the trigger is pulled for the next shot.

The breech locking system is the familiar Browning dropping barrel, but using a shaped cam beneath the chamber to lower the rear of the barrel and using a squared block formed around the chamber to lock into the ejection opening in the slide instead of the original lugs locking into recesses machined into the slide. The system adopted by Glock is easier to manufacture than the multiple-lug system and gives a very strong lock-up to the breech.

The original Glock design is the

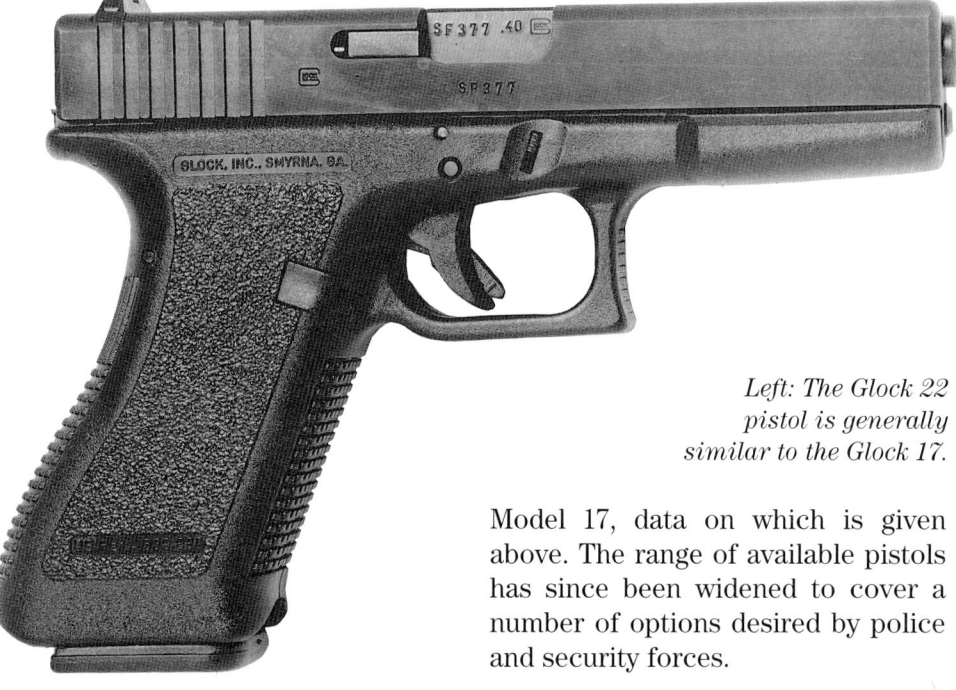

Left: The Glock 22 pistol is generally similar to the Glock 17.

Model 17, data on which is given above. The range of available pistols has since been widened to cover a number of options desired by police and security forces.

Hammerli 215 Target Auto Pistol

Above: The Hammerli target pistol.

Manufacturer Hammerli SA, Lenzberg, Switzerland
Type Blowback semi-automatic target
Caliber .22 Long Rifle RF
Barrel Variable
Weight Variable
Magazine Capacity 8 rounds

The Hammerli company have been in the target pistol business for many years and produce some of the world's finest competition weapons. Unfortunately, due to the strength of the Swiss franc they tend to be very expensive outside Switzerland, which does nothing for Hammerli's sales. As a result they decided to produce a weapon which, while remaining high quality, would be competitive in price.

The Model 215 resembles the older Model 208 in being a chunky semi-automatic using a heavy fixed barrel and a short recoiling slide moving in short frame rails. The trigger guard is a separate component and acts as a slide latch. The rear sight is held on a saddle unit which locks to the outside of the frame and straddles the recoiling slide. Since this would prevent gripping the slide in the normal way, it is made with extended sides which stretch forward, alongside the barrel, and have finger grips for cocking and unloading. The sight saddle unit has to be removed to strip the pistol, but the construction is such that it automatically returns to the pre-set zero when replaced. The pistol is hammer fired. The grips are of hard wood, anatomically shaped and have an adjustable palm rest.

The front sight blade can be easily changed, and blades of various widths are available; the rear sight can also be changed for different widths of slot and is fully adjustable. The trigger pull is smooth, with a consistent pull-off point. A balance weight is fitted beneath the muzzle; it can be adjusted or changed by use of an Allen key.

On the range this pistol performs as Hammerli products are expected to perform, firing with absolute accuracy and reliability. The only concession to price has been in the external finish which is not quite so luxurious as in previous products, but the performance is in no way diminished.

Heckler & Koch Model P7 (PSP)

Manufacturer Heckler & Koch GmbH, D-7238 Oberndorf/Neckar, Germany
Type Delayed blowback, semi-automatic
Caliber 9mm Parabellum
Barrel 4.13in (105mm)
Weight (empty) 27.7oz (785gm)
Magazine Capacity 8 rounds

This unusual pistol can be used rapidly, with neither a safety catch nor a cocking hammer delaying matters, yet it is totally safe while being carried loaded.

The P7 (originally called the PSP for 'Polizei Selbstlader Pistole') is a pocket or holster weapon, relatively small, but firing a powerful cartridge. For this reason it demands some form of breech locking, and this is done by gas pressure. The slide has the usual recoil spring beneath it, with a guide rod inside the spring. But this guide rod is carefully machined and as the slide recoils it moves inside a close-fitting cylinder lying in the frame above the trigger. A port between this cylinder and the barrel allows high-pressure gas to flow in and fill the

Below: The Heckler & Koch 9mm Model P7.

Right: The Heckler & Koch P9S semi-automatic.

cylinder when the pistol is fired; this pressure resists the rearward movement of the recoil spring guide rod, so delaying the rearward movement of the slide. Once the bullet has left the barrel and the gas pressure drops, the rod can move back, forcing the gas out of the cylinder and into the barrel and thence out to atmosphere. Thereafter the action is that of any other blowback automatic pistol.

In order to carry the weapon safely in a loaded condition, the firing pin is not cocked during the recoil stroke as is usual; instead it is controlled by a grip forming the front edge of the butt. When the firer grasps the butt and squeezes this grip, the firing pin is cocked; there is no need for him to keep squeezing, since the grip engages in the cocked position. Once he releases his grip, however, the pistol is de-cocked. It can thus be carried safely with a round in the chamber and brought into action with no delay; if, once uncocked, the shooter drops it, it is uncocked before it hits the floor.

The sights are fixed, but the foresight can be changed and the rear sight moved sideways to zero the weapon. Both sights have inlaid white dots to assist in aligning in poor visibility and it is possible to have 'Betalight' luminous markers fitted for night firing. Disassembly of this distinctive pistol is easy, though it requires the use of a special stripping tool.

Heckler & Koch P9S Auto Pistol

Manufacturer Heckler & Koch GmbH, D-7238 Oberndorf/Neckar, Germany
Type Locked breech double-action semi-automatic
Caliber 9mm Parabellum
Barrel 4in (102mm)
Weight (empty) 30.8oz (875gm)
Magazine Capacity 9 rounds

The Heckler & Koch P9S is a military and police pistol using an unusual breech locking system derived from the company's highly successful G3 rifle. The P9S has been adopted by German armed forces and police forces and has been widely sold throughout the world. Some have been manufactured in 7.65mm Parabellum chambering and also in .45 ACP chambering for export to the U.S.A., but the 9mm Parabellum version is by far the most common.

The roller locking system for the breech relies on a two-part breech block which is held close by two small rollers which engage in recesses in the barrel extension. The rollers are carried on the forward, lightweight, portion of the block which is actually part of the slide. When the pistol is fired, the light portion, impelled by the pressure on the cartridge case, attempts to move backwards, but the inertia of the slide keeps the rollers forced outwards and the block section locked to the barrel. As the inward pressure on the rollers, due to the pressure on the forward section of the block, gradually overcomes the inertia of the slide, so the bullet speeds up the barrel and leaves, allowing chamber pressure to drop to safe levels before the rollers move in and the slide and breech block assembly is free to move.

The pistol has an internal hammer, with a protruding indicator pin at the rear of the frame which extends when the hammer is cocked. There is a thumb-operated hammer release and re-cocking lever on the left side, allowing the hammer to be lowered under control on to a loaded chamber, or rapidly cocked from the 'down' position. The barrel has a 'polygonal bore' in which the four grooves (6in .45 ACP caliber) are merged into the rest of the bore so that the final result resembles a flattened circle. The manufacturers claim that this reduces friction and bullet deformation and promotes a somewhat higher velocity.

Two variant models exist: the P9, now discontinued, was the same pistol but with conventional single-action lock; the P9S 'Sport' Competition Model has a longer barrel with balance weight, adjustable trigger stop, fine-adjustment rear sight and an anatomical wooden grip. The barrel is 5.5in (140mm) long, leading to a slight increase in muzzle velocity; with barrel counterweight fitted and a full magazine it weighs 45.2oz (1290gm).

Jericho

Manufacturer Ta'as Israel Industries, Ramat Hasharon, Israel
Type Recoil-operated, semi-automatic, double-action
Caliber 9mm Parabellum or .41 Action Express
Barrel 4.40in (112mm)
Weight 39oz (1103gm)
Magazine Capacity 16 rounds (9mm) or 11 rounds (.41AE)

The Jericho's family resemblance to the Desert Eagle is entirely cosmetic; under the skin the operation is entirely different. The Jericho is a conventional recoil-operated pistol using the Browning tilting barrel controlled by a cam beneath the chamber. Indeed, much of it is bought from Tanfoglio of Italy, Ta'as Israel Industries being responsible for clothing the barrel and trigger mechanism in a body designed to resemble the Desert Eagle. One result of this cosmetic change is that the slide is designed to ride inside the frame, instead of the more usual method of riding outside the frame. Though somewhat more difficult and expensive to make, this system gives the slide better support and is generally agreed to provide better inherent accuracy.

There is a slide-mounted safety catch which also functions as a hammer de-cocking lever, and this is duplicated on both sides of the slide for the benefit of left-handed users. A conversion kit is available, to alter the pistol from 9mm to .41 calibers or vice versa; the components (barrel, return spring and magazine) are supplied with the pistol and are color-coded so that it is difficult to assemble the pistol wrongly.

Right: A stripped-down Jericho semi-automatic.

Korth .357 Magnum

Manufacturer Willi Korth Sportwaffen-Herst, D-2418 Ratzeburg, Germany
Type Six-shot, double-action, solid-frame
Caliber .357 Magnum
Barrel 3in (76mm); 6in (152mm)
Weight 35oz (992gm) with 3in barrel

Above and left: Exterior and interior views of the Korth .357 Magnum.

The firm of Willi Korth is little known outside Germany; it is a subsidiary of the Dynamit-Nobel group and has produced limited numbers of sporting weapons in the past. It is now exporting a revolver which, at well over $1000, must qualify as the most expensive handgun in existence.

The Korth .357 Magnum is a conventional solid frame pistol with swing-out cylinder with some likeness to the Colt Python. Under the skin, however, there are some interesting differences. The barrel, for example, is a separate component shrouded within a steel jacket which also forms the extractor rod shroud. The barrel screws into the frame, the jacket passes over it, and the whole assembly is then secured by a barrel nut on the muzzle.

The cylinder crane is released by pushing a serrated catch on the right side of the hammer, which presses forward the ejector rod and allows the crane to move. Once open, the cylinder can be slipped from the crane by depressing a spring latch. The clearance between the face of the cylinder and the rear of the barrel is minimal, so that gas leak is negligible, but this does mean the interface must be cleaned regularly.

The firing pin is a separate component, mounted in the frame, and there is a safety system linked to the trigger which prevents the pin being struck by the hammer unless the trigger is pulled. The trigger action is smooth, if a trifle heavy at double-action, but the let-off point is clean and crisp. The trigger is adjustable for travel.

The foresight is a conventional ramp blade, while the rear sight is a notch, adjustable for windage and elevation. The grip fills the hand well and gives good control of the pistol when firing. Finish is excellent, the metal being well blued and the grips being high-grade walnut, while hammer, trigger and barrel lock nut are chromium-plated.

In use the Korth is pleasant to shoot and as accurate as might be expected, capable of delivering tight groups in single-action mode, slightly larger in double-action. So far as performance goes, I would say that it is on a par with other high-quality revolvers; the finish, inside and out is excellent, the design good; but I cannot honestly see where the high price is justified in any concrete manner. But then again, one could perhaps make the same sort of observation about some breeds of cameras and automobiles which carry a high price tag but still sell all they can make.

Left: The Llama 'Comanche' revolver.

Llama 'Comanche' Revolver

Manufacturer Gabilondo y Cia, Vitoria, Spain
Type Six-shot, solid frame, double-action
Caliber .357 Magnum
Barrel 4in (102mm) or 6in (152mm)
Weight 31oz (880gm)

The Gabilondo company began business in 1904 making cheap pocket revolvers; during World War One it moved to cheap automatic pistols, and then in the early 1930s began making a line of good quality autos under the 'Llama' trade name. Revolvers were added after World War Two, using the Llama name for the best models and the name 'Ruby' for the cheaper ones.

The 'Comanche' has been on sale for some time, but deserves mention as the top pistol in the line-up. It is a conventional solid frame double-action revolver bearing more than a passing resemblance to the Smith & Wesson pattern. The finish is excellent, a smooth and lustrous blue with well-checkered walnut grips of good hand-filling shape. Both single- and double-action trigger pulls are smooth, with crisp let-off. There is a ramp front sight with a square-notch rear sight which is adjustable for both elevation and windage.

The interior of the pistol is to the same standard as the exterior, and the double-action trigger is smooth and not of excessive tension, while the single-action let-off is crisp and consistent. Accuracy is good, and in practical use will group as closely as the skill of the owner allows.

Right: The Manurhin MR73 revolver.

Manurhin Model MR73 Revolver

Manufacturer Giat Industries, F-78034, Versailles-Satory, France
Type 6-shot solid-frame double-action revolver
Caliber .357 Magnum or 9mm Parabellum
Barrel 2.5in (63.5mm); 3in (76.2mm); 4in (102mm); 5.25in (134mm); 6in (152mm) and 8in (203mm)
Weight (empty) 31.4oz (890gm) (3in barrel)

This is a compact revolver basically intended for police use, though the longer-barreled versions can also be bought in competition form. They are currently used by French police and security agencies and are commercially sold.

The MR73 is a conventional solid-frame revolver with swing-out cylinder. In 'combat' form (ie with 2.5, 3 or 4in barrels) it has the usual fixed blade and notch sights. In competition form (ie with 4, 5.25, 6 and 8in barrels) an adjustable rear sight is provided. The cylinder is removeable and can be replaced by a special cylinder which chambers the 9mm Parabellum rimless cartridge; in this case the cartridges must be loaded with a special spring clip in order to position them correctly and also to ensure that the empty cases are ejected properly. The standard cylinder is designed for use with rimmed .357 Magnum or .38 Special cartridges.

The lockwork is fairly conventional and there is a safety bar which prevents the firing pin striking a cartridge unless the trigger is pulled. The linkage between trigger and hammer spring, via the rebound slide, is engineered so that the load felt by the trigger finger remains almost constant throughout the double-action pull.

Merrill Single Shot Pistol

Manufacturer Merrill Co., Fullerton, CA 92631, U.S.A.
Type Single shot
Caliber Various
Barrel 9in (228mm) or 12in (305mm)
Weight ca. 68oz (1920gm)

Single shot pistols are less common today than in years gone by, when 'saloon' and 'parlor' pistols firing low-power ammunition were a popular source of amusement. Today the single shot survives for two principle purposes; specialized target shooting and hunting, and the Merrill will perform either of these very well indeed.

The Merrill uses a stainless steel frame and standing breech, to which is hinged the barrel, fixed so that it drops down to expose the chamber for loading. As the barrel is opened, so it automatically cocks the striker, and as it is closed so an automatic safety comes into play, locking the trigger and firing pin. This safety can only be released by pressing the safety lever at the top of the left hand grip plate with the thumb. To cater for left-handed shooters, a left-handed model is available which has the safety on the other side.

The barrel unit can be in carbon or stainless steel, and is easily interchanged since the hinge-bolt is an Allen-type socket screw. Barrels in over a dozen calibers, from .22RF upwards, can be obtained, and they can be in either smooth 'bull' contour or with ventilated ribs. Two standard lengths are used, nine or 12 inches.

The front sight is a blade, the rear a Patridge-type notch, fully adjustable. The sight normally provided is of Micro manufacture, but other makes can be supplied to order. Trigger pull is adjustable by a set-screw at the rear of the frame.

The accuracy of the Merrill is beyond reproach; in virtually any caliber it should be possible to make one-inch groups at 25 yards and in the larger calibers this makes an excellent hunting or silhouette-shooting weapon.

The Resolver

Manufacturer SITES SpA, Turin, Italy
Type Blowback or short recoil (see below)
Caliber .380 Auto, 9mm Parabellum or .40 S&W
Barrel 5.9-6.3in (150-160mm)
Weight 19-23oz (550-650gm)
Magazine Capacity 8 or 9 rounds

Some people have to carry pistols for self-protection all day but are usually given something heavy which, eventually, they get tired of carrying. So one day they leave it behind, and that's the day they need it. Moreover, many of these people are not weapons experts; in an emergency they do not want to have to remember to take off the safety, cock the weapon, take up the correct grip ... they want to pull out the pistol, point it at the enemy and start shooting. The Resolver has been designed for these people. Finally, the designer of the Resolver considered that there was no good reason for a large magazine capacity; if you haven't disposed of the criminal in eight shots, you are unlikely to do so with 15, should you live that long.

There are two models. The basic .380 Resolver fires the .380 Auto cartridge (also called 9mm Short in Europe) and is a simple blowback automatic. There is no manual safety device, and the trigger mechanism is self-cocking. It is light and slim (only 0.65 inch thick) and can be carried all day without inconvenience, and when required, all that is necessary is to

RUGER MARK II AUTO PISTOL

Left: The Resolver M380.

The Sturm Ruger company virtually made its name with its 'Standard' .22 automatic pistol which was first introduced in 1949 and has been the firm's anchor ever since. At the end of 1981, with over one million of this and its target version the 'Mark One' sold, it was announced that an improved version, the 'Mark II', would be marketed during 1982.

The Mark II maintains the same basic form and appearance as its predecessor, a blowback pistol using a fixed barrel and a bolt which reciprocates within a tubular receiver; several component parts are, in fact, interchangeable between old and new models. The changes are minor in form but add up to significant improvements; the trigger has been changed in material and shape, and its pivot system has been redesigned so that it is now possible to retract the bolt to unload or examine the chamber while the safety is applied and with the sear firmly locked; the magazine has been reworked and now accepts 10 rounds instead of the former nine; the rear of the receiver

draw it and pull the trigger. For those countries where the law demands a safety catch, one can be provided; but there is, of course, no need to use it.

Generally speaking, the 9mm Short bullet is enough to deter the casual robber; but for those people who feel that a more powerful cartridge may be needed, the M9/M40 Resolver is available. This is a locked-breech pistol which can be had in 9mm Parabellum or .40 S&W calibers. Breech locking is by the usual Browning tilting barrel system, but the dimensions have still been kept to the minimum and this weapon is very little larger than the .380 blowback, being only 19.8mm (less than three-quarters of an inch) wide. On request it can be chambered for other cartridges, including the .38 Super Auto, 7.62mm Tokarev and .32 Auto.

Left: The Ruger Mark II Auto Pistol.

Ruger Mark II Auto Pistol

Manufacturer Sturm, Ruger & Co., Southport, CT 06490, U.S.A.
Type Blowback semi-automatic
Caliber .22 Long Rifle RF
Barrel 4.75in (120mm)
Weight (empty) 36oz (1019gm)
Magazine Capacity 10 rounds

has been cut away on each side so that it is now easier to grasp the bolt retraction ears; and a new bolt hold-open device has been adopted. The old model used the safety catch as a hold-open device, but the Mark II has a small catch above the left grip which, when depressed, allows the bolt to close after it has been held open by the magazine follower after the last shot has gone.

An impressive weapon, the Mark II Ruger Auto Pistol is available in Standard models with fixed sights and with 4.75in or 6in barrel lengths, a Target model with fully adjustable sights and a 6in barrel, and a 'Bull Barrel' model with adjustable sights and a heavy 5in barrel.

Ruger P-89

Right: The Ruger P-89.

Manufacturer Sturm, Ruger & Co. Inc., Southport, CT 06490, U.S.A.
Type Recoil-operated semi-automatic, double-action
Caliber 9mm Parabellum
Barrel 4.49in (114mm)
Weight 32oz (907gm)
Magazine Capacity 15 rounds

Sturm, Ruger & Co. began with a .22 automatic pistol and then built up a high reputation for excellent revolvers. In 1987 they announced a military-style automatic pistol, the P-85, and since then it has been steadily improved and is now the P-89. Mechanically, it used the familiar Browning link swivel to draw down the rear end of the barrel as the slide and barrel recoil after firing, but instead of using lugs above the barrel to lock to the slide, the Ruger design uses a squared section around the chamber which locks into the ejection slot in the slide. The barrel is of stainless steel, as are the hammer, trigger and most internal components. The frame is of lightweight aluminum alloy, hardened to withstand wear and finished in matt black. The slide is of chrome-moly steel, also finished in matt black. A safety catch is on the rear of the slide; this can be used by either hand and, when applied, locks the firing pin, blocks the hammer and disconnects the trigger.

The firing mechanism is double-action, the trigger guard being large enough to allow firing in a gloved hand and reverse-curved so as to provide a grip for the non-firing hand. The magazine release is in the forward edge of the butt and can be operated by either hand.

A number of variations have been developed in response to demand:
KP89 This model is the same as the basic Model P-89 but with a stainless steel slide.
De-Cocker P89 This has a de-cocking lever on the slide in place of the usual safety catch. When pressed, this blocks the firing pin and lowers the hammer. Thereafter the pistol can be fired by a double-action pull on the trigger or by thumb-cocking the hammer and firing single-action.
Double-Action-Only P-89 This mechanism can only be fired by pulling through on the trigger; after each shot the hammer follows the slide back and comes to rest in the down position.
KP90DAC Similar to the De-Cocker P-89, this is chambered for the .45 ACP cartridge.
KP91DAC Like the KP90DAC, but chambered for the 10mm Auto cartridge.

Ruger Redhawk Revolver

Manufacturer Sturm, Ruger & Co., Southport, CT 06490, U.S.A.
Type Solid frame double-action 6-shot revolver
Caliber .44 Magnum
Barrel 7.5in (190mm)
Weight 52oz (1474gm)

Sturm Ruger have acquired a fine reputation for their heavy revolvers, and this is one of their masterpieces.

The Redhawk is a conventional double-action solid frame revolver made of stainless steel, with the cylinder swinging out on a crane for loading and ejection. The cylinder has ample metal on the outside of the chambers and is securely locked by an additional lug in the crane which engages into the frame, as well as the usual ejector rod locking points. A small but important detail is that the cylinder locking notches are located off the axis of the chambers so that they are not liable to weaken the chamber walls. The barrel is ribbed and both the rib and the ejector rod shroud are forged in one piece with the barrel. The foresight is of blued steel with a red insert, and the backsight, also of blued steel, is a Patridge type notch with a white line around it and is capable of adjustment for both windage and elevation.

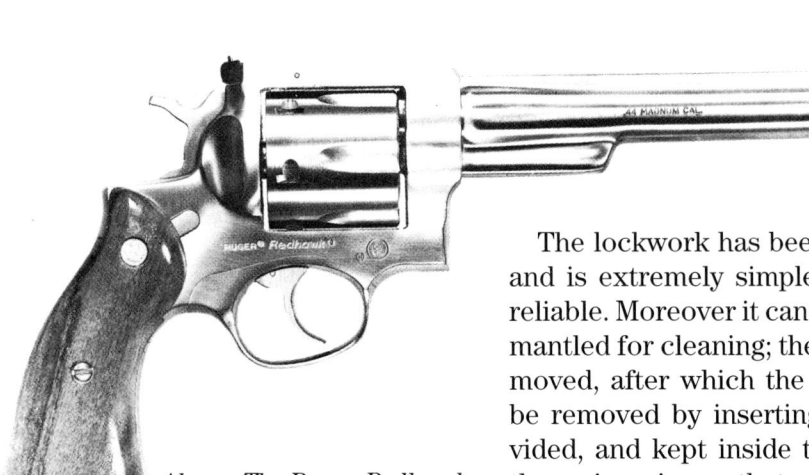

Above: The Ruger Redhawk.

The lockwork has been redesigned and is extremely simple, robust and reliable. Moreover it can be easily dismantled for cleaning; the grips are removed, after which the hammer can be removed by inserting a pin (provided, and kept inside the grip) into the mainspring so that when the ham-

Left: The Armi Renato Gamba .38Sp.

Below: The SAB G90 semi-automatic.

mer is cocked, tension is taken off it and the pivot can be removed and the hammer slipped free. The mainspring can now be removed, and by pulling on a stud behind the trigger guard the entire trigger guard and trigger mechanism can be taken from the frame. There is a rising transfer bar which acts as an intermediary between the hammer and the firing pin only when the trigger is correctly pressed, so that the pistol cannot be accidentally discharged.

On the range, this elegant pistol performs well; like any .44 Magnum it is a handful, but the weight and size allow good control and it is capable of close groups at all ranges. For day-to-day practise the .44 Special can be used, although the sights require altering; with this loading one can shoot all day without discomfort.

SAB Trident Super Revolver

Manufacturer Sociéte Armi Bresciane Srl, Gardone Val Trompia, Italy
Type 6-shot double-action solid frame revolver
Caliber .38 Special
Barrel 4in (102mm)
Weight (empty) 25.4oz (720gm)

This is a conventional design of solid frame revolver with swing out cylinder and rod ejection. The grip is well-proportioned to fill the hand and the barrel is slab-sided to lighten it, which results in a particularly well-balanced weapon. The foresight is mounted on a ventilated rib and the back-sight is fully adjustable for elevation and windage. The finish is in bright blueing, with well-checkered walnut grips, and the workmanship is good.

SAB HSc80 Auto Pistol

Manufacturer Sociéte Armi Bresciane Srl, Gardone Val Trompia, Italy
Type Blowback, double-action, semi-automatic
Caliber 7.65mm ACP, 9mm Short or 9mm Police
Barrel 3.34in (85mm)
Weight (unloaded) 24.7oz (700gm)
Magazine Capacity 13 rounds

The Sociéte Armi Bresciane of Gardone Val Trompia, Italy is a relatively new company in the firearms field. They obtained a license from Mauser to manufacture the Mauser HSc automatic pistol, a prewar design, and have done this for some time. They have now made some improvements to the design. The butt has been lengthened, allowing the magazine capacity to be increased to 13 rounds, and the frame has been altered to give the trigger guard a recessed curve on its forward edge so as to make it suitable for a two-handed grip. The pistol can be obtained chambered for 7.65mm ACP, 9mm Short or 9mm Police cartridges. It retains the

double-action feature of the original HSc, is a simple blowback, and in 9mm Police caliber would appear to be a sound pistol for use by police or security forces or for home defense.

Semmerling LM-4 Pistol

Manufacturer Semmerling Corp., Newton, MA 02160, U.S.A.
Type Manual repeating pistol
Caliber .45 ACP
Barrel 3.656in (92.8mm)
Weight (empty) 26.5oz (751gm)
Magazine Capacity 4 rounds

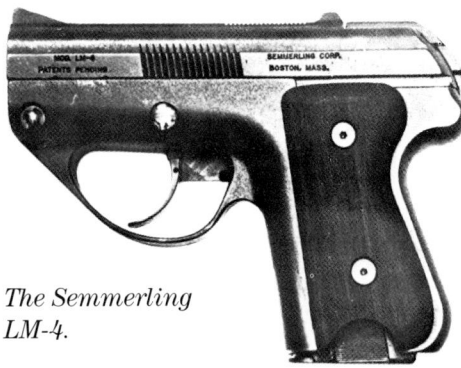

The Semmerling LM-4.

This is one of the most unusual pistols in existence, a pistol designed solely as a defensive weapon and using a unique mechanical action. It is also one of the strongest and probably the most expensive .45 – the last quoted price was $748. Manufacture ceased in the late 1980s, but the unusual features of the pistol make it a desirable addition to any collection.

The Semmerling looks like an an automatic but is actually hand-operated. The frame carries a heavy standing breech and the four-round magazine and trigger mechanism; on the forward section of the frame is the barrel unit which can slide forward, exposing the chamber. When it is manually pushed forward and pulled back, the chamber slides over the top round in the magazine and the breech is closed. Pulling the trigger now brings up a lock to hold the barrel in place during firing and then cocks and releases the hammer to fire the cartridge. The firer then pushes and pulls once more on the barrel, first ejecting the fired case and then reloading the fresh round.

This all sounds very difficult, but with practice it all works very well; the light weight and small size of the LM-4 demand a two-handed grip, and thus the free hand is ready to perform the reloading movement. This can be done by thumb pressure on the serrated area on top of the barrel, or by grasping the side serrations. The firer must remember to release the trigger, however, since as long as the trigger is pressed, the barrel is securely locked to the breech; conversely, if the breech is not properly closed, then the trigger cannot move and the pistol cannot be fired.

There is no manual safety; however, there is a slight possibility that in drawing the pistol from a holster the barrel could be pulled forward, and to guard against this there is a 'holster lock' lever on the right side which can be set to hold the barrel firmly closed. It is automatically disengaged as the trigger is pulled to fire the first shot. The sights compromise a fixed blade front and square notch rear.

The recoil is quite violent, but accurate shooting in combat is no problem. It should only be used with standard military or jacketed commercial .45 ACP ammunition, and handloading should be done carefully so as not to exceed standard pressure levels.

Sig-Hammerli Model 240 Pistol

Manufacturer Collaboration between Schweizerische Industrie Gesellschaft, Neuhausen-Am-Rheinfalls, Switzerland and Hammerli SA, Lenzburg, Switzerland
Type Target, locked-breech, semi-automatic.
Caliber .38 Special
Barrel 5.81in (148mm)
Weight (empty) 43.5oz (1233gm)
Magazine Capacity 5 rounds

This is a highly-specialized pistol intended for one purpose only, making holes in targets with supreme accuracy, and that only in international-class formal contests. It is not intended for combat shooting, either real or simulated, or casual plinking at vermin.

The P-240 might be said to be a SIG P-210 which has been worked over by the Hammerli people to give it the accuracy desired. SIG are without peers for producing well-built and fitted automatic pistols, while Hammerli, as we have pointed out elsewhere, have a long history of producing prize-winning match pistols, and the combination is unbeatable.

The 240 uses the now-standard Browning cam breech lock system in which the barrel is withdrawn from engagement with the slide by a shaped cam beneath the breech. Having said that, one has to add that in this case the machining and fit is to the finest tolerances and the muzzle is shaped to fit closely into the slide. The slide itself, in SIG fashion, rides inside the frame, a method which gives good support to the moving parts. The barrel is rifled to very close tolerances, which is part of the secret of its accuracy, and the loading ramp is particularly carefully contoured since this pistol fires only one type of ammuni-

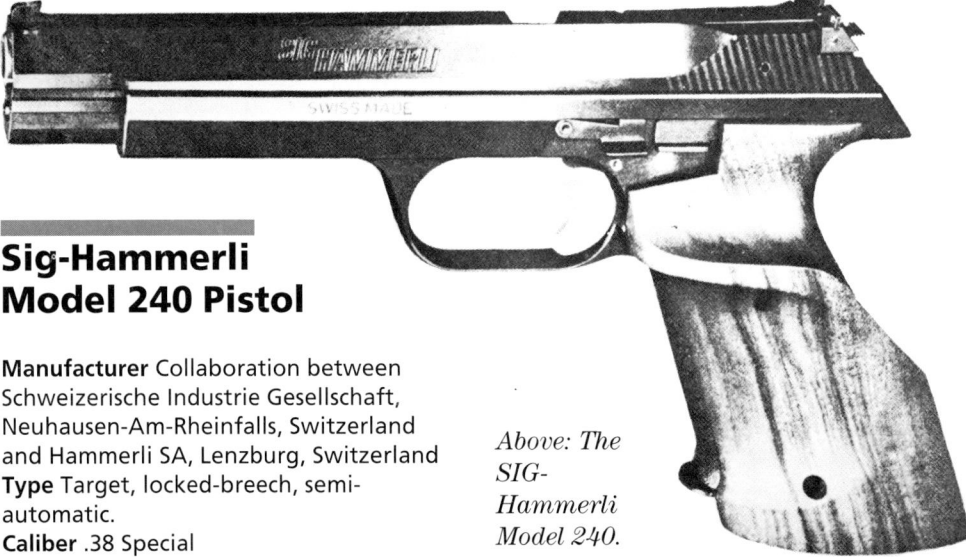

Above: The SIG-Hammerli Model 240.

tion, the .38 Special Wadcutter, a most unusual cartridge to find in an automatic but one with enormous potential for accuracy.

The grip is large, plain wood, and with a palm rest, giving an excellent grip, and the whole pistol is large and muzzle-heavy, promoting a firm and steady aim. The wide trigger is fully adjustable for tension, slack and over-travel, with a clean and consistent let-off. The foresight is a blade, the rear sight a square notch adjustable for elevation and windage.

The accuracy of this gun is beyond question; to put it plainly, it is capable of whatever accuracy the shooter can bring to it, and quoting figures would be meaningless.

Sig-Sauer Model P225 Auto Pistol

Manufacturer J. P. Sauer & Son, Eckernforde, Germany; Schweizerische Industriegesellschaft Neuhausen-Am-Rheinfalls, Switzerland
Type Locked breech, double-action, semi-automatic
Caliber 9mm Parabellum
Barrel 3.85in (98mm)
Weight (empty) 26.1oz (740gm)
Magazine Capacity 8 rounds

This pistol was designed by SIG (Schweizer Industrie Gesellschaft) of Neuhausen-Rheinfalls, Switzerland and was first announced in 1978. Due to the restrictions placed on arms sales by the Swiss Government, SIG have entered into agreements with J. P. Sauer & Son of Germany so that the SIG designs can be manufactured by Sauer, this giving them an export market since the German government's regulations are much less restrictive. The Swiss-manufactured pistols have been adopted by the Swiss police, while those made in Germany, the 'Pistoles 6', have been adopted by the German Border Police, Customs Administration, and six regional police forces.

The P225 is a slightly smaller and slightly modified version of the earlier P220. It uses the well-known Browning link method of breech locking, using a shaped cam to withdraw the barrel from engagement with the slide. Its principal feature is the incorporation of improved safety devices, and there is no applied safety, so that the weapon can be brought into action very rapidly. Once the pistol has been loaded by operating the slide, the hammer can be safely lowered by pressing on the de-cocking lever on the left side of the frame. The firing pin is securely locked by a spring-loaded pin which passes through it, but the hammer is stopped short of striking the pin. To fire, the trigger is pulled through to raise the hammer and then release it; as the hammer reaches the full-cocked position, a safety lever is rotated by the trigger bar. This rises beneath the firing pin and pushes the locking pin up and clear of the hole, so that as the hammer drops the firing pin is free to move when struck. As soon as the slide moves on recoil, the disconnector allows the firing pin safety pin to drop back into place and the pin is again securely locked.

The design is well balanced and the P225 performs well on the range. Like all SIG products the finish is immaculate, and quality control is such that parts from Swiss or German pistols are freely interchangeable.

Right: The SIG-Sauer P-229 semi-automatic.

Sig-Sauer P-229

Manufacturer Schweizerische Industriegesellschaft, Neuhausen-Am-Rheinfalls, Switzerland
J.P. Sauer & Son, Eckernforde, Germany
Type Recoil-operated semi-automatic, double-action
Caliber .40 S&W or 9mm Parabellum
Barrel 3.85in (98mm)
Weight 30.5oz (865gm)
Magazine Capacity 12 rounds (13 rounds in 9mm)

The Swiss Industrial Company (SIG) have produced some of the best pistols in the world, but the Swiss neutrality laws make the export of weapons very difficult; as one Swiss said, "We are only allowed to sell guns to people who don't want them." As a result, SIG set up a combined operation with the German company of J. P. Sauer & Son, an old-established and well-respected company, so that Sauer can make SIG pistols and sell them into countries where the Swiss cannot.

The P-229 developed from earlier designs; this series began with the P-220 which more or less set the general pattern: a recoil-operated pistol using a shaped cam beneath the breech to pull down the rear of the barrel, thus disengaging a squared-off section around the chamber from its lock in the ejection port of the slide, SIG were the pioneers of this system, which is gradually replacing the original Browning system of machined lugs on the barrel mating with slots in the slide. The P-220 was a full-sized pistol adopted by the Swiss Army as their Model 75.

SIG-SAUER P-230

Next came the P-225, which was slightly smaller and lighter than the P-220 and which had improved safety features including an automatic firing pin safety, decocking lever, drop safety device, but no applied safety catch, so that it can be brought into action very quickly indeed. In late 1980, when the U.S. Army advertised for a new pistol, SIG modified the P-225 to meet the American requirements, resulting in the P-226; the principal change was the addition of an ambidextrous magazine catch and a 15-round magazine capacity. Although not adopted by the U.S. armed forces, the P-226 was widely purchased by police and security agencies.

The P-228 came next, a compact pistol, smaller than the other members of the family but with a 13-round magazine capacity. And finally came the P-229, which is virtually the same as the P-228 but chambered for the .40 Smith & Wesson cartridge. Developed primarily for police use, it has high-contrast sights and the usual automatic firing pin safety, drop safety and de-cocking lever. The basic P-229 has a steel slide and aluminum alloy frame; the P-229SL is similar but with the slide in stainless steel; and this version is also available in 9mm Parabellum caliber. (In effect, this latter model is a P-228 with stainless steel slide.)

commercial sale.

The P230 is a simple blowback weapon with double-action lockwork and is provided with a de-cocking lever on the left side, by means of which the hammer can be lowered on a loaded chamber. As with the P225 the firing pin is securely locked at all times except for the instant that the hammer is released by the trigger. There is no manual safety catch.

The various caliber types are identical in appearance and major dimensions but there are differences in weight; the 7.65mm and 9mm Short versions have an alloy frame and there is only 5 gm difference between them. But the 9mm Police version, firing a more powerful cartridge, uses a steel frame which adds 170gm, and also has a heavier slide so as to reduce the recoil force, adding another 70gm to make the total weight 690gm or 24.3oz.

The 9mm Police (9 × 18mm) cartridge is a special round developed in Germany in order to obtain the maximum possible performance from an unlocked-breech weapon. It is not yet commercially manufactured in the U.S.A.

Smith & Wesson Distinguished Combat Magnum

since before the start of the century, but it incorporates one new feature, their 'L' frame. Smith & Wesson have long categorized their pistols according to the size of the frame, the smaller and lighter weapons using the 'K' and the very large revolvers the 'N'; the 'L' falls between these, giving additional strength and size to cope with today's magnum ammunition but not increasing the size by an inordinate amount.

There are, in fact, four distinct models in this range; the Model 586 comes in steel with a blued finish and has 4in or 6in (nominal – the actual lengths are as quoted above) barrel lengths. The Model 686 is similar but in stainless steel with a satin finish. Both models have adjustable rear sights. Model 581 is steel, blued, with a 4in barrel and fixed frame notch rear sight, while the Model 581 is the same but in stainless steel with satin finish.

There are certain refinements; revolvers with 4in barrels and 'target accessories', and all revolvers with 6in barrels are furnished with a trigger stop; the 'standard' 4in barrel models – ie the 581 and 681 – will not have a trigger stop. The 586 and 686 are fitted with Goncalo Alves checkered target grips cut away for use with a speed loader, while the 581 and 681 have straightforward checkered walnut grips.

SIG-Sauer P230 Auto Pistol

Manufacturer J. P. Sauer & Son, Eckernforde, Germany
Type Blowback semi-automatic
Caliber 7.65mm/.32 ACP; 9mm Short/.380; 9mm Police
Barrel 3.62in (92mm)
Weight (empty) 16.2oz (460gm) in 9mm Short
Magazine Capacity 8 rounds (7.65mm); 9 rounds (9mm caliber)

This is another Swiss-designed, German-manufactured fruit of the cooperation between SIG and J. P. Sauer & Son. It is used by a number of European police forces and enjoys a wide

Manufacturer Smith & Wesson, Springfield, MA, 01101, U.S.A.
Type Six-shot, solid frame, double-action revolver
Caliber .357 Magnum/.38 Special
Barrel 4³⁄₈in (110mm); 5⁷⁄₈in (149mm)
Weight (empty) 4in barrel: 42oz (1190gm) 6in barrel: 46oz (1304gm)

Like all Smith & Wesson products, this pistol is beautifully finished and absolutely reliable. It is a conventional enough double-action revolver of the type they have been producing

Above: The Smith & Wesson Distinguished Combat Magnum.

Right: A Smith & Wesson Third Generation auto pistol.

Smith & Wesson have said that they developed these revolvers from lessons learned in Police Combat Competitions, and on the range this appears to be borne out in practice. The trigger is wide and smooth, with a good double-action movement and a crisp let-off in the single-action mode. The pistol balances well, comes quickly to the aim and is as accurate as anyone could wish. There is sufficient weight and good balance to prevent excessive throw-off after firing, so that the shooter can quickly regain his point of aim. For practical shooting contests, or for service, it would be hard to fault this weapon.

Smith & Wesson Third Generation Auto Pistols

Manufacturer Smith & Wesson Inc., Springfield, MA, 01101, U.S.A.
Type Recoil-operated, semi-automatic, double-action
Caliber 9mm Parabellum
Barrel 4.0in (101.6mm)
Weight 28.5oz (808gm)
Magazine Capacity 14 rounds
(Data for Model 5903)

This series of pistols has completely replaced earlier models and has been designed with the assistance of many U.S. law enforcement agencies, who were encouraged to make suggestions and criticisms. Features incorporated in these new pistols include fixed barrel bushes for better accuracy and simpler stripping, an improved trigger pull, three-dot sights, wrap-around grips, a bevelled magazine aperture for quicker reloading, and a triple safety system incorporating an automatic firing pin safety, an ambidextrous manual safety catch and a magazine safety.

The 9mm **5900 Series** can be considered as the baseline series. There are three models, the 5903, 5904 and 5906; the '03 has an alloy frame and stainless steel slide, the '04 an aluminum frame, carbon steel slide and stainless steel barrel and is finished in blue, and the '06 is entirely of stainless steel and is satin-finished. All are fitted with wrap-around grips, adjustable sights are optional, and all have the same 4-inch barrel.

The 9mm **3900 Series** generally resembles the 5900 series but is slimmer, lighter and with a smaller magazine capacity.

The 9mm **6900 Series** has a reverse-curved trigger-guard. It is larger and uses the same length of barrel but has a 12-round magazine.

The **Model 4006** generally resembles the 5906 but is chambered for the .40 Smith & Wesson cartridge and has a magazine capacity of 11 rounds.

The **4500 Series** is chambered for the .45 ACP cartridge and adds the power of a well-proven cartridge to the other advantages of the Third Generation system.

The **Model 1000 Series** resembles the 5900 series but is chambered for the 10mm Auto cartridge. The Model 1076 is specially made for the FBI and does not have a safety catch on the slide but instead, a frame-mounted de-cocking lever.

All models have fixed sights as standard, and most are available with adjustable rear sights as an option.

Sphinx AT-2000

Manufacturer Sphinx Engineering, Porrentruy, Switzerland
Type Recoil-operated, semi-automatic, double-action
Caliber 9mm Parabellum or .41 Action Express
Barrel 4.53in (115mm)
Weight 35.2oz (1000gm)
Magazine Capacity 15 rounds (9mm) or 11 rounds (.41 AE)

Below: The Sphinx AT-2000.

Above: The Sphinx AT-2000PDA.

This was originally the ITM 2000 pistol, announced in 1984, but ITM was bought by Sphinx Engineering and the pistol re-named accordingly. In fact, it originated as a licensed copy of the Czechoslovakian CZ-75 pistol, but over the years there have been a number of small changes in detail and various improvements, to the point that the AT-2000 can now be considered as a completely independent design. Assembly tolerances and finish have been greatly improved, and the dimensions of the barrel have been slightly changed so that it is no longer possible to interchange a Czech CZ-75 barrel. Barrels are now made in Germany by Peters Stahl and have exceptional accuracy and resistance to wear.

The AT-2000 series are therefore recoil-operated pistols using the usual type of Browning dropping barrel for their breech lock. The safety catch can be applied whether the pistol is cocked or uncocked, and in 1987 an automatic firing pin safety system was introduced, preventing any movement of the firing pin except during the final few degrees of trigger movement prior to releasing the hammer. Recent designs have an ambidextrous safety catch and, if desired, the slide stop pin can be fitted to the right of the frame, a refinement seen on no other pistol.

The pistol was originally designed for the 9mm Parabellum cartridge but was one of the first to accept the .41 Action Express round and a conversion kit was supplied to permit a change of caliber. Since the .41 AE uses the same rim diameter as the 9mm Parabellum, only the barrel, return spring and magazine need be changed.

The basic model of the range is the **AT-2000S**, a full-sized holster pistol by police and military use. The **AT-2000P** is a shorter and lighter version designed by Sphinx; except for the dimensions (93mm barrel, 910 grams weight) it is the same as the 2000S and a similar 9mm/.41 conversion kit is available.

The **AT-2000H** is the 'hideaway' version, mechanically similar to the other members of the family but even smaller than the 2000P, weighing only 740 grams, with an 87mm barrel and a 10-shot magazine. Normally supplied in 9mm Parabellum caliber, it can be converted to either .41 Action Express or the new 9mm Action Express, and a patented design of magazine has been developed which will accept and feed all three calibers without the need for change.

The **AT-2000SDA, 2000PDA** and **2000HDA** are the same as the three pistols described above, but, as the 'DA' suffix indicates, are arranged so as to fire in the 'double-action only' or self-cocking mode. The pistols are automatically de-cocked and made safe after each shot, but pulling the trigger will raise the hammer, disconnect the automatic firing pin safety and drop the hammer to fire the weapon. These pistols have the same ability to interchange between 9mm Parabellum and .41 AE calibers as the original versions.

The **AT-2000R** is similar to the double-action-only DA models but has the additional ability to be thumb-cocked to allow single-action firing when required. In normal use the hammer always falls to the safe position, but stands sufficiently clear of the slide to be pulled back by the thumb for a more deliberate shot. This 'R' variation can be applied to any of the three standard 2000 models, thus producing the 'PR', 'SR' or 'HR' varieties.

Spitfire Mark II

Manufacturer JSL Ltd, Hereford, England
Type Recoil-operated semi-automatic, double-action
Caliber 9mm Parabellum or 9 × 21mm IMI
Barrel 3.7in (94mm)
Weight 35.2oz (1000gm)
Magazine Capacity 15 rounds

The Spitfire is another derivative of the Czechoslovakian CZ-75, but, like the Sphinx 2000, has undergone a number of modifications in the course of its development, so that it can now be considered a completely different weapon.

The Spitfire is a conventional recoil-operated pistol using the Browning tilting barrel, controlled by a cam beneath the chamber and locked by lugs above the chamber engaging in recesses in the slide. The entire pistol, except for the grip surfaces and springs, is made from investment-cast and machined stainless steel, and machining is done on computer-controlled machines to a tolerance of 5

SPITFIRE MARK II

Two types of the Spitfire Mark II, including the Competition Model (below).

microns. This produces a pistol which is tight throughout, with no looseness in the fit of components and a very crisp trigger pull.

The sights are fully adjustable for elevation and windage and produce a clear picture. Three models are currently produced: the **Standard** with fixed sights; the **Stirling** with adjustable rear sight, and the **Competition Model** with fully adjustable sights and a muzzle compensator. All models are available in either 9mm Parabellum or 9 × 21mm chambering, the latter being particularly recommended for competition shooting, since it appears to be somewhat more accurate than the Parabellum round.

The Standard model has been tested by various military and police authorities and is in wide use as a police pistol in Europe.

Star Model BKM Auto Pistol

Manufacturer 'Star', B. Echeverria, Eibar, Spain
Type Locked breech, semi-automatic
Caliber 9mm Parabellum
Barrel 3.9in (100mm)
Weight 26oz (737gm)
Magazine Capacity 8 rounds

The Star line of 9mm automatic pistols has generally been developed along military lines, but in the late 1970s, with the 9mm Parabellum cartridge beginning to become popular in the U.S.A., they were prevailed upon to produce a smaller weapon, one more suited to concealment for personal defense. Their answer was the BKM.

With an overall length of just over seven inches and weighing less than two pounds when loaded, this meets the specification, but the result is something of a handful. A light alloy frame helps to keep the weight down, but the combination of short-barrel, light weight and the 9mm Parabellum cartridge means recoil and muzzle blast both heavier than average; this is particularly noticeable when firing some types of European military 9mm ammunition. It is rather more acceptable when using commercial 'Luger' loadings.

The finish is excellent, with blued slide, anodized black frame, and well-checkered walnut grips. The foresight is the usual blade and the rear a square notch which is rather too narrow for easy alinement in a hurry. The rear sight may be drifted sideways in its notch for zeroing but there is no other adjustment. The breech locking is by the traditional Browning-Colt swinging link, though there is only one locking lug on top of the barrel to engage with the slide. It is worth noting that the firing pin is not an inertia type, and this pistol should never have the hammer lowered on to a loaded chamber.

In practical use the BKM delivers good accuracy for such a short barrel, giving two to three inch groups at 25 yards quite regularly. Like many autos it tends to be fussy over its ammunition, and several brands should be checked for their compatability before deciding which to use. Once the recoil and noise are mastered, the BKM becomes an extension of the hand, and is well-suited to the defensive role.

Star Model FR Target Pistol

Manufacturer 'Star', B. Echeverria, Eibar, Spain
Type Blowback, semi-automatic
Caliber .22 Long Rifle RF
Barrel 7in (178mm)
Weight (empty) 29oz (820gm)
Magazine Capacity 10 rounds

The number of target shooters who cut their teeth on the Star Model F target pistol in years gone by must be astronomical; it was cheap, reliable and sufficiently accurate to satisfy the beginner at target work and it also made a very satisfactory 'fun gun'. Unfortunately Echeverria found more lucrative things to do in the early 1960s and stopped making it. They have now returned to this field with the new 'Model FR' which is simply the old Model F revived and somewhat better made.

This is a basic blowback pistol, having a heavy barrel fixed into the frame and a slide which has a front arms frame which traps the recoil spring beneath the barrel. It is simple to dismantle; one merely pulls the slide slightly back, presses the dismantling button above the left grip, lifts the slide and slips it off forward, over the barrel. End of dismantling; nothing further is needed.

There is an external hammer and a safety catch which locks the slide while disconnecting the trigger. A hold-open catch ensures that the slide stays to the rear after firing the last shot in the magazine; with a new magazine in, the slide can be closed by pressing this catch or by simply pulling it back and releasing it. The foresight is on a ramp and is adjustable for elevation; the rear sight, a square notch, is adjustable for windage. Balance weights are available, which can be attached to the barrel to adjust the point of balance for the individual shooter.

Altogether the FR is a good beginner's pistol which will provide accuracy enough to satisfy many shooters for their entire career.

Below: The Star Model FR Target Pistol.

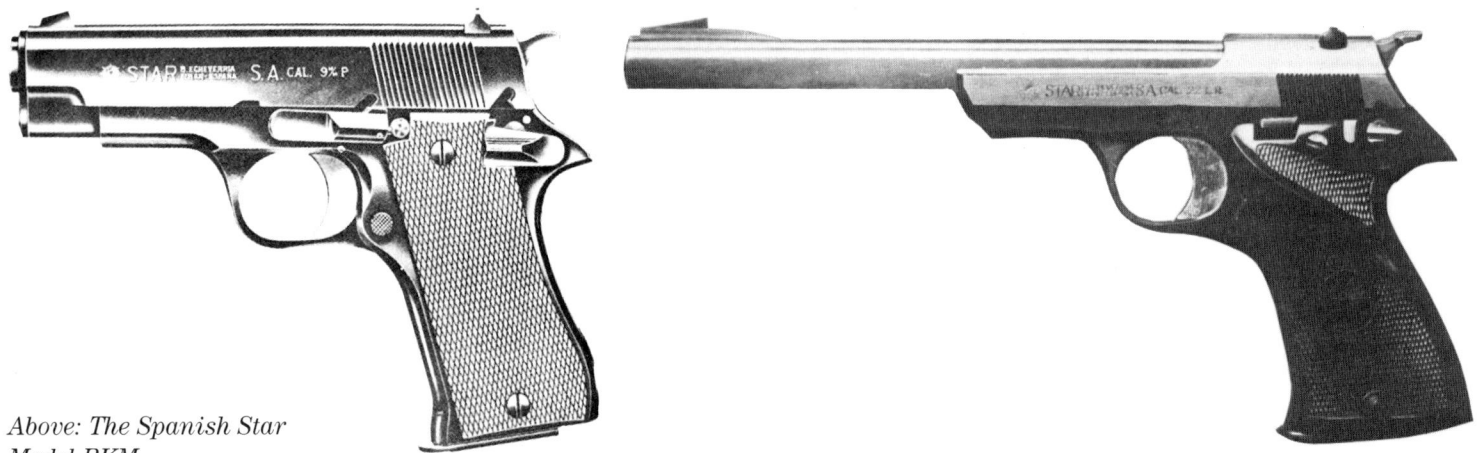

Above: The Spanish Star Model BKM.

Above: The compact Star Model PD.

Star Model PD

Manufacturer 'Star', B. Echeverria, Eibar, Spain
Type Locked breech semi-automatic
Caliber .45 ACP
Barrel 3.94in (100mm)
Weight 25oz (710gm)
Magazine Capacity 6 rounds

The venerable U. S. Government Colt M1911A1 pistol is a splendid weapon for stopping malefactors, but it is rather bulky and heavy; as a result there has long been a tendency to develop lighter and smaller pistols firing the .45 ACP cartridge. Many have been short-lived hack-and-chop jobs done on the basic Colt, but some have been designed from the ground up, as it were, and have been considerably more successful.

The Star PD is one of the earliest of this group and probably the most long-lived. In order to bring the size down there have been some changes from the basic Colt-Browning swinging link breech locking system; there is only one interlocking lug and notch holding slide and barrel together, and the recoil spring and guide rod are an assembled unit instead of separate components. The frame is of alloy, and there is no grip safety. The foresight is a blade and the rear sight a fully adjustable leaf with open notch.

The PD is much lighter than the Colt M1911A1 and, consequently, rather more difficult to control, though it is not uncomfortable to shoot. Due to the short barrel the velocity and muzzle energy is less than in full-sized pistols but there is still ample stopping power, and the PD is a sensible gun for those who need a potent but concealable pistol.

Sterling Mark II Auto

Manufacturer Sterling Arms Corp., Lockport, NY 14094, U.S.A.
Type Blowback, double-action, semi-automatic
Caliber .380 Auto/9mm Short
Barrel 3.56in (90.5mm)
Weight 25.5oz (723gm)
Magazine Capacity 8 rounds

The .380 Auto, or 9mm Short as it is known in Europe, is a somewhat under-rated cartridge. It has served as a police cartridge throughout Europe for several decades and as a military cartridge too. The bullet will deliver something in the order of 165 foot-pounds of energy at the muzzle, which is sufficient to make most people stop and think, and it is also less likely to ricochet than higher powered cartridges such as the 9mm Parabellum. For many years it was just about the most powerful cartridge which could be managed in a blowback action without going to extremes, another point which counted in its favor.

The Sterling is one of the few .380 automatic pistols made in the U.S.A.; it is an inexpensive pistol and the standard of finish reflects its price, but there is nothing wrong with its quality of construction and it is surprisingly accurate. The action is a straightforward blowback with an external hammer, and with double-action trigger. There is a slide-mounted safety which, when operated, moves a steel barrier behind the firing pin, so that should the hammer fall it cannot discharge a cartridge. Once the safety is on, the hammer may be lowered by controlling it with the thumb while pressing the trigger; thereafter the pistol can be fired by releasing the safety and pulling the trigger to cock and drop the hammer. Once the first shot has been fired, subsequent shots are in single-action mode, the recoiling slide cocking the hammer.

The foresight is a fixed blade, the rear-sight, a square notch adjustable for elevation and windage. The Sterling is comfortable to fire and can deliver consistent three- to four-inch groups at 25 yards range.

TA 382

Manufacturer Fratelli Tanfoglio SpA, Gardone Val Trompia, Italy
Type Blowback, semi-automatic
Caliber .380/9mm Short: .32 ACP/7.65mm
Barrel 3.75in (95mm)
Weight 28oz (794gm)
Magazine Capacity 11 rounds (.380); 12 rounds (.32)

Under the name Tanfoglio & Sabotti this company exported large numbers of inexpensive auto pistols to the U.S.A. in the 1950s, one of them being a .25 auto called the 'Titan'. The 1968 Gun Control Act stopped this trade and shortly afterwards there was news of an American company being set up to import component parts and assemble them in the U.S. This does not seem to have prospered particularly well, and now Tanfoglio (Sabotti having left the concern) have completely rebuilt the Titan into the TA 382 and are marketing it in the U.S.A.

The new pistol follows the current

Above: The TA 382 by Tanfoglio.

fashion in having a magazine larger than was previously considered normal during its first production run, but apart from that it is of conventional design, somewhat resembling Beretta from its use of an open-topped slide. The safety catch on the left side of the frame, above the trigger, locks the trigger. In addition to this there is a magazine safety and a half-cock notch on the hammer. The frame safety catch also doubles as a stripping catch; when turned to the 'safe' position the slide can be pulled back and lifted off the frame at its rear end, then slid forward to clear the barrel. With the catch in the 'fire' position dismantling is impossible.

The sights are roughly what one might expect in this sort of pistol; a blade at the front and a fixed notch at the rear, mounted in a block which can be knocked sideways for windage correction when zeroing. Accuracy is likewise average for the class, about four-inch groups at 25 yards. On the whole the TA 382 is a reliable and robust workaday pistol.

Tanfoglio TA90

Manufacturer Fratelli Tanfoglio SpA, Gardone Val Trompia, Italy
Type Recoil-operated semi-automatic, double-action
Caliber 9mm Parabellum, 9 × 21mm IMI, .40 S&W, .41 Action Express, 10mm Auto, .45ACP
Barrel 4.7in (120mm)
Weight 35.8oz (1015gm)
Magazine Capacity 15 rounds (9mm)

The Tanfoglio company have manufactured pocket pistols for some years, but in the 1980s decided to market a military-style heavy-caliber pistol; like many others, they chose the Czech CZ-75 as their model, though since then several variants have been developed.

The basic pistol of the Tanfoglio range is the TA-90, a conventional 9mm pistol using the Browning tipping barrel system of breech locking, controlled by a fixed cam beneath the breech and locking into the slide by two lugs above the chamber. The frame is of cast steel, while the slide and barrel are machined from forged steel. All models are supplied in black finish or hard chromed and are also available with frame and slide in stainless steel.

On the standard models there is a manual safety catch on the slide which locks the firing pin and also disconnects the hammer and trigger. On the 'Combat' models there is a frame-mounted safety catch which allows the weapon to be carried cocked and locked. All models are double-action, but there is no provision for de-cocking the hammer on any of them.

The TA90 is paralleled by the TA40, TA41, TA10 and TA45, and the only difference lies in the caliber, which can be deduced from the model numbers. There are also 'Combat' versions of all these models, differing only in the safety arrangement, as described above.

The 'Baby Standard' models are compact versions of the standard, differing only in dimensions; they have a 90mm barrel and weigh about 30oz (850 gm) empty.

The 'Baby Combat' models resemble the Baby Standard but have the Combat safety arrangement. All the Baby models are available in the same range of calibers as the full-sized Standard and Combat models.

Below: The Tanfoglio TA90.

The Taurus PT-92 (top) and PT-99 pistols.

Taurus PT-92 and PT-99 Auto Pistols

Manufacturer Forjas Taurus SA, Estrada do Forte 511, CP44, Porto Alegre RS, Brazil
Type Locked breech, double-action semi-automatic
Caliber 9mm Parabellum
Barrel 4.9in (125mm)
Weight (empty) 34oz (964gm)
Magazine Capacity 15 rounds

These two pistols bear a considerable resemblance to two Beretta designs, and it would appear that they are based on Beretta models but with slight modifications, and made under license in Brazil. They are currently being offered on the commercial market in the Americas and they have been adopted by Brazilian military and security forces.

The PT-92 and PT-99 are virtually identical, the difference being that the 92 uses fixed sights and is intended as a service or combat weapon, while the

99 has wooden grips and adjustable rear sights and is intended for target shooting. The general form is that of the Beretta Model 92, a locked breech pistol using a variation of the Walther P-38 dropping block to lock barrel and receiver together during firing. The principal change is in the trigger guard, the front edge of which has a reverse curve which is serrated to provide a good grip for the popular two-handed grasp. The magazine is slightly different from the Beretta design, having a number of small holes in the rear face through which the cartridge contents can be counted.

The workmanship and finish of the Taurus pistols is very good, and they are of above-average accuracy for basic military pistols. The adjustable-sight model, once zeroed, is very good, being capable of off-hand two-inch groups at 25 yards in the hands of moderately-practised shooters.

Thompson-Center Super 14 Contender

Manufacturer Thompson-Center Arms Ltd., Rochester, NH 03867, U.S.A.
Type Single shot pistol
Caliber Various
Barrel 14in (355mm)
Weight ca 46oz (1315gm)

The Thompson-Center single shot pistol has been in existence since the late 1960s and has proved a very successful design. It has been made available in almost every possible caliber at various times; the company is a small one and staffed by practical men who, if they see a trend, can rapidly produce barrels to suit. Thus in the days when .17 caliber was all the rage, they produced several .17 chamberings, and when the fashion died away they abandoned them. It would profit us little to tabulate all the variations that have existed. The latest model, the Super 14, is intended principally for silhouette shooting, though it is likely to appeal also to hunters who prefer to use handguns.

The Super 14 would appear to have gained its name from the combination of several powerful chamberings and a 14in barrel; it is available in .22LR, .222 Rem, 7mm TCU, .30-30 win, .35 Rem Maximum, .44 Magnum, 10mm Auto and .445 Magnum.

The basic design has changed little over the years. The Contender is still an elegant single-shot with a standing breech and a barrel which hinges down for loading. The Super 14 has a new grip, designed to provide a more firm anchorage when firing heavy loads, and a nicely-shaped fore end which is designed for a two-handed hold.

The foresight is a blade, while the rear sight can be had in two forms, open notch or aperture, both fully adjustable for elevation and windage. The long and heavy barrel gives good balance and a long sight base, so that the pistol is certainly capable of as much accuracy as the shooter is likely to bring to it. Fired from a rest at 50 yards, groups between three and four inches are easily obtainable, though some care should be taken in selecting the ammunition.

Uberti Single Action Revolver

Manufacturer Aldo Uberti, SpA, Brescia, Italy
Type Six shot, solid frame, single-action
Caliber .45 Colt
Barrel 7.5in (190mm)
Weight 40oz (1134gm)

This is not exactly new, though it reappears under a new name every few months. In the 1960s the 'spaghetti western' movies and the quick-draw craze appear to have hit Italy and several companies began making cheap and cheerful copies of the Colt 1873 'Frontier' to meet the demand.

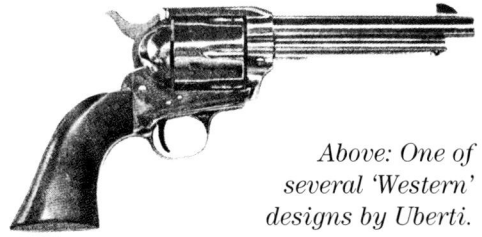

Above: One of several 'Western' designs by Uberti.

One or two of them realized that there could be something better in this, and seeing that there was a large demand for good single-action revolvers (since Colt had stopped making theirs) began making good quality pistols and exporting them. Uberti are one of the best, and their products have appeared under their own name, under the names of various importers in the U.S. (eg Mitchell Arms Corp, Costa Mesa, CA.; Western Arms, Santa Fe, NM; Iver Johnson, Middlesex, NJ; and many more), and under various brand names – Cattleman, Buckhorn, Trailblazer and so forth.

The Uberti standard .45 uses a 7.5in barrel on a nicely color-hardened frame with brass trigger guard and solid walnut grip. The foresight is a serrated blade on a ramp, the backsight a square notch with adjustment for elevation and windage. The finish, both in appearance and in fit of the cylinder, is excellent, and the single-action trigger 'breaks' very cleanly with a consistent feel. It is capable of very good accuracy, provided some care is taken over selecting compatible ammunition; groups of under two inches at 25 yards are possible when rest-fired.

The Uberti design can be had in a wide variety of caliber and barrel length options; .44 Magnum and .357 Magnum chamberings are offered, and barrel lengths of 4.75, 5.5, 7.5, 10, 12 and 18 inches are possible; with the latter a shoulder stock is available.

Left: The Thompson-Center Super 14 Contender.

4.5mm Underwater Pistol

Manufacturer Russian state arsenals
Type Multi-barrel repeater
Caliber 4.5mm special
Barrel About 8.25in (210mm)
Weight 33.5oz (995gm)
Magazine Capacity 4 rounds

Weapons designed for underwater use by frogmen have been in the inventories of major armies for some years, but are not publicized, and the first such weapon to be seen at an international arms exhibition was this Russian pistol, first shown in 1992. Conventional firearms do not perform well under water, for various technical reasons, and thus the design of this pistol is quite unlike any weapon used on land.

There are four barrels, arranged in a block so that they can be tipped down to expose the breech end for loading. The round of ammunition is a drag-stabilized dart 115mm long, the rear end being secured inside a cartridge case of fairly conventional shape. Four rounds are held together by a clip, so that the whole clip can be handled as one unit and the four rounds slipped into the four barrels. The barrels are then folded down and locked to the breech, which contains a self-cocking firing mechanism which fires each round in succession for four pulls of the trigger. The cartridge contains a piston which, when the powder explodes, is driven forward and launches the dart from the barrel; the piston is stopped by the bottle-neck of the cartridge so that no gas escapes into the water.

The darts are sufficiently accurate to strike within a 150mm (6in) circle at 100 meters range when fired in air, and the short-range under water accuracy is said to be comparable. The effective underwater range varies according to the depth and water pressure; at five meters depth the dart has lethal effect at 17 meters range, while at 40 meters depth the effective range is only six meters. At these ranges the darts are capable of penetrating all types of wet or dry suit, face-masks and helmets. And, of course, they can be used as self-protection weapons against the more dangerous types of fish and mammals liable to be encountered during underwater activities.

The Russians have also developed a 5.66m underwater rifle using a dart cartridge. With approximately double the range of the pistol, it is a semi-automatic weapon which uses a similar mechanism to the Kalashnikov rifle.

Unique DES-69U Target Auto Pistol

Manufacturer Unique SA, France
Type Blowback, semi-automatic
Caliber .22 Long Rifle RF
Barrel 6in (152mm)
Weight 37oz (1050gm) (without weights)
Magazine Capacity 5 rounds

This is another specialized weapon, specially tailored to suit the requirements of the European 'Standard Pistol' match, which is based on the U.S. National Match rules. The dimensions of the weapon and such parameters as sight radius, trigger pull and weight are all closely regulated, so that the manufacturer's job is to produce the most accurate machine within those tolerances that he can.

The Unique DES-69 is one of the best known stock European pistols for this type of contest and it is made by a company who have been in the pistol business since 1923. It has a long record of successes and will be seen on almost every pistol range.

The DES-69 is a simple blowback using a heavy fixed barrel and a short breech-block/slide with long 'wings' which run alongside the barrel and are serrated to provide finger grips for retracting the slide. The wooden grip is anatomically shaped, with palm rest, and frame and grip run back, over the web of the thumb, to form a support for the rear sight, so as to take advantage of the maximum limits for sight radius of 8.6 inches (220mm). The construction is such that the barrel 'sits' low in the hand, and since all mechanical movement is confined to a short space above the grip, there is minimal disturbance of aim with each shot. Balance weights of 150, 260 or 350gm are provided and can be secured to the barrel, forward of the slide.

The pistol is hammer fired, the hammer operating in a well between the breech and the sight unit, though it is possible to reach it for thumb-cocking. The five-round magazines are loaded through the bottom of the butt in the usual way, and there is a magazine release button low on the grip. The trigger is fully adjustable for reach, pull weight, slack and backlash, and the sear spring is also capable of adjustment, so that the shooter can tune the pull-off.

On the range the DES-69 is capable of ultimate accuracy, but most shooters agree that it should be tested with various brands of ammunition in order to find one which is ballistically suited. Once this is determined, half-inch groups at 25 yards should be possible.

Above: The Unique DES-69 target pistol, with the various balance weights.

Walther Model GSP-C Target Pistol

Manufacturer Carl Walther GmbH Sportwaffenfabrik, Ulm, West Germany
Type Blowback, semi-automatic
Caliber .32 S&W Long
Barrel 4.2in (107mm)
Weight 2.875lbs (1305gm)
Magazine Capacity 5 rounds

This is the latest of a series of pistols developed by Walther for various types of pistol competition. The International Shooting Union (UIT) standard pistol contest has .32 as the minimum caliber, and since it is obviously advantageous to use the lowest caliber so as to have the least recoil and disturbance of aim, the .32 Smith & Wesson long cartridge became popular in Europe as a competition round. Walther had developed their GSP pistol for .22 Long Rifle rimfire, and seeing the rise of interest in .32 S&W, they modified the design to centrefire and produced the GSP-C.

The pistol has a fixed barrel and a reciprocating bolt which works inside the square receiver. A box magazine fits ahead of the trigger guard, which helps, with the heavy barrel block, to keep the weight forward and thus arrive at the balance preferred by contestants. The rimmed cartridge might be expected to give problems in feeding from the magazine, but this has been overcome by raking the magazine rather sharply so that the rounds are loaded with the rims ahead of each other; feeding is thus smooth and feed jams are unknown.

The wooden grips are angular in appearance but fit the hand well and there is a palm rest on the right side. The foresight is a blade, interchangeable for others of different height and thickness, while the rear sight is a leaf with square notch, fully adjustable for elevation and windage. The trigger assembly is an interchangeable unit; there are adjustments for slack, trigger position, travel and weight of pull within certain limits; if these limits do not suit the firer he can change the unit for one with a different range of pull tension and begin adjusting again. The trigger unit can also be replaced by a special training unit which has a ratchet device and gives five 'dry shots' for every winding.

Accuracy is what one would expect from a pistol of this type and quality; groups fractionally over one inch at 25 yards when fired from a rest. Certainly the pistol will be capable of as much accuracy as the firer will be able to put into it.

Above: The Walther GSP-C target pistol.

Walther Model P5 Auto Pistol

Manufacturer Carl Walther GmbH, Post Box 4325, D-7900 Ulm, Germany
Type Locked breech double-action semi-automatic
Caliber 9mm Parabellum
Barrel 3.5in (90mm)
Weight (empty) 28oz (795gm)
Magazine Capacity 8 rounds

This is virtually an updated version of the well-known Walther P-38, used by the German Army from 1938 to 1945 and afterwards, as the P-1, adopted by the Bundeswehr. Like the Heckler & Koch P7 it was designed in response to demands from the West German police for a pistol which combined rapid response with total safety. Walther took the well-proven locking system of the P-38 and wrapped a completely new configuration of pistol round it, incorporating several new safety features.

The P5 has an enveloping slide, but the barrel is semi-fixed and breech locking uses the familiar dropping block of the P-38, in which a locking plate holds slide and barrel together during a short recoil, after which the plate descends and the slide is free to move backwards. An external hammer is cocked during this movement. However, the double-action now incorporates a large thumb-lever which in one movement activates all the safety devices and drops the hammer safely on a loaded chamber. From this position the firer needs only to pull the trigger to fire the pistol; there is no manual safety catch to be operated.

Safety relies on the fact that until the very moment of firing the firing pin is held aligned with a recess on the face of the hammer; thus if the hammer should accidentally fall it will surround the firing pin head without touching it. In addition, the firing pin is never aligned with the solid part of the hammer except at the instant the hammer is released by the action of the trigger. There is also a disconnector which ensures that the trigger cannot affect the hammer unless the slide is closed and the breech securely locked.

When the trigger is pulled it begins to cock the hammer, and as the hammer reaches full cock so a trip lever is extended upwards and forces the firing pin into alignment with the hammer's solid face just as the hammer is released. If the hammer is thumb-cocked, or cocked by the action of the slide, then the releasing action of the trigger will still cause the trip lever to rise and align the firing pin.

The P5 has been adopted by the Netherlands Police and by the police forces of Baden-Wurttemburg and Rheinland-Pfalz in Germany.

Walther P-88

Manufacturer Carl Walther Waffenfabrik, Ulm, Germany
Type Recoil-operated semi-automatic, double-action
Caliber 9mm Parabellum or 9 × 21mm IMI
Barrel 4in (102mm)
Weight 31.7oz (900gm)
Magazine Capacity 15 rounds

Walther pistols have been well-known since the 1920s, and they were the first to make a success of the double-action trigger system using a de-cocking device. Their first major caliber locked-breech pistol was the Pistole 38, designed for the German Army and

WALTHER PP SUPER AUTO PISTOL

Above: The Walther P-88 compact.

first issued in 1939, and this used a block locking system which has been used by all Walther heavy-caliber pistols ever since, as well as being adopted by Beretta and other manufacturers. The P-38 is still manufactured, having been re-adopted by the reconstituted German Army in 1955 as the Pistole 1.

In the middle 1980s, however, with competition from newer manufacturers eroding their markets, Walther decided on a totally new pistol and developed the P-99; in doing so they broke with tradition and abandoned the locking block system and the familiar open barrel and short slide which was almost their trademark.

The P-88 is a conventional design, using an enveloping slide and locking the breech by means of the familiar Browning tilting barrel, controlled by a cam beneath the chamber and locking to the slide by a squared section around the chamber engaging with the ejection slot in the slide. The trigger mechanism is double-action, with an ambidextrous de-cocking lever mounted on both sides of the frame. There is also an ambidextrous magazine catch in the front edge of the butt.

Safety is achieved by a complicated firing pin arrangement: the firing pin normally rests at an angle, and the face of the hammer is recessed so that should it accidentally fall, the end of the firing pin enters the recess and there is thus no pressure on the pin and no danger of firing. When the trigger is pulled the rear end of the firing pin is moved upwards until it is lined up with the solid portion of the hammer face and is held there while the trigger releases the hammer and the hammer falls, striking the firing pin and firing the shot. As soon as the slide begins to move backwards after the shot, the trigger connection is broken and the firing pin drops back to its safe position, to remain there until the trigger is pressed once more.

There is thus no way by which the firing pin can be driven forward except when the trigger is being correctly pulled with the intention of firing a shot.

The P-88 is normally supplied in 9mm Parabellum chambering; it can, though, be supplied in 9×21mm IMI chambering should this be required.

Walther PP Super Auto Pistol

Manufacturer Carl Walther Sportwaffenfabrik, Ulm, Germany
Type Blowback, double-action, semi-automatic
Caliber 9mm Police
Barrel 3.62in (92mm)
Weight (empty) 30oz (850gm)
Magazine Capacity 7 rounds

The Walther PP (Polizei Pistole) is well-known around the world and has been the source of inspiration for a number of copyists for many years; in spite of its age it still sets the standard for the rest and sells as fast as Walther can make it. It is an elegant design, reliable and accurate, and it pioneered a double-action lock which has rarely been surpassed for smoothness of operation. In the mid-1970s Walther decided to give it a face-lift and a new caliber in order to keep up with the changing demands of police authorities in Europe; though not exactly new, this pistol is so little-known outside Germany that we feel it is worth bringing into sharper focus.

The PP Super uses the same basic mechanism as the older PP but has an entirely new frame and slide assembly and is chambered for the 9mm Police (or 9mm × 18mm) cartridge, a round devised in Germany in order to obtain the maximum power from a blowback pistol, combined with good stopping power and a low risk of ricochet for use by police in urban areas. The frame is slightly longer, the slide longer and more 'squared-off' at its front end. The grips are carefully molded to a hand-filling shape and provided with a thumb-rest; wooden grips of similar contour can be had as an alternative. The trigger guard has been made slightly larger and with a vertical front edge to facilitate a two-handed grip of the pistol. The front sight blade has a night-aiming luminous spot in its rear face, while the rear sight is a square notch adjustable for windage and with a central luminous patch which can be aligned with the front spot in poor light.

The most significant change has been in the safety arrangements. In the old PP the safety catch on the slide dropped the hammer, locked the firing pin, and locked the trigger. With the pistol loaded, pressing the safety dropped the hammer and left everything locked; to fire, it was necessary to push the safety up and then pull the trigger to double-action the hammer to cock and drop. In the PP Super the safety locking function has been omitted; the safety catch is now only a decocking lever, and once the pistol is loaded this lever is pressed down; this rotates a block in front of a shoulder on the firing pin and releases the hammer. The firing pin is capable of vertical movement, and at this time is forced down in its housing by a spring, so that its end is aligned with a recess on the face of the hammer. Thus when the hammer falls, the face strikes the rear of the slide while the recess surrounds the firing pin but does not touch it. If the trigger is now pulled, the hammer begins to rise to the cocked position, while a linkage forces the firing pin upwards in its housing, against the spring. This lifts it clear of the safety block and lines the end of the pin up with the solid face of the hammer, so that when the hammer falls, the pin goes forward to fire the cartridge. It is thus unnecessary to move the safety catch when firing in a hurry. This arrangement may sound somewhat unsafe, but it should be remembered that this is a weapon intended for use by police and similar well-trained people, so that some degree of short-cutting is acceptable.

Wichita Mark 40 Target Pistol

Manufacturer Wichita Arms, 333 Lulu, PO Box 11371, Wichita, KS 67211, U.S.A.
Type Bolt-action single shot target pistol
Caliber .308 Winchester (7.62mm NATO)
Barrel 13in (330mm)
Weight (empty) 4.5lbs (2.04kg)

This is a highly-specialized pistol known more specifically as a 'Silhouette Pistol' since it is primarily designed for the competitions organized under the rules of the International Handgun Metallic Silhouette Association. Briefly, these involve shooting high velocity ammunition against life-like animal silhouettes at long ranges; there is, though, no reason why this pistol should not make a good hunting weapon, fitted with suitable sights.

The Mark 40 pistol uses an aluminum receiver which has a steel insert for attachment of the barrel; within the receiver slides a breech bolt using three lugs to lock into the breech, giving an extremely secure lock. The bolt handle is on the left side of the pistol, and has a flattened and turned-down handle which can be operated by the shooter's left hand while he retains his hold on the pistol with his

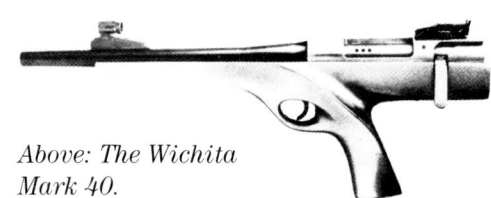

Above: The Wichita Mark 40.

right. There are three holes in the bolt which will allow a safe venting of gas should a primer be punctured.

The stock of the pistol is of glass fiber-reinforced plastic and is shaped into a comfortable pistol grip with a thumb rest. The trigger is fully adjustable for travel and weight of pull and is smooth in action with a crisp let-off point.

The sights consist of a tubular front with post insert and an open rear with arcuate notch; the two combine to form the 'Wichita Multi-Quick' system in which the front sight can be adjusted in elevation and the rear sight for both elevation and windage. The rear sight has a knurled adjusting knob which can be used to set predetermined values once these have been established by zeroing and the sight settings recorded by tightening specified screws in the rear sight unit. The front sight can be used for making corrections on the day to compensate for minor meteorological and other changes.

In practical use the pistol is heavy, but necessarily so when one considers that this is firing a full-sized rifle cartridge. The sights are clear and the pistol is extremely accurate; indeed, some observers have said that it really needs a telescope sight to bring out its full potential, though this, of course, is going beyond what the designer set out to do. For its specified purpose the Mark 40 sets a very high standard and reaches it admirably. Like most target weapons it needs to be fired with various types of ammunition to decide which suits it (and the shooter) best, but with this question settled, two-inch groups at 100 yards are well within its capability. It can be obtained chambered for a specialized 'wildcat' cartridge, the 7mm IHMSA, a round developed for silhouette shooting and based on the .308 Winchester case.

Right: The Walther PP Super.

RIFLES

AAI Advanced Combat Rifle

Manufacturer AAI Corporation, Baltimore, MD., U.S.A.
Type Gas-operated, semi-automatic and three-round bursts
Caliber 5.56mm special
Barrel 20.6in (525mm)
Weight 7.78lbs (3.53kg)
Magazine Capacity 30 rounds

The American search for an Advanced Combat Rifle (ACR) began in the early 1980s with the decision to seek a new rifle design for adoption in about 1995. Multi-million-dollar contracts were awarded to a number of companies to develop caseless rifles, and, later, further contracts to other companies to examine non-caseless solutions. The designers were given a free hand within broad limits of weight and size, the primary stipulation being that the rifle had to give 100 percent improvement in first round hit probability over the current M16A1 rifle.

Eventually, in 1989, four candidate weapons were tested, from Heckler & Koch of Germany, Colt and the AAI Corporation of the U.S.A., and Steyr-Mannlicher of Austria. Testing was prolonged and expensive, and at the end of it the U.S. Army decided that while all the candidate rifles showed merit, none provided the quantum leap in performance that was desired. The program was placed on hold in 1990, and that was that. However, the various designs are worth study, because they suggest the way that the next generation of rifles might go, as and when the armies of the world show sufficient interest.

The AAI rifle, compared to some of the others, looks quite conventional; but it actually fires fin-stabilized fléchettes, dart-like projectiles, at the high velocity of 4600 feet per second (1400 m/sec) and cannot fire conventional ammunition. The rifle is driven by a gas piston, and although full details of the breech mechanism have not been revealed, it is said to be derived from an earlier AAI design which, in its most efficient form, used a three-chambered breech unit which moved very quickly in and out of engagement with the barrel to allow very fast cycling of a three-round burst. There is no provision for full automatic fire.

A four-power optical sight is fitted, with iron sights as backup, and the muzzle carries a rather unusual compensator/muzzle brake which has been specially designed to work with fléchettes.

The barrel is rifled with a very slow twist – one turn in 85 inches – which gives the fléchette a degree of roll stabilization and helps accuracy. The fléchette idea is not new; several makers, including AAI, experimented with fléchettes as rifle projectiles in the 1960s, but at that time the materials and construction of the fléchette cartridge was not particularly good. By now new materials and improved technology has made the fléchette concept more acceptable, and the AAI rifle was considered a good design, although not sufficiently accurate for the purpose intended.

Anschutz Model 54 Silhouette Rifle

Manufacturer J. G. Anschutz GmbH, Ulm, West Germany
Type Bolt-action, single shot
Caliber .22 Long Rifle RF
Barrel 21.63in (550mm)
Weight 7.92lb (3.59kg)

Previous pages: U.S. Seals come ashore. The man in the foreground carries a M16A2

Top and above: Two views of the AAI Advanced Combat Rifle.

The Anschutz Model 54 rimfire target rifle has been in production for some time, but this is a specially developed model intended to suit the growing sport of 'silhouette shooting' in which metal silhouettes of various animals are engaged at long range from the standing position, the idea being to approximate to hunting conditions. In smallbore silhouette shooting the targets are scaled down and the ranges are shorter than those used in full-bore contests, but the basic features remain the same.

The principal difference between this and 'prone' target rifles lies in the shape of the stock, which has a deep pistol grip and a high Monte Carlo comb so that the sights fall to the eye with minimum neck-twisting and the shooter can get a really firm grip on the rifle. The stock material is walnut, well finished and liberally stippled wherever the hand is likely to need to grip.

The bolt is substantial, and the trigger can be adjusted for first pressure and tension. The muzzle is counter-bored to protect the edges of the rifling, and no sights are provided. The receiver is grooved to accept telescope mounts, which are the standard means of sighting in this type of shooting and the reason for the high comb of the stock.

The barrel is almost an inch in external diameter and heavy, and as might be expected the accuracy of this rifle is beyond reproach. Fired from a rest at 50 yards it should give groups well under an inch in diameter with almost any brand of ammunition, and if care is taken to match ammunition to rifle, then successive shots will practically go through the same hole.

Barrett Light Fifty M82A1

Manufacturer Barrett Firearms Manufacturing Inc., Murfreesboro, Tennessee, U.S.A.
Type Recoil-operated, semi-automatic
Caliber .50in
Barrel 29in (737mm)
Weight 28.4lbs (12.9kg)

The Barrett rifle was one of the first successful designs in an entirely new field which appeared in the 1980s. Generally referred to as a 'long range sniping rifle', its purpose is not sniping at enemy personnel but at vulnerable high-technology equipment. The scenario envisaged for this type of weapon is a two or three-man infiltration party which can slip through enemy lines, set up on a hill perhaps a mile away from a forward radar station or a fighter airstrip or a communications center, and then, by a few well-aimed and powerful shots, wreck the equipment. The rifle can then be abandoned and the men make their escape; the loss of a few thousand dollars' worth of rifle is trifling against the destruction of half-a-dozen fighter aircraft or a vital air defense radar.

The Light Fifty is a semi-automatic rifle firing the .50in Browning heavy machine gun cartridge and is capable of making accurate hits on ranges up to 1800 yards, depending upon the type of target. The barrel and locked bolt recoil about 25mm in the frame on firing, which absorbs a good deal of the recoil force, making the rifle about as comfortable to fire as a normal big-game rifle. An accelerator arm un-

Above: The Anschutz Model 54 target rifle.

Left: The Barrett Light Fifty M82A1.

BARRETT MODEL 90

locks the bolt, though the recoil continues for another 20mm or so. The barrel then stops and the bolt continues rearwards to extract and eject the empty case. The barrel is returned to its forward position by a spring, after which another spring drives the bolt forward, stripping a fresh cartridge from the magazine and chambering it; finally, the bolt rotates and locks into the chamber.

The barrel is fitted with a high-efficiency muzzle brake, which reduces the recoil by some 65 percent, and an adjustable bipod is fitted. A 10x telescope sight is fitted as standard, and this has a special sighting reticle which is calibrated to the particular ammunition. The manufacturers recommend using the armor-piercing explosive/incendiary bullet for maximum target effect, but the rifle will fire any type of standard Browning ammunition.

The Barrett Light Fifty has been used by the U.S. Army, Navy and Marine Corps and it is also in use by several agencies as a device for dealing with explosive ordnance – terrorist bombs and unexploded bombs – which can be destroyed from a safe range by one shot.

Barrett Model 90

Manufacturer Barrett Firearms Manufacturing Inc., Murfreesboro, Tennessee, U.S.A.
Type Bolt-action repeating rifle
Caliber .50in
Barrel 29in (736mm)
Weight 22lbs (9.98kg)

The Model 90 is a simpler weapon than the Barrett Light Fifty, being a bolt-action magazine rifle. This change in mechanism has been accompanied by other modifications, resulting in a weapon which is shorter and lighter than the semi-automatic Light Fifty. It is in 'bullpup' form, with the action well back in the stock; the chamber is under the firer's cheek, so as to accommodate the maximum length of barrel within the minimum overall length. A very efficient muzzle brake is fitted, together with a special absorbent butt pad, reducing the felt recoil to a manageable level.

There are no iron sights on the Model 90, nor is any sight provided as standard, but the top of the receiver is dovetailed to accept most types of sighting telescope or night vision sight. In general terms, the Model 90 will do anything the Light Fifty will do, but is a more convenient load to carry for long distances.

Beretta 70/90

Manufacturer Pietro Beretta SpA, Gardone Val Trompia, Italy
Type Gas-operated, selective fire
Caliber 5.56mm (.223)
Barrel 17.7in (450mm)
Weight 8.4lbs (3.8kg)

The Beretta 70/90 system was developed to meet the Italian Army's requirements for a modern assault rifle, and was taken into service in 1990. The system consists of four weapons: the assault rifle AR70/90 for infantry, the carbine SC70/90 for Special Forces, the special carbine (short) SCS70/90 for mechanized troops, and the light machine gun AS70/90 for use as the infantry squad automatic weapon.

The AR70/90 is an improved version of an earlier 5.56mm design, the 70/223, and its design was influenced by experience with that weapon. Certain weaknesses in the earlier design were corrected, and a number of new features introduced. The method of operation is the usual modern system of a bolt carrier with a rotating bolt driven by a gas piston mounted in a cylinder above the barrel. As the gas follows the bullet up the barrel, a small amount is tapped off to drive the piston backwards. This pushes the bolt carrier, and a cam path in the carrier rotates the bolt to unlock it, after which carrier and bolt run back, extracting the empty case and ejecting it. A spring then drives the carrier and piston forward again, collecting a cartridge from the magazine and chambering it, and as the carrier comes to rest, so the cam rotates the bolt to lock it into the chamber. A hammer mechanism, controlled by the trigger is left cocked ready to fire.

The trigger mechanism has a selector lever which allows single shots, three-round bursts for a single pressure of the trigger, or sustained automatic fire. Optionally, fire can be restricted to single shots and three-round bursts.

The rifle feeds from a 30-round magazine, and the magazine housing is NATO-standard so that it will accept magazines from other NATO-standard rifles such as the M16 or the British L85.

A carrying handle is fitted above the receiver, clipped in place and holding a luminous source for illuminating the sights at night. The handle can be removed, leaving a dovetailed receiver cover which will accept most types of night vision or telescopic sight.

The carbine SC70/90 differs from the rifle only in having a folding butt, while the short carbine SCS70/90 also has a shorter barrel and is thus slightly lighter. The machine gun version AR70/90 has a heavier barrel, surrounded by a perforated handguard, fixing points for vehicle or tripod mounting, a bipod folded beneath the handguard and a different butt with a shoulder rest and facilities for gripping it more firmly. As with the rifle and carbines, it is possible to launch grenades from the muzzle of the machine gun.

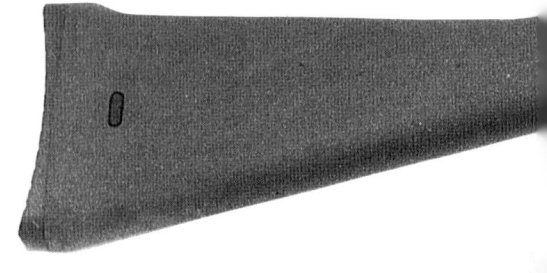

Calico M-900S Carbine

Manufacturer Calico Inc., Bakersfield, CA, U.S.A.
Type Delayed blowback, semi-automatic
Caliber 9mm Parabellum
Barrel 16.1in (409mm)
Weight 7.06lbs (2.87kg), loaded, with 50-round magazine
Magazine Capacity: 50 or 100 rounds

The Calico carbine is part of a complete weapon system which contains pistols, sub-machine guns and carbines, all of which operate upon the same principles. They are unusual weapons, principally because of their magazine system, which allows a very large capacity magazine to fit into a compact space.

The company began by developing a helical-feed magazine for a .22 rifle in 1985. They then produced improved versions to accept 9mm parabellum cartridges, and from this went on to develop a number of different weapons in this caliber which have

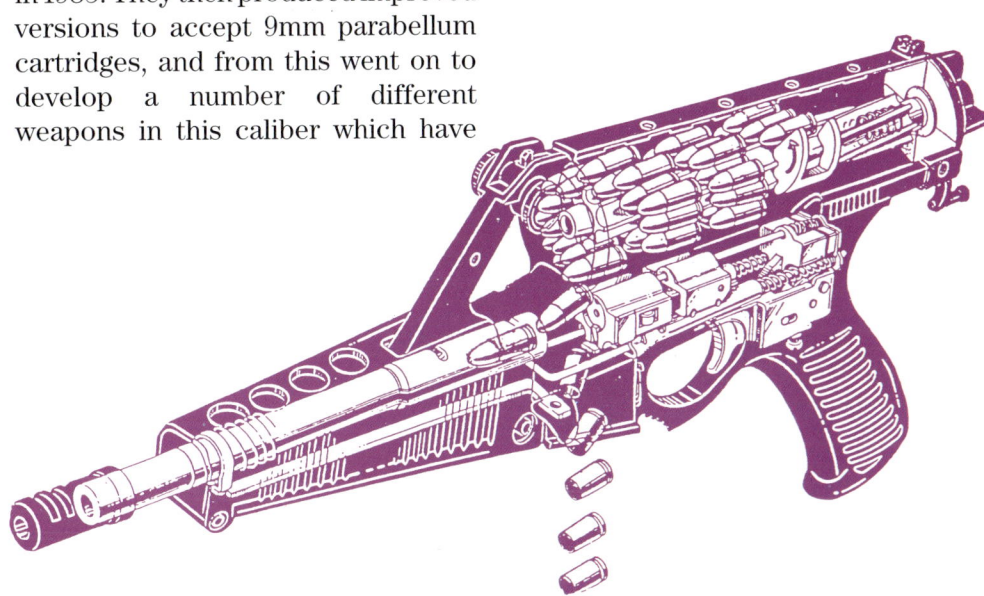

Below: The Calico M-900S Carbine.

Left: The Beretta SCS70/90.

Left: The standard Beretta AR70/90.

CALICO M-900S CARBINE

Above: The Carl Gustav AK5 assault rifle.

Above: The Calico M-900S Carbine.

been adopted by several military and security forces round the world.

The helical magazine is a plastic moulding only 57mm in diameter. Using a staggered helix principle, the rounds are driven forward along a fluted cartridge carrier as they press against the helical walls of the magazine. The driving pressure is provided by a torsion spring. The cartridges are fed one by one to a feed port, from where they are guided into the top-loading chamber of the weapon. Loading the magazine is easily done, and a 50-round magazine can be loaded in 22 seconds.

The receiver is of cast aluminum, with steel inserts in areas subject to wear. The breech is closed by a roller-locked bolt of similar design to that used in the Heckler & Koch and CETME assault rifles and submachine guns, which allows the weapon to fire from a closed bolt and delays bolt opening long enough for the bullet to leave the muzzle, and the chamber pressure to drop to a safe level. Ejection of the spent case is downward, in front of the trigger guard, and it is possible to fit a cloth 'brass catcher' to collect the fired cases.

In spite of the long barrel, the 178mm sight base is relatively short, the rear sight forms part of the magazine and the foresight is mounted on an elevated base at the front end of the magazine. The rear sight flips between a notch and an aperture, and the front sight is adjustable for elevation and windage.

The 100-round magazine fits in exactly the same place as the 50-round, but extends backwards over the stock; it also adds 1.69 lbs (0.77kg) to the weight of the loaded weapon.

CETME MODEL L ASSAULT RIFLE

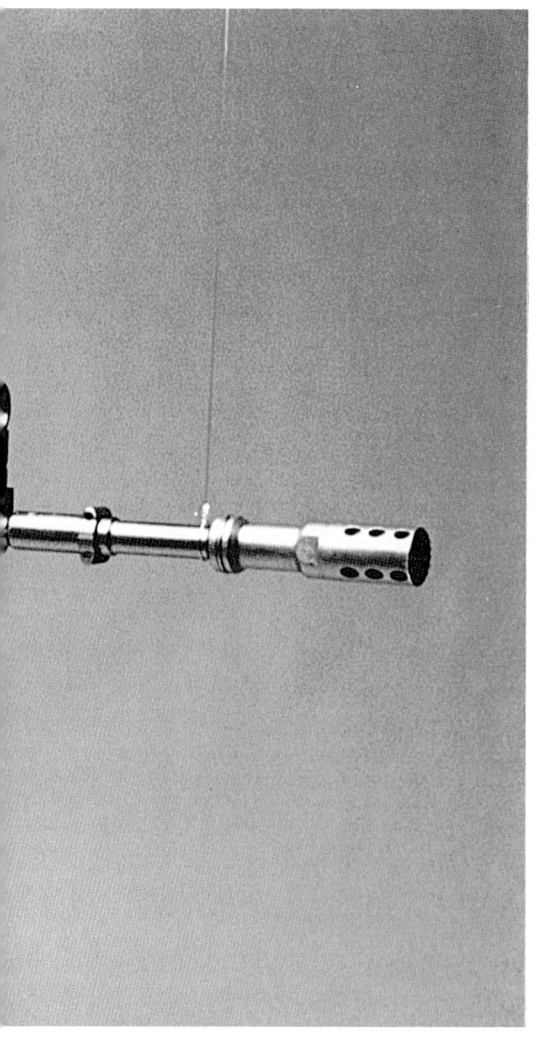

Carl Gustav AK5

Manufacturer Bofors Ordnance, Eskilstuna, Sweden
Type Gas-operated, selective fire
Caliber 5.56mm (.223)
Barrel 17.7in (450mm)
Weight 8.6lbs (3.90kg)
Magazine Capacity 30 rounds

The Carl Gustav AK5 assault rifle is a good example of how a stock weapon can be modified to suit the requirements of a particular purchaser, provided, of course, that he purchases enough of them.

In the mid-1970s the Swedish Army began looking for a new assault rifle to replace its existing 7.62mm weapons. All the available designs were studied, and the choice reduced to either the Israeli Galil or the Belgian FN-FNC. A quantity of each was bought and subjected to long technical and troop trials in 1979/80, and as a result of this the Galil was dropped and the FNC selected as being capable of further development to what the Swedes required. Their principal concern was to have a rifle which would withstand the severe northern climate; extreme cold places unusual stresses on a firearm, and handling weapons in cold conditions often demands modifications.

More trials took place, with changes being made to prototype FNC designs, until finally the Army was satisfied, and in 1985 the AK5 was finally approved for adoption.

The changes from the original FNC did not affect the basic mechanism; that remained the same gas-operated rotating bolt type. But the three-round burst mechanism was removed, leaving only the choice of single shots or automatic fire at 650 rounds per minute. The greatest changes were strengthening parts such as the butt, bolt, extractor, handguard, gas block, cocking handle, selector switch and sling swivels. The cocking handle and trigger guard were enlarged so that they could be operated easily by a man wearing heavy gloves, and the handguard was increased in size for the same reason.

The sights are a simple two-position flip with apertures for 250 and 400 meter ranges, and the front sight is hooded to reduce reflection. Optical and electro-optical sights can, of course, be fitted. The surface finish is for a gun of this type; the metal is first sand-blasted, then Parkerised, and finally has a coat of dark green enamel baked on.

CETME Model L Assault Rifle

Manufacturer Centro de Estudios Tecnicas de Materiales Especiale (CETME), Madrid 46, Spain
Type Delayed blowback, selective fire
Caliber 5.56mm (.223)
Barrel 15.75in (400mm)
Weight 7.49lbs (3.4kg)
Magazine Capacity 20 rounds
Cyclic rate of fire 750 rounds/minute

CETME is the Spanish government research and development establishment, and in the early 1950s a Herr Vorgrimmler went to work there. Vorgrimmler worked for Mauser during World War Two, particularly on their Sturmgewehr 45 project which was never completed, and he adapted the Mauser design to produce the first CETME rifle. Several countries showed interest in this, and eventually the Germans obtained a license; with some working over by Heckler & Koch it became the G3. Meanwhile CETME continued development and their 7.62mm 'Model C' was adopted by the Spanish Army. In conformity with the general move to smaller calibers they have now developed a 5.56mm rifle, the Model L, and this was evaluated by the Spanish Army and became their new service rifle.

As might have been inferred from the reference to the G3 above, the

Below: The CETME Model L assault rifle.

Above: The CETME L's structure is mainly plastic.

CETME relies upon the same divided bolt and roller locking system as the Heckler & Koch rifles. CETME have made one important addition, though, in the form of a spring-loaded locking lever in the bolt assembly which adds resistance to the initial opening movement of the bolt. No reason has been given for this, but it is likely that the increased unit pressure on the smaller base of the 5.56mm case led to too-fast initial opening and stretched or blown cases.

The structure of the rifle is largely plastic, with a sheet metal receiver. There is a selector on the left side which gives single shots, three-round burst fire or full automatic fire. The standard magazine is a 20-round model, but 10- and 30-round alternatives are available. The foresight is an adjustable post, between protective wings, and the rear sight is a rotating disc with a notch for 100m and apertures for 200, 300 and 400 meters. A mount base is incorporated and may be used for optical or electro-optical sights.

In addition to the standard rifle there is a short model which has a 12.6in (320mm) barrel and a telescoping metal butt.

Colt Advanced Combat Rifle

Manufacturer Colt's Manufacturing Co. Inc., Hartford, CT, U.S.A.
Type Gas-operated, selective fire
Caliber 5.56mm (.223)
Barrel not known
Weight 7.28lbs (3.306kg)
Magazine Capacity 30 rounds

The Colt entrant for the Advanced Combat Rifle program was, quite simply, a progressive improvement upon their existing M16A2 service rifle, but designed to fire a new 'duplex' cartridge carrying two bullets instead of the usual one; it can also fire the standard 5.56mm cartridge, and this is recommended for long-range shooting. For ranges up to 325 meters the Duplex round gives a higher chance of a hit; the theory is that the leading bullet goes where it is aimed, but the second bullet has a slightly random dispersion about the point of aim which is intended to compensate for any human error. Or, in plain words, if you miss with the aimed shot, you might get lucky with the random one. This idea was tested in the 1960s, and Duplex ammunition was used in Vietnam with some success. As with fléchette ammunition, the past 30 years have seen some design improvements so that one can now expect better performance.

The Colt ACR is gas-operated and uses exactly the same rotating bolt system as the M16A2. The handguard, pistol grip and buttstock have all been redesigned to improve handling, and the handguard incorporates a top rib which allows instinctive shooting in a manner similar to handling a shotgun. The barrel is fitted with a very advanced muzzle brake/compensator which, together with a new oil-spring buffer in the receiver, reduces recoil to about 40 percent of that of a standard M16A2 rifle. The firing mechanism permits single shots and full automatic fire, but there is no three-round burst facility.

A 3.5-power optical sight is provided, and two-range flip iron sights are fitted. The U.S. Army tests showed that the Colt ACR improved upon the M16A2, but not sufficiently to make it worthwhile contemplating a complete change of equipment.

Colt M16A2 Assault Rifle

Manufacturer Colt's Manufacturing Co., Inc. Hartford, CT, U.S.A.
Type Gas-operated, selective fire
Caliber 5.56mm NATO
Barrel 20.07in (510mm)
Weight 7.5lbs (3.40kg)
Magazine Capacity 20 or 30 rounds
Rate of fire 700 to 900 rounds per minute

The M16A2 is the current service rifle of the U.S. Armed Forces and of some 55 other countries. It is the latest version of a weapon which has been the U.S. standard since 1967 and it has a well-earned combat reputation.

Like the original M16A1, the M16A2 is a gas-operated automatic rifle using a direct gas blast to drive back the bolt carrier; this causes the bolt to be rotated and unlocked, then drawn back to eject the spent case and cock the firing hammer, after which a spring returns the bolt, loading a fresh round and leaving the hammer cocked. The rifle is built in 'straight line' form, the butt lying on the axis of the barrel, so that there is little lever action to lift the muzzle onto the air on recoil, as happens with rifles having conventional sloped butts. This, together with the relatively low recoil energy of the 5.56mm cartridge means that the rifle does not deviate far from its point of aim and can be quickly brought back for a second shot. On automatic fire the muzzle climb is minimal, putting the maximum number of rounds into the target area.

The firing mechanism can provide single shots, automatic fire or three-round bursts, according to the user's requirement. The U.S. Army's M16A2s can fire single shots and automatic fire; the version adopted by the Canadian Army as their C7 rifle is adjusted to give single shots and three-round bursts, without the automatic facility. The rifle can be fitted with the M203 grenade launcher, and the muzzle is to NATO standard dimensions so that any NATO-approved rifle grenade may be fired.

Left: The Colt Advanced Combat Rifle.

CZECH CZ58 ASSAULT RIFLE

Czech CZ58 Assault Rifle

Manufacturer Czeskoslovenska Zbrojovka, Uhersky Brod, Czechoslovakia
Type Gas-operated, selective fire
Caliber 7.62 × 39mm Soviet
Barrel 15.78in (401mm)
Weight 6.92lbs (3.14kg)
Magazine Capacity 30 rounds
Cyclic rate of fire 800 rounds/minute

Although there is a superficial resemblance to the Kalashnikov AK47, the CZ58 is a totally different weapon, designed and built in Czechoslovakia and owing nothing to Russian design. With low production costs in comparison with rifles of a similar specification, the CZ58 was standard issue for the Czech army for many years. In its original form it was even of a different caliber to the rest of the Warsaw Pact countries, but this was thought too much of a deviationist measure, and it was re-chambered to fire the standard Communist 7.62mm short cartridge.

The rifle is gas-operated, using a chrome-plated short-stroke piston; this strikes the bolt carrier a sharp blow, sufficient to send it backwards. After a short free travel the breech lock is freed from engagement with the receiver and the bolt is withdrawn from the chamber by the movement of the carrier. The locking of the breech is done by a hinged plate beneath the carrier which closely resembles the locking system used on the Walther P-38 automatic pistol. Firing is done by a hollow hammer tube which lies in the bolt and is propelled by a spring; when released by the sear, the hammer flies forward and strikes a floating firing pin. It is cocked by being caught by the sear during the recoil movement; indeed, if the firing pin was attached, the whole assembly would be called a striker.

The stock and fore end of the rifle are of wood-powder-reinforced plastic material, with a polished finish, and the metal work is blued or phosphated. The receiver is machined from the solid, and has a sheet steel cover. The rear sight is a tangent V-notch mounted on a steel block welded to the receiver and acting as a gas piston rod guide. The foresight is a post with protective ears, set well above the muzzle.

The CZ58 is light and robust, with a degree of internal finish which is sufficient for the job in hand, but without excessive frills. It is a highly satisfactory military rifle, and the folding-butt variation appears to be used in place of submachine guns in the Czech Army.

Above: The Daewoo 5.56mm K2 rifle.

Daewoo K2

Manufacturer Daewoo Precision Industries Ltd, Pusan, South Korea
Type Gas-operated, selective fire
Caliber 5.56mm (.223)
Barrel 18.3in (465mm)
Weight 7.18lbs (3.26kg)
Magazine Capacity 30 rounds

The Daewoo company gained experience in manufacturing rifles by making the U.S. M16 under license for the South Korean Army. Once the initial requirements had been met, the company set about developing their own design. After a series of prototypes and limited-production models, the K2 has become the standard South Korean Army rifle.

The mechanism is the usual gas piston driving a bolt carrier holding a rotating bolt. A selector lever permits firing single shots, three-round bursts or automatic fire. The receiver is made from two aluminum alloy forgings, and the plastic butt is hinged so as to fold round to the right of the receiver, making the weapon more compact for carrying inside a vehicle.

There are two unique features about this rifle. The three-round burst mechanism does not re-set itself when the trigger is released. When the trigger is pressed for a second time, the burst picks up from where the last one stopped. This could be a trifle off-putting if you expect three rounds and only get one. The sights are also unusual; the rear sight is a two-position flip unit, but instead of two apertures for two ranges it has one aperture for daylight shooting, and the other flip has a notch and two white spots for night firing. Range adjustment is performed by turning a cam beneath the sight mount, so lifting the entire unit; the maximum range setting is 600 metres.

The barrel is rifled with one turn of the rifling in nine inches; this allows good shooting from either the older U.S. M193 ammunition (which normally uses one turn in 12 inches) or from the newer NATO-standard SS109 ammunition (which normally uses one turn in seven inches).

DESTROYER HEAVY SNIPING RIFLE

Left: The Czech CZ58 assault rifle.

Below: The Destroyer heavy sniping rifle.

Destroyer Heavy Sniping Rifle

Manufacturer Istvan Fellegi, Miskolo, Hungary
Type Recoil-operated semi-authomatic
Caliber 0.57mm (14.5mm)
Barrel 53.15in (1358mm)
Weight 37.5lbs (17kg)
Magazine Capacity 5 rounds

When the .50 heavy sniping rifles began to appear in the U.S.A., one or two people wondered what sort of performance these might have if they were given a really potent cartridge. The same question arose in Hungary, and when Istvan Fellegi completed the development of the Destroyer rifle in 12.7mm caliber, he set about developing an improved model firing the powerful ex-Soviet 14.5mm cartridge.

This cartridge was devised during World War Two for an anti-tank rifle, and it was so effective that it remained in use against light German armor throughout the war, long after every other country had abandoned anti-tank rifles as being useless. The 994 grain (64.4 grams) bullet has a core of tungsten carbide, a muzzle velocity of 1000 meters per second, and is capable of penetrating 16mm of armor steel at 1000 meters range.

Such a cartridge will, of course, produce a tremendous recoil, and the Destroyer has been built to minimize this as much as possible. There is a large muzzle brake, and the entire receiver and barrel can recoil inside the supporting frame of the rifle, damped down by a hydraulic record buffer. The butt is heavily padded, and while the effect on the firer is a good deal more severe than any ordinary rifle, it is tolerable to a trained soldier.

The rifle is semi-automatic, reloading automatically after every shot. The barrel and receiver recoil within the support frame for a short distance, after which the unit comes to a stop and the bolt is then unlocked and free to move backwards due to the momentum of the recoil. It loads a heavy return spring, then goes forward again, collecting a cartridge from the magazine and loading it into the chamber. The bolt then locks and the entire unit then runs back to the firing position. The rifle is automatically cocked during the recoil stroke and the next shot can be fired as soon as the firer has taken aim once more.

Dragunov SVD

Manufacturer Soviet State Arsenal, Izhevsk, CIS
Type Gas-operated, semi-automatic
Caliber 7.62mm Russian M1891
Barrel 24.5in (622mm)
Weight 9.5lbs (4.3kg) with sight
Magazine Capacity 10 rounds

The Dragunov SVD rifle has been the standard Soviet Army sniping rifle since 1965, and it was also adopted by the other armies of the Warsaw Pact, as well as being copied by Chinese, Egyptian, Iraqi and Yugoslavian makers. The Soviets were the first to adopt a semi-automatic rifle for sniping purposes, at a time when all other armies considered that semi-automatics were not sufficiently accurate for this role.

The operation of the Dragunov is, in principle, the same as that of the Kalashnikov rifle, using a gas piston and rotating bolt. But there are two very significant differences. Firstly there is no provision for automatic fire, since this is unnecessary on a sniping rifle. And secondly, the gas piston action is different. The Kalashnikov, like most gas-operated military rifles, uses a long stroke piston which gives a great reserve of power for dealing with dirt and sticky cartridge cases, but which shifts the balance of the rifle as it moves. This is not conducive to accuracy, and so the Dragunov uses a short-stroke piston which only moves a fraction of an inch and gives the bolt carrier a sharp blow, imparting enough momentum to drive it back and initiate the reloading cycle. One is entitled to assume that a sniper will keep his rifle clean and lubricated and be fussy about his ammunition, so the reserve of power is not necessary.

The cartridge is virtually an antique – the rimmed 7.62mm full-power round introduced with the Mosin-Nagant bolt-action rifle in 1891 – but it is an accurate and powerful round, which is what counts in this role. As with all rimmed cartridges there is a danger of jamming if the rims override each other, but the magazine is carefully made with guide ribs to control the cartridges and jams are extremely rare. (One report says that the design of the magazine took more time than any other part of the rifle, an indication of the importance of reliable feed.)

The standard sight is the four-power PSO-1, a somewhat clumsy but robust design with adequate optics. It also incorporates a 'Metascope', a small electronic device capable of detecting infra-red light at night and thus warning the sniper of being under observation. Unfortunately modern infra-red sights do not need IR illumination, and thus this device is no longer of much use.

With the recent change in the political climate, it can be expected that numbers of Dragunov rifles, not necessarily of Russian manufacture, will appear on the commercial market around the world.

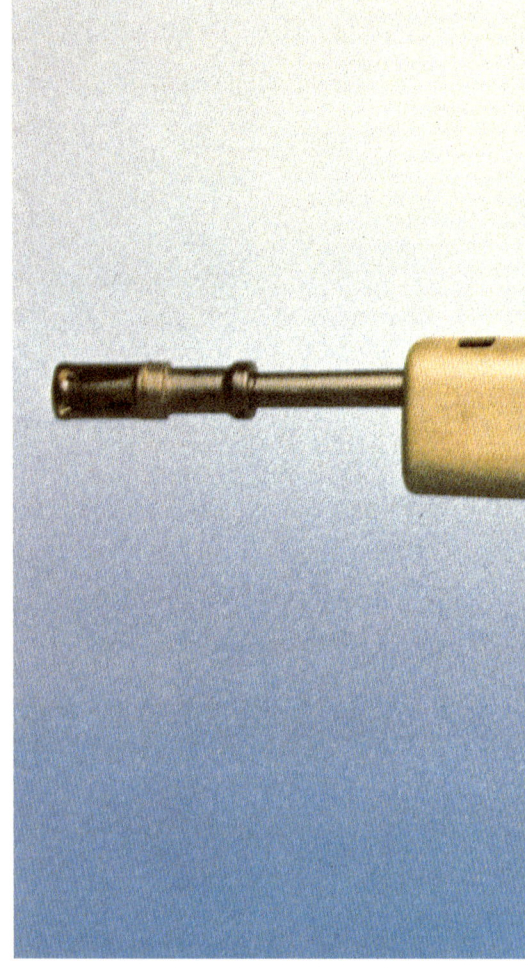

Below: The Dragunov SVD rifle.

Enfield L85A1 Individual Weapon

Manufacturer Royal Small Arms Factory, Nottingham, England
Type Gas-operated, selective fire
Caliber 5.56mm (.223)
Barrel 20.4in (518mm)
Weight 8.20lbs (3.72kg)
Magazine Capacity 20 rounds
Cyclic rate of fire 800 rounds/minute

The British Army began looking for an automatic rifle in about 1910, but the research program was interrupted several times and it was not until 1950 that a design was finally approved. Just as it was about to go into production, though, the politicians got into the act and the design was dropped in favour of the Belgian FN-FAL and the 7.62mm NATO cartridge. When this rifle began to be outdated, Enfield began designing once more, this time with a new cartridge of 4.85mm caliber, ready for the 1978 NATO small arms trials. Their 1950 model,

ENFIELD L85A1 INDIVIDUAL WEAPON

Above and below: The Enfield SA-80 Individual Weapon.

ENFIELD L85A1 INDIVIDUAL WEAPON

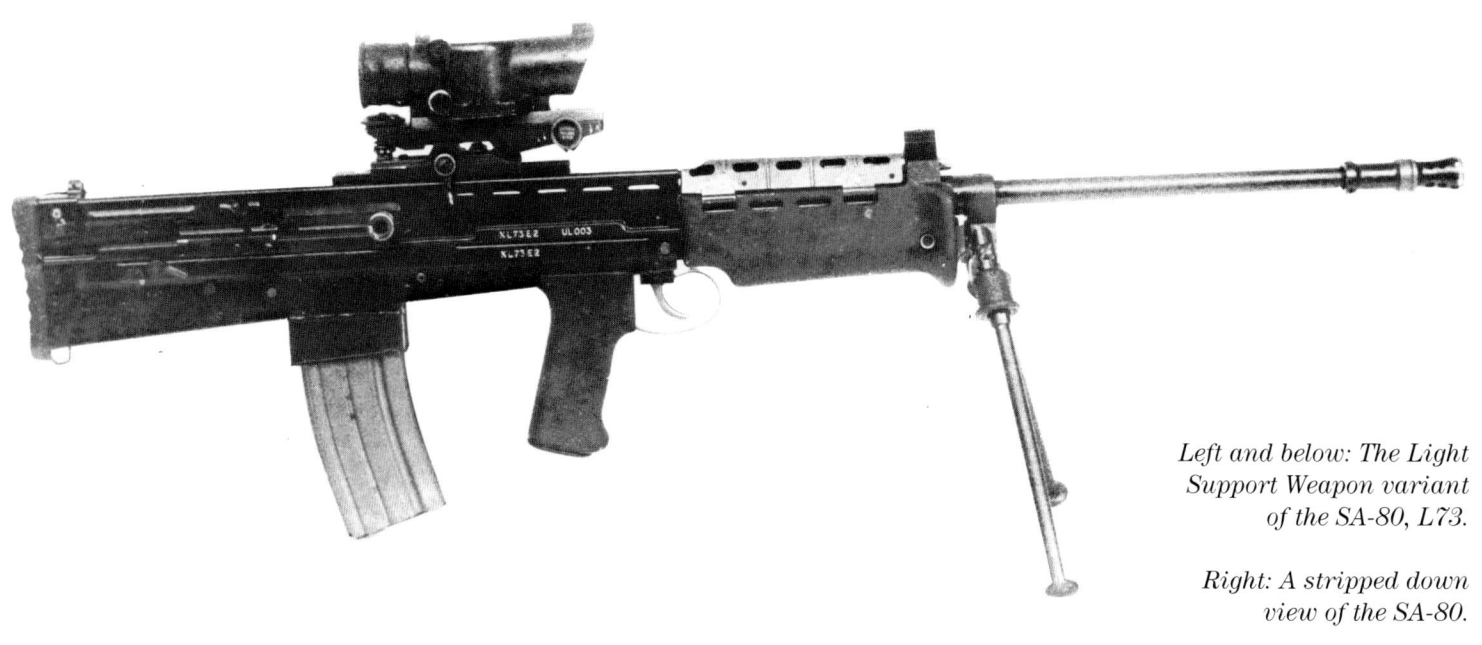

Left and below: The Light Support Weapon variant of the SA-80, L73.

Right: A stripped down view of the SA-80.

the EM1, had been dropped because it could not be reworked into 7.62mm caliber (from 2.80) when the need arose, so the designers of the new rifle were wise enough to build it so that it could be recalibered if necessary. When the NATO trial decided on 5.56mm as the next standard caliber their foresight paid off; the Enfield design was rejigged to 5.56mm and has now been approved for service. It is believed that a number of pre-production models were evaluated in combat during the 1982 Falkland Islands campaign. The rifle was adopted for use by the British Army in the mid-1980s.

The Enfield 'Individual Weapon' is a conventional gas-piston-operated design, using a rotating bolt in a carrier which rides on two guide rods. It is of 'bullpup' layout, the magazine being well behind the trigger and the action lying under the firer's cheek. The receiver is a pressed-steel component which requires little machining since the guide rods control the bolt's movement. The furniture is of sturdy plastic, and the gas system has a three-position regulator giving normal use, extra power for fouled actions, and in closed position for grenade launching.

The standard sight is the 'SUIT' or

ERMA EM1/EGM1 CARBINE

'Sight Unit, Infantry, Trilux,' a short optical telescope containing an illuminating source for shooting in bad light. This is a sealed unit and adjustments for elevation and windage are carried out on its supporting bracket. On top of the SUIT unit there are emergency iron sights; there are no sights on the body of the rifle, though a foresight blade and a two-aperture backsight can be fitted if desired.

The Enfield rifle is extremely easy to shoot, popular with soldiers and very accurate; in spite of its compactness, the bullpup layout ensures a good barrel length, and the latest models will be rifled to suit the new SS109 NATO standard 5.56mm bullet. There is also a heavy-barrelled version with a bipod which is intended as the squad automatic weapon; this rejoices in the name 'L86 Light Support Weapon'.

Erma EM1 and EGM1 Carbines

Manufacturer Ermawerke GmbH, Dachau, D-8080 Germany
Type Blowback, semi-automatic
Caliber .22 Long Rifle RF
Barrel 18in (457mm)
Weight 5.5lbs (2.49kg)
Magazine Capacity 10 rounds

The U.S. Army's M1 Carbine of World War Two had a mysterious charisma which made people lust after it, even though it was a pretty dismal combat weapon at anything over 50 yards range. As a result there have been numerous lookalikes over the years, and the German Erma company, renowned for military weapons in days gone by, have now produced a pair of

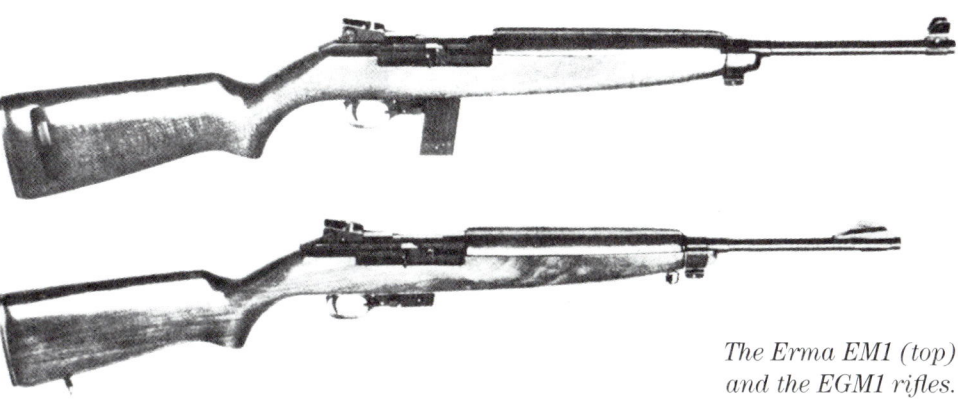

The Erma EM1 (top) and the EGM1 rifles.

.22 rimfire carbines which look almost like carbon copies of the 'real thing'.

There are two models which are mechanically identical; the EM1 is the 'standard' and is almost indistinguishable from an M1; the EGM1 is the 'de luxe' version fitted with a sporterized walnut stock. The receiver is of alloy, blackened to match the finish of the steel barrel, and the cocking handle operating rod vanishes forward into the woodwork just as did that of the M1, but has nothing on the forward end except the return spring and its guide rod; the bolt is a straightforward blowback action. Since there is thus no need to revolve the bolt, the connection between cocking handle and bolt is not so complex as that of the M1. Firing is performed by a spring-driven firing pin which has a bent protruding below the bolt to be caught by the sear on the reloading stroke.

The carbines are equipped with replicas of the original sights; a front blade between protective ears, and a rear aperture 'battle' sight. They are efficient within their capabilities, and on the range the carbine showed itself to be capable of sufficient accuracy for its purpose in life, which is eminently that of a 'fun gun' for casual plinking or vermin shooting at moderate ranges. It is light, handy, reliable if cleaned regularly of the grease and fouling which 'shooting' .22 ammunition generates, and good value for money.

Erma EG73 Carbine

Manufacturer Ermawerke GmbH, D-8080 Dachau, Germany
Type Lever-action, rimfire, magazine
Caliber .22 Winchester Magnum RF
Barrel 19.5in (495mm)
Weight 5.5lbs (2.49kg)
Magazine Capacity 12 rounds

Although the experts are fond of telling us that lever-action carbines are inherently inaccurate, up until now nobody has told the carbines anything of the sort and they still go on shooting straight. There is no doubt that there is a great visual appeal in the classic saddle-gun lines of straight stock and short fore-end, with the barrel and tubular magazine in front, and as long as this appeal remains, gunmakers are going to produce them and sell them.

The Ermawerke of Germany have had considerable experience in weapon design and construction, and one of their latest offerings is this Magnum carbine. Its lines follow the classic Winchester, though the action is entirely their own, with a solid-topped receiver. The bolt is unlocked and retracted by full 90° swing of the under-lever, and in doing so it cocks the external hammer and lifts a fresh cartridge from the magazine. Pulling the lever back chambers the round and locks the bolt, ready to fire. The action is exceptionally smooth, being made to fine tolerances and well fitted, and the quietness will be appreciated by hunters.

The magazine is of steel, unlikely to be accidentally dented, and holds 12 cartridges, after which a 13th can be loaded into the breech. The foresight is a post concealed in a hood, while the rear sight is a notch on a step-adjustable leaf. There is no windage adjustment as such, though the sight can be moved sideways in its mounting for zeroing. The only safety device is the usual half-cock notch on the hammer.

The stock is of walnut and well finished, the steel of the barrel, magazine and action, is blued and polished, and the whole weapon makes an attractive and functional package.

Fabrique Nationale FNC Rifle

Manufacturer Fabrique Nationale d'Armes de Guerre, Herstal, Belgium
Type Gas-operated, selective fire
Caliber 5.56mm (.223)
Barrel 17.7in (450mm)
Weight 8.37lbs (3.80kg)
Magazine Capacity 30 rounds
Cyclic rate of fire 650 rounds/minute

Some years ago the FN company developed a 5.56mm rifle which they called the 'CAL' (Carabine Automatique Legère), anticipating that 5.56mm would become popular as a

Above: The Erma EG73 carbine.

FINNBIATHLON .22

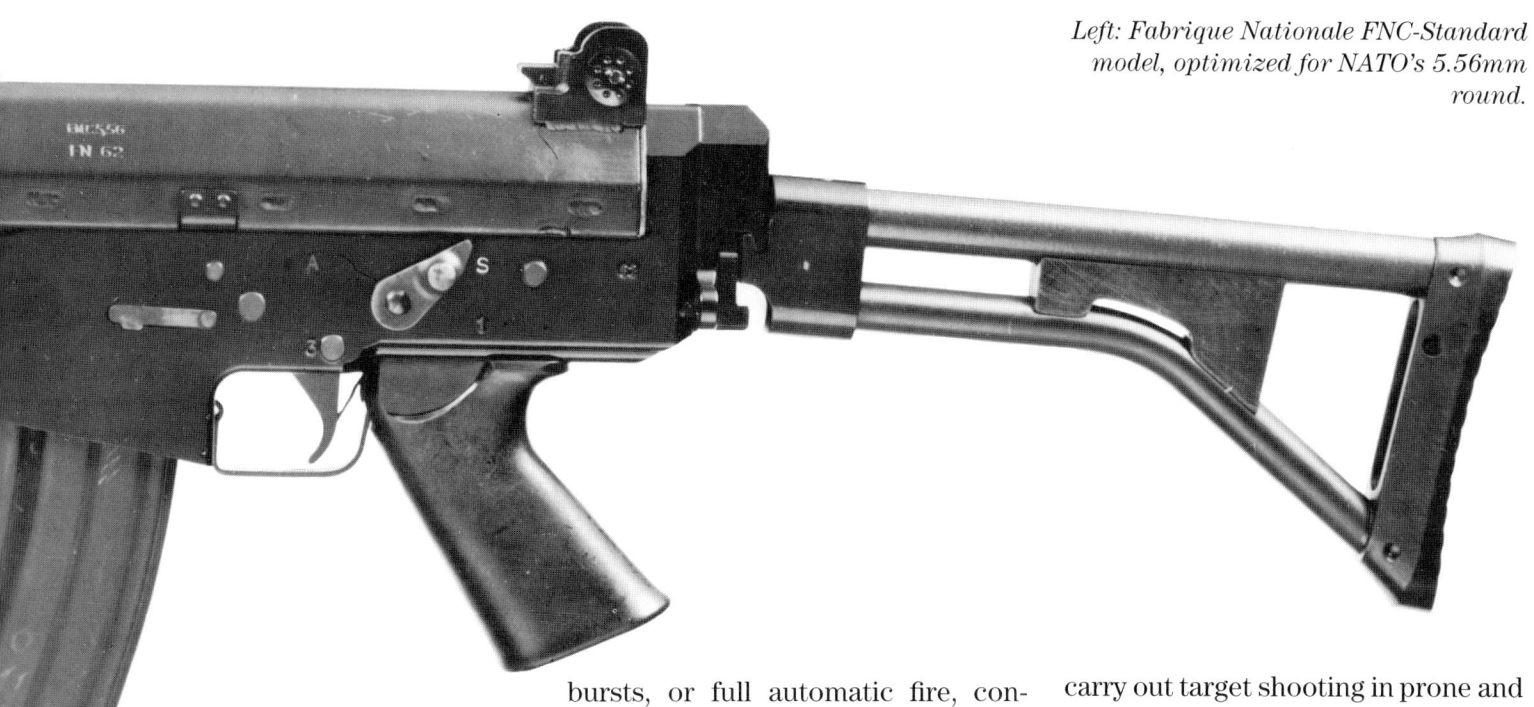

Left: Fabrique Nationale FNC-Standard model, optimized for NATO's 5.56mm round.

military caliber; they were right, but it took longer than they thought and the CAL was rather in advance of its time. Several armies bought small quantities for evaluation, and their reports, together with FN's own expertise, suggested that it should be possible to develop a cheaper and better design; this FN did, the result being the FNC. It has undergone extensive military trials in Sweden and in some NATO armies, and the Indonesian Army has adopted it for service.

The FNC makes extensive use of pressed steel and plastic components; it follows the general pattern of FN automatic rifles and the body opens on a front hinge pin to allow the working parts to be withdrawn to the rear. Operation is by gas tapped from the barrel and fed to a conventional gas cylinder above the barrel. The gas piston is driven back to strike a bolt carrier which contains the usual type of two-lug rotating bolt. The bolt and carrier are among the few components in the FNC which demand precision machining. The gas cylinder has a two-port regulator which can be switched from the normal position to admit more gas when operating under adverse conditions.

The trigger mechanism allows selection of single shots, three-round bursts, or full automatic fire, controlled by a selector switch on the left side. The box magazine is interchangeable with that of the U. S. M16A1 rifle, and both can be folded alongside the receiver either for transport or to make the weapon more compact for use in the submachine gun role.

The barrel is rifled one turn in 32 calibers, much tighter than previous 5.56mm weapons, and is optimized for use with the Belgian SS109 bullet, which has been selected as NATO standard. With this ammunition the three-round burst will deliver shots dispersed by 70cm at 500m range, and will penetrate the standard U.S. Army steel helmet at over 1000 yards. The standard sights consist of a front post and a flip aperture rear sight set for 250m and 400m, but the rifle can accept all types of telescope, image intensifying and thermal imaging sights for sniping or night use.

Finnbiathlon .22

Manufacturer Tampereen Asepaja Oy, SF-33100, Tampere 10, Finland
Type Bolt-action, magazine, rimfire
Caliber .22 Long Rifle RF
Barrel 22.8in (580mm)
Weight 9.25lbs (4.2kg)
Magazine Capacity 5 rounds

The Biathlon event is an Olympic contest which involves skiing across country and stopping four times to carry out target shooting in prone and standing positions; the whole affair is intended to simulate a hunting expedition in the frozen North. When it was first invented, by the Scandinavians many years ago, it probably did; the contestants used military rifles and fired at realistically varying ranges. Since it has been absorbed into the artificial world of Olympic sports, however, the rifle has become a .22 rimfire and the range is fixed at 50 yards. Needless to say, as soon as it became an organized sport, the sportsmen began looking for an edge and a highly specialized design of rifle has resulted.

The Finnbiathlon is a good example of this rare class, and it exhibits some unusual features. Its angular appearance makes it obvious that it is a target rifle, but the unusual collection of straps mark it out as something out of the ordinary. These are the carrying slings which allow it to be slung from both shoulders and worn in the middle of the back; pointing up, so as to be out of the way when skiing; the sling ends in cords which can be passed through any pair of eight holes in the butt, so adjusting the height of the carry.

The bolt action is also unusual, being a straight pull type; these are exceptionally rare in modern weapons. The T-shaped handle is simply pulled straight back and pushed forward again, a sleeve with cam track taking

GALIL ASSAULT RIFLE

Left: Galil sniper's rifle.

care of rotating the bolt. This leads to a very fast action and one which gives minimal aim disturbance when performed at the shoulder, both desirable features in the Biathlon where time is at a premium. Another unusual item is a 'snow guard' around the muzzle, which prevents the sights or barrel becoming blocked with snow during traveling or even when diving for the ground for the prone shoots. When the muzzle is closed off, so are the sights, so there is no danger of accidentally loosing off a round.

The trigger is adjustable for tension and position, and is a two-pressure military type. The rear sight is an aperture type, fully adjustable for elevation and windage, while the front sight is a hooded aperture. Weights can be fitted inside the fore end in order to achieve the desired balance, the maximum additions taking the overall weight of the rifle up to 11lbs. As a final touch, the fore end has four slots in its right side into which four loaded magazines can be fitted, their bases out, so that they can be rapidly reached and changed during the progress of the event.

The center ring of the Biathlon target is 40mm in diameter (1.56in) and the rifle is quite capable of putting a string of shots into this at 50 meters. Its accuracy is first class, giving half- to three-quarter-inch groups at that range when fired from a rest. But of course, shooting a string of five from the standing position after traveling across miles of snow isn't exactly shooting from a rest.

Galil Assault Rifle

Manufacturer Israeli Military Industries, Tel Aviv, Israel
Type Gas-operated, selective fire
Caliber 5.56mm (.223)
Barrel 20.6in (524mm)
Weight 8.8lbs (4.0kg)
Magazine Capacity 35 rounds
Cyclic rate of fire 650 rounds/minute

The Israeli Army decided to adopt the 5.56mm cartridge after the Six-Day War of 1967, and in the following two years every 5.56mm rifle in existence was bought and tested. In view of their location, much emphasis was placed on reliability under hot dusty conditions. Of the various models tested, the Galil, designed by Israel Galil and Yaacov Lior, most closely met the requirements and development went ahead; it was approved for adoption in 1972 but it was some time before it actually got into service and it is not, even now, a universal issue throughout the Israeli armed forces. It has been exported to some other countries, however.

The Galil has been designed to fill the place of three weapons – the rifle, the sub-machine gun and the squad automatic or light machine gun. It can also fire a variety of grenades, and a short-barreled version has been developed for use by Special Forces.

Mechanically, the Galil leans heavily on the Kalashnikov; it uses a similar method of gas operation, with a cylinder above the barrel, and a similar gas piston-cum-bolt carrier assembly. The bolt has two locking lugs and a cam pin which follows a track in the carrier which drives it to rotate for locking and unlocking. The cocking lever is attached to the bolt carrier so that it can be used for positive bolt closure in the event of fouling, and the change lever for single shot or automatic fire is on the right; when moved to the 'safe' position it closes up the cocking handle slot against dust and also restricts the movement of the handle and bolt. The trigger and firing mechanism use a hammer and are very reminiscent of the Garand design.

The Galil may be found with a wood or plastic stock and handguard (Model ARM), or with a folding metal stock and plastic handguard (Model AR); the ARM is fitted with bipod and carrying handle for use as the squad automatic. There is also the Model SAR which resembles the AR but has a shorter (13in – 332mm) barrel.

The foresight is a post, adjustable for elevation for zeroing and concealed within a ring shroud, and a flip-over rear sight set for 300m and 500m ranges. Both sights have auxiliary night sights folded down behind them; when raised, these exhibit three white or pale green spots of light, generated by 'Betalight' radiological sources. To sight the weapon the three dots are lined up horizontally and the centre one alined with the target. The barrel has a flash hider which doubles as a grenade launching spigot, and the bipod joint incorporates a wire-cutter.

In service the Galil appears to have lived up to its expectations; it is simple, robust and accurate and it can withstand desert conditions probably better than any other comparable rifle.

Gepard Heavy Sniping Rifle

Manufacturer Istvan Fellegi, Miskolo, Hungary
Type Bolt-action, single shot
Caliber 0.50in (12.7mm)
Barrel 43.3in (1100mm)
Weight 35.2lbs (16kg)

HECKLER & KOCH G-11

Right: The Advanced Combat Rifle version of Heckler & Koch's G-11.

Bottom: The Gepard Heavy Sniping Rifle.

The Hungarian Gepard rifle is a rather peculiar design which first appeared in the West in 1990. It is a single-shot weapon, without a magazine, so that firing each round is a slow business. The pistol grip actually acts as the handle of the breech bolt and contains a very simple hammer and firing pin mechanism. To load, the pistol grip is twisted sideways to unlock the lugs on the bolt from meting recesses in the barrel, and the grip and bolt are then removed completely from the weapon. The cartridge is then inserted into the exposed chamber and the grip and bolt are replaced and twisted back so as to lock the breech securely. The hammer is cocked and then the trigger is pressed to fire the round.

The cartridge is the ex-Soviet 12.7mm machine gun round, roughly equivalent to the U.S. .50 Browning machine gun cartridge. It delivers a heavy bullet, and, as a result, generates a heavy recoil in the gun. The Gepard's barrel is fitted with a high-efficiency muzzle brake, which helps to reduce the recoil to manageable proportions. There is also a resilient butt pad and cheek piece to avoid injury to the firer. The rifle is usually supported on a simple adjustable bipod, but standard Warsaw Pact machine gun tripods can also be used.

The cartridge is sufficiently accurate to give a 300mm (12 inch) group with five shots at 600 meters range. The bullet is capable of penetrating 30mm of rolled steel armor plate at 100 meters, dropping to 15mm at 600 meters. The effective range is claimed to be up to 2000 meters against vehicles and similar large targets, 1200 meters against personnel.

Heckler & Koch G-11

Manufacturer Heckler & Koch GmbH, Oberndorf Am Neckar, Germany
Type Gas-operated, selective fire
Caliber 4.73mm
Barrel 21.25in (540mm)
Weight 8lbs (3.65kg)
Magazine Capacity 45 rounds

HECKLER & KOCH G-11

This is probably the most revolutionary weapon to appear anywhere in the past 40 years or more, involving a totally new type of mechanism and a caseless cartridge. It was planned to be adopted by the West German Army in 1990, but events overtook it, and the G-11 and the company who developed it were among the first victims of the 'peace dividend'.

The design began in the late 1960s when the West German Army, looking ahead, asked for new rifle designs. They laid down few conditions except that it had to be able to fire a three-round burst with dispersion of not more than two mils between each bullet impact. This meant that at 500 metres the extreme spread between the three shots had to be under one metre – and we are talking abut a three-round burst, not three individual aimed shots. Heckler & Koch soon realized that this meant a rate of fire in excess of 2000 rounds a minute in order to get three rounds off before the barrel moved from the point of aim, and this, in turn, meant devising a totally new mechanical solution.

Their first move was to develop a caseless cartridge, in association with Dynamit Nobel. This has two advantages: it is lighter than a conventional brass-cased round, so the soldier can carry more of them; and the rifle mechanism no longer has to cater for the extraction and ejection of the spent case. This development took time; the first design was a block of nitro-cellulose propellant and plastic binder, with a bullet in the front and a combustible cap in the rear. It worked, but overheated the rifle, leading to cook-off problems in which a round loaded into a hot chamber suffered spontaneous combustion from the induced heat. The problem was eventually overcome by the development of a new 'High Ignition Temperature Propellant' which requires a temperature some 100 degrees C higher than nitro-cellulose before it cooks off.

The mechanism in the rifle is complex, but can be summed up by saying that it is a rotating breechblock with a chamber bored in it. This revolves in line with the barrel. By operating an external knob the chamber is turned vertically, and a cartridge is fed in from the magazine, which lies above the barrel. Another turn of the knob and the block is rotated so that the chamber lies behind the barrel. Pressing the trigger allows a firing pin to strike the cap; cap and propellant are entirely consumed and the bullet is driven out of the barrel. Gas is tapped from the barrel and the power used to rotate the breechblock, collect a fresh round and rotate it again ready for the next shot. To unload, the knob is turned backwards and the cartridge drops out through a hole in the bottom of the rifle.

As might be imagined, the greatest problem to be overcome in this design is sealing the breech so that all the gas drives the bullet out and does not escape between the chamber and the barrel; the precise details are secret, but they appear to be very similar to the sealing of a Wankel automobile engine.

The mechanism, together with the barrel, is completely concealed within an all-enveloping plastic casing. This is formed into a butt, into a pistol grip and into a carrying handle which also contains a low-power optical sight with illuminated reticle for night firing. When a shot is fired the entire mechanism recoils about an inch inside this casing, being damped by buffer springs. As a result the recoil is felt more as a gentle push than as a violent blow.

If the selector switch is turned to the three-round burst position, the sequence of events for the first shot is the same as for a single shot. But as the first shot is fired and the mechanism begins to move backwards in recoil, control is assumed by an automatic device which now operates the bolt to load and fire a second shot while the system is still moving backwards. The second shot adds to the rearward momentum, and the third shot is chambered and fired. Only then does the system complete the recoil stroke and return to the forward position. In this case the recoil is about 2.5 inches, but the blow to the firer's shoulder is still not excessive. The noise of the three shots merges into one rasping report and the three bullets have left the barrel before the firer feels any recoil and before the barrel has started to move off the aim.

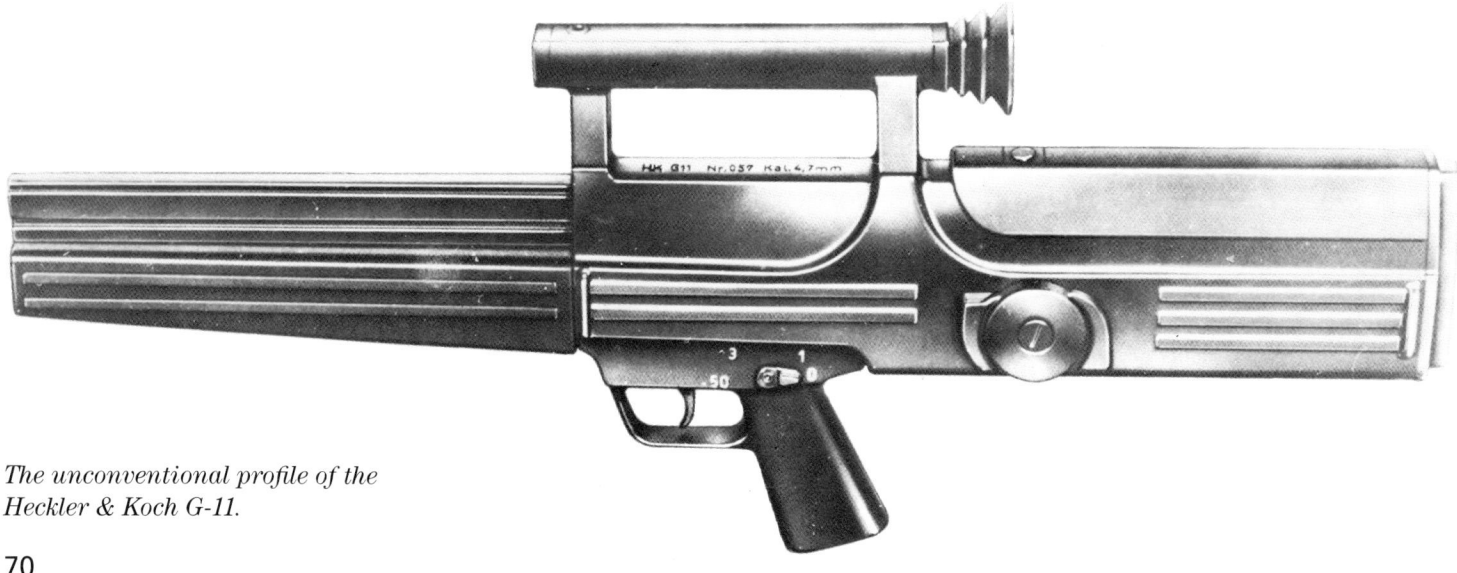

The unconventional profile of the Heckler & Koch G-11.

Left: The Heckler & Koch HK81 rifle.

In this way the demand for burst accuracy has been met.

At automatic fire the high-speed mechanism is out of action and the rifle merely repeats the single shot movement at a rate of about 600 rounds per minute. Here the individual recoils can be felt, but the internal buffering keeps most of the shots in the target area.

A slightly modified version of the G-11 was put forward as a candidate for the U.S. Army's Advanced Combat Rifle project. It performed well, but, as with all the other contestants, failed to provide the demanded 100 percent improvement over the M16A2. At much the same time as this trial was under way the re-unification of Germany took place, and the German government was faced with the problem of finding money to fund the economic recovery of the eastern provinces. As usual, the defense budget was the first target, and the contract for the G-11 was canceled. Instead of equipping the German Army with the new rifle, only about 1000 were purchased for use by Special Forces. Heckler & Koch had been relying upon this promised contract to recoup their enormous developmental expenses, and when the contract failed, so did the company. They were eventually bought by Royal Ordnance of Britain, and the G-11 rifle production was canceled. Whether this revolutionary weapon will ever see general issue is an open question; at the present time, it appears unlikely.

Heckler & Koch HK81 Rifle

Manufacturer Heckler & Koch GmbH, Oberndorf Am Neckar, Germany
Type Delayed blowback, selective fire
Caliber 7.62mm NATO
Barrel 17.7in (450mm)
Weight 19.05lbs (8.65kg) (with bipod and telescope sight)
Magazine Capacity 5, 20 or 30 rounds
Cyclic rate of fire 800 rounds/minute

European police forces now regularly confront armed criminals, so it is not surprising that the public's attitudes towards armed police are gradually changing.

The HK81 rifle is an interesting example of how gunmakers are tailoring their products to suit the special requirements of police forces, and it is also a lesson in how to acquire firepower without upsetting the populace at large.

On the face of it the HK81 is little more than the basic G3 military rifle with a few small changes. It uses the same two-part, roller-locked bolt which every H&K weapon shares, but the barrel is somewhat heavier than the military standard and is carefully fitted so that the rifle is capable of extremely high accuracy. There is also a light but strong bipod attached to the fore-end so that the rifle can be rested during long periods of surveillance. While iron sights (front hooded post and rear aperture) are fitted, the rifle is always supplied with a variable-power telescope sight. The trigger mechanism can be either a standard military two-stage trigger or an adjustable set trigger for increased accuracy. So the basic weapon is a robust and highly accurate sniping or general-purpose rifle.

Above the trigger, however, there is a change lever which allows automatic fire; and on the right side of the rifle there is a release for the quick-change barrel. So the HK81 can also function as a light machine gun, using the 30-round magazine. Thus while the police force has ostensibly bought rifles, it has in fact equipped itself with machine guns.

Further, by changing the barrel and bolt the gun can be rapidly converted to fire either the 7.62mm × 39 cartridge or the 5.56mm × 45 cartridge should the need arise. And by removing the magazine housing and replacing it with a belt adapter, it can be turned into a belt-fed machine gun in any of the three calibers. As if this were not enough, a laser projector can be fitted, placing a spot of light on the target to permit accurate aiming at night; image-intensifying sights can be fitted to the telescope mount; tear gas grenades can be projected from the flash hider (which doubles as a grenade-launching spigot), and there is even a tripod mount for heavy duty.

The HK81 is a remarkable example of versatility; it is also a depressing example of the lengths to which European police forces are being driven by political extremists.

Heckler & Koch HK91

Manufacturer Heckler & Koch GmbH, Oberndorf Am Neckar, Germany
Type Delayed blowback, semi-automatic
Caliber 7.62mm NATO (.308 Winchester)
Barrel 19in (482mm)
Weight 10.25lbs (4.65kg)
Magazine Capacity 20 rounds

The German Army's service rifle, the Heckler & Koch G3 is widely distributed throughout the world and enjoys a high reputation for serviceability. It is too well-known to warrant a separate entry here, but it is perhaps worth reminding readers that it is descended from the Mauser design of Sturmgewehr developed in 1945, whisked off to Spain to become the original CETME, and later returned to Germany and polished into G3 form. Like many military rifles of today, the G3 has a selective fire option which prevents it being legally acquired by sport shooters, and therefore Heckler & Koch have developed a semi-automatic-only version, which sells as the Model 91.

The HK91 is typical of today's military firearms, having a stamped steel receiver, plastic fore end, butt and pistol grip, and a very simple takedown procedure. The bolt moves on ribs formed in the receiver walls, and the barrel is pinned into the receiver. Above the barrel is a tubular sleeve carrying the cocking handle and bolt extension. The bolt is Heckler & Koch's renowned two-piece unit with roller locking, described elsewhere in these pages, which delays the opening of the breech long enough for the bullet to clear the muzzle, after which the action is straightforward blowback. One problem with blowback action is that the initial extraction of the cartridge tends to be somewhat abrupt, and this can cause trouble with necked high pressure cases. The HK91 uses a grooved chamber to allow gas to flow back down the grooves to the outside of the case and so 'float' it on a layer of gas, making extraction more easy and generally foolproof. The cases are ejected streaked with carbon and generally looking rather sorry, but experience has shown that they are perfectly safe to reload several times.

The sights are standard Bundeswehr service pattern, a post inside a ring for the foresight and a rotating rear sight with apertures for 200, 300 and 400 meters. There is also an open notch 'battle sight', and the entire rear sight unit can be adjusted to compensate for individual zeroing and for differences in ammunition.

The standard model uses a fixed plastic butt; there is also a version with telescoping metal buttstock. There is also the HK93, similar to the 91 but chambered for the 5.56mm cartridge.

The accuracy of the HK91 is rather better than average for this class of rifle; it will generally make four- to five-inch groups at 200 yards with European service ammunition, rather worse with other types. With handloaded ammunition it should be possible to get slightly under four inches if a telescope sight is used.

Heckler & Koch HK270

Manufacturer Heckler & Koch GmbH, Oberndorf Am Neckar, Germany
Type Blowback semi-automatic
Caliber .22 Long Rifle RF
Barrel 19.7in (500mm)
Weight 5.5lbs (2.5kg)
Magazine Capacity 2, 5 or 20 rounds

This sporting rifle from Heckler & Koch has an interesting amalgamation of civil and military features and there is a suggestion that it may have originated in a design for a military training rifle. However it started, the resulting rifle is one of their best, being light, rapid, accurate and extremely popular.

The 270 is a conventional sporting rimfire model, using a plain blowback bolt action. The stock is of walnut and might be called 'semi-Monte Carlo', since while the comb is fairly high there is no prominent cheek rest. Its finish is excellent and it complements the well-blued finish of the metalwork.

The magazine enters beneath the action; as with other German designs, regulations restrict the home market to a two-round box, but larger magazines are provided for export, the five-round as standard and the 20-round as an optional alternative or extra.

The foresight is a ring shroud containing a diaphragm unit carrying a central post; by removing a pin this diaphragm can be changed for different thicknesses and heights of post. The rear sight is the standard Germany Army G3 sight, which is the

Left: The Heckler & Koch G-3 rifle, the basis for the HK81.

Above: The Heckler & Koch HK270 semi-automatic rifle.

clue to its possible military training origin. This is an aperture sight which can be varied for set ranges by rotating an obliquely-set drum. The whole sight can be adjusted for elevation and windage very easily by use of a special tool supplied with the rifle. In addition, the receiver top is grooved for a telescope mount.

The 270 is by no means a target rifle, but on the other hand it should not be dismissed simply as a 'fun gun' either. Once zeroed it is capable of impressive accuracy and it makes an excellent hunting weapon for the vermin and small game found in Europe.

Heckler & Koch HK300

Manufacturer Heckler & Koch GmbH, Oberndorf Am Neckar, Germany
Type Blowback, semi-automatic
Caliber .22 Winchester Magnum RF
Barrel 19.7in (500mm)
Weight 5.7lbs (2.59kg)
Magazine Capacity 2, 5 or 15 rounds

The HK300 might be called a 'de luxe' version of the 270; it is built to take a more powerful cartridge, but retains the same basic blowback mechanism and is generally to a higher standard of fit and finish. The manufacturers claim that it is 'Specially intended for the close season and for hunting small predatory game and controlling stray domestic animals.'
The stock is of walnut, well checkered and oil-finished, and with a cheek rest on the butt. The barrel is somewhat heavier than that of the 270, as befits the heavier cartridge, but the bolt mechanism is basically the same. The sights comprise a front blade set on a ramp and adjustable for elevation, and an open blade rearsight adjustable for windage. The receiver top is slotted to take the HK05 universal telescope mount, which can be attached or removed in seconds, firmly locked in place by a lever, and retains the zero whenever replaced. As with other German designs, there is a two-round magazine for the domestic market and five or 15-round models for export.

The combination of heavier barrel and .22 Magnum cartridge have produced a rifle of superlative accuracy, capable of stretching most marksmen to their utmost ability.

Heckler & Koch HK770

Manufacturer Heckler & Koch GmbH, Oberndorf Am Neckar, Germany
Type Delayed blowback semi-automatic
Caliber .308 Winchester (7.62mm NATO)
Barrel 19.7in (500mm)
Weight 7.04lbs (3.20kg)
Magazine Capacity 2, 3 or 10 rounds

Thanks to somewhat more intelligent gun legislation than the rest of Europe and to their natural advantages in respect of forests and hunting areas, the Germans still have a thriving home market for firearms which helps to form a sound base for their export activities. Most German gunmakers, irrespective of their primary product, have an eye to this home market and ensure that they have a suitable product, if only to remind people of their existence. Thus it comes about that Heckler & Koch, generally associated in most non-German minds with military firearms, have an impressive range of sporting weapons, and the Model 770 is the civilian equipment of the well-known G3 military rifle.

In saying that we do not imply that it is a conversion for civil purposes; this role is played by the HK91 already discussed, but this sort of conversion is less popular in Europe than in the U.S.A. The HK770 is a well-built sporting rifle and looks it; its military heritage is only seen in the mechanical arrangements, which include the same two-part roller-locked breech block.

The 770 is a handsome weapon, with a graceful walnut stock, finely checkered and well finished. The receiver has a somewhat unusual steel cover over the bolt mechanism, and there is a folding cocking handle on the right side. A box magazine is inserted beneath the action; in Germany this is restricted to a model holding two rounds, to comply with various regulations, but for export, magazines holding 5 or 10 rounds can be provided. The magazine retaining catch is in the front of the trigger guard and the safety is on the left side, just above the trigger area.

The foresight is a flat-topped blade adjustable for elevation, while the rear sight is an open notch, adjustable for elevation and windage. The top surface of the 'upper receiver' (receiver top cover) is prepared for H&K's HK05 Claw Mount which will accept virtually any type of telescope mount.

On the range the 770 performs extremely well; those unaccustomed to

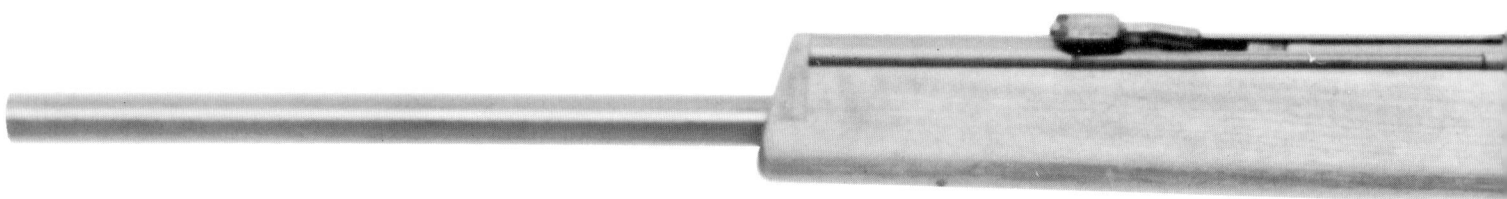

Above: The Heckler & Koch PSG-1 sniping rifle.

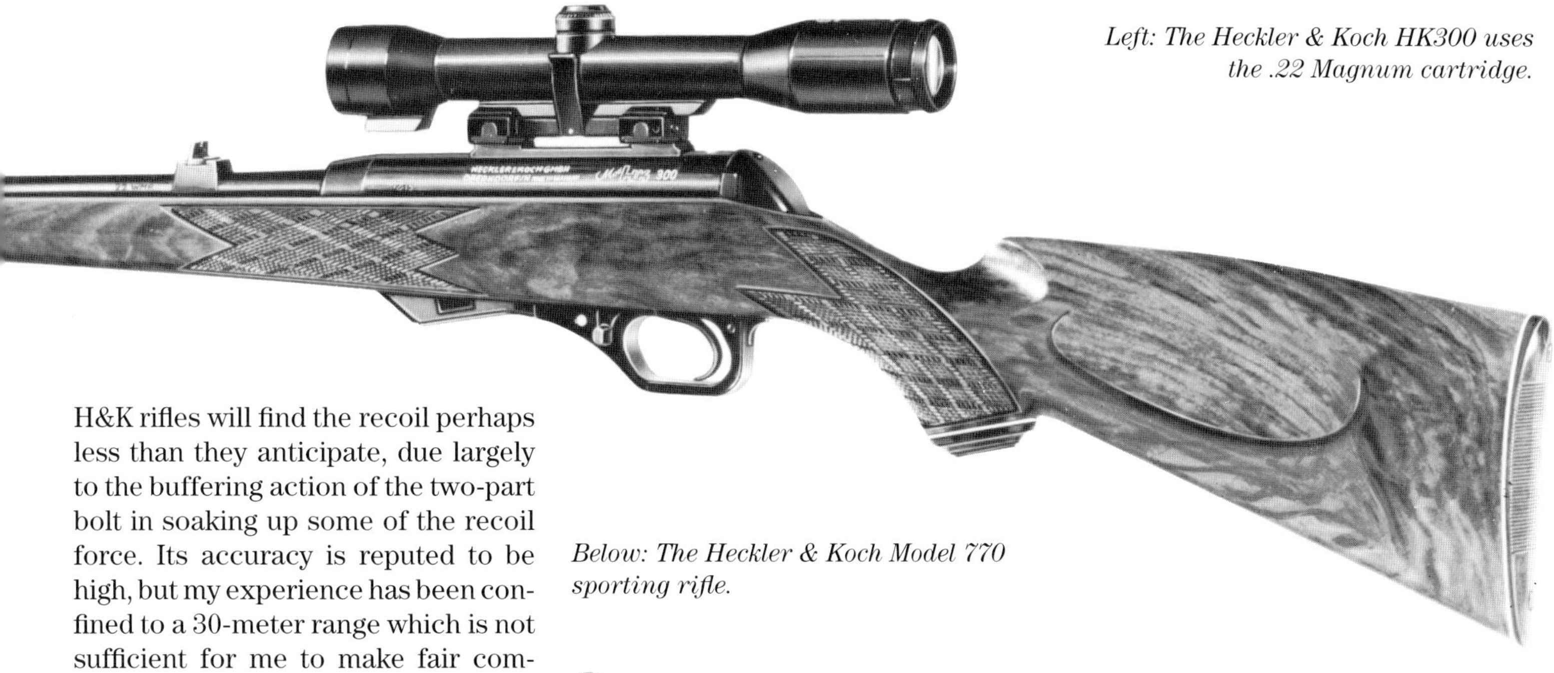

HECKLER & KOCH PSG-1 SNIPING RIFLE

Left: The Heckler & Koch HK300 uses the .22 Magnum cartridge.

H&K rifles will find the recoil perhaps less than they anticipate, due largely to the buffering action of the two-part bolt in soaking up some of the recoil force. Its accuracy is reputed to be high, but my experience has been confined to a 30-meter range which is not sufficient for me to make fair comment. One major advantage over most semi-automatics derived from military design is that the vast production of the G3 and its allied models over the years enables this rifle to be turned out to a high standard of manufacture but at a most competitive price.

There are two parallel models to this; the HK630 is chambered for .223 Remington (5.56mm) cartridges, and the HK940 for the .30-06 cartridge. Apart from small differences in barrel length to accommodate the differing ballistics of the cartridges they are substantially the same as the 770.

Below: The Heckler & Koch Model 770 sporting rifle.

Heckler & Koch PSG-1 Sniping Rifle

Manufacturer Heckler & Koch GmbH, Oberndorf Am Neckar, Germany
Type Semi-automatic, delayed blowback, magazine
Caliber 7.62mm NATO (.308 Winchester)
Barrel 25.6in (650mm)
Weight 15.8lbs (7.2kg)
Magazine Capacity 5 rounds

This rifle has been developed by Heckler & Koch to satisfy the current demand from military and police authorities for a high-precision weapon for use by snipers and skilled marksmen. It uses the standard basic breech mechanism in which the bolt is a two-part unit and its opening is delayed by a roller-locking system. In this way the rifle's operation is already familiar to most service personnel and its repair and maintenance present no fresh problems.

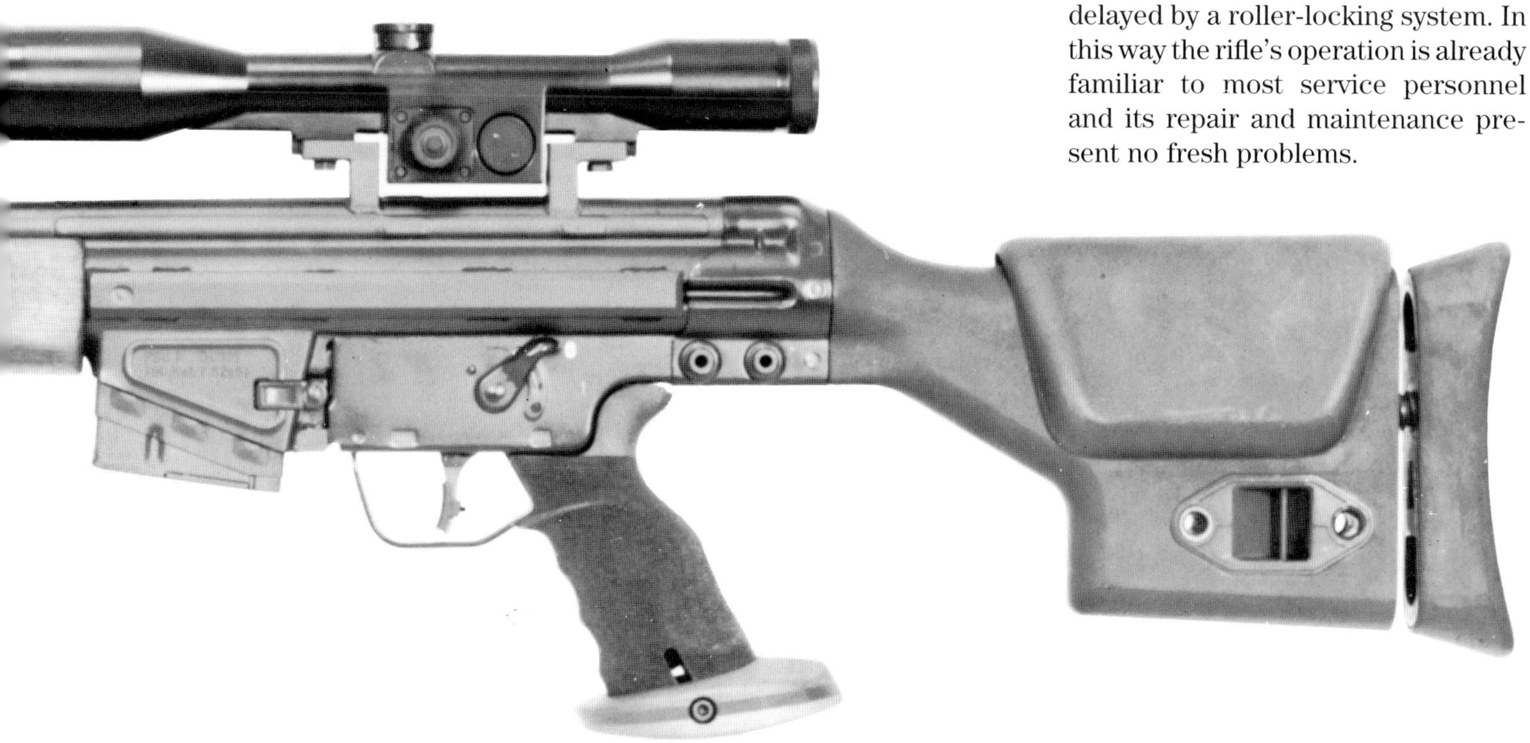

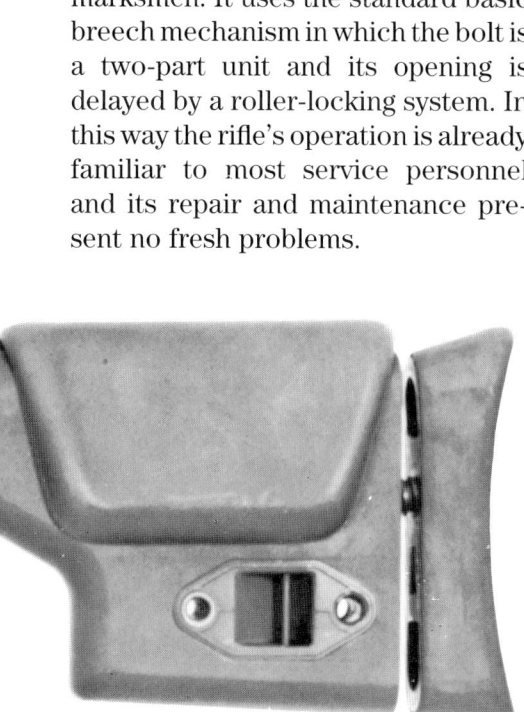

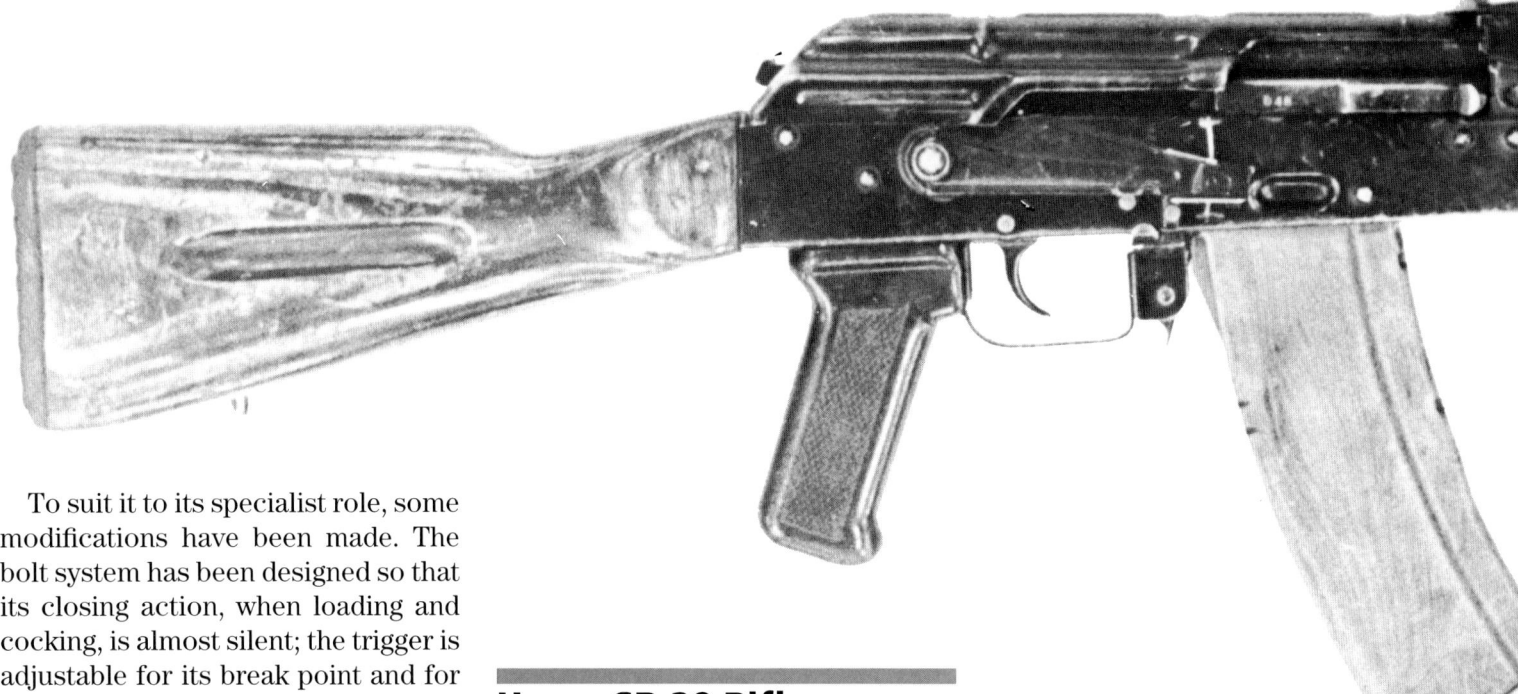

Below: The ubiquitous AK-74.

To suit it to its specialist role, some modifications have been made. The bolt system has been designed so that its closing action, when loading and cocking, is almost silent; the trigger is adjustable for its break point and for width; the abruptly-contoured stock is adjustable for length and for height of the cheek-piece; there is a T-rail underneath the fore end which permits the mounting of a hand-stop, a sling or even a light bipod or tripod; and the weapon is equipped with a telescope sight as standard. This has been carefully designed to suit the weapon and is unusual in that adjustments for elevation and azimuth are made by movement of the internal optical system, giving a high degree of precision; one click of either adjustment will move the bullet strike 1cm at 100m range.

The PSG-1 is heavy but well-balanced, and it shoots extremely accurately; 10 shots in a two-inch circle at 300 yards is well within its capabilities, though as with any other precision weapon it is best to test it with several makes of ammunition and bullet weights to find the one which suits it best. The PSG-1 has only recently been announced, and so far as I am aware there have been no major sales, though several German police authorities are evaluating it.

Heym SR-20 Rifle

Manufacturer Fried. W. Heym, D-8732 Munnerstadt, Germany
Type Bolt-action, center-fire, magazine
Caliber .270 Winchester
Barrel 20.5in (520mm)
Weight 6.5lb (2.94kg)
Magazine Capacity 5 rounds

Friedrich Heym is a long-established German gunmaker whose principal fame comes from his hand-built sporting guns – rifles, shotguns, drillings – which are virtually tailor-made for his clients. But for those with less wealth, he also makes a stock rifle which can be bought off the shelf – though even this has sufficient variations of barrel length and caliber to be able to suit almost all applicants.

The SR-20 is basically a Mauser action, but furnished in three lengths to suit short, medium and magnum cartridge lengths. It is assembled to three possible barrel lengths; 20.5in (520mm), 24in (610mm) and 26in (660mm); generally the three barrel lengths parallel the actions, the two shorter lengths being found with either of the two shorter actions and the 26in with the magnum action, but this is not immutable and Heym will marry whatever barrel and action you wish.

The shortest barrels are usually stocked to the muzzle in Mannlicher carbine style, while the longer ones are partially stocked in the usual sporting rifle manner. Whatever the stock type it will be of high-grade walnut, oil-finished and hand checkered, fitted to the barrel and action in a faultless manner. The sights are usually a front post with removable hood, and a rear notch fully adjustable for elevation and windage. The receivers are always drilled and tapped for telescope mounts. The trigger is fully adjustable, and the magazine has a hinged floor-plate released by a catch in the trigger guard. There is a three-position safety catch which gives the shooter a choice of 'bolt & trigger locked,' 'trigger only locked' and 'all free' positions.

Heym rifles will group to two minutes of arc as they come from the box. They are not inexpensive weapons by any standard of comparison, but the customer gets an accurate weapon, beautifully hand-finished and flawless in operation.

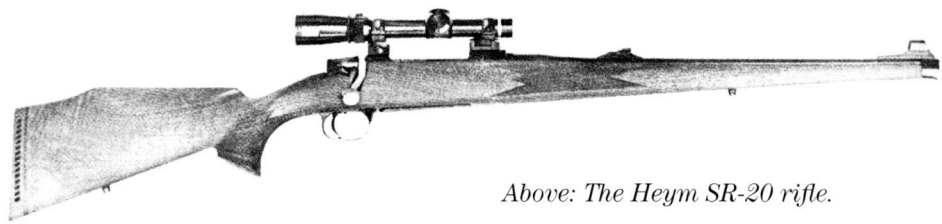

Above: The Heym SR-20 rifle.

KALASHNIKOV AK-74

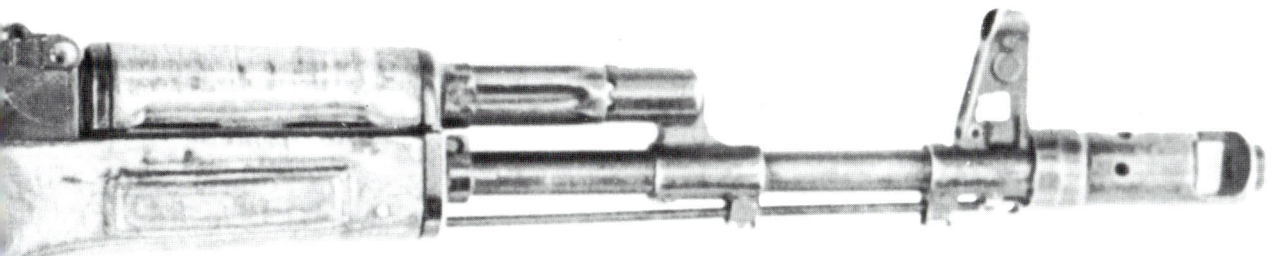

Below: The forerunner of the AK-74, the AK-47.

Kalashnikov AK-74

Manufacturer Soviet State Arsenals
Type Gas-operated, selective fire
Caliber 5.4mm
Barrel 15.75in (400mm)
Weight 7.93lbs (3.60kg)
Magazine Capacity 40 rounds
Cyclic rate of fire 650 rounds/minute

It was to be expected that with the western nations turning to small calibers for their military rifles, the Soviets would eventually follow suit. They had developed a necked-down version of their standard 7.62mm M43 cartridge with a 5.56mm bullet in the 1960s, though this appears never to have had any military applications other than as a research vehicle. What was also to be expected was that when they did move, it would be to a caliber and chambering entirely unlike anything in the west and totally incompatible with any capitalist weapon system.

The resulting rifle was first seen by outsiders in 1979, since when numbers of them have become available to western agencies (mainly from Afghanistan). In general the AK-74 is a modified AK-47 insofar as it uses the same receiver and stock, pistol grip, trigger unit and general configuration. The bolt is smaller, but the bolt carrier and gas piston are the same. The magazine is of thick and tough plastic, thick so that it can fit into the AK-47 magazine housing without demanding any modification. It holds 10 more of the smaller cartridges than did the AK-47 magazine. The wooden fore end grip has a horizontal groove, useful as a recognition feature if nothing else.

The most obvious change is in the addition of a muzzle brake, designed to divert some of the ejected gases sideways and upwards to counter recoil and upward climb during automatic fire. In this it appears to be very successful, since numbers of tests have shown that the rifle can be controlled quite well when firing automatic, the recoil force having been reduced to a level approximately that of a .22 rimfire sporting rifle. Unfortunately, muzzle brakes are a two-edged sword; they make life easier for the shooter, but they make life difficult for the men next to him, diverting the muzzle blast sideways, and Soviet medical publications have printed one or two articles on the dangers of ear damage on firing ranges with the new rifle.

The new cartridge is conventional enough, the case being slightly shorter and fatter than the .223. The bullet weighs 53 grains, is fully jacketed and boat-tailed and has a muzzle velocity of 900 meters/second (2950 ft/sec). This is rather low for this class of weapon, but appears to be adequate for combat purposes. Internally, the bullet is remarkable for having a vacant space in the nose; the major part of the core is mild steel, with a short lead section at the front. This combination appears to facilitate expansion, bent noses and tumbling on impact so as to deliver a severe wound. It is also somewhat complicated to mass-produce with any accuracy. The rifling twist is very steep – one turn in 26 calibers – and the rifling is bevelled on its leading edge so as not to incise the bullet jacket during its travel up the bore. Tracer and armor-piercing bullets have also been reported, though there is no information available on the penetration ability of the armor-piercing type.

Two types of rifle have been seen; the standard AK-74 has a wooden butt, while the AK-74S has a folding steel butt and appears to be issued to paratroopers and special forces only. The AK-74 replaced the AK-47 in Soviet service, and was adopted by other members of the former Warsaw Pact.

Kimber Model 82

Manufacturer Kimber of Oregon, Clackamas, OR 97015, U.S.A.
Type Bolt-action, rimfire, magazine
Caliber .22 Long Rifle RF
Barrel 22.5in (572mm)
Weight 6.56lbs (2.97kg)
Magazine Capacity 5 or 10 rounds

The bolt action .22 rifle was common in the U.S.A. in years gone by, but in the past decade American makers have become extremely scarce, and in order to remedy this the Kimber company was formed for the sole purpose of making and selling this rifle.

The Model 82 is well finished and elegantly checkered – even the buttplate. The receiver is tubular, milled from the solid, and attached firmly to the one-piece trigger and magazine housing. The bolt is sturdy and the handle positioned above the trigger, while the trigger is easily adjustable for pressure and over-travel. Five- or ten-round magazines are available; the five-round fits flush with the bottom of the fore end and is released by a small catch at its rear. Even the trigger guard has been milled from solid metal and not stamped from sheet steel as some sort of afterthought. The rifle can be supplied with sights to choice, but the normal case is for it to have no iron sights but grooves for Kimber telescope mounts. The barrel is heavy, extremely well finished inside and out, and with the chamber dimensions on the low side of the permitted tolerances. Accuracy is excellent; half-inch groups at 50 yards, firing from a rest, are easily attained, provided one takes the trouble to try various brands of ammunition to discover that which is best suited.

Marlin Model 375 Rifle

Manufacturer Marlin Firearms Co., North Haven, CT 06473, U.S.A.
Type Lever action, center fire, magazine
Caliber .375 Winchester
Barrel 20in (508mm)
Weight 6.75lbs (3.06kg)
Magazine Capacity 5 rounds

John Mahon Marlin began making lever-action rifles and carbines in 1881 and the fact that the company he founded is still making them is sufficient proof of the excellence. There have been some small changes, but since 1889 the significant feature of the Marlin has been the solid top to the receiver and the side ejection port.

The Marlin Model 375 gets its nomenclature from being chambered for the .375 Winchester cartridge, which was introduced specifically for use in lever-action rifles in order to give them a medium-to-high powered round for use in forests and close country. Note that it is a rifle rather than a carbine; the barrel is much longer than the magazine tube and the whole weapon is three to four inches longer than the average carbine.

The Marlin action retains the solid top receiver and has a cylindrical bolt which, on operating the lever, comes out from the rear of the receiver to cock the external hammer. At the same time the cartridge lifter pivots to raise a fresh round from the magazine, and on the return stroke the bolt chambers the round, is locked, and the rifle is ready to fire.

Below: The Marlin Model 375 rifle.

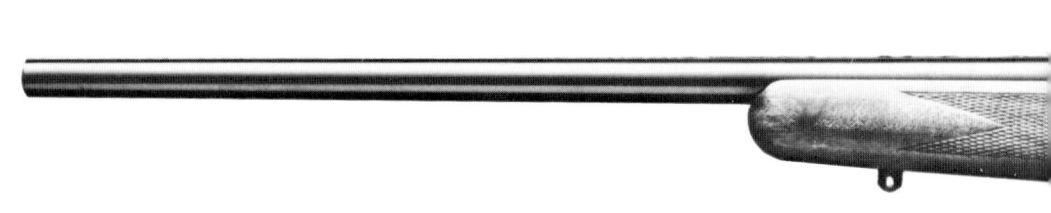

Above: The Kimber Model 82 bolt-action rifle.

MAUSER SP66 SNIPER'S RIFLE

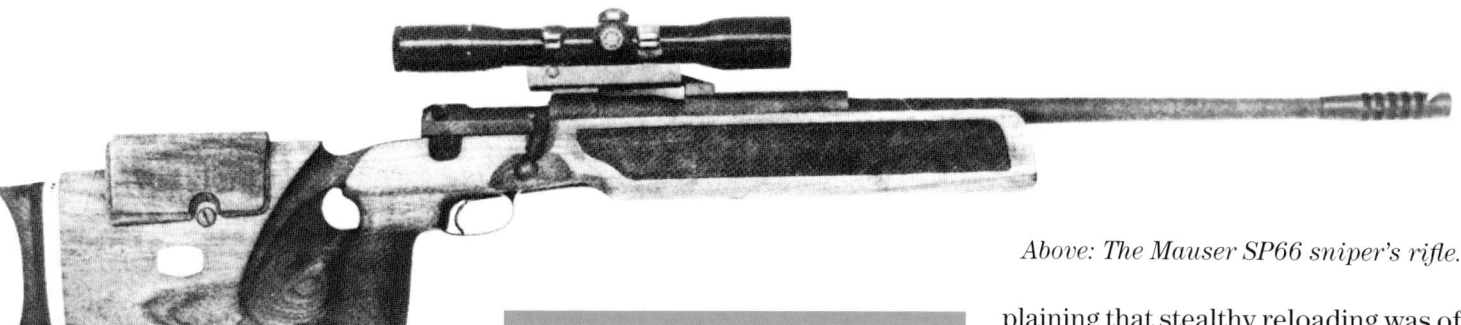

Above: The Mauser SP66 sniper's rifle.

One advantage of the solid top and side ejection Marlin is that it makes life easier for fitting a telescope, and the receiver is factory drilled and tapped for a mount. Marlin have also aided telescope shooters by making an extension hammer spur which protrudes to one side (either side, to choice) so that there is no danger of trapping the thumb between hammer and telescope when cocking or lowering the hammer. Iron sights re fitted, a gold-bead foresight and a step-adjustable rear sight with a rotatable insert which provides a choice of four notches.

The short magazine makes the rifle somewhat lighter at the muzzle than one normally expects with lever-actions, though this certainly helps when attempting to follow a moving target. Accuracy leans heavily upon the ammunition in use, but with the correct choice made, then groups between two and three inches are possible at 100 yards for the moderately practised shooter.

Mauser SP66 Sniper's Rifle

Manufacturer Mauser-Werke Oberndorf GmbH, Oberndorf am Neckar, Germany
Type Bolt-action, magazine
Caliber 7.62mm NATO
Barrel 26.7in (670mm)
Magazine Capacity 3 rounds

When the armies of the world adopted semi-automatic rifles, most of them slapped a telescope on those which proved-out best in their acceptance tests and issued them to snipers. The theory was that semi-autos made good sniping weapons since the firer did not have to move his arm to operate the bolt and therefore was less likely to disclose his position. This seems to have arisen because of the Soviet Army's policy of giving semi-autos to snipers during World War Two, but in my view the reason for this was more that their semi-autos were somewhat temperamental unless properly looked after, and a sniper is more likely to devote care to his rifle than the average front line soldier. In any event, after some years the snipers of the Western armies began complaining that stealthy reloading was of little use unless you could hit the target in the first place, and that military semi-autos, no matter how good, were simply not accurate enough for sniping purposes. As a result, there has been a gradual move back to bolt action rifles for snipers, and this Mauser is the issue for the German and at least a dozen other armies.

In appearance you would be excused for thinking that it is a high quality match rifle; the stock is strictly functional and non-military, with a near-vertical pistol grip, thumb-hole, deep comb and adjustable cheek-rest and deep stippled fore end. All this, of course, simply permits the sniper to get the best 'hold' he possibly can, which is half the battle. The action is a short Mauser bolt locking into the receiver with forward lugs and feeding from an integral three-round magazine concealed within the depth of the fore end. The bolt handle is at the forward end of the bolt, just behind the locking lugs, so that it is close to the trigger and reduces the action length to about half the normal. The firing pin spring is stronger than normal to give a fast movement to the striker and the 'lock time' (the time between pressing the trigger and the exit of the bullet from the muzzle) is about half of that with a conventional Mauser action.

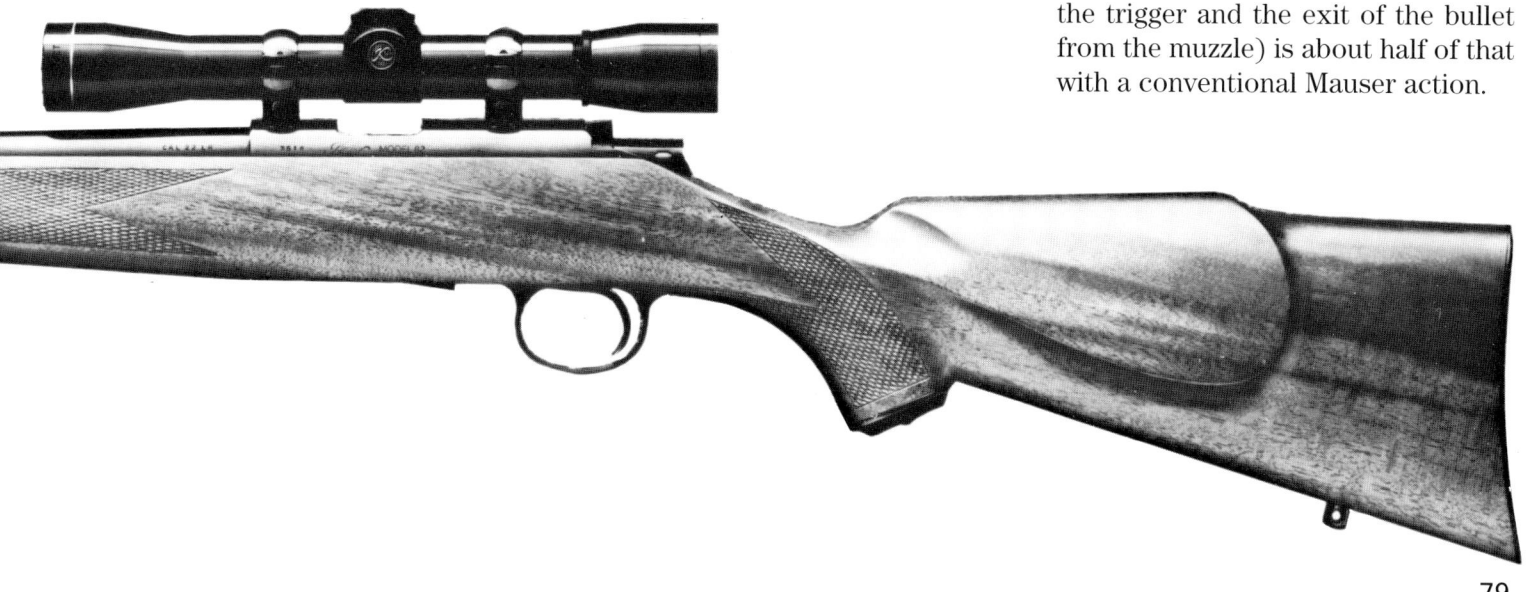

No sights are fitted; the user is expected to specify what he wants and the receiver is then adapted to it; Mauser recommend using a Zeiss Diavari optical telescope or a Varo or similar image-intensifying sight. The muzzle is fitted with a complex muzzle brake and flash hider which is designed to prevent the firer being dazzled by his own flash at night, a feature of particular importance when image-intensifying sights are in use.

I have been unable to fire the rifle, but reports indicate that its inherent accuracy is well in excess of the capabilities of stock military ammunition. Most countries are now taking steps to produce special batches of cartridges which have been more carefully assembled than the regular run-of-the mill issue ammunition, for use solely by snipers, and with this available, the Mauser will undoubtedly come into its own.

Mossberg RM-7

Manufacturer O. F. Mossberg & Sons, North Haven, CT 06473, U.S.A.
Type Bolt-action, center-fire, magazine
Caliber .30-06; 7mm Remington Magnum
Barrel 22in (560mm)
Weight 7.87lbs (3.57kg)
Magazine Capacity 4 rounds

Mossberg are well-known for the long series of shotguns and rimfire rifles produced by the company since before the turn of the century; their center-fire rifles are less well-known outside the U.S.A. This is their latest center-fire model, and one which repays study.

The appearance is conventional, with a conservatively styled walnut stock having a graceful pistol grip and good crisp checkering. Two heavy steel crosspins go through the stock behind the recoil shoulder and magazine in order to reinforce it.

The bolt is of Mossberg's own design using four front lugs for very positive locking and with the body fluted, with polished bearing surfaces, to ensure smooth action. The bolt knob is checkered for a firm grip, and there is a prominent safety catch on the bolt sleeve where it can be easily operated by the right thumb.

The magazine is unusual in being a rotary type, though not totally mechanical as, say, the Mannlicher-Schoenauer. The magazine has a curved inner wall against which the cartridges ride, propelled by a sprung follower arm which tracks them round their curved path to deliver them to the feedway. There is a magazine release lever which permits the contents to be emptied without having to work the bolt; the bolt is opened and the lever pressed, withdrawing the stop arm and allowing the follower to

push the cartridges out and into the feedway where they can be removed.

The foresight is a gold bead on a ramp; the rear sight an open folding leaf in the mid-position, capable of adjustment for elevation and windage. The receiver is factory drilled and tapped for telescope mounts.

Accuracy is good, averaging two-inch groups when rest-fired at 100 yards, and the rifle is well-balanced and handy in practical use.

Musgrave Model 90

Manufacturer Musgrave (Pty) Ltd, Bloemfontein, South Africa
Type Bolt-action repeater
Caliber Available in .243, .270, .308, .30-06, 7×57mm and 7×64mm
Barrel 24in (610mm)
Weight 9.25lb (4.2kg) approximately
Magazine Capacity 4 rounds

The Musgrave company was established in 1950 and soon built up a reputation for accurate, robust and elegant sporting rifles for South African hunters and target shooters. With the easing of the political situation, their rifles are now becoming available in other countries and are well worth consideration.

All their major-caliber sporting rifles are based upon a modified Mauser bolt system, machined from steel forgings and with sufficient strength to cater for the most powerful cartridges. The 'flagship' rifle is the Model 90, which is available in Standard, De Luxe, Light and Magnum models.

Some of the design features of the Model 90 are based on the Mauser K98 and Winchester Model 70. The Standard model is fitted with a sporter stock with cheek rest and butt pad. The bolt action is the Musgrave variation of the Mauser, notable for its safety catch being mounted on top of the striker cover at the rear of the bolt, where it is convenient to the thumb and easily visible. Iron sights are fit-

Left: A quartet of Musgrave bolt-action rifles. From the top: The Model 90, Model 93, K98 de Luxe, and K98 light.

ted, the adjustable rear sight ahead of the chamber and the front sight being hooded; the receiver is also drilled and tapped ready for a Weaver telescope sight mount.

The magazine is, in Mauser style, integral within the rifle stock. As noted above, the rifle can be chambered for various popular sporting cartridges, though the magazine capacity remains the same for all.

The De Luxe Model 90 is mechanically the same as the Standard, but with a selected walnut stock and a generally higher quality of finish; the company can engrave virtually any form of decoration to order.

The Light Model 90 has a lightweight walnut stock with 'Schnabel' fore end and the barrel is some 50mm shorter than the standard rifle. Mechanically it is the same as the Standard, but weighs 2.2lbs (1kg) less.

The Magnum Model 92 differs in being chambered for the .375 H&H, .300 Winchester or 7mm Remington Magnum cartridges; it therefore has a longer action and trigger guard. Otherwise it uses the same type of bolt action as the Standard rifle, is fitted with a walnut stock with cheekpiece and recoil pad, and weighs 8.1lbs (3.66kg). This rifle has become very popular among big-game hunters in South Africa due to its combination of high power, accuracy and light weight.

Musgrave also manufacture a series of sporting rifles based on the Mauser Kar98 military bolt action rifle. These rifles are less expensive, more 'working' rifles than the Model 90, and are widely used throughout Africa.

Nikko Model 7000

Manufacturer Nikko Firearms Co., Tochigi, Japan
Type Bolt-action, center-fire, magazine
Caliber Various
Barrel 24in (610mm) or 26in (660mm)
Weight 8.5lbs (3.86kg) with 24in barrel
Magazine Capacity 3 (Magnum) or 5 (regular)

Although ostensibly manufactured in Japan, this is something of an international weapon; the action is made in Japan, the barrel in Belgium, and the wood for the stocks comes from the U.S.A. The whole design is very much tailored for the American market.

The action is a five-lug bolt having an opening arc of 60°, the lugs being at the rear end of the bolt. The bolt body is nicely engine-turned, the face is counterbored, and the firing pin cocks on opening. There is a sliding safety catch alongside the rear of the bolt which locks the trigger but leaves the bolt free to be operated.

The stock is quite heavy and amply-proportioned; there is a high Monte Carlo comb and cheekpiece and the finish is good, if glossy. The interior fit and finish is not so good.

The magazine has a spring-loaded floor plate and a release catch at the front of the trigger guard. Sights are provided only on two calibers, .375 and .458; all others are without sights and are drilled and tapped for telescope mounts. Calibers available run from .22-250 to .458 Winchester Magnum and include all the commercial standards currently available.

I have been unable to fire this rifle, and reports from other sources are mixed; the general opinion seems to be that as it comes, the barrel is not always well bedded, giving rise to inconsistent shooting, but that with a little adjustment this can be overcome, resulting in a very good hunting rifle at a reasonable price.

Parker-Hale M85

Manufacturer Gibbs Rifle Co. Inc., Martinsburg, West Virginia, U.S.A.
Type Bolt-action repeater
Caliber 7.62mm NATO (.308 Winchester)
Barrel 27.5in (700mm)
Weight 12.56lbs (5.7kg) with sight
Magazine Capacity 10 rounds

The Parker-Hale company of Birmingham, England, has a long history of making small arms and accessories for sporting shooters. In the early 1960s they began making major-caliber rifles based on Mauser-type actions purchased from Spain. In the early 1980s their 7.62mm Model 82 was selected as the service sniper rifle by Australia, Canada and New Zealand. They then developed the Model 85 for the British Army sniping rifle trials, but it was not selected. In 1990 the company decided to give up their rifle business and concentrate on other things, and the patents and rights to the Parker-Hale rifles were purchased by Navy Arms of the U.S.A., whose subsidiary, the Gibbs Rifle Company now manufactures the Parker-Hale range.

The M85 is a highly accurate and reliable rifle designed to give a 100 percent first round hit probability up to 600 yards range, and is capable of accurate shooting to ranges well in excess of that. The action is basically that of the Mauser 1898 rifle, immensely strong and thoroughly tested over the century. Iron sights for ranges up to 900 yards are fitted, and the receiver is prepared for a telescope or electro-optical night vision sight.

The muzzle is threaded to accept a suppressor which can be used with supersonic or reduced velocity ammunition and eliminates all muzzle flash and firing signature and also reduces the recoil. The butt-stock is fully adjustable and there is a quick-detach bipod attached to the fore end.

Remington Model Six Slide Action

Manufacturer Remington Arms Co., Ilion, New York, 13357, U.S.A.
Type Pump-action, center-fire, magazine
Caliber Various
Barrel 22in (560mm)
Weight 7.5lbs (3.40kg)
Magazine Capacity 4 rounds

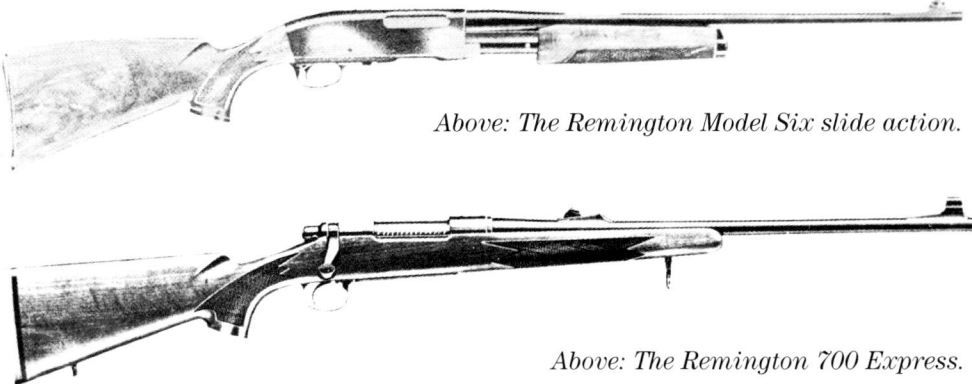

Above: The Remington Model Six slide action.

Above: The Remington 700 Express.

Slide action guns ('pump guns' or 'trombone guns') are usually associated, at least in Europe, with low-powered .22 rimfire rifles or with shotguns, but providing the design is properly done there is no reason why the system should not be used with high powered rifles. Remington, though, seem to be the only people to have made a success of it, and they have featured a center-fire slide action rifle in their catalogs for several years. The Model Six is the latest version, introduced in 1981 and replacing the earlier Model 760.

One advantage of the slide action, if only a cosmetic one, is the 'streamlined' shape of the receiver, which flows from the line of the stock. This box-like receiver is immensely strong and has an ejection slot in the right side. The box magazine enters below the receiver. Below the barrel is a rod assembly which acts as a bearing surface for the slide grip to move upon. When the slide is operated, a connecting link cams the breech block out of engagement with a locking recess in the receiver, then withdraws it, ejecting the spent case. The forward stroke then propels the block forward to load the cartridge and cams the block into the locking recess. By careful design of the leverages the action can be made very smooth and it barely disturbs the aim; the only defect is that there is no mechanical gain to deal with the occasional sticky case.

The Model 760 has a checkered walnut Monte Carlo stock with pistol grip, and the slide grip is of similar material. The foresight is a gold beat on a matt ramp, while the rear sight is open, step-adjustable for elevation and also adjustable for windage. The receiver is factory drilled and tapped for telescope mounts.

The rifle is available in 6mm, .243, .270, .30-06 and .308 calibers, and its accuracy is good, with groups of just over two inches at 100 yards. In view of the extraction hazard, it pays to try a variety of ammunition to find which particular brand suits this rifle.

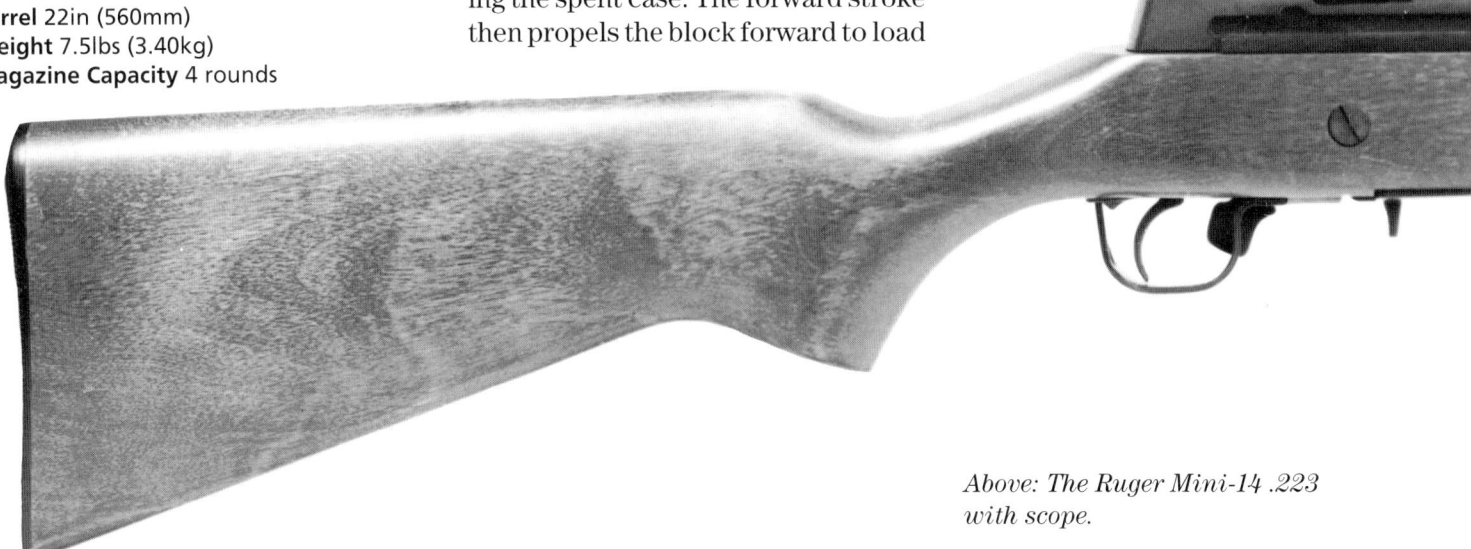

Above: The Ruger Mini-14 .223 with scope.

Remington Model 700 7mm Express

Manufacturer Remington Arms Co., Bridgeport, CT 06602, U.S.A.
Type Bolt-action, center-fire, magazine
Caliber 7mm Remington Express
Barrel 22in (559mm)
Weight 7.25lbs (3.29kg)
Magazine Capacity 5 rounds

The 7mm Remington Express cartridge is the new name for what used to be the .280 Remington; dimensionally identical, the new version has improved ballistics and Remington are promoting it as a long-range hunting cartridge. And the best way of doing that is to produce a good rifle to shoot it from, hence the Model 700 in 7mm Express.

The Model 700 has been in production for some time in a wide variety of calibers from .17 to .458, so it is a thoroughly proven design. Elegantly proportioned and well-finished, with a Monte-Carlo stock and inlaid fore end, the Model 700 balances well and comes easily to the shoulder. The action is basically a Mauser bolt, amply strong for this loading, while the barrel is smoothly tapered and appears to be light in weight, which probably accounts for the good balance.

The front sight is a post set on a ramp, hooded to obviate glare, and can be drift-set to compensate when zeroing. The rear sight is open, adjustable for elevation and windage. The receiver has been factory drilled and tapped for mounting any type of telescope sight mount base or for the addition of more specialized receiver sights.

The 7mm Express cartridge generates some 2800 feet per second (853 meters/sec) muzzle velocity in this rifle, and 200 meters is the theoretical cross-over point at which bullet and sight line should coincide. As a result the rifle shoots particularly well at that range and is capable of producing better than four-inch groups straight from the box and with factory ammunition.

Rossi Model 92SRC Carbine

Manufacturer Amadeo Rossi Lda., São Leopoldo, Brazil
Type Lever-action, tubular magazine
Caliber .357 Magnum
Barrel 20in (508mm)
Weight (empty) 5.94lbs (2.69kg)
Magazine Capacity 8 rounds

In the days of the Old West the carbine chambered for a handgun cartridge (or vice versa, as you prefer) was the common saddle gun, but the concept seems to have withered over the years, with the riflemen looking to more exotic calibers and better ballistic efficiency. But there is still a good case for the combination, especially in those parts of the world where there is a need for a general-purpose rifle with no frills. Rossi's Carbine enjoys good sales.

The 92SRC makes no bones about being an almost identical copy of the Winchester Model of 1892 in appearance, though there are some minor differences internally. The receiver is an investment casting, attached to a steel barrel, and the woodwork is well-fitted and polished while the metalwork is well blued. The breech mechanism is the traditional Winchester lever action, feeding from the tubular magazine beneath the barrel. This holds 8 rounds of .357; but the weapon can be used with .38 Special cartridges, and nine of these can be accommodated in the magazine. The foresight is a blade, while the rear sight is open, with step adjustment for elevation and capable of being drifted sideways for windage and drift zeroing.

The carbine appears to be somewhat touchy about ammunition; naturally, with a tubular magazine only flat-nosed bullets should be used, but different brands appeared to have tolerances which did not mate well with the tolerances of, for example, the cartridge guides in the breech. Length is also fairly critical, and while factory loads mostly work well, hand-loads need to be tailored to suit the characteristics of the breech. The accuracy is adequate, with two-inch groups at 50 yards possible with the right ammunition.

Ruger Mini-14 Series

Manufacturer Sturm Ruger & Co., Southport, CT 06490, U.S.A.
Type Gas-operated, semi-auto or selective fire
Caliber .223 (5.56mm)
Barrel 18.5in (470mm)
Weight 6.39lbs (2.9kg)
Magazine Capacity 5, 10, 20 or 30 rounds
Cyclic rate of fire 750 rounds/min (AC556 &556K only)

Sturm Ruger & Co introduced their Mini-14 carbine in 1973, a lightweight weapon using the well-proven Garand system of gas operation and rotating bolt, allied to the .223 cartridge. As might be imagined, such a useful combination of reliability and light weight, allied to a modern service cartridge, attracted several military and para-military forces to the extent that Sturm Ruger have developed some specific variants of the Mini-14 for use by such agencies. In the expectation

RUGER MINI-14 SERIES

that readers might be less familiar with these models, we append some notes on them.

The **Ruger Mini-14/20GB Infantry Rifle** is a conversion of the standard Mini-14 to meet general military standards. The front sight is protected, moved back on the barrel, and incorporates a bayonet lug; there is a flash hider on the muzzle, and the handguard is of heat-resistant glass-fiber reinforced plastic material. The flash hider is shaped so as to function as a grenade launching spigot. In other respects, and in general dimensions and weight, the Infantry Rifle version is the same as the commercial Mini-14 and is available in blued steel or stainless steel.

The **AC-556 Selective Fire Weapon** resembles the Mini-14/20 Infantry Rifle but incorporates modifications to the trigger mechanism to permit the firing of single shots, three-round bursts or full automatic fire.

The **AC-556K Selective Fire Weapon** is the AC-556 modified to have a steel folding stock, a pistol grip, and a shorter (16.7in or 425mm) barrel. Due to the added weight of the stock the complete weapon now weighs 6.9lbs (3.15kg). It is a particularly compact model, well suited to airborne or armored troops. These models are only for sale to law enforcement agencies or governments.

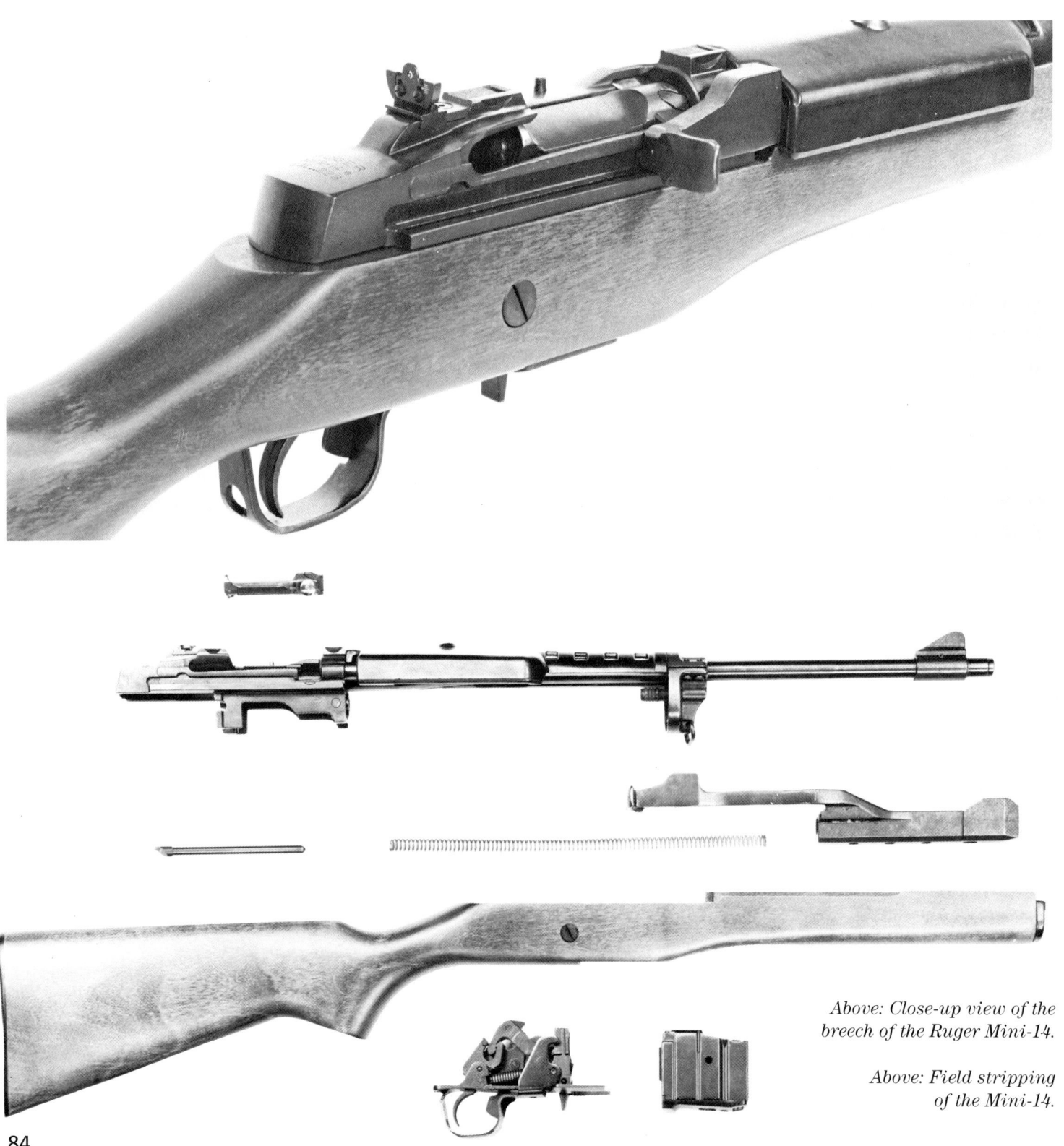

Above: Close-up view of the breech of the Ruger Mini-14.

Above: Field stripping of the Mini-14.

ST. ETIENNE 'FA-MAS' ASSAULT RIFLE

Above: The St. Etienne FA-MAS assault rifle.

St. Etienne 'FA-MAS' Assault Rifle

Manufacturer Manufacture d'Armes de St. Etienne, St. Etienne, France
Type Delayed blowback, selective fire
Caliber 5.56mm (.223)
Barrel 19.2in (488mm)
Weight 8.73lbs (3.96kg)
Magazine Capacity 25 rounds
Cyclic rate of fire 950 rounds/minute

The peculiar shape of this rifle has led to it being nicknamed 'The Trumpet' by today's *poilus*, and in the hands of a well-built soldier it looks like a toy. But it is a very efficient and ingenious design, and production at St. Etienne placed it in the hands of every French soldier by 1990. At first it was only seen in service use with paratroops, but infantry units are now being equipped and trained, and it eventually became the standard 'personal weapon' acting as rifle, carbine or sub-machine gun.

The system of operation relies upon delayed blowback of the breech block and carrier. The carrier has two 'delay arms' which, when the bolt is closed, contact a hardened steel rod lying across the receiver. When the rifle fires, the cartridge case attempts to move back against the face of the bolt; this movement is transferred to the carrier, but when this attempts to move, the delay arms, held against the cross-bar, resist. They now have to rotate on their pivot, so that their upper section moves back and, in doing so, begin to move the bolt carrier backwards. But the differing lengths of the two sections of the delay arms ensures a mechanical disadvantage which delays the movement. When the arms have moved about 45° they clear the cross-bar and the bolt and carrier now move to the rear, ejecting the spent case. In order to avoid hard extraction, the chamber has longitudinal grooves machined in it so that the fired case is 'floated' on a layer of gas during the extraction phase.

The rifle is a bullpup design, the bolt and chamber being alongside the firer's face and the trigger ahead of the magazine; this permits a long barrel in a short rifle, since the otherwise wasted length of a naked butt is avoided. The butt carries a buffer unit in its upper surface so as to cushion the recoil, and there is a rubber recoil pad. The bolt can have its extractor moved across, and the butt cheek-piece can also be moved, so that the rifle can be quickly adapted to left or right-handed firers. The cocking handle lies centrally, underneath the carrying handle; this handle is of plastic and grooved; within it lies the sights, a blade foresight and an adjustable aperture rear sight calibrated to 300 meters.

The firer can select single shots, three-round bursts or full automatic fire; the three-round burst mechanism is separate from the rest of the trigger group so that should it fail the remaining options are still available. This means that there has to be two separate controls, one for fire selection and one for burst selection, but careful training avoids any problems with this. The rifle can also be readily adapted for firing grenades, and there is a light bipod which folds beneath the handle and steadies the rifle when firing automatic.

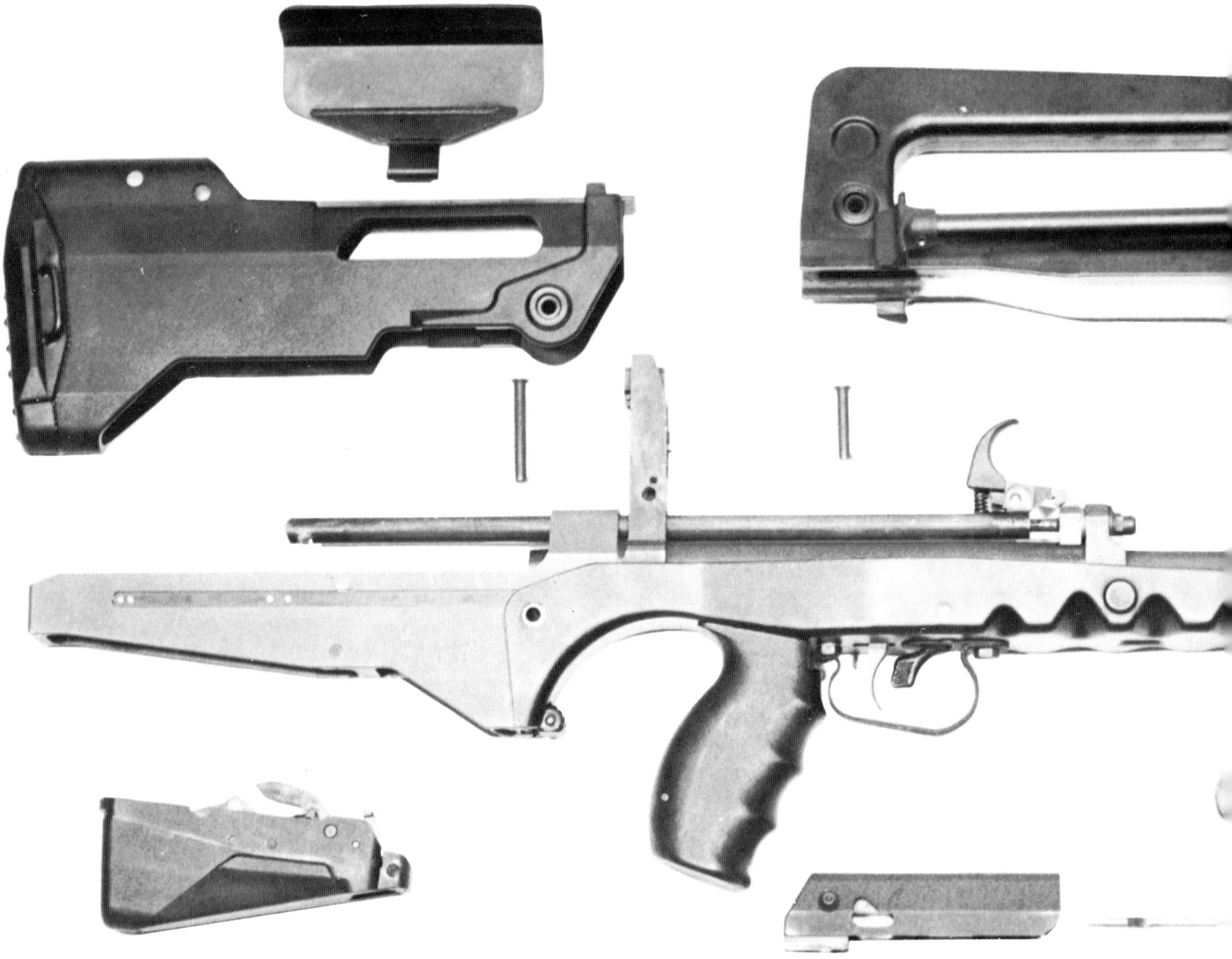

The FA-MAS (which means 'Fusil Automatique, Manufacture d'Armes St. Etienne) is comfortable to fire. It is very accurate at battle ranges and is easily controlled during burst fire. Its length allows it to be used in the submachine gun role quite effectively, and its adoption by the French Army increased the basic squad's fire power and also reduced the variety of weapons carried.

Sako P-72

Manufacturer Oy Sako AB, SF-11100 Riihimaki 10, Finland
Type Bolt-action, magazine
Caliber .22 Long Rifle RF
Barrel 23.375in (594mm)
Weight 6.53lbs (2.96kg)
Magazine Capacity 5 rounds

Sako have been making firearms for many years, concentrating particularly on center-fire sporting rifles in their export markets, but they have always made .22 rimfire rifles for home consumption. They have now begun exporting this rimfire rifle and, as well as making it in the standard .22 Long Rifle chambering, offer models in .22 Winchester Magnum RF and a center-fire version in .22 Hornet.

The general appearance echoes the lines of their larger-caliber sporting rifles, and the Sako is definitely not intended as a child's first gun or a plinker. The action gives the impression of immense strength, the bolt having two extractors and two locking lugs, while both receiver and bolt are large by conventional .22 rimfire

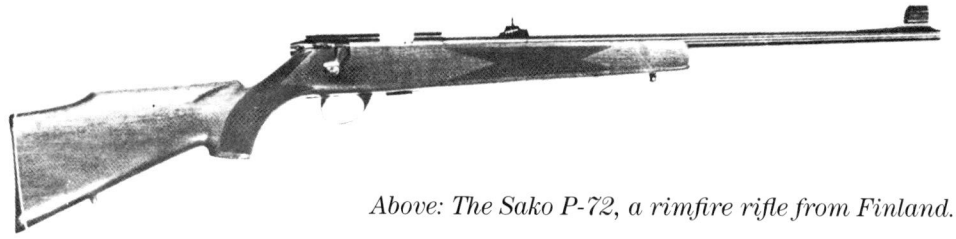

Above: The Sako P-72, a rimfire rifle from Finland.

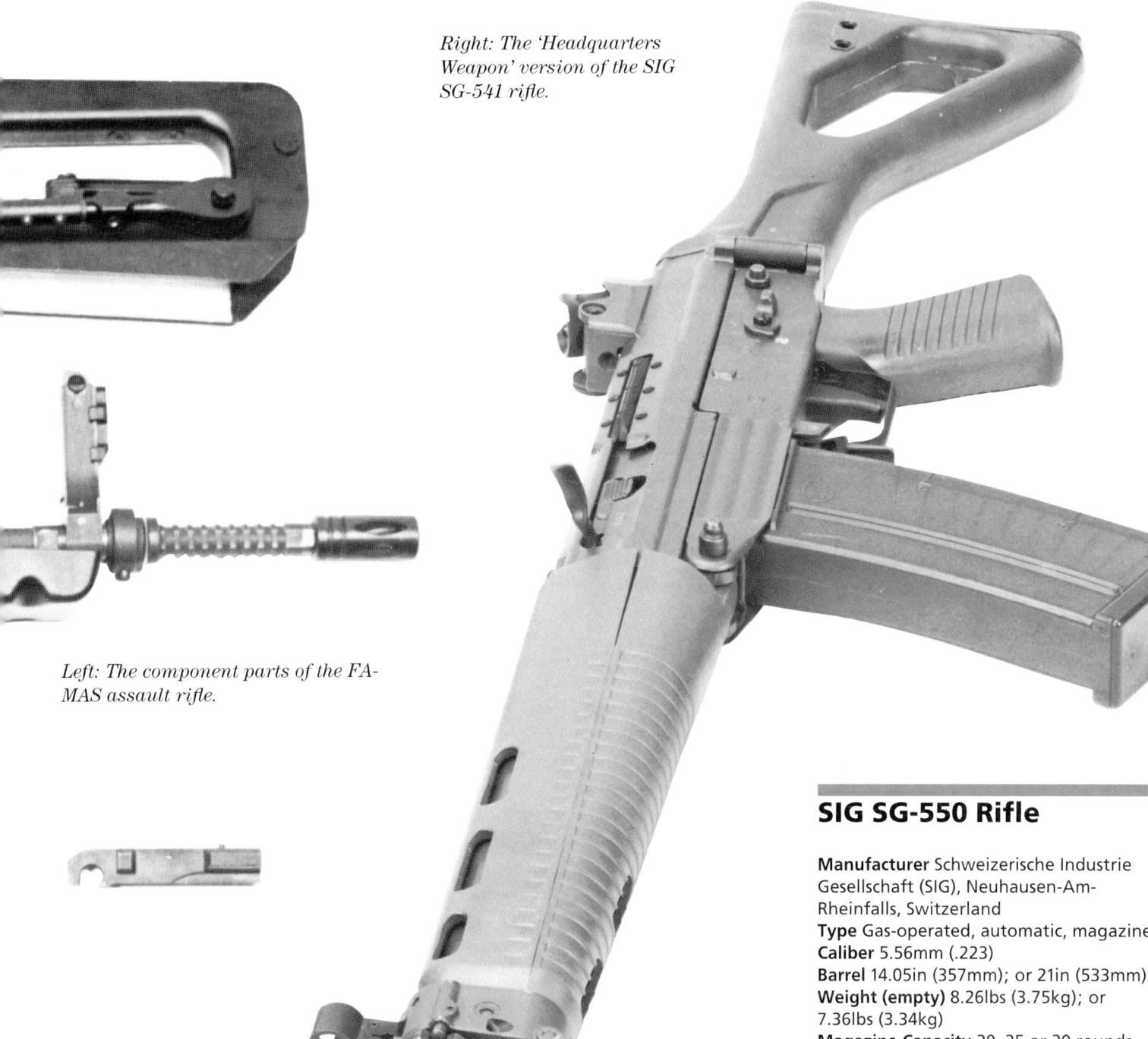

Right: The 'Headquarters Weapon' version of the SIG SG-541 rifle.

Left: The component parts of the FA-MAS assault rifle.

SIG SG-550 Rifle

Manufacturer Schweizerische Industrie Gesellschaft (SIG), Neuhausen-Am-Rheinfalls, Switzerland
Type Gas-operated, automatic, magazine
Caliber 5.56mm (.223)
Barrel 14.05in (357mm); or 21in (533mm)
Weight (empty) 8.26lbs (3.75kg); or 7.36lbs (3.34kg)
Magazine Capacity 20, 25 or 30 rounds
Cyclic rate of fire 750 rounds/minute

The Swiss Army has used a powerful 7.5mm cartridge since the turn of the century, but in recent years it decided to investigate a lighter caliber and asked both its own Federal Arsenal at Berne and the SIG Company to develop some new rifles in smaller calibers. As a result both establishments produced prototypes in 5.56mm and in a new 6.45mm caliber; government testing eliminated the 6.45mm round and the SIG 550 became the Swiss service rifle in 1990.

The SIG 550 is their answer to the request and as well as being formally adopted it is now available for com-

standards. The bolt is an interesting three-piece design in which the firing pin floats free, held back by its own spring, and the cocking piece, driven by the mainspring, is released by the sear to strike the pin. The cocking piece is retracted as the bolt lever is lifted to open the bolt, so that the firing pin spring moves the pin back before the chamber is opened.

The stock is checkered and oil-finished, and there is a substantial pistol grip; the comb of the Monte Carlo butt is somewhat low, though this may be an individual impression.

The sights incorporate the Williams Guide Line and comprise a ramped front sight with hooded bead and an open rear sight adjustable for windage and elevation; the receiver also has dovetail bases for a telescope.

Accuracy is good, one-inch groups at 50 yards being accomplished from a rest. I have seen reports of misfeeding but was unable to fire sufficient rounds to make any conclusions of my own.

SIG SG-550 RIFLE

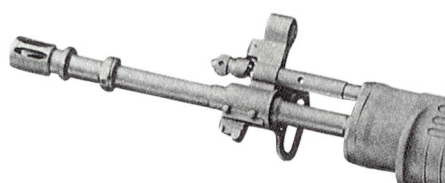

mercial sale to approved customers. It is a conventional gas-piston-operated rifle using a rotating bolt inside a bolt carrier. High-quality plastic material has been used for the folding stock and the fore-end guard, and also for the transparent magazine. Two lengths are available; the longer model is the 'Assault Rifle' while the shorter model is known as the 'Headquarters Weapon' and, with the butt folded, can be used in the sub-machine-gun role.

The sights are an aperture rear and blade front, with luminous dots for night sighting; there are mounting points for a telescope or for a variety of electro-optical sight units. There is a three-round burst facility, plus single shots or full automatic fire, and a light bipod can be fitted to steady the weapon when used in the squad automatic role.

Left: The SIG SG3000 sniper's rifle.

Below: The SIG SG551 assault rifle.

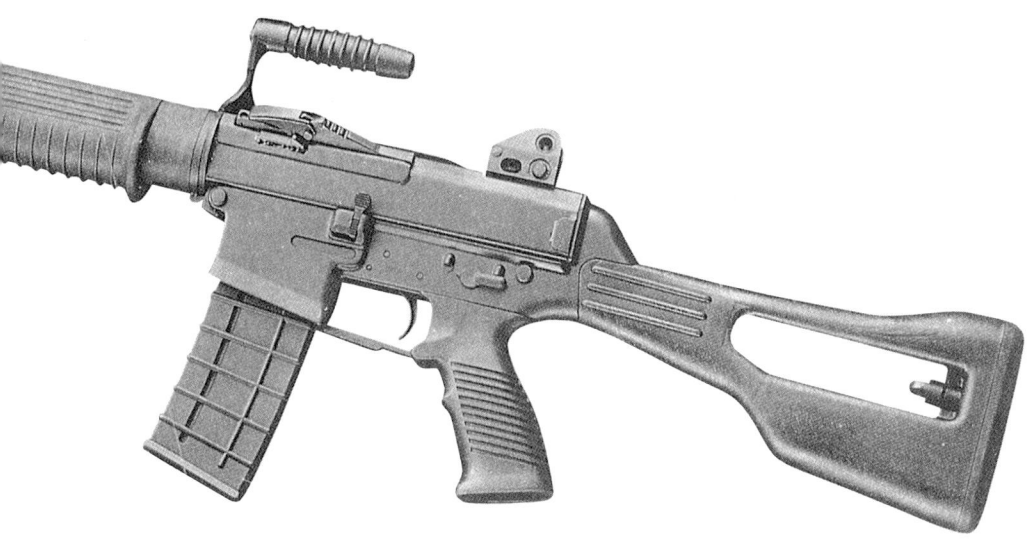

Left: The SR88A assault rifle.

Singapore Assault Rifle SR88A

Manufacturer Chartered Firearms Industries Ltd, Singapore
Type Gas-operated, selective fire
Caliber 5.56mm (.223)
Barrel 18.1in (460mm)
Weight 8.11lbs (3.68kg)
Magazine Capacity 30 rounds

Chartered Firearms Industries began rifle manufacture by making the U.S. M16A1 rifle under license from Colt for the Singapore Armed Forces. They saw that there was a potential market in the Far East for a modern assault rifle, and since they could not market the M16, set about making a rifle of their own. In 1980 a design from Sterling Armaments of Britain went into production as the SAR80 rifle; it has gone through two stages of modification and improvement to reach the present SR88A model.

The SR88A, like its predecessors, uses the conventional gas piston, bolt carrier and rotating bolt method of operation. The lower receiver is an aluminum forging, the upper receiver a steel pressing, and the stock is of glass-fiber reinforced nylon. The bolt group assembly is in modular form and consists of the bolt, carrier, buffer springs and rods. The bolt has seven locking lugs, and the bolt is always kept forward in its carrier by the firing pin spring, a concept which allows for rapid assembly after cleaning and little risk of the bolt falling free during stripping.

The barrel is held to the receiver by a locknut and detent system and is oriented to the receiver by special slots in the barrel extension, so simplifying accurate assembly. The gas system consists of a chrome-plated regulator and a long-stroke piston assembly connected to the bolt carrier. The regulator has three positions, two which provide different amounts of gas and the third which shuts off the gas flow so that the rifle can be used for launching grenades.

The standard rifle has a fixed butt; where compactness is important it can be fitted with a telescoping butt. There is also a carbine version for airborne and other troops who need a more portable weapon. This has a 292mm barrel and a telescoping butt, but is otherwise to the same general design as the standard rifle. There is also an interesting sub-machine gun variant, chambered for the 9mm Parabellum cartridge and with a different barrel and bolt assembly. The bolt is not locked in this model and it operates as a simple blowback weapon. In appearance it is exactly the same as the short carbine, except for a thinner magazine which holds 32 rounds.

Squibman M-16 Rifle

Manufacturer Squires, Bingham Mfg. Co., Marikina, Philippines
Type Semi-automatic, blowback
Caliber .22 Long Rifle RF
Barrel 16in (406mm)
Weight 6lbs (2.72kg)
Magazine Capacity 15 rounds

'Squibman' is the brand name of the Squires Bingham Company and they have produced a variety of rifles, shotguns and pistols under this name. Their M-16 is one of several attempts to make a cheap rimfire weapon which resembles a combat rifle.

The configuration of the rifle is, as the title implies, based upon that of the American M-16, though the detail execution is considerably different. There is the 'straight-line' stock layout, the carrying handle with rear sight, the elevated foresight and the muzzle flash hider. But the mechanism is a simple blowback unit and the barrel and receiver are in a tubular assembly which simply drops into the stock. Below is the pistol grip and magazine housing assembly.

The stock is of mahogany, finished in ebony black, while the metal components are either blackened steel or anodized alloy. The rear sight is a fixed elevation aperture, adjustable for windage.

The M-16 shoots quite well, with acceptable accuracy, and makes a good general purpose 'fun gun' or vermin shooter. The design has not copied the M-16 so slavishly as to finish up with bad proportioning, as have some others, and there is sufficient length of butt to allow the rifle to be held comfortably and firmly.

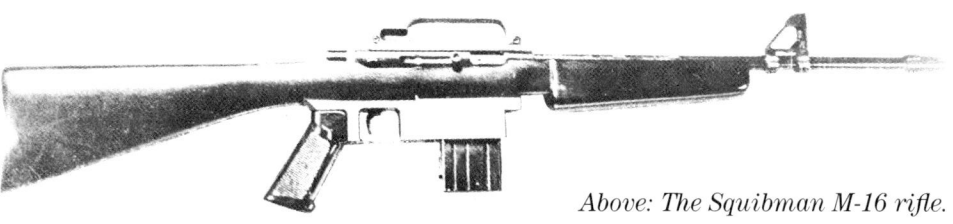

Above: The Squibman M-16 rifle.

Steyr Advanced Combat Rifle

Manufacturer Steyr-Mannlicher GmbH, Steyr, Austria
Type Gas-operated, selective fire
Caliber 5.56mm synthetic case fléchette
Barrel 21.25in (540mm)
Weight 7.12lbs (3.23kg) without magazine and sight
Magazine Capacity 24 rounds

The Steyr-Mannlicher entrant for the U.S. Advanced Combat Rifle competition was considered to be an excellent example of modern technology, but, like the other entries it could not reach the 100 percent improvement over the M16A2 demanded by the U.S. Army. The company have said that it represents their view of the next generation of assault rifles and they will continue to develop it privately and will probably offer it for consideration some time early in the next century.

The rifle uses a gas system to actuate the breech mechanism, which is quite unusual and which is built around the special cartridge. This cartridge is of plastic, a plain cylinder with the priming composition arranged in a ring around the inside of the case, just ahead of the base. A fin-stabilized fléchette lies inside the case, its fins positioned by the primer ring and the body held by a polycarbonate sabot, and surrounded by propellant.

The breech consists of a block which carries the chamber. At the commencement of firing an operating arm is held back against a spring. On pulling the trigger this arm is released to run forward, take a cartridge from the magazine and load it into the chamber. The chamber then rises vertically to a position behind the barrel, where it is locked by a spring catch. Above the chamber is a fixed firing pin, pointing downwards, and as the chamber rises so this firing pin passes through a hole in the chamber block and, just as the chamber aligns with the barrel and locks, strikes the ring primer and fires the cartridge. The fléchette is driven up the barrel; gas, tapped from the barrel into a surrounding chamber, drives back a piston which is actually a sleeve around the barrel. This drives the operating arm back, unlocking the chamber and lowering it to the loading position. As the trigger is pressed for the next shot, so the arm goes forward again, and the cartridge entering the chamber pushes out the spent plastic case of the previous round, ejecting it forward from the weapon. There is no rim on the plastic case, so no obstacle to this forward ejection.

Above: Steyr's AMR 5075.

The rifle is a bullpup design, with the magazine almost at the rear of the stock. The mechanism is enclosed in a plastic outer casing, there being something of a family resemblance between this and their well-known AUG rifle. A carrying handle above the weapon is extended almost to the muzzle, so acting as a sighting rib for snap shooting, and iron sights are fitted; a telescope can be quickly attached to the carrying handle. The barrel is rifled with a twist of one turn in 85 inches, giving roll stabilization to the fléchette to improve accuracy.

The only real defect of the design, as revealed in the U.S. tests, is that the fléchette tends to leave the cartridge at varying chamber pressures, due to inconsistent strength in the plastic cartridge case. Varying pressures mean varying muzzle velocities and changes in trajectory from shot to shot, so that accuracy suffers. This, however, is simply a question of testing various materials and assembly methods until a consistent release pressure can be obtained, and it is probable that Steyr have already solved this, ready to offer the rifle to the next applicant.

Steyr AMR 5075 Anti-Matériel Rifle

Manufacturer Steyr-Mannlicher GmbH, Steyr, Austria
Type long recoil, semi-automatic
Caliber 14.5mm Special
Barrel 47.25in (1200mm) smoothbore
Weight 44lbs (20kg) approximately
Magazine Capacity 5 rounds

It will be recalled (see the Barrett rifle above) that the 1980s saw a sudden interest in the development of heavy sniping rifles, primarily intended for the destruction of vulnerable high-technology equipment. Unfortunately

STEYR ARMEE-UNIVERSAL-GEWEHR

the word 'sniping' suggests anti-personnel shooting, which gave many people a completely wrong idea about the function of these weapons. Steyr-Mannlicher avoided this by carefully calling this weapon an 'anti-matériel' rifle.

The AMR 5075 is a heavyweight precision rifle for a long-range attack of vulnerable equipment. It uses the long

Below: The Steyr AUG assault rifle.

recoil system of operation; barrel and bolt recoil locked together for almost ten inches, after which the bolt is unlocked and held while the barrel runs back to the forward position. The bolt is then released to run forward, collect a cartridge, load it and then lock into the chamber by rotating.

This long recoil movement helps to absorb some of the recoil force; more is absorbed by a multi-baffle muzzle brake of high efficiency, and the entire barrel recoils inside a sleeve-type hydro-pneumatic recoil system which is more like the sort of thing found on artillery weapons than anything generally associated with rifles. All these reduction methods cut the felt recoil to a level which is little more than that of a conventional service rifle.

This is necessary, because the cartridge is a very powerful design. Instead of building the weapon around an existing cartridge, Steyr designed the cartridge to do what was wanted and then designed the weapon to suit. The cartridge case is of part-plastic construction and carries a 36-gram (1.25 ounce) tungsten fléchette which has a muzzle velocity of 4920 ft/sec (1500 m/sec) and an effective range up to 2000 meters, depending upon the type of target. At 800 meters range this fléchette has penetrated 40mm of rolled steel armor and then shattered behind the plate to give severe fragmentation damage.

The weapon is supported on a bipod, attached to the recoil cradle, and there is a 10-power telescope sight fitted as standard. A box magazine is inserted from the right side; on the prototype this held five rounds, but an eight-round magazine has since been developed. Other options for the future are automatic fire at a low rate, and the adoption of a rifled barrel so as to be able to take advantage of other ammunition designs.

The AMR 5075 was first shown publicly in 1990; this, unfortunately, was just the time when severe economies were beginning to be felt in the military world, and though a great deal of interest was expressed, no army has so far decided to adopt the weapon. Meanwhile Steyr go on refining it, and we may be sure that we have not heard the last of this potent design.

Steyr Armee-Universal-Gewehr

Manufacturer Steyr-Mannlicher GmbH, Steyr, Austria
Type Gas-operated, selective fire
Caliber 5.56mm (.223)
Barrel Various
Weight 7.9lbs (3.6kg) (508mm barrel)
Magazine Capacity 30 rounds
Cyclic rate of fire 650 rounds/minute

STEYR ARMEE-UNIVERSAL-GEWEHR

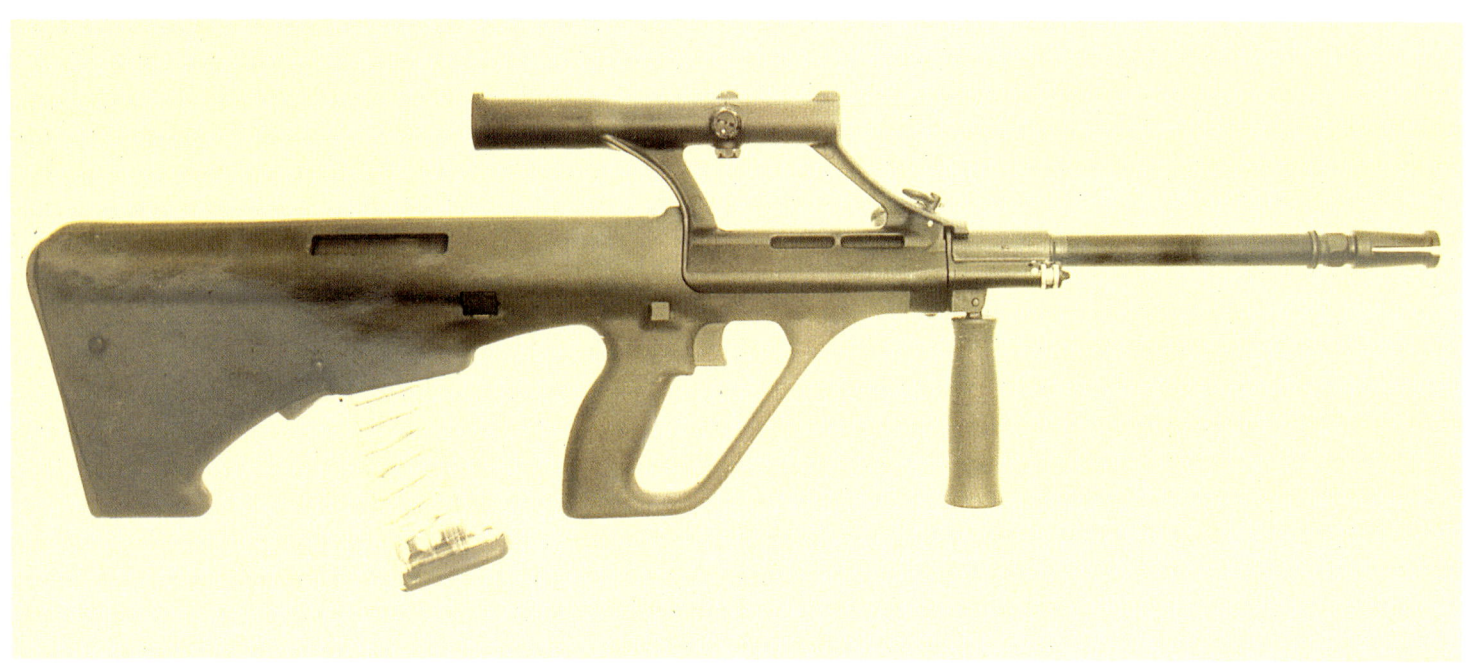

Above: Steyr's SSG-69 fitted with a suppressor.

Right: The Steyr AUG with alternative barrels. From top to bottom: the squad machine gun, rifle, carbine, and submachine gun barrels.

Below, far right: The futuristic lines of the Steyr AUG.

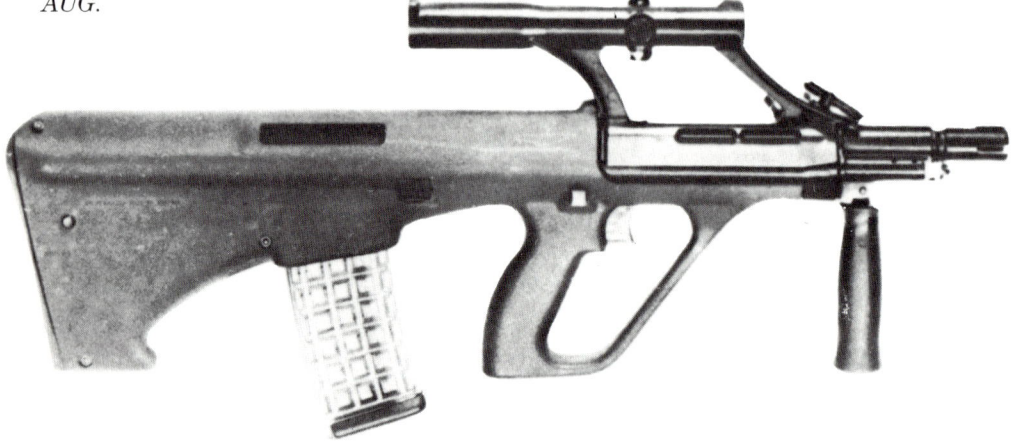

The Steyr AUG gets its name from its ability to be configured in four different ways, depending upon the length of the barrel and the presence or absence of a bipod. The basic mechanism, receiver and stock remain the same in all cases.

In appearance the AUG is, to say the least, futuristic, the plastic stock material and shape giving it the appearance of a toy or something from a space program. But its performance puts it well into the front rank of contemporary assault rifles and it has already been adopted by the armies of Austria, Argentina, Saudi Arabia and Tunisia, with others currently making evaluations and comparisons preparatory to possible orders.

The plastic stock unit forms a major part of the weapon; the principal feature is the main pistol grip with an enormous trigger guard which accepts the whole hand. Behind this is the magazine and its housing and release, and then the shoulder stock. It follows from this sequence that the AUG is a 'bullpup', having the action under the firer's cheek and the trigger well forward of the bolt and magazine.

The receiver unit is an aluminum die-casting which includes the seating for the barrel, bearings for the two bolt guides, the carrying handle and the optical sight. The bolt is the usual rotating multi-lug type held in a carrier, and this carrier moves back and forth on two machined steel bolt guide rods which are held in the receiver; thus there is no direct contact between receiver and bolt and therefore no need for expensive machining of the boltway. The return springs are concealed within the guide rods; in addition the left-hand rod acts with the cocking lever to operate the bolt when loading, and right-hand rod acts as the gas piston.

The barrel unit consists of the barrel, gas port and cylinder, gas regulator and a folding forward hand grip.

This grip can be used to change barrels, since the barrel locks into the receiver by interrupted lugs. Once the barrel is aligned, the gas cylinder unit, which carries a short-stroke piston, lines up with the right-hand bolt guide rod. One might expect some degree of imbalance with the gas impulse working off-axis, but in practice there is no torque effect and no deviation of shooting is detectable.

The magazine is a clear plastic unit, so that its contents can be seen at all times. The trigger group, containing the safety and selective fire mechanism, is a removable unit, much of it plastic. Selective fire is achieved by trigger pressure; a light pressure gives single shots, a harder pressure automatic fire. Again, this is something which, at first, one would expect to lead to inaccuracy, but once the technique is mastered it gives no trouble and automatic fire can be delivered as accurately with the AUG as with any other comparable rifle.

The various models are as follows: 'Commando' with 14in (315mm) barrel; 'Machine Carbine' with 16in (407mm) barrel; 'Assault Rifle' (the standard version) with 20in (508mm) barrel; and the 'Heavy Barrel Rifle' or 'Squad Automatic Weapon' with 24in (610mm) barrel and bipod. All models can be modified by removing the receiver casting and replacing it with another type which carries a low telescope mount instead of the optical sight and integral telescope; this is intended to cater for sniping telescopes or night vision sights.

Firing the AUG holds no surprises; it can be set up for left or right-hand firing very quickly by changing the ejector to one or other side of the bolt and rotating the ejection port cover in the butt to expose the port on the selected side. For those not accustomed to bullpup rifles, the weight distribution feels strange and distinctly light at the muzzle, but this is soon mastered and the rifle is extremely handy for use in quick combat situations. Accuracy is as good as, if not slightly better, than most other rifles of this caliber. The rifling is one turn in 41 calibers, tighter than the usual 1/54, which suggests that it will shoot equally well with a wide variety of service ammunition types.

Steyr-Mannlicher SSG-69 Sniper's Rifle

Manufacturer Steyr-Mannlicher GmbH, Steyr, Austria
Type Bolt-action, magazine
Caliber 7.62mm NATO
Barrel 25.6in (650mm)
Weight 8.6lbs (3.9kg)
Magazine Capacity 5 rounds

I have previously commented upon the recent rise in the use of bolt-action rifles for military sniping, replacing the earlier semi-automatics. One of the first to make this move was the Austrian Army, and the Steyr SSG-69 was the weapon developed to their specification.

When this rifle first appeared, most commentators suggested that it was simply the Greek Army Mannlicher-Schoenauer Model 1900 revived, but this was a gross simplification. In the first place the bolt is unusual in having its six locking lugs, in three pairs, at the rear and not in the front; in theory this is liable to give rise to compression stresses in the bolt and consequent inaccuracy, but in practice it seems not to matter. By way of compensation the barrel is set extremely deeply into the receiver and the receiver itself is strengthened, so that the whole assembly is rock-rigid.

The magazine is the Schoenauer rotating spool type, not seen on a military rifle since the aforementioned 1900 model, and it can be quickly removed from the bottom of the stock by squeezing in two grips on its base. The rear face of the magazine is closed by a transparent panel, so that the firer can slip the magazine out and, without moving it, can check on its contents and replace it. There is a specially-adapted 10-round box

STEYR-MANNLICHER SSG-69 SNIPER'S RIFLE

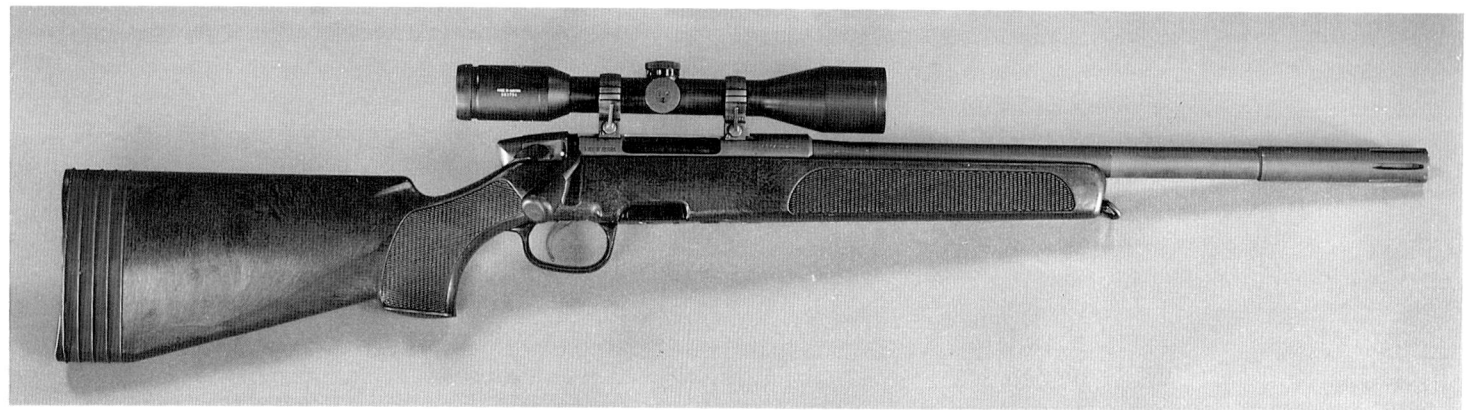

Above: The police version of the Steyr-Mannlicher SSG-69 sniper's rifle.

magazine which will fit in place of the spool should this be desired.

Iron sights are fitted for emergency use, a blade foresight and 'V' notch backsight. In normal use this weapon will be aimed by a telescope and the receiver is ribbed to take the Kahles 'Helia 6S2' which is standard issue. The same mounting can also be used for infra-red or image-intensifying night sights.

The stock and butt are made of olive-drab self-colored glass-reinforced fiber plastic material which is rot-resistant, impervious to rain, and fairly resistant to casual impact damage. It is also less likely to be seen than a wooden stock and has a matted surface which gives a good grip at all points, though the pistol grip and fore end have additional stippling.

In use this weapon is very accurate, giving 3½-inch groups at 30 yards, though as with most rifles of this type the accuracy relies greatly upon the quality of the military-grade ammunition. It is now available commercially, with a walnut stock and Walther match-grade adjustable sights; it makes an excellent full-bore match rifle.

Above: The Valmet M76 assault rifle.

Stirling M-20 Rifle

Manufacturer Squires, Bingham Mfg Co., Marikina, Philippines
Type Semi-automatic, blowback
Caliber .22 Long Rifle RF
Barrel 19.5in (495mm)
Weight 6lbs (2.72kg)
Magazine Capacity 15 rounds

The Stirling is another product of the Philippine Islands company of Squires Bingham. It is, in essence, the same blowback action used in their 'Squibman M-16' combat-style rifle but installed into a more conventional form of stock.

The stock is of Philippine mahogany; the standard model is sanded and oil finished while the De Luxe Model has the grain well figured and is with a polished finish. Both have machined checkering on pistol grip and fore end, and butt pads and pistol grip caps with white spacers; the De Luxe model also has the fore end capped.

The mechanism is a straightforward blowback bolt working in a tubular receiver attached behind the barrel; the trigger mechanism and magazine housing are fitted through the stock, and the box magazine goes in from beneath. There is a combined muzzle brake and compensator, though just how much of its effect is practical and how much cosmetic is a moot point in this caliber. The whole of the mechanism can be removed from the stock by simply taking out one screw, after which disassembly into the various component parts for cleaning is very simple.

The Stirling is a sound little rifle, excellent for vermin and general plinking and sufficiently accurate for all practical purposes. It is well finished, and of first-class material, and the manufacture and assembly appears to be to a high standard for a reasonably-priced weapon.

Valmet M76 Rifle

Manufacturer Valmet Oy, Jyvaskyla, Finland
Type Gas-operated, selective fire
Caliber 7.62 × 39mm Soviet
Barrel 16.5in (420mm)
Weight 7.7lbs (3.5kg)
Magazine Capacity 15 or 30 rounds
Cyclic rate of fire 650 rounds/minute

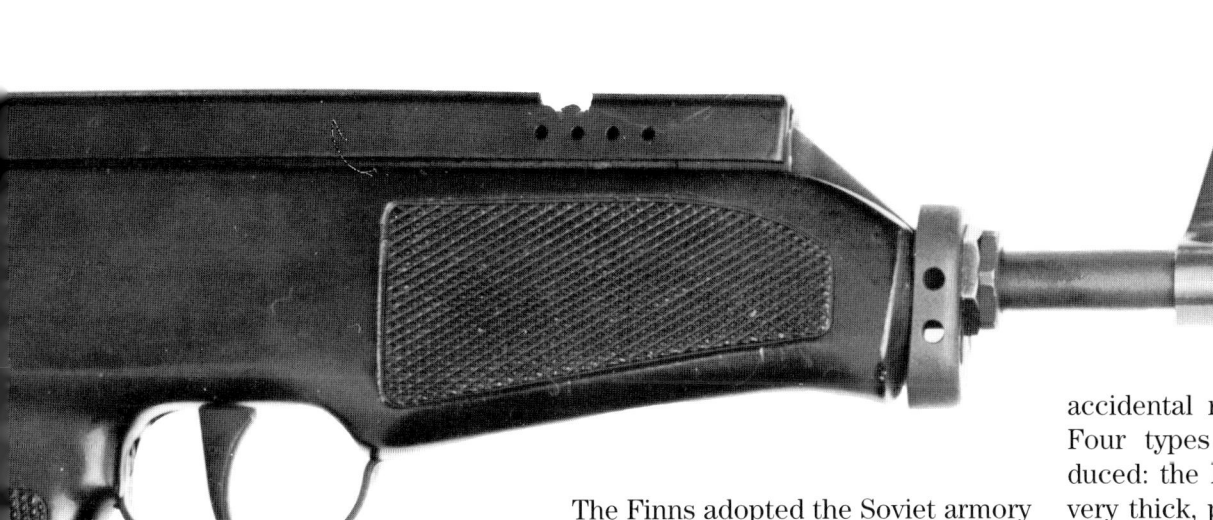

The Finns adopted the Soviet armory at the end of the war and the Kalashnikov AK47 rifle in the early 1950s. However, like the Czechs, they have ideas of their own on what a good rifle consists of, and in a few years time they were at work modifying the Kalashnikov design. They have now gone through three stages of change and their latest version is known as the M-76. Though it looks like a standard Kalashnikov (though with far better exterior finish) there are some major differences. It has been adopted by the forces of Qatar, in the Middle East, and a semi-automatic-only version is sold as a sporting rifle in the U.S.A.

The receiver is of stamped steel rivetted together, and there is no wood whatever in the construction; the pistol grip and fore end are of steel, covered in plastic. Earlier versions (M60 and M62) have cooling holes in the fore end, but these have been omitted on the M76. There is a three-pronged flash hider on the muzzle, one prong of which carries a bayonet lug. The foresight is a hooded, adjustable, post, while the back sight is an aperture type protected by two wings. Instead of using the Soviet position in front of the chamber, the Finnish rear sight, being an aperture, is at the rear end of the receiver. It is also fitted with Tritium light beads for night aiming.

The trigger guard has no forward part, so that heavily-gloved fingers can get in to the trigger; there is a hinged bar at the front end to prevent accidental release of the magazine. Four types of butt-stock are produced: the M76T has a tubular unit, very thick, plastic-covered and rigid; the M76F has a folding skeleton butt; the M76M has a plastic stock of conventional appearance, and the M76W has, unusually, a wooden butt.

In 1981 Valmet announced the existence of a new experimental rifle, the M76 Short; this uses the same Kalashnikov mechanism of the M76 but fitted into a bullpup stock. It is chambered for the 5.56mm cartridge. The stock of the prototype is entirely of wood, but it is said that if the rifle were to go into production, then a plastic stock would be developed. However, the Finnish army showed no interest and the design was abandoned.

AKSU-74

Previous pages: The Bushman 'Individual Defense Weapon,' in action.

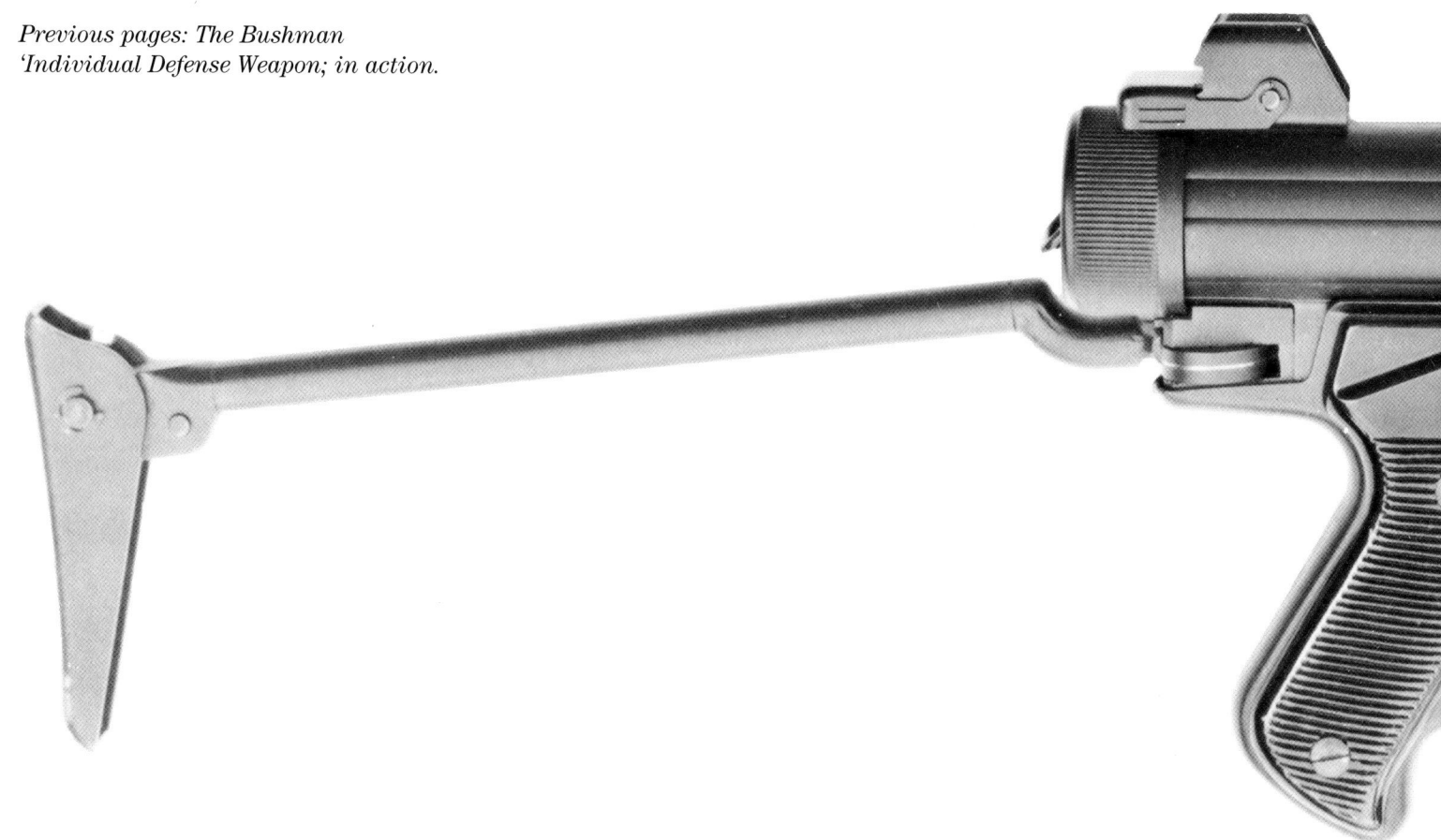

AKSU-74

Manufacturer State Rifle Factory, Izhevsk, Russia
Type Gas-operated, selective fire
Caliber 5.45mm
Barrel 7.87in (200mm)
Weight ca. 6.5lbs (3kg)
Magazine Capacity 30 rounds
Cyclic rate of fire 800 rounds/minute

When the Soviets adopted the Kalashnikov 7.62mm rifle, they abandoned their submachine guns, but in later years realized that they had been a little too hasty and needed a more compact weapon for occupants of vehicles. Their first attempt was to shorten the AK47 rifle, but this proved to be almost uncontrollable at automatic fire. At about this time they adopted the 5.45mm caliber for a new generation of Kalashnikov rifles and machine guns, and shortly afterwards set about making a compact model in the new caliber. The result was the AKSU-74, which was first revealed to the West in 1982 when a specimen was captured in Afghanistan.

The AKSU retains the basic method of operation of the familiar AK47 rifle, using a gas piston and a rotating bolt, but the shortening of the barrel introduced several complications. The 5.45mm cartridge was designed to be fired in a long-barrelled rifle, and the gas system of the Kalashnikov taps its gas from a position about two-thirds of the way up the barrel. Since the AKSU barrel is so short, all the gas generated in the cartridge would not have time to expend its energy and there would be a prominent muzzle flame and considerable blast. Therefore, a bulbous muzzle attachment can be seen, which acts as an expansion chamber for the emerging gas and muffles the flash and blast. It also helps to balance the internal pressure so that it is possible to tap off gas for the gas system closer to the breech than in other weapons.

A skeleton butt is fitted, which folds to the left side of the weapon, reducing the overall length to about 16.5 inches. The magazine is similar to that used with the AK-74 rifle, but has strengthening ribs molded into its front edge and is made of a lamination of sheet steel and plastic material. The receiver top cover is hinged to the gas block and lifts up to permit stripping the weapon; this differs from all other Kalashnikov designs, in which the top cover lifts off completely.

The AKSU is an ingenious design, but in many eyes somewhat overpowerful for the self-defense role for which it is intended. However, it does mean that the design and operation is already familiar to any soldier who knows the AK series of rifles – which was every Soviet soldier – and, unlike submachine guns, it does not require its own particular type of ammunition, happily firing the standard rifle cartridges.

Beretta Model 12S

Manufacturer Armi Beretta SpA, Gardone Val Trompia, Italy
Type Blowback, selective fire
Caliber 9mm Parabellum
Barrel 7.87in (200mm)
Weight (empty) 7.05lbs (3.2kg)
Magazine Capacity 20, 32 or 40 rounds
Cyclic rate of fire 550 rounds/minute

The Beretta Model 12 submachine gun has been in use by several armies since the late 1950s and has been produced under license in Indonesia and

BERETTA MODEL 12S

Above: The Beretta 12A, a slight modification to a highly-respected design.

Below: The Model 12S field stripped.

Brazil. Beretta have now brought it up to date in a new and slightly modified version which has been issued to the Italian forces and has also been exported to Tunisia and other countries.

The basic Model 12 is a sheet steel submachine gun of outstanding robustness and simplicity. The breech block is of the 'overhung' type and surrounds the barrel at the moment of firing, while the pistol grips, magazine housing and trigger housing are all in one piece. There is a grip safety in the pistol grip which ensures that the bolt cannot move unless the weapon is being properly held in the firing position. It has a reputation for smooth action and controllable fire, largely

BERETTA MODEL 12S

due to its balance and the fact that most of the barrel is inside the receiver so that the turning movement about the forward pistol grip is very small.

The Model 12S differs in having the fire selector and safety catch in a single lever unit, instead of two; the front sight has been made adjustable for windage and elevation; the attachment of the receiver rear cap has been strengthened and its locking catch moved to the top of the receiver for easier visual checking; the butt plate of the folding metal stock has been modified by the addition of a catch which ensures positive locking folded or unfolded position.

Though these are relatively small changes, they have made a positive difference to the weapon and turned a good design into a better one.

Top and right: The Beretta 12S is a weapon with a long service record. It was first introduced in the 1950s.

Above: The Model 12 with its butt folded.

BUSHMAN IDW

Bushman IDW

Manufacturer Bushman Ltd, Frogmore, St. Albans, England
Type Blowback, regulated
Caliber 9mm Parabellum
Barrel 3.25in (82.5mm)
Weight (empty) 6.4lbs (2.92kg)
Magazine Capacity 20, 28 or 32 rounds
Cyclic rate of fire 450 rounds/minute

The Bushman is described as an 'Individual Defense Weapon' (IDW) and is exceptionally small, no more than 10.8 inches (276mm) long. It can be easily concealed and carried, though it is rather heavier than might be expected from its size.

The Bushman introduced an entirely new idea into automatic weapons. Hitherto, it has been usual to build a weapon and then find out how fast it fires; if the rate of fire is too high or too low, then adjustments are made to the weight of the bolt, the strength of the return spring and other features in order to approach the desired figure. But the desired figure was no more than a figure which the designer felt was right; it had no scientific or technical origin. As a result most submachine guns are difficult to keep on target, since the vibration of the weapon and the muzzle blast combine to lift the muzzle during automatic fire, and the shots fly harmlessly into the air.

The designer of the Bushman reasoned that like most mechanical devices, a submachine gun would have a 'natural frequency' at which it would fire smoothly, without vibration and without the muzzle climbing. He developed an electronic control unit which arrested the bolt for a fraction of a second as it recoiled, and then released it. Being electronic, this device could be adjusted from infinitely slow to the full natural speed of the weapon, and it was simply a question of experimenting to find the natural frequency once the weapon had been designed.

Above left and left: Two views of the Bushman IDW, one of the smallest submachine guns in existence.

The result is one of the smallest submachine guns in existence, little larger than an automatic pistol, which can be fired one-handed at a full automatic rate of 450 rounds a minute and which puts all the bullets into the target area. The weapon does not jump; it merely rocks slightly in the hand.

The Bushman is heavy for its size, being machined from forged steel, using modern computer-controlled machine tools. It is a blowback weapon, and without the delaying mechanism would have a natural rate of fire of about 1400 rounds per minute, at which rate it would be almost uncontrollable and certainly incapable of being fired one-handed. But the regulator arrests the bolt momentarily after each shot and then, instructed by a micro-chip, releases it at the correct time to give the desired rate of fire.

The electronic control principle has also been applied to some existing submachine gun designs, with equally good effect. At the time of writing the Bushman has just entered production, and it will be interesting to see where it will be adopted.

Above: The CETME Ameli 5.56mm machine gun.

CETME Ameli 5.56mm Machine Gun

Manufacturer Santa Barbara SA, Madrid, Spain
Type Delayed blowback, automatic
Caliber 5.56mm
Barrel 15.75in (400mm)
Weight 11.5lbs (5.2kg)
Magazine Capacity 200-round belt
Cyclic rate of fire 900 rounds/minute

CETME (Centro de Estudios Tecnicos de Materiales Especiales) is a design and research establishment set up by the Spanish government in the early 1950s, and many of the original staff were refugees from Germany with experience in gun design. As a result, one can trace the original parentage of some of their designs right back to the Mauserwerke of 1943/45, and by the look of this weapon, to some other wartime design establishments as well: the Ameli looks very much like a miniaturised German MG42.

The Ameli was designed in the early 1980s for the Spanish Army, and it was one of the earliest 5.56mm machine

CETME AMELI 5.56MM MACHINE GUN

guns to enter service with any army. As with most of the weapons developed by CETME, it uses a delayed blowback system relying upon a roller locking system much the same as that used in the Model L rifle and in the Heckler & Koch rifles and machine guns. A two-part bolt is used, and as it closes, the rear section forces two rollers outwards into grooves in the receiver. On firing, the forward portion of the bolt cannot move back until these rollers have been withdrawn, which is done by pressure of inclined faces and delays the opening of the bolt long enough to let the bullet leave the muzzle.

The barrel lies within a perforated barrel jacket which has a long slot in the right side. A quick-release lever unlocks the barrel and forces the breech end out of the slot so that it can be grasped and pulled out of its front bearing. A fresh, cool, barrel can then be inserted, and a trained squad can change the barrel in under five seconds.

Feed is by means of a disintegrating-link belt; as each round is loaded from the belt the link falls free, so that there is no problem of what to do with the empty belt as it comes out of the gun. The rate of fire can be adjusted between 800 and 1200 rounds per minute to suit the particular role; the Ameli can be used either as a light squad automatic, when the high rate of fire is generally selected, or as a tripod-mounted company support weapon, where the low rate of fire is more appropriate.

The Ameli is currently in use by the Spanish Army, and has been assessed by several others. It is manufactured by Santa Barbara, the state armaments company, since, unusually, CETME do not possess any manufacturing capacity.

CHINESE TYPE 64 SILENCED

Chinese Type 64 Silenced

Manufacturer Chinese State Arsenal
Type Blowback, selective fire, silenced
Caliber 7.62mm Soviet Pistol
Barrel 9.6in (244mm)
Weight (empty) 7.5lbs (3.4kg)
Magazine Capacity 30 rounds
Cyclic rate of fire Not known

This weapon is far from new, its Type number being an indication of its date into service, but it was not generally known in the west until the latter 1970s. It is completely Chinese-designed and constructed and appears to be an amalgam of ideas taken from various European designs. So far as is known, the Type 64 is only used by the Chinese Communist Army.

The basic mechanism is that of the Soviet PPS-43, a plain blowback weapon using a stamped and welded steel receiver to house a very basic bolt and return spring. The trigger mechanism, which incorporates a selective fire mechanism, is a copy of that used on the Bren machine gun, several hundred of which, in 7.92mm Mauser caliber, were made in Canada and supplied to China during the 1939-45 war. The chamber is fluted, a step probably devised to ease extraction with the necked cartridge case, and the curved magazine fits into the bottom of the receiver.

The forward section of the barrel is perforated with four rows of holes which follow the rifling grooves, after which there are a series of disc-shaped baffles with a central hole through which the bullet passes. This whole assembly is surrounded by a jacket which forms the external 'barrel' section of the weapon. The result is unique because it is a rare example of a weapon designed from scratch as a silenced gun, and not one which has had the silencer added as an afterthought or modification. It is moderately effective, though not so efficient in silencing as the British Sterling or American Ingram designs, but it has the added bonus of being an efficient flash hider, so that the result is a useful weapon for ambushes and guerrilla operations. The principal drawback is the loss of velocity due to the escape of gas through the barrel vents; this is intended to reduce the bullet to subsonic speed, but obviously has a deleterious effect on its range and penetrative power.

Above and right: Two views of the Ameli 5.56 machine gun.

Above: The Chinese Type 64 silenced submachine gun, without magazine.

FAMAE SAF

Manufacturer FAMAE, Santiago, Chile
Type Blowback, selective fire
Caliber 9mm Parabellum
Barrel 7.87in (200mm)
Weight (empty) 6.4lbs (2.9kg)
Magazine Capacity 30 rounds
Cyclic rate of fire 1300 rounds/minute

Like the Steyr submachine gun, the SAF is based upon an assault rifle design, though in this case with much more modification. In the 1980s the FAMAE factory (the Chilean government small arms factory) obtained a license to manufacture the Swiss SIG 540 assault rifle. This is a 5.56mm locked-breech weapon of fairly conventional pattern, and is the standard

FN P-90 PERSONAL DEFENSE WEAPON

Left and below left: The Chilean-manufactured FAMAE SAF, available with either fixed or folding butt. Based on the Swiss SIG540 assault rifle, the SAF is standard Chilean army issue.

Chilean service rifle. Having set up the machinery to make this rifle, FAMAE looked at the design and decided to adapt what they could of the rifle to a submachine gun.

The general design, the receiver, stock and fore-end, is that of the rifle, though shortened. The rotating bolt breech closing system was modified to a simple blowback bolt, but the rifle's hammer mechanism was retained, so that, like the AUG 9 Para, this weapon fires from a closed bolt. The actual mechanism was altered, however, to allow for single shots, automatic fire or three-round bursts, the latter being somewhat unusual on submachine guns.

A new 9mm barrel was designed and fitted. The magazine was made in translucent plastic so that the contents can be seen at any time; it is also fitted with protruding lugs on one side and keyhole-like slots on the other, so that two or three magazines can be clipped together. One can be inserted into the magazine housing on the weapon, leaving the others exposed. When the first magazine is empty, it is simple to slip it out, shift the lot sideways and slip a fresh magazine into position – far quicker than withdrawing a fresh magazine from a pouch and fitting it in place, then having to pick up the old magazine.

Three models of the SAF are made; the standard model with a fixed plastic butt; standard with a side-folding tubular metal butt; and a silenced model with an integral silencer and folding butt.

There is also the 'Mini-SAF' with a much shorter barrel, no shoulder stock and a forward handgrip. It can use the standard 30-round magazine but a special 20-round magazine gives additional compactness. The whole weapon is only 12 inches long and is ideal for stealth work like bodyguard and covert operations.

FN P-90 Personal Defense Weapon

Manufacturer FN Herstal SA, Herstal, Belgium
Type Blowback, selective fire
Caliber 5.7 × 28mm SS90
Barrel
Weight 7lbs (3.02kg) with full magazine
Magazine Capacity 50 rounds
Cyclic rate of fire 900 rounds/minute

This unique weapon was developed by FN Herstal (originally, and perhaps better, known as Fabrique National of Liège) as a result of a very careful analysis of weapons usage in modern armies. This showed that only the assault infantry – which is perhaps about one-eighth of an army – actually needs a powerful (and expensive) assault rifle. The other seven-eighths are troops who serve other weapons – artillery, rockets or tanks, for example – or are service, communication or supply troops; none of these expect to use a rifle as their primary job, but they need a weapon for self-defense should the gun position be attacked or the ration column ambushed. Pistols and submachine guns are traditionally the weapon for these troops, but both these require training and constant practice to get the best out of them. A low-recoil weapon with a reasonable self-defense range and sufficient power to defeat body armor was required, one which was simple and instinctive in its use.

The P-90 broke new ground in weapon design. The shape is unusual, with a forward grip which can be held with both hands when the weapon is fired from the shoulder, or simply by one hand with the butt tucked into the hip. It is a blowback, firing a specially-designed cartridge which is more like a small rifle cartridge than the usual type of submachine gun round. The magazine lies on top of the receiver,

Below: The FN P-90 PDW.

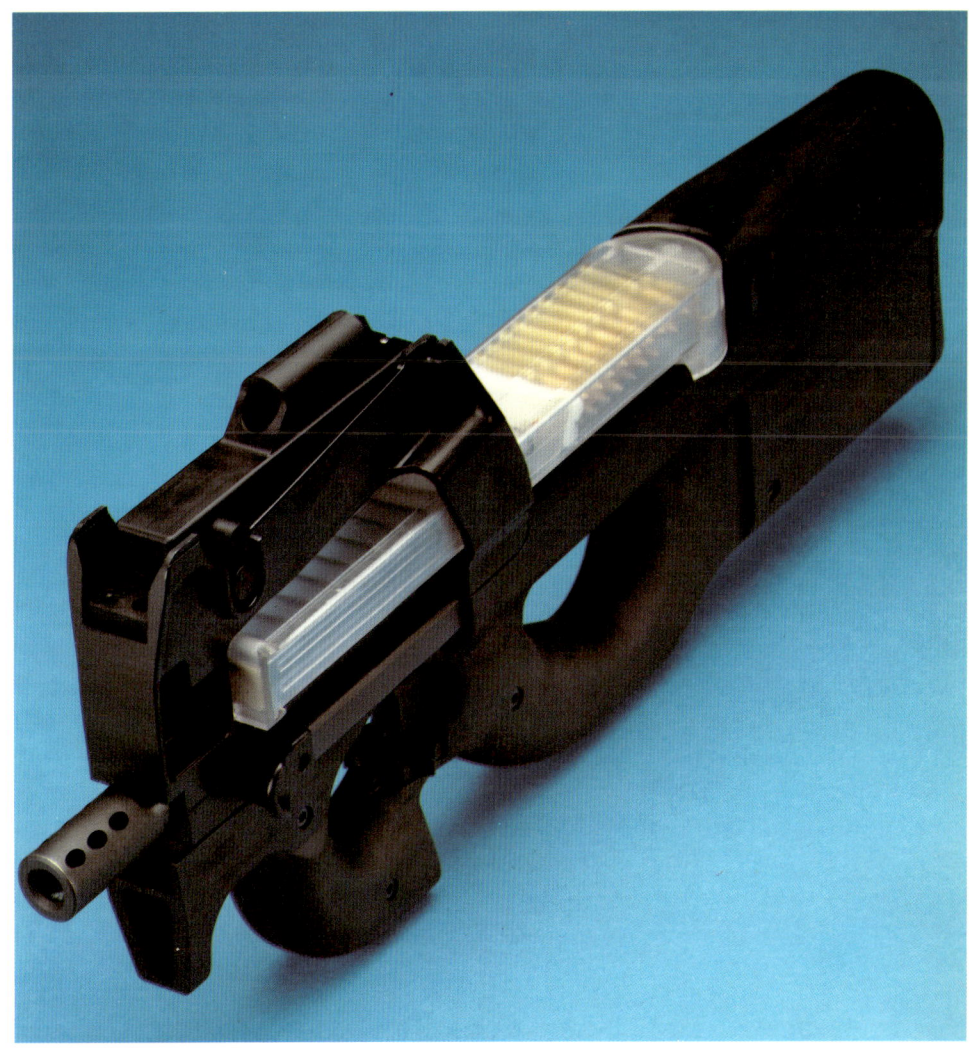

FN P-90 PERSONAL DEFENSE WEAPON

with the cartridges lying across the axis of the weapon and feeding through a turntable which turns them through 90 degrees and guides them into the feedway in front of the bolt. Ejection is downwards, through the hollow pistol grip.

A collimating optical sight is fitted, which can be used with both eyes open and projects an image of a circle and central dot on to the view of the target. There are also two sets of iron sights, so that both right- and left-handed firers find it easy to aim.

The bullet has a synthetic core and metal jacket; it is capable of piercing 30 layers of Kevlar fabric (as used in bullet-proof vests) at 100 meters range and a standard steel helmet at 150 meters. In spite of this, the recoil energy is about two-thirds of the 9mm Parabellum round and the weapon is quite easily controlled during automatic fire.

The P-90 has been adopted by a number of military forces since its introduction in 1992.

Left and below: The compact FN P-90.

FN 'Minimi' Machine Gun

Manufacturer Fabrique Nationale d'Armes de Guerre, Herstal, Belgium
Type Gas-operated light machine gun
Caliber 5.56mm (.223)
Barrel 18.3in (465mm)
Weight 14.32lbs (6.5kg)
Magazine Capacity 30 rounds, or belts
Cyclic rate of fire 850 rounds/minute

Top and above: Two views of the FN 'Minimi' machine gun.

When Fabrique Nationale developed their 5.56mm CAL rifle in the late 1960s, they felt it logical to continue work and develop a 5.56mm machine gun to accompany it. In fact the CAL was somewhat ahead of its time, and has since been replaced by the FNC, an improved design, but the 'Minimi' machine gun appeared in 1974 and was well-timed to catch the first stirring of enthusiasm for the 5.56 caliber. It has been adopted by the armies of Belgium, Indonesia, Thailand and other countries and also approved for the U.S. Army as the M249 Squad Automatic Weapon (SAW).

The Minimi is of conventional type, using gas tapped from the barrel to drive a piston which propels a bolt carrier. This contains a rotating bolt which is unlocked by cam action. The unusual feature of the Minimi is its feed system; it is capable of feeding from a box magazine or from a belt. The bolt is provided with two sets of feed horns which will strip cartridges either from an overhead belt or from a side-mounted magazine, while a simple mechanism prevents any attempt to feed both at once. Thus the gun can be normally operated as a belt-feed weapon but in an emergency

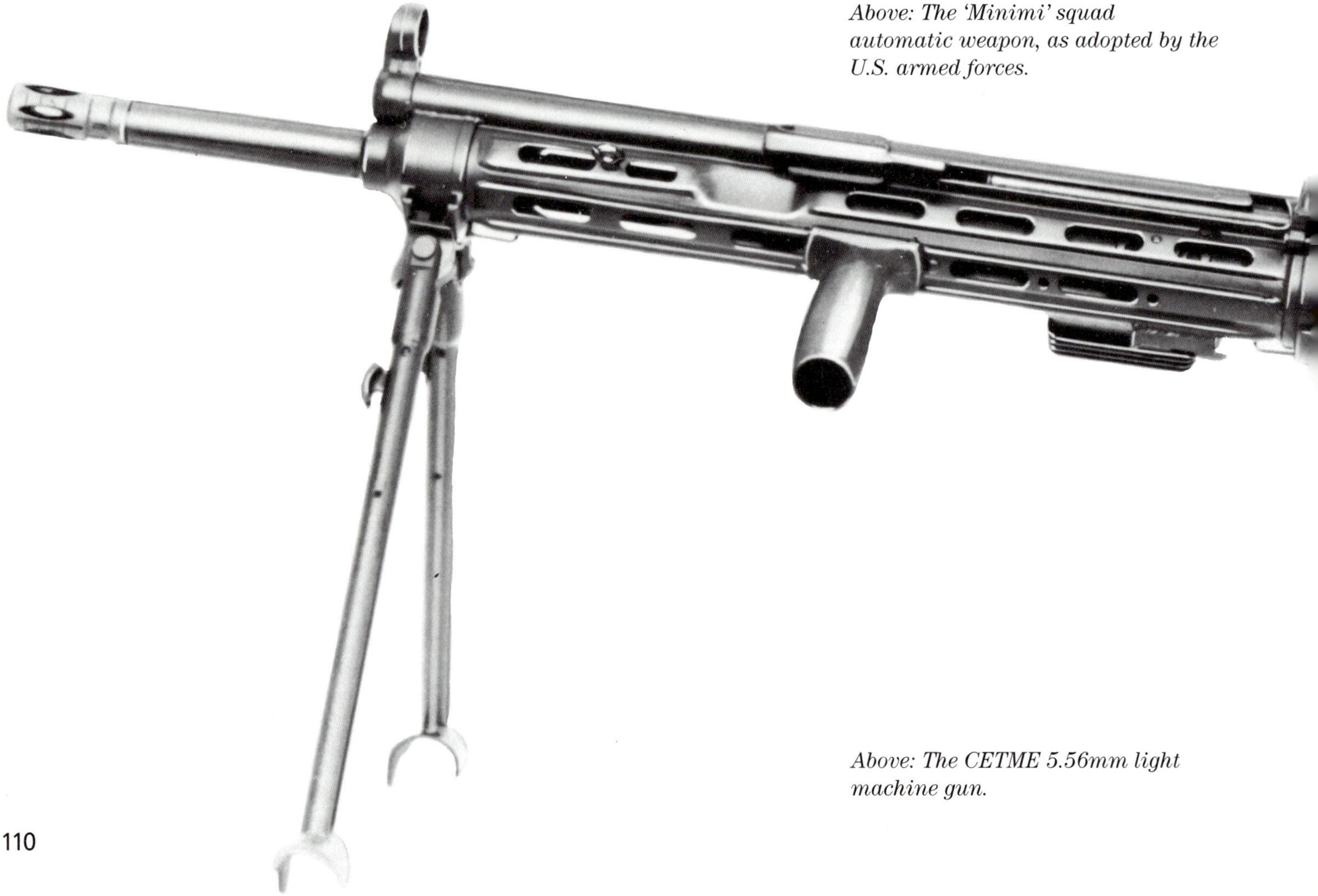

FN 'MINIMI' MACHINE GUN

Above: The 'Minimi' squad automatic weapon, as adopted by the U.S. armed forces.

Above: The CETME 5.56mm light machine gun.

HECKLER & KOCH HK21A1 GP MACHINE GUN

can be fed from the standard M16A1 30-round box. The belt is carried in a transparent box which acts as a carrier when not on the gun and then locks securely to the gun when installed for feeding. Two sizes are available, one for 100 rounds and one for 200 rounds.

The standard model has a fixed metal butt; there is a variant model for airborne or special forces which has a shorter barrel (335mm) and a folding metal butt. Both types have quick-release barrels so that they can be changed when over-heating. The standard sights consist of a protected blade mounted on the gas regulator and an elevation-adjustable aperture rear sight. The receiver will also accept NATO standard mounts for image-intensifying sights.

Trials by the U.S. Army, preparatory to accepting it for the SAWS program, showed the Minimi to be remarkably free from stoppages and breakages during prolonged firing. By adopting the Minimi the U.S. Army looks like having a good light machine gun for the first time in its history.

Above: The 'Minimi' in action.

Heckler & Koch HK21A1 GP Machine Gun

Manufacturer Heckler & Koch GmbH, Oberndorf-Am-Neckar, Germany
Type Delayed blowback general-purpose automatic
Caliber 7.62mm NATO
Barrel 17.7in (450mm)
Weight 17.63lbs (8kg)
Magazine Capacity Belt feed
Cyclic rate of fire 900 rounds/minute

The HK21A1 is the latest development of the HK21 gun, which has been in military service for some years, and the aim has been to produce a one-man machine gun which will improve the firepower of the infantry squad without adding to their logistic load. As well as being the squad light gun it can be tripod-mounted and used as a company support weapon.

The layout of the gun is similar to the company's rifle design, and it uses the same roller-locked delayed blowback breech mechanism. A major change has been to do away with the magazine-loading option and make

this a belt-fed-only gun. The belt feed unit has been redesigned to make belt loading much quicker than previously. The barrel can be quickly changed by cocking the weapon, releasing the barrel latch, and then easing the barrel forward and sideways through a slot in the ventilated barrel guard. There is a bipod which can be mounted in the usual place, at the front end of the jacket, or can be moved to a position just in front of the feed unit, at the center of balance, if preferred.

A variety of specialized mountings are available; there is a spring-buffered tripod with panoramic sight for support fire roles; a column mount which fits on light vehicles and uses spring balancing gear to take the weight of the gun; and two different 360° tracks for ground, vehicle or anti-aircraft defense.

The HK21A1 is understood to have been purchased by several African and Asian armies, but no firm details have been released.

Heckler & Koch MP5

Manufacturer Heckler & Koch GmbH, Oberndorf-Am-Neckar, Germany
Type Delayed blowback, selective fire
Caliber 9mm Parabellum
Barrel 8.8in (225mm)
Weight (empty) 5.4lbs (2.45kg)
Magazine Capacity 15 or 30 rounds
Cyclic rate of fire 650 rounds/minute

The Heckler & Koch company made their G3 rifle the foundation of their business and by adapting its mechanism they have parlayed it into a number of formats. This submachine gun is somewhat unusual in that it uses a delayed blowback mode of operation and incorporates the roller-locked breech mechanism used in the G3 rifle to do it. As a result several of the parts of the MP5 are common to the G3 rifle, a point which has attractions for military procurement officers. The MP5 is in use by German police and Border Guards, by the Swiss and Dutch and several other police and military forces, and has also been seen in the hands of the British Special Air Service operating against terrorists.

The two-part breech block of the MP5 locks the forward section by two rollers, forced out into recesses in the receiver by the forward motion of the rear section during the closing movement. The force on the cartridge base, on firing, attempts to drive the for-

This page: Two variants of the Heckler & Koch MP5: at top, with retractable stock; and the ultra-short type.

HUGHES CHAIN GUN

Above: The Hughes Chain Gun mounted on a Bradley infantry fighting vehicle.

ward section back, but it cannot move immediately, so keeping the breech closed, and does not move until the heavy rear section of the bolt has begun to move back and so left space for the rollers to be forced inwards by the inclined faces of their recesses. Once the bolt is free, it recoils backwards in the usual manner to complete the extracting and reloading cycle.

There are a number of variations on the basic model, which is known as the MP5A2 and has a plastic buttstock and fore end. The MP5A3 has a telescoping metal buttstock. The MP5SD has a permanently-fixed silencer around the barrel and sub-divides into three versions – MP5SD1 with no butt, MP5SD2 with fixed plastic butt, and MP5SD3 with telescoping butt. The MP5K is a specially shortened version for concealed use by anti-terrorist squads and similar people; it can also be fitted inside a special briefcase for use by bodyguards; it can be fired from this concealment and performs faultlessly, the empty cases being carefully channelled and collected so as not to bounce around and jam the weapon. There are also attachments to permit these various models to be fired from ball-mounts in armored vehicles or from specially-developed turrets.

Hughes Chain Gun® Machine Gun

Manufacturer Hughes Helicopters, Culver City, CA90230, U.S.A.
Type Mechanical, belt fed, machine gun
Caliber 7.62mm NATO
Barrel 22in (558mm)
Weight 29.1lbs (13.2kg)
Magazine Capacity Belt fed
Cyclic rate of fire Variable up to 600 rounds/minute

Mechanical machine guns are as old as the industry, names like Gatling, Gardner and Nordenfelt having been prominent in this field in the 1870s, but with the development of the self-powered Maxim they were rendered obsolescent. They reappeared when it became obvious that only mechanical solutions could provide the high rate of fire demanded by modern aerial combat, and the Gatling was revived as the electrically-driven 'Vulcan' aircraft cannon. But for land force use they seemed to be out of the question until Hughes perfected this design, one of the most significant developments in small arms technology in the last fifty years. It has been adopted in 7.62mm caliber as a tank and armored vehicle gun by the U.S. and British armies and is likely to be taken into use by several others in the future. In 25mm and 30mm caliber it is in use by the U.S. forces as a helicopter weapon and has also been evaluated by the British Army as armament for their 'Fox' armored car.

The heart of the Chain Gun is a loop of commercial roller chain which lies on the bottom of the receiver and is driven round by a gear, driven by an electric motor. Attached to this chain is a lug which engages in the bolt carrier, so that as the chain moves forward, along one side of the receiver, so the carrier is moved forward, a cartridge is fed into the breech, and the bolt is rotated and locked. As the chain lug moves, following the loop path, across the front of the receiver there is no motion of the bolt carrier; the breech stays locked and the cartridge is fired. Then as the chain lug turns the corner and begins to run back, down the other side of the receiver, the bolt is unlocked and opened, the carrier pulled back, the case ejected. As the chain lug makes its fourth side of the receiver, again there is no motion on the carrier and there is a brief pause which permits cooling of the open barrel.

The delay, or 'dwell', with the closed bolt acts as a safety in case of a hangfire (delayed ignition of the cartridge), and if the cartridge has not fired by the time the lug has made its crossing, the gun stops and the operator has to restart it, thus giving ample time for the longest hangfire to discharge itself safely. If the round is a misfire, then once the gun is re-started the dud round is extracted and ejected safely. Ejection is done down a forward-facing tube, since this gun is designed for use in armored vehicles and the empties (and any unfired rounds) are thrown clear of the turret. Since the gun is sealed, fumes cannot escape into the vehicle but are ejected either through a jacket sleeve around the barrel or through the ejector tube, keeping the air in the tank relatively clean.

It will be apparent that the rate of fire is infinitely variable by simply controlling the speed of the drive motor, though in practice the controls are such that either single shots or 600 rpm are available. The Chain Gun also has the advantage of providing positive mechanical lift for the ammunition belt, instead of relying upon recoil of the gun's moving parts to actuate the feed. This, together with the precise control and inter-operation of the entire operating cycle, makes the Chain Gun one of the most reliable and smoothly-operating machine guns in existence.

M60E3 Lightweight Assault Machine Gun

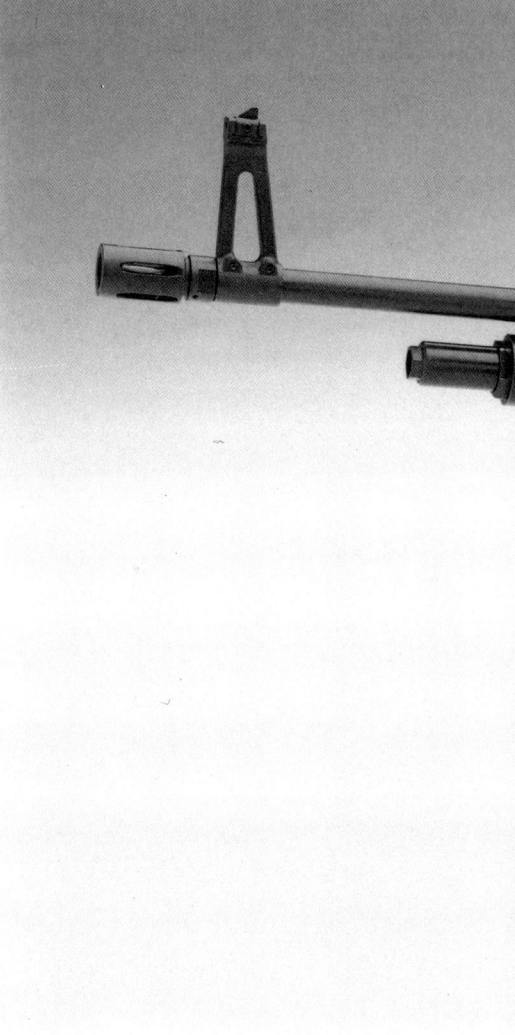

Manufacturer Saco Defense Inc, Saco, Maine, U.S.A.
Type Gas-operated, automatic
Caliber 7.62mm
Barrel 22in (560mm)
Weight 19.4lbs (8.8kg)
Magazine Capacity unlimited link belt
Cyclic rate of fire 500-650 rounds/minute

The M60 machine gun was adopted by the U.S. Army in the late 1950s and served as a general-purpose machine gun, bipod-mounted as the squad automatic, or tripod-mounted as the company support gun. It was somewhat heavy and had a number of design faults which took some time to cure, and in the 1980s the U.S. forces requested a lighter version for use by rapid intervention troops and light infantry. The M60E3 was developed to fill this requirement, which it has done with considerable success.

The weapon uses a rotating bolt which is mounted on a post at the end of the gas piston assembly. As the piston is driven back, this post, acting in

Above: The 7.62mm version of the Hughes Chain Gun for co-axial mounting on an armored vehicle.

Above: The M60E3 lightweight assault machine gun.

a curved camway in the body of the bolt, rotates the bolt to unlock it from the chamber. It then drives the bolt back; it is prevented from rotating by the locking lugs riding in grooves in the receiver. A buffer spring halts the rearward movement, and then the assembly runs forward, the bolt collecting a fresh round from the feedway and loading it into the chamber. As the bolt reaches the end of the grooves, the post and cam path rotate it to lock, and the post, continuing forward, strikes the firing pin in the bolt and fires the round. The backward and forward movement of the bolt is also used to grip the feed belt and move it across the gun.

The changes in the basic M60 design which turned it into the M60E3 are the fitting of a lightweight barrel, adding a light bipod, a carrying handle attached to the barrel, a forward hand grip for firing from the hip or shoulder, and some improvements to the feed and gas systems. Two optional barrels are also available, a lightweight short barrel for the utmost compactness, and a heavy barrel for missions which demand sustained firing. These may be interchanged with the standard barrel without the need for any further adjustment. There is also a conversion kit which allows any older M60 to be converted to the M60E3 specification.

In 1992 the Saco company announced the development of the 'M60E3 Enhanced' machine gun. This is generally similar to the M60E3 but has an improved bipod, improved forward hand grip and heat shield, a hinged shoulder rest to give the firer better control when firing from the bipod, and a new design of sling attachment to prevent the sling coming into contact with a hot barrel.

A variety of fire control systems are available for these weapons, including optical and electro-optical sights for night or day use, laser aiming spotlights, laser rangefinders and similar devices. All these can be attached to or detached from the gun without loss of zero, using specially-developed U.S. Army mounts.

Model 62 Machine Gun

Manufacturer Sumitomo Heavy Industries, Tokyo, Japan
Type Gas-operated, automatic
Caliber 7.62mm
Barrel 20.6in (524mm)
Weight 23.6lbs (10.7kg)
Magazine Capacity Belt
Cyclic rate of fire 600 rounds/minute

The Model 62 is the standard machine gun of the Japanese Self-Defense Force and has some unusual features. It is a general-purpose gun, used on a

Above: Israel's Negev light machine gun.

bipod as the squad automatic and on a tripod as a heavy-support weapon.

The gun is gas-operated, having the usual cylinder and piston below the barrel. The rear end of the piston rod carries a vertical post, to which is attached the firing pin. This post fits into a slot in the breech-block and thus as the piston moves, so it drives the block backwards and forwards. As the block closes the breech, the piston rod continues moving, and a ramp on the end of the rod forces up the rear end of the breech-block until two lugs on its sides are wedged into recesses in the side of the receiver, so locking the breech firmly closed. The last forward movement of the piston carries the firing pin forward to strike the cap and fire the cartridge.

The quick-change barrel is automatically locked in place so long as the top cover of the receiver is closed. Opening the cover unlocks the barrel, so that it can be removed and a new barrel inserted; it also prevents the bolt from rising in order to lock, so that there is no chance that the firing pin can possibly line up with the chamber and thus accidentally fire a shot while the barrel is being removed or the cover open.

Extraction of the spent case is not done by the usual sort of spring-loaded extractor; the cartridge is located in the chamber by a spring-loaded stud which presses into the extractor groove from below. As the bolt is unlocked, so a claw-like arm drops and engages with the cartridge rim, and as the bolt moves back so the cartridge is pulled out of the chamber and ejected.

Feed is from a disintegrating-link belt. A feed arm inside the top cover is driven by the movement of the bolt, and pulls the belt across in two steps, corresponding to the backward and forward movement of the bolt as each shot is fired.

A somewhat heavier version of this weapon, known as the Model 74, is used as a co-axial machine gun in armored vehicles.

Negev Light Machine Gun

Manufacturer Ta'as Israel Industries, Ramat Hasharon, Israel
Type Gas-operated, selective fire
Caliber 5.56mm
Barrel 18.1in (460mm)
Weight 15.9lbs (7.2kg) empty
Magazine Capacity 30-round magazine or belt
Cyclic rate of fire 650-950 rounds/minute

The Israel Defense Force adopted a heavy-barrelled version of their standard Galil rifle as their squad automatic weapon and used it for several years, but in the late 1980s decided that a more purpose-built light machine gun would be preferable. One drawback of the heavy Galil was its fixed barrel, which made overheating, particularly in the Middle Eastern climate, an ever-present problem.

The Negev is a conventional enough weapon, using gas to drive a bolt

'SCORPION' MACHINE PISTOL

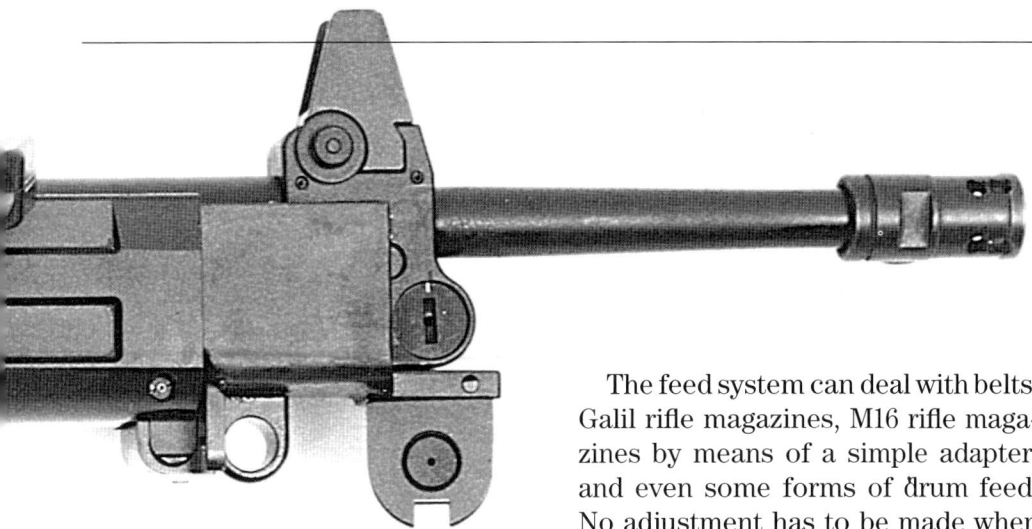

carrier which contains a cam-operated rotating bolt. The bolt locks into a barrel extension, to which a quick-change barrel is attached by interrupted lugs. Thus, as soon as the barrel begins to overheat it can be rapidly changed for a fresh one, and the hot barrel allowed to cool. It also fires from an open bolt; the bolt is kept back by the trigger mechanism when the trigger is released, so that air can flow through the barrel and into the interior of the receiver and thus assist in cooling between bursts of fire.

The feed system can deal with belts, Galil rifle magazines, M16 rifle magazines by means of a simple adapter, and even some forms of drum feed. No adjustment has to be made when changing from one system to another, and there are safeguards to ensure that in the heat of battle, nobody tries to load from two sorts of feed at once.

The gas regulator has three positions; in normal conditions position one gives a rate of fire of 650-800 rounds per minute; position two gives a rate of 800-950 rounds per minute, or, in dusty or dirty conditions, can be used to give more power to overcome fouling. The third position shuts off the gas to the gas system in order to permit grenades to be launched from the muzzle.

The Negev can be used as a light machine gun or it can be fitted with a shorter (330mm) barrel to act as an assault machine gun or rifle. The gun can be easily and quickly stripped into six sub-assemblies, including the bipod. All parts, including the quick-change barrels, are fully interchangeable, and the receiver is prepared for sight mounts to accept any kind of optical or electro-optical sight.

'Scorpion' Machine Pistol

Manufacturer Czech State Arsenals
Type Blowback, selective fire
Caliber .32 ACP (7.65mm) (but see text)
Barrel 4.4in (112mm)
Weight 3.50lbs (1.59kg)
Magazine Capacity 10 or 20 rounds
Cyclic rate of fire 840 rounds/minute

Like the Czech CZ58 rifle mentioned elsewhere, this is not a new weapon but it deserves a mention for two reasons; firstly because it is a unique miniature submachine gun, and secondly because it is appearing more

Above: The Czech 'Scorpion' machine pistol in .32ACP caliber.
Left: The silenced version of the 'Scorpion.'

'SCORPION' MACHINE PISTOL

and more often in the hands of terrorists and revolutionaries, largely because of its small size and concentrated firepower. In its original form it was of somewhat limited legitimate application; it was then increased in caliber to give it a wider military role, and was adopted and manufactured in Yugoslavia. (The two are easily distinguished, since Czech production has a wooden pistol grip and Yugoslavian models have plastic grips.) It equipped various units of the Czech and Yugoslavian armies and has been exported to various African states with Communist connections. How these weapons find their way into terrorist hands is not for us to suggest.

The original Scorpion (or CZ61) is the .32 caliber model, and it was designed as a light weapon capable of being holster-carried by crews of armored vehicles, as a self-defense weapon. The small bullet is hardly a combat projectile, but as a last-ditch weapon for use by the crew of a stalled tank, it has some validity. The mechanism is a simple blowback bolt, and a change lever allows single shots or automatic fire. In either mode it can be fired one-handed, or the wire stock can be unfolded to allow its use as a shoulder weapon. It is unpleasant to fire from the hip since the empty cases are ejected vertically and usually hit the firer in the face.

The light bolt and weak recoil spring would led to an unacceptably high rate of fire if left to themselves, and so a rate reducer is fitted into the pistol grip. As the bolt reaches the end of its rearward travel it is held by a catch; during the rearward movement the bolt trips a light plunger and drives it down inside the pistol grip, against a spring. This light plunger passes through a heavy weight and passes some of its energy to the weight, causing it to begin to move down. The plunger reaches the bottom of the grip and its spring sends it back, where it meets the descending weight and passes through it; this acts as a retardant to the plunger. Eventually the plunger reaches the top of the grip once more and releases the bolt catch, allowing it to go forward and fire the next round. This all sounds very time-consuming, but in fact it cuts the rate down to 840 rounds per minute, so the travel of the plunger is all over in about .0012 of a second.

Later models of the Scorpion were chambered for different cartridges; the CZ64 fires the .380 Auto (9mm Short) cartridge; the CZ65 fires the 9mm Soviet (Makarov) cartridge; and the CZ68 is chambered for the 9mm Parabellum round. There has been little published about these variants and few have been seen outside Czechoslovakia. The CZ68 is, as might be expected, somewhat larger than the other models.

Singapore Ultimax 100

Manufacturer Chartered Industries of Singapore, Singapore
Type Gas-operated, automatic
Caliber 5.56mm (.223)
Barrel 20in (508mm)
Weight 10.8lbs (4.9kg) with bipod
Magazine Capacity 20, 30 or 100 rounds
Cyclic rate of fire 520 rounds/minute

Having successfully manufactured M16 rifles, M203 grenade launchers and then their own rifle (described elsewhere in these pages), CIS of Singapore, moved by the U.S. Army's SAW (Squad Automatic Weapon) program of the 1970s, decided to make their own machine gun and offer it for test. They originally called it the SAW, though in this case it meant 'Section Machine Gun', but this was soon changed to 'Ultimax 100', largely because of the unusual 100-round magazine. Work began in 1980, but before the design could be perfected the U.S. Army had selected the FN Minimi as their light machine gun. Nevertheless, the Ultimax proved to be an excellent weapon and was

Right: The Ultimax 100, named after its 100-round magazine.

Below: The Ultimax 100 fitted with drum magazine.

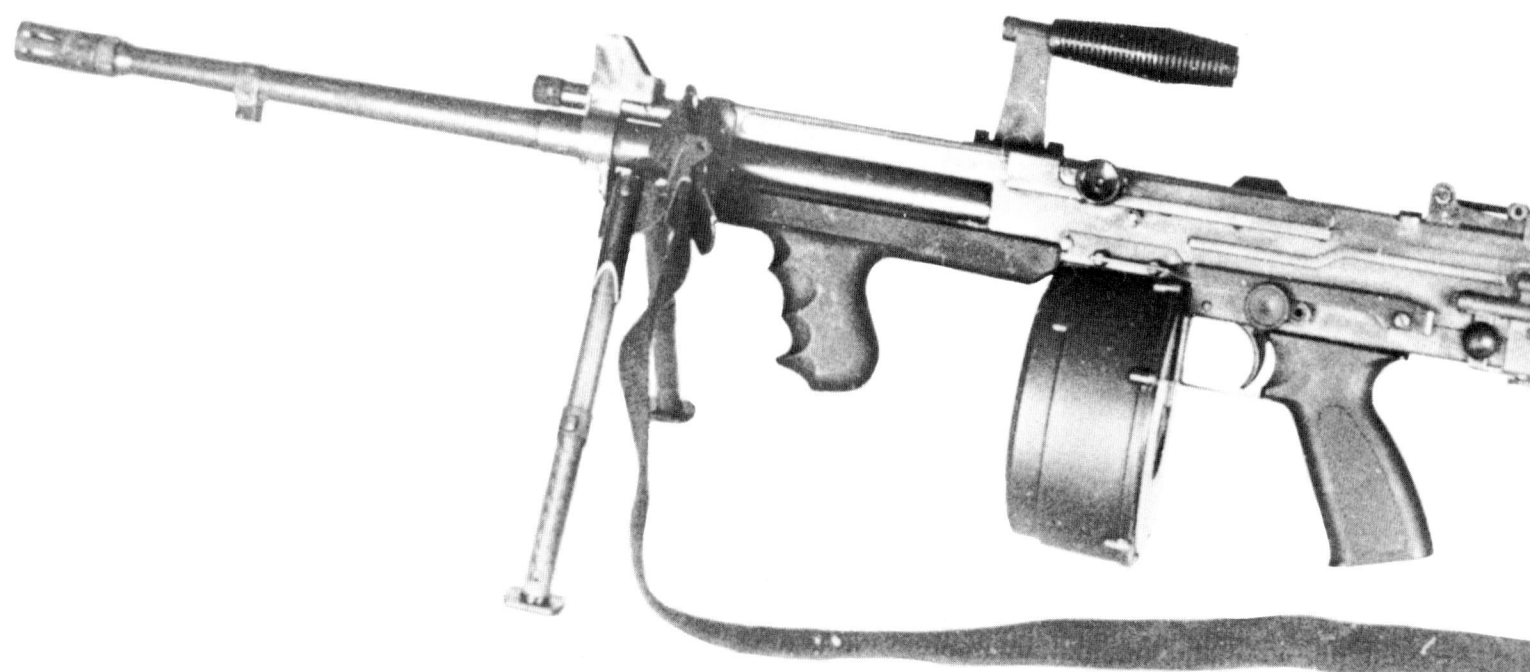

SINGAPORE ULTIMAX 100

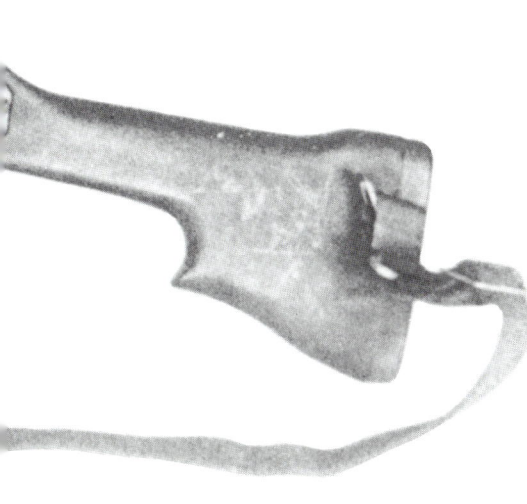

adopted by the Singapore Armed Forces and has been sold to various countries in the Far East where it has performed well.

The Ultimax 100 is a fairly conventional gas-operated gun, using a piston to drive a bolt carrier which holds a rotating bolt. It fires from the open bolt position and only fires automatic – single shots are not possible except by careful taps on the trigger, the slow rate of fire helping here. The first model (Mark I) had a quick-change barrel which proved not to be very quick in practice, and it has been dropped. The Mark II uses a heavy fixed barrel capable of firing 500 continuous rounds without heat damage problems. The Mark III has a similarly heavy barrel but one which can be quickly changed when circumstances dictate.

There are various magazines; 20- or 30-round box magazines can be used, or a special 100-round plastic drum. With any of these the weapon can be fired from the shoulder or the hip under complete control. The sights are fully adjustable for windage and elevation and are graduated up to 1000 meters, a somewhat optimistic marking with 5.56mm ammunition. At shorter ranges to 400-500 meters, though, it is steady, holds well on the target and is as accurate as any of its competitors.

Soviet PK Machine Gun

Manufacturer Soviet State Arsenals
Type Gas-operated, belt fed, machine gun
Caliber 7.62mm Soviet Nagant M1891
Barrel 25.9in (658mm)
Weight 19.84lbs (9kg)
Magazine Capacity 100, 200 or 250-round belt
Cyclic rate of fire 700 rounds/minute

Since the 1920s the principal Soviet infantry machine gun was a Degtyarev design, using a locking system based on flaps forced into notches in the receiver by the forward movement of the firing pin. But when the Kalashnikov rifle became the Soviet standard, it was thought advisable to develop a Kalashnikov-based machine gun, if only for commonality of parts and manufacture. As a result, the 'PK' series ('Pulyemet Kalashnikova') appeared in the mid-1960s and was in universal use throughout the armies of the former Warsaw Pact.

In fact, although the PK uses the same type of bolt carrier and rotating bolt as the Kalashnikov rifle, other parts of the mechanism have been 'borrowed' from other designs; thus, the feed system has been taken from the Goryunov machine gun, as has the method of changing the barrel; the method of using the gas piston to drive the belt feed mechanism comes from a Czechoslovakian design; and the trigger has been taken from the

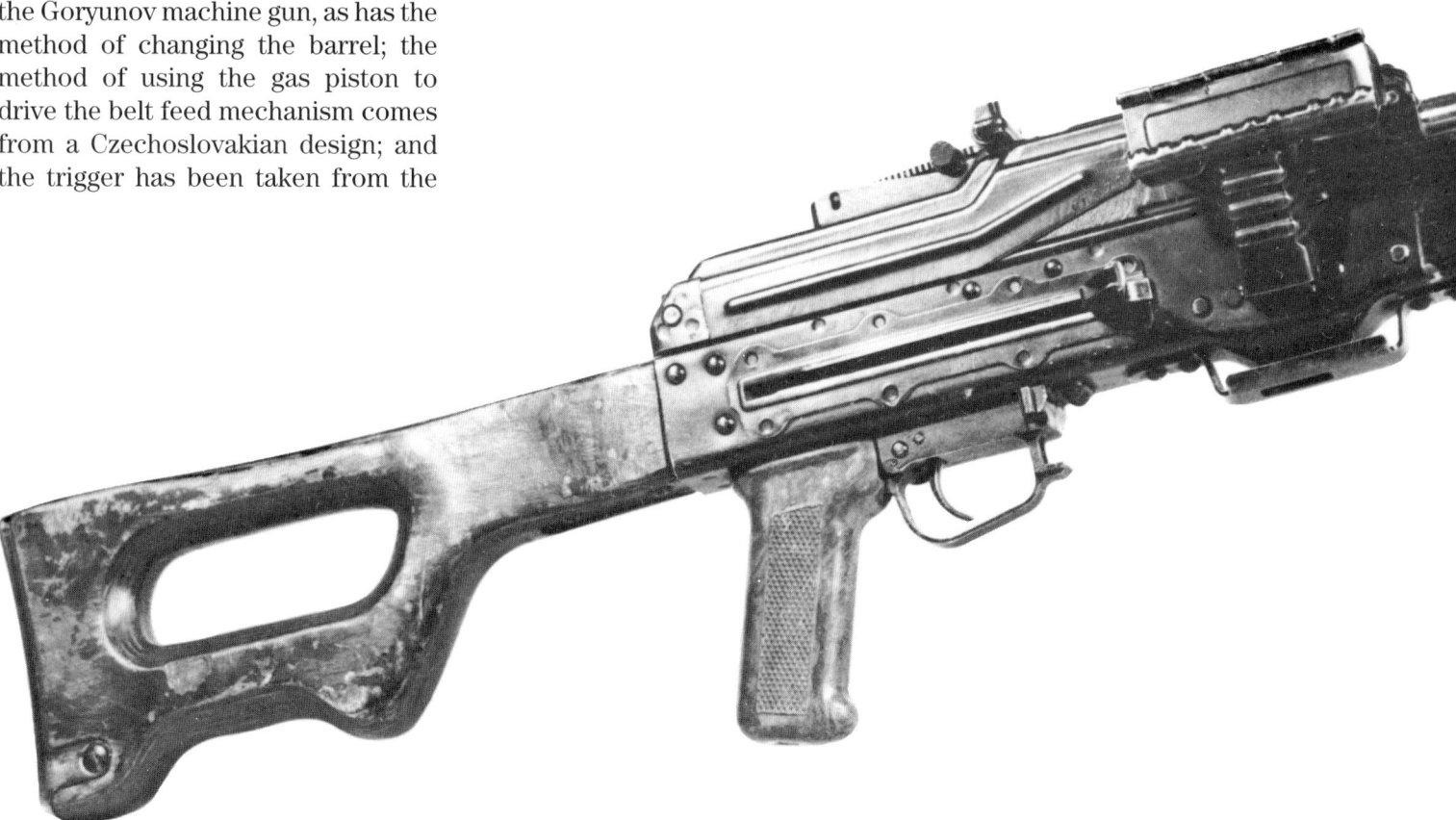

SPECTRE M-4

older Degtyarev guns. One benefit of this is that the various parts should all be well understood by the troops and armorers, and the result is a useful weapon, but it would have probably been better had it been designed for a more modern, rimless, cartridge instead of the ancient rimmed round dating from 1891. Nevertheless, this is a good long range cartridge and it gives the weapon ample power to reach out with accuracy.

The PK was the Soviet Army's first 'general purpose' machine gun, a concept widely adopted elsewhere but long resisted by the Soviets since they were reluctant to discard anything and had a vast collection of old medium machine guns to wear out before adopting the PK. The basic design has been parlayed into several versions, each slightly different and for a specific role; the PK is the basic gun on a bipod, the squad automatic; the PKS is the same gun but with a light tripod, making it the company medium machine gun; the PKT is the PK altered for installation as the coaxial gun in a tank; the sights, stock, pistol grip and trigger, and bipod are removed and a solenoid firing mechanism installed; the PKM is a 'product improved' PK with stamped metal feed cover, unfluted and lighter barrel and a hinged butt rest; the PKMS is the PKM on a tripod; and the PKB is the PKM with bipod, butt and trigger mechanism removed and twin spade grips fitted, for use as a pintle-mounted gun on armored vehicles.

Left: The Spectre M-4 first appeared in the early 1980s.

Above: The Russian PK squad machine gun.

Spectre M-4

Manufacturer Sites SpA, Turin, Italy
Type Blowback, selective fire, double-action
Caliber 9mm Parabellum
Barrel 5.12in (130mm)
Weight 6.4lbs (2.9kg)
Magazine Capacity 30 or 50 rounds
Cyclic rate of fire 850 rounds/minute

This submachine gun appeared in 1983 and has a number of unusual features. The designer set out to develop a weapon which could be used in an instinctive and automatic manner, so that the user could open fire instantly without having to consider the safety condition or perform any action other than pulling the trigger. The intention was to provide a weapon for anti-terrorist police and others who need to carry a weapon daily but may not be called upon to use it except at rare intervals; and when that time comes, it has to be ready for use without hesitation.

SPECTRE M-4

The Spectre looks conventional enough, with a pressed steel receiver and barrel jacket, and a butt which folds to lie along the top of the receiver. The magazine fits into a housing ahead of the trigger and is the first unusual feature; it contains four columns of cartridges instead of the usual two. This means that the 30-round magazine is no longer than a conventional 20-round, and the 50-round no longer than a normal 30-round.

The operation is also unusual. After inserting a magazine, the cocking handle is pulled back and released in the normal way. But instead of the bolt remaining back, it runs forward and chambers a cartridge. A 'hammer unit' remains at the rear of the receiver; but pressing a de-cocking lever allows this unit to run forward under control and stop a short distance behind the bolt. The weapon is now perfectly safe to carry, and will not fire if dropped or mishandled. But as soon

SPECTRE M-4

Above: The compact look of the M-4.

Left: The Spectre M-4 in action on the firing range.

Below left: A stripped-down view of the M-4.

Above: The long-barreled version of the M-4, the Spectre Carbine.

as it becomes necessary to fire, all that needs to be done is to squeeze the trigger. This will retract the hammer unit from its rest position and then release it with sufficient force to hit the firing pin in the bolt and fire the cartridge in the chamber, after which the action is automatic until the trigger is released.

Since the bolt is always closed when the gun is at rest, it might be expected that the barrel will heat up when firing and not cool very quickly; this is countered by a forced draught air system, operated by the movement of the bolt, which pumps air through and around the barrel while firing.

The basic Spectre submachine gun is accompanied by three variant models; the 'Spectre PCC' (Police Compact Carbine) which fires single shots only and has a longer barrel; it can also be fitted with a silencer. The Spectre Carbine is long-barreled and fires only single shots. And the Spectre Pistol is the basic Spectre but without a stock or fore-grip, and fires single shots only. The Police Carbine and Pistol versions are available in .40 Smith & Wesson caliber as well as in 9mm Parabellum.

STAR Z-84

Star Z-84

Manufacturer Star Bonifacio Echeverria & Cia, Eibar, Spain
Type Blowback, selective fire
Caliber 9mm Parabellum
Barrel 8.45in (215mm)
Weight 6.6lbs (3kg)
Magazine Capacity 25 or 30 rounds
Cyclic rate of fire 600 rounds/minute

Star is one of the oldest of Spanish small arms manufacturers, and they have been making submachine guns since the 1930s. Since 1945 a succession of their weapons has equipped the Spanish armed forces, and the latest of these is the Z-84, introduced in the mid-1980s.

The Z-84 was developed with a view to correcting one or two deficiencies in earlier models and also to reduce the cost and complexity of manufacture. Much use has been made of steel stampings and investment casting. The feed system has been carefully engineered so that it will feed both jacketed and soft-point bullets without faltering, and its resistance to water damage has led to it being adopted as an assault weapon by Spanish marine and commando units.

The gun fires from an open bolt, using the system of 'advanced primer ignition' in which the cartridge is actually fired while the bolt is still loading it into the breech. This means that the explosion force must first arrest the forward movement of the bolt, then reverse it, and then blow it to the rear. Without this feature the bolt would have to be much heavier and the weapon correspondingly larger.

The bolt is recessed, so that it wraps around the chamber end of the barrel at the instant of firing; this allows for a maximum barrel length in a compact overall length and also reduces the distance needed for the bolt to recoil. The center of balance is above the pistol grip, so that it is possible to fire the weapon single-handed with good stability. The magazine fits into the pistol grip, so that the balance of the weapon does not change as the ammunition is used and it is possible to change magazines, even in the dark, very quickly.

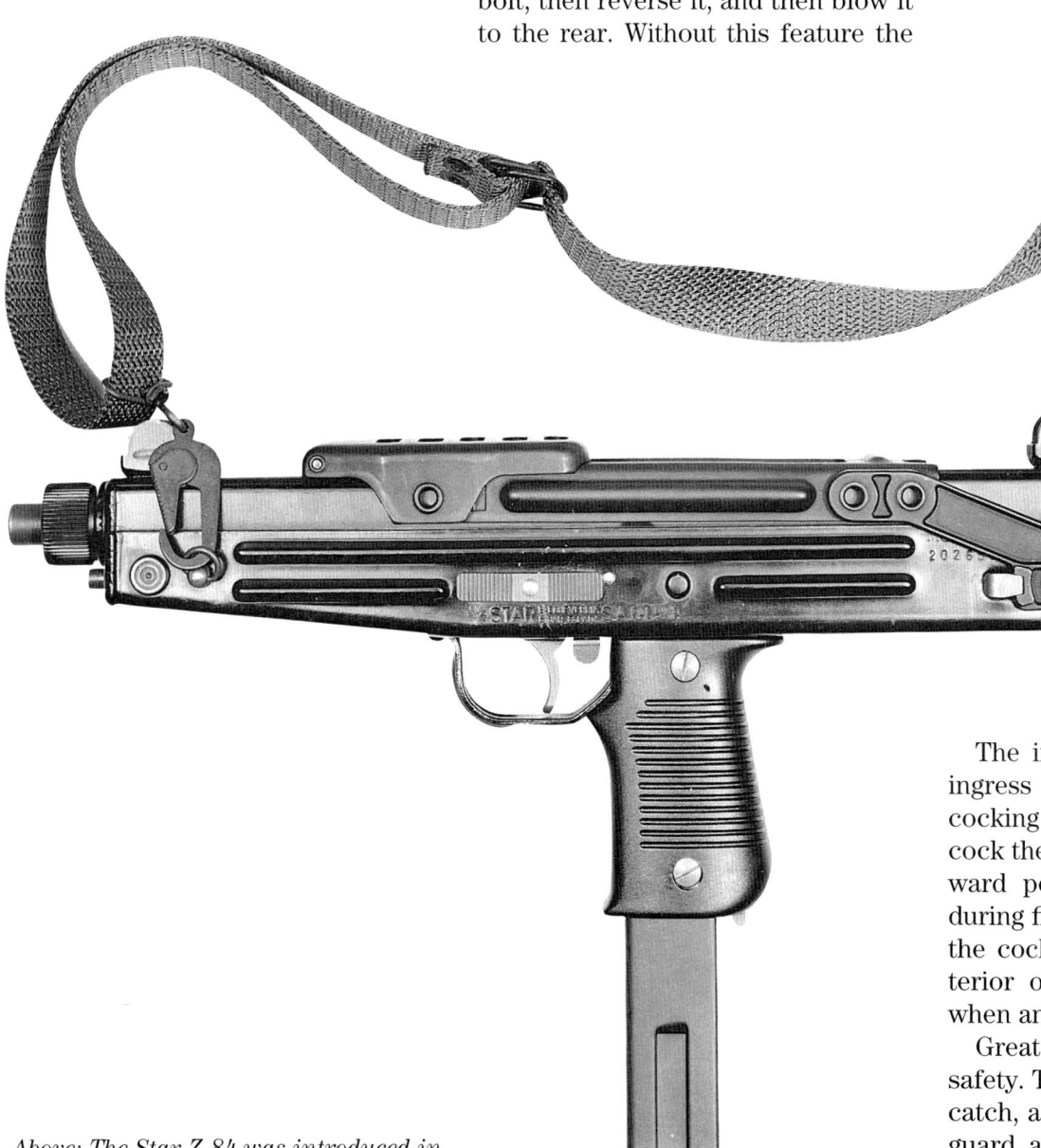

Above: The Star Z-84 was introduced in the early 1980s.

The interior is sealed against the ingress of dust and dirt; after the cocking handle is pulled to initially cock the weapon, it returns to its forward position and does not move during firing. There is a dust cover in the cocking handle slot, and the interior of the weapon is only open when an empty case is being ejected.

Great attention has been paid to safety. There is a conventional safety catch, a sliding button in the triggerguard, and there are also three safety notches on the bolt so that should the hand slip while cocking, the bolt cannot run forward and load a cartridge. An automatic safety lock is applied whenever the bolt is at rest, so that dropping the weapon cannot jar the bolt into loading and firing; this is automatically withdrawn when the weapon is cocked and remains out of action while firing.

The Z-84 is a well-thought-out design and has been sold to numerous military and security forces outside Spain.

Steyr AUG 9 Para

Manufacturer Steyr-Mannlicher GmbH, Steyr, Austria
Type Blowback, selective fire
Caliber 9mm Parabellum
Barrel 16.5in (420mm)
Weight (empty) 7.25lbs (3.3kg)
Magazine Capacity 25 or 32 rounds
Cyclic rate of fire 650-750 rounds/minute

The Steyr AUG rifle was the first 'modular' design: the barrel, receiver, firing mechanism can all be changed to configure the weapon into whatever sort of rifle is wanted. By an extension of this principle, Steyr pioneered a trend which is now becoming more common, of converting what is basically a locked-breech rifle into a blowback submachine gun.

The AUG 9 Para is based on the standard AUG rifle by changing the barrel for one of 9mm caliber; changing the bolt assembly for a simple blowback unit; and changing the magazine housing by fitting an adapter to take a narrower magazine holding the 9mm Parabellum pistol cartridge.

The result is a submachine gun with a longer barrel than normal for this type of weapon, and one which fires from a closed bolt. Both these features improve accuracy, and the longer barrel produces a rather higher muzzle velocity than is usual in this caliber.

The 'closed bolt' feature means that when the magazine is inserted and the cocking handle pulled back and released, the bolt runs forward and chambers a cartridge, leaving the hammer cocked ready to fire. On pulling the trigger in the usual type of submachine gun, the bolt runs forward, loads the chamber and then fires. There is therefore a sudden shift of balance due to the movement of the bolt and, as a result, a first-round hit is unlikely. With the AUG 9 Para, pulling the trigger simply releases the hammer; nothing else moves and the weapon stays steady at the aim, so that first-round hits are the rule rather than the exception.

The company originally marketed a conversion kit, allowing anyone with an AUG to convert it to a submachine gun. Later, however, this was withdrawn and only brand-new weapons were sold, since it appeared that even a simple conversion was beyond the skill of some users.

A separate barrel fitted with an efficient silencer is also available; this can be exchanged for the normal barrel by simply pressing a catch and twisting the front handle sideways to unlock the interrupted lugs of the barrel from the receiver. As with the rifle, the basic model has a carrying handle with a low-power optical sight, but it is possible to change the receiver to one with a sight mount and thus fit night vision or other specialist sights.

Above: The Steyr AUG 9 Para, based on the standard AUG rifle, is shown here with a silencer.

STEYR TMP

STEYR TMP

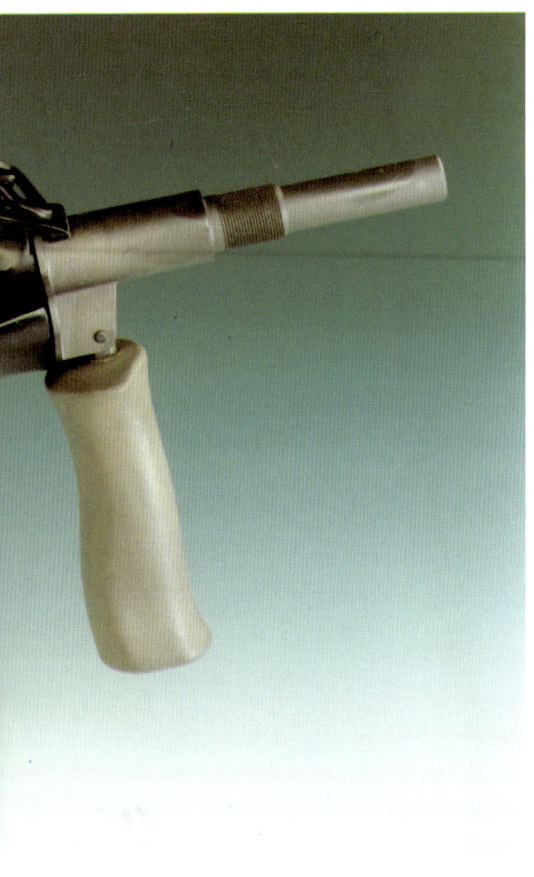

Above: The Steyr AUG 9 Para in standard configuration.

Left: Indonesian troops get to grips with the Steyr AUG on the firing range.

Steyr TMP (Tactical Machine Pistol)

Manufacturer Steyr-Mannlicher AG, Steyr, Austria
Type Recoil-operated, selective fire
Caliber 9mm Parabellum
Barrel 5.12in (130mm)
Weight 2.86lbs (1.3kg)
Magazine Capacity 15 or 20 rounds
Cyclic rate of fire ca 600 rounds/minute

The Steyr Tactical Machine Pistol belongs in the emerging group of 'Personal Defense Weapons' – short, stockless, and closer to being an enlarged pistol than a down-sized submachine gun. Indeed, a variant model which does away with the front handgrip and only fires single shots is called the 'Special Purpose Pistol' (SPP) and is classed as a pistol.

The TMP is a locked-breech weapon firing the 9mm Parabellum cartridge. There are only 41 component parts, and the frame and top cover are made from a synthetic plastic which is sufficiently strong to be able to do without steel inserts to support the bolt. The breech is locked and unlocked by rotation of the barrel, a system which Steyr pioneered in the early years of the century but which they ceased to use after 1918. A lug beneath the barrel engages in a groove in the frame. On firing, the barrel and breech block recoil still locked together, the lug sliding down the groove. The groove then spirals, and as the cam follows this track, so the barrel is revolved until the bolt lugs are unlocked from the chamber. The barrel is then held while the bolt runs back and then forward again to chamber a fresh round. Bolt and barrel then go forward, and the cam track again revolves the barrel to lock the breech.

Single shots or automatic fire are provided by a two-stage trigger, similar to that used on the Steyr AUG rifle. The first pressure on the trigger fires single shots; pulling through against the pressure of an auxiliary spring delivers automatic fire. There is a three-position cross-bolt safety catch which has a central position giving semi-automatic fire only, so providing additional control.

Although there is no butt-stock, and no provision for fitting one, the forward handgrip permits adequate control of the weapon, and short bursts can be fired with considerable accuracy after a little practice. Single shots can be fired with one hand quite easily; it is only slightly heavier than a Colt .45 automatic pistol and somewhat lighter than most larger-caliber revolvers.

Initially made in 9mm caliber, production in .40 Smith & Wesson caliber has now begun, and there are plans for a modular system of interchangeable parts which will allow the TMP to be converted to fire 9mm Steyr, 10mm Auto or .41 Action Express cartridges.

Above: The Steyr TMP (Tactical Machine Pistol).

Steyr MPi 69

Below: The Steyr MPi 69 field-stripped.
Right: The MPi 69, similar in look to the Uzi.

Steyr MPi 69

Manufacturer Steyr-Daimler-Puch AG, A-4400 Steyr, Austria
Type Blowback, selective fire
Caliber 9mm Parabellum
Barrel 10.2in (260mm)
Weight (empty) 6.46lbs (2.93kg)
Magazine Capacity 25 or 32 rounds
Cyclic rate of fire 550 rounds/minute

This submachine gun resembles the Uzi in some respects, but is a totally different and rather simpler design. It is currently in use by a number or armies and police forces throughout Europe and the rest of the world.

The receiver is formed from bent and welded sheet steel and is carried in the frame unit, steel with a molded nylon covering. The magazine feeds in through the pistol grip, a convenient system in the dark, and the bolt is of the 'wrap-around' or 'telescoped' type in which the actual bolt face is well back within the bolt and much of the bolt mass is in front of the breech at the moment of firing. This system allows the maximum mass for the minimum bolt stroke and assists in producing a compact weapon. Cocking is performed by pulling on the carrying sling, which is attached, at the forward end, to the cocking knob. This, at first sight, is open to abuse, but a bracket, welded to the top of the receiver, ensures that the cocking action can only be performed when the sling is held at right-angles to the receiver, on the left-hand side. The normal pull from the top of the weapon, as when slinging it over the shoulder, cannot move the cocking-piece.

There is a safety catch in the form of a cross-bolt above the trigger which locks the trigger when set to safe; it is a three-position bolt; when pushed across to the right, so that a white 'S' protrudes, it is safe; when pushed across to the left so that a red 'F' protrudes, it is set for automatic fire. There is also a half-way position in which single shots are possible. This safety catch is a weak piece of design in my view since except by memorizing, it is impossible to know what the state is in darkness; it would be better to have one end ribbed or knurled.

The third position is, in any case, superfluous; with the selector set for automatic fire a light squeeze on the trigger fires a single shot, and this can be repeated as often as wanted. To fire bursts, a heavier squeeze is required. There is no need to reset the selector lever at all, and I can only assume that the central position has been put there as a safety feature during initial training, so that an over-enthusiastic squeeze will not produce a runaway gun. This two-stage trigger is also to be found on the Steyr AUG rifle, and takes some getting used to; I have found it a hindrance to accurate shooting in the automatic mode.

The MPi 69 is easy to strip and re-assemble, taking no more than 15 seconds in either direction for a trained soldier. Strictures on the safety and trigger apart, it is a well-designed, simple and robust weapon, and provided soldiers are trained to its peculiarities, a highly effective one.

STEYR MPi 69

Uzi Semi-automatic Carbine

Manufacturer Israeli Military Industries, Tel Aviv, Israel
Type Blowback, semi-automatic
Caliber 9mm Parabellum
Barrel 16.1in (410mm)
Weight 8.5lbs (3.85kg)
Magazine Capacity 25 or 32 rounds

The Israeli-developed and manufactured 'Uzi' submachine gun is probably one of the best-known modern weapons of its class. During its 30 years of military service many countries have bought it for their armies and even more for their police and security services. Undoubtedly many less well-connected gun buffs would like to have one for their collections, but the law tends to frown upon privately-owned machine guns; as a result IMI spent a good deal of time in redesigning the Uzi so that it became a repeater, firing single shots only, and yet was impossible to modify back into full-automatic form.

The resulting weapon came on the market in 1981 and the only visual difference from a service Uzi is the length of the barrel, some six inches longer than the military version. There are internal differences, within the receiver, which change the method of operation and which also prevent substitution of standard military components, so that it is impossible to swap parts and so change it back into a full-automatic weapon. In addition the mechanism is now altered so that the Uzi fires from a closed bolt, instead of an open bolt; this makes good sense for a single-shot weapon since it helps accuracy, and there is no need to have the bolt stay open so as to allow cooling air to go through the barrel during pauses in firing.

The Uzi is built up from steel pressings and turnings, with grip and fore-end in black plastic. The folding steel butt is used, and stripping the weapon is extremely simple. The foresight is a post which is adjustable for windage and elevation for purposes of zeroing, and there is a special tool for this pur-

UZI SEMI-AUTOMATIC CARBINE

Left: The folding stock version of the Uzi.

Below: Uzis with fixed stocks.

Above: The Uzi in German hands.

pose. The rear sight is a simple two-position flip aperture with settings for 100 and 200 meters.

Although the 9mm Parabellum cartridge is not one which would instinctively commend itself to anyone searching for the ultimate in accuracy, it has to be said that this long-bareled Uzi performs remarkably well, consistently making five-shot groups around one-and-a-half inches at 25 yards. As a home defense weapon it has an authoritative air and the accuracy to back it up, and when not in use the makers provide a dummy barrel of service length.

SHOT GUNS

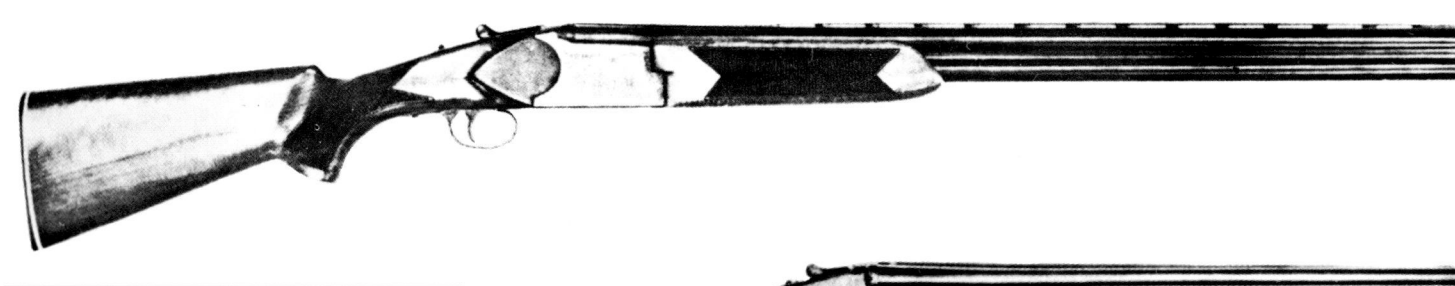

Astra Models 650 & 750 Shotguns

Manufacturer Astra-Unceta y Cia, Guernica, Spain
Type Superposed, single or double trigger
Gage 12
Barrel 28in (711mm)
Weight 7.34lbs (3.33kg)

Astra-Unceta are widely-known for their pistols, but rather less well-known outside Europe for their sporting guns, a state of affairs they are now seeking to remedy. Their home market has been satisfied by conventional single and double guns for some years, but they have now developed an over-and-under specifically for export.

The Models 650 and 750 differ in their trigger arrangement; the 650 has double triggers, while the 750 has a single trigger with a selector to permit firing either barrel first. Either can be had with automatic ejectors or with manual extractors. The barrels are bored to modified and full choke.

The gun is well-finished, with a walnut stock with pistol grip, and well-executed checkering on stock and fore end. The receiver is neatly roll-engraved, the fit of metal to wood is first-class, and the barrels are well polished and blued. The receiver body is somewhat deep, due to the use of bottom bolting, but this leaves ample room for the hammers and firing pins and the selective trigger mechanism, so that the component parts are robustly proportioned and easily reached for repair or adjustment. The firing pin holes in the standing breech have removable bushings. The barrels are surmounted by a ventilated rib with a gold bead front sight.

The Astra gun handles well and delivers consistent patterns. For its price it is a sound and reliable gun which should give long service.

AYA Model 25 Shotgun

Manufacturer Aguirre & Aranzabal, Eibar, Spain
Type Double, side-by-side
Gage 12
Barrels 25in (635mm)
Weight 6.25lbs (2.83kg)

AYA have a long and good reputation for the production of shotguns to a wide variety of specifications, ranging from 'working guns' to 'best guns', and their Model 25 is a classic side-by-side in the English tradition.

The walnut stock is straight, without a pistol grip, and is lightened by two longitudinal holes plugged at the butt end; both it and the short and tapering fore end are well finished and carefully checkered. The barrels are light and shorter than is usual, so that the principal weight lies in the center of the gun and it balances well.

The action uses internal hammers and double triggers, and the smooth stock permits the hand to be moved rapidly to shift triggers between shots. The top lever opens the gun and sets the automatic safety, while the action of opening the gun cocks the hammers. As the gun is closed, so the ejectors are cocked and the double underbolt locks the gun firmly. The barrels are usually provided with modified choke on the right and full on the left, and these produce tight patterns.

These short, light, and centrally-balanced guns are not to everyone's taste; in broad terms this gun has been based on, if not copied from, the Churchill Model XXV of London, and Churchill had his own ideas on what constituted a good gun and on how to shoot it.

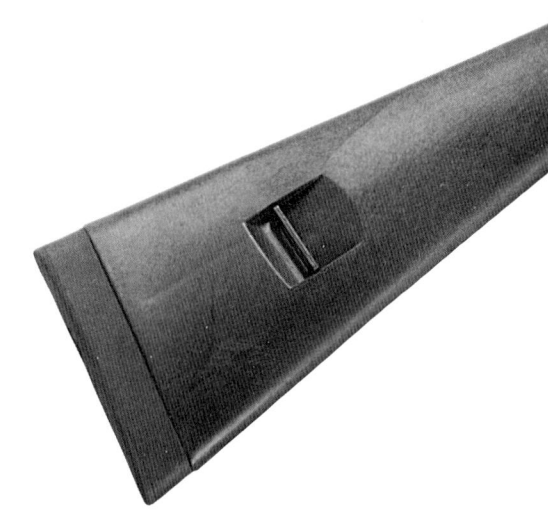

Benelli Auto-loading Shotgun

Manufacturer Benelli Armi SpA, I-61029 Urbino, Italy
Type Recoil-operated auto-loader
Gage 12 or 20
Barrel 25.6in (650mm), 27.6in (700mm)
Weight 7lbs (3.18kg)
  (12-ga, 27.6in barrel)
Magazine capacity 3 or 4 rounds

The Benelli looks like any other automatic shotgun, but underneath the skin is a most unusual mechanism, much different to the usual long-recoil system pioneered by Browning and copied by almost everybody since then. It is well-known in Europe but a recent newcomer to the U.S.A. and deserves closer inspection.

The breech bolt of the Benelli is a two-part unit, the two being separated

BENELLI M3 SUPER 90 SHOTGUN

Pages 132-133: Hunting in the Alps with a Beretta over-and-under shotgun.
Above left: The Astra 750 over-and-under 12-gage.
Below left: The Spanish AYA Model 25.

Below: The Benelli M3 Super 90.

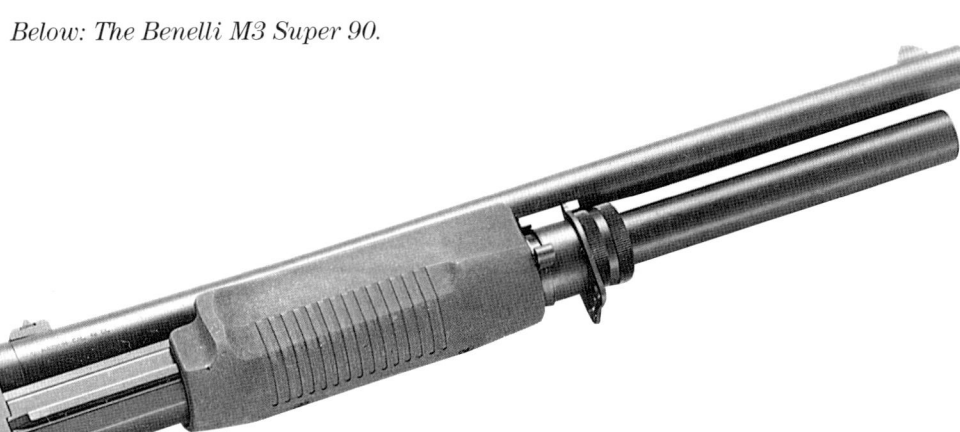

Benelli M3 Super 90 Shotgun

Manufacturer Benelli Armi SpA, Urbino, Italy
Type Convertible semi-auto or slide action
Gage 12
Barrel 19.7in (500mm)
Weight 7.7lbs (3.50kg)

This shotgun was specially designed by Benelli to meet the needs of law enforcement and anti-terrorist squads. The Super 90 uses a rotating bolt locking system and works in such a way that the user can select either semi-automatic fire or manual pump action by simply pressing the command lever set into the front of the handguard. To fire in the semi-automatic mode this lever is turned anti-clockwise and moved forward so as to lock the handguard to the barrel connecting ring. Once set in this mode, the gun operates using the two-part inertia bolt mechanism described elsewhere.

For pump action the command lever is turned anti-clockwise and pulled backwards. This frees the handguard so that it can be pushed back and forwards in the usual slide or pump action manner to load and unload the gun. When set in the slide-action mode, the inertia spring is locked out of action and it is impossible for the gun to fire semi-automatically.

by a coil spring. Attached to the bolt head is a locking bar which trails beneath the bolt assembly and drops into a recess in the receiver so as to hold the breech closed during firing. When the shot is fired, the recoil drives the gun backwards; the bolt body's inertia causes it to remain stationary in space, so that it actually moves forward in relation to the rest of the gun. This compresses the spring and also holds the locking bar firmly down. This movement occupies the time during which the shot charge is passing up the barrel and leaving the muzzle, so that by the time the spring is fully compressed and the bolt body has stopped moving, breech pressure has dropped to a safe level. Now the spring reasserts itself, forces the bolt body back, and this lifts the locking bar from its recess. The complete bolt is now free to be driven back by the residual pressure inside the chamber, extracting and ejecting the spent case. The bolt's movement compresses a return spring and cocks the gun, after which the spring drives the bolt back, loading the next cartridge, the locking bar drops into place and the gun is ready again.

An interesting bonus of this system is that if cartridges with different loadings are used, the recoil force changes and so does the relative compression of the bolt spring, so that there is a self-regulating effect which gives fractionally greater delay in opening for heavier charges.

The Benelli is well-finished, with an aluminum lower section to the receiver, a steel upper section, and well-checkered walnut stock and fore end. The steel parts are highly polished and well blued, while the aluminum portion of the receiver is finished in matching black. The gun handles well and delivers a good pattern. Various choices of choke are available in the two barrel lengths.

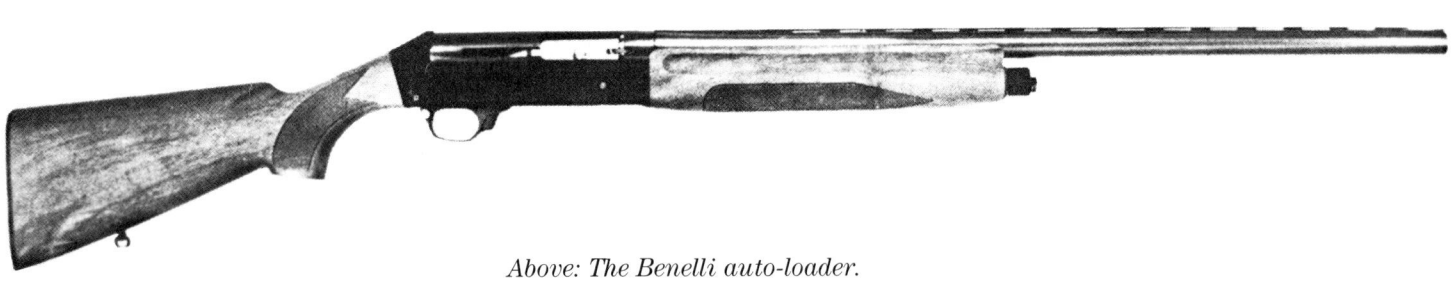

Above: The Benelli auto-loader.

Above: The M3T Convertible variant of Benelli's Super 90.

Below: The firing mechanism of the M3T.

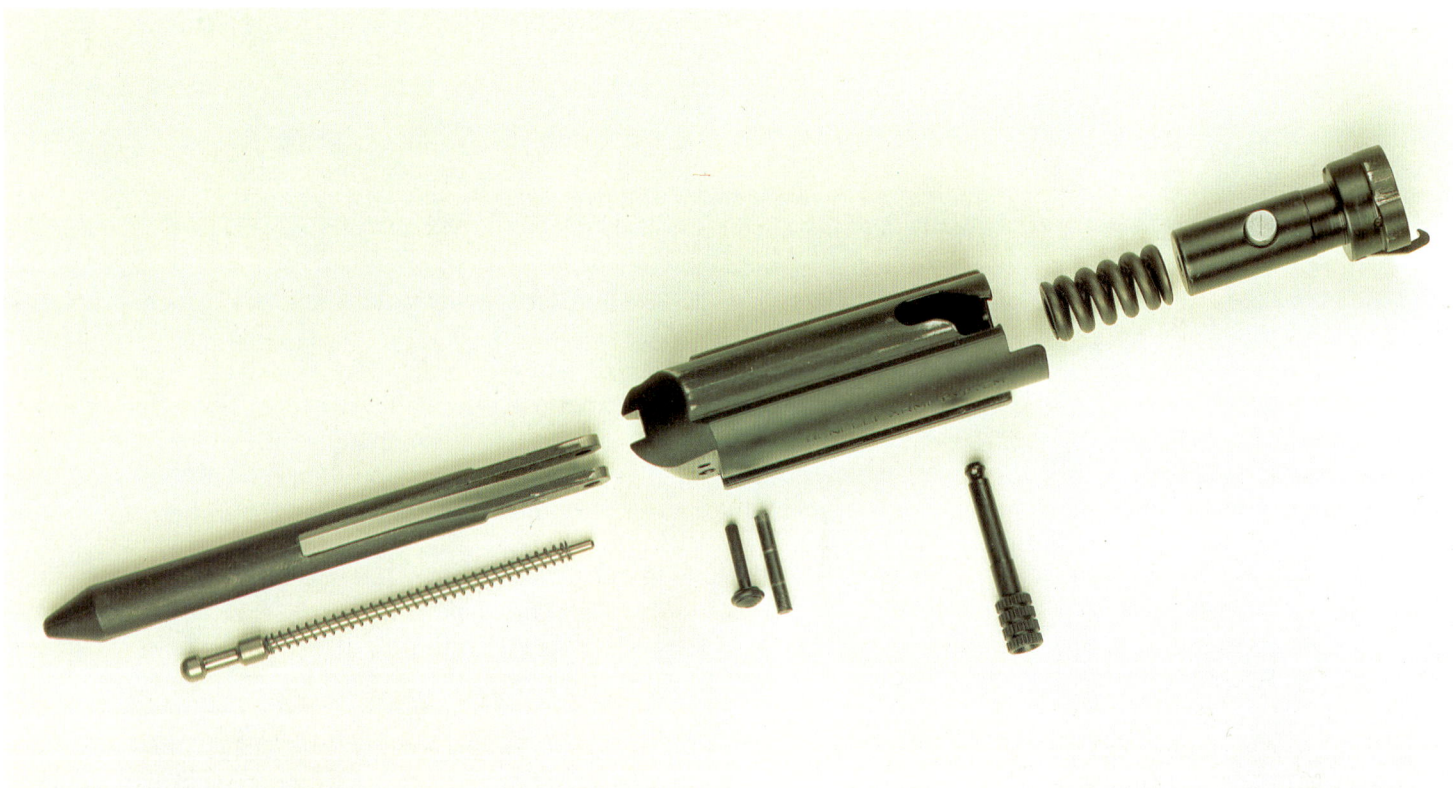

As with other slide-action shotguns, the bolt of the Super 90 remains open after the last round in the magazine had been fired, both in semi-automatic and slide modes.

The upper receiver is of alloy steel, the lower receiver of 'Ergal' special aluminum alloy. The alloy steel barrel is cylinder bored and chromium plated, the outer surface being blued. The stock and handguard are in Rilsan synthetic material, reinforced with glassfiber. The foresight is fixed, and the rearsight is adjustable for windage.

In addition to the standard Super 90, there are a number of variant models. The Super 90 Combat is the same as the Super 90 standard but has special 'ghost ring' sights which allows the shooter to keep both eyes open while taking aim. He focuses on the foresight, and the rear sight becomes a softly defined 'ghost ring' image around it. This new sighting system ensures fast and accurate target acquisition and is now in use by many law enforcement agencies.

The 'Special Application' Model 90 is intended for easy carriage in cars; the barrel is shortened to 14 inches (355mm) and the magazine capacity reduced to five rounds. It also has a folding skeleton stock which folds forward, across the top of the receiver, to act as a carrying handle.

The most recent variation is the M3T Convertible, which is the standard Super 90 with the folding stock of the Special Application model. It is normally supplied with the 500mm barrel and 7-shot magazine, but on special order can be built with a 13.3 inch (340mm) barrel and 5-shot magazine, making it even more compact than the Special Application model. The M3 Super 90 family is extremely versatile, being capable of firing rifled slugs, buckshot (lead or rubber) or birdshot cartridges, CS or CN tear gas grenades, smoke bombs and signaling flares.

Bentley Model 30 Shotgun

Manufacturer Squires, Bingham Mfg. Co., Marikina, Philippines
Type Slide action repeater
Gage 12
Barrel 30in (762mm) (but see text)
Weight 7lbs (2.17kg)
Magazine capacity 5 rounds

The Bentley is another trade name of the Philippine Company of Squires Bingham. The Model 30 is the basic term for three quite distinctly different models.

The 'Model 30 Standard' is a conventional hunting slide-action gun, rather long in the barrel but otherwise unremarkable. The length of barrel does give it a useful long-range capability, which may well be useful on its home ground. The stock and fore end are of figured Philippine mahogany, oil-finished, while the receiver and barrel are blacked and polished, the bolt showing an engine-turned finish through the ejection port. The action is normal slide, a tilting bolt locking into the roof of the receiver. The standard form of barrel is with full choke, but a 26in. barrel bored improved cylinder or a 28in. modified choke can be obtained to special order.

The Model 30 Skeet has the same mechanism but uses a 24in. barrel, with a muzzle compensator and a special 'skeet choke' designed to get the optimum pattern at skeet ranges. The finish is to a higher standard than on the hunting gun, with a polished and varnished surface to the woodwork, a more hand-filling fore end, and checkering on pistol grip and fore end. This appears to be a very handy gun for rapid movement, and the muzzle compensator would diminish the throw-off and blast from such a short barrel.

The third model is somewhat specialized, the 'Model 30 Riot'. In general form this resembles the hunting gun, with plain stock and fore end (though with vertical ribbing to assist grip) but with a shorter 20in barrel which is cylindrical bored. This also has sling swivels on butt and magazine tube nose to permit it being carried slung.

All three Bentley guns are soundly made of good material and would appear to be good working guns in their particular roles.

Beretta 304 Semi-Automatic Shotgun

Manufacturer Pietro Beretta SpA, Gardone Val Trompia, Italy
Type Semi-automatic, gas-operated
Gage 12
Barrel 28in (711mm)
Weight 6.4lbs (2.9kg)
Magazine capacity 3 rounds

The Beretta family have been in the arms business since the 15th century, starting as barrel-makers and moving into making complete guns. Their work was divided between sporting and military, though biased towards the latter, but after the fall of Napoleon and in the years of the 'Long Peace' in Europe, the company moved into the mass manufacture of sporting weapons. Today, they are one of the largest firearms manufacturers in the world, and they have adopted the most up-to-date technology to ensure that their products combine the high-

Below: The Beretta 304 semi-automatic.

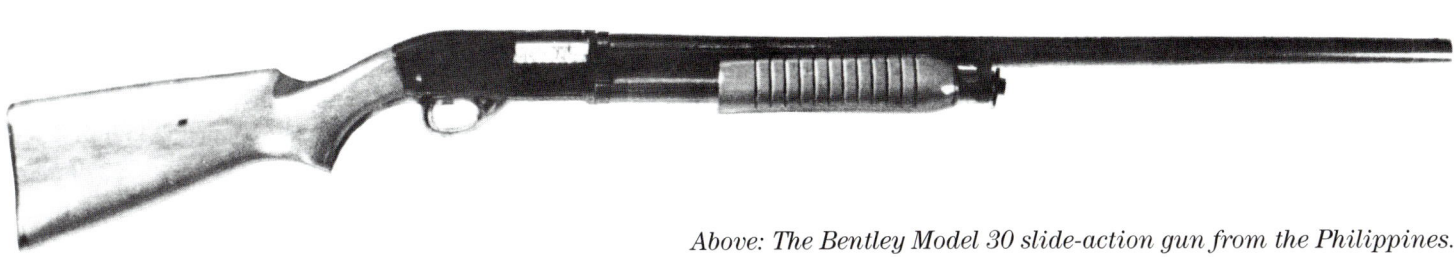

Above: The Bentley Model 30 slide-action gun from the Philippines.

BERETTA 687 EELL SHOTGUN

est quality with attractive price.

The 304 is a lightweight gas-actuated weapon using a light alloy (aluminum/zirconium) which it is claimed, is as strong as steel, but only 65 percent of the weight. The barrel is, of course, cold hammer-forged from high-grade Cr-Mo-Ni steel and is internally chrome-plated, which should give it a very long life. The barrels are fitted with the Beretta style of interchangeable chokes so that the user can adjust the shot pattern to his own preference.

When the gun is fired, some of the propellant gas is tapped off to drive a stainless steel gas piston; this operates a rod sleeve which unlocks the breech bolt by means of a falling block. The bolt goes back against a recoil spring while the block actuates a lifter to bring the next cartridge in line with the breech. The spring then drives the bolt forward and loads the cartridge, the block rises and the bolt is securely locked ready for the next shot. The gas system is self-regulating, so that cartridges of varying power can be used without affecting the regularity or reliability of the reloading operation. There is a safety catch in the trigger guard, and there is also a cut-off which isolates the magazine, turning the weapon into a single-shot action.

The stock and fore end are well-finished and fit the hand comfortably; the stock can be adjusted for drop and cast-off by a spacer which fits between the stock and the receiver, so that it should be possible to adjust the fit of the gun to virtually any user.

There are a number of variants of the 304 either on the market or in course of development, including various barrel lengths, varying degrees of finish, and field, sporter and trap configurations.

Beretta 687 EELL Shotgun

Manufacturer Pietro Beretta SpA, Gardone Val Trompia, Italy
Type Double barrel, superposed
Gage 12
Barrel 30in (762mm)
Weight 7.05lbs (3.20kg)

The Beretta 680-series family of over-and-under guns is a most prolific one, with choices of 12 or 20-gage, 28 or 30 inch (710 or 762mm) barrels, and a variety of degrees of decoration and finish. The 687 EELL is the top-of-the-line gun.

The two barrels are forged from Cr-Mo-Ni steel, joined by a ventilated rib and surmounted by a flat sighting rib. They are fitted with the Beretta Mobilchoke which allows the user to change the degree of choke to suit his own

BERETTA 687 EELL SHOTGUN

Below: The Beretta 687 EELL.

Right: The beautifully-finished Beretta 687 EELL.

average drop, and with a well-shaped and checkered pistol grip.

The gun is slightly muzzle heavy, which some shooters prefer, and which could always be adjusted by a competent gunsmith if desired. However, even as it comes from the maker it handles admirably; it points well, shoots accurately and delivers a well-distributed shot pattern, which, really, is all anyone asks of a sporting gun.

preferences. The action is also of high-quality steel and of Beretta's own design, using two pins mounted in the walls of the action body rather than the more usual full-width hinge pin. Locking is done by conical bolts which move out from the face of the action and fit into recesses in the barrel block. All these pins and bolts are replaceable with oversize units as and when they begin to wear.

The box-locks are covered by engraved sideplates which add greatly to the gun's appearance as well as providing a certain amount of weight to the action area. The stock is of American walnut, well tapered, of

Above: The Beretta 687 EELL.

Browning Custom 325 Shotgun

Manufacturer Miroku Firearms Co., Kochi, Japan
Type Double-barreled, superposed
Gage 12
Barrels 30in (762mm)
Weight 7.5lbs (3.4kg)

The question of who invented the over-and-under shotgun will be argued until Doomsday, but the parentage of this one is firmly established; it is the latest in a long line of similar guns stemming from the one designed by John M. Browning in the early 1920s and, in one variation or another, made by Browning ever since.

The Custom 325 is a well-built and well-finished gun, equally suited to trap or field use. The stock has a full pistol grip and a 'Schnabel' fore-end (with a little lip which positions the hand and prevents it slipping forward). There is a safety catch on the top strap which also acts as a barrel selector for the single-trigger mechanism, which utilizes recoil to re-set after the first shot.

The gun balances well, the center of balance being approximately in the hinge pin, making it quick to point and easily handled. The barrels are surmounted by a wide rib with a shallow center channel, giving a good visual aid to aiming and, as is usual with Browning products, the rich blue finish is immaculate. The chambers are for 2.25in. cartridges, and the shot pattern is even and well-distributed.

Above right and right: Browning designs have been acquired by a number of companies around the world. The Browning Custom 325 is made in Japan and possesses the high-quality finish and attention to detail for which the Browning name is justly famous.

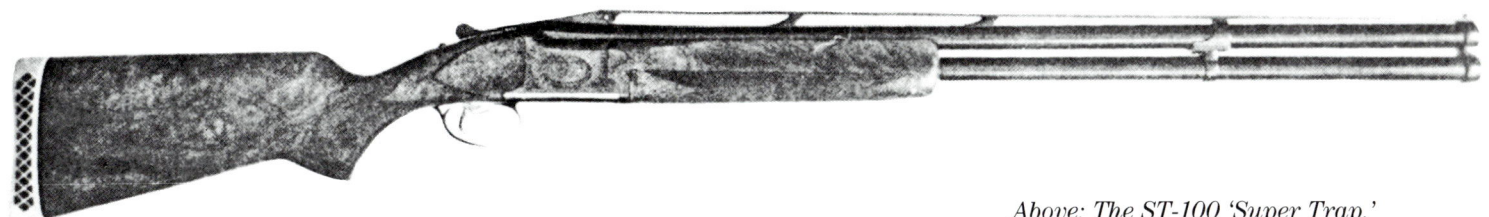

Above: The ST-100 'Super Trap.'

Browning ST-100 Shotgun

Manufacturer Fabrique Nationale Herstal SA, Herstal, Belgium
Type Double-barreled, superposed
Gage 12
Barrels 29.9in (760mm)
Weight 8.06lbs (3.65kg)

This is marketed as a 'Trap Gun' and in Europe is known as the 'Super Trap 80' model. It is unusual in that it is possible to vary the parallelism of the barrels so as to vary the placement of the patterns from each barrel.

The ST-100's barrels are not joined by a rib, as are most over-and-under guns, but are distinctly separated except for the breech lump and a band around the muzzles. About eight inches behind the muzzles there is a linking wedge between the barrels which can be adjusted into any one of five positions, so altering the set of the barrels and shifting the shot patterns. A table in the instruction book gives the theoretical differences, but practical tests show that while the sense of the shift follows the table, the exact distance may vary slightly.

This apart, the rest of the gun is conventional except for the ventilated rib which is attached by five supports and is capable of flexing, necessary because of the barrel adjustment feature. The single trigger is mechanically operated, rather than by inertia, to select the second barrel. The degree of choke can be selected from various options; the top barrel is always full, while the other can be had in steps from modified to full.

The gun delivers tight patterns from either barrel and the inter-barrel adjustment works well, though it needs to be checked by firing. Finish is good, and in keeping with the Browning standards of excellence.

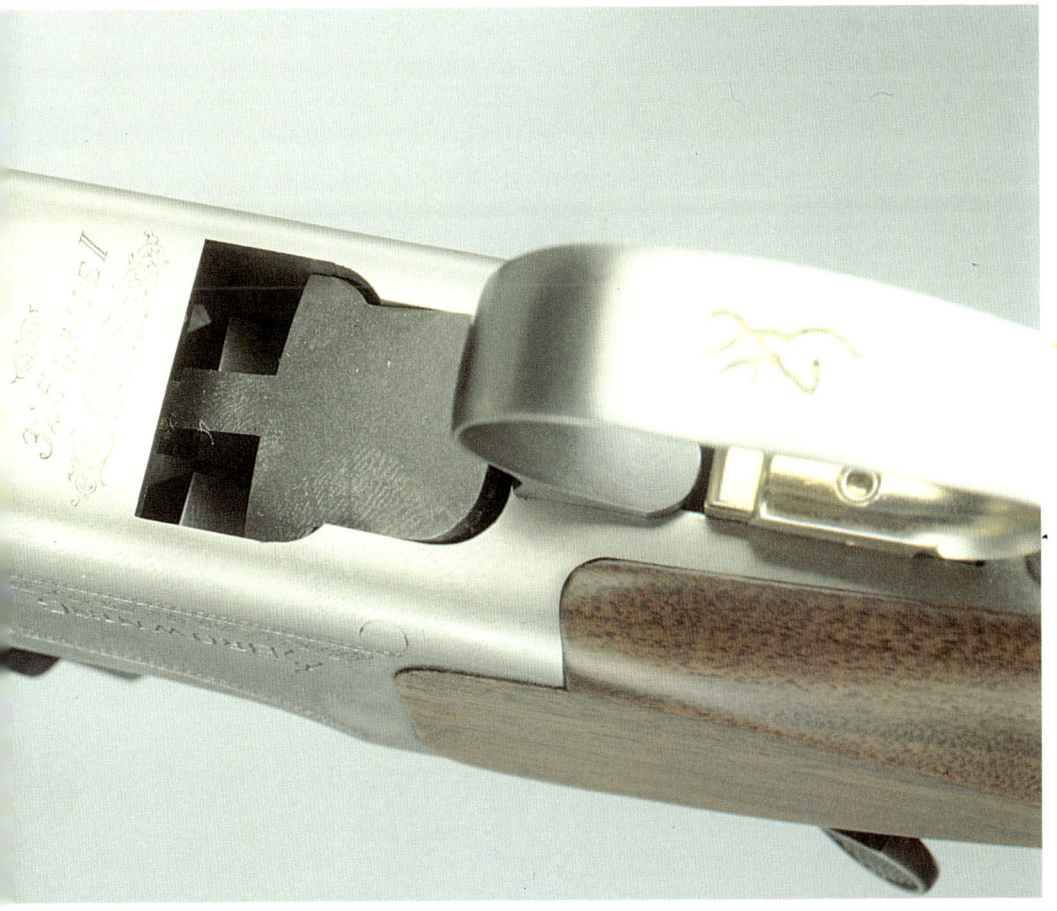

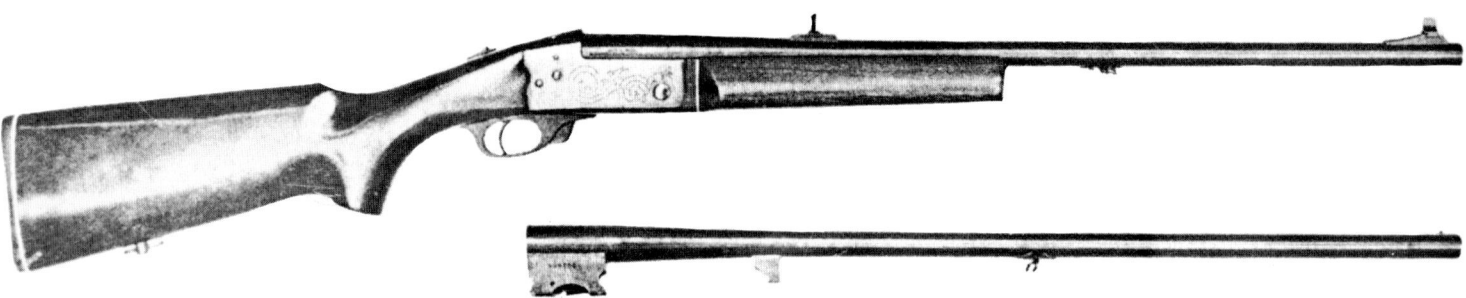

Above: The CBC Combination Gun, shown here with shot and rifle barrels.

CBC Combination Gun

Manufacturer Companhia Brasiliero de Cartouchoes, São Paulo, Brazil
Type Rifle-shotgun combination
Calibers .30-30 and 20-gage
Barrels Shotgun: 28in (711mm)
Rifle: 26in (660mm)
Weights 6.78lbs (3.07kg)
Rifle: 8.28lbs (3.75kg)

This interesting and unusual weapon is the product of a company better-known for ammunition than for firearms, though it has considerable domestic sales of shotguns to its credit. The Combination Gun is a basic action to which either a 20-gage shotgun barrel or a .30-30 rifle barrel can be quickly mounted, and it seems to be an eminently sensible working weapon for anyone living in the wilds.

The basic action is a concealed hammer, similar to that of a shotgun and carried in a simple receiver unit. To this the barrel can be attached by simply hooking the lump over the cross-pin and attaching the fore-end by means of a spring latch. The result is tight-fitting, and the action can be dropped open for loading by pressing on a catch in the front of the trigger guard.

The rifle barrel is provided with a ramp front and adjustable folding leaf rear sight, as well as having standard grooves for mounting a telescope sight. The shotgun barrel has a simple front sight bead. One advantage of this sort of action is that it suits both right- and left-handed shooters equally well.

The shotgun delivers good patterns with consistency, while the rifle barrel is as accurate as most shooters would ask, giving three-inch groups at 100 yards from rest. Altogether this is a well-thought-out combination, practical and robust, capable of adequate accuracy, and remarkably inexpensive for what it gives.

IAB Premier Skeet Shotgun

Manufacturer Industria Armi Bresciane SpA, Marcheno, Italy
Type Superposed double, single trigger
Gage 12
Barrels 26.8in (680mm)
Weight 7.68lbs (3.48kg)

The IAB company is one of the younger Italian gunmaking concerns, numbers of which have begun to prosper in northern Italy. There is a long tradition of fine metal-working and gunmaking in this region, and small companies have realized that they can aim for specialist areas of the market with high-class products and succeed where the big companies cannot compete. Over the past decade IAB have specialized in first-class competition shotguns and have won a long string of international prizes.

The appearance of the IAB Premier Skeet is impressive; oiled-finish walnut of best grade, well-executed hand checkering, fine engraving on the receiver, and a high polish and blue on the rest of the metalwork allied with meticulous fit on the parts is indicative of the care this company lavish on their products.

The mechanism uses strikers, rather than hammers, and has an inertia-operated selector on the single trigger mechanism. This is fixed to fire the lower barrel with the first pull, then the upper, and the sequence cannot be changed. The gun is opened by the usual top lever which clears a single cross-bolt; dropping the barrels cocks the strikers, and closing the gun cocks the ejectors. The safety is manually operated.

The barrels are bored with what the makers call their 'enlarged skeet choke,' a form of recessed choke in which the transition is very abrupt, with a step-form which acts as a trap for debris from the shot wads. This is not difficult to clean but it should be borne in mind, since a built-up of debris can play havoc with patterns. Patterning is extremely consistent at Skeet ranges, and there can be no doubt that this gun has earned its place in the competitive world.

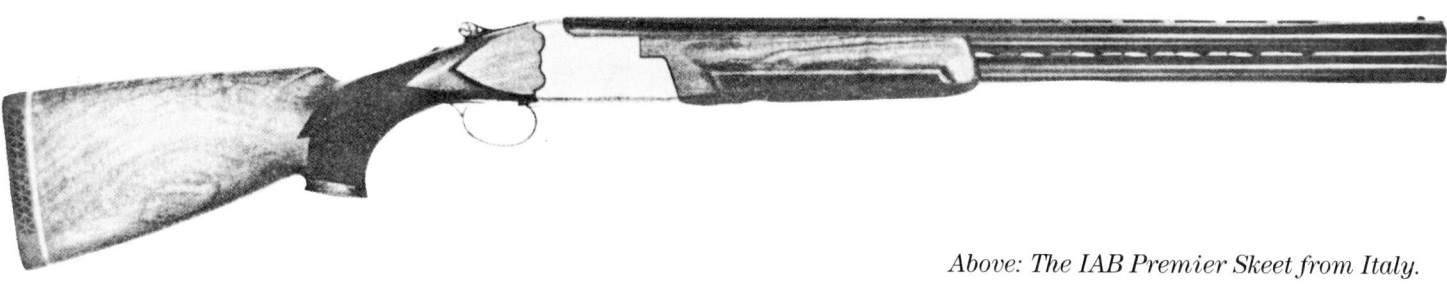

Above: The IAB Premier Skeet from Italy.

JACKHAMMER COMBAT SHOTGUN

*Above: The Jackhammer Mark 3-A2.
Left: The Mark 3-A1 version.*

Jackhammer Combat Shotgun

Manufacturer Mark Three, Albuquerque, New Mexico, U.S.A.
Type Automatic revolver, gas-operated
Gage 12
Barrel 20.6in (525mm)
Weight 10.07lbs (4.57kg)
Magazine capacity 10 rounds
Cyclic rate of fire 240 rounds/minute

The Jackhammer is an automatic, gas-operated, 12-gage shotgun which uses a pre-loaded rotating cylinder as its magazine. The cylinder has grooves incised on its outer surface which are engaged by a stud on an operating rod, so that as the rod moves back and forth, so it rotates the cylinder. This is a very similar system to that employed in the Webley-Fosbery automatic revolver. The barrel is floating, and is driven forward by gas pressure as each shot is fired. It is then returned by a spring and gives movement to the cylinder-operating rod. This movement of the barrel also disconnects the barrel from its gas-tight seal with the cylinder, allowing the cylinder to be turned to bring the next chamber in line; on the return stroke the barrel re-seals itself into the chamber mouth.

The barrel, flash eliminator, return spring and 'Autobolt' (the patented name for the cylinder operating rod) are all of high-quality steel. The rest of the weapon is almost all of synthetic material, a new material by DuPont called Rynite SST.

The cylinder, called by the makers

LANBER SPORTING 97LCH

the 'Ammo Cassette' is also of Rynite SST, contains 10 cartridges, and is sealed with a shrink-film plastic, color-coded to indicate the type of ammunition loaded. The seal is removed by a pull-strip and the cassette slips straight into the weapon and engages the operating system. The weapon is then cocked by the sliding action of the fore-end, and is ready to fire. Once the cassette has been emptied, a simple movement of the fore-end releases it to fall clear and allow a new cassette to be loaded. It is not possible to load single cartridges into the weapon, and empty cases are not ejected while firing.

The Jackhammer's 'Ammo Cassette'.

A de-cocking lever, inside the buttstock, allows the hammer to be safely lowered when the gun is loaded; it can then be carried quite safely. When required, the hammer can be re-cocked silently by using the same lever.

Although the chambers are for the standard shotgun cartridge, the receiver has been strengthened so that a specially-developed cartridge known as the 'Jack Shot' can be fired. This special cartridge operates at a much higher pressure than sporting ammunition and allows special loadings such as fléchettes, armor penetrators, preformed fragmenting projectiles or canister loadings, or even simply larger charges of conventional lead shot to be fired safely.

Development of the Jackhammer has now been completed, and the weapon is being studied by various official agencies. Meanwhile the company is working on more specialized ammunition options and a sound suppressor which will be relatively inexpensive and which can be discarded after a limited life.

Lanber Sporting 97LCH Shotgun

Manufacturer Armas Lanber SA, Zaldibar, Spain
Type Double-barreled, superposed
Gage 12
Barrels 28in (710mm)
Weight 7.5lbs (3.4kg)

The Lanber company of Spain has, over the past 20 years, built up a very good reputation for middle-price shotguns throughout Europe and is now beginning to export them farther afield. Their current range includes four grades of over-and-under guns (Expert, Aventura, Aventura Light, Rivaland Sporting) and three grades of semi-automatic (Victoria I, II and IV), which between them cater for practically any shooting requirement.

The Sporting 97LCH is their current 'best-seller,' particularly in the trap-shooting fraternity. The barrels are of high-grade steel and fitted into the usual monobloc breech end which carries the ejectors and locking system. The barrels are joined by a ventilated rib and the sighting rib has a slight taper and a white front beat, giving a very well-defined sight picture. The bores are somewhat loose, at 18.6mm diameter, rather unusual on a European gun, but tending to reduce recoil slightly as well as shot deformation.

The action is of steel and uses twin stud hinges, as on the Beretta system described elsewhere, rather than the more usual full-width hinge pin. One

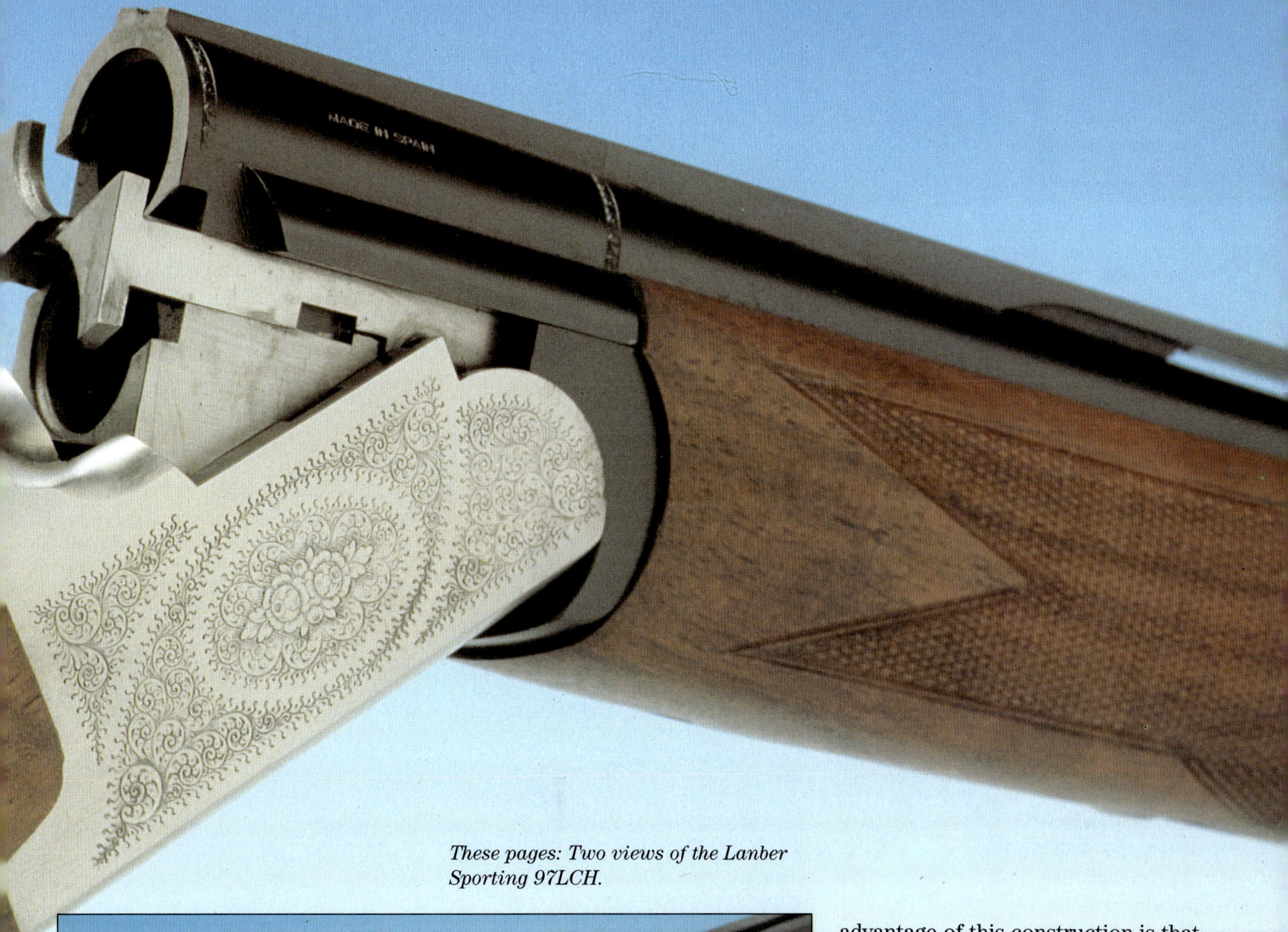

These pages: Two views of the Lanber Sporting 97LCH.

advantage of this construction is that it reduces the height of the action and gives the entire gun a sleeker appearance. A combined safety catch and barrel selector is mounted on the action backstrap, just behind the top lever. The action locks to the barrels by a full-width flat bolt which engages on a groove on the barrel block. The action side-plates are machine-engraved with a decorative pattern.

The barrels are fitted with multi-chokes, and five different chokes are provided with each gun. The multi-choke units fit unobtrusively; there is a slight enlargement of the muzzles to make room for them, but this is scarcely noticeable.

The Lanber handles well, shoots accurately and with good pattern, and well merits its popularity.

LELAND MODEL 210 SHOTGUN

Above: The high-quality Leland Model 210.

Leland Model 210 Shotgun

Manufacturer Union Armera, Eibar, Spain
Type Side-by-side double, hammerless
Gage 12, 16, 20 or 28
Barrels 26, 27 or 28in (660, 685 or 711mm)
Weight 6.625lbs (3kg) (28in barrels)

Though made in Spain this takes its name from being imported into the U.S.A. by Leland Firearms of West Orange, NJ; it is known under the maker's name in Europe. The Union Armera has been making shotguns for very many years and has a wide domestic market for all qualities of gun. The Model 210 is a basic side-by-side modeled on the classic English 'game gun'. It is reasonably priced, fitting about half-way in the Union Armera catalog.

The gun has an elegant appearance, using the English style of straight stock and splinter fore end. The wood is good quality walnut, hand-checkered and oil-finished, while the receiver and fittings are nicely scroll-engraved and color case-hardened. The side-plates can be removed, and the interior of the lockwork is polished and engine-turned. The fit of metal to wood is very well done. The action is locked by a Purdey triple bolt, somewhat unusual nowadays, and there are automatic ejectors.

The standard gun is in 12-gage with 26-inch barrels having improved cylinder and modified choke; it is also possible to have the longer barrels with modified and full choke. The other gages noted are also available, and while the normal chamber length is 2.75 inches, 3 inch chambers can be specified at extra cost.

The Model 210 balances well, feels good, and delivers consistent patterns. The workmanship is good and most observers consider the gun represents value for money.

Luigi Franchi Model 610 Autoloader

Manufacturer Luigi Franchi SpA, Brescia, Italy
Type Gas-operated auto-loader
Gage 12
Barrel 26, 28 or 30 in (660, 710 or 760mm)
Weight around 7lbs (3.17kg)
Magazine capacity 5 rounds

The Luigi Franchi company is an old-established one with a high reputation for shotguns in Europe and elsewhere.

The Model 610 is a gas-operated auto-loader of conventional pattern, the bolt being locked to the barrel extension until freed by the action of the gas piston concealed in the fore end, along with the tubular magazine. The stock design features a flowing pistol grip which permits a rearward placement of the trigger hand, something which many shooters prefer, and the stock has rather less drop than is common. The finish is excellent, the stock and fore end in nicely-figured walnut with good hand checkering, and the aluminum receiver blacked and etched with a floral pattern.

The gun is well-balanced, allowing rapid movement when at the shoulder, and the recoil is, as usual with gas-operated weapons, damped down to an acceptable level. It delivers consistent patterns, and there is a choice of improved, modified or full choke available. For what you get, the Franchi is remarkably inexpensive, and with the company's reputation for workmanship, we would expect it to deliver flawless performance for many years. The 610 is an improvement on the earlier Model 500 and incorporates the Franchi "Variopress" system of gas regulation, which allows cartridges of varying power and length to be fixed without affecting the gas operation. A de luxe model, the 610 VS Luxe is also available.

Luigi Franchi SPAS Shotgun

Manufacturer Luigi Franchi SpA, I-25020 Fornaci, Italy
Type Automatic, combat-type
Gage 12
Barrel 19.68in (500mm)
Weight (empty) 7.05lbs (3.20kg)
Magazine capacity 8 rounds

LUIGI FRANCHI SPAS SHOTGUN

Luigi Franchi are well-known for sporting shotguns of the highest quality, but their SPAS (Special Purpose Automatic Shotgun) series will be rather less well-known outside Italy. It was designed for police and military use and aims to be rather more efficient in that role than conventional civil shotguns which were designed with sporting use in mind and have been 'misappropriated' to police use. The firm claim that their design gives good accuracy with little training; instant hits in all kinds of employment; great firepower; the ability to launch grenades if required; and low maintenance.

The basic SPAS Model 11 is a short-barreled semi-automatic shotgun with a folding butt which has been configured so that it can be locked under the armpit and allow the gun to be used one-handed. The receiver is of light alloy, while the barrel and gas cylinder have been hard-chromed to reduce the risk of corrosion. All the external surfaces are sand-blasted and phosphated black.

An unusual provision is for the gas cylinder to be shut off, converting the weapon to a slide-action repeater; the fore end can be unlocked to act as the reloading slide in this mode, which is designed for use with certain types of light ammunition which will not cycle the gas action reliably.

The barrel is cylinder bored and spreads a normal shot charge to about three feet at 130 feet range, reducing the need for precise aiming. The automatic action will fire about four shots per second, and at this rate of fire, with standard buckshot loadings, it is possible to put 48 pellets per second into a one-yard-square target at 130 foot range. At this range the pellets have about 50 percent more striking energy than a .32 pistol bullet.

There is a wide range of ammunition available for security use, from buckshot and solid slug to tear-gas rounds which fire a small plastic container of CS gas to 170-yards range. There is a launching attachment which fits the muzzle and which permits the firing of grenades to 150m range, and there is also a 'shot spreader' attachment which fits on the muzzle and breaks up the shot pattern to give much greater short-range spread, an option designed for indoor use.

The SPAS Model 12 differs slightly from the Model 11; it has an additional grip safety in the forward edge of the pistol grip, an improved and strengthened butt stock, and a reshaped fore end. The barrel is slightly shorter but the weapon weighs almost exactly one pound more than the Model 11.

Far left: The Luigi Franchi SPAS 12.

Below: The SPAS 12 pictured with folded butt.

Bottom: The SPAS Model 11 Riot Gun ready for use.

PIOTTI SIDELOCK SHOTGUN

Piotti Sidelock Shotgun

Manufacturer Piotti Armi, Gardone Val Trompia, Italy
Type Double-barreled, side-by-side
Gage 12
Barrels 28in (710mm)
Weight 6.6lbs (2.99kg)

The Piotti company is an old-established family firm who have a reputation for producing high-quality sporting guns at a reasonable price. Their quality is attested to by the fact that they are generally imported into other countries by top-class gunmakers rather than import-export companies.

As might be expected, the quality of fit and finish of Piotti guns is excellent. The blue is deep and lustrous, the wood fine-grained, well-figured and finished, and the fit of every part is perfect. The engraving is exceptional and covers the sideplates, bottom, trigger-guard, breeches, top strap and backstrap with ornate and tasteful designs.

The barrels are built independently, the tubes and breech lump being of the same piece of metal, and are then brazed together. There is a central rib and the barrels are choked improved and half-choke.

The action is a sidelock, with double triggers, the sideplates being silver polished, though color case-hardened plates are an available option. As usual, the second trigger breaks at a slightly higher pressure than the first, though both are very smooth and with a well-defined let-off point. For those who prefer it, a single trigger is an option.

The stock may be of straight handgrip type or pistol grip, to choice. In either case the wood is of high quality and the finish excellent, with firm and clean checkering. As might be expected, the gun handles and shoots extremely well.

Left: The handsome Piotti sidelock. This shotgun not only looks handsome, it also handles well and shoots extremely accurately.

Remington 11-87 Premier Skeet Shotgun

Manufacturer Remington Arms, Wilmington, Delaware, U.S.A.
Type Automatic, gas-operated
Gage 12
Barrel 25.5in (648mm)
Weight 7.5lbs (3.4kg)

Introduced in 1987, the 11-87 Premier Skeet is intended, as the name implies, for clay pigeon shooting, and it has gained a good reputation in this field for its accuracy, handiness and low recoil.

Remington automatic shotguns are gas-operated, tapping off a proportion of the propellant gas to drive a piston rearwards and so operate the bolt and reloading mechanism. In most of the Remington 11-87 series, the gas is self-regulating, so that virtually any cartridge capable of fitting inside the chamber will operate the action satisfactorily. The Premier Skeet mode, however, is regulated for 70mm cartridges only, and firing smaller charges may not result in successful reloading. This might be a disadvantage in field shooting, but since this gun is purely for one type of sport using one type of cartridge, it is an acceptable restriction and it does allow the gas system to be easily 'tuned' for the most trouble-free, reliable and consistent performance.

The barrel is fitted for a multi-choke, and three are supplied with the gun, allowing the owner to set the shot pattern to his preference. The mechanism cycles smoothly; pulling back the cocking handle locks the action open until released by a carrier release catch on the loading ramp. With the chamber loaded, the magazine can then have two cartridges fed in from underneath the action.

The stock is a full pistol-grip with cut checkering. It is of standard 'skeet' length, just short of 14 inches (350mm) and with an average amount of drop. There is no form of adjustment, and no options, but most shooters are happy with this length. There is a rubber recoil pad, and a synthetic protective coating to the wood. Metal parts are in a black satin finish.

Altogether, the 11-87 Premier Skeet is a sound, no-nonsense tool for competition shooting, and is particularly recommended for beginners in the game.

REMINGTON 11-87 PREMIER SKEET SHOTGUN

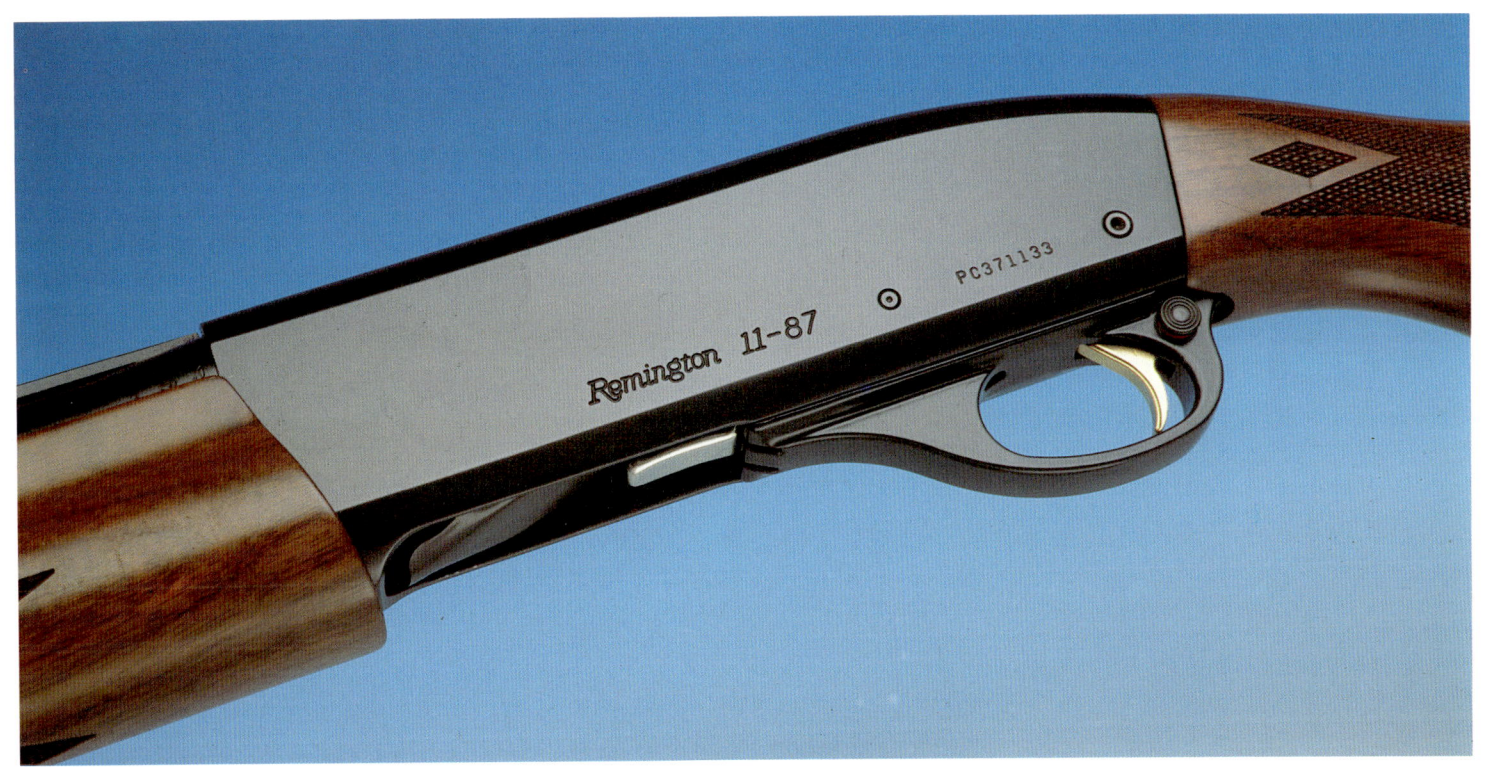

Above and left: The Remington 11-87 Premier Skeet, a sound and reliable shotgun for competition shooting.

RIZZINI MULTICHOKE SHOTGUN

Rizzini Multichoke Shotgun

Manufacturer B. Rizzini, Marcheno, Italy
Type Double-barreled, superposed
Gage 12
Barrels 28in (710mm)
Weight 8lbs (3.62kg)

The Rizzini company is another of those old-established family firms operating in the traditional gunmaking area around Brescia in northern Italy. Most such firms tend to aim at one particular area of the shooting market, but Rizzini covers the entire range of quality, making on the one hand entry-level economy guns for practical shooters, and on the other hand, luxurious hand-crafted, custom-built guns. Their wide rfange of products has ensured their survival in an area where small firms must fight for their living.

The Multichoke is one of the inexpensive guns, but there is nothing cheap or shoddy about it. The barrels are of best steel, built on the monobloc system in which the two barrels are inserted into a chamber block. They are separated by a ventilated rib, with another ventilated rib above the barrel carrying a translucent red bead foresight and a white bead center sight. They are prepared for multichokes, four of which are supplied with the gun, together with a key for unscrewing and replacing them.

The action uses coil springs, common with Italian guns, and a recoil-operated single trigger which tends to be on the light side. A barrel selector-cum-safety catch lies on the backstrap. Locking is done by the usual bolt engaging in a slot, but into the monobloc below the lower barrel, and the barrels are hinged on side pins rather than on a full-width hinge pin. The sideplates and under surface are machine engraved with a traditional sporting motif.

The stock is of average drop, protected by a synthetic finish, and the fore-end is a hand-filling design with finger grooves. As a basic beginner's gun the Rizzini represents good value.

Above and left: Two views of the Rizzini Multichoke, a basic beginner's gun representing excellent value.

Right: A close-up shot of the barrels of the Multichoke.

153

Rossi 'Squire' Shotgun

Manufacturer Amadeo Rossi SA, São Paulo, Brazil
Type Side-by-side double, hammerless
Gage 12, 20 or .410
Barrels 26in (660mm) or 28in (711mm)
Weight 7.75lbs (3.51kg) (12-ga)

Amadeo Rossi are a Brazilian company who, over the past 20 or 50 years have built up something of an export trade, particularly in revolvers. This hammerless shotgun first appeared in the 1960s and has recently been improved.

The 'Squire' is an unpretentious gun, designed to be used rather than admired. The stock and fore-end are of some local hardwood, plainly finished to resemble walnut and without checkering or decoration. The metal is well polished and blued, and the fit, though not to the highest standards, is perfectly serviceable. The mechanism of the lock is robust and the manufacturer's aim has been to produce a design capable of machine production and using as many interchangeable parts as possible. This at least has the virtue of delivering a sound gun at a reasonable price.

The 12- and 20-gage guns are well balanced full-sized weapons; the .410, as might be expected, is on a reduced scale and weighs rather less. We are, in fact, rather surprised that Rossi find it profitable to make a .410 gun since the current fashion appears to be moving away to the 29-gage when a light weapon is required. Nevertheless, at whatever gage is chosen the Rossi functions reliably and shoots well, delivering consistent patterns to the point of aim.

Rottweil Super Trap Combination Gun

Manufacturer Deutsche Jagdpatronenfabrik GmbH, Rottweil, Germany
Type Combination single or superposed
Gage 12
Barrels Single: 34in (864mm); double: 32in (812mm)
Weight 8.75lbs (3.96kg)

The phrase 'combination gun' means different things to different people; to workaday farmers it can mean interchangeable rifle and shotgun barrels, to upland shooters it can mean simple interchangeable barrels with different degrees of choke. But to International Trap competition shooters it means a gun which is specifically designed for their peculiar requirements and which can shift from a double over-and-under to a single barrel on call, so as to fit the various types of contest. On the face of it this sounds easy, but a look at this Rottweil gun shows that some careful thought and ingenious design is necessary to make a success of it.

The basic stock and receiver is no more than that; to it must be added first the barrel of choice and then the appropriate trigger unit. With the single barrel, there is (obviously) a single trigger; with the over-and-under set there is a selective single trigger, inertia operated and with a button which allows selection of the first barrel. The trigger units slip in and out and exhibit precise workmanship; the hammer coil springs are encased in telescoping steel tubes for alignment and protection, and all metal surfaces are polished clean of tool marks.

Each barrel set has a ventilated rib which stands well clear to avoid heat mirages, and the single barrel has a short balance tube beneath it so that whichever barrel is fitted the gun always weighs and balances the same. The same fore end will fit either barrel set. The stock and fore end are in satin-finished French walnut with excellent hand-checkering, while every metal surface is immaculately finished. The bores are hand-honed, test-fired, and re-worked if necessary at the factory in order to produce absolutely flawless patterns. The result of this careful hand-fitting shows up in its performance, which is beyond criticism; it also shows up in the price, which reflects the excellence of this product.

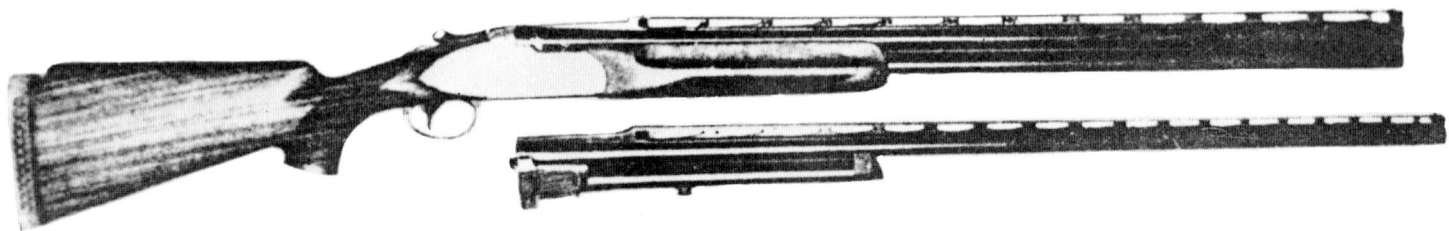

Above: The Rottweil 'Super Trap' allows the use of single or superposed double barrels.

Left: The Rossi 'Squire,' shoots well, delivering consistent patterns.

Ruger Red Label Shotgun

Manufacturer Sturm Ruger & Co. Inc., Southport, Connecticut, U.S.A.
Type Double-barreled, superposed
Gage 12 or 20
Barrels 26 or 28in (660 or 710mm)
Weight 7.5lbs (3.4kg) in 12-ga.

Sturm Ruger have been well-known for their handguns since the late 1940s; in the late 1960s they began work on a shotgun design. First shown in prototype form in 1971, it was progressively developed and perfected, and went on sale in 20-gage in 1978. A 12-gage was added in 1982, and although the basic design has remained unchanged, there have been a number of small improvements from time to time as refinements have been added.

The Ruger uses some patented design features, notably the positioning of the locking bolt between the bores so as to obtain a low-set profile, and the inertia-locking single-trigger mechanism which can be set to fire either the upper or lower barrel firs. There are rebounding hammers and a hammer interruptor to guard against accidental discharge when the gun is cocked and set to safe; when set to fire, the interruptor is only moved by positive action of the trigger. The action body may be of blued or stainless steel to choice.

Below: The open breech of the Ruger 12-gage.

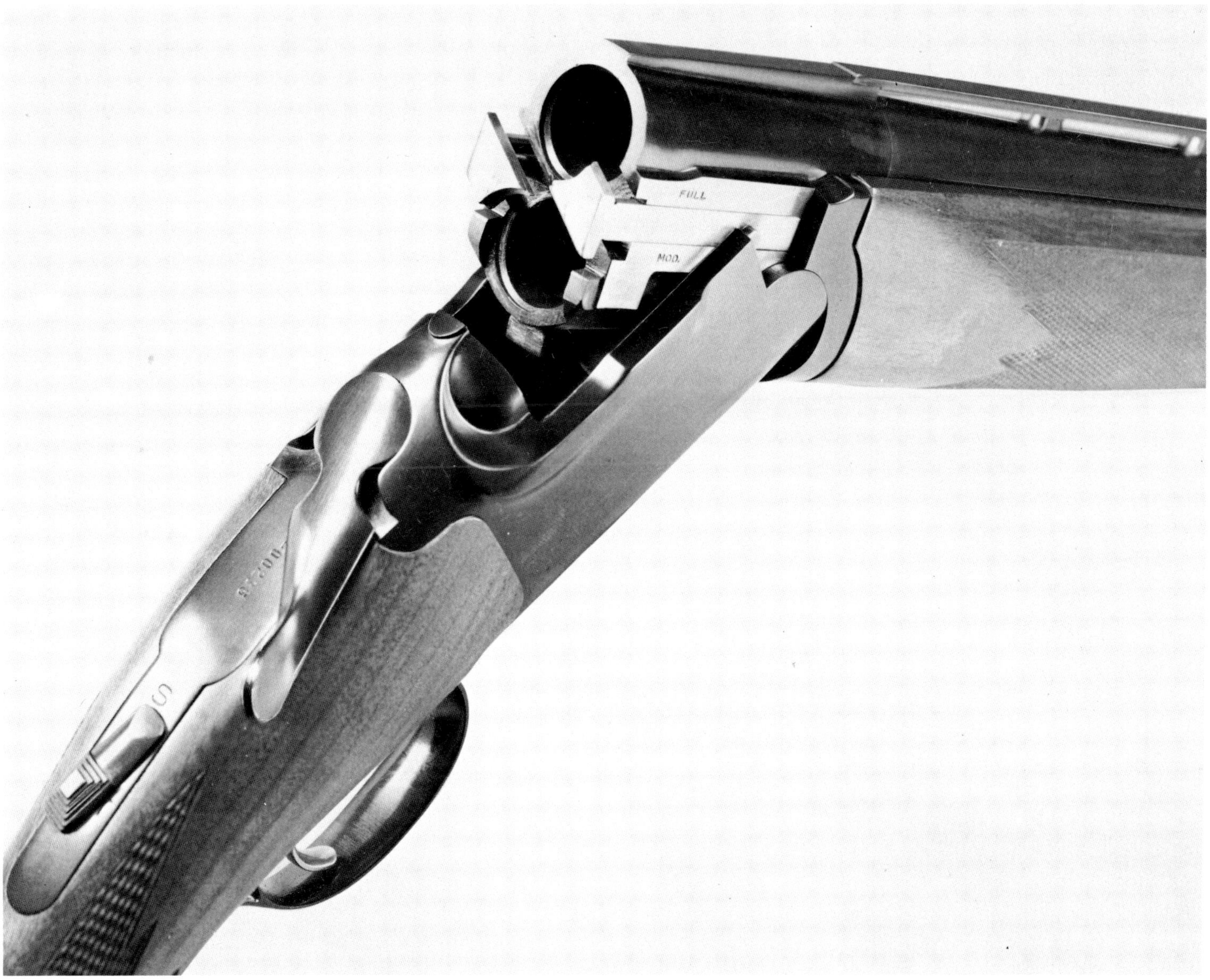

RUGER RED LABEL SHOTGUN

The hammer-forged Cr-Mo steel barrels are silver-soldered into the breech end monobloc, into which go the ejector mechanism and the trunnion pins which form the barrel pivot. There is a ventilated rub with glare-free top and a brass foresight bead. Stock and fore end are of American walnut, well-figured and neatly hand-checkered. The muzzles are fitted for multi-chokes, five of which are supplied with the gun, together with a key for fitting and removing them.

In the field the Red Label is a well-balanced, accurate gun with light, but not too sensitive, trigger and moderate recoil. It can be used equally well for game or competition shooting, and for the person restricted to using one gun, the Ruger should cover every eventuality.

These pages: Two views of the Ruger Red Label, a well-balanced and accurate shotgun that can be used in many different types of competition shooting.

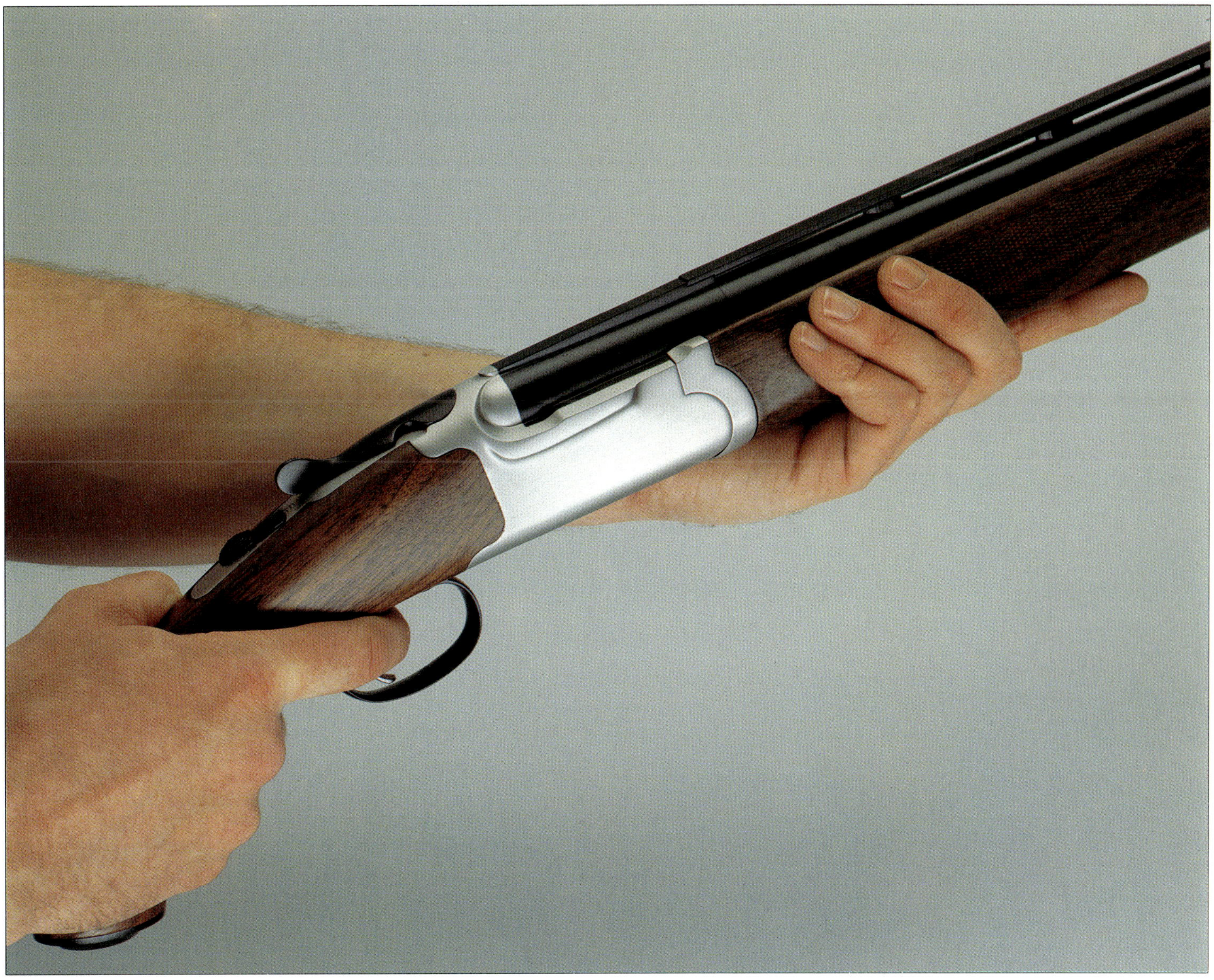

RUGER RED LABEL SHOTGUN

157

S.A.B. 'London' Shotgun

Manufacturer Societe Armi Bresciane Srl., Gardone Val Trompia, Italy
Type Side-by-side double, automatic ejector
Gage 12 or 20
Barrels 26.7in (680mm) or 27.5in (700mm)
Weight 6.62lbs (3kg) (26in barrels)

S.A.B. build a number of grades of shotgun and the 'London' model is their top line; as the name implies, it sets out to duplicate the type and quality made famous by the London gunmakers, and it achieves this very well.

The 'London' comes in a traditional gun case, leather-covered and baize-lined, into which the dismantled gun and its cleaning gear fit neatly. The gun itself is elegantly finished with an English-style straight stock in European walnut, oil-finished, the case-hardened receiver is neatly engraved, as are the trigger guard, top lever and other components, the barrels are well polished and blued, and the fitting of metal to wood is excellent. The front trigger is hinged so as not to trap the finger on the second trigger during recoil, the firing pin holes are bushed, and the matted top rib is finished by a white metal front bead.

The stock has a slight cast-off and little drop, making it perhaps best suited to those small of stature. Fired with light loadings it is comfortable to shoot, but heavier loadings tend to punish the firer due to the low weight of the gun. Nevertheless, this low weight has its advantages when carrying the gun all day, and it is quick and accurate in coming to the shoulder and pointing.

Viking Arms SOS Shotgun

Manufacturer Viking Arms Ltd., Harrogate, England
Type Slide action repeater
Gage 12
Barrel 24.25in (616mm)
Weight 7.43lbs (3.37kg)
Magazine capacity 7 rounds

The shotgun has evolved into certain well-known shapes over the years, and the appearance of something new comes as a shock to most people. The Viking gun is designed along the lines of the modern assault rifle, with a 'straight-line' stock and a carrying-handle-cum-sight unit which requires an equally high-set foresight. The makers suggest it as a 'defense' gun rather than as a purely sporting gun, and I have little doubt that the appearance of this weapon on some European shoots would result in a rapid request for the bearer to leave.

But leaving visual impressions aside, the Viking is a well-made weapon with certain definite 'plus' points. It has an unusually large magazine for a slide-action gun, and since the barrel is cylinder-bored it makes a good gun for firing solid slugs. The sights assist in this, though they are not capable of being adjusted without the aid of a gunsmith. As a trap gun or as a sporting gun the shape takes some getting used to, and it does not come to the shoulder as easily as a traditional shape, though doubtless practice would improve this.

The straight-line configuration helps to control recoil, the gun appearing to jump less and be rapidly recovered, though this is only of value when firing against an immobile target. There is the possibility that the gun would be attractive to police or security forces; it is certainly reliable and accurate, simple to dismantle and maintain, all features making it attractive for service use, and it is comparatively inexpensive. An optional butt of conventional form will be available in the near future so that it will be possible to convert it into a more normal-looking pump gun for 'social' occasions.

Viking Suhl Shotgun

Manufacturer Viking Arms Ltd., Harrogate, England
Type Side-by-side double, non-ejector
Gage 12
Barrels 28in (711mm)
Weight 6.56lbs (2.97kg)

Suhl, in Thuringia, was once the heart of the German gunmaking industry, but when Germany was divided in 1945 it vanished behind the Iron Curtain and the independent gunsmiths were amalgamated into impersonal state-controlled cooperatives. The quality was still apparent, but the individuality of different makers vanished. The Viking shotgun was one of these products. Since the reformation of Germany, the various state organizations are being slowly dismantled, but at the time of writing it is not entirely clear how the former Ernst Thalmann Gunmaking Cooperative is being split up, and therefore we list the gun under the name of the British importer.

In an age when manufacturers vie with each other to make more and more luxurious products at higher

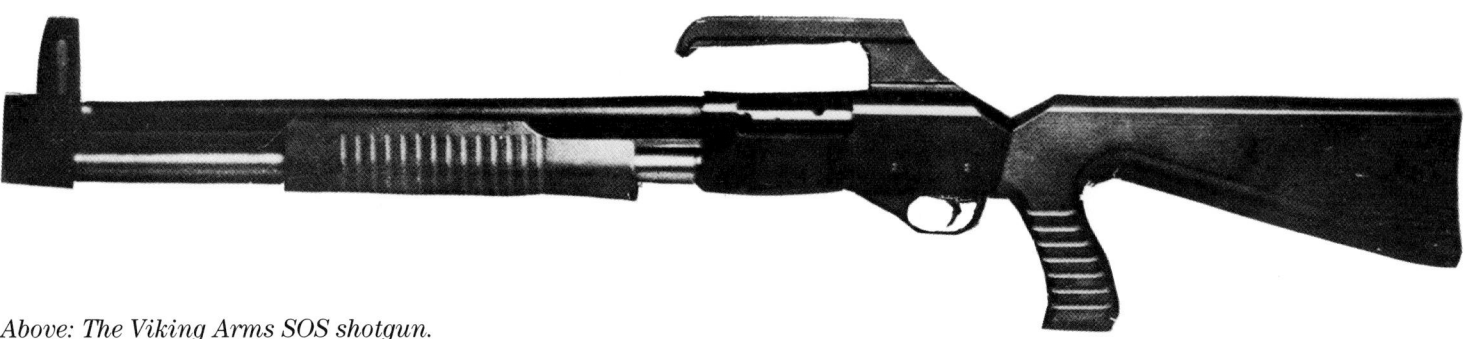

Above: The Viking Arms SOS shotgun.

VIKING SUHL SHOTGUN

and higher prices, the Suhl shotgun comes as a welcome surprise; it is an unpretentious 'working gun', with no concessions to elegance. The walnut stock has a half-pistol grip, the fore end is machine-checkered, but the finish is good and the fit of the gun to the stock is excellent. The action is a double-bolted box-lock, color case-hardened and without decoration, but it works smoothly, the trigger pull is crisp and consistent, and the whole action is tight and sound.

The barrels are bored quarter and three-quarter choke on Continental standards, closer to half and full-choke to western ideas, but the patterns are good and consistent. It handles well, the stock being cast-off for right-handed shooting, and gives the impression of a no-nonsense gun which will stand years of hard use.

This page: The Ruger 12 gauge shotgun.

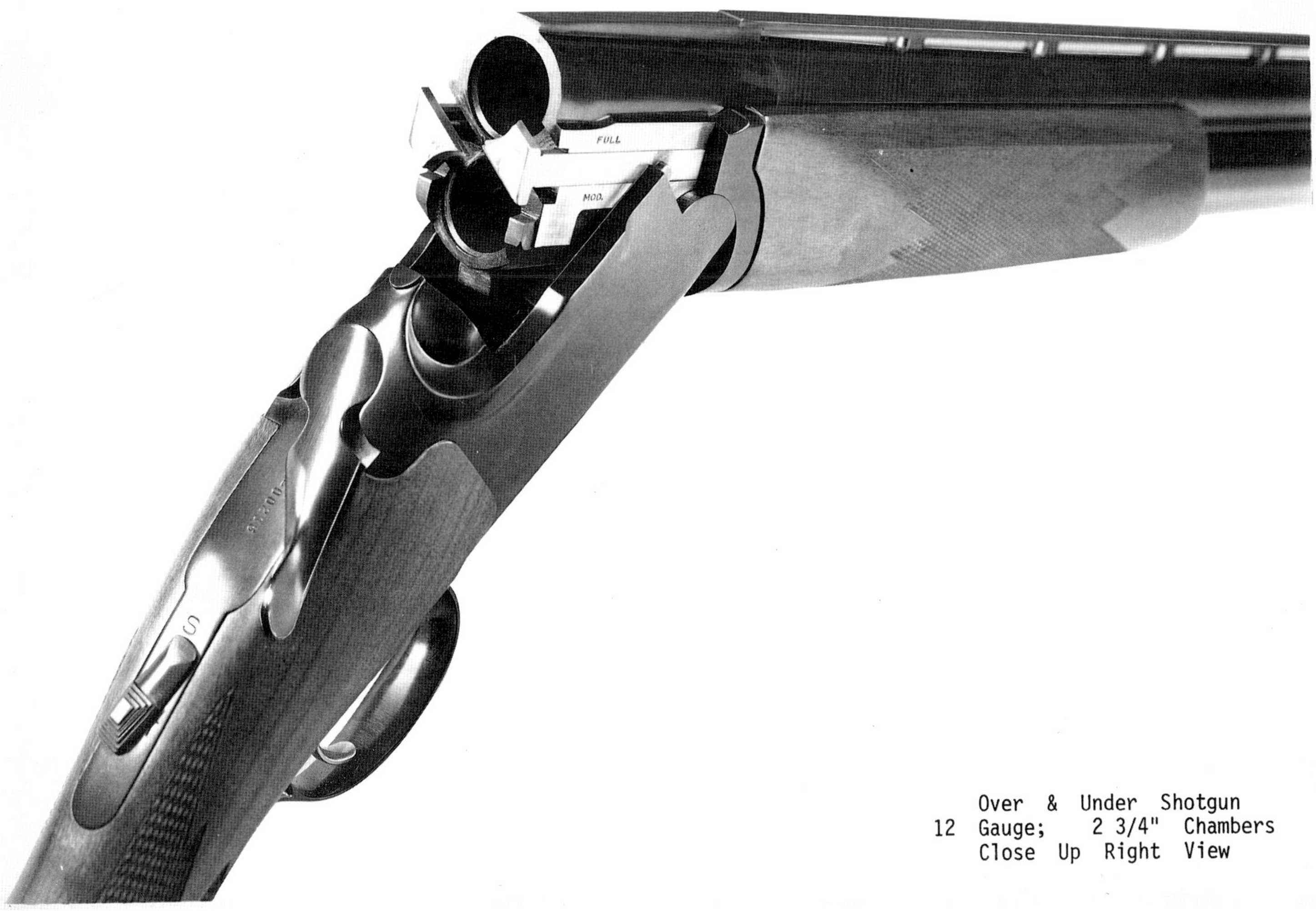

```
         Over  &  Under  Shotgun
12  Gauge;    2 3/4"  Chambers
     Close  Up  Right  View
```

Acknowledgments

The author and publisher would like to thank Design 23, Susan Brown for production, and Judith Millidge the editor, for their help in the preparation of this book. Most of the photographs are from the author's collection or have been supplied by the manufacturers and our thanks are due to them. Additional material was provided by the individuals and organizations listed below.

BPL: 77

Guns and Shooting Magazine/Dave Page: 138-139, 140-141 (all 3), 144-145 (both), 148-149, 150, 151, 152-153 (all 3), 155, 156-157 (both)

Jacques Lenaerts: 61 below, 69 below

Reuters/Bettmann: 9 top

The Research House: 1, 2-3, 6-7, 8, 10 (below) 12, 21, 28, 50-51, 72, 85

H P White Laboratory: 143 (both), 144